CHILTON BOOK COMPANY

REPAIR & TUNE-UP GUIDE

CHEVROLET MID-SIZE 1964-86

All U.S. and Canadian models of Chevelle • El Camino • Laguna S-3 • Malibu, Malibu SS • Monte Carlo, Monte Carlo SS

D1522863

President LAWRENCE A. FORNASIERI
Vice President and General Manager JOHN P. KUSHNERICK
Executive Editor KERRY A. FREEMAN, S.A.E.
Senior Editor RICHARD J. RIVELE, S.A.E.
Editor RICHARD T. SMITH

CHILTON BOOK COMPANY
Radnor, Pennsylvania
19089

SAFETY NOTICE

Proper service and repair procedures are vital to the safe, reliable operation of all motor vehicles, as well as the personal safety of those performing repairs. This book outlines procedures for servicing and repairing vehicles using safe, effective methods. The procedures contain many NOTES, CAUTIONS and WARNINGS which should be followed along with standard safety procedures to eliminate the possibility of personal injury or improper service which could damage the vehicle or compromise its safety.

It is important to note that repair procedures and techniques, tools and parts for servicing motor vehicles, as well as the skill and experience of the individual performing the work vary widely. It is not possible to anticipate all of the conceivable ways or conditions under which vehicles may be serviced, or to provide cautions as to all of the possible hazards that may result. Standard and accepted safety precautions and equipment should be used when handling toxic or flammable fluids, and safety goggles or other protection should be used during cutting, grinding, chiseling, prying, or any other process that can cause material removal or projectiles.

Some procedures require the use of tools specially designed for a specific purpose. Before substituting another tool or procedure, you must be completely satisfied that neither your personal safety, nor the performance of the vehicle will be endangered.

Although information in this guide is based on industry sources and is as complete as possible at the time of publication, the possibility exists that the manufacturer made later changes which could not be included here. While striving for total accuracy, Chilton Book Company cannot assume responsibility for any errors, changes, or omissions that may occur in the compilation of this data.

PART NUMBERS

Part numbers listed in this reference are not recommendations by Chilton for any product by brand name. They are references that can be used with interchange manuals and aftermarket supplier catalogs to locate each brand supplier's discrete part number.

SPECIAL TOOLS

Special tools are recommended by the vehicle manufacturer to perform their specific job. Use has been kept to a minimum, but where absolutely necessary, they are referred to in the text by the part number of the tool manufacturer. These tools can be purchased, under the appropriate part number, from the Service Tool Division, Kent-Moore Corporation, 29784 Little Mack, Roseville, MI 48066-2298, or an equivalent tool can be purchased locally from a tool supplier or parts outlet. Before substituting any tool for the one recommended, read the SAFETY NOTICE at the top of this page.

ACKNOWLEDGMENTS

The Chilton Book Company expresses its appreciation to the Chevrolet Motor Division, General Motors Corporation, Detroit, Michigan for their generous assistance.

Information has been selected from Chevrolet shop manuals, owners manuals, service bulletins, and technical training manuals.

Manufactured in the United States of America
    4567890   543210987

Chilton Repair & Tune-Up Guide: Chevrolet Mid-Size 1964–86
ISBN 0-8019-7677-4 pbk.
Library of Congress Catalog Card No. 85-47968

CONTENTS

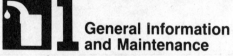

Quick Reference Specifications For Your Vehicle

Fill in this chart with the most commonly used specifications for your vehicle. Specifications can be found in Chapters 1 through 3 or on the tune-up decal under the hood of the vehicle.

Tune-Up

Firing Order_____

Spark Plugs:

    Type_____

    Gap (in.)_____

Torque (ft. lbs.)_____

Idle Speed (rpm)_____

Ignition Timing (°)_____

    Vacuum or Electronic Advance (Connected/Disconnected)_____

Valve Clearance (in.)

    Intake_____   **Exhaust**_____

Capacities

Engine Oil Type (API Rating)_____

    With Filter Change (qts)_____

    Without Filter Change (qts)_____

Cooling System (qts)_____

Manual Transmission (pts)_____

    Type_____

Automatic Transmission (pts)_____

    Type_____

Front Differential (pts)_____

    Type_____

Rear Differential (pts)_____

    Type_____

Transfer Case (pts)_____

    Type_____

FREQUENTLY REPLACED PARTS

Use these spaces to record the part numbers of frequently replaced parts.

PCV VALVE	OIL FILTER	AIR FILTER	FUEL FILTER
Type_____	**Type**_____	**Type**_____	**Type**_____
Part No._____	**Part No.**_____	**Part No.**_____	**Part No.**_____

General Information and Maintenance

HOW TO USE THIS BOOK

This book is divided into ten easy to follow chapters, avoiding "mechanic's jargon" and highlighting important procedures with illustrations wherever possible. As time goes by, you'll probably find that some chapters such as Chapter 2 (Tune Up) naturally accumulate more dirty fingerprints than others, but everything from engine rebuilding to waxing the car is covered here. Of course, even professional mechanics won't attempt a repair without the proper tools and a thorough knowledge of the work required. This is why operations like rebuilding your transmission or rear axle assembly are not covered here—they require a range of special tools which are too expensive, and a technical knowledge too extensive to be useful to you, the owner/mechanic.

Before loosing a single nut, read through the entire section you are dealing with and make sure you have the time, tools, and replacement parts necessary to do the job. This will save you much frustration, many hassles, and possibly a walk to the bus stop Monday morning because you needed a part or were without a tool Saturday afternoon. Remember, too, that auto parts stores sometimes have to order certain parts, so it's wise to run through a procedure and make a couple phone calls to be sure a part will be available when you need it.

Each section begins with a brief description of the particular system and the basic theory behind it. When repairs involve a level of technical know-how beyond most owner/mechanics, we tell you how to remove the part and replace it with a new or rebuilt unit. This way you can at least save the cost of labor, and the percentage that is often placed on top of the retail cost of new parts.

There are a few basic mechanic's rules that should be followed when working on any car:

1. Left side of the car means the driver's side; right side is the passenger's side.

2. Most screws, bolts, and nuts are "right handed"—they are tightened by turning clockwise and removed by turning counterclockwise.

3. *Never* crawl under a vehicle supported only by a jack—jack up the car, then support it with jackstands!

4. *Never* smoke or position an exposed flame near the battery or any part of the fuel system.

5. *Never* operate an engine in a closed room.

6. Use common sense during all operations.

TOOLS AND EQUIPMENT

The following list contains the basic tools needed to perform most of the maintenance and repair work covered in this book. The nut, bolts and thread sizes in your Chevrolet are mostly standard U.S. sizes (S.A.E.) in the 1964 through '76 models, and a combination of standard U.S. sizes (S.A.E.) and metric sizes in the 1977 and later models. Most of the later models covered here use metric fasteners and thread sizes exclusively on their engines, transmissions and drive axles. It's a good idea to check your particular model for the types of fasteners used on various assemblies.

1. One set each of both metric and S.A.E. sockets, including a ⅝ in. spark plug socket. Various length socket drive extensions and universals are also very helpful, but you'll probably acquire these as you need them. Ratchet handles are available in ¼, ⅜ and ½ in. drives, and will fit both metric and S.A.E. sockets (just make sure that your sockets are the proper drive size for the ratchet handled you buy).

2. One set each of metric and S.A.E. "combination" (one end open and one end box) wrenches.

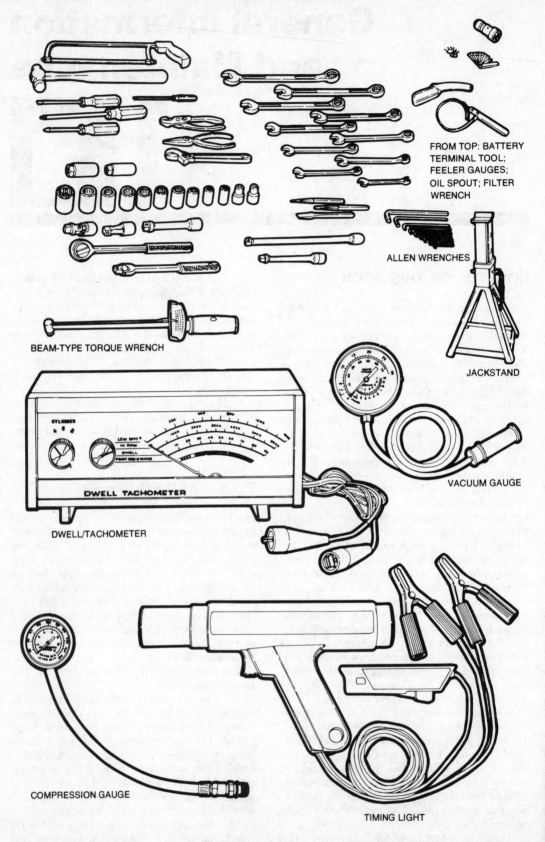

FROM TOP: BATTERY TERMINAL TOOL; FEELER GAUGES; OIL SPOUT; FILTER WRENCH

ALLEN WRENCHES

JACKSTAND

BEAM-TYPE TORQUE WRENCH

VACUUM GAUGE

DWELL TACHOMETER

DWELL/TACHOMETER

COMPRESSION GAUGE

TIMING LIGHT

You need only a basic assortment of hand tools and test instruments for most maintenance and repair jobs

3. Wire-type spark plug feeler gauge.

4. Blade-type feeler gauge for ignition and valve settings.

5. Slot and Phillips head screwdrivers in various sizes.

6. Oil filter strap wrench, necessary for removing oil filters (*never* used, though, for installing the filters).

7. Oil can filler spout, for pouring fresh oil from quart oil cans.

8. Pair of slip-lock pliers.

9. Pair of vise-type pliers.

10. Adjustable wrench.

11. At least two sturdy jackstands for working underneath the car—any other type of support (bricks, wood and especially cinderblocks) is just plain dangerous.

12. Timing light, preferably a DC battery hookup type, and preferably an inductive type for use on cars with electronic ignition.

This is an adequate set of tools, and the more work you do yourself on your car, the larger you'll find the set growing—a pair of pliers here, a wrench or two there. It makes more sense to have a comprehensive set of basic tools as listed above, and then to acquire more along the line as you need them, then to go out and plunk down big money for a professional size set you may never use. In addition to these basic tools, there are several other tools and gauges you may find useful.

Special Tools

• A hydraulic floor jack of at least 1½ ton capacity. If you are serious about maintaining your own car, then a floor jack is as necessary as a spark plug socket. The greatly increased utility, strength, and safety of a hydraulic floor jack makes it pay for itself many times over through the years.

• A compression gauge. The screw-in type is slower to use but it eliminates the possibility of a faulty reading due to escaping pressure.

• A manifold vacuum gauge, very useful in troubleshooting ignition and emissions problems.

• A drop light, to light up the work area (make sure yours is Underwriter's approved, and has a shielded bulb).

• A volt/ohm meter, used for determining whether or not there is current in a wire. These are handy for use if a wire is broken somewhere and are especially necessary for working on today's electronics-laden vehicles.

As a final note, a torque wrench is necessary for all but the most basic work—it should even be used when installing spark plugs. The more common beam-type models are perfectly ade-

quate and are usually much less expensive than the more precise "click" type (on which you pre-set the torque and the wrench "clicks" when that setting arrives on the fastener you are torquing).

NOTE: *Special tools are occasionally necessary to perform a specific job or are recommended to make a job easier. Their use has been kept to a minimum. When a special tool is indicated, it will be referred to by a manufacturer's part number, and, where possible, an illustration of the tool will be provided so that an equivalent tool may be used. The tool manufacturer and address is; Service Tool Division Kent-Moore 29784 Little Mack Roseville, MI 48066-2298*

SERVICING YOUR CAR SAFELY

It is virtually impossible to anticipate all of the hazards involved with automotive maintenance and service, but care and common sense will prevent most accidents.

The rules of safety for mechanics range from "don't smoke around gasoline," to "use the proper tool for the job." The trick to avoiding injuries is to develop safe work habits and take every possible precaution.

Dos

• Do keep a fire extinguisher and first aid kit within easy reach.

• Do wear safety glasses or goggles when cutting, drilling, grinding or prying, even if you have 20-20 vision. If you wear glasses for the sake of vision, they should be made of hardened glass that can serve also as safety glasses, or wear safety goggles over your regular glasses.

• Do shield your eyes whenever you work around the battery. Batteries contain sulphuric acid. In case of contact with the eyes or skin, flush the area with water or a mixture of water and baking soda and get medical attention immediately.

• Do use safety stands for any undercar service. Jacks are for raising vehicles; safety stands are for making sure the vehicle stays raised until you want it to come down. Whenever the car is raised, block the wheels remaining on the ground and set the parking brake.

• Do use adequate ventilation when working with any chemicals or hazardous materials. Like carbon monoxide, the asbestos dust resulting from brake lining wear can be poisonous in sufficient quantities.

• Do disconnect the negative battery cable when working on the electrical system. The

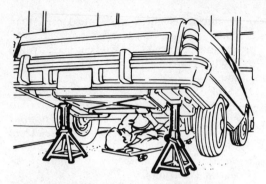

Always use jackstands when supporting the car; never use cinder blocks or tire changing jacks

secondary ignition system can contain up to 40,000 volts.

• Do follow manufacturer's directions whenever working with potentially hazardous materials. Both brake fluid and antifreeze are poisonous if taken internally.

• Do properly maintain your tools. Loose hammerheads, mushroomed punches and chisels, frayed or poorly grounded electrical cords, excessively worn screwdrivers, spread wrenches (open end), cracked sockets, slipping ratchets, or faulty droplight sockets can cause accidents.

• Likewise, keep your tools clean; a greasy wrench can slip off a bolt head, ruining the bolt and often ruining your knuckles in the process.

• Do use the proper size and type of tool for the job being done.

• Do when possible, pull on a wrench handle rather than push on it, and adjust your stance to prevent a fall.

• Do be sure that adjustable wrenches are tightly closed on the nut or bolt and pulled so that the face is on the side of the fixed jaw.

• Do select a wrench or socket that fits the nut or bolt. The wrench or socket should sit straight, not cocked.

• Do strike squarely with a hammer; avoid glancing blows.

• Do set the parking brake and block the drive wheels if the work requires the engine running.

Don'ts

• Don't run the engine in a garage or anywhere else without proper ventilation—EVER! Carbon monoxide is poisonous; it takes a long time to leave the human body and you can build up a deadly supply of it in your system by simply breathing in a little every day. You may not realize you are slowly poisoning yourself. Always use power vents, windows, fans or open the garage doors.

• Don't work around moving parts while wearing a necktie or other loose clothing. Short sleeves are much safer than long, loose sleeves; hard-toed shoes with neoprene soles protect your toes and give a better grip on slippery surfaces. Jewelry such as watches, fancy belt buckles, beads or body adornment of any kind is not safe working around a car. Long hair should be tied back under a hat or cap.

• Don't use pockets for toolboxes. A fall or bump can drive a screwdriver deep into your body. Even a wiping cloth hanging from the back pocket can wrap around a spinning shaft or fan.

• Don't smoke when working around gasoline, cleaning solvent or other flammable material.

• Don't smoke when working around the battery. When the battery is being charged, it gives off explosive hydrogen gas.

• Don't use gasoline to wash your hands; there are excellent soaps available. Gasoline may contain lead, and lead can enter the body through a cut, accumulating in the body until you are very ill. Gasoline also removes all the natural oils from the skin so that bone dry hands will suck up oil and grease.

• Don't service the air conditioning system unless you are equipped with the necessary tools and training. The refrigerant, R-12, is extremely cold when compressed, and when released into the air will instantly freeze any surface it contacts, including your eyes. Although the refrigerant is normally non-toxic, R-12 becomes a deadly poisonous gas in the presence of an open flame. One good whiff of the vapors from burning refrigerant can be fatal.

• Don't use screwdrivers for anything other than driving screws! A screwdriver used as a prying tool can snap when you least expect it, causing injuries. At the very least, you'll ruin a good screwdriver.

• Don't use a bumper jack (that little ratchet, scissors, or pantograph jack supplied with the car) for anything other than changing a flat! These jacks are only intended for emergency use out on the road; they are NOT designed as a maintenance tool. If you are serious about maintaining your car yourself, invest in a hydraulic floor jack of at least 1½ ton capacity, and at least two sturdy jackstands.

SERIAL NUMBER IDENTIFICATION

Vehicle Identification Number
(VIN) Plate

The 1964–67 vehicle serial number is stamped on a vehicle identification plate, attached to the left front door hinge pillar. On 1968 and later cars, the Vehicle Identification Number (VIN) is stamped on a plate located on the top left-hand side of the instrument panel, so it can be seen by looking through the windshield.

The VIN is a thirteen digit (1968–80) or seventeen digit (1981 and later) sequence of numbers and letters important for ordering parts and for servicing.

NOTE: *Model years appear in the VIN as the last digit of each particular year (6 is 1976, 8 is 1978, etc.) until 1980 (which is A). This is the final year under the thirteen digit code.*

Vehicle serial number for 1964–67, found on left front door pillar

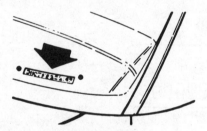

VIN location on 1968 and later cars

The seventeen digit VIN begins with 1981 (B) and continues 1982 (C), 1983 (D), etc.

Engine Serial Number

The engine serial number shows the manufacturing plant signified by a letter (F for Flint, T for Tonawanda, etc.), the month of manufacture, the day of manufacture, and the transmis-

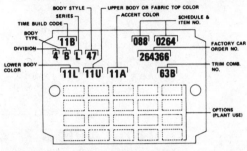

Body number plate—Canadian models

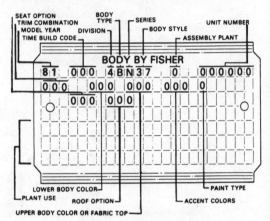

Body number plate—U.S. models

Vehicle Identification Number (VIN)

It is important for servicing and ordering parts to be certain of the vehicle and engine identification. The VIN (vehicle identification number) is a 13 or 17 digit number visible through the windshield on the driver's side of the dash and contains the vehicle and engine identification codes. It can be interpreted as follows:

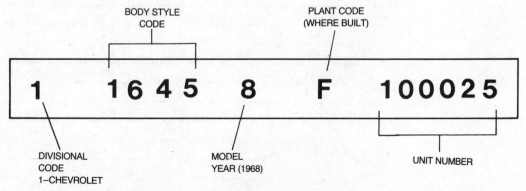

Thirteen digit VIN, 1968–71

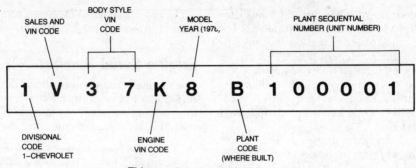

Thirteen digit VIN, 1972–80

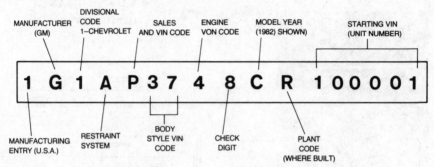

Seventeen digit VIN, 1981 and later

1976–80

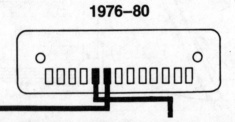

Model Year Code		Engine Code					
			Displacement				
Code	Year	Code	Cu. In.	Liters	Cyl.	Carb.	Eng. Mfg.
6	'76	D	250	4.1	6	1	Chev.
		G	262	4.3	6	2	Chev.
		Q	305	5.0	8	2	Chev.
		V	350	5.7	8	2	Chev.
		L	350	5.7	8	4	Chev.
		U	400	6.6	8	4	Chev.
		S	454	7.4	8	4	Chev.
7	'77	D	250	4.1	6	1	Chev.
		U	305	5.0	8	2	Chev.
		L	350	5.7	8	4	Chev.
8	'78	M	200	3.3	6	2	Chev.
		A	231	3.8	6	2	Buick
		D	250	4.1	6	1	Chev.

1976–80 (cont.)

Model Year Code		Engine Code					
			Displacement				
Code	Year	Code	Cu. In.	Liters	Cyl.	Carb.	Eng. Mfg.
		U	305	5.0	8	2	Chev.
		L	350	5.7	8	4	Chev.
9	'79	M	200	3.3	6	2	Chev.
		A	231	3.8	6	2	Buick
		D	250	4.1	6	1	Chev.
		J	267	4.4	8	2	Chev.
		G	305	5.0	8	2	Chev.
		H	305	5.0	8	4	Chev.
		L	350	5.7	8	4	Chev.
A	'80	K	229	3.8	6	2	Chev.
		A	231	3.8	6	2	Buick
		3	231	3.8	6	Turbo	Buick
		J	267	4.4	8	2	Chev.
		H	305	5.0	8	4	Chev.
		N	350	5.7	8	Diesel	Olds.

The thirteen digit Vehicle Identification Number can be used to determine engine application and model year. The sixth digit indicates the model year, and the fifth digit identifies the factory installed engine.

1981–86

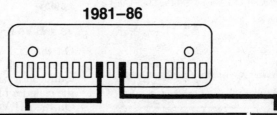

Engine Code						Model Year Code	
Code	Cu. In.	Liters	Cyl.	Carb.	Eng. Mfg.	Code	Year
K	229	3.8	6	2	Chev.	B	81
9	229	3.8	6	2	Chev.	C	82
A	231	3.8	6	2	Buick	D	83
3	231	3.8	6	Turbo	Buick	E	84
Z	262	4.3	6	TBI	Chev.	F	85
V	263	4.3	6	Diesel	Olds.	G	86
J	267	4.4	8	2	Chev.		
G	305	5.0	8	4	Chev.		
H	305	5.0	8	4	Chev.		
7	305	5.0	8	4	Chev.		
6	350	5.7	8	4	Chev.		
N	350	5.7	8	Diesel	Chev.		

The seventeen digit Vehicle Identification Number can be used to determine engine application and model year. The tenth digit indicates the model year, and the eighth digit identifies the factory installed engine.

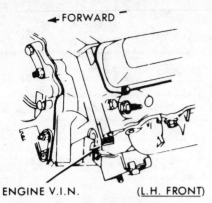

Engine VIN location, V6 and V8 Diesels

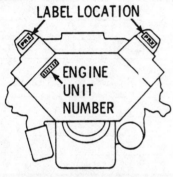

Some 305 and 350 V8s have VIN codes here

VIN label (decal) locations, 231 V6

sion and engine type represented by a two or three-letter code. A typical engine serial number would be F1005FA. The F represents the manufacturing plant (Flint), the 10 signifies the month of manufacture (October), 05 signifies the day of manufacture and FA signifies the engine and transmission type. Beginning with 1968 models, a VIN is stamped on the cylinder block next to the engine serial number. The VIN (up to 1971) is the same as the vehicle serial number stamped on the instrument panel except that it does not include the four numbers representing body style.

In 1972, the VIN changed somewhat. A typical VIN for a 1972 Chevelle might be: 1Q87F2F000001 identifying this particular car

as the first (000001) 1972 Chevelle to roll off the Flint assembly line. It includes the manufacturer's identity number (number 1 representing Chevrolet products), a series code letter (Q representing Camaro in this particular instance), a two-digit body style number (87 representing 2 dr. Sport Coupe), an engine code letter (letters listed below), a one-digit model year number (2 representing 1972), an assembly plant letter (F signifying Flint), and a unit number signifying order of production. According to the VIN, this car had a 307 cu in. engine with two-barrel carburetor represented by the engine code letter "F."

This basic format is utilized through the 1981 model year, although specific letter/number designations may change from year to year.

Inline 6 Cylinder Engines

On six-cylinder engines, the serial number is found on a pad at the front right-hand side of the cylinder block, just to the rear of the distributor.

Engine serial number location—inline six cylinder engine

V8 and V6 Engines

On the 229 V6 (1967–84), 265 V6 (1985 and later) and all V8 engines, the serial number is found on a pad at the front right hand side of the cylinder block, just below the cylinder head. On the 231 V6, the number can be found on a pad on the left side of the cylinder block, where it meets the transmission.

229 V6 (1967–84), 265 V6 (1985 and later) and all V8 engine serial number location—just below right-hand valve cover, stamped on engine block

Transmission Serial Number

A transmission serial number is stamped on each transmission. Beginning with 1968 models, a

Engine Identification
1964–70

Engine identification code letter follows immediately after engine serial number.
6 Cyl.—pad at front right-hand side of cylinder block at rear of distributor.
V8—Pad at front right-hand side of cylinder block.

No. Cyls.	Cu. In. Displ.	Type	Year and Code						
			1964	1965	1966	1967	1968	1969	1970
6	194	M.T.	GF, G	AA	AA				
6	194	HDC	GG, GB	AC	AC				
6	194	AC	GM, GK	AG	AG				
6	194	HDC, AC	GN, GL	AH	AH				
6	194	Taxi	GH, GK	AK					
6	194	PG	K, KB	AL	AL				
6	194	PG, Taxi	KC, KD	AN					
6	194	PG, AC	KJ, KH	AR	AR				
6	194	w/ex. EM			AS				
6	194	w/ex. EM, AC			AT				
6	194	PG, w/ex. EM			AX				
6	194	PG, w/ex. EM, AC			AY				
6	230	HDC				BC	BC	BC	
6	230	HDC, AC				BB	BB	BB	
6	230	PG					BF	BF	
6	230	PG, w/ex. EM	BN		BL			AN	
6	230	Hyd., AC						AR	
6	230	PG, w/ex. EM, AC			BM				
6	230	Hyd.						AD	
6	230	w/ex. EM			BN				
6	230	w/ex. EM, AC			BO				
6	230	PG, PCV, AC	BP						
6	230	M.T.		CA	CA	CA	BA	AM	
6	230	M.T.	LM	CB	CB				
6	230	3 Spd. AC	LN, LL			CB		AP	
6	230	PG		CC	CC	CC			
6	230	PG, AC	BM	CD	CD	CD	BH	AQ	
6	250	3 Spd. or OD				CM	CM	BE	CCL
6	250	3 Spd. AC				CN	CN	BF	
6	250	3 Spd. or OD w/ex. EM				CO			
6	250	3 Spd. AC w/ex. EM				CP			
6	250	PG				CQ	CQ	BB	CCM
6	250	PG, AC				CR	CR	BC	
6	250	Hyd.						BD	CCK
6	250	PG, w/ex. EM				CS			
6	250	Hyd., AC						BH	
6	250	PG, AC w/ex. EM				CT			
8	283	3 Spd.	J	DA	DA	DA			
8	283	4 Spd.	JA	DB	DB	DB			
8	283	PG	JD	DE	DF	DE			
8	283	3 Spd., 4 Bbl.	JH	DG	DG				
8	283	PG, 4 Bbl.	JG	DH	DH				
8	283	w/ex. EM			DI	DI			
8	283	PG, w/ex. EM			DJ	DJ			
8	283	4 Spd., w/ex. EM			DK	DK			
8	283	4 Bbl., w/ex. EM			DL				
8	283	PG, 4 Bbl., w/ex. EM			DM				
8	283	HDC				DN			
8	307	Hyd.						DD	CNF
8	307	M.T.					DA	DA	CNC
8	307	4 Spd.					DE	DE	CND
8	307	PG					DB	DC	CNE
8	307	HDC					DN		
8	327	M.T.	JQ	EA	EA	EA	EA		
8	327	HP	JR	EB					
8	327	w/ex. EM			EB	EB			
8	327	SHP	JS	EC				ES	
8	327	PG, w/ex. EM			EC	EC			
8	327	w/T. Ign.	JT	ED					
8	327	3 or 4 Spd. (325 H.P.)				EP			

Engine Identification
1964–70 (cont.)

Engine identification code letter follows immediately after engine serial number.
6 Cyl.—pad at front right-hand side of cylinder block at rear of distributor.
V8—Pad at front right-hand side of cylinder block.

No. Cyls.	Cu. In. Displ.	Type	_____ Year and Code _____						
			1964	1965	1966	1967	1968	1969	1970
8	327	HDC, 3 or 4 Spd. w/ex. EM (325 H.P.)				ER			
8	327	HDC (325 H.P.)				ES	ES		
8	327	HDC (275 H.P.)				ED	ED		
8	327	PG	SR	EE	EE	EE	EE		
8	327	PG, HP	SS	EF					
8	350	M.T.						HA	
8	350	Hyd.						HB	
8	350	2-BBL.						HC	
8	350	2-BBL., Hyd.						HD	
8	350	PG						HE	CNM(250)
8	350	PG, 2-BBL.						HF	
8	350	M.T.						HP	CNI(250)
8	350	M.T.						HR	CNJ(300)
8	350	PG						HR	CNK(300)
8	350	Hyd.						HS	CRE(300)
8	396	HDC			ED	ED	ED	ED	
8	396	HP			EF	EF	EF	JC	
8	396	SHP					EG	JD	
8	396	w/ex. EM			EH	EH			
8	396	HP, w/ex. EM			EJ	EJ			
8	396	PG			EK	EK	EK	EK	
8	396	PG, HP			EL	EL	EL	EL	
8	396	PG, w/ex. EM			EM	EM			
8	396	PG, HP, w/ex. EM			EN	EN			
8	396	Hyd. (325 H.P.)				ET	ET	ET	
8	396	Hyd. (350 H.P.)				EU	EU	EU	
8	396	w/ex. EM (325 H.P.)				EV			
8	396	w/ex. EM (350 H.P.)				EW			
8	396	M.T.						JA	CZX(265), CTX(350), CKT(375) CKO(375)
8	396	HP, 3-sp. Hyd. 400						JE	
8	396	Hyd. 400						JK	CTW(350)
8	396	SHP, Hyd. 400. (#–CKP only)						KF	CTY(375), CKP(375) CKU(375)
8	396	M.T.						KG	
8	396	Hyd. 400						KH	CKN(325)
8	396	M.T., HP						KB	
8	396	M.T.						JV	
8	396	SHP, M.T.						KD	
8	396	M.T.						KI	
8	396	M.T., HDC							CTZ(350), CKQ(375)
8	400	M.T. (330 H.P.)							CKR
8	400	M.T., HDC (330 H.P.)							CKS
8	454	M.T. (390 H.P.)							CRN, CRT
8	454	Hyd. 400 (390 H.P.)							CRQ
8	454	Hyd. 400 (450 H.P.)							CRR
8	454	Hyd. 400 #(450 H.P.)							CRS
8	454	M.T. (450 H.P.)							CRV

AC—air conditioned.
HDC—heavy duty clutch.
HP—high performance.
SHP—special high performance.
M.T.—manual transmission.

OD—overdrive.
PG—powerglide transmission.
PCV—positive crankcase ventilation.
w/ex. EM—with exhaust emission

w/T. Ign.—with transistor ignition.
4 Bbl.—four barrel carburetor.
Hyd.—Hydramatic.
#—Aluminum heads.

Engine Identification
1971–75

Engine identification code letter follows immediately after engine serial number.
6 Cyl.—Pad at front right-hand side of cylinder block at rear of distributor.
V8—Pad at front right-hand side of cylinder block.

No. Cyls.	Cu. In. Displ.	Type	Year and Code				
			1971	1972	1973	1974	1975
6	250	PG		CBJ			
6	250	T.H.			CCA	CCX	
6	250	M.T.	CAA	CBG	CCC	CCR	D
6	250	M.T., w/NB2			CCD		
6	250	T.H., w/NB2			CCB	CCW	
8	307	T.H.		CTK	CMA		
8	307	M.T.			CHB		
8	307	PG		CKH			
8	307	M.T.	CCA	CKG			
8	300	T.H., w/NB2			CHC		
8	350	M.T.		CKK, CKA	CKA, CKB		
8	350	2-BBL., M.T.				CMC	H
8	350	2-BBL., T.H.				CMA	
8	350	PG		CKB, CDB			
8	350	T.H.		CT, CKD	CKL, CKJ		
8	350	M.T.	CGA(245)				
8	350	PG	CGB(245)				
8	350	M.T.	CGK(270)				
8	350	T.H. 350	CGL(270) CJD(270)				
8	350	M.T.	CJJ(270)				
8	350	M.T., w/NB2		CKC, CKH			
8	350	T.H., w/NB2		CKD, CKK		CKD	
8	350	3-spd., 4-BBL.				CKH	J, T
8	400	T.H., 4-BBL.				CTC	U
8	400	T.H., 4-BBL., California				CTA	
8	402	M.T., HDC (330 hp)		CLA, CLS			
8	402	T.H. 400 (Mk. IV)	CLB	CLB			
8	402	4-spd. (Mk. IV)	CLL				
8	402	M.T. Police (Mk. IV)	CLR				
8	402	M.T. (Mk. IV)	CLS				
8	402	M.T. (Mk. IV)	CPR				
8	400	M.T. (Mk. IV)	CPA CPG CPD CPP	CPA			
8	454	T.H. 400 (450 hp)		CPD			
8	454	M.T.			CWA	CWA	
8	454	T.H.			CWB	CWX	
8	454	M.T., w/NB2			CWC		
8	454	T.H. w/NB2			CWD	CWD	

AC—air conditioned
HDC—heavy duty clutch
HP—high performance
M.T.—manual transmission
OD—overdrive

PG—powerglide transmission
PCV—positive crankcase ventilation
w/ex. EM—with exhaust emission
w/T. Ign.—with transistor ignition

4-BBL.—four-barrel carburetor
T.H.—Turbo Hydra-Matic
#—Aluminum heads
NB2—Calif. only

VIN is stamped on each cylinder block and on every transmission, in addition to the serial number. The VIN is the same as the vehicle serial number stamped on the instrument panel except that it does not include the four numbers representing body style. The location of the transmission serial number on each transmission is as follows:

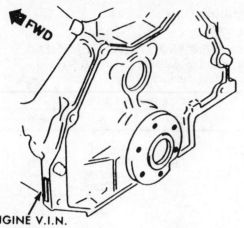

ENGINE V.I.N.

231 V6 engine serial number—at extreme left rear of cylinder block

Serial number location—Turbo Hydra-Matic

Serial number location—Saginaw 3 and 4 speed

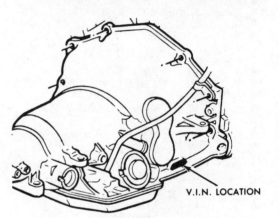

V.I.N. LOCATION

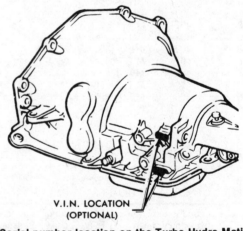

V.I.N. LOCATION (OPTIONAL)

Serial number location on the Turbo Hydra-Matic 350 and 350C

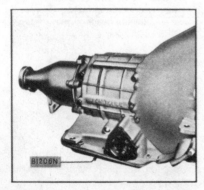

Serial number location on the Powerglide

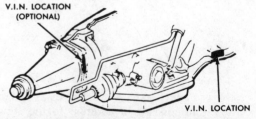

V.I.N. LOCATION (OPTIONAL)

V.I.N. LOCATION

Serial number location on the Turbo Hydra-Matic 200 and 250

Manual Transmissions 1964–86

	Year																						
	64	65	66	67	68	69	70	71	72	73	74	75	76	77	78	79	80	81	82	83	84	85	86
Muncie 3-speed	✓																						
Muncie 3-speed, Fully Synchronized		✓																					
Saginaw 3-speed, Fully Synchronized						✓	✓	✓	✓	✓	✓	✓	✓	✓	✓	✓	✓	✓	✓	✓			
Muncie 4-Speed	✓	✓	✓	✓	✓	✓	✓	✓	✓	✓	✓	✓	✓	✓	✓	✓	✓	✓					
Saginaw 4-Speed		✓	✓	✓	✓	✓	✓	✓	✓	✓	✓	✓											
Warner T-16, 3-Speed			✓	✓	✓																		
Warner T-10, 4-Speed, Overdrive													✓	✓	✓	✓	✓	✓	✓	✓			
Saginaw 4-Speed, Overdrive													✓	✓	✓	✓	✓	✓	✓	✓	✓		
Muncie 4-Speed, Overdrive													✓	✓	✓	✓							
Warner T-50, 5-Speed														✓	✓	✓							
Warner 5-Speed, Overdrive																					✓	✓	✓

Automatic Transmissions 1964–86

	Year																						
	64	65	66	67	68	69	70	71	72	73	74	75	76	77	78	79	80	81	82	83	84	85	86
Power Glide	✓	✓	✓	✓	✓	✓	✓	✓	✓														
Turbo Hydramatic 350						✓	✓	✓	✓	✓	✓	✓	✓	✓	✓	✓	✓	✓					
Turbo Hydramatic 400			✓	✓	✓	✓	✓	✓	✓	✓	✓	✓	✓	✓	✓	✓	✓	✓					
Turbo Hydramatic 200				✓	✓	✓	✓							✓	✓								
Turbo Hydramatic 250											✓	✓	✓	✓	✓								
Turbo Hydramatic 200C																			✓	✓	✓	✓	✓
Turbo Hydramatic 250C																			✓	✓	✓	✓	
Turbo Hydramatic 350C 4-speed																	✓	✓	✓	✓	✓		
Turbo Hydramatic 200-4R overdrive 4-speed															✓	✓	✓	✓	✓	✓	✓	✓	✓
Turbo Hydramatic 700-R4																				✓	✓	✓	
Turbo Hydramatic 700C-R4, overdrive																							✓
Turbo Hydramatic 350C 3-speed																			✓	✓			

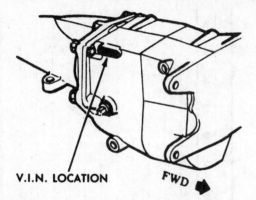

V.I.N. LOCATION FWD ➡

Manual transmission serial number location—
1979–81

Rear Axle Identification

The axle identification number is located either on a metal tag (attached to the rear of the differential) or stamped onto the front right-side of the axle tube, about three inches outboard from the differential cover.

For servicing the rear axle, the third letter must be known, which is the manufacturers identity. The codes are: "B" for Buick, "C" for Buffalo, "G" for Chevrolet-Gear and Axle, "K" or "M" for GM of Canada, "O" for Oldsmobile, "P" for Pontiac and "W" for Warren.

On all late model vehicles, the axle ratios are designed to meet emission standards for areas of operation.

Vehicle Emission Control Information Label

The Vehicle Emission Control Information Label is located in the engine compartment (fan shroud, radiator support, hood underside, etc.) of every vehicle produced by General Motors. The label contains important emission specifications and setting procedures, as well as a vacuum hose schematic with various emissions components identified.

When servicing your Chevrolet, this label should always be checked for up-to-date information pertaining specifically to your car.

NOTE: *Always follow the timing procedures on this label when adjusting ignition timing.*

ROUTINE MAINTENANCE

Air Cleaner

The air cleaner has a dual purpose. It not only filters the air going to the carburetor, but also acts as a flame arrester if the engine should backfire through the carburetor. If an engine

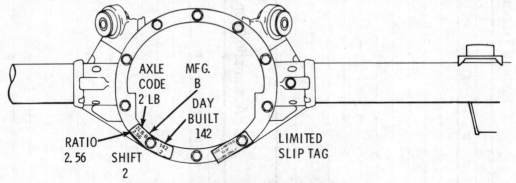

AXLE CODE MFG. B DAY BUILT 142
RATIO 2.56 SHIFT 2 LIMITED SLIP TAG

AXLE CODE LOCATION "B" AXLE

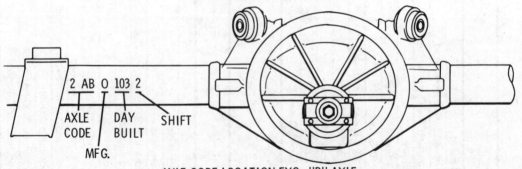

2 AB O 103 2
AXLE CODE DAY BUILT SHIFT MFG.

AXLE CODE LOCATION EXC. "B" AXLE

View of the rear axle identification numbers.

Typical emissions decal, 1979 231 V6 shown. Located under hood

Rear Axle Identification and Ratio
1964–86

Codes	64	65	66	67	68	69	70	71	72	73	74	75	76	77	78	79	80	81	82	83	84	85	86
AA																			2.56				
AB														2.56	2.73	2.73	2.73	2.73	2.73	2.73	2.73	2.73	2.73
AC										2.73	2.73	2.73	2.73	2.73		3.08	3.08	3.08				3.08	3.08
AD										3.08	3.08	3.08	3.08			3.23	3.23						
AE																				3.42			
AF														3.08									
AG															2.93	2.93		2.93					
AH												2.56	2.56			2.29	2.29	2.29	2.29	2.29	2.29	2.29	2.29
AJ										3.42	3.42	3.42				2.41	2.41	2.41	2.41	2.41	2.41	2.41	2.41
AL																2.73							
AS																					3.42		
AT																		2.29	2.29	2.29	2.29		
AU																							
AV																3.08	3.08	3.08	3.08	3.08	3.08	3.08	3.08
AW																		2.93					
AX															2.73	2.73	2.73	2.73	2.73	2.73	2.73	2.73	2.73
AY																2.56	2.56	2.56	2.56			2.56	2.56
AZ															2.41	2.41	2.41	2.41	2.41	2.41	2.41	2.41	2.41
BA															2.56	2.56							
BB															2.73	2.73	2.73	2.73	2.73	2.73	2.73	2.73	2.73
BC																3.08		3.08				3.08	3.08
BD																3.23							
BG															2.93	2.93		2.93					

BH	2.29	2.29	2.29	2.29	2.29	2.29	2.29	2.29	2.29	2.29		
BJ	2.41	2.41	2.41	2.41	2.41	2.41	2.41	2.41	2.41	2.41		
BL	2.73											
BS	3.42											
BT	2.29	2.29	2.29	2.29								
BU	3.23											
BV	3.08	3.08	3.08	3.08	3.08	3.08						
BW	2.93											
BY	2.73	2.73	2.73	2.73	2.73	2.73	2.73	2.56	2.56	2.56	2.56	2.56
BZ	2.41	2.41	2.41	2.41	2.41	2.41	2.41	2.41	2.41	2.41		
CA	3.08	3.08	3.08	3.08	3.08							
CB	3.36	3.36	3.36	3.36	3.36							
CC	3.73	3.73	3.73	3.73	2.73	2.73	2.73					
CD	3.07	3.07	3.07	3.07	3.08	3.08	2.73					
CE	3.08	3.08	3.08	3.08								
CF	3.31	3.31	3.31	3.31	3.31	3.31	3.08					
CG	3.36	3.36	3.36	3.36								
CH	3.70	2.73	2.73	2.73	2.73							
CI	3.73	3.73	3.73	3.73								
CJ	3.07	3.07	2.56	3.42	3.42	3.42						
CK	3.07	3.07	3.07	2.56								
CL	3.08	3.08	2.56									
CM	3.08	3.08	2.56									
CN	3.31	3.31	3.31	2.56								
CO	3.31	3.31	3.31	2.56								
CP	3.36	3.36	2.73	2.73								

Rear Axle Identification and Ratio (cont.)
1964–86

Codes	64	65	66	67	68	69	70	71	72	73	74	75	76	77	78	79	80	81	82	83	84	85	86
CQ	3.36	3.36	3.36			2.56																	
CR	3.70	3.70	3.70	3.70	3.70																		
CS	3.70	3.70	3.70			2.56																	
CT	3.73	3.73	3.73	3.73		2.73																	
CU	3.73	3.73	3.73	3.73	3.73																		
CV	3.70	3.70	3.70	3.70	3.70																		
CW	3.31	3.31	3.31	3.31	3.31	3.31	3.31	3.31	3.31														
CX	3.07	3.07	3.07	3.07	3.07	3.07																	
CY					3.07																		
CZ					2.73																		
CCA							3.08																
CCD							3.07																
CCE							3.08																
CCF							3.31																
CCH							2.73																
CCN							2.56																
CCO							2.56																
CCP							2.73																
CCW							3.31																
CCX							3.07																
CGA							2.56																
CGB							2.56																
CGC							2.73																
CGD							2.73																

Code			
CGG	3.36		
CGI	3.36		
CKC	2.73		
CKD	2.73		
CKF	3.55		
CKJ	3.55		
CKK	4.10		
CRJ	2.56		
CRK	2.56		
CRU	3.31		
CRV	3.31		
CRW	4.10		
FH	2.73	2.73	
FI	2.73	2.73	
FJ	3.08	3.08	
FK	3.08	3.08	
FL	3.36	3.36	
FM	3.36	3.36	
FN	3.55	3.55	
FO	3.55	3.55	
FP	3.70		
FQ	3.70		
GA			2.56
GB	2.73	2.73	2.56
GC	2.73	2.73	2.73
GD	2.73	2.73	2.73

Rear Axle Identification and Ratio (cont.)
1964–86

Codes	64	65	66	67	68	69	70	71	72	73	74	75	76	77	78	79	80	81	82	83	84	85	86
GE	2.73	2.73																					
GF								3.08	3.08														
GG								3.36	3.36														
GH								2.73	2.73														
GI								3.36	3.36														
GN								3.08	3.08														
KA					3.55	3.55																	
KB					3.55	3.55																	
KC					2.73	2.73																	
KD					2.73	2.73	2.73	2.73															
KE						2.73																	
KF			3.55	3.55	3.55	3.55																	
KG			3.55	3.55	3.08	3.08																	
KH			3.55	3.55	3.08	3.08																	
KI			2.73		3.36	3.36																	
KJ			3.55	3.55	3.55	3.55																	
KK			4.10	4.10	4.10	4.10																	
KL			4.10	4.10	3.36	3.36																	
KM			4.56	4.56	4.56	4.56																	
KN			4.56	4.56	3.55	3.55																	
KO			4.88	4.88	4.88	4.88																	
KP			4.88	4.88	3.55	3.55																	
KW					2.73																		

KX	3.07	3.07	
KY	3.31		
KZ	3.31		
K2	3.55		
K3	3.55		
K4	3.73		
K5	3.73		
K6	4.10		
K7	4.56		
K8	4.88		
PC	2.41		
RA	2.29	2.29	2.29
RB		2.41	2.29
RC	2.56	2.56	
RD	2.73	2.73	2.73
RF	3.08		
RU	3.31	3.31	
RV	3.31	3.31	
RW	4.10	4.10	
RX	2.73	2.73	2.73
SC	2.29		
SC	2.41		
SC	3.08		

Rear Axle Identification and Ratio (cont.) 1964–86

Codes	64	65	66	67	68	69	70	71	72	73	74	75	76	77	78	79	80	81	82	83	84	85	86
WA												2.73	2.73										
WB										2.73	2.73												
WC										3.08	3.08	3.08	3.08										
WE										3.42	3.42	3.42											
XA										2.73	2.73	2.73	2.73										
XB										2.73	2.73												
XC										3.08	3.08	3.08	3.08										
XE										3.42	3.42	3.42											
ZE														2.73									
ZJ														3.08									
ZW														2.73									
ZY														3.08									

Unscrew the wing nut and remove the cover

Using a clean rag or paper towel, wipe out the inside of the air cleaner

Remove and discard the old filter

Check the small crankcase breather

maintenance procedure requires the temporary removal of the air cleaner, remove it; otherwise, never run the engine without it. Operating a car without its air cleaner results in some throaty sounds from the carburetor giving the impression of increased power but will only cause trouble. Unfiltered air to the carburetor will eventually result in a dirty, inefficient carburetor and engine. A dirty carburetor increases the chances of carburetor backfire and, without the protection of an air cleaner, fire becomes a probable danger. The air cleaner as-

sembly consists of the air cleaner itself, which is the large metal container that fits over the carburetor, the element (paper or polyurethane) contained within, and the flame arrester located in the base of the air cleaner. If your car is equipped with the paper element, it should be inspected at its first 12,000 miles, rechecked every 6,000 miles thereafter, and replaced after 24,000 miles. The 1975 and later air cleaners should be replaced at 30,000 mile intervals if the paper type (V6 and V8), and 15,000 miles if the oil wetted type (inline six). Inspections and replacements should be more frequent if the car is operated in a dirty, dusty environment. When inspecting the element, look for dust leaks, holes or an overly dirty appearance. If the element is excessively dirty, it may cause a reduction in clean air intake. If air has trouble getting through a dirty element, the carburetor fuel mixture will become richer (more gas, less air), the idle will be rougher, and the exhaust smoke will be noticeably black. To check the effectiveness of your paper element, remove the air cleaner assembly and, if the idle increases, then the element is restricting airflow and should be replaced. If a polyurethane element is installed, clean or replace it every 12,000 miles. If you choose to clean it, do so with kerosene or another suitable solvent. Squeeze out all of the solvent, soak in engine oil, and then squeeze out the oil using a clean, dry cloth to remove the excess. The flame arrester, located at the base of the carburetor, should be cleaned in solvent (kerosene) once every 12,000 miles.

Gasoline Fuel Filter

There are three types of fuel filters; internal (in the carburetor fitting), inline (in the fuel line) and in-tank (the sock on the fuel pickup tube).

CAUTION: *Before removing any component of the fuel system, refer to the "Fuel*

Pressure Release" procedures in this section and release the fuel pressure.

REMOVAL AND INSTALLATION

Internal Filter

The carburetor inlet fuel filter should be replaced every 12,000 miles (15,000 miles for 1975 and later models) or more often if necessary.

1. Disconnect the fuel line connection at the fuel inlet filter nut on the carburetor.

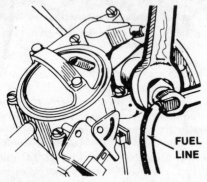

FUEL LINE

The fuel filter is located behind the large fuel line inlet nut on the carburetor

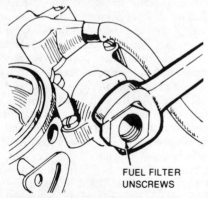

FUEL FILTER UNSCREWS

Remove the retaining nut and the filter will pop out under spring pressure

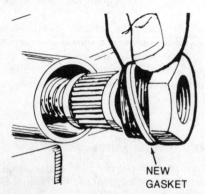

NEW GASKET

Install the new filter and spring. Certain early models use a bronze filter element, but most are made of paper

2. Remove the fuel inlet filter nut from the carburetor.

3. Remove the filter and the spring.

NOTE: *If a check valve is not present with the filter, one must be installed when the filter is replaced.*

4. Install the spring, filter and check valve (must face the fuel line), then reverse the removal procedures.

5. Start the engine and check for leaks.

Inline Filter

1. Disconnect the fuel lines.

2. Remove the fuel filter from the retainer or mounting bolt.

3. To install, reverse the removal procedures. Start the engine and check for leaks.

NOTE: *The filter has an arrow (fuel flow direction) on the side of the case, be sure to install it correctly in the system, with the arrow facing away from the fuel tank.*

In-Tank Filter

To service the in-tank fuel filter, refer to the "Electric Fuel Pump Removal and Installation" procedures in Chapter 4.

FUEL PRESSURE RELEASE

Carbureted

To release the fuel pressure on the carbureted system, remove and replace the fuel tank cap.

Throttle Body Injection (TBI); Electronic Fuel Injection (EFI)

To release the fuel pressure on the TBI system, remove the fuel pump fuse from the fuse panel, start and operate the engine until it stalls, then replace the fuse.

NOTE: *The 1985 V6 TBI engine has a bleeder screw, located on the pressure regulator, to reduce the pressure in the fuel system.*

Diesel Fuel Filter

The diesel fuel filter is mounted on the rear of the intake manifold, and is larger than that on a gasoline engine because diesel fuel generally is "dirtier" (has more suspended particles) than gasoline.

The diesel fuel filter should be changed every 30,000 miles or two years.

REMOVAL AND INSTALLATION

1. With the engine cool, place absorbent rags underneath the fuel line fittings at the filter.

2. Disconnect the fuel lines from the filter.

3. Unbolt the filter from its bracket.

4. Install the new filter. Start the engine and check for leaks. Run the engine for about two

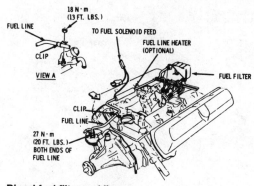

Diesel fuel filter and lines

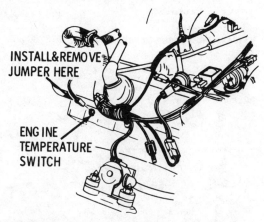

HDCA solenoid connection, diesels

minutes, then shut the engine off for the same amount of time to allow any trapped air in the injection system to blood off.

The GM diesel cars also have a fuel filter inside the fuel tank which is maintenance-free.

NOTE: *If the filter element ever becomes clogged, the engine will stop. This stoppage is usually preceded by a hesitation or sluggish running. General Motors recommends that after changing the diesel fuel filter, the Housing Pressure Cold Advance be activated manually, if the engine temperature is about 125°F. Activating the H.P.C.A. will reduce engine cranking time.*

To activate the H.P.C.A. solenoid, disconnect the two-lead connector at the engine temperature switch and bridge the connector with a jumper. After the engine is running, remove the jumper and reconnect the connector to the engine temperature switch. When the new filter element is installed, start the engine and check for leaks.

Positive Crankcase Ventilation Valve (PCV)

The crankcase ventilation system (PCV) must be operating properly in order to allow evapo-

ration of fuel vapors and water from the crankcase. This system should be checked at every oil change and serviced after one year or 12,000 miles. The PCV valve is replaced after 2 years or 24,000 miles. For 1975 and later cars, the service interval has been upgraded to one year or 15,000 miles, with PCV valve replacement scheduled for two years or 30,000 miles. Normal service entails cleaning the passages of the system hoses with solvent, inspecting them for cracks and breaks, and replacing them as necessary. The PCV valve contains a check valve and, when working properly, this valve will make a rattling sound when the outside case is tapped. If it fails to rattle, then it is probably stuck in a closed position and needs to be replaced.

The PCV system is designed to prevent the emission of gases from the crankcase into the atmosphere. It does this by connecting a crankcase outlet (valve cover, oil filler tube, back of engine) to the intake manifold with a hose. The crankcase gases travel through the hose to the intake manifold where they are returned to the combustion chamber to be burned. If

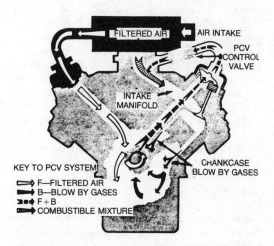

PCV system schematic; V8 engine (others similar)

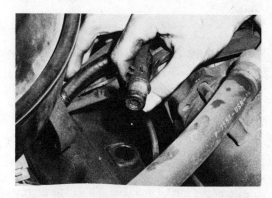

Pulling out the PCV valve from the rocker cover

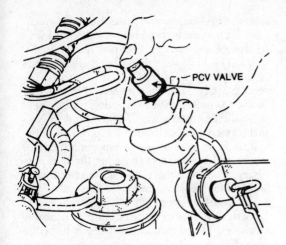

Checking PCV valve for vacuum

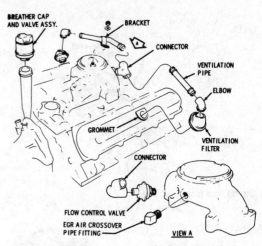

V8 diesel crankcase ventilation system, 1978—80

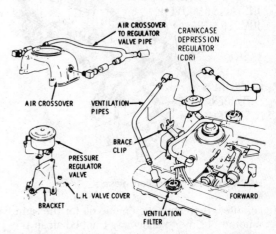

V8 diesel crankcase ventilation system, 1981—84

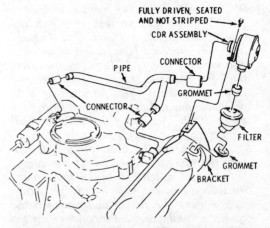

V6 diesel crankcase ventilation system, 1982—84

maintained properly, this system reduces condensation in the crankcase and the resultant formation of harmful acids and oil dilution. A clogged PCV valve will often cause a slow or rough idle due to a richer fuel mixture. A car equipped with a PCV system has air going through a hose to the intake manifold from an outlet at the valve cover, oil filler tube, or rear of the engine. To compensate for this extra air going to the manifold, carburetor specifications require a richer (more gas) mixture at the carburetor. If the PCV valve or hose is clogged, this air doesn't go to the intake manifold and the fuel mixture is too rich. A rough, slow idle results. The valve should be checked before making any carburetor adjustments. Disconnect the valve from the engine or merely clamp the hose shut. If the engine speed decreases less than 50 rpm, the valve is clogged and should be replaced. If the engine speed decreases much more than 50 rpm, then the valve is good. The PCV valve is an inexpensive item and it is suggested that it be replaced. If the new valve doesn't noticeably improve engine idle, the problem might be a restriction in the PCV hose. For further details on PCV valve operation see Chapter 4.

Crankcase Depression Regulator and Flow Control Valve

V8 and V6 Diesel Engines

The Crankcase Depression Regulator (CDR), found on 1981—84 diesels, and the flow control valve, used from 1978—80 are designed to scavenge crankcase vapors in basically the same manner as the PCV valve on gasoline engines. The valves are located either on the left rear corner of the intake manifold (CDR), or on the rear of the intake crossover pipe (flow control valve). On each system there are two ventilation filters, one per valve cover.

The filter assemblies should be cleaned every 15,000 miles by simply prying them carefully from the valve covers (be aware of the grom-

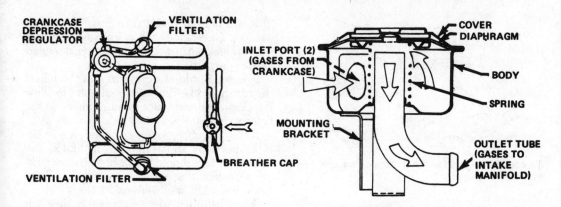

DIESEL CRANKCASE VENTILATION SYSTEM   **CRANKCASE DEPRESSION REGULATOR**

Diesel crankcase ventilation and crankcase depression regulator cutaway, 1980–84

mets underneath), and washing them out in solvent. The ventilation pipes and tubes should also be cleaned. Both the CDR and flow control valves should also be cleaned every 30,000 miles (the cover can be removed from the CDR; the flow control valve can simply be flushed with solvent). Dry each valve, filter, and hose with compressed air before installation.

NOTE: *Do not attempt to test the crankcase controls on these diesels. Instead, clean the valve cover filter assembly and vent pipes and check the vent pipes.*

Replace the breather cap assembly every 30,000 miles. Replace all rubber fittings as required every 15,000 miles.

Evaporative Emissions Control System

This system, standard since 1970, eliminates the release of unburned fuel vapors into the atmosphere. The only periodic maintenance required is an occasional check of the connecting lines of the system for kinks or other damage and deterioration. Lines should only be replaced with quality fuel line or special hose marked "evap." On the 1970–71 vehicles, every 12,000 miles or 12 months, the filter in the bottom of the carbon canister which is located in the engine compartment should be removed and replaced. On 1972–1976 vehicles, this service interval is 24,000 miles or 24 months. For 1977 and later vehicles, the mileage interval has been increased to 30,000 miles, while the time interval remains the same. For further details on the Evaporative Control System please refer to Chapter 4.

FILTER REPLACEMENT

1. Tag and disconnect all hoses connected to the charcoal canister.
2. Loosen the retaining clamps and then lift out the canister.
3. Grasp the filter in the bottom of the canister with your fingers and pull it out. Replace it with a new one.
4. Installation of the remaining components is in the reverse order of removal.

Battery

SPECIFIC GRAVITY (EXCEPT "MAINTENANCE FREE" BATTERIES)

Check the battery fluid level (except in Maintenance Free batteries) at least once a month, more often in hot weather or during extended periods of travel. The electrolyte level should be up to the bottom of the split ring in each cell. All batteries are equipped with an "eye" in the cap of one cell. If the "eye" glows or has an amber color to it, this means that the level is low and only distilled water should be added. Do not add anything else to the battery. If the

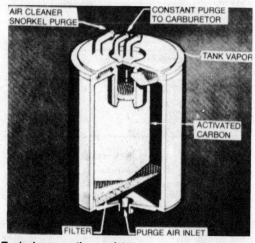

Typical evaporation canister

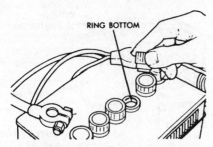

Fill each battery cell to the bottom of the split ring with distilled water

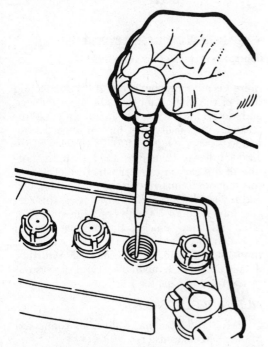

The specific gravity of the battery can be checked with a simple float-type hydrometer

Battery State of Charge at Room Temperature

Specific Gravity Reading	Charged Condition
1.260–1.280	Fully Charged
1.230–1.250	¾ Charged
1.200–1.220	½ Charged
1.170–1.190	¼ Charged
1.140–1.160	Almost no Charge
1.110–1.130	No Charge

"eye" has a dark appearance the battery electrolyte level is high enough. It is also wise to check each cell individually.

At least once a year, check the specific gravity of the battery. It should be between 1.20–1.26. Clean and tighten the clamps and apply a thin coat of petroleum jelly to the terminals.

This will help to retard corrosion. The terminals can be cleaned with a stiff wire brush or with an inexpensive terminal cleaner designed for this purpose.

If water is added during freezing weather, the car should be driven several miles to allow the electrolyte and water to mix. Otherwise the battery could freeze.

If the battery becomes corroded, a solution of baking soda and water will neutralize the corrosion. This should be washed off after making sure that the caps are securely in place. Rinse the solution off with cold water.

Some batteries were equipped with a felt terminal washer. This should be saturated with engine oil approximately every 6,000 miles. This will also help to retard corrosion.

If a "fast" charger is used while the battery is in the car, disconnect the battery before connecting the charger.

NOTE: *Keep flame or sparks away from the battery; it gives off explosive hydrogen gas.*

TESTING THE MAINTENANCE-FREE BATTERY

All later model cars are equipped with maintenance-free batteries, which do not require normal attention as far as fluid level checks are concerned. However, the terminals require periodic cleaning, which should be performed at least once a year.

The sealed-top battery cannot be checked for charge in the normal manner, since there is no provision for access to the electrolyte. To check the condition of the battery:

1. If the indicator eye on top of the battery is dark, the battery has enough fluid. If the eye is light, the electrolyte fluid is too low and the battery must be replaced.

2. If a green dot appears in the middle of the eye, the battery is sufficiently charged. Proceed to Step 4. If no green dot is visible, charge the battery as in Step 3.

3. Charge the battery at this rate:

Charging Rate Amps	Time
75	40 min
50	1 hr
25	2 hr
10	5 hr

CAUTION: *Do not charge the battery for more than 50 amp/hours. If the green dot appears, or if electrolyte squirts out of the vent hole, stop the charge and proceed to Step 4.*

It may be necessary to tip the battery from side to side to get the green dot to appear after charging.

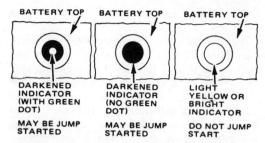

DARKENED INDICATOR (WITH GREEN DOT)	DARKENED INDICATOR (NO GREEN DOT)	LIGHT YELLOW OR BRIGHT INDICATOR
MAY BE JUMP STARTED	MAY BE JUMP STARTED	DO NOT JUMP START

Maintenance-free batteries contain their own built in hydrometer

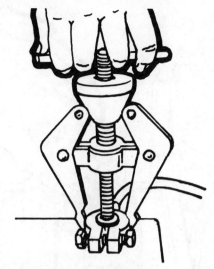

Pullers make clamp removal easier

4. Connect a battery load tester and a voltmeter across the battery terminals (the battery cables should be disconnected from the battery). Apply a 300 amp load to the battery for 15 seconds to remove the surface charge. Remove the load.

5. Wait 15 seconds to allow the battery to recover. Apply the appropriate test load, as specified in the following chart: Apply the load for 15 seconds while reading the voltage. Disconnect the load.

Battery	Test Load
Y85-4	130 amps
R85-5	170 amps
R87-5	210 amps
R89-5	230 amps

6. Check the results against the following chart. If the battery voltage is at or above the specified voltage for the temperature listed, the battery is good. If the voltage falls below what's listed, the battery should be replaced.

Temperature (°F)	Minimum Voltage
70 or above	9.6
60	9.5
50	9.4
40	9.3
30	9.1
20	8.9
10	8.7
0	8.5

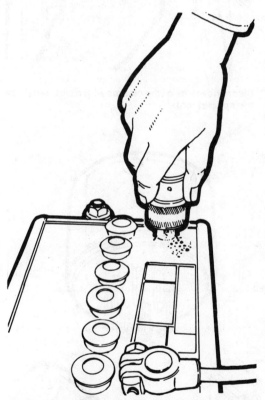

Clean the posts with a wire brush, or a terminal cleaner made for the purpose (shown)

CABLES AND CLAMPS

Once a year, the battery terminals and the cable clamps should be cleaned. Loosen the clamps and remove the cables, negative cable first. On batteries with posts on top, the use of a puller specially made for the purpose is recommended. These are inexpensive, and available in auto parts stores. Side terminal battery cables are secured with a bolt.

Clean the cable clamps and the battery terminal with a wire brush, until all corrosion, grease, etc. is removed and the metal is shiny. It is especially important to clean the inside of the clamp thoroughly, since a small deposit of foreign material or oxidation will prevent a sound electrical connection and inhibit either starting or charging. Special tools are available for cleaning these parts, one type for conventional

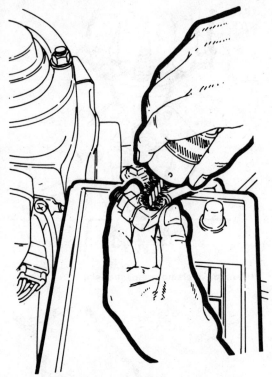

Clean the inside of the clamps with a wire brush, or the special tool

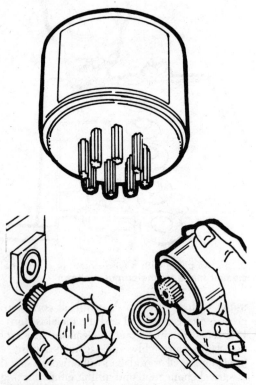

Special tools are also available for cleaning the posts and clamps on side terminal batteries

batteries and another type for side terminal batteries.

Before installing the cables, loosen the battery hold-down clamp or strap, remove the battery and check the battery tray. Clear it of any debris, and check it for soundness. Rust should be wire brushed away, and the metal given a coat of anti-rust paint. Replace the battery and tighten the hold-down clamp or strap securely, but be careful not to overtighten, which will crack the battery case.

After the clamps and terminals are clean, reinstall the cables, negative cable last; do not hammer on the clamps to install. Tighten the clamps securely, but do not distort them. Give the clamps and terminals a thin external coat of grease after installation, to retard corrosion.

Check the cables at the same time that the terminals are cleaned. If the cable insulation is cracked or broken, or if the ends are frayed, the cable should be replaced with a new cable of the same length and gauge.

NOTE: *Keep flame or sparks away from the battery; it gives off explosive hydrogen gas. Battery electrolyte contains sulphuric acid. If you should splash any on your skin or in your eyes, flush the affected area with plenty of clear water; if it lands in your eyes, get medical help immediately.*

REPLACEMENT

When it becomes necessary to replace the battery, select a battery with a rating equal to or greater than the battery originally installed. Deterioration, embrittlement and just plain aging of the battery cables, starter motor, and associated wires makes the battery's job harder in successive years. The slow increase in electrical resistance over time makes it prudent to install a new battery with a greater capacity than the old. Details on battery removal and installation are covered in Chapter 3.

Manifold Heat Control Valve (Heat Riser) 1964–74

This valve is located in the exhaust manifold under the carburetor on in-line engines, and in either the right or left side exhaust manifold on V engines. It can be identified by looking for an external thermostatic spring and weight, and hinge pins that run through the walls of the manifold. Check the valve for free operation every 6,000 miles and, if it binds or is frozen, free it up with a solvent.

NOTE: *Certain early engines had the heat riser built into the manifold and could only be repaired by replacing the entire manifold.*

Typical heat riser valve (6 cyl shown)

Early Fuel Evaporation (EFE) System 1975 and Later

This is a more effective form of heat riser which is vacuum actuated. It is used on all models built in 1975 and later. It heats incoming mixture during the engine warm-up process, utilizing a ribbed heat exchanger of thin metal that is located in the intake manifold. This pre-heating allows the choke to open more rapidly, thus reducing emissions. Problems in this system might be indicated by poor engine operation during warm-up.

This valve should be checked initially at 6 months/7,500 miles, and, thereafter, at 18 months/22,500 mile intervals.

To check, move the valve through its full stroke by hand, making sure that the linkage does not bind and is properly connected. If the valve sticks, free it with a solvent. Also check that all vacuum hoses are properly connected

and free of cracks or breaks. Replace hoses or broken or bent linkage parts as necessary.

Belts

TENSION CHECKING AND ADJUSTMENT

Check the drive belts every 7,500 miles or six months for evidence of wear such as cracking, fraying, and incorrect tension. Determine belt tension at a point halfway between the pulleys by pressing on the belt with moderate thumb pressure. If the distance between the pulleys (measured from the center of each pulley) is 13–16 in., the belt should deflect ½ in. at the halfway point or ¼ in. if the distance is 7–10 in. If the deflection is found to be too much or too little, loosen the mounting bolts and make the adjustments.

NOTE: *The replacement of the inner belt on multi-belted engines may require the removal of the outer belts.*

Before you attempt to adjust any of your engine's belts, you should take an old rag soaked in solvent and clean the mounting bolts of any road grime which has accumulated there. On some of the harder-to-reach bolts, an application of penetrating oil will make them easier to loosen. When you're adjusting belts, especially on late model V8's with air conditioning and power steering, it would be especially helpful to have a variety of socket extensions and universals to get to those hard-to-reach bolts.

NOTE: *When adjusting the air pump belt, if you are using a pry bar, make sure that you pry against the cast iron end cover and not against the aluminum housing. Excessive force on the housing itself will damage it.*

Hoses

Upper and lower radiator hoses and all heater hoses should be checked for deterioration, leaks and loose hose clamps every 15,000 miles.

REMOVAL AND INSTALLATION

1. Drain the radiator as detailed later in this chapter.

2. Loosen the hose clamps at each end of the hose to be removed.

3. Working the hose back and forth, slide it off its connection and then install a new hose if necessary.

4. Position the hose clamps at least ¼ in. from the end of the hose and tighten them.

NOTE: *Always make sure that the hose clamps are beyond the bead and place in the center of the clamping surface before tightening them.*

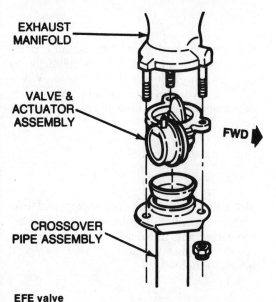

EXHAUST MANIFOLD

VALVE & ACTUATOR ASSEMBLY

FWD ▶

CROSSOVER PIPE ASSEMBLY

EFE valve

HOW TO SPOT WORN V-BELTS

V-Belts are vital to efficient engine operation—they drive the fan, water pump and other accessories. They require little maintenance (occasional tightening) but they will not last forever. Slipping or failure of the V-belt will lead to overheating. If your V-belt looks like any of these, it should be replaced.

This belt has deep cracks, which cause it to flex. Too much flexing leads to heat build-up and premature failure. These cracks can be caused by using the belt on a pulley that is too small. Notched belts are available for small diameter pulleys.

Cracking or weathering

Oil and grease on a belt can cause the belt's rubber compounds to soften and separate from the reinforcing cords that hold the belt together. The belt will first slip, then finally fail altogether.

Softening (grease and oil)

Glazing is caused by a belt that is slipping. A slipping belt can cause a run-down battery, erratic power steering, overheating or poor accessory performance. The more the belt slips, the more glazing will be built up on the surface of the belt. The more the belt is glazed, the more it will slip. If the glazing is light, tighten the belt.

Glazing

The cover of this belt is worn off and is peeling away. The reinforcing cords will begin to wear and the belt will shortly break. When the belt cover wears in spots or has a rough jagged appearance, check the pulley grooves for roughness.

Worn cover

This belt is on the verge of breaking and leaving you stranded. The layers of the belt are separating and the reinforcing cords are exposed. It's just a matter of time before it breaks completely.

Separation

HOW TO SPOT BAD HOSES

Both the upper and lower radiator hoses are called upon to perform difficult jobs in an inhospitable environment. They are subject to nearly 18 psi at under hood temperatures often over 280°F., and must circulate nearly 7500 gallons of coolant an hour—3 good reasons to have good hoses.

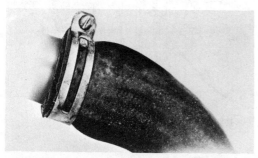

Swollen hose

A good test for any hose is to feel it for soft or spongy spots. Frequently these will appear as swollen areas of the hose. The most likely cause is oil soaking. This hose could burst at any time, when hot or under pressure.

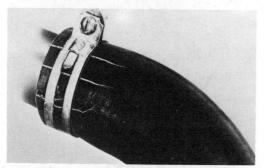

Cracked hose

Cracked hoses can usually be seen but feel the hoses to be sure they have not hardened; a prime cause of cracking. This hose has cracked down to the reinforcing cords and could split at any of the cracks.

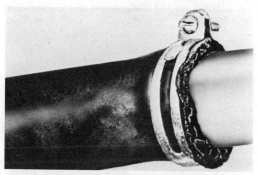

Frayed hose end (due to weak clamp)

Weakened clamps frequently are the cause of hose and cooling system failure. The connection between the pipe and hose has deteriorated enough to allow coolant to escape when the engine is hot.

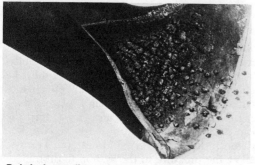

Debris in cooling system

Debris, rust and scale in the cooling system can cause the inside of a hose to weaken. This can usually be felt on the outside of the hose as soft or thinner areas.

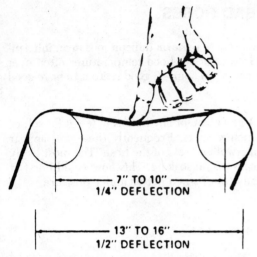

A gauge is recommended, but you can check the belt tension with thumb pressure

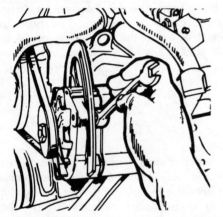

To adjust belt tension or to replace belts, first loosen the component's mounting and adjusting bolts slightly

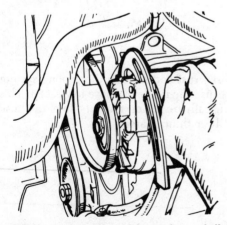

Push the component toward the engine and slip off the belt

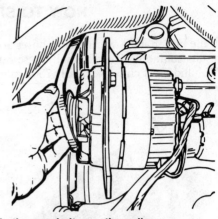

Slip the new belt over the pulley

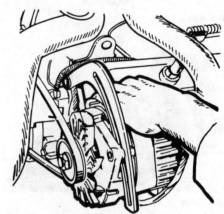

Pull outward on the component and tighten the mounting bolts

Cooling System

Dealing with the cooling system can be a dangerous matter unless the proper precautions are observed. It is best to check the coolant level in the radiator when the engine is cold. On early models this is accomplished by carefully removing the radiator cap and checking that the coolant is within 2 in. of the bottom of the filler neck. On later models, the cooling system has, as one of its components, a coolant recovery tank. If the coolant level is at or near the "FULL COLD" line (engine cold) or the "FULL HOT" line (engine hot), the level is satisfactory. Always be certain that the filler caps on both the radiator and the recovery tank are closed tightly.

In the event that the coolant level must be checked when the engine is hot on engines without a coolant recovery tank, place a thick rag over the radiator cap and slowly turn the cap counterclockwise until it reaches the first detent. Allow all hot steam to escape. This will allow the pressure in the system to drop gradually, preventing an explosion of hot coolant.

On models without a coolant recovery tank, the coolant level should be about 2 in. below the filler neck (engine cold)

If the engine is hot, cover the radiator cap with a rag

Some radiator caps have pressure release levers

When the hissing noise stops, remove the cap the rest of the way.

If the coolant level is found to be low, add a 50/50 mixture of ethylene glycol-based antifreeze and clean water. On older models, coolant must be added through the radiator filler neck. On newer models with the recovery tank, coolant may be added either through the filler neck on the radiator or directly into the recovery tank.

CAUTION: *Never add coolant to a hot engine unless it is running. If it is not running you run the risk of cracking the engine block.*

If the coolant level is chronically low or rusty, refer to Chapter 10 for diagnosis of the problem.

The radiator hoses and clamps and the radiator cap should be checked at the same time as the coolant level. The radiator cap gasket should be checked for any obvious tears, cracks or swelling, or any signs of incorrect seating in the radiator filler neck.

Air Conditioning

Regular maintenance for the air conditioning system includes periodic checks of the drive belt tension. In addition, the system should be operated for at least five minutes every month. This ensures an adequate supply of lubricant to the bearings and also helps to prevent the seals an hoses from drying out. To do this comfortably in the winter months, turn the air conditioning on, the temperature control lever to the WARM or HI position and turn the blower fan to its highest setting. This will engage the compressor, circulating lubricating oils within the system, but prevent the discharge of cold air. The system should also be checked for proper refrigerant charge using the procedure given below.

NOTE: *This book contains simple testing procedures for your vehicles air conditioning system. More comprehensive testing, diagnosis and service procedures may be found in CHILTON'S GUIDE TO AIR CONDITIONING SERVICE AND REPAIR, book part number 7580, available at most book stores and auto parts stores or available directly from Chilton Co.*

SYSTEM CHECKS

CAUTION: *Do not attempt to charge or discharge the refrigerant system unless you are thoroughly familiar with its operation and the hazards involved. The compressed refrigerant used in the air conditioning system expands and evaporates (boils) into the atmosphere at a temperature of −21.7°F (−29.8°C) or less. This will freeze any surface that it comes in contact with, including your eyes. In addition, the refrigerant decomposes into a poisonous gas in the presence of flame.*

1964–77 cars with factory installed air conditioners have a sight glass for checking the refrigerant charge. The sight glass is on top of the VIR (valves-in-receiver) which is located in the front of the engine compartment, usually on the left side of the radiator.

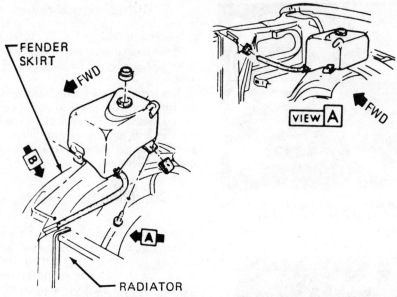

The coolant recovery tank is mounted on the right fender skirt

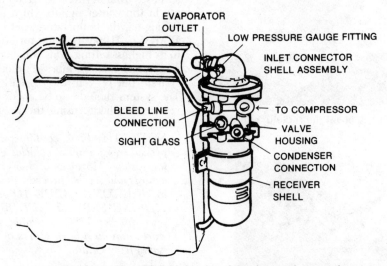

Air conditioning VIR assembly showing sight glass and connections

1978 and later models utilize a different system which does not include a sight glass.

NOTE: *If your car is equipped with an aftermarket air conditioner, the following system checks may not apply. Contact the manufacturer of the unit for instructions on system checks.*

1964–77

This test works best if the outside air temperature is warm (above 70°F).

1. Place the automatic transmission in Park or the manual in Neutral. Set the parking brake.

2. With the help of a friend, run the engine at a fast idle (about 1500 rpm).

3. Set the controls for maximum cold with the blower on high.

4. Look at the sight glass on top of the VIR. If a steady stream of bubbles is present in the sight glass, the system is low on charge. Very likely there is a leak in the system.

5. If no bubbles are present, the system is either fully charged or completely empty. Feel the high and low pressure lines at the compressor, if no appreciable temperature difference is felt, the system is empty or nearly so.

6. If one hose is warm (high pressure) and the other is cold (low pressure), the system may be OK. However, you are probably making these tests because there is something wrong

with the air conditioner, so proceed to the next step.

7. Either disconnect the compressor clutch wire or have a friend in the car turn the fan control on and off to operate the compressor clutch. Watch the sight glass.

8. If bubbles appear when the clutch is disengaged and disappear when it is engaged, the system is properly charged.

9. If the refrigerant takes more than 45 seconds to bubble when the clutch is disengaged, the system is more than likely overcharged. This condition will usually result in poor cooling at low speeds.

NOTE: *If it is determined that the system has a leak, it should be repaired as soon as possible. Leaks may allow moisture to enter the system, causing an expensive rust problem.*

1978 and Later

The air conditioning system on these cars has no sight glass.

1. Run the engine until it reaches normal operating temperature.

2. Open the hood and all doors.

3. Turn the air conditioning on, move the temperature selector to the first detent to the right of COLD (outside air) and then turn the blower on HI.

4. Idle the engine at 1000 rpm.

5. Feel the temperature of the evaporator inlet and the accumulator outlet with the compressor clutch engaged.

6. Both lines should be cold. If the inlet pipe is colder than the outlet pipe, the system is low on charge. Do not attempt to charge the system yourself.

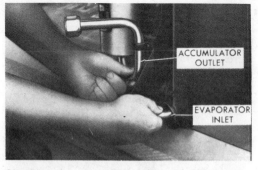

Checking the evaporator inlet and the accumulator outlet line temperatures—1978 and later

Windshield Wipers

For maximum effectiveness and longest element life, the windshield and wiper blades should be kept clean. Dirt, tree sap, road tar and so on will cause streaking, smearing and blade deterioration if left on the glass. It is advisable to wash the windshield carefully with a commercial glass cleaner at least once a month. Wipe off the rubber blades with the wet rag afterwards. Do not attempt to move the wipers back and forth by hand; damage to the motor and drive mechanism will result.

If the blades are found to be cracked, broken or torn, they should be replaced immediately. Replacement intervals will vary with usage, although ozone deterioration usually limits blade life to about one year. If the wiper pattern is smeared or streaked, or if the blade chatters across the glass, the blades should be replaced. It is easiest and most sensible to replace them in pairs.

There are basically three different types of wiper blade refills, which differ in their method of replacement. One type has two release buttons, approximately one-third of the way up from the ends of the blade frame. Pushing the buttons down releases a lock and allows the rubber blade to be removed from the frame. The new blade slides back into the frame and locks in place.

The second type of refill has two metal tabs which are unlocked by squeezing them together. The rubber blade can then be withdrawn from the frame jaws. A new one is installed by inserting it into the front frame jaws and sliding it rearward to engage the remaining frame jaws. There are usually four jaws; be certain when installing that the refill is engaged in all of them. At the end of its travel, the tabs will lock into place on the front jaws of the wiper blade frame.

The third type is a refill made from polycarbonate. The refill has a simple locking device at one end which flexes downward out of the groove into which the jaws of the holder fit, allowing easy release. By sliding the new refill through all the jaws and pushing through the slight resistance when it reaches the end of its travel, the refill will lock into position.

Regardless of the type of refill used, make sure that all the frame jaws are engaged as the refill is pushed into place and locked. The metal blade holder and frame will scratch the glass if allowed to touch it.

Tires

INFLATION

Tires should be checked weekly for proper air pressure. A chart, located either in the glove compartment or on the driver's or passenger's door, gives the recommended inflation pressures. Maximum fuel economy and tire life will result if the pressure is maintained at the highest figure given on the chart. Pressures should

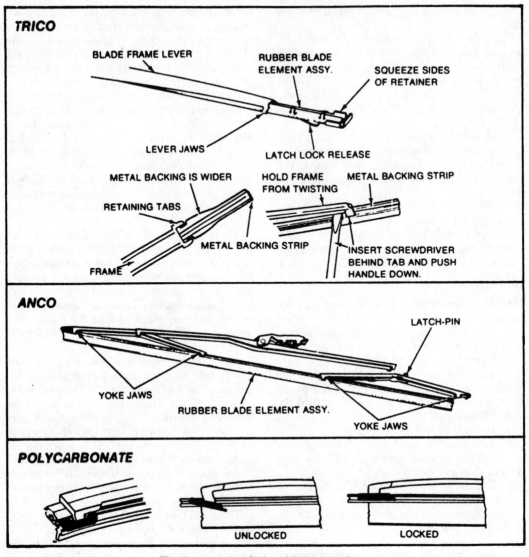

TRICO

BLADE FRAME LEVER

RUBBER BLADE ELEMENT ASSY.

SQUEEZE SIDES OF RETAINER

LEVER JAWS

LATCH LOCK RELEASE

METAL BACKING IS WIDER

HOLD FRAME FROM TWISTING

METAL BACKING STRIP

RETAINING TABS

METAL BACKING STRIP

FRAME

INSERT SCREWDRIVER BEHIND TAB AND PUSH HANDLE DOWN.

ANCO

LATCH-PIN

YOKE JAWS

RUBBER BLADE ELEMENT ASSY.

YOKE JAWS

POLYCARBONATE

UNLOCKED

LOCKED

The three types of wiper blade retention

Tread wear indicators will appear when the tire is worn out

be checked before driving since pressure can increase as much as six pounds per square inch (psi) due to heat buildup. It is a good idea to have your own accurate pressure gauge, because not all gauges on service station air pumps

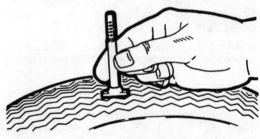

Tread depth can be checked with an inexpensive gauge

A penny works as well as anything for checking tire tread depth; when you can see the top of Lincoln's head, it's time for a new tire

can be trusted. When checking pressures, do not neglect the spare tire. Note that some spare tires require pressures considerably higher than those used in the other tires.

While you are about the task of checking air pressure, inspect the tire treads for cuts, bruises and other damage. Check the air valves to be sure that they are tight. Replace any missing valve caps.

Check the tires for uneven wear that might indicate the need for front end alignment or tire rotation. Tires should be replaced when a tread wear indicator appears as a solid band across the tread.

TIRE DESIGN

When buying new tires, give some thought to the following points, especially if you are considering a switch to larger tires or a different profile series:

1. All four tires must be of the same construction type. This rule cannot be violated,

Radial, bias, and bias-belted tires must not be mixed.

2. The wheels should be the correct width for the tire. Tire dealers have charts of tire and rim compatibility. A mistmatch will cause sloppy handling and rapid tire wear. The tread width should match the rim width (inside bead to inside bead) within an inch. For radial tires, the rim should be 80% or less of the tire (not tread) width.

3. The height (mounted diameter) of the new tires can change speedometer accuracy, engine speed at a given road speed, fuel mileage, acceleration, and ground clearance. Tire manufacturers furnish full measurement specifications.

4. The spare tire should be usable, at least for short distance and low speed operation, with the new tires.

5. There shouldn't be any body interference when loaded, on bumps, or in turns.

TIRE ROTATION

Tire rotation is recommended every 6,000 miles or so, to obtain maximum tire wear. The pattern you use depends on whether or not your car has a usable spare. Radial tires should not be cross-switched (from one side of the car to the other); they last longer if their direction of rotation is not changed. Snow tires sometimes have directional arrows molded into the side of the carcass; the arrow shows the direction of rotation. They will wear very rapidly if the rotation is reversed. Studded tires will lose their studs if their rotational direction is reversed.

NOTE: *Mark the wheel position or direction of rotation on radial tires or studded snow tires before removing them.*

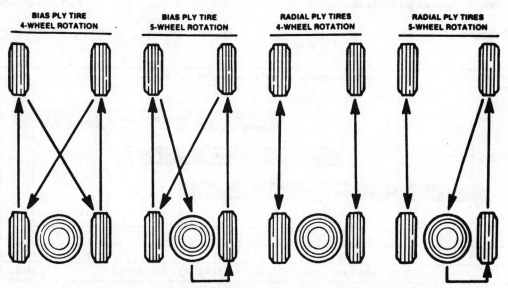

Tire rotation diagrams; note that radials should not be cross-switched

STORAGE

Store the tires at the proper inflation pressure if they are mounted on wheels. Keep them in a cool dry place, laid on their sides. If the tires are stored in the garage or basement, do not let them stand on a concrete floor; set them on strips of wood.

FLUIDS AND LUBRICANTS

Oil and Fuel Recommendations

Oil

The SAE (Society of Automotive Engineers) grade number indicates the viscosity of the engine oil and thus its ability to lubricate at a given temperature. The lower the SAE grade number, the lighter the oil; the lower the viscosity, the easier it is to crank the engine in cold weather.

Oil viscosities should be chosen from those oils recommended for the lowest anticipated temperatures during the oil change interval.

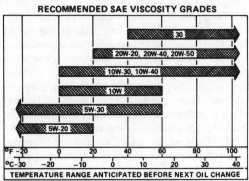

RECOMMENDED SAE VISCOSITY GRADES

NOTICE: Do not use SAE 5W-20 oils for continuous high-speed driving.

Oil viscosity chart

Multi-viscosity oils (10W-30, 20W-50 etc.) offer the important advantage of being adaptable to temperature extremes. They allow easy starting at low temperatures, yet they give good protection at high speeds and engine temperatures. This is a decided advantage in changeable climates or in long distance touring.

The API (American Petroleum Institute) designation indicates the classification of engine oil used under certain given operating conditions. Only oils designated for use "Service SE" should be used. Oils of the SE type perform a variety of functions inside the engine in addition to their basic function as a lubricant. Through a balanced system of metallic detergents and polymeric dispersants, the oil prevents the formation of high and low temperature deposits and also keeps sludge and particles of dirt in suspension. Acids, particularly sulfuric acid, as well as other byproducts of combustion, are neutralized. Both the SAE grade number and the API designation can be found on top of the oil can.

For recommended oil viscosities, refer to the chart.

NOTE: *As of late 1980, the API has come out with a new designation of motor oil, SF. Oils designated for use "Service SF" are equally acceptable in your car.*

CAUTION: *Non-detergent or straight mineral oils should not be used in your car.*

Synthetic Oil

There are excellent synthetic and fuel-efficient oils available that, under the right circumstances, can help provide better fuel mileage and better engine protection. However, these advantages come at a price, which can be three or four times the price per quart of conventional motor oils.

Before pouring any synthetic oils into your

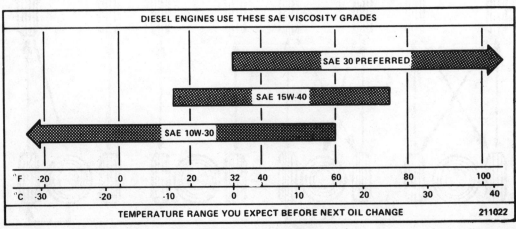

DIESEL ENGINES USE THESE SAE VISCOSITY GRADES

SAE 30 PREFERRED

SAE 15W-40

SAE 10W-30

TEMPERATURE RANGE YOU EXPECT BEFORE NEXT OIL CHANGE

211022

Diesel oil viscosity chart

car's engine, you should consider the condition of the engine and the type of driving you do. Also, check the car's warranty conditions regarding the use of synthetics.

Generally, it is best to avoid the use of synthetic oil in both brand new and older, high mileage engines. New engines require a proper break-in, and the synthetics are so "slippery" that they can prevent this; most manufacturers recommend that you wait at least 5,000 miles before switching to a synthetic oil. Conversely, older engines are looser and tend to "use" more oil; synthetics will slip past worn parts more readily than regular oil, and will be used up faster. If your car already leaks and/or "uses" oil (due to worn parts and bad seals or gaskets), it will leak and use more with a slippery synthetic inside.

Consider your type of driving. If most of your accumulated mileage is on the highway at higher, steadier speeds, a synthetic oil will reduce friction and probably help deliver better fuel mileage. Under such ideal highway conditions, the oil change interval can be extended, as long as the oil filter will operate effectively for the extended life of the oil. If the filter can't do its job for this extended period, dirt and sludge will build up in your engine's crankcase, sump, oil pump and lines, no matter what type of oil is used. If using synthetic oil in this manner, you should continue to change the oil filter at the recommended intervals.

Cars used under harder, stop-and-go, short hop circumstances should always be serviced more frequently, and for these cars synthetic oil may not be a wise investment. Because of the necessary shorter change interval needed for this type of driving, you cannot take advantage of the long recommended change interval of most synthetic oils.

Finally, most synthetic oils are not compatible with conventional oils and cannot be added to them. This means you should always carry a couple of quarts of synthetic oil with you while on a long trip, as not all service stations carry this oil.

Fuel

GASOLINE

All 1964–74 models are designed to run on either regular or premium grade fuel depending upon the particular engine's compression ratio. All engines having a compression ratio of 9.0:1 or less can run efficiently on regular gasoline, while any engines with a higher ratio must use premium fuel. All 1975 and later models have been designed to run on unleaded fuel. The use of a leaded fuel in a car requiring unleaded fuel will plug the catalytic converter and

render it inoperative. It will also increase exhaust backpressure to the point where engine output will be severely reduced. In all cases, the minimum octane rating of the unleaded fuel being used must be at least 91 RON (87 CLC). All unleaded fuels sold in the U.S. are required to meet this minimum rating.

The use of a fuel too low in octane (a measurement of anti-knock quality) will result in spark knock. Since many factors such as altitude, terrain, air temperature and humidity affect operating efficiency, knocking may result even though the recommended fuel is being used. If persistent knocking occurs, it may be necessary to switch to a higher grade of fuel. Continuous or heavy knocking may result in engine damage.

NOTE: *Your engine's fuel requirement can change with time, mainly due to carbon buildup, which will in turn change the compression ratio. If your engine pings, knocks, or diesels (runs with the ignition off) switch to a higher grade of fuel. Sometimes just changing brands will cure the problem. If it becomes necessary to retard the timing from the specifications, don't change it more than a few degrees. Retarded timing will reduce power output and fuel mileage, in addition to making the engine run hotter.*

DIESEL FUEL

Fuel makers produce two grades of diesel fuel, No. 1 and No. 2, for use in automotive diesel engines. Generally speaking, No. 2 fuel is recommended over No. 1 for driving in temperatures above 20°F. In fact, in many areas, No. 2 diesel is the only fuel available. By comparison, No. 2 diesel fuel is less volatile than No. 1 fuel, and gives better fuel economy. No 2 fuel is also a better injection pump lubricant.

Two important characteristics of diesel fuel are its cetane number and its viscosity.

The cetane number of a diesel fuel refers to the ease with which a diesel fuel ignites. High cetane numbers mean that the fuel will ignite with relative ease or that it ignites well at low temperatures. Naturally, the lower the cetane number, the higher the temperature must be to ignite the fuel. Most commercial fuels have cetane numbers that range from 35 to 65. No. 1 diesel fuel generally has a higher cetane rating than No. 2 fuel.

Viscosity is the ability of a liquid, in this case diesel fuel, to flow. Using straight No. 2 diesel fuel below 20°F can cause problems, because this fuel tends to become cloudy, meaning wax crystals begin forming in the fuel (20°F is often called the "cloud point" for No. 2 fuel). In extreme cold weather, No. 2 fuel can stop flowing altogether. In either case, fuel flow is restricted, which can result in a "no start" condition or poor engine performance. Fuel manufacturers often "winterize" No. 2 diesel fuel by using various fuel additives and blends (No. 1 diesel fuel, kerosene, etc.) to lower its winter-time viscosity. Generally speaking, though, No. 1 diesel fuel is more satisfactory in extremely cold weather.

NOTE: *No. 1 and No. 2 diesel fuels will mix and burn with no ill effects, although the engine manufacturer will undoubtedly recommend one or the other. Consult the owner's manual for information.*

Depending on local climate, most fuel manufacturers make winterized No. 2 fuel available seasonally.

Many automobile manufacturers (Oldsmobile, for example) publish pamphlets giving the locations of diesel fuel stations nationwide. Contact the local dealer for information.

NOTE: *Do not substitute home heating oil for automotive diesel fuel.*

While in some cases, home heating oil refinement levels equal those of diesel fuel, many times they are far below diesel engine requirements. The result of using "dirty" home heating oil will be a clogged fuel system, in which case the entire system may have to be dismantled and cleaned.

One more word on diesel fuels. Don't thin diesel fuel with gasoline in cold weather. The lighter gasoline, which is more explosive, will cause rough running at the very least, and may cause extensive damage if enough is used.

Engine

OIL LEVEL CHECK

Every time you stop for fuel, check the engine oil as follows:

1. Make sure the car is parked on level ground.

2. When checking the oil level it is best for the engine to be at normal operating temperature, although checking the oil immediately after stopping will lead to a false reading. Wait a few minutes after turning off the engine to allow the oil to drain back into the crankcase.

3. Open the hood and locate the dipstick which will be on either the right or left side depending upon your particular engine. Pull the dipstick from its tube, wipe it clean and then reinsert it.

4. Pull the dipstick out again and, holding it horizontally, read the oil level. The oil should be between the "FULL" and "ADD" marks on the dipstick. If the oil is below the "ADD" mark, add oil of the proper viscosity through the capped opening in the top of the cylinder head cover. See the "Oil and Fuel Recommenda-

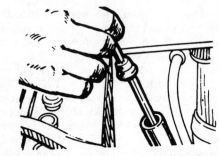

The oil level is checked with the dipstick

The oil level should be between the 'ADD' and 'FULL' marks on the dipstick

tions" chart in this chapter for the proper viscosity and rating of oil to use.

5. Replace the dipstick and check the oil level again after adding any oil. Be careful not to over fill the crankcase. Approximately one quart of oil will raise the level from the "ADD" mark to the "FULL" mark. Excess oil will generally be consumed at an accelerated rate.

OIL AND FILTER CHANGE

The oil should be changed every four months or 6,000 miles on all 1964–74 models. On 1975–78 models, the interval is six months or 7,500 miles. 1979 and later models increased the time interval to 12 months while keeping the mileage (7,500) the same (Diesel interval is 5,000 miles). Make sure that you change the oil based on whichever interval comes first.

The oil drain plug is located on the bottom of the oil pan (bottom of the engine, underneath the car). The oil filter is located on the right side of the inline six cylinder engine and on the left side of all other engines.

The mileage figures given are the Chevrolet recommended intervals assuming normal driving and conditions. If your car is used under dusty, polluted or off-road conditions, change the oil and filter more often than specified. The same goes for cars driven in stop-and-go traffic or only for short distances at a time. Always drain the engine oil after the engine has been running long enough to bring it up to normal operating temperature. Hot oil will flow easier and more contaminants will be removed along with the oil than if it were drained cold. To change the oil and filter:

1. Run the engine until it reaches normal operating temperature.

2. Jack up the front of the car and support it on safety stands.

3. Slide a drain pan of at least 6 quarts capacity under the oil pan.

4. Loosen the drain plug. Turn the plug out by hand. By keeping an inward pressure on the plug as you unscrew it, oil won't escape past the threads and you can remove it without being burned by hot oil.

5. Allow the oil to drain completely and then install the drain plug. Don't overtighten the plug, or you'll be buying a new pan or a trick replacement plug for stripped threads.

6. Using a strap wrench, remove the oil filter. Keep in mind that it's holding about one quart of dirty, hot oil.

7. Empty the old filter into the drain pan and dispose of the filter.

8. Using a clean rag, wipe off the filter adapter on the engine block. Be sure that the rag doesn't leave any lint which could clog an oil passage.

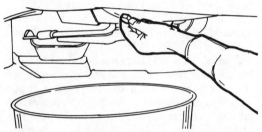

By keeping an inward pressure on the plug as you unscrew it, oil won't escape past the threads

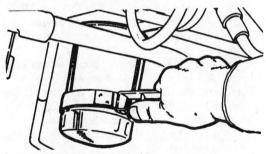

Remove the oil filter with a strap wrench

Coat the new oil filter gasket with clean oil

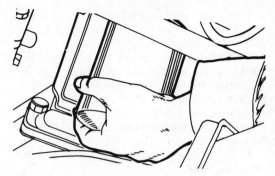

Install the new oil filter by hand

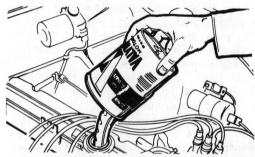

Add oil through the capped opening in the cylinder head cover

9. Coat the rubber gasket on the filter with fresh oil. Spin it onto the engine *by hand;* when the gasket touches the adapter surface, give it another ½–¾ turn. No more, or you'll squash the gasket and it will leak.

10. Refill the engine with the correct amount of fresh oil. See the "Capacities" chart.

11. Check the oil level on the dipstick. It is normal for the level to be a bit above the full mark. Start the engine and allow it to idle for a few minutes.

CAUTION: *Do not run the engine above idle speed until it has built up oil pressure, indicated when the oil light goes out.*

12. Shut off the engine, allow the oil to drain for a minute, and check the oil level. Check around the filter and drain plug for any leaks, and correct as necessary.

Manual Transmission

FLUID RECOMMENDATIONS AND LEVEL CHECK

The oil in the manual transmission should be checked at least every 6,000 miles for 1964–74 models or every 7,500 miles for all 1975–81 models.

1. With the car parked on a level surface, remove the filler plug from the side of the transmission housing.

2. If the lubricant begins to trickle out of the hole, there is enough and you need not go any

further. Otherwise, carefully insert your finger (watch out for sharp threads) and check to see if the oil is up to the edge of the hole.

3. If not, add oil through the hole until the level is at the edge of the hole. Most gear lubricants come in a plastic squeeze bottle with a nozzle; making additions simple. You can also use a common kitchen baster. Use only standard GL-5 hypoid-type gear oil—SAE 80W or SAE 80W/90.

4. Replace the filler plug, run the engine and check for leaks.

DRAIN AND REFILL

There is no recommended interval for the manual transmission but it is always a good idea to change the fluid if you have purchased the car used or if it has been driven in water high enough to reach the axles.

1. The oil must be hot before it is drained. Drive the car until the engine reaches normal operating temperature.

2. Remove the filler plug to provide a vent.

3. Place a large container underneath the transmission and then remove the drain plug.

4. Allow the oil to drain completely. Clean off the drain plug and replace it; tighten it until it is just snug.

5. Fill the transmission with the proper lubricant as detailed earlier in this chapter. Refer to the "Capacities" chart for the correct amount of lubricant.

6. When the oil level is up to the edge of the filler hole, replace the filler plug. Drive the car for a few minutes, stop, and check for any leaks.

Automatic Transmission

FLUID RECOMMENDATIONS AND LEVEL CHECK

Check the automatic transmission fluid level at least every 6,000 miles (7,500 miles for 1975 and later models). The dipstick can be found in the rear of the engine compartment. The fluid level should be checked only when the transmission is hot (normal operating temperature). The transmission is considered hot after about 20 miles of highway driving.

1. Park the car on a level surface with the engine idling. Shift the transmission into Neutral and set the parking brake.

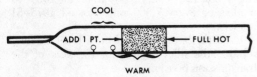

Automatic transmission dipstick marks; the proper level is within the shaded area

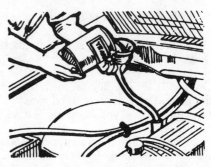

Add automatic transmission fluid through the dipstick tube

2. Remove the dipstick, wipe it clean and then reinsert it firmly. Be sure that it has been pushed all the way in. Remove the dipstick again and check the fluid level while holding it horizontally. With the engine running, the fluid level should be between the second notch and the "FULL HOT" line. If the fluid must be checked when it is cool, the level should be between the first and second notches.

3. If the fluid level is below the second notch (engine hot) or the first notch (engine cold), add DEXRON® (1964–75) or DEXRON® II (1976 and later) automatic transmission fluid through the dipstick tube. This is easily done with the aid of a funnel. Check the level often as you are filling the transmission. Be extremely careful not to overfill it. Overfilling will cause slippage, seal damage and overheating. Approximately one pint of ATF will raise the fluid level from one notch/line to the other.

NOTE: *Always use DEXRON® or DEXRON® II AFT. The use of AFT Type F or any other fluid will cause severe damage to the transmission.*

The fluid on the dipstick should always be a bright red color. If it is discolored (brown or black), or smells burnt, serious transmission troubles, probably due to overheating, should be suspected. The transmission should be inspected by a qualified technician to locate the cause of the burnt fluid.

DRAIN AND REFILL PAN AND FILTER SERVICE

The procedures for automatic transmission fluid drain and refill, filter change and band adjustment are all detailed in Chapter 6.

Rear Axle

FLUID RECOMMENDATIONS AND LEVEL CHECK

The oil in the differential should be checked at least every 6,000 miles (7,500 miles for 1975 and later models).

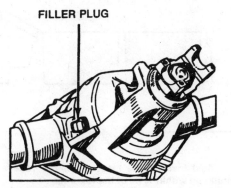

FILLER PLUG

Remove the filler plug to check the lubricant level in the rear axle

1. With the car on a level surface, remove the filler plug from the front side of the differential.

2. If the oil begins to trickle out of the hole, there is enough. Otherwise, carefully insert your finger (watch out for sharp threads) into the hole and check that the oil is up to the bottom edge of the filler hole.

3. If not, add oil through the hole until the level is at the edge of the hole. Most gear oils come in a plastic squeeze bottle with a nozzle; making additions is simple. You can also use a common kitchen baster. Use only standard GL-5 hypoid-type gear oil—SAE 80W or SAE 80W/90.

NOTE: *On all models equipped with the positraction/limited slip rear axle, GM recommends that you use only the special lubricant which is available at your local Chevrolet parts department.*

DRAIN AND REFILL

There is no recommended change interval for the rear axle but it is always a good idea to change the fluid if you have purchased the car used or if it has been driven in water high enough to reach the axle.

1. Park the car on a level surface and set the parking brake.

2. Remove the filler plug.

3. Place a large container underneath the rear axle.

4. Unscrew the retaining bolts and remove the rear cover. This will allow the lubricant to drain out into the container.

5. Install the rear cover using a new gasket and sealant. Tighten the retaining bolts in a crosswise pattern.

6. Refill with the proper grade and quantity of lubricant as detailed earlier in this chapter. Replace the filler plug, run the car and then check for any leaks.

Cooling System

FLUID RECOMMENDATION

When adding or changing the fluid in the system, create a 50/50 mixture of high quality ethylene glycol antifreeze and water.

LEVEL CHECK

The fluid level may be checked by observing the fluid level marks of the recovery tank. The level should be below the "ADD" mark when the system is cold. At normal operating temperatures, the level should be between the "ADD" and the "FULL" marks. Only add coolant to bring the level to the "FULL" mark.

CAUTION: *Should it be necessary to remove the radiator cap, make sure that the*

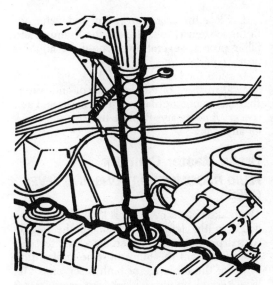

Coolant protection can be checked with a simple, float-type tester

The system should be pressure tested at least once a year

system has had time to cool, reducing the internal pressure.

DRAIN, FLUSH AND REFILL

The cooling system should be drained, thoroughly flushed and refilled at least every 30,000 miles or 24 months. These operations should be done with the engine cold.

1. Remove the radiator and recovery tank caps. Run the engine until the upper radiator hose gets hot. this means that the thermostat is open and the coolant is flowing through the system.

2. Turn the engine "OFF" and place a large container under the radiator. Open the drain valve at the bottom of the radiator. Open the block drain plugs to speed up the draining process.

3. Close the drain valves and add water until the system is full. Repeat the draining and filling process several times, until the liquid is nearly colorless.

4. After the last draining, fill the system with a 50/50 mixture of ethylene glycol and water. Run the engine until the system is hot and add coolant, if necessary. Replace the caps and check for any leaks.

Brake Master Cylinder

FLUID RECOMMENDATIONS AND LEVEL CHECK

The brake master cylinder is located under the hood, in the left rear section of the engine compartment. It is divided into two sections (reservoirs) and the fluid must be kept within ¼ in. of the top edge of both reservoirs. The level should be checked at least every 6,000 miles (7,500 miles for 1975 and later models).

NOTE: *Any sudden decrease in the level of fluid indicates a possible leak in the system and should be checked out immediately.*

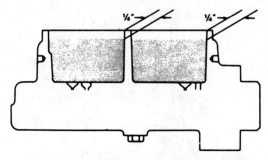

The fluid level in the master cylinder reservoir should be within ¼ in. of the top edge

To check the fluid level, simply pry off the retaining bar and then lift off the top cover of the master cylinder. When making additions of brake fluid, use only fresh, uncontaminated brake fluid which meets or exceeds DOT 3 standards. Be careful not to spill any brake fluid on painted surfaces, as it eats paint. Do not allow the brake fluid container or the master cylinder reservoir to remain open any longer than necessary; brake fluid absorbs moisture from the air, reducing its effectiveness and causing corrosion in the lines.

NOTE: *The reservoir cover on some later models (1978 and later) may be without a retaining bail. If so, simply pry the cover off with your fingers.*

Power Steering Pump

FLUID RECOMMENDATIONS AND LEVEL CHECKS

Power steering fluid level should be checked at least once every 6,000 miles (7,500 miles for 1975 and later models). To prevent possible overfilling, check the fluid level only when the fluid has warmed to operating temperatures and the wheels are turned straight ahead. If the level is low, fill the pump reservoir with DEXRON®

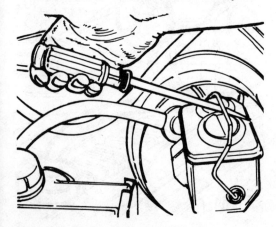

Pry the retaining bail from the master cylinder reservoir cap to check the fluid level

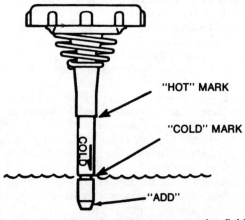

"HOT" MARK

"COLD" MARK

"ADD"

Use the dipstick to check the power steering fluid

Automatic Transmission Fluid on 1976 and earlier cars. 1977 and later cars require GM power steering fluid, until the fluid level measures "full" on the reservoir dipstick. Low fluid level usually produces a moaning sound as the wheels are turned (especially when standing still or parking) and increases steering wheel effort.

Chassis Greasing

Chassis greasing can be performed with a pressurized grease gun or it can be performed at home by using a hand-operated grease gun. Wipe the grease fittings clean before greasing in order to prevent the possibility of forcing any dirt into the component.

Body Lubrication

Transaxle Shift Linkage

Lubricate the manual transaxle shift linkage contact points with the EP grease used for chassis greasing, which should meet G.M. specification 6031M. The automatic transaxle linkage should be lubricated with clean engine oil.

Hood Latch and Hinges

Clean the latch surfaces and apply clean engine oil to the latch pilot bolts and the spring anchor. Use the engine oil to lubricate the hood hinges as well. Use a chassis grease to lubricate all the pivot points in the latch release mechanism.

Door Hinges

The gas tank filler door, car door, and rear hatch or trunk lid hinges should be wiped clean and lubricated with clean engine oil. Silicone spray also works well on these parts, but must be applied more often. Use engine oil to lubricate the trunk or hatch lock mechanism and the lock bolt and striker. The door lock cylinders can be lubricated easily with a shot of silicone spary or

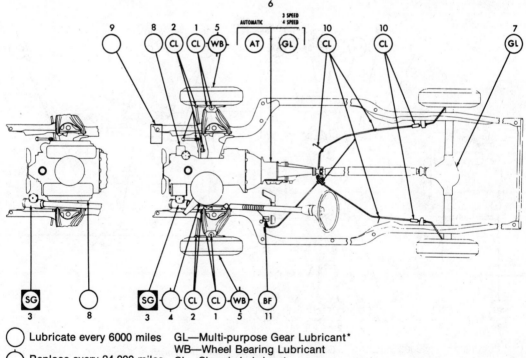

Lubricate every 6000 miles

Replace every 24,000 miles

Check for grease leakage every 36,000 miles

*. Refill Positraction Rear Axle with Special Positraction Rear Axle Lubricant Only.

GL—Multi-purpose Gear Lubricant*
WB—Wheel Bearing Lubricant
CL—Chassis Lubricant

AT —DEXRON® Automatic Transmission Fluid
BF —Hydraulic Brake Fluid
SG —Steering Gear Lubricant

1. Front suspension
2. Steering linkage
3. Steering gear
4. Air cleaner
5. Front wheel bearings
6. Transmission
7. Rear axle
8. Oil filter
9. Battery
10. Parking brake
11. Brake master cylinder

Chassis lubrication—1972–74

Recommended Lubricants

Item	Lubricant
Engine Oil (Gasoline)	API "SE", "SF/CC" or "SF/CD"
Engine Oil (Diesel)	API "SF/CC", "SF/CD" or "SE/CC"
Manual Transmission	SAE 80W GL-5 or SAE 80W/90 GL-5
Automatic Transmission	DEXRON® or DEXRON® II ATF
Rear Axle–Standard	SAE 80W GL-5 or SAE 80W/90 GL-5
Positraction/Limited Slip	GM Part #1052271 or 1052272
Power Steering Reservoir	DEXRON® ATF—1964–76 Power Steering Fluid—1977 and later
Brake Fluid	DOT 3
Antifreeze	Ethylene Glycol
Front Wheel Bearings	GM Wheel Bearing Grease
Clutch Linkage	Engine Oil
Hood and Door Hinges	Engine Oil
Chassis Lubrication	NLGI #1 or NLGI #2
Lock Cylinders	WD-40 or Powdered Graphite

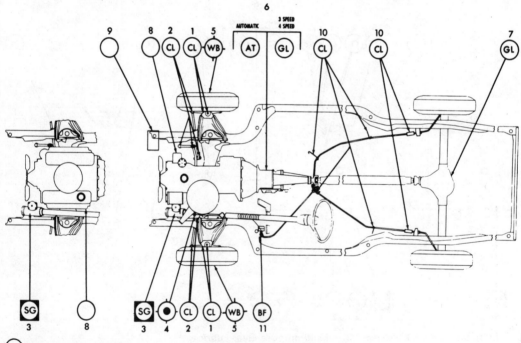

Lubricate every 6000 miles

Replace every 12,000 miles

Replace every 24,000 miles

Check for grease leakage every 36,000 miles

GL —Multi-purpose Gear Lubricant*
WB—Wheel Bearing Lubricant
CL —Chassis Lubricant

AT —DEXRON® Automatic Transmission Fluid
BF —Hydraulic Brake Fluid
SG—Steering Gear Lubricant

*Refill Positraction Rear Axle with Special Positraction Rear Axle Lubricant Only.

1. Front suspension
2. Steering linkage
3. Steering gear
4. Air cleaner
5. Front wheel bearings
6. Transmission
*7. Rear axle
8. Oil filter
9. Battery
10. Parking brake
11. Brake master cylinder

Chassis lubrication—1975 and later

Capacities

Year	Engine No. Cyl Displacement (cu in.)	Engine Crankcase Add 1 qt for New Filter	Transmission Pts to Refill After Draining			Drive Axle (pts)	Gasoline Tank (gals)	Cooling System (qts)	
			Manual					With Heater	With A/C
			3-Speed	4-Speed	Automatic●				
1964	6-194 6-230	4	2	—	15.2①	3.5	20	11.5	12
	8-283	4	2	2.5	15.2①	3.5	20	17	18
	8-327	4	2	2.5	15.2①	3.5	20	16②	18②
1965	6-194 6-230	4	2	—	15.2①	4	20	12	12
	8-283	4	2	2.5	15.2①	4	20	17	18
	8-327	4	2	2.5	15.2①	4	20	16②	18②
1966	6-194	4	2	—	6③	3.5	20	12	12
	6-230	4	2	2.5	6③	3.5	20	12	12
	8-283	4	2	2.5	6③	3.5	20	16	18
	8-327	4	3④	3	6.5③	3.5⑤	20	15	17⑥
	8-396	4	3④	3	6.5③	3.5⑤	20	23	23
1967	6-230	4	3④	3④	6③	3.5	20	14	14
	6-250	4	3④	3④	6③	3.5	20	13	14
	8-283	4	3④	3④	6③	3.5	20	16	17
	8-327	4	3④	3④	6③	3.5	20	15	18
	8-396	4	3④	3④	6③	3.5	20	23	23
1968	6-230	4	3④	3④	6③	3.5	20	12	12
	6-250	4	3④	3④	6③	3.5	20	12	12
	8-307	4	3④	3④	6③	3.5	20	17	17
	8-327	4	2.5	3④	6③	3.5	20	16	16
	8-350	4	2.5	3④	6③	3.5	20	16	16
	8-396	4	2.5	3④	6⑦③	3.5	20	23	23
1969	6-230	4	3④	—	6⑧③	3.5⑤	20	13	13
	6-250	4	3④	—	6⑧③	3.5⑤	20	13	13
	8-307	4	3④	3④	6⑧③	3.5⑤	20	17	18
	8-350	4	3④	3④	6⑧③	3.5⑤	20	16	17
	8-396	4	3④	3④	8③	3.5⑤	20	23	24
1970	6-230	4	3	—	6⑧③	3.75⑨	20⑩	12	13
	6-250	4	3	—	6⑧③	3.75⑨	20⑩	12	13
	8-307	4	3	—	6⑧③	3.75⑨	20⑩	15	16
	8-350	4	3	3	6.5⑧⑪③	3.75⑨	20⑩	16	16
	8-400	4	3	3	8③	3.75⑨	20⑩	16	16
	8-396	4	3	3	8③	3.75⑨	20⑩	23	24
	8-402	4	3	3	8③	3.75⑨	20⑩	23	24
	8-454	4	3	3	8③	3.75⑨	20⑩	22	23
1971	6-250	4	3	—	6③	3.75	19⑩	12	—
	8-307	4	3	—	6⑧③	3.75	19⑩	15	16
	8-350	4	3	3	6.5⑧③	3.75	19⑩	16	16

Capacities (cont.)

Year	Engine No. Cyl Displacement (cu in.)	Engine Crankcase Add 1 qt for New Filter	Manual 3-Speed	Manual 4-Speed	Automatic●	Drive Axle (pts)	Gasoline Tank (gals)	Cooling System With Heater (qts)	Cooling System With A/C (qts)
	8-402	4	3	3	8③	3.75	19⑩	23	23
	8-454	4	—	3	8③	3.75	19⑩	22	23
1972	6-250	4	3	—	6⑧③	4.25	19⑩	12	—
	8-307	4	3	—	6⑧③	4.25	19⑩	15	16
	8-350	4	3	3	6.5⑧③	4.25	19⑩	16	16
	8-402	4	—	3	8③	4.25⑫	19⑩	24	24
	8-454	4	—	3	8③	4.25⑫	19⑩	23	24
1973	6-250	4	3	—	6⑧③	4.25	22	12.5	—
	8-307	4	3	—	5③	4.25	22	16	17
	8-350	4	3	3	5③	4.25	22	16	17
	8-454	4	—	3	8③	4.25⑫	22	23	24
1974	6-250	4	3	—	8③	4.25	22	12.5	—
	8-350	4	3	3	8③	4.25	22	16	17
	8-400	4	—	—	8③	4.25⑫	22	16	17
	8-454	4	—	3	9③	4.9	22	23	24
1975	6-250	4	3	—	8③	4.25	22	14	16
	8-350	4	3	3	8③	4.25	22	17	18
	8-400	4	—	—	8③	4.25⑫	22	17⑬	18
	8-454	4	—	3	9③	4.9	22	23	23
1976–77	6-250	4	3	—	8③	4.25	22	15	17
	8-305	4	3	—	8③	4.25	22	17	18
	8-350	4	—	3	8③	4.25	22	17	18
	8-400	4	—	—	8③	4.25	22	17	18
1978	V6-200	4	3	—	6③	3.5	⑯	16.8	18.8
	V6-231	4⑮	3	3	6③	3.5	⑯	14.7	14.7
	6-250	4	3	—	6③	3.5	⑯	14.6	14.6
	8-305	4	—	3	6③	3.5⑭	⑯	19.2	19.2
	8-350	4	—	3	6③	3.5⑭	⑯	19.2	19.2
1979	V6-200	4	3	—	8③	3.25	18	18.5	18.5
	V6-231	4⑮	3	—	8③	3.25	18	15.5	15.5
	8-267	4	—	3.4	8③	3.25	18	19.2	19.2
	8-305	4	—	3.4	8③	3.5⑭	18	19.2	19.2
	8-350	4	—	3.4	8③	3.5⑭	18	19.2	19.2
1980–81	V6-229	4⑮	3	—	8③⑰	3.25	18	18.5	18.5
	V6-231	4⑮	3	—	8③⑰	3.25	18	15.5	15.5
	8-267	4	—	—	8③⑱	3.25	18	21	21
	8-305	4	—	3.4	8③⑱	3.5⑭	18	19	19
1982–84	V6-229	4⑮	—	—	7⑲	3.5⑭	⑬⑳	12㉑	13㉑
	V6-231	4⑮	—	—	7⑲	3.5⑭	⑬⑳	12㉑	13㉑

Capacities (cont.)

Year	Engine No. Cyl Displacement (cu in.)	Engine Crankcase Add 1 qt for New Filter	Transmission Pts to Refill After Draining			Drive Axle (pts)	Gasoline Tank (gals)	Cooling System (qts)	
			Manual					With Heater	With A/C
			3-Speed	4-Speed	Automatic●				
	8-267	4	—	—	7 [19]	3.5 [14]	[13][20]	16.75	16.75 [22]
	8-305	4	—	—	7 [19]	3.5 [14]	[13][20]	15.5	15.5 [22]
	8-350	4	—	—	7 [19]	3.5 [14]	[13][20]	19.2	19.2
	V6-263 Diesel	6	—	—	7 [19]	3.5 [14]	[20]	13.4	14.4
	V8-350 Diesel	6	—	—	7 [19]	3.5 [14]	[20]	18.3	19.3
1985–86	V6-262	4 [15]	—	—	7 [23]	3.5 [14]	17.6	12	12
	V8-305	4 [15]	—	—	7 [23]	3.5 [14]	18.1	16.3	16.3

●Specifications do not include torque converter
[1] Figure given is for dry refill
[2] 18 qts—300 hp eng., 19 qts—350 hp eng.
[3] Figure given is for drain and refill
[4] 3.5 pts with heavy duty trans.
[5] 4 pts with 8.875 in. ring gear
[6] 16 qts—350 hp eng.
[7] 8 pts—THM 400
[8] 5 pts—THM 350
[9] 4.25 pts with 8.875 in. ring gear
[10] 18 gals—station wagon
[11] 8 pts—360 hp eng.
[12] 4.9 pts with 8.875 in. ring gear
[13] 18 gals—Monte Carlo
[14] 4.25 pts—8.5 in. ring gear; 5.4 pts. with 8.75 in. ring gear
[15] Figure is the same with or without a filter change
[16] 18.1—Malibu, El Camino
   18.2—Malibu station wagon
   17.5—Monte Carlo
[17] 7.0 pts—1981
[18] 6.0 pts—1981
[19] 6.0 pts—THM 350
[20] 25 gals—Malibu
   22 gals—Malibu station wagon
   27 gals—Diesel coupe
   22 gals—Diesel station wagon
[21] Chevrolet-built V6; 15 qts. (heater) and 16 qts. (A/C) with Buick V6
[22] Monte Carlo 21 qts, 267 V8; 19 qts 305 V8
[23] 10.0 pts—THM 700-4R

one of the many dry penetrating lubricants commercially available.

Parking Brake Linkage

Use chassis grease on the parking brake cable where it contacts the guides, links, levers, and pulleys. The grease should be a water resistant one for durability under the car.

Accelerator Linkage

Lubricate the carburetor stud, carburetor lever, and the accelerator pedal lever at the support inside the car with clean engine oil.

Wheel Bearings

Once very 12 months or 12,000 miles, clean and repack wheel bearings with a wheel bearing grease. Use only enough grease to completely coat the rollers. Remove any excess grease from the exposed surface of the hub and seal.

It is important that wheel bearings be properly adjusted after installation. Improperly adjusted wheel bearings can cause steering instability, front-end shimmy and wander, and increased tire wear. For complete lubrication

JUMP STARTING A DEAD BATTERY

The chemical reaction in a battery produces explosive hydrogen gas. This is the safe way to jump start a dead battery, reducing the chances of an accidental spark that could cause an explosion.

Jump Starting Precautions

1. Be sure both batteries are of the same voltage.
2. Be sure both batteries are of the same polarity (have the same grounded terminal).
3. Be sure the vehicles are not touching.
4. Be sure the vent cap holes are not obstructed.
5. Do not smoke or allow sparks around the battery.
6. In cold weather, check for frozen electrolyte in the battery.
7. Do not allow electrolyte on your skin or clothing.
8. Be sure the electrolyte is not frozen.

Jump Starting Procedure

1. Determine voltages of the two batteries; they must be the same.
2. Bring the starting vehicle close (they must not touch) so that the batteries can be reached easily.
3. Turn off all accessories and both engines. Put both cars in Neutral or Park and set the handbrake.
4. Cover the cell caps with a rag—do not cover terminals.
5. If the terminals on the run-down battery are heavily corroded, clean them.
6. Identify the positive and negative posts on both batteries and connect the cables in the order shown.
7. Start the engine of the starting vehicle and run it at fast idle. Try to start the car with the dead battery. Crank it for no more than 10 seconds at a time and let it cool off for 20 seconds in between tries.
8. If it doesn't start in 3 tries, there is something else wrong.
9. Disconnect the cables in the reverse order.
10. Replace the cell covers and dispose of the rags.

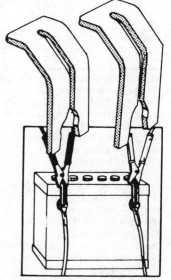

Side terminal batteries occasionally pose a problem when connecting jumper cables. There frequently isn't enough room to clamp the cables without touching sheet metal. Side terminal adaptors are available to alleviate this problem and should be removed after use.

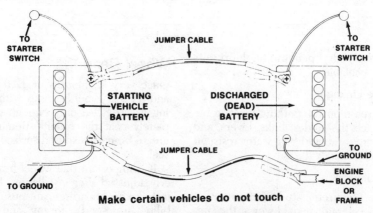

TO STARTER SWITCH

JUMPER CABLE

TO STARTER SWITCH

STARTING VEHICLE BATTERY

DISCHARGED (DEAD) BATTERY

TO GROUND

JUMPER CABLE

TO GROUND

ENGINE BLOCK OR FRAME

Make certain vehicles do not touch

This hook-up for negative ground cars only

Maintenance Intervals
Gasoline Engined Cars—1970–76

Interval At Which Services Are To Be Performed	Service
LUBRICATION AND GENERAL MAINTENANCE	
Every 6 months or 7,500 miles	*CHASSIS-Lubricate ●*FLUID LEVELS-Check *ENGINE OIL-Change
At first oil change-then every 2nd	*ENGINE OIL FILTER-Replace (V-6 Replace each oil change)
See Explanation of Maintenance Schedule	TIRES-Rotate DIFFERENTIAL
Every 12 months	AIR CONDITIONING SYSTEM-Check charge & hose condition. TEMPMATIC AIR FILTER-Replace every other year.
Every 12 months or 15,000 miles	*COOLING SYSTEM-See Explanation of Maintenance Schedule
Every 30,000 miles	WHEEL BEARINGS-Clean and repack *AUTOMATIC TRANS.-Change fluid and service filter MANUAL STEERING GEAR-Check seals CLUTCH CROSS SHAFT-Lubricate
SAFETY MAINTENANCE	
Every 6 months or 7,500 miles	TIRES AND WHEELS-Check condition *EXHAUST SYSTEM-Check condition of system *DRIVE BELTS-Ck. cond. & adjustment. Replace every 30,000 miles FRONT AND REAR SUSPENSION & STEERING SYSTEM-Ck. cond. BRAKES AND POWER STEERING-Check all lines and hoses
Every 12 months or 15,000 miles	DRUM BRAKES AND PARKING BRAKE-Check condition of linings; adjust parking brake THROTTLE LINKAGE-Check operation and condition UNDERBODY-Flush and check condition BUMPERS-Check condition
EMISSION CONTROL MAINTENANCE	
At 1st 6 months or 7,500 miles-then at 18 month/22,500 mile Intervals Thereafter	THERMOSTATICALLY CONTROLLED AIR CLEANER-Check operation CARBURETOR CHOKE-Check operation ENGINE IDLE SPEED ADJUSTMENT EFE VALVE-Check operation CARBURETOR-Torque attaching bolts or nuts to manifold
Every 12 months or 15,000 miles	CARBURETOR FUEL INLET FILTER-Replace VACUUM ADVANCE SYSTEM AND HOSES-Check oper. PCV SYSTEMS-See Explanation of Maintenance Schedule
Every 18 months or 22,500 miles	IDLE STOP SOLENOID OR DASHPOT-Check operation SPARK PLUG AND IGNITION COIL WIRES-Inspect and clean
Every 22,500 miles	SPARK PLUGS-Replace ENGINE TIMING ADJUSTMENT & DISTRIBUTOR CHECK
Every 24 months or 30,000 miles	ECS SYSTEM-See Explanation of Maintenance Schedule FUEL CAP, TANK AND LINES-Check condition
Every 30,000 miles	AIR CLEANER ELEMENT-Replace

*Also Required Emission Control Maintenance
●Also a Safety Service

Maintenance Intervals
Gasoline Engined Cars—1977 and Later

When to Perform Services (Months or Miles, Whichever Occurs First)	Services
LUBRICATION AND GENERAL MAINTENANCE	
Every 12 months or 7,500 miles (12 000 km)	●CHASSIS-Lubricate ●FLUID LEVELS-Check CLUTCH PEDAL FREE TRAVEL-Check/Adjust
See Explanation of Maintenance Schedule	*ENGINE OIL-Change *ENGINE OIL FILTER-Replace TIRES-Rotation (Radial Tires) REAR AXLE OR FINAL DRIVE-Check lube
Every 12 months or 15,000 miles (24 000 km)	*COOLING SYSTEM-See Explanation of Maintenance Schedule
Every 30,000 miles (48 000 km)	WHEEL BEARINGS-Repack CLUTCH CROSS SHAFT-Lubricate
See Explanation	AUTOMATIC TRANSMISSION-Change fluid and service filter
SAFETY MAINTENANCE	
Every 12 months or 7,500 miles (12 000 km)	TIRES, WHEELS AND DISC BRAKES-Check condition *EXHAUST SYSTEM-Check condition SUSPENSION & STEERING SYSTEM-Check condition BRAKES AND POWER STEERING-Check all lines and hoses
Every 12 months or 15,000 miles (24 000 km)	*DRIVE BELTS-Check condition and adjustment (1) DRUM BRAKES AND PARKING BRAKE-Check condition of linings; adjust parking brake THROTTLE LINKAGE-Check operation and condition BUMPERS-Check condition *FUEL CAP, TANK AND LINES-Check
EMISSION CONTROL MAINTENANCE	
At first 6 MOnths or 7,500 Miles (12 000 km)–Then at 24-Month/ 30,000 Mile (48 000 km) Intervals as Indicated in Log, Except Choke Which Requires Service at 45,000 Miles (72 000 km)	CARBURETOR CHOKE & HOSES-Check (2) ENGINE IDLE SPEED-Check adjustment (2) EFE SYSTEM-Check operation (If so equipped) CARBURETOR-Torque attaching bolts or nuts to manifold (2)
Every 30,000 miles (48 000 km)	THERMOSTATICALLY CONTROLLED AIR CLEANER-Check operation VACUUM ADVANCE SYSTEM AND HOSES-Check (3) SPARK PLUG WIRES-Check IDLE STOP SOLENOID AND/OR DASH POT OR ISC-Check operation SPARK PLUGS-Replace (2) ENGINE TIMING ADJUSTMENT AND DISTRIBUTOR-Check AIR CLEANER AND PCV FILTER ELEMENT-Replace (2) PCV VALVE-Replace EGR VALVE-Service

●Also a Safety Service
*Also an Emission Control Service
(1) In California, a separately driven air pump belt check is recommended but not required at 15,000 miles (24 000 km) and 45,000 miles (72 000 km).
(2) Only these emission control maintenance items are considered to be required maintenance as defined by the California Air Resources Board (ARB) regulation and are, according to such regulation, the minimum maintenance an owner in California must perform to fulfill the minimum requirements of the emission warranty. All other emission maintenance items are recommended maintenance as defined by such regulation. General Motors urges that all emission control maintenance items be performed.
(3) Not applicable on vehicles equipped with electronic spark timing (EST).

Maintenance Intervals
Diesel Engined Cars

When to Perform Services (Months or Miles, Whichever Occurs First)	Services
LUBRICATION AND GENERAL MAINTENANCE	
Every 5,000 Miles (8 000 km)	*ENGINE OIL-Change *OIL FILTER-Change ●CHASSIS-Lubricate ●FLUID LEVELS-Check
See Explanation	TIRES-Rotation REAR AXLE OR FINAL DRIVE-Check lube
Every 12 months or 15,000 miles (24 000 km) Every 30,000 miles (48 000 km)	*COOLING SYSTEM-Check *CRANKCASE VENTILATION-Service WHEEL BEARINGS-Repack
See Explanation	AUTOMATIC TRANSMISSION-Change fluid and filter
SAFETY MAINTENANCE	
At first 5,000 miles (8 000 km) Then at 15,000/30,000/45,000 miles	*EXHAUST SYSTEM-Check condition
Every 12 months or 10,000 miles (16 000 km)	TIRES, WHEEL AND DISC BRAKE-Check SUSPENSION AND STEERING-Check BRAKES AND POWER STEERING-Check
Every 5,000 Miles (8 000 km)	*DRIVE BELTS-Check condition and adjustment
Every 12 months or 15,000 miles (24 000 km)	DRUM BRAKES AND PARKING BRAKE-Check THROTTLE LINKAGE-Check operation BUMPERS-Check condition
EMISSION CONTROL MAINTENANCE	
At first 5,000 miles (8 000 km) Then at 15,000/30,000/45,000 miles	EXHAUST PRESSURE REGULATOR VALVE
At first 5,000 miles (8 000 km) Then at 30,000 miles (48 000 km)	ENGINE IDLE SPEED-Adjust
Every 30,000 miles (48 000 km)	AIR CLEANER-Replace FUEL FILTER-Replace

●Also a Safety Service
*Also on Emission Control Service

and adjustment procedures, see the "Wheel Bearing" section in Chapter 9.

PUSHING AND TOWING

Push Starting

This is the last recommended method of starting a car and should be used only in an extreme case. Chances of body damage are high, so be sure that the pushcar's bumper does not override your bumper. If your Chevrolet has an automatic transmission it cannot be push started. In an emergency, you can start a manual transmission car by pushing. With the bumpers evenly matched, get in your car, switch on the ignition, and place the gearshift in Second or Third gear—do not engage the clutch. Start off slowly. When the speed of the car reaches about 15–20 mph, release the clutch.

Towing

The car can be towed safely (with the transmission in Neutral) from the front at speeds of 35 mph or less. The car must either be towed with the rear wheels off the ground or the driveshaft disconnected if: towing speeds are to be over 35 mph, or towing distance is over 50 miles, or transmission or rear axle problems exist.

When towing the car on its front wheels, the steering wheel must be secured in a straight-ahead position and the steering column unlocked. Tire-to-ground clearance should not exceed 6 in. during towing.

JACKING

The standard jack utilizes slots in the bumper to raise the car. The jack supplied with the car should never be used for any service operation other than tire changing. Never get under the car while it is supported by only a jack. Always block the wheels when changing tires.

The service operations in this book often require that one end or the other, or both, of the car be raised and safely supported. The ideal method, of course, would be a hydraulic hoist. Since this is beyond both the resource and requirement of the do-it-yourselfer, a small hydraulic, screw or scissors jack will suffice for the procedures in this guide. Two sturdy jackstands should be acquired if you intend to work under the car at any time. An alternate method of raising the car would be drive-on ramps. These are available commercially or can be fabricated from heavy boards or steel. Be sure to block the wheels when using ramps. Never use concrete blocks to support the car. They may break if the load is not evenly distributed.

Regardless of the method of jacking or hoisting the car, there are only certain areas of the undercarriage and suspension you can safely use to support it. See the illustration below, and make sure that only the shaded areas are used.

In addition, be especially careful on vehicles built after 1974 that you do not damage the catalytic converter. Remember that various cross braces and supports on a lift can sometimes contact lowhanging parts of the car.

HOW TO BUY A USED CAR

Many people believe that a two or three year old used car is a better buy than a new car. This may be true; the new car suffers the heaviest depreciation in the first two years, but is not old enough to present a lot of costly repair problems. Whatever the age of the used car you might want to buy, this section and a little patience will help you select one that should be safe and dependable.

Tips

1. First decide what model you want, and how much you want to spend.
2. Check the used car lots and your local newspaper ads. Privately owned cars are usually less expensive, however you will not get a warranty that, in most cases, comes with a used car purchased from a lot.
3. Never shop at night. The glare of the lights make it easy to miss faults on the body caused by accident or rust repair.

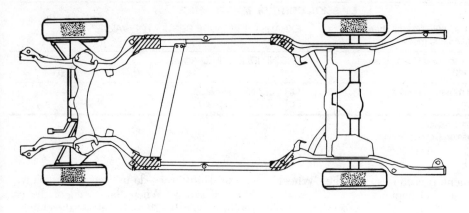

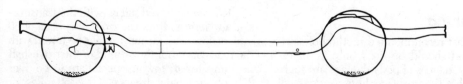

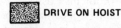 **DRIVE ON HOIST**

▨ **FLOOR JACK OR JOIST LIFT: DO NOT LIFT AT REAR AXLE WHEN EQUIPPED WITH REAR STABILIZER.**

Vehicle hoisting and jacking points

4. Try to get the name and phone number of the previous owner. Contact him/her and ask about the car. If the owner of the lot refuses this information, look for a car somewhere else.

A private seller can tell you about the car and maintenance. Remember, however, there's no law requiring honesty from private citizens selling used cars. There is a law that forbids the tampering with or turning back the odometer mileage. This includes both the private citizen and the lot owner. The law also requires that the seller or anyone transferring ownership of the car must provide the buyer with a signed statement indicating the mileage on the odometer at the time of transfer.

5. Write down the year, model and serial number before you buy any used car. Then dial 1-800-424-9393, the toll free number of the National Highway Traffic Safety Administration, and ask if the car has ever been included on any manufacturer's recall list. If so, make sure the needed repairs were made.

6. Use the "Used Car Checklist" in this section and check all the items on the used car you are considering. Some items are more important than others. You know how much money you can afford for repairs, and, depending on the price of the car, may consider doing any needed work yourself. Beware, however, of trouble in areas that will affect operation, safety or emission. Problems in the "Used Car Checklist" break down as follows:

1–8: Two or more problems in these areas indicate a lack of maintenance. You should be ware.

9–13: Indicates a lack of proper care, however, these can usually be corrected with a tune-up or relatively simple parts replacement.

14–17: Problems in the engine or transmission can be very expensive. Walk away from any car with problems in both of these areas.

7. If you are satisfied with the apparent condition of the car, take it to an independent diagnostic center or mechanic for a complete check. If you have a state inspection program, have it inspected immediately before purchase, or specify on the bill of sale that the sale is conditional on passing state inspection.

8. Road test the car—refer to the "Road Test Checklist" in this section. If your original evaluation and the road test agree—the rest is up to you.

Used Car Checklist

NOTE: *The numbers on the illustrations refer to the numbers on this checklist.*

1. *Mileage:* Average mileage is about 12,000 miles per year. More than average mileage may indicate hard usage. 1975 and later catalytic converter equipped models may need converter service at 50,000 miles.

2. *Paint:* Check around the tailpipe, molding and windows for overspray indicating that the car has been repainted.

3. *Rust:* Check fenders, doors, rocker panels, window moldings, wheelwells, floorboards, under floormats, and in the trunk for signs of rust. Any rest at all will be a problem. There is no way to check the spread of rust, except to replace the part or panel.

4. *Body appearance:* Check the moldings, bumpers, grille, vinyl roof, glass, doors, trunk

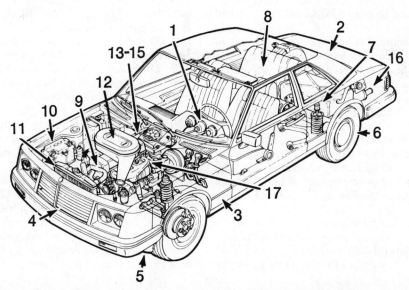

You should check these points when buying a used car. The "Used Car Checklist" gives an explanation of the numbered items

lid and body panels for general overall condition. Check for misalignment, loose holdown clips, ripples, scratches in glass, rips or patches in the top. Mismatched paint, welding in the trunk, severe misalignment of body panels or ripples may indicate crash work.

5. *Leaks:* Get down and look under the car. There are no normal "leaks", other than water from the air conditioning condenser.

6. *Tires:* Check the tire air pressure. A common trick is to pump the tire pressure up to make the car roll easier. Check the tread wear, open the trunk and check the spare too. Uneven wear is a clue that the front end needs alignment. See the troubleshooting chapter for clues to the causes of tire wear.

7. *Shock absorbers:* Check the shock absorbers by forcing downward sharply on each corner of the car. Good shocks will not allow the car to bounce more than twice after you let go.

8. *Interior:* Check the entire interior. You're looking for an interior condition that agrees with the overall condition of the car. Reasonable wear is expected, but be suspicious of new seatcovers on sagging seats, new pedal pads, and worn armrests. These indicate an attempt to cover up hard use. Pull back the carpets and look for evidence of water leaks or flooding. Look for missing hardware, door handles, control knobs etc. Check lights and signal operations. Make sure all accessories (air conditioner, heater, radio etc.) work. Check windshield wiper operation.

9. *Belts and Hoses:* Open the hood and check all belts and hoses for wear, cracks or weak spots.

10. *Battery:* Low electrolyte level, corroded terminals and/or cracked case indicate a lack of maintenance.

11. *Radiator:* Look for corrosion or rust in the coolant indicating a lack of maintenance.

12. *Air filter:* A dirty air filter usually means a lack of maintenance.

13. *Ignition Wires:* Check the ignition wires for cracks, burned spots, or wear. Worn wires will have to be replaced.

14. *Oil level:* If the oil level is low, chances are the engine uses oil or leaks. Beware of water in the oil (cracked block), excessively thick oil (used to quiet a noisy engine), or thin, dirty oil with a distinct gasoline smell (internal engine problems).

15. *Automatic Transmission:* Pull the transmission dipstick out when the engine is running. The level should read "Full", and the fluid should be clear or bright red. Dark brown or black fluid that has distinct burnt odor, signals a transmission in need of repair or overhaul.

16. *Exhaust:* check the color of the exhaust smoke. blue smoke indicates, among other problems, worn rings; black smoke can indicate burnt valves or carburetor problems. Check the exhaust system for leaks; it can be expensive to replace.

17. *Spark Plugs:* Remove one of the spark plugs (the most accessible will do). An engine in good condition will show plugs with a light tan or gray deposit on the firing tip. See the color Tune-Up tips section for spark plug conditions.

Road Test Check List

1. *Engine Performance:* The car should be peppy whether cold or warm, with adequate power and good pickup. It should respond smoothly through the gears.

2. *Brakes:* they should provide quick, firm stops with no noise, pulling or brake fade.

3. *Steering:* Sure control with no binding, harshness, or looseness and no shimmy in the wheel should be expected. Noise or vibration from the steering wheel when turning the car means trouble.

4. *Clutch (Manual Transmission):* clutch action should give quick, smooth response with easy shifting. The clutch pedal should have about 1–1½ inches of free-play before it disengages the clutch. Start the engine, set the parking brake, put the transmission in first gear and slowly release the clutch pedal. The engine should begin to stall when the pedal is one-half to three-quarters of the way up.

5. *Automatic Transmission:* The transmission should shift rapidly and smoothly, with no noise, hesitation, or slipping.

6. *Differential:* No noise or thumps should be present. Differentials have no "normal" leaks.

7. *Driveshaft, Universal Joints:* Vibration and noise could mean driveshaft problems. Clicking at low speed or coast conditions means worn U-joints.

8. *Suspension:* Try hitting bumps at different speeds. A car that bounces has weak shock absorbers. Clunks mean worn bushings or ball joints.

9. *Frame:* Wet the tires and drive in a straight line. Tracks should show two straight lines, not four. Four tire tracks indicate a frame bent by collision damage. If the tires can't be wet for this purpose, have a friend drive along behind you and see if the car appears to be traveling in a straight line.

TUNE-UP PROCEDURES

In order to extract the full measure of performance and economy from your engine it is essential that it is properly turned at regular intervals. A regular tune-up will keep your car's engine running smoothly and will prevent the annoying breakdowns and poor performance associated with an untuned engine.

NOTE: *All 1964–74 models use a conventional breaker point ignition system. In 1975, Chevrolet switched to a full electronic ignition system known as HEI.*

A complete tune-up should be performed at least every 15,000 miles (12,000 miles for early models) or twelve months, whichever comes first.

NOTE: *1981 and later models have increased their interval to 30,000 miles.*

This interval should be halved if the car is operated under severe conditions such as trailer towing, prolonged idling, start-and-stop driving, or if starting or running problems are noticed. It is assumed that the routine maintenance described in Chapter 1 has been kept up, as this will have a decided effect on the results of a tune-up. All of the applicable steps of a tune-up should be followed in order, as the result is a commulative one.

If the specifications on the underhood tune-up sticker in the engine compartment of your car disagree with the "Tune-Up Specifications" chart in this chapter, the figures on the sticker must be used. The sticker often reflects changes made during the production run.

Spark Plugs

A typical spark plug consists of a metal shell surrounding a ceramic insulator. A metal electrode extends downward through the center of the insulator and protrudes a short distance.

Located at the end of the plug and attached to the side of the outer metal shell is the side electrode. This side electrode bends in at 90° so its tip is even with, and parallel to, the tip of the center electrode. This distance between

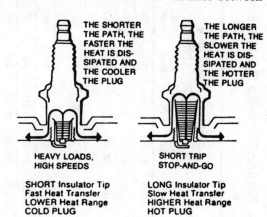

THE SHORTER THE PATH, THE FASTER THE HEAT IS DISSIPATED AND THE COOLER THE PLUG

THE LONGER THE PATH, THE SLOWER THE HEAT IS DISSIPATED AND THE HOTTER THE PLUG

HEAVY LOADS, HIGH SPEEDS

SHORT TRIP STOP-AND-GO

SHORT Insulator Tip
Fast Heat Transfer
LOWER Heat Range
COLD PLUG

LONG Insulator Tip
Slow Heat Transfer
HIGHER Heat Range
HOT PLUG

Spark plug heat range

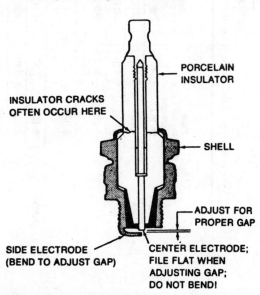

PORCELAIN INSULATOR

INSULATOR CRACKS OFTEN OCCUR HERE

SHELL

ADJUST FOR PROPER GAP

SIDE ELECTRODE (BEND TO ADJUST GAP)

CENTER ELECTRODE; FILE FLAT WHEN ADJUSTING GAP; DO NOT BEND!

Cross section of a spark plug

Gasoline Engine Tune-Up Specifications

When analyzing the compression test results, look for uniformity among cylinders rather than specific pressures.

Year	Engine No. Cyl Displacement (cu in.)	hp	Spark Plugs Type	Gap (in.)	Distributor Point Dwell (deg)	Point Gap (in.)	Ignition Timing ▲(deg)■● Man Trans	Auto Trans	●Valves■ Intake Opens (deg)	Fuel Pump Pressure (psi)	●Idle Speed▲* Man Trans	Auto Trans
1964	6-194	120	46N	0.035	31–34	0.019	8B	8B	62	4½–6	500②	500②
	6-230	155	46N	0.035	31–34	0.019	4B	4B	62	4½–6	500②	500②
	8-283	195, 220	45	0.035	28–32	0.019	4B	4B	32½	5¼–6½	500②	500②
	8-327	250, 300	44	0.035	28–32	0.019	8B	8B	32½	5¼–6½	500②	500②
1965	6-194	120	46N	0.035	31–34	0.019	8B	8B	62	4½–6	500②	500②
	6-230	140	46N	0.035	31–34	0.019	4B	4B	62	4½–6	500②	500②
	8-283	195, 280	45	0.035	28–32	0.019	4B	4B	32½	5¼–6½	500②	500②
	8-327	250, 300	44	0.035	28–32	0.019	8B	8B	32½	5¼–6½	500②	500②
	8-327	350	44	0.035	28–32	0.019	10B	—	54	5–6½	750②	750②
1966	6-194	120	46N	0.035	31–45	0.019	8B	8B	62	4½–6	500②	500②
	6-194①	120	46N	0.035	31–34	0.019	3B	8B	62	4½–6	700②	600②
	6-230	140	46N	0.035	31–34	0.019	4B	4B	62	4½–6	500②	500②
	6-230①	140	46N	0.035	31–34	0.019	4B	4B	62	4½–6	700②	600②
	8-283	195	45	0.035	28–32	0.019	4B	4B	32½	5¼–6½	500②	500②
	8-283①	220	45	0.035	28–32	0.019	4B	4B	32½	5¼–6½	700②	600②
	8-327	275	44	0.035	28–32	0.019	8B	8B	32½	5¼–6½	500②	500②
	8-327①	275	44	0.035	28–32	0.019	8B	2A	32½	5–6½	700②	600②
	8-327	350	44	0.035	28–32	0.019	10B	—	54	5–6½	750②	750②
	8-396	325	43N	0.035	28–32	0.019	4B	4B	40	5–6½	500②	500②

Year	Engine											
1966	8-396	360	43N	0.035	28–32	0.019	4B	4B	56	5–6½	550②	550②
	8-396	375	R-43N	0.035	28–32	0.019	4B	—	44	5–8½	750	—
1967	6-230	140	46N	0.035	31–34	0.019	4B	4B	62	3½–4½	500②	500②
	6-230①	140	46N	0.035	31–34	0.019	4B	4B	62	3½–4½	700	500
	6-250	155	46N	0.035	31–34	0.019	4B	4B	62	3½–4½	500②	500②
	6-250①	155	46N	0.035	31–34	0.019	4B	4B	62	3½–4½	700	500
	8-283	195	45	0.035	28–32	0.019	4B	4B	38	5–6½	500②	500②
	8-283①	195	45	0.035	28–32	0.019	TDC	4B	38	5–6½	700	600
	8-327	275	44	0.035	28–32	0.019	8B	8B	38	5¼–6½	500②	500②
	8-327①	275	44	0.035	28–32	0.019	6B	6B	38	5¼–6½	700	600
	8-327	325	44	0.035	28–32	0.019	10B	—	54	5–6½	700②	—
	8-327①	325	44	0.035	28–32	0.019	10B	—	54	5–6½	750②	—
	8-396	325	43N	0.035	28–32	0.019	4B	4B	40	5–6½	500②	500②
	8-396①	325	43N	0.035	28–32	0.019	4B	4B	40	5–6½	700②	500②
	396	350	43N	0.035	28–32	0.019	4B	4B	56	7¼–8½	550②	550②
	396①	350	43N	0.035	28–32	0.019	4B	4B	56	7¼–8½	700②	500②
	8-396	375	R-43N	0.035	28–32	0.019	4B	—	44	5–8½	750	—
1968	6-230	140	46N	0.035	31–34	0.019	TDC	4B	16	3½–4½	700	500②/400
	6-250	155	46N	0.035	31–34	0.019	TDC	4B	16	3½–4½	700	500②/400
	8-307	200	45S	0.035	28–32	0.019	2B	2B	28	5–6½	700	600
	8-327	275	44	0.035	28–32	0.019	TDC	4B	28	5–6½	700	600
	8-327	325	44	0.035	28–32	0.019	4B	—	40	5–6½	750②	—
	8-396	325	43N	0.035	28–32	0.019	4B	4B	28	5–6½	700②	600②
	8-396	350	43N	0.035	28–32	0.019	TDC	4B	40	7¼–8½	700②	600
	8-396	375	R-43N	0.035	28–32	0.019	4B	—	44	5–8½	750	—
1969	6-230	140	R-46N	0.035	31–34	0.019	TDC	4B	16	3–4½	700	550/400

Gasoline Engine Tune-Up Specifications (cont.)

When analyzing the compression test results, look for uniformity among cylinders rather than specific pressures.

Year	Engine No. Cyl Displacement (cu in.)	hp	Spark Plugs Type	Gap (in.)	Distributor Point Dwell (deg)	Point Gap (in.)	Ignition Timing ▲(deg)■● Man Trans	Auto Trans	●Valves■ Intake Opens (deg)	Fuel Pump Pressure (psi)	●Idle Speed ▲* Man Trans	Auto Trans
1969	6-250	155	R-46N	0.035	31–34	0.019	TDC	4B	16	3-4½	700	550/400②
	8-307	200	R-45S	0.035	28-32	0.019	2B	2B	28	5-6½	700	600
	8-350	250	R-44	0.035	28-32	0.019	TDC	4B	28	5-6½	700	600
	8-350	300	R-44	0.035	28-32	0.019	TDC	4B	28	5-6½	700	600
	8-396	325	R-44N	0.035	28-32	0.019	4B	4B	28	5-8½	800	600
	8-396	350	R-43N	0.035	28-32	0.019	TDC	4B	56	5-8½	800	600
	8-396	375	R-43N	0.035	28-32	0.019	4B	4B	44	5-8½	750	750/400
1970	6-250	155	R-46T	0.035	31–34	0.019	TDC	4B	16	3-4½	750	600/400
	8-307	200	R-43	0.035	28-32	0.019	2B	8B	28	5-6½	700	600/450
	8-350	250	R-44	0.035	28-32	0.019	TDC	4B	28	5-6½	750	600/450
	8-350	300	R-44	0.035	28-32	0.019	TDC	4B	28	5-6½	700	600
	8-396	350	R-44T	0.035	28-32	0.019	TDC	4B	56	5-8½	700	600
	8-396	375	R-43T	0.035	28-32	0.019	4B	4B	NA	5-8½	750	700
	8-400	265	R-44	0.035	28-32	0.019	4B	8B	28	5-8½	700	600/450
	8-402	330	R-44T	0.035	28-32	0.019	4B	4B	28	5-8½	700	600
	8-454	360	R-43T	0.035	28-32	0.019	6B	6B	56	5-8½	700	600
	8-454	390	R-43T	0.035	28-32	0.019	6B	6B	NA	5-8½	700	600
	8-454	450	R-43T	0.035	28-32	0.019	4B	4B	NA	5-8½	700	700

Year	Engine											
1971	6-250	145	R-46TS	0.035	31–34	0.019	4B	4B	16	3½–4½	550	500
	8-307	200	R-45TS	0.035	29–31	0.019	4B	8B	28	5–6½	600	550
	8-350	245	R-45TS	0.035	29–31	0.019	2B	6B	28	7–8½	600	550
	8-350	270	R-44TS	0.035	29–31	0.019	4B	8B	28	7–8½	600	550
	8-400	255	R-44TS	0.035	29–31	0.019	4B	8B	28	7–8½	600	550
	8-402	300	R-44TS	0.035	29–31	0.019	8B	8B	28	7–8½	600	600
	8-454	365	R-42TS	0.035	29–31	0.019	8B	8B	56	7–8½	600	600
	8-454	425	R-42TS	0.035	29–31	0.019	8B	12B	44	7–8½	700	700
1972	6-250	110	R-46TS	0.035	31–34	0.019	4B	4B	16	3½–4½	700	600
	8-307	130	R-44T	0.035	29–31	0.019	4B	8B	28	5–6½	900	600
	8-350	165	R-44T	0.035	29–31	0.019	6B	6B	28	7–8½	900	600
	8-350	175	R-44T	0.035	29–31	0.019	4B	8B	28	7–8½	800	600
	8-402	240	R-44T	0.035	29–31	0.019	8B	8B	30	7–8½	750	600
	8-454	270	R-44T	0.035	29–31	0.019	8B	8B	56	7–8½	750	600
1973	6-250	100	R-46T	0.035	31–34	0.019	6B	6B	16	3½–4½	700/450	600/450
	8-307	115	R-44T	0.035	29–31	0.019	4B	8B	28	5–6½	900/450	600/450
	8-350	145	R-44T	0.035	29–31	0.019	8B	8B	28	7–8½	900/450	600/450
	8-350	175	R-44T	0.035	29–31	0.019	8B	12B	28	7–8½	900/450	600/450
	8-454	245	R-44T	0.035	29–31	0.019	10B	10B	55	7–8½	900/450	600/450
1974	6-250	100	R-46T	0.035	31–34	0.019	6B	6B	16	4–5	800/450	600/450
	8-350	145	R-44T	0.035	29–31	0.019	4B	8B	28	7½–9	900/450	600/450
	8-350	160	R-44T	0.035	29–31	0.019	4B	8B	44	7½–9	900/450	600/450
	8-400	150	R-44T	0.035	29–31	0.019	—	8B	28	7½–9	—	600/450

Gasoline Engine Tune-Up Specifications (cont.)

When analyzing the compression test results, look for uniformity among cylinders rather than specific pressures.

Year	Engine No. Cyl Displacement (cu in.)	hp	Spark Plugs Type	Spark Plugs Gap (in.)	Distributor Point Dwell (deg)	Distributor Point Gap (in.)	Ignition Timing ▲(deg)■● Man Trans	Ignition Timing ▲(deg)■● Auto Trans	●Valves■ Intake Opens (deg)	Fuel Pump Pressure (psi)	●Idle Speed▲* Man Trans	●Idle Speed▲* Auto Trans
1974	8-400	180	R-44T	0.035	29-31	0.019	—	8B	44	7½-9	—	600/450
	8-454	235	R-44T	0.035	29-31	0.019	10B	10B	55	7½-9	800/450	600/450
1975	6-250	105	R-46TX	0.060	Electronic		10B	10B	16	4-5	850/425	550/425 (600/425)
	8-350	145	R-44TX	0.060	Electronic		6B	6B	28	7½-9	800	600
	8-350	155	R-44TX	0.060	Electronic		—	6B	28	7½-9	—	600
	8-400	175	R-44TX	0.060	Electronic		—	8B	28	7½-9	—	600
	8-454	215	R-44TX	0.060	Electronic		—	16B	55	7½-9	—	600/500
1976	6-250	105	R-46TS	0.035	Electronic		6B	6B	16	3½-4½	850	550 (600)
	8-305	140	R-45TS	0.045	Electronic		—	8B (TDC)	28	7-8½	—	600
	8-350	145	R-45TS	0.045	Electronic		—	6B	28	7-8½	—	600
	8-350	165	R-45TS	0.045	Electronic		—	8B (6B)	28	7-8½	—	600
	8-400	175	R-45TS	0.045	Electronic		—	8B	28	7-8½	—	600
1977	6-250	110	R-46TS	0.035	Electronic		6B @ 850	8B @ 600	16	4-5	750	550
	8-305	145	R-45TS	0.045	Electronic		—	8B @ 500	28	7½-9	—	500

Year	Engine	HP	Spark Plug	Gap	Distributor						
1977	8-350	170	R-45TS	0.045	Electronic	—	8B @ 500	28	7½-9	—	500
1978	6-200	95	R-45TS	0.045	Electronic	8B	8B	28	7.5-9	700	600
	6-231	105	R46TSX	0.060	Electronic	15B	15B	17	6-7	600	500
	8-305	145	R-45TS	0.045	Electronic	4B	④	28	7.5-9	600	500
	8-350	170	R-45TS	0.045	Electronic	—	8B	2B	7.5-9	—	500
1979	6-200	all	R-45TS	0.045	Electronic	8B	14B	34	4.5-6.0	700	600
	6-231	all	R-46TSX	0.060	Electronic	15B	15B	16	4.2-5.7	600	500
	8-267	all	R-45TS	0.045	Electronic	4B	10B	2B	7.5-9.0	600	500
	8-305	all	R-43TS	0.045	Electronic	4B	4B	28	7.5-9.0	600	500
	8-350	all	R-43TS	0.045	Electronic	—	8B	2B	7.5-9.0	—	500
1980	6-229	115	R-T5TS ⑤	0.045	Electronic	8B	12B	42	4.5-6.0	700	600
	6-231	110	R-45TSX	0.060	Electronic	—	15B	16	4.25-5.75	—	560 (600)
	6-231 Turbo	170	R-45TSX	0.060	Electronic	—	15B	16	4.25-5.75	—	550 (600)
	8-267	120	R-45TS	0.045	Electronic	—	4B	28	7.5-9.0	—	500
	8-305	155	R-45TS	0.045	Electronic	4B	4B	28	7.5-9.0	700	500 (550)
1981	6-229	110	R-45TS	0.045	Electronic	6B	6B	42	4.5-6.0	⑥	⑥
	6-231	110	R-45TS8	0.080	Electronic	—	15B	16	4.25-5.75	—	⑥
	6-231 Turbo	170	R-45TS	0.040	Electronic	—	15B	16	4.25-5.75	—	⑥
	8-267	115	R-45TS	0.045	Electronic	—	6B	28	7.5-9.0	—	500
	8-305	150	R-45TS	0.045	Electronic	6B	6B	28	7.5-9.0	700	500
1982–84	6-229	110	R-45TS	0.045	Electronic	—	6B ⑥	42	4.5-6.0	—	⑥
	6-231	110	R-45TS	0.045	Electronic	—	15B ⑥	16	4.5-6.0	—	⑥
	8-267	115	R-45TS	0.045	Electronic	—	6B ⑥	44	7.5-9.0	—	⑥
	8-305	145 ⑦	R-45TS	0.045	Electronic	—	6B ⑥	44	7.5-9.0	—	⑥

Gasoline Engine Tune-Up Specifications (cont.)

When analyzing the compression test results, look for uniformity among cylinders rather than specific pressures.

Year	Engine No. Cyl Displacement (cu in.)	hp	Spark Plugs		Distributor		Ignition Timing ▲ (deg)■●		●Valves■ Intake Opens (deg)	Fuel Pump Pressure (psi)	●Idle Speed ▲*	
			Type	Gap (in.)	Point Dwell (deg)	Point Gap (in.)	Man Trans	Auto Trans			Man Trans	Auto Trans
1985–86	6-262	130	R-43CTS	0.035	Electronic		—	⑥	44	9-13	—	⑥
	8-305	150⑧	R-45TS	0.045	Electronic		—	⑥	44	5.5-6.5	—	⑥
1986	6-262	140	R-43TS	0.035	Electronic		—	⑥	44	9-13	—	⑥
	8-305	150⑧	R-43TS	0.035	Electronic		—	⑥	44	5.5-6.5	—	⑥

NOTE: The underhood specification sticker often reflects tune-up specification changes made in production. Sticker figures must be used if they disagree with those in this chart.

▲ See text for procedure
● Figures in parentheses indicate California
■ All figures Before Top Dead Center
* When two idle speed figures are separated by a slash, the lower figure is with the idle speed solenoid disconnected
NA Not Available
① Equipped with the Air Injection Reactor system
② A/C on
③ Lower figure is with idle solenoid disconnected
④ 49 states—4B
   Calif.—6B
   High alt.—8B
⑤ With A/T—R-45TS
⑥ See underhood specifications sticker
⑦ 150 hp, 1983–84
⑧ 180 hp—SS Model

Diesel Engine Tune-Up Specifications

Year	Eng V.I.N. Code	Engine No. Cyl. Displacement (Cu. in.)	Eng. Mfg.	Fuel Pump Pressure (psi)	Compression (lbs)▲	Ignition Timing (deg) Auto. Trans.	Intake Valve Opens (deg)	Idle Speed● (rpm)
'80	N	8-350	Olds.	5.5–6.5	275 min.	5B ②	16	750/600
'81–'84	N	8-350	Olds.	5.5–6.5	275 min.	①	16	①
'82–'84	V	V6-263	Olds.	5.5–6.5	275 min.	①	16	①

NOTE: The underhood specifications sticker often reflects changes made in production. Sticker figures must be used if they disagree with those in this chart.
① See underhood specifications sticker.
② Static.
● Where two idle speed figures appear separated by a slash, the first is idle speed with solenoid energized; the second is with solenoid disconnected.
▲ The lowest cylinder reading should not be less than 70% of the highest cylinder reading.

these two electrodes (measured in thousandths of an inch) is called spark plug gap. The spark plug in no way produces a spark but merely provides a gap across which the current can arc. The coil produces 20,000–25,000 V (the HEI transistorized ignition produces considerably more voltage than the standard type, approximately 50,000 volts), which travels to the distributor where it is distributed through the spark plug wires to the plugs. The current passes along the center electrode and jumps the gap to the side electrode and, in so doing, ignites the air/fuel mixture in the combustion chamber. All plugs used since 1969 have a resistor built into the center electrode to reduce interference to any nearby radio and television receivers. The resistor also cuts down on erosion of plug electrodes caused by excessively long sparking. Resistor spark plug wiring is original equipment on all models.

Spark plug life and efficiency depend upon the condition of the engine and the temperatures to which the plug is exposed. Combustion chamber temperatures are affected by many factors such as compression ratio of the engine, fuel/air mixtures, exhaust emission equipment, and the type of driving you do. Spark plugs are designed and classified by number according to the heat range at which they will operate most efficiently. The amount of heat that the plug absorbs is determined by the length of the lower insulator. The longer the insulator (it extends farther into the engine), the hotter the plug will operate; the shorter it is, the cooler it will operate. A plug that has a short path for heat transfer and remains too cool will quickly accumulate deposits of oil and carbon since it is not hot enough to burn them off. This leads to plug fouling and consequently to misfiring. A plug that has a long path for heat transfer will have no deposits but, due to the excessive heat, the electrodes will burn away quickly and, in some instances, pre-ignition may result. Pre-

ignition takes place when plug tips get so hot that they glow sufficiently to ignite the fuel/air mixture before the spark does. This early ignition will usually cause a pinging (sounding much like castanets) during low speeds and heavy loads. Inn severe cases, the heat may become enough to start the fuel/air mixture burning throughout the combustion chamber rather than just to the front of the plug as in normal operation. At this time, the piston is rising in the cylinder making its compression stroke. The burning mass is compressed and an explosion results producing tremendous pressure. Something has to give, and it does—pistons are often damaged. Obviously, this detonation (explosion) is a destructive condition that can be avoided by installing a spark plug designed and specified for your particular engine.

A set of spark plugs usually requires replacement after 10,000–12,000 miles depending on the type of driving (this interval has been increased to 22,500 miles for all 1975–79 models and 30,000 miles for all 1980 and later models). The electrode on a new spark plug has a sharp edge but, with use, this edge becomes rounded by erosion causing the plug gap to increase. In normal operation, plug gap increases about 0.001 in. in every 1,000–2,000 miles. As the gap increases, the plug's voltage requirement also increases. It requires a greater voltage to jump the wider gap and about two to three times as much voltage to fire a plug at high speeds and acceleration than at idle.

The higher voltage produced by the HEI ignition coil is one of the primary reasons for the prolonged replacement interval for spark plugs in 1975 and later cars. A consistently hotter spark prevents the fouling of plugs for much longer than could normally be expected; this spark is also able to jump across a larger gap more efficiently than a spark from a conventional system. However, even plugs used with the HEI system wear after time in the engine.

Worn plugs become obvious during acceleration. Voltage requirement is greatest during acceleration and a plug with an enlarged gap may require move voltage than the coil is able to produce. As a result, the engine misses and sputters until acceleration is reduced. Reducing acceleration reduces the plug's voltage requirement and the engine runs smoother. Slow, city driving is hard on plugs. The long periods of idle experienced in traffic creates an overly rich gas mixture. The engine isn't running fast enough to completely burn the gas and, consequently, the plugs are fouled with gas deposits and engine idle becomes rough. In many cases, driving under the right conditions can effectively clean these fouled plugs.

NOTE: *There are several reasons why a spark plug will foul and you can usually learn which is at fault by just looking at the plug. A few of the most common reasons for plug fouling, and a description of the fouled plug's appearance, can be found in the color insert in this book.*

Accelerate your car to the speed where the engine begins to miss and then slow down to the point where the engine smooths out. Run at this speed for a few minutes and then accelerate again to the point of engine miss. With each repetition this engine miss should occur at increasingly higher speeds and then disappear altogether. Do not attempt to shortcut this procedure by hard acceleration. This approach will compound problems by fusing deposits into a hard permanent glaze. Dirty, fouled plugs may be cleaned by sandblasting. Many shops have a spark plug sandblaster. After sandblasting, the electrode should be filed to a sharp, square shape and then gapped to specifications. Gapping a plug too close will produce a rough idle while gapping it too wide will increase its voltage requirement and cause missing at high speeds and during acceleration.

The type of driving you do may require a change in spark plug heat range. If the majority of your driving is done in the city and rarely at high speeds, plug fouling may necessitate changing to a plug with a heat range one number higher than that specified by the car manufacturer. For example, a 1970 Chevelle with a 350 cu in. (300 hp) engine requires an R44 plug. Frequent city driving may foul these plugs making engine operation rough. An R45 is the next hottest plug in the AC heat range (the higher the AC number, the hotter the plug) and its insulator is longer than the R44 so that it can absorb and retain more heat than the shorter R44. This hotter R45 burns off deposits even at low city speeds but would be too hot for prolonged turnpike driving. Using this plug at high speeds would create dangerous pre-

ignition. On the other hand, if the aforementioned Chevelle were used almost exclusively for long distance high speed driving, the specified R44 might to be too hot resulting in rapid electrode wear and dangerous pre-ignition. In this case, it might be wise to change to a colder R43. If the car is used for abnormal driving (as in the examples above), or the engine has been modified for higher performance, then a change to a plug of a different heat range may be necessary. For a modified car it is always wise to go to a colder plug as a protection against pre-ignition. It will require more frequent plug cleaning, but destructive detonation during acceleration will be avoided.

REMOVAL

When you're removing spark plugs, you should work on one at a time. Don't start by removing the plug wires all at once because unless you number them, they're going to get mixed up. On some models though, it will be more convenient for you to remove all the wires before you start to work on the plugs. If this is necessary, take a minute before you begin and number the wires with tape before you take them off. The time you spend here will pay off later on.

1. Twist the spark plug boot and remove the boot from the plug. You may also use a plug wire removal tool designed especially for this purpose. *Do not pull on the wire itself.* When the wire has been removed, take a wire brush and clean the area around the plug. Make sure that all the grime is removed so that none will enter the cylinder after the plug has been removed.

2. Remove the plug using the proper size

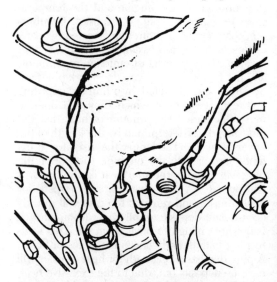

Twist and pull on the rubber boot to remove the spark plug wires; never pull on the wire itself

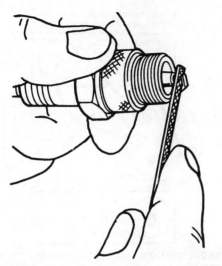

Plugs that are in good condition can be filed and re-used

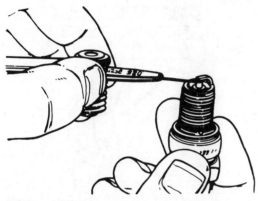

Always use a wire gauge to check the electrode gap

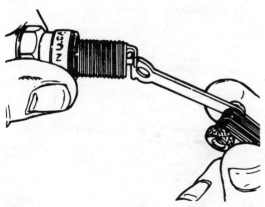

Adjust the electrode gap by bending the side electrode

socket, extensions, and universals as necessary. For all 1964–69 engines, and all V8s 1964–71, use a $^{13}/_{16}$ in. spark plug socket. Six-cylinder engines from 1970 and V8s from 1972 are equipped with tapered seat plugs which require a $^5/_8$ in. socket.

3. If removing the plug is difficult, drip some penetrating oil on the plug threads, allow it to work, then remove the plug. Also, be sure that the socket is straight on the plug, especially on those hard to reach plugs.

INSPECTION

Check the plugs for deposits and wear. If they are not going to be replaced, clean the plugs thoroughly. Remember that any kind of deposit will decrease the efficiency of the plug. Plugs can be cleaned on a spark plug cleaning machine, which can sometimes be found in service stations, or you can do an acceptable job of cleaning with a stiff brush. If the plugs are cleaned, the electrodes must be filed flat. Use an ignition points file, not an emery board or the like, which will leave deposits. The electrodes must be filed perfectly flat with sharp edges; rounded edges reduce the spark plug voltage by as much as 50%.

Check spark plug gap before installation. The ground electrode (the L-shaped one connected to the body of the plug) must be parallel to the center electrode and the specified size wire gauge (see "Tune-Up Specifications") should pass through the gap with a slight drag. Always check the gap on new plugs, too; they are not always set correctly at the factory. Do not use a flat feeler gauge when measuring the gap, because the reading will be inaccurate. Wire gapping tools usually have a bending tool attached. Use that to adjust the side electrode until the proper distance is obtained. *Absolutely never bend the center electrode.* Also, be careful not to bend the side electrode too far or too often; it may weaken and break off within the engine, requiring removal of the cylinder head to retrieve it.

INSTALLATION

1. Lubricate the threads of the spark plugs with a drop of oil. Install the plugs and tighten them hand-tight. Take care not to cross-thread them.

2. Tighten the spark plugs with the socket. Do not apply the same amount of force you would use for a bolt; just snug them in. If a torque wrench is available, tighten to 11–15 ft. lbs.

3. Install the wires on their respective plugs. Make sure the wires are firmly connected. You will be able to feel them click into place.

CHECKING AND REPLACING SPARK PLUG WIRES

Every 15,000 miles, inspect the spark plug wires for burns, cuts, or breaks in the insulation.

Check the boots and the nipples on the distributor cap. Replace any damaged wiring.

Every 45,000 miles or so, the resistance of the wires should be checked with an ohmeter. Wires with excessive resistance will cause misfiring, and may make the engine difficult to start in damp weather. Generally, the useful life of the cables is 45,000–60,000 miles.

To check resistance, remove the distributor cap, leaving the wires in place. Connect one lead of an ohmmeter to an electrode within the cap; connect the other lead to the corresponding spark plug terminal (remove it from the spark plug for this test). Replace any wire which shows a resistance over 30,000 ohms. A chart in Chapter 10 gives resistance values and function of length. Generally speaking, however, resistance should not be over 25,000 ohms, and 30,000 ohms must be considered the outer limit of acceptability.

It should be remembered that resistance is also a function of length; the longer the wire, the greater the resistance. Thus, if the wires on your car are longer than the factory originals, resistance will be higher, quite possibly outside these limits.

When installing new wires, replace them one at a time to avoid mixups. Start by replacing the longest one first. Install the boot firmly over the spark plug. Route the wire over the same path as the original. Insert the nipple firmly onto the tower on the distributor cap, then install the cap cover and latches to secure the wires.

NOTE: *For further information on the spark plug wires, refer to the color insert on Spark Plug Analysis.*

FIRING ORDERS

To avoid confusion, remove and tag the wires one at a time, for replacement.

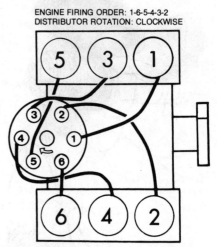

ENGINE FIRING ORDER: 1-6-5-4-3-2
DISTRIBUTOR ROTATION: CLOCKWISE

The 200 (1978–79), 229 (1980–83) and 262 (1984 and later) V6 firing order

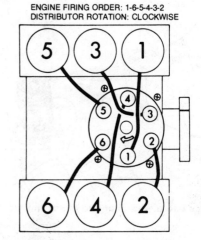

ENGINE FIRING ORDER: 1-6-5-4-3-2
DISTRIBUTOR ROTATION: CLOCKWISE

The 231 (1980–83) V6 firing order

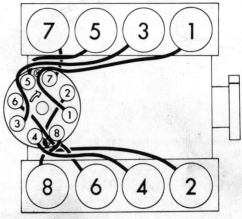

ENGINE FIRING ORDER: 1-8-4-3-6-5-7-2
DISTRIBUTOR ROTATION: CLOCKWISE

1967–74 V8 firing order

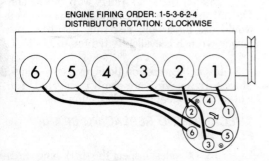

ENGINE FIRING ORDER: 1-5-3-6-2-4
DISTRIBUTOR ROTATION: CLOCKWISE

Inline 6 cyl (1964–79) firing order

ENGINE FIRING ORDER: 1-8-4-3-6-5-7-2
DISTRIBUTOR ROTATION: CLOCKWISE

1975 and later V8 firing order

Breaker Points and Condenser

The points function as a circuit breaker for the primary circuit of the ignition system. The ignition coil must boost the 12 volts of electrical pressure supplied by the battery to as much as 25,000 volts in order to fire the plugs. To do this, the coil depends on the points and the condenser to make a clean break in the primary circuit.

The coil has both primary and secondary circuits. When the ignition is turned on, the battery supplies voltage through the coil and onto the points. The points are connected to ground, completing the primary circuit. As the current passes through the coil, a magnetic field is created in the iron center core of the coil. When the cam in the distributor turns, the points open, breaking the primary circuit. The magnetic field in the primary circuit of the coil then collapses and cuts through the secondary circuit windings around the iron core. Because of the physical principle called "electromagnetic induction," the battery voltage is increased to a level sufficient to fire the spark plugs.

When the points open, the electrical charge in the primary circuit tries to jump the gap created between the two open contacts of the points. If this electrical charge were not transferred elsewhere, the metal contacts of the points would start to change rapidly.

The function of the condenser is to absorb excessive voltage from the points when they open and thus prevent the points from becoming pitted or burned.

If you have ever wondered why it is necessary to tune-up your engine occasionally, consider the fact that the ignition system must complete the above cycle each time a spark plug fires. On a four-cylinder, four-cycle engine, two

of the four plugs must fire once for every engine revolution. If the idle speed of your engine is 800 revolutions per minute (800 rpm), the breaker points open and close two times for each revolution. For every minute your engine idles, your points open and close 1,600 times ($2 \times 800 = 1,600$). And that is just at idle. What about at 60 mph?

There are two ways to check breaker point gap: with a feeler gauge or with a dwell meter. Either way you set the points, you are adjusting the amount of time (in degrees of distributor rotation) that the points will remain open. If you adjust the points with a feeler gauge, you are setting the maximum amount the points will open when the rubbing block on the points is on a high point of the distributor cam. When you adjust the points with a dwell meter, you are measuring the number of degrees (of distributor cam rotation) that the points will remain closed before they start to open as a high point of the distributor cam approaches the rubbing block of the points.

If you still do not understand how the points function, take a friend, go outside, and remove the distributor cap from your engine. Have your friend operate the starter (make sure that the transmission is not in gear) as you look at the exposed parts of the distributor.

There are two rules that should always be followed when adjusting or replacing points. *The points and condenser are a matched set; never replace one without replacing the other. If you change the point gap or dwell of the engine, you also change the ignition timing. Therefore, if you adjust the points, you must also adjust the timing.*

REMOVAL AND INSTALLATION
1964–74

The usual procedure is to replace the condenser each time the point set is replaced. Although this is not always necessary, it is easy to do at this time and the cost is negligible. Every time you adjust or replace the breaker points, the ignition timing must be checked and, if necessary, adjusted. No special equipment other than a feeler gauge is required for point replacement or adjustment, but a dwell meter is strongly advised. A magnetic screwdriver is handy to prevent the small points and condenser screws from falling down into the distributor.

Point sets using the push-in type wiring terminal should be used on those distributors equipped with an R.F.I. (Radio Frequency Interference) shield (1970–74). Points using a lockscrew-type terminal may short out due to contact between the shield and the screw.

The six cylinder distributor cap is retained by two captive screws

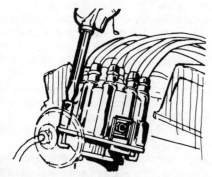

The eight cylinder distributor cap has spring latches

1. Push down on the spring-loaded V8 distributor cap retaining screws and give them a half-turn to release. Unscrew the captive six-cylinder cap retaining screws. Remove the cap. You might have to unclip or detach some or all of the plug wires to remove the cap. If so, number the wires and the cap from removal.

2. Clean the cap inside and out with a clean rag. Check for cracks and carbon paths. A carbon path shows up as a dark line, usually from one of the cap sockets or inside terminals to a ground. Check the condition of the carbon button inside the center of the cap and the inside terminals. Replace the cap as necessary. Carbon paths cannot usually be successfully scraped off. It is better to replace the cap.

3. Pull the six-cylinder rotor up and off the shaft. Remove the two screws and lift the round V8 rotor off. There is less danger of losing the screws if you just back them out all the way and lift them off with the rotor. Clean off the metal outer tip if it is burned or corroded. Don't file it. Replace the rotor as necessary or if one came with your tune-up kit.

4. Remove the radio frequency interference shield if your distributor has one. Watch out for those little screws! The factory says that the points don't need to be replaced if they are only slightly rough or pitted. However, sad experience shows that it is more economical and

reliable in the long run to replace the point set while the distributor is open, than to have to do this at a later (and possibly more inconvenient) time.

5. Pull one of the two wire terminals from the point assembly. One wire comes from the condenser and the other comes from within the distributor. The terminals are usually held in place by spring tension only. There might be a clamp screw securing the terminals on some older versions. There is also available a one-piece point/condenser assembly for V8s. The radio frequency interference shield isn't needed with this set. Loosen the point set hold-down screw(s). Be very careful not to drop any of these little screws inside the distributor. If this happens, the distributor will probably have to be removed to get at the screw. If the hold-down screw is lost elsewhere, it must be replaced with one that is no longer than the original to avoid interference with the distributor workings. Remove the point set, even if it is to be reused.

6. If the points are to be reused, clean them with a few strokes of a special point file. This is done with the points removed to prevent tiny metal filings from getting into the distributor. Don't use sandpaper or emery cloth; they will cause rapid point burning.

7. Loosen the condenser hold-down screw and slide the condenser out of the clamp. This

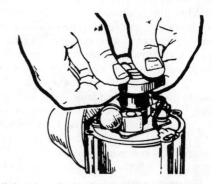

Pull the six cylinder rotor straight up to remove it

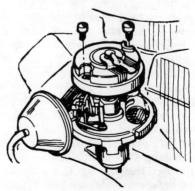

The eight cylinder rotor is held on by two screws

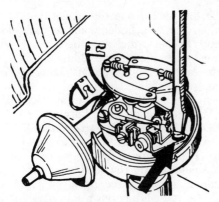

The points are retained by screws; use a magnetic screwdriver to avoid losing them

The condenser is held in place by a screw and a clamp

will save you a struggle with the clamp, condenser, and the tiny screw when you install the new one. If you have the type of clamp that is permanently fastened to the condenser, remove the screw and the condenser. Don't lose the screw.

8. Attend to the distributor cam lubricator. If you have the round kind, turn it around on its shaft at the first tune-up and replace it at the second. If you have the long kind, switch ends at the first tune-up and replace it at the second.

NOTE: *Don't oil or grease the lubricator. The foam is impregnated with a special lubricant.*

If you didn't get any lubricator at all, or if it looks like someone took it off, don't worry. You don't really need it. Just rub a matchhead size dab of grease on the cam lobes.

9. Install the new condenser. If you left the clamp in place, just slide the new condenser into the clamp.

10. Replace the point set and tighten the screws on a V8. Leave the screw slightly loose on a six. Replace the two wire terminals, making sure that the wires don't interfere with anything. Some V8 distributors have a ground wire that must go under one of the screws.

11. Check that the contacts meet squarely.

If they don't, bend the tab supporting the fixed contact.

NOTE: *If you are installing preset points on a V8, go ahead to Step 16. If they are preset, it will say so on the package. It would be a good idea to make a quick check on point gap, anyway. Sometimes those preset points aren't.*

12. Turn the engine until a high point on the cam that opens the points contacts the rubbing block on the point arm. You can turn the engine by hand if you can get a wrench on the crankshaft pulley nut, or you can grasp the fan belt and turn the engine with the spark plugs removed.

CAUTION: *If you try turning the engine by hand, be very careful not to get your fingers pinched in the pulleys.*

On a stick-shift you can push it forward in High gear. Another alternative is to bump the starter switch or use a remote starter switch.

13. On a six, there is a screwdriver slot near the contacts. Insert a screwdriver and lever the points open or closed until they appear to be at about the gap specified in the "Tune-Up Specifications." On a V8, simply insert a 1/8 in. allen wrench into the adjustment screw and turn. The wrench sometimes comes with a tune-up kit.

14. Insert the correct size feeler gauge and

Install the point set on the breaker plate and then attach the wires

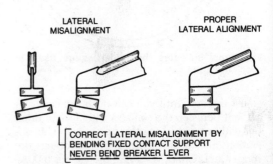

LATERAL MISALIGNMENT   PROPER LATERAL ALIGNMENT

CORRECT LATERAL MISALIGNMENT BY BENDING FIXED CONTACT SUPPORT NEVER BEND BREAKER LEVER

Check the points for proper alignment after installation

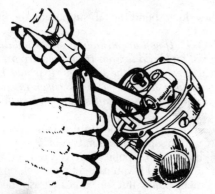

Use a screwdriver to lever the points closer to-gether or farther apart on the six cylinder models

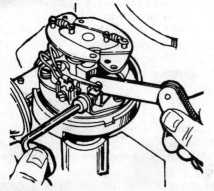

You will need an Allen wrench to adjust the point gap on the V8 engine

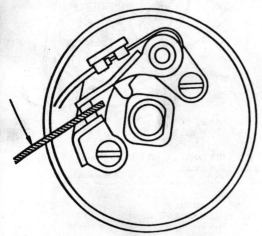

The arrow indicates the feeler gauge used to check the point gap

adjust the gap until you can push the gauge in and out between the contacts with a slight drag, but without disturbing the point arm. This operation takes a bit of experience to obtain the correct feel. Check by trying the gauges 0.001–0.002 larger and smaller than the setting size. The larger one should disturb the point arm,

while the smaller one should not drag at all. Tighten the six-cylinder point set hold-down screw. Recheck the gap, because it often changes when the screw is tightened.

15. After all the point adjustments are complete, pull a white index card through (between) the contacts to remove any traces of oil. Oil will cause rapid contact burning.

NOTE: *You can adjust six-cylinder dwell at this point, if you wish. Refer to Step 18.*

16. Replace the radio frequency interference shield, if any. You don't need it if you are installing the one-piece point/condenser set. Push the rotor firmly down into place. It will only go on one way. Tighten the V8 rotor screws. If the rotor is not installed properly, it will probably break when the starter is operated.

17. Replace the distributor cap.

18. If a dwell meter is available, check the dwell. The dwell meter hookup is shown in the "Troubleshooting" chapter.

NOTE: *This hookup may not apply to electronic, capacitive discharge, or other special ignition systems. Some dwell meters won't work at all with such systems.*

1975 and Later

These engines use the breakerless HEI (High Energy Ignition) system. Since there is no mechanical contact, there is no wear or need for periodic service. There is an item in the distributor that resembles a condenser; it is a radio interference suppression capacitor which requires no service.

Dwell Angle

Dwell angle is the amount of time (measured in degrees of distributor cam rotation) that the contact points remain closed. Initial point gap determines dwell angle. If the points are set too wide they open gradually and dwell angle (the time they remain closed) is small. This wide

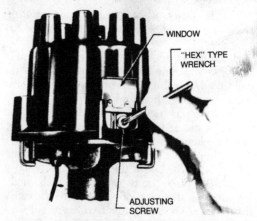

To set the dwell on a V8, lift the window and then turn the adjusting screw

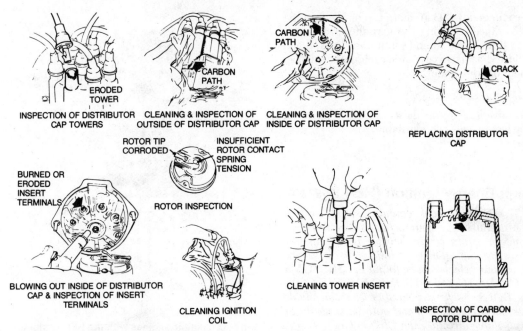

INSPECTION OF DISTRIBUTOR CAP TOWERS

CLEANING & INSPECTION OF OUTSIDE OF DISTRIBUTOR CAP

CLEANING & INSPECTION OF INSIDE OF DISTRIBUTOR CAP

REPLACING DISTRIBUTOR CAP

ROTOR INSPECTION

BLOWING OUT INSIDE OF DISTRIBUTOR CAP & INSPECTION OF INSERT TERMINALS

CLEANING IGNITION COIL

CLEANING TOWER INSERT

INSPECTION OF CARBON ROTOR BUTTON

Inspection points for the distributor, rotor, cap and coil

gap causes excessive arcing at the points and, because of this, point burning. This small dwell doesn't give the coil sufficient time to build up maximum energy and so coil output decreases. If the points are set too close, the dwell is increased but the points may bounce at higher speeds and the idle becomes rough and starting is made harder. The wider the point opening, the smaller the dwell and the smaller the gap, the larger the dwell. Adjusting the dwell by making the initial point gap setting with a feeler gauge is sufficient to get the car started but a finer adjustment should be made. A dwell meter is needed to check the adjustment.

Connect the red lead (positive) wire of the meter to the distributor primary wire connection on the positive (+) side of the coil, and the black ground (negative) wire of the meter to a good ground on the engine. The dwell angle may be checked either with the engine cranking or running, although the reading will be more accurate if the engine is running. With the engine cranking, the reading will fluctuate between zero degrees dwell and the maximum figure for that angle. While cranking, the maximum figure is the correct one.

NOTE: *Dwell angle is permanently set electronically on HEI distributors, requiring no adjustment or checking.*

ADJUSTMENT

1964–74

Dwell can be checked with the engine running or cranking. Decrease dwell by increasing the point gap; increase by decreasing the gap. Dwell angle is simply the number of degrees of distributor shaft rotation during which the points stay closed. Theoretically, if the point gap is correct, the dwell should also be correct or nearly so. Adjustment with a dwell meter produces more exact, consistent results since it is a dynamic adjustment. If dwell varies more than 3 degrees from idle speed to 1,750 engine rpm, the distributor is worn.

1. To adjust dwell on a six, trial and error point adjustments are required. On a V8, simply open the metal window on the distributor and insert a ⅛ in. allen wrench. Turn until the meter shows the correct reading. Be sure to snap the window closed.

2. An approximate dwell adjustment can be made without a meter on a V8. Turn the adjusting screw clockwise until the engine begins to misfire, then turn it out ½ turn.

3. If the engine won't start, check:

   a. That all the spark plug wires are in place.

   b. That the rotor has been installed.

   c. That the two (or three) wires inside the distributor are connected.

   d. That the points open and close when the engine turns.

   e. That the gap is correct and the hold-down screw (on a six) is tight.

4. After the first 200 miles or so on a new set of points, the point gap often closes up due to initial rubbing block wear. For best performance, recheck the dwell (or gap) at this time. This quick initial wear is the reason the factory

recommends 0.003 in. more gap on new points.

5. Since changing the gap affects the ignition timing, the timing should be checked and adjusted as necessary after each point replacement or adjustment.

1974 and Later

The dwell angle on these models is preset at the factory and not adjustable.

High Energy Ignition (HEI) System

NOTE: *This book contains simple testing procedures for your vehicle's electronic ignition. More comprehensive testing in this system and other electronic control systems on your vehicle can be found in CHILTON'S GUIDE TO ELECTRONIC ENGINE CONTROLS, book part number 7535, available at most book stores and auto parts stores or available directly from Chilton Co.*

The General Motors HEI system is a pulse-triggered, transistor-controlled, inductive discharge ignition system. Except on inline six-cylinder models through 1977, the entire HEI system is contained within the distributor cap. Inline six-cylinder engines through 1977 have an external coil. Otherwise, the systems are the same.

The distributor, in addition to housing the mechanical and vacuum advance mechanisms, contains the ignition coil (except on some inline six engines), the electronic control module, and the magnetic pick-up assembly contains a permanent magnet, a pole piece with internal "teeth," and a pick-up coil (not to be confused with the ignition coil).

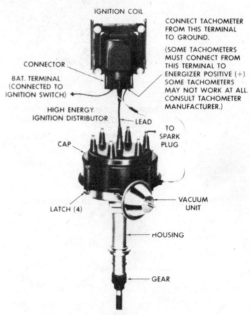

Early six cylinder engines with the HEI distributor had an external coil

For 1981 and later an HEI distributor with Electronic Spark Timing is used (for more information on EST, refer to Chapter 4). This system uses a one piece distributor with the ignition coil mounted in the distributor cap, similar to 1980.

All spark timing changes in the 1981 and later distributors are done electronically by the Electronic Control Module (ECM) which moniters information from various engine sensors, computes the desired spark timing and then signals the distributor to change the timing accordingly. No vacuum or mechanical advance systems are used whatsoever.

V8 HEI distributor components—1975–80 (1978–80 6-cyl. similar)

In the HEI system, as in other electronic ignition systems, the breaker points have been replaced with an electronic switch—a transistor—which is located *within* the control module. This switching transistor performs the same function the points did in a conventional ignition system; it simply turns coil primary current on and off at the correct time. Essentially then, electronic and conventional ignition systems operate on the same principle.

The module which houses the switching transistor is controlled (turned on and off) by a magnetically generated impulse induced in the pick-up coil. When the teeth of the rotating timer align with the teeth of the pole piece, the induced voltage in the pick-up coil signals the electronic module to open the coil primary circuit. The primary current then decreases, and a high voltage is induced in the ignition coil secondary windings which is then directed through the rotor and high voltage leads (spark plug wires) to fire the spark plugs.

In essence then, the pick-up coil module system simply replaces the conventional breaker points and condenser. The condenser found within the distributor is for radio suppression purposes only and has nothing to do with the ignition process. The module automatically controls the dwell period, increasing it with increasing engine speed. Since dwell is automatically controlled, it cannot be adjusted. The module itself is non-adjustable and non-repairable and must be replaced if found defective.

HEI SYSTEM PRECAUTIONS

Before going on to troubleshooting, it might be a good idea to take note of the following precautions:

Timing Light Use

Inductive pick-up timing lights are the best kind to use with HEI. Timing lights which connect between the spark plug and the spark plug wire occasionally (not always) give false readings.

Spark Plug Wires

The plug wires used with HEI systems are of a different construction than conventional wires.

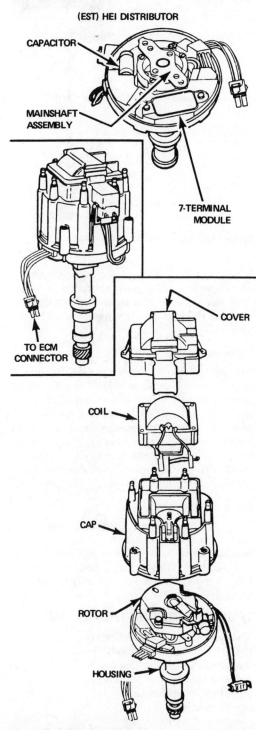

HEI EST distributor components—1981 (note absence of vacuum advance unit)

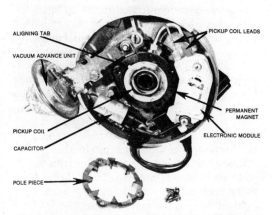

All HEI circuitry is contained within the distributor body (1980 shown)

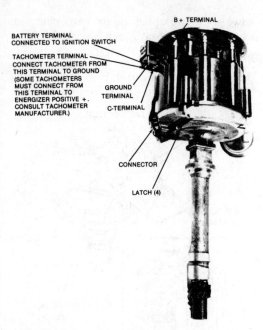

BATTERY TERMINAL
CONNECTED TO IGNITION SWITCH

TACHOMETER TERMINAL
CONNECT TACHOMETER FROM
THIS TERMINAL TO GROUND
(SOME TACHOMETERS
MUST CONNECT FROM
THIS TERMINAL TO
ENERGIZER POSITIVE +.
CONSULT TACHOMETER
MANUFACTURER.)

B + TERMINAL

GROUND
TERMINAL

C-TERMINAL

CONNECTOR

LATCH (4)

Typical HEI distributor connections

When replacing them, make sure you get the correct wires, since conventional wires won't carry the voltage. Also, handle them carefully to avoid cracking or splitting them and *never* pierce them.

Tachometer Use

Not all tachometers will operate or indicate correctly when used on a HEI system. While some tachometers may give a reading, this does not necessarily mean the reading is correct. In addition, some tachometers hook up differently from others. If you can't figure out whether or not your tachometer will work on your car, check with the tachometer manufacturer. Dwell readings, or course, have no significance at all.

HEI System Testers

Instruments designed specifically for testing HEI systems are available from several tool manufacturers. Some of these will even test the module itself. However, the tests given in the following section will require only an ohmmeter and a voltmeter.

TROUBLESHOOTING THE HEI SYSTEM

The symptoms of a defective component within the HEI system are exactly the same as those you would encounter in a conventional system. Some of these symptoms are:

- Hard or no Starting
- Rough Idle
- Poor Fuel Economy
- Engine misses under load or while accelerating

If you suspect a problem in your ignition system, there are certain preliminary checks which you should carry out before you begin to check the electronic portions of the system. First, it is extremely important to make sure the vehicle battery is in a good state of charge. A defective or poorly charged battery will cause the various components of the ignition system to read incorrectly when they are being tested. Second, make sure all wiring connections are clean and tight, not only at the battery, but also at the distributor cap, ignition coil, and at the electronic control module.

Since the only change between electronic and conventional ignition systems is in the distributor component area, it is imperative to check the secondary ignition circuit first. If the secondary circuit checks out properly, then the engine condition is probably not the fault of the ignition system. To check the secondary ignition system, perform a simple spark test. Remove one of the plug wires and insert some sort of extension in the plug socket. An old spark plug with the ground electrode removed makes a good extension. Hold the wire and extension about ¼ in. away from the block and crank the engine. If a normal spark occurs, then the problem is most likely *not* in the ignition system. Check for fuel system problems, or fouled spark plugs.

If, however, there is no spark or a weak spark, then further ignition system testing will have to be done. Troubleshooting techniques fall into two categories, depending on the nature of the problem. The categories are (1) Engine cranks, but won't start or (2) Engine runs, but runs rough or cuts out. To begin with, let's consider the first case.

Engine Fails to Start

If the engine won't start, perform a spark test as described earlier. This will narrow the problem area down considerably. If no spark occurs, check for the presence of normal battery voltage of the battery (BAT) terminal in the distributor cap. The ignition switch must be in the "on" position for this test. Either a voltmeter or a test light may be used for this test. Connect the test light wire to ground and the probe end to the BAT terminal at the distributor. If the light comes on, you have voltage to the distributor. If the light fails to come on, this indicates an open circuit in the ignition primary wiring leading to the distributor. In this case, you will have to check wiring continuity back to the ignition switch using a test light. If there is battery voltage at the BAT terminal, but no spark at the plugs, then the problem lies within the distributor assembly.

HEI Plug Wire Resistance Chart

Wire Length	Minimum	Maximum
0–15 inches	3000 ohms	10,000 ohms
15–25 inches	4000 ohms	15,000 ohms
25–35 inches	6000 ohms	20,000 ohms
Over 35 inches		25,000 ohms

Go on to the distributor components test section.

Engine Runs, But Runs Rough or Cuts Out

1. Make sure the plug wires are in good shape first. There should be no obvious cracks or breaks. You can check the plug wires with an ohmmeter, but *do not* pierce the wires with a probe. Check the chart for the correct plug wire resistance.

2. If the plug wires are OK, remove the cap assembly and check of moisture, cracks, chips, or carbon tracks, or any other high voltage leaks or failures. Replace the cap if any defects are found. Make sure the timer wheel rotates when the engine is cranked. If everything is all right so far, go on to the distributor components test section following.

DISTRIBUTOR COMPONENTS TESTING

If the trouble has been narrowed down to the units within the distributor, the following tests

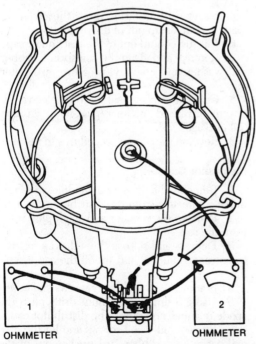

Ohmmeter 1 shows the primary coil resistance connection. Ohmmeter 2 shows the secondary resistance connection (1980 shown, most models similar)

can help pinpoint the defective component. An ohmmeter with both high and low ranges should be used. These tests are made with the cap assembly removed and the battery wire disconnected. If a tachometer is connected to the TACH terminal, disconnect it before making these tests.

1. Connect an ohmmeter between the TACH and BAT terminals in the distributor cap. The primary coil resistance should be less than one ohm.

2. To check the coil secondary resistance, connect an ohmmeter between the rotor button and BAT terminal. Note the reading. Connect the ohmmeter between the rotor button and the TACH terminal. Note the reading. The resistance in both cases should be between 6,000 and 30,000 ohms. Be sure to test between the rotor button and both the BAT and TACH terminals.

3. Replace the coil *only* if the readings in Step 1 and Step 2 are infinite.

NOTE: *These resistance checks will not disclose shorted coil windings. This condition can only be detected with scope analysis or a suitably designed coil tester. If these in-*

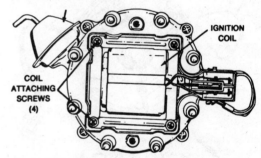

The coil on all but the 1975–77 six cylinder engine is accessible by removing the four attaching screws

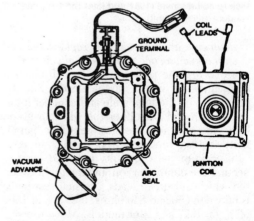

Check the condition of the arc seal under the coil

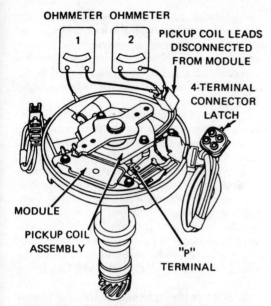

Ohmmeter 1 shows the connections for testing the pickup coil. Ohmmeter 2 shows the connections for testing the pickup coil continuity (1980 shown, most models similar)

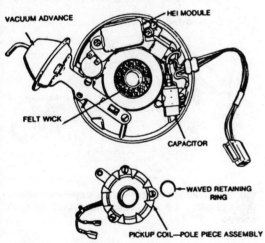

Pickup coil removal (1981 and later models have no vacuum advance unit)

struments are unavailable, replace the coil with a known good coil as a final coil test.

4. To test the pick-up coil, first disconnect the white and green module leads. Set the ohmmeter on the high scale and connect it between a ground and either the white or green lead. Any resistance measurement *less* than infinity requires replacement of the pick-up coil.

5. Pick-up coil continuity is tested by connecting the ohmmeter (on low range) between the white and green leads. Normal resistance is between 650 and 850 ohms, or 500 and 1500 ohms on 1977 and later models. Move the vacuum advance arm while performing this test.

This will detect any break in coil continuity. Such a condition can cause intermittent misfiring. Replace the pick-up if the reading is outside the specified limits.

6. If no defects have been found at this time, you still have a problem, then the module will have to be checked. If you do not have access to a module tester, the only possible alternative is a substitution test. If the module fails the substitution test, replace it.

HEI SYSTEM MAINTENANCE

Except for periodic checks of the spark plug wires, and an occasional check of the distributor cap for cracks (see Steps 1 and 2 under "Engine Runs, But Runs Rough or Cuts Out" for details), no maintenance is required on the HEI System. No periodic lubrication is necessary; engine oil lubricates the lower bushing, and an oil-filled reservoir lubricates the upper bushing.

COMPONENT REPLACEMENT

Integral Ignition Coil

1. Disconnect the feed and module wire terminal connectors from the distributor cap.
2. Remove the ignition set retainer.
3. Remove the 4 coil cover-to-distributor cap screws and the coil cover.
4. Remove the 4 coil-to-distributor cap screws.
5. Using a blunt drift, press the coil wire spade terminals up out of distributor cap.
6. Lift the coil up out of the distributor cap.
7. Remove and clean the coil spring, rubber seal washer and coil cavity of the distributor cap.
8. Coat the rubber seal with a dielectric lubricant furnished in the replacement ignition coil package.
9. Reverse the above procedures to install.

Distributor Cap

1. Remove the feed and module wire terminal connectors from the distributor cap.
2. Remove the retainer and spark plug wires from the cap.
3. Depress and release the 4 distributor cap-to-housing retainers and lift off the cap assembly.
4. Remove the 4 coil cover screws and cover.
5. Using a finger or a blunt drift, push the spade terminals up out of the distributor cap.
6. Remove all 4 coil screws and lift the coil, coil spring and rubber seal washer out of the cap coil cavity.
7. Using a new distributor cap, reverse the above procedures to assemble being sure to

clean and lubricate the rubber seal washer with dielectric lubricant.

Rotor

1. Disconnect the feed and module wire connectors from the distributor.
2. Depress and release the 4 distributor cap-to-housing retainers and lift off the cap assembly.
3. Remove the two rotor attaching screws and rotor.
4. Reverse the above procedure to install.

Vacuum Advance (1975–80)

1. Remove the distributor cap and rotor as previously described.
2. Disconnect the vacuum hose from the vacuum advance unit.
3. Remove the two vacuum advance retaining screws, pull the advance unit outward, rotate and disengage the operating rod from its tang.
4. Reverse the above procedure to install.

Module

1. Remove the distributor cap and rotor as previously described.
2. Disconnect the harness connector and pick-up coil spade connectors from the module. Be careful not to damage the wires when removing the connector.
3. Remove the two screws and module from the distributor housing.
4. Coat the bottom of the new module with dielectric lubricant supplied with the new module. Reverse the above procedure to install.

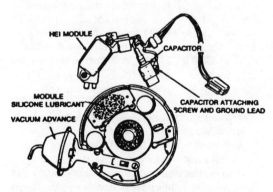

Module replacement, be sure to coat the mating surfaces with silicone lubricant

HEI SYSTEM TACHOMETER HOOKUP

There is a terminal marked TACH on the distributor cap. Connect one tachometer lead to this terminal and the other lead to a ground. On some tachometers, the leads must be connected to the TACH terminal and to the battery positive terminal.

CAUTION: *Never ground the TACH terminal; serious module and ignition coil damage will result. If there is any doubt as to the correct tachometer hookup, check with the tachometer manufacturer.*

1975–77 models with a six cylinder engine utilize an HEI distributor with an external coil. For these particular vehicles, connect one tachometer lead to the TACH terminal on the ignition coil and connect the other one to a suitable ground.

Ignition Timing

Ignition timing is the measurement, in degrees of crankshaft rotation, of the point at which the spark plugs fire in each of the cylinders. It is measured in degrees before or after Top Dead Center (TDC) of the compression stroke.

Because it takes a fraction of a second for the spark plug to ignite the mixture in the cylinder, the spark plug must fire a little before the piston reaches TDC. Otherwise, the mixture will not be completely ignited as the piston passes TDC and the full power of the explosion will not be used by the engine.

The timing measurement is given in degrees of crankshaft rotation before the piston reaches TDC (BTDC). If the setting for the ignition timing is 5° BTDC, the spark plug must fire 5° before each piston reaches TDC. This only holds true, however, when the engine is at idle speed.

As the engine speed increases, the pistons go faster. The spark plugs have to ignite the fuel even sooner if it is to be completely ignited when the piston reaches TDC. To do this, the distributor has two means to advance the timing of the spark as the engine speed increases. This is accomplished by centrifugal weights within the distributor, and a vacuum dia-

Typical ignition timing marks

phragm mounted on the side of the distributor.

If the ignition is set too far advanced (BTDC), the ignition and expansion of the fuel in the cylinder will occur too soon and tend to force the piston down while it is still traveling up. This causes engine ping. If the ignition spark is set too far retarded, after TDC (ATDC), the piston will have already passed TDC and started on its way down when the fuel is ignited. This will cause the piston to be forced down for only a portion of its travel. This will result in poor engine performance and lack of power.

Timing marks consist of a notch on the rim of the crankshaft pulley and a scale of degrees attached to the front of the engine. The notch corresponds to the position of the piston in the number 1 cylinder. A stroboscopic (dynamic) timing light is used, which is hooked into the circuit of the No. 1 cylinder spark plug. Every time the spark plug fires, the timing light flashes. By aiming the timing light at the timing marks, the exact position of the piston within the cylinder can be read, since the stroboscopic flash makes the mark on the pulley appear to be standing still. Proper timing is indicated when the notch is aligned with the correct number on the scale.

There are three basic types of timing lights available. The first is a simple neon bulb with two wire connections (one for the spark plug and one for the plug wire, connecting the light in series). This type of light is quite dim, and must be held closely to the marks to be seen, but it is quite inexpensive. The second type of light operates from the car's battery. Two alligator clips connect to the battery terminals, while a third wire connects to the spark plug with an adapter. This type of light is more expensive, but the xenon bulb provides a nice bright flash which can even be seen in sunlight. The third type replaces the battery source with 110 volt house current. Some timing lights have other functions built into them, such as dwell meters, tachometers, or remote starting switches. These are convenient, in that they reduce the tangle of wires under the hood, but may duplicate the functions of tools you already have.

If your car has electronic ignition, you should use a timing light with an inductive pickup. This pickup simply clamps onto the No. 1 spark plug wire, eliminating the adapter. It is not susceptible to crossfiring or false triggering, which may occur with a conventional light, due to the greater voltages produced by electronic ignition.

CHECKING AND ADJUSTMENT

1. Warm the engine to normal operating temperature. Shut off the engine and connect the timing light to the No. 1 spark plug (left front on V8 and V6 or front on an inline 6 cyl.). Do not, under any circumstances, pierce a wire to hook up a light.

2. Clean off the timing marks and mark the pulley or damper notch and the timing scale with white chalk or paint. The timing notch on the damper or pulley can be elusive. Bump the engine around with the starter or turn the crankshaft with a wrench on the front pulley bolt to get it to an accessible position.

3. Disconnect and plug the vacuum advance hose (if equipped) at the distributor, to prevent any distributor advance. The vacuum line is the rubber hose connected to the metal cone-shaped canister on the side of the distributor. A short screw, pencil, or a golf tee can be used to plug the hose.

NOTE: *1981 models with Electronic Spark Timing have no vacuum advance, therefore you may skip the previous step, but you must disconnect the four terminal EST connector before going on.*

4. Start the engine and adjust the idle speed to that specified in the "Tune-Up Specifications" chart. Some cars require that the timing be set with the transmission in Neutral. You can disconnect the idle solenoid, if any, to get the speed down. Otherwise, adjust the idle speed screw. This is to prevent any centrifugal advance of timing in the distributor.

The tachometer hookup for cars 1964–74 is the same as that shown for the dwell meter in the "Tune-Up" section. On 1975–77 HEI systems, the tachometer connects to the TACH terminal on the distributor for V8s, or on the coil for sixes, and to a ground. For 1978 and later models, all tachometer connections are to the TACH terminal. Some tachometers must connect to the TACH terminal and to the positive battery terminal. Some tachometers won't work at all with HEI. Consult the tachometer manufacturer if the instructions supplied with the unit do not give the proper connection.

CAUTION: *Never ground the HEI TACH terminal; serious system damage will result, including module burnout.*

5. Aim the timing light at the timing marks, Be careful not to touch the fan, which may appear to be standing still. Keep your clothes and hair, and the light's wires clear of the fan, belts and pulleys. If the pulley or damper notch isn't aligned with the proper timing mark (see the "Tune-Up Specifications" chart), the timing will have to be adjusted.

NOTE: *TDC or Top Dead Center corresponds to 0 degrees; B, or BTDC, or Before Top Dead Center, may be shown as BEFORE; A or ATDC, or After Top Dead Center, may be shown as AFTER.*

6. Loosen the distributor base clamp locknut. You can buy special wrenches which make this task a lot easier on V8s and V6s. Turn the distributor slowly to adjust the timing, holding it by the body and not the cap. Turn the distributor in the direction of rotor rotation (found in the "Firing Order" illustration in this Chapter) to retard, and against the direction to advance.

NOTE: *The 231 V6 engine has two timing marks on the crankshaft pulley. One timing mark is ⅛ in. wide and the other, four inches away, is ¹⁄₁₆ in. wide. The smaller mark is used for setting the timing with a hand-held timing light. The larger mark is used with the magnetic probe and is only of use to a dealer or garage. Make sure you set the timing using the smaller mark.*

7. Tighten the locknut. Check the timing, in case the distributor moved as you tightened it.

8. Replace the distributor vacuum hose, if removed. Correct the idle speed.

9. Shut off the engine and disconnect the light.

Valve Lash

Hydraulic valve lifters rarely require adjustment, and are not adjusted as part of a normal tune-up. All adjustment procedures concerning them will be found in Chapter 3.

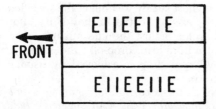

Valve arrangement, Chevrolet small-block V8

Inline six cylinder valve arrangement

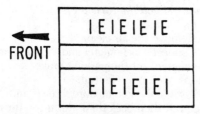

Big-block V8 valve arrangement

Solid Lifters (1964–71)

Before adjusting solid lifters, thoroughly warm the engine. The solid lifters are generally found on certain high-performance engines.

ENGINE RUNNING

1. Run the engine to reach normal operating temperature.

2. Remove the valve covers and gaskets by tapping the end of the cover rearward. Do not attempt to pry the cover off.

3. To avoid being splashed with hot oil, use oil deflector clips. Place one each oil hole in the rocker arm.

4. Measure between the rocker arm and the valve stem with a flat feeler gauge, then adjust the rocker arm stud nut until clearance agrees with the specifications in the chart.

5. After adjusting all the valves, stop the engine, clean the gasket surfaces, and install the valve covers with new gaskets.

Oil deflector clips will prevent splatter when adjusting the valves with the engine running

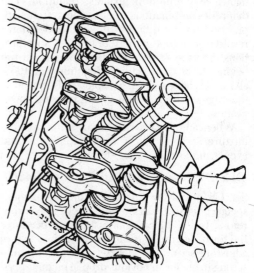

Adjusting the solid valve lifters

ENGINE NOT RUNNING

These are initial adjustments usually required after assembling an engine or doing a valve job. They should be followed up by an adjustment with the engine running as described above.

1. Set the engine to the No. 1 firing position.

2. Adjust the clearance between the valve stems and the rocker arms with a feeler gauge. Check the Chart for the proper clearance. Adjust the following valves in the No. 1 firing position: Intake No. 2, 7, Exhaust No. 4, 8.

3. Turn the crankshaft one-half revolution clockwise. Adjust the following valves: Intake No. 1, 8, Exhaust No. 3, 6.

4. Turn the crankshaft one-half revolution clockwise to No. 6 firing position. Adjust the following valves in the No. 6 firing position: Intake No. 3, 4, Exhaust No. 5, 7.

5. Turn the crankshaft one-half revolution clockwise. Adjust the following valves: Intake No. 5, 6, Exhaust No. 1, 2.

6. Run the engine until the normal operating temperature is reached. Reset all clearances, using the procedure listed above under "Engine Running."

Hydraulic Lifters—1972 and Later

All models, with the exception of those few already discussed, use a hydraulic tappet system with adjustable rocker mounting nuts to obtain zero lash. No periodic adjustment is necessary.

Carburetor

Idle mixture and speed adjustments are critical aspects of exhaust emission control. It is important that all tune-up instructions be carefully followed to ensure satisfactory engine performance and minimum exhaust pollution. The different combinations of emission systems application on the different engine models have resulted in a great variety of tune-up specifications. See the "Tune-Up Specifications" at the beginning of this section. Beginning in 1968, all models have a decal conspicuously placed in the engine compartment giving tune-up specifications.

When adjusting a carburetor with two idle mixture screws, adjust them alternately and evenly, unless otherwise stated.

IDLE SPEED AND MIXTURE ADJUSTMENT

See Chapter 4 for illustrations and adjustment specifications of Carter and Rochester carburetors. In the following adjustment procedures the term "lean roll" means turning the mixture adjusting screws in (clockwise) from optimum setting to obtain an obvious drop in engine speed (usually 20 rpm).

1964–66

Turn the idle screw(s) slightly *in* to seat, and then back out 1½ turns (3 when equipped with A.I.R.). Do not turn the idle mixture screws tightly against their seats or you could damage them. With the engine idling at operating temperature (air cleaner on, preheater valve and choke valve wide open), adjust the idle speed to the specified (automatic transmission in Drive; manual in Neutral).

Adjust the mixture screw to obtain the highest steady idle speed, then adjust the idle speed screw to the specified rpm. Adjust the mixture screw *in* to obtain a 20 rpm drop, then back the screw out ¼ turn. Repeat this operation on the second mixture, if so equipped. Readjust the idle speed screw as necessary until the specified rpm is reached.

1967 Without Air

Adjust with air cleaner removed.

1. Remove the air cleaner.

2. Connect a tachometer and vacuum gauge to the engine, set the parking brake, and place the transmission in Neutral.

3. Turn in the idle mixture screws until they *gently* seat, then back out 1½ turns.

4. Start the engine and allow it to come to the normal operating temperature. Make sure the choke is fully open, then adjust the idle speed screw to obtain the specified idle speed (automatic in Drive, manual in Neutral).

5. Adjust the idle mixture screw(s) to obtain the highest steady vacuum at the specified idle speed, except for the Rochester BV. For this carburetor, adjust the idle mixture screw out ¼ turn from lean "drop-off," the point where a 20–30 rpm drop is achieved by leaning the mixture.

NOTE: *On carburetors having a hot idle compensator valve (A/C models), hold the brass valve down with a pencil while making the mixture adjustment.*

6. Repeat Steps four and five if necessary.

7. Turn off the engine, remove the gauges, and install the air cleaner.

1967 With Air

Adjust with the air cleaner removed.

NOTE: *During this adjustment, air conditioning should be turned off on 327 and 350 cu in. engines.*

1. Remove the air cleaner.

2. Connect a tachometer and a vacuum gauge to the engine, set the parking brake, and place the transmission in Neutral.

3. Turn in the idle mixture screw(s) until they *gently* seat, then back them out three turns.

4. Start the engine and allow it to reach nor-

mal operating temperature. Make sure the choke is fully open, then adjust the idle speed screw(s) to obtain the specified idle speed (automatic in Drive, manual in Neutral).

5. Turn the idle mixture screw(s) clockwise (in) to the point where a 20–30 rmp drop in speed is achieved—this is the lean "drop off" point. Back out the screws ¼ turn from this point.

6. Repeat Steps four and five if necessary.

7. Turn off the engine, remove the gauges, and install the air cleaner.

1968–69

Adjust with the air cleaner installed.

NOTE: *Turn off the air conditioner (if applicable) unless your car is a 1968 model with the 6 cylinder engine and automatic transmission. These cars should have the air conditioner turned on when setting the idle.*

1. Turn in the idle mixture screw(s) until they seat gently, then back them out three turns.

2. Start the engine and allow it to reach operating temperature. Make sure the choke is fully open and the preheater valve is open, then adjust the idle speed screw to obtain the specified idle speed (automatic in Drive, manual in Neutral).

3. Adjust the idle mixture screw(s) to obtain the highest steady idle speed, then readjust the idle speed screw to obtain the specified speed. On cars with an idle stop solenoid adjust as follows:

a. Adjust the idle speed to 500 RPM (6) or 600 rpm (1968 V8) by turning the hex on the solenoid plunger. Refer to the tune-up decal in the engine compartment for 1969 idle speeds.

b. Disconnect the wire at the solenoid. This allows the throttle lever to seat against the idle screw.

c. Adjust the idle screw to obtain 400 rpm (1968), then reconnect the wire. On 1969 models, adjust the idle to that specified on the tune-up decal in the engine compartment.

4. Adjust one mixture screw to obtain a 20 rpm drop in idle speed, and back out the screw ¼ turn from this point.

5. Repeat Steps three and four for the second mixture screw (if so equipped).

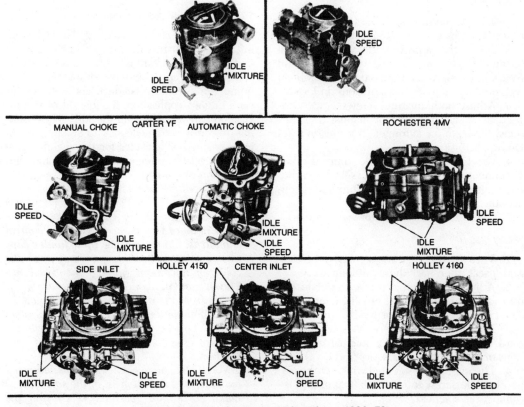

Idle speed and mixture screw location—1964–72

6. Readjust the idle speed to obtain the specified idle speed.

1970—Initial Adjustments

Adjust with the air cleaner installed.

1. Disconnect the fuel tank line from the vapor canister (EEC).

2. Connect a tachometer to the engine, start the engine and allow it to reach operating temperature. Make sure the choke and preheater valves are fully open.

3. Turn off the air conditioner and set the parking brake. Disconnect and plug the distributor vacuum line.

4. Make the following adjustments:

6-250

1. Turn in the mixture screw until it *gently* seats, then back out the screw four turns.

2. Adjust the solenoid screw to obtain 830 rpm for manual transmissions (in Neutral) or 630 rpm for automatic transmissions (in Drive).

3. Adjust the mixture screw to obtain 750 rpm for manual transmissions (in Neutral) or 600 rpm for automatic transmissions (in Drive).

4. Disconnect the solenoid wire and set the idle speed to 400 rpm, then reconnect it.

5. Reconnect the distributor vacuum line.

V8-307, 400

1. Turn in the mixture screws until they seat *gently*, then back them out four turns.

2. Adjust the carburetor idle speed screw to obtain 800 rpm for manual transmissions (in Neutral), or adjust the solenoid screw to obtain 630 rpm for automatic transmissions (in Drive).

3. Adjust both mixture screws equally inward to obtain 700 rpm for manual transmissions, 600 rpm for automatic transmissions (in Drive).

4. On cars with automatic transmissions, disconnect the solenoid wire, set the carburetor idle screw to obtain 450 rpm and reconnect the solenoid.

5. Reconnect the distributor vacuum line.

V8-350 (250 HP)

1. Turn in the mixture screws until they *gently* seat, then back them out four turns.

2. Adjust the solenoid screw to obtain 830 rpm for manual transmissions (in neutral), or 630 rpm for automatic transmissions (in Drive).

3. Adjust both mixture screws equally inward to obtain 750 rpm for manual transmissions or 600 rpm for automatics (in Drive).

4. Disconnect the solenoid wire, set the carburetor idle screw to obtain 450 rpm, and reconnect the solenoid.

5. Reconnect the distributor vacuum line.

V8-350 (300 HP), 402 (330 HP)

1. Turn in both mixture screws until they *gently* seat, then back them out four turns.

2. Adjust the carburetor idle screw to obtain 775 rpm for manual transmissions, 630 rpm for automatics (in Drive).

3. Adjust the mixture screws equally to obtain 700 rpm for manual transmissions, 600 rpm for automatics (in Drive).

4. Reconnect the distributor vacuum line.

V8-402 (350 HP), 454

1. Turn in both mixture screws until they *gently* seat, then back them out four turns.

2. Adjust the carburetor idle screw to obtain 700 rpm for manual transmissions or 630 rpm for automatics (in Drive).

3. For cars with automatic transmissions: adjust the mixture screws equally to obtain 600 rpm with the transmission in Drive.

4. For cars with manual transmissions: turn in *one* mixture screw until the speed drops to 400 rpm, then adjust the carburetor idle screw to obtain 700 rpm. Turn in the *other* mixture screw until the speed drops 400 rpm, then regain 700 rpm by adjusting the carburetor idle screw.

5. Reconnect the distributor vacuum line.

1971–72—Initial Adjustments

Adjust with air cleaner installed. The following initial idle adjustments are part of the normal engine tune-up. There is a tune-up decal placed conspicuously in the engine compartment outlining the specific procedure and settings for each engine application. Follow all of the instructions when adjusting the idle. These tuning procedures are necessary to obtain the delicate balance of variables for the maintenance of both reliable engine performance and efficient exhaust emission control.

NOTE: *All engines have limiter caps on the mixture adjusting screws. The idle mixture is preset and the limiter caps installed at the factory in order to meet emission control standards. Do not remove these limiter caps unless all other possible causes of poor idle condition have been thoroughly checked out. The solenoid used on 1971 carburetors is different from the one used on earlier models. The Combination Emission Control System (C.E.C.) solenoid valve regulates distributor vacuum as a function of transmission gear position.*

CAUTION: *The C.E.C. solenoid is adjusted only after: 1) replacement of the solenoid, 2) major carburetor overhaul, or 3) after the throttle body is removed or replaced.*

All initial adjustments described below are made:

1. With the engine warmed up and running.

2. With the choke fully open.

3. With the fuel tank line disconnected from the Evaporative Emission canister on all models.

4. With the vacuum hose disconnected at the distributor and plugged.

Be sure to reconnect the distributor vacuum hose and to connect the fuel tank-to-evaporative emission canister line or install the gas cap when idle adjustments are complete.

6-250

1. Adjust the carburetor idle speed screw to obtain 550 rpm (700 rpm for 1972) for manual transmissions (in Neutral) or 550 rpm (600 rpm for 1972) for automatics (in Drive). *Do not adjust the solenoid screw.* Using the solenoid screw to set idle or incorrectly adjusting it may result in a decrease in engine braking.

2. Reconnect the vapor line and distributor vacuum advance line.

V8-307 AND 350 (2-BBL)

1. On 1971 models, adjust the carburetor idle speed screw to obtain 600 rpm for manual transmission (in Neutral) with the air conditioning turned off, or 550 rpm for automatic transmissions (in Drive) with the air conditioning turned on. *Do not adjust the solenoid screw.* On 1972 models, turn the air conditioning off and adjust the idle stop solenoid screw to obtain 900 rpm for manual transmissions (in Neu-

tral) or 600 rpm for automatics (in Drive). Place the transmission in Park or Neutral and adjust the fast idle cam screw to get 1,850 rpm on 307 engines and 2,200 rpm on 350 engines.

2. Reconnect the vapor line and distributor vacuum advance line.

V8-350 (4-BBL)

1. On 1971 models, adjust the carburetor idle speed screw to obtain 600 rpm for manual transmissions (in Neutral) with the air conditioning turned off, or 550 rpm for automatics (in Drive) with the air conditioning turned on. *Do not adjust the solenoid screw.* On 1972 models, turn the air conditioning off and adjust the idle stop solenoid screw to get 800 rpm for manual transmissions (in Neutral) or 600 rpm for automatic transmissions (in Drive).

2. For both 1971 and 1972 models, place the fast idle cam follower on the second step of the fast idle cam, turn the air conditioning off and adjust the fast idle to 1,350 rpm for manual transmissions (in Neutral) or 1,500 rpm for automatics (in Park).

3. Reconnect the vapor line and the distributor vacuum advance line on all models.

V8-402, 454

1. On 1971 models, turn off the air conditioner and adjust the carburetor idle speed screw to obtain 600 rpm with manual transmissions in Neutral and automatics in Drive. *Do not adjust the solenoid screw.* On 1972 cars, turn off the air conditioning and adjust the idle stop solenoid screw to 800 rpm (in Neutral) for man-

ROCHESTER CARBURETORS

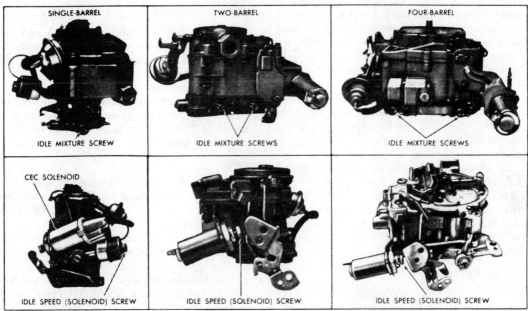

Idle speed and mixture screw location—1973–75

IDLE MIXTURE SCREW

IDLE SPEED SOLENOID SCREW

Idle speed and mixture screw location—1972 Holley 4150

ual transmissions and 600 rpm (in Drive) for automatics.

2. On both 1971 and 1972 cars, place the fast idle cam follower on the second step of the fast idle cam, turn off the air conditioner and adjust the fast idle to 1,350 rpm for manual transmissions (in Neutral) or 1,500 rpm for automatics (in Park).

3. Reconnect the vapor line and the distributor vacuum line on 1971 and 1972 cars.

1973—Initial Adjustments

All models are equipped with idle limiter caps and idle solenoids. Disconnect the fuel tank line from the evaporative canister. The engine must be running at operating temperature, choke off, parking brake on, and rear wheels blocked. Disconnect the distributor vacuum hose and plug it. After adjustment, reconnect the vacuum and evaporative hoses.

6-250

Adjust the idle stop solenoid for 700 rpm on manual transmission models or 600 rpm on automatics (in Drive). On manual models, make no attempt to adjust the CEC solenoid (the larger of the two carburetor solenoids) or a decrease in engine braking could result.

V8-307 & 350, 400 (2-BBL)

1. With the air conditioning Off, adjust the idle stop solenoid screw for a speed of 900 rpm on manual models; 600 rpm for automatics in Drive.

2. Disconnect the idle stop solenoid electrical connector and adjust the idle speed screw (screw resting on lower step of the cam) for 450 rpm on all 307 cu in. engines, 400 rpm on 350 and 400 engines with automatic transmissions, or 500 rpm on 350 and 400 u in. engine with manual transmissions.

V8-350, 400 (4-BBL)

1. Adjust the idle stop solenoid screw to 900 rpm (manual), 600 rpm (automatic in Drive).

2. Connect the distributor vacuum hose and position the fast idle cam follower on the top step of the fast idle cam (turn air conditioning off) and adjust the fast idle to 1300 rpm on manual transmission 350 engines; 1600 rpm for all automatics in Park.

V8-454

1. With the air conditioning off, adjust the idle stop solenoid screw to 900 rpm for the manual transmission; 700 rpm with the automatic transmission in Drive.

2. Connect the distributor vacuum hose and place fast idle cam follower on the top step of the fast idle cam. Adjust the fast idle to 1300 rpm for manual transmission; and 1600 rpm for automatic transmissions (in Park).

1974

The same preliminary adjustments as for 1973 apply.

6-250

1. Using the hex nut on the end of the solenoid body, turn the entire solenoid to get 850 rpm for the manual transmission; 600 rpm for automatic transmissions in Drive.

V8-350, 400 (2-BBL)

1. Turn the air conditioning off. Adjust the idle stop solenoid screw for 900 rpm on manual; 600 rpm on automatic (in Drive).

2. De-energize the solenoid and adjust the carburetor idle cam screw (on low step of cam) for 400 rpm on automatic models (in Drive); 500 rpm on 350 engines with manual transmission.

V8-350, 400 (4-BBL)

1. Turn the air conditioning off. Adjust the idle stop solenoid screw for 900 rpm on manual transmission models; 600 rpm on automatic (in Drive).

2. Connect the distributor vacuum hose. Position the fast idle cam follower on the top step of the fast idle cam and adjust the fast idle speed to 1300 rpm on manual; 1600 on automatic (in Park).

V8-454

1. With the air conditioning off, adjust the idle stop solenoid screw for 800 rpm with the manual transmission; 600 with the automatic transmission in Drive.

2. Reconnect the distributor vacuum advance hose and place the fast idle cam follower on the top step of the fast idle cam. With the air conditioning off, adjust the fast idle to 1600 rpm for manual transmissions; 1500 rpm for all automatics in Park.

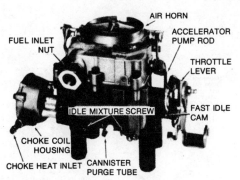

Idle mixture screw location—1976–77 2GC

1975–76

6-250 (1-BBL)

1. Idle speed is adjusted with the engine at normal operating temperature, air cleaner on, choke open, and air conditioning off (air conditioning on—1976 automatic transmission models). Hook up a tachometer to the engine.

2. Block the rear wheels and apply the parking brake.

3. Disconnect the fuel tank hose from the evaporative canister.

4. Disconnect and plug the distributor vacuum advance hose.

5. Start the engine and check the ignition timing. Adjust if necessary. Reconnect the vacuum hose. To adjust the idle speed, turn the solenoid in or out to obtain the higher of the two specifications listed on the decal. With the automatic transmission in Drive or the manual transmission in Neutral, disconnect the solenoid electrical connector and turn the ⅛ in. Allen screw in the end of the solenoid body to the lower idle speed.

6. Place the shift lever in Drive on cars with automatic transmissions and have an assistant apply the brakes. On cars with manual transmissions, put it into Neutral.

7. Cut the tab off the mixture limiter cap, but don't remove the cap. Turn the screw counterclockwise until the highest idle speed is reached.

8. Set the idle speed to the higher of the two listed idle speeds by turning the solenoid in or out.

9. Check the tachometer and turn the mixture screw clockwise until the idle speed is at the lower of the two listed idle speeds.

10. Shut off the engine, remove the tachometer, and reconnect the carbon canister hose.

V8-350; 1975 (2-BBL)
V8-305; 1976 (2-BBL)

1. Idle speed is adjusted with the engine at normal operating temperature, air cleaner on,

choke open, and air conditioning off. Hook up a tachometer to the engine.

2. Block the rear wheels and apply the parking brake.

3. Disconnect the fuel tank hose from the evaporative canister.

4. Disconnect and plug the distributor vacuum advance hose.

5. Start the engine and check the ignition timing. Adjust if necessary. Reconnect the vacuum hose.

6. Adjust the idle speed screw to the specified rpm. If the figures given in the "Tune-Up Specifications" chart differ from those on the tune-up decal, those on the decal take precedence. Automatic transmissions should be in Drive, manual transmissions should be in Neutral.

CAUTION: *Make doubly sure that the rear wheels are blocked and the parking brake applied.*

7. Adjust the idle speed to the higher of the two figures on the tune-up decal. Back out the two mixture screws equally until the highest idle is reached. Reset the speed if necessary to the higher one on the tune-up decal. Next, turn the screws in equally until the lower of the two figures on the decal is obtained.

8. Shut off engine, reconnect hose to evaporative canister, and remove blocks from wheels.

V8-350, 400, 454

1975 four-barrel carburetors are equipped with idle stop solenoids. There are two idle speeds, one with the solenoid energized and second with the solenoid de-energized. Both are set with the solenoid. The slower speed (solenoid de-energized) is necessary to prevent dieseling by allowing the throttle plates to close further than at a normal idle speed.

1. Idle speed is set with the engine at normal operating temperature, air cleaner on, choke open, and air conditioning off. Hook up a tachometer to the engine.

2. Block the rear wheels and apply the parking brake.

3. Disconnect the fuel tank hose from the evaporative canister.

4. Disconnect and plug the distributor vacuum advance hose.

5. Start the engine and check the ignition timing. Adjust if necessary. Reconnect the vacuum hose.

6. Disconnect the electrical connector at the idle solenoid.

7. Set the transmission in Drive. Adjust the low idle speed screw for the lower of the two figures given for idle speed.

CAUTION: *Make sure that the drive wheels*

are blocked and the parking brake is applied.

8. Reconnect the idle solenoid and open the throttle slightly to extend the solenoid plunger.

9. Turn the solenoid plunger screw in or out to obtain the higher of the two idle speed figures (this is normal curb-idle).

10. To adjust the mixture, break off the limiter caps. Make sure that the idle is at the higher of the two speeds listed on the decal. Turn the mixture screws out equally to obtain the highest idle. Reset the idle speed with the plunger screw if necessary. Turn the mixture screws in until the lower of the two figures on the decal is obtained.

11. Shut off engine, remove blocks from drive wheels, and reconnect hose to evaporative canister.

NOTE: *For 1976, the idle solenoid has been dropped. To adjust the idle, follow the preceding Steps 1–5. Skip Steps 6, 7, and 8, then follow Steps 9 and 10, adjusting the idle speed screw.*

1977

1. First satisfy all the following requirements:

    A. Set parking brake and block drive wheels.

    B. Bring the engine to operating temperature.

    C. Remove the air cleaner for access, but make sure all hoses stay connected.

    D. Consult the Emission Control Information label under the hood, and disconnect and plug hoses as required by the instructions there.

    E. Connect an accurate tach to the engine.

2. Set ignition timing as described above.

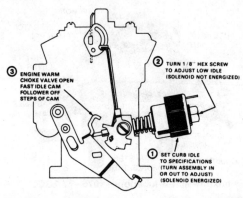

Idle speed adjustment screw location—1976–79 1 BBL

3. Remove the cap(s) from the idle mixture screw(s). Remove caps carefully, to prevent bending these screws.

4. Turn in the screw(s) till they seat *very lightly,* then back screw(s) out just far enough to permit the engine to run.

5. Put automatic transmission in Drive.

6. Back out screw(s) ⅛ turn at a time, going alternately from screw to screw after each ⅛ turn where there are two screws, until the highest possible idle speed is achieved. Then, set the idle speed as follows: 250 CID engine with manual transmission—950; with automatic—575; with automatic in California—640; with automatic used in higher altitude area—650; 305 V8 with manual transmission—650; with automatic—550; standard 350 V8, manual transmission—800; standard 350 V8 with automatic—550; 350 V8 used at high altitudes—650.

7. After setting the idle speed, repeat the mixture adjustment to ensure that mixture is at the point where highest idle speed is obtained. Then, if idle speed has increased, repeat idle speed adjustment of Step 6.

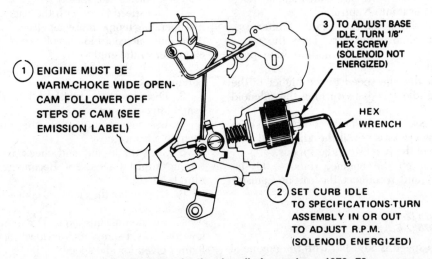

Idle speed adjustment for the six cylinder engine—1976–78

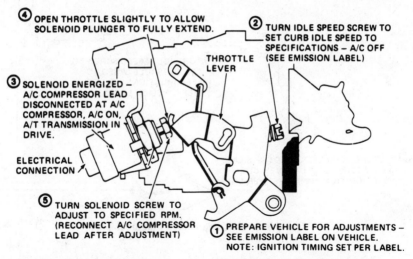

④ OPEN THROTTLE SLIGHTLY TO ALLOW SOLENOID PLUNGER TO FULLY EXTEND.

② TURN IDLE SPEED SCREW TO SET CURB IDLE SPEED TO SPECIFICATIONS – A/C OFF (SEE EMISSION LABEL)

THROTTLE LEVER

③ SOLENOID ENERGIZED – A/C COMPRESSOR LEAD DISCONNECTED AT A/C COMPRESSOR, A/C ON, A/T TRANSMISSION IN DRIVE.

ELECTRICAL CONNECTION

⑤ TURN SOLENOID SCREW TO ADJUST TO SPECIFIED RPM. (RECONNECT A/C COMPRESSOR LEAD AFTER ADJUSTMENT)

① PREPARE VEHICLE FOR ADJUSTMENTS – SEE EMISSION LABEL ON VEHICLE. NOTE: IGNITION TIMING SET PER LABEL.

Idle speed adjustment for the the V8, 4 BBL with solenoid—1977

8. Now, turn screw(s) in, going evenly in ⅛ turn increments where there are two, until the following idle speeds are obtained: 250 CID engine with manual transmission—750; with automatic—550; with automatic in California—600; with automatic used in high altitude areas—600; 305 V8 with manual transmission—600; with automatic—500; standard 350 V8, manual transmission—700; standard 350 V8 with automatic—500; 350 V8 used at high altitudes—600.

9. Reset idle speed to the value shown on the engine compartment sticker, if that differs from the final setting in the step above.

10. Check and adjust fast idle as described on the engine compartment sticker. See Chapter 4.

11. Reconnect any vacuum hoses that were disconnected for the procedure, and install the air cleaner.

12. If idle speed has changed, reset according to the engine compartment sticker. Disconnect tach.

1978 and Later

1978 and later models have sealed idle mixture screws; in most cases these are concealed under staked-in plugs. Idle mixture is adjustable only during carburetor overhaul, and requires the addition of propane as an artificial mixture enrichener.

See the emission control label in the engine compartment for procedures and specifications not supplied here. Prepare the car for adjustment (engine warm, choke open, fast idle screw off the fast idle cam) as per the label instructions.

1BBL

1. Run the engine to normal operating temperature.

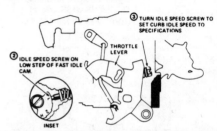

① PREPARE VEHICLE FOR ADJUSTMENTS

③ TURN IDLE SPEED SCREW TO SET CURB IDLE SPEED TO SPECIFICATIONS

THROTTLE LEVER

② IDLE SPEED SCREW ON LOW STEP OF FAST IDLE CAM.

INSET

Idle speed adjustment for the V8, 4 BBL without solenoid—1977

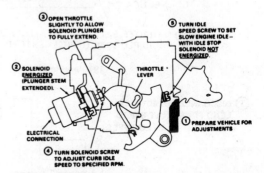

③ OPEN THROTTLE SLIGHTLY TO ALLOW SOLENOID PLUNGER TO FULLY EXTEND.

⑤ TURN IDLE SPEED SCREW TO SET SLOW ENGINE IDLE – WITH IDLE STOP SOLENOID NOT ENERGIZED.

② SOLENOID ENERGIZED (PLUNGER STEM EXTENDED).

THROTTLE LEVER

ELECTRICAL CONNECTION

④ TURN SOLENOID SCREW TO ADJUST CURB IDLE SPEED TO SPECIFIED RPM.

① PREPARE VEHICLE FOR ADJUSTMENTS

Idle speed adjustment for the 2 BBL with solenoid—1978–79

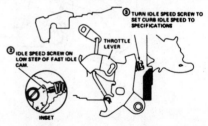

① PREPARE VEHICLE FOR ADJUSTMENTS

③ TURN IDLE SPEED SCREW TO SET CURB IDLE SPEED TO SPECIFICATIONS

THROTTLE LEVER

② IDLE SPEED SCREW ON LOW STEP OF FAST IDLE CAM.

INSET

Idle speed adjustment for the 2 BBL without solenoid—1978–79

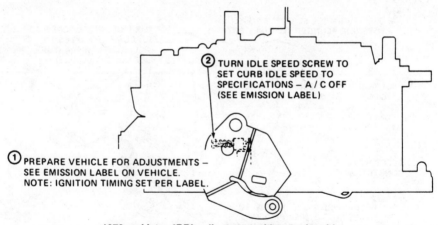

② TURN IDLE SPEED SCREW TO SET CURB IDLE SPEED TO SPECIFICATIONS – A / C OFF (SEE EMISSION LABEL)

① PREPARE VEHICLE FOR ADJUSTMENTS – SEE EMISSION LABEL ON VEHICLE. NOTE: IGNITION TIMING SET PER LABEL.

1979 and later 4BBL adjustment without solenoid

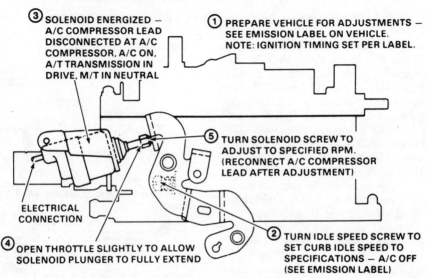

③ SOLENOID ENERGIZED – A/C COMPRESSOR LEAD DISCONNECTED AT A/C COMPRESSOR, A/C ON, A/T TRANSMISSION IN DRIVE, M/T IN NEUTRAL

① PREPARE VEHICLE FOR ADJUSTMENTS – SEE EMISSION LABEL ON VEHICLE. NOTE: IGNITION TIMING SET PER LABEL.

⑤ TURN SOLENOID SCREW TO ADJUST TO SPECIFIED RPM. (RECONNECT A/C COMPRESSOR LEAD AFTER ADJUSTMENT)

ELECTRICAL CONNECTION

④ OPEN THROTTLE SLIGHTLY TO ALLOW SOLENOID PLUNGER TO FULLY EXTEND

② TURN IDLE SPEED SCREW TO SET CURB IDLE SPEED TO SPECIFICATIONS – A/C OFF (SEE EMISSION LABEL)

1979 and later 4BBL adjustment with solenoid

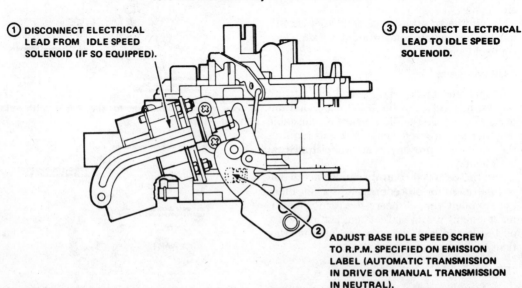

① DISCONNECT ELECTRICAL LEAD FROM IDLE SPEED SOLENOID (IF SO EQUIPPED).

③ RECONNECT ELECTRICAL LEAD TO IDLE SPEED SOLENOID.

② ADJUST BASE IDLE SPEED SCREW TO R.P.M. SPECIFIED ON EMISSION LABEL (AUTOMATIC TRANSMISSION IN DRIVE OR MANUAL TRANSMISSION IN NEUTRAL).

Idle speed adjustment with solenoid—1980 2 BBL

A/C IDLE SPEED ADJUSTMENT (ON VEHICLE)

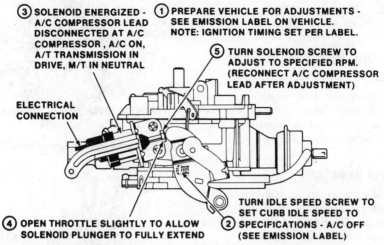

③ SOLENOID ENERGIZED - A/C COMPRESSOR LEAD DISCONNECTED AT A/C COMPRESSOR , A/C ON, A/T TRANSMISSION IN DRIVE, M/T IN NEUTRAL

① PREPARE VEHICLE FOR ADJUSTMENTS - SEE EMISSION LABEL ON VEHICLE. NOTE: IGNITION TIMING SET PER LABEL.

⑤ TURN SOLENOID SCREW TO ADJUST TO SPECIFIED RPM. (RECONNECT A/C COMPRESSOR LEAD AFTER ADJUSTMENT)

ELECTRICAL CONNECTION

TURN IDLE SPEED SCREW TO SET CURB IDLE SPEED TO

④ OPEN THROTTLE SLIGHTLY TO ALLOW SOLENOID PLUNGER TO FULLY EXTEND

② SPECIFICATIONS - A/C OFF (SEE EMISSION LABEL)

Idle speed adjustment without solenoid—1980 2 BBL

2. Make sure that the choke is fully opened.

3. Turn the A/C Off and disconnect the vacuum line at the vapor canister. Plug the line.

4. Set the parking brake, block the drive wheels and place the transmission in Drive (AT) or Neutral (MT). Connect a tachometer to the engine according to the manufacturer's instructions.

5. Turn the solenoid assembly to achieve the solenoid-on speed.

6. Disconnect the solenoid wire and turn the ⅛ inch hex screw in the solenoid end, to achieve the solenoid-off speed.

7. Remove the tachometer, connect the canister vacuum line and shut off the engine.

2 BBL AND 4 BBL (ALL BUT V8-350)

1. Run the engine to normal operating temperature.

2. Make sure that the choke is fully opened, turn the A/C off, set the parking brake, block the drive wheels and connect a tachometer to the engine according to the manufacturer's instructions.

3. Disconnect and plug the vacuum hoses at the EGR valve and the vapor canister.

4. Place the transmission in Park (AT) or Neutral (MT).

5. Disconnect and plug the vacuum advance hose at the distributor. Check and adjust the timing.

6. Connect the distributor vacuum line.

7. Manual transmission cars without A/C and without solenoid: place the idle speed screw on the low step of the fast idle cam and turn the screw to achieve the specified idle speed.

8. If equipped with A/C: set the idle speed screw to the specified rpm. Disconnect the compressor clutch wire and turn the A/C On. Open the throttle momentarily to extend the solenoid plunger. Turn the solenoid screw to obtain the specified rpm.

9. Automatic transmission cars without A/C; manual transmission cars without A/C, solenoid-equipped carburetor: momentarily open the throttle to extend the solenoid plunger. Turn the solenoid screw to obtain the specified rpm. Disconnect the solenoid wire and turn the idle speed screw to obtain the slow engine idle speed.

V8-350

1. Run the engine to normal operating temperature.

2. Set the parking brake and block the drive wheels.

3. Connect a tachometer to the engine according to the manufacturer's instructions.

4. Disconnect and plug the purge hose at the vapor canister. Disconnect and plug the EGR vacuum hose at the EGR valve.

5. Turn the A/C Off.

6. Place the transmission in Park (AT) or Neutral (MT).

7. Disconnect and plug the vacuum advance line at the distributor. Check and adjust the timing.

8. Connect the vacuum advance line. Place the automatic transmission in Drive.

9. Manual transmission cars without A/C: adjust the idle stop screw to obtain the specified rpm. If equipped with A/C: with the A/C Off, adjust the idle stop screw to obtain the specified rpm. Disconnect the compressor clutch wire and turn the A/C On. Open the throttle slightly to allow the solenoid plunger

to extend. Turn the solenoid screw to obtain the solenoid rpm listed on the underhood emission sticker.

10. Connect all hoses and remove the tachometer.

Throttle Body Injection (TBI)

1985 and Later

The throttle body injected vehicles are controlled by a computer which supplies the correct amount of fuel during all engine operating conditions; no adjustment is necessary.

Diesel Fuel Injection

NOTE: *GM diesel engines are equipped with Roosa-Master, CAV Lucas, or Stanodyne injection pumps. The Roosa-Master and Stanodyne pumps are nearly identical.*

IDLE SPEED ADJUSTMENT

A special tachometer with an RPM counter suitable for the 263 V6 and 350 V8 diesels is necessary for this adjustment; a standard tach suitable for gasoline engines will not work.

1. Place the transmission in Park, block the rear wheels and firmly set the parking brake.

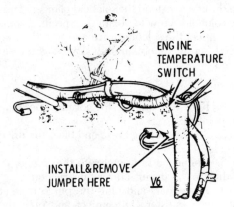

Fast idle temperature switch, V6 diesel

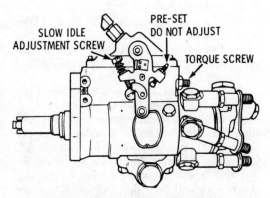

CAV-Lucas injection pump slow idle screw

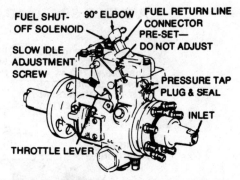

Roosa-Master injection pump slow idle screw

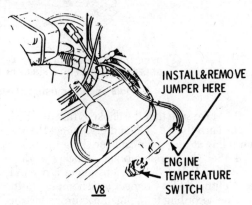

Fast idle temperature switch (V8 diesel)

V6 diesel fast idle solenoid

2. If necessary, adjust the throttle linkage as described in Chapter 6.

3. Start the engine and allow it to warm up for 10–15 minutes.

4. Shut off the engine and remove the air cleaner assembly.

5. Clean off any grime from the timing probe holder on the front cover; also clean off the crankshaft balancer rim.

6. Install the magnetic probe end of the tachometer fully into the timing probe holder. Complete the remaining tachometer connections according to the tach manufacturer's instructions.

7. On the V6 diesel, disconnect that A/C compressor clutch lead at the compressor (if equipped with A/C).

8. Make sure all electrical accessories are OFF.

NOTE: *At no time should either the steering wheel or brake pedal be touched.*

9. Start the engine and place the transmission in Drive (after first making sure the parking brake is firmly applied).

10. Check the slow idle speed reading against the one printed on the underhood emissions sticker. Reset if necessary.

11. Unplug the connector from the fast idle cold advance (engine temperature) switch, and install a jumper wire between the connector terminals.

NOTE: *DO NOT allow the jumper to ground.*

12. Check the fast idle speed and reset if necessary according to the specification printed on the underhood emissions sticker.

13. Remove the jumper wire and reconnect it to the temperature switch.

14. Recheck the slow idle speed and reset if necessary.

15. Shut off the engine.

16. Reconnect the leads at the generator and A/C compressor.

17. Disconnect and remove the tachometer.

18. If equipped with cruise control, adjust the servo throttle rod to minimum slack, then put the clip in the first free hole closest to the bellcrank or throttle lever.

19. Install the air cleaner assembly.

Engine and Engine Overhaul

3

UNDERSTANDING THE ENGINE ELECTRICAL SYSTEM

The engine electrical system can be broken down into three separate and distinct systems—(1) the starting system; (2) the charging system; (3) the ignition system.

Battery and Starting System

The battery is the first link in the chain of mechanisms which work together to provide cranking of the automobile engine. In most modern cars, the battery is a lead-acid electrochemical device consisting of six two-volt (2V) subsections connected in series so the unit is capable of producing approximately 12V of electrical pressure. Each subsection, or cell, consists of a series of positive and negative plates held a short distance apart in a solution of sulfuric acid and water. The two types of plates are of dissimilar metals. This causes a chemical reaction to be set up, and it is this reaction which produces current flow from the battery when its positive and negative terminals are connected to an electrical appliance such as a lamp or motor. The continued transfer of electrons would eventually convert the sulfuric acid in the electrolyte to water, and make the two plates identical in chemical composition. As electrical energy is removed from the battery, its voltage output tends to drop. Thus, measuring battery voltage and battery electrolyte composition are two ways of checking the ability of the unit to supply power. During the starting of the engine, electrical energy is removed from the battery. However, if the charging circuit is in good condition and the operating conditions are normal, the power removed from the battery will be replaced by the generator (or alternator) which will force electrons back through the battery, reversing the normal flow, and restoring the battery to its original chemical state.

The battery and starting motor are linked by very heavy electrical cables designed to minimize resistance to the flow of current. Generally, the major power supply cable that leaves the battery goes directly to the starter, while other electrical system needs are supplied by a smaller cable. During the starter operation, power flows from the battery to the starter and is grounded through the car's frame and the battery's negative ground strap.

The starting motor is a specially designed, direct current electric motor capable of producing a very great amount of power for its size. One thing that allows the motor to produce a great deal of power is its tremendous rotating speed. It drives the engine through a tiny pinion gear (attached to the starter's armature), which drives the very large flywheel ring gear at a greatly reduced speed. Another factor allowing it to produce so much power is that only intermittent operation is required of it. Thus, little allowance for air circulation is required, and the windings can be built into a very small space.

The starter solenoid is a magnetic device which employs the small current supplied by the starting switch circuit of the ignition switch. This magnetic action moves a plunger which mechanically engages the starter and electrically closes the heavy switch which connects it to the battery. The starting switch circuit consists of the starting switch contained within the ignition switch, a transmission neutral safety switch or clutch pedal switch, and the wiring necessary to connect these with the starter solenoid or relay.

A pinion, which is a small gear, is mounted to a one-way drive clutch. This clutch is splined to the starter armature shaft. When the ignition switch is moved to the "start" position, the solenoid plunger slides the pinion toward the flywheel ring gear via a collar and spring. If the teeth on the pinion and flywheel match properly, the pinion will engage the flywheel immediately. If the gear teeth butt one another, the spring will be compressed and will force the gears to mesh as soon as the starter turns far enough to allow them to do so. As the solenoid plunger reaches the end of its travel, it closes the contacts that connect the battery and starter and then the engine is cranked.

As soon as the engine starts, the flywheel ring gear begins turning fast enough to drive the pinion at an extremely high rate of speed. At this point, the one-way clutch begins allowing the pinion to spin faster than the starter shaft so that the starter will not operate at excessive speed. When the ignition switch is released from the starter position, the solenoid is de-energized, and a spring contained within the solenoid assembly pulls the gear out of mesh and interrupts the current flow to the starter.

Some starters employ a separate relay, mounted away from the starter, to switch the motor and solenoid current on and off. The relay thus replaces the solenoid electrical switch, but does not eliminate the need for a solenoid mounted on the starter used to mechanically engage the starter drive gears. The relay is used to reduce the amount of current the starting switch must carry.

The Charging System

The automobile charging system provides electrical power for operation of the vehicle's ignition and starting systems and all the electrical accessories. The battery serves as an electrical surge or storage tank, storing (in chemical form) the energy originally produced by the engine-driven generator. The system also provides a means of regulating generator output to protect the battery from being overcharged and to avoid excessive voltage to the accessories.

The storage battery is a chemical device incorporating parallel lead plates in a tank containing a sulfuric acid-water solution. Adjacent plates are slightly dissimilar, and the chemical reaction of the two dissimilar plates produces electrical energy when the battery is connected to a load such as the starter motor. The chemical reaction is reversible, so that when the generator is producing a voltage (electrical pressure) greater than that produced by the battery, electricity is forced into the battery, and the battery is returned to its fully charged state.

The vehicle's generator is driven mechanically, through V belts, by the engine crankshaft. It consists of two coils of fine wire, one stationary (the "stator"), and one movable (the "rotor"). The rotor may also be known as the "armature" and consists of fine wire wrapped around an iron core which is mounted on a shaft. The electricity which flows through the two coils of wire (provided initially by the battery in some cases) creates an intense magnetic field around both rotor and stator, and the interaction between the two fields creates voltage, allowing the generator to power the accessories and charge the battery.

There are two types of generators; the earlier is the direct current (DC) type. The current produced by the DC generator is generated in the armature and carried off the spinning armature by stationary brushes contacting the commutator. The commutator is a series of smooth metal contact plates on the end of the armature. The commutator plates, which are separated from one another by a very short gap, are connected to the armature circuits so that current will flow in one direction only in the wires carrying the generator output. The generator stator consists of two stationary coils of wire which draw some of the output current of the generator to form a powerful magnetic field and create the interaction of fields which generates the voltage. The generator field is wired in series with the regulator.

Newer automobiles use alternating current generators or "alternators" because they are more efficient, can be rotated at higher speeds, and have fewer brush problems. In an alternator, the field rotates while all the current produced passes only through the stator windings. The brushes bear against continuous slip rings rather than a commutator. This causes the current produced to periodically reverse the direction of its flow. Diodes (electrical one-way switches) block the flow of current from traveling in the wrong direction. A series of diodes is wired together to permit the alternating flow of the stator to be converted to a pulsating, but unidirectional flow at the alternator output. The alternator's field is wired in series with the voltage regulator.

The regulator consists of several circuits. Each circuit has a core, or magnetic coil of wire, which operates a switch. Each switch is connected to ground through one or more resistors. The coil of wire responds directly to system voltage. When the voltage reaches the required level, the magnetic field created by the winding of wire closes the switch and inserts a resistance into the generator field circuit, thus reducing the output. The contacts of the switch cycle open and close many times each second to precisely control voltage.

While alternators are self-limiting as far as maximum current is concerned. DC generators employ a current regulating circuit which responds directly to the total amount of current flowing through the generator circuit rather than to the output voltage. The current regulator is similar to the voltage regulator except all system current must flow through the energizing coil on its way to the various accessories.

SAFETY PRECAUTIONS

Observing these precautions will ensure safe handling of the electrical system components, and will avoid damage to the vehicle's electrical system:

a. Be *absolutely* sure of the polarity of a booster battery before making connections. Connect the cables positive to positive, and negative to negative. Connect positive cables first and then make the last connection to a ground on the body of the booster vehicle so that arcing cannot ignite hydrogen gas that may have accumulated near the battery. Even momentary connection of a booster battery with the polarity reversed will damage alternator diodes.

b. Disconnect both vehicle battery cables before attempting to charge a battery.

c. Never ground the alternator or generator output or battery terminal. Be cautious when using metal tools around a battery to avoid creating a short circuit between the terminals.

d. Never ground the field circuit between the alternator and regulator.

e. Never run an alternator or generator without load unless the field circuit is disconnected.

f. Never attempt to polarize an alternator.

g. Keep the regulator cover in place when taking voltage and current limiter readings.

h. Use insulated tools when adjusting the regulator.

i. Whenever DC generator-to-regulator wires have been disconnected, the generator *must* be repolarized. To do this with an externally grounded, light duty generator, momentarily place a jumper wire between the battery terminal and the generator terminal of the regulator. With an internally grounded heavy duty unit, disconnect the wire to the regulator field terminal and touch the regulator battery terminal with it.

ENGINE ELECTRICAL

High Energy Ignition (HEI) Distributor

The Delco-Remy High Energy Ignition (HEI) System is a breakerless, pulse triggered, transistor controlled, inductive discharge ignition system available as an option in 1974 and standard in 1975.

There are only nine external electrical connections; the ignition switch feed wire, and the eight spark plug leads. On eight cylinder models through 1977, and all 1978 and later models, the ignition coil is located with the distributor cap, connecting directly to the rotor.

The magnetic pick-up assembly located inside the distributor contains a permanent magnet, a pole piece with internal teeth, and a pick-up coil. When the teeth of the rotating timer core and pole piece align, an induced voltage in the pick-up coil signals the electronic module to open the coil primary circuit. As the primary current decreases, a high voltage is induced in the secondary windings of the ignition coil, directing a spark through the rotor and high voltage leads to fire the spark plugs. The dwell period is automatically controlled by the electronic module and is increased with increasing engine rpm. The HEI System features a longer spark duration which is instrumental in firing lean and EGR diluted fuel/air mixtures. The condenser (capacitor) located within the HEI distributor is provided for noise (static) suppression purposes only and is not a regularly replaced ignition system component.

As already noted in Chapter 2, 1981 models continue to use the HEI distributor although it now incorporates an Electronic Spark Timing System (for more information on EST, please refer to Chapter 4). With the new EST system, all spark timing changes are performed electronically by the Electronic Control Module (ECM) which moniters information from various engine sensors, computes the desired spark timing accordingly. Because all timing changes are controlled electronically, no vacuum or mechanical advance systems are used whatsoever.

Ignition Coil

TESTING

1964–74

PRIMARY CIRCUIT WITH VOLTMETER

A quick, tentative check of the 12 volt ignition primary circuit (including ballast resistor) can be made with a simple voltmeter, as follows:

1. With engine at operating temperature, but stopped, and the distributor side of the ignition coil grounded with a jumper wire, hook up a voltmeter between the ignition coil (switch side) and a good ground.

2. Jiggle the ignition switch (switch on) and watch the meter. An unstable needle will indicate a defective ignition switch.

3. With ignition switch on (engine stopped)

the voltmeter should read 5.5 to 7 volts for 12-volt systems.

4. Crank the engine. Voltmeter should read at least 9 volts during cranking period.

5. Now remove the jumper wire from the coil. Start the engine. Voltmeter should read from 9.0 volts to 11.5 volts (depending upon generator output) while running.

PRIMARY CIRCUIT WITH OHMMETER

To check ignition coil resistance, primary side, switch ohmmeter to low scale. Connect the ohmmeter leads across the primary terminals of the coil and read the low ohms scale.

Coils requiring ballast resistors should read about 1.0 ohm resistance. 12-volt coils, not requiring external ballast resistors, should read about 4.0 ohms resistance.

SECONDARY CIRCUIT WITH OHMMETER

To check ignition coil resistance, secondary side, switch ohmmeter to high scale. Connect one test lead to the distributor cap end of the coil secondary cable. Connect the other test lead to the distributor terminal of the coil. A coil in satisfactory condition should show between 4K and 8K on the scale. Some special coils (Mallory, etc.) may show a resistance as high as 13 K. If the reading is much lower than 4 K, the coil probably has shorted secondary turns. If the reading is extremely high (40 K or more) the secondary winding is either open, there is a bad connection at the coil terminal, or resistance is high in the cable.

If both primary and secondary windings of the coil test good, but the ignition system is still unsatisfactory, check the system further.

1975 and Later

An ohmmeter with both high and low ranges should be used. These tests are made with the cap assembly removed and the battery wire disconnected. If a tachometer is connected to the TACH terminal, disconnect it before making these tests.

1. Connect an ohmmeter between the TACH and BAT terminals in the distributor cap. The primary coil resistance should be less than one ohm.

2. To check the coil secondary resistance, connect an ohmmeter between the rotor button and the BAT terminal. Note the reading. Connect the ohmmeter between the rotor button and the TACH terminal. Note the reading. The resistance in both cases should be between 6,000 and 30,000 ohms. Be sure to test between the rotor button and both the BAT and TACH terminals.

3. Replace the coil *only* if the readings in Step 1 and Step 2 are infinite.

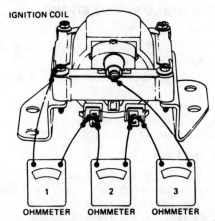

IGNITION COIL

To test HEI ignition coil on external coil models, attach an ohmmeter as shown: Test 1, use high scale. Reading should be very high or infinite. Test 2, use low scale. Reading should be very low or zero. Test 3, use high scale. Reading should not be infinite. If any test proves otherwise, replace coil.

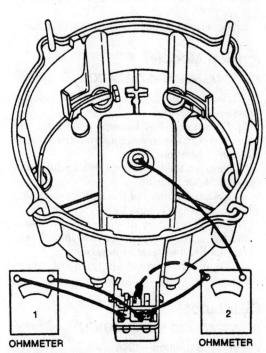

Ohmmeter 1 shows the primary coil resistance connection. Ohmmeter 2 shows the secondary resistance connection (1980 shown, most models similar)

NOTE: *These resistance checks will not disclose shorted coil windings. This condition can only be detected with scope analysis or a suitable designed coil tester. If these instruments are unavailable, replace the coil with a known good coil as a final coil test.*

REMOVAL AND INSTALLATION
1964–74

1. Remove the ignition switch-to-coil lead from the coil.
2. Unfasten the distributor leads from the coil.
3. Remove the screws which secure the coil to the engine and lift it off.
4. Installation is the reverse of removal.

1975 and Later

1. Disconnect the feed and module wire terminal connectors from the distributor cap.
2. Remove the ignition wire set retainer.
3. Remove the 4 coil cover-to-distributor cap screws and the coil cover.
4. Remove the 4 coil-to-distributor cap screws.
5. Using a blunt drift, press the coil wire spade terminals up out of distributor cap.
6. Lift the coil up out of the distributor cap.
7. Remove and clean the coil spring, rubber seal washer and coil cavity of the distributor cap.
8. Reverse the above procedures to install.

Ignition Module
REMOVAL AND INSTALLATION

1. Remove the distributor cap and rotor as previously described.
2. Disconnect the harness connector and pick-up coil spade connectors from the module (note their positions).
3. Remove the two screws and module from the distributor housing.
4. Coat the bottom of the new module with silicone dielectric compound
   NOTE: *If a five terminal or seven terminal module is replaced, the ignition timing must be checked and reset as necessary.*
5. To install, reverse the removal procedures.

Distributor
REMOVAL AND INSTALLATION
Points-Type Ignition—1964–74

1. Remove the distributor cap and position it out of the way.
2. Disconnect the primary coil wire and the vacuum advance hose.
3. Scribe a mark on the distributor body and the engine block showing their relationship. Mark the distributor housing to show the direction in which the rotor is pointing. Note the positioning of the vacuum advance unit.
4. Remove the hold-down bolt and clamp and remove the distributor.

5. To install the distributor with the engine undisturbed:
   a. Reinsert the distributor into its opening, aligning the previously made marks on the housing and the engine block.
   b. The rotor may have to be turned either way a slight amount to align the rotor-to-housing marks.
   c. Install the retaining clamp and bolt. Install the distributor cap, primary wire or electrical connector, and the vacuum hose.
   d. Start the engine and check the ignition timing.
6. To install the distributor with the engine disturbed:
   a. Turn the engine to bring the No. 1 piston to the top of its compression stroke. This may be determined by inserting a rag into the No. 1 spark plug hole and slowly turning the engine over. When the timing mark on the crankshaft pulley aligns with the 0 on the timing scale and the rag is blown out by compression, the No. 1 piston is at top dead center (TDC).
   NOTE: *On Mark IV (big block) V8 engines there is a punch mark on the distributor drive gear which indicates the rotor position. Thus, the distributor may be installed with the cap in place. Align the punch mark 2° clockwise from the No. 1 cap terminal, then rotate the distributor body 1/8 turn counterclockwise and push the distributor down into the block.*
   b. Install the distributor to the engine block so that the vacuum advance unit points in the correct direction.
   c. Turn the rotor so that it will point to the No. 1 terminal in the cap.
   d. Install the distributor into the engine block. It may be necessary to turn the rotor a little in either direction in order to engage the gears.
   e. Tap the starter a few times to ensure that the oil pump shaft is mated to the distributor shaft.
   f. Bring the engine to No. 1 TDC again and check to see that the rotor is indeed pointing toward the No. 1 terminal of the cap.
   g. After correct positioning is assured, turn the distributor housing so that the points are just opening. Tighten the retaining clamp.
   h. Install the cap and primary wire. Check the ignition timing. Install the vacuum hose.

HEI Distributor—1975 and later

1. Disconnect the ground cable from the battery.
2. Tag and disconnect the feed and module terminal connectors from the distributor cap.

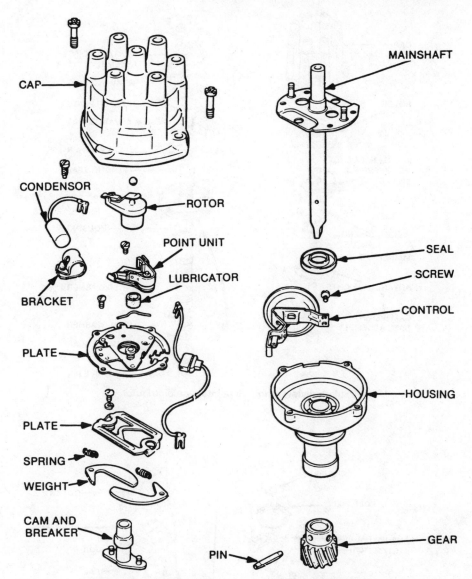

Exploded view of the six cylinder points-type distributor

3. Disconnect the hose at the vacuum advance (1975–80 only).

4. Depress and release the 4 distributor cap-to-housing retainers and lift off the cap assembly.

5. Using crayon or chalk, make locating marks on the rotor and module and on the distributor housing and engine for installation purposes.

6. Loosen and remove the distributor clamp bolt and clamp, and lift the distributor out of the engine. Noting the relative position of the rotor and module alignment marks, make a second mark on the rotor to align it with the mark on the module.

UNDISTURBED ENGINE

1. With a new O-ring on the distributor housing and the second mark on the rotor

aligned with the mark on the module, install the distributor, taking care to align the mark on the housing with the one on the engine. It may be necessary to lift the distributor and turn the rotor slightly to align the gears and the oil pump driveshaft.

2. With the respective marks aligned, install the clamp and bolt finger-tight.

3. Install and secure the distributor cap.

4. Connect the feed and module connectors to the distributor cap.

5. Connect a timing light to the engine and plug the vacuum hose.

6. Connect the ground cable to the battery.

7. Start the engine and set the timing.

8. Turn the engine off and tighten the distributor clamp bolt. Disconnect the timing light

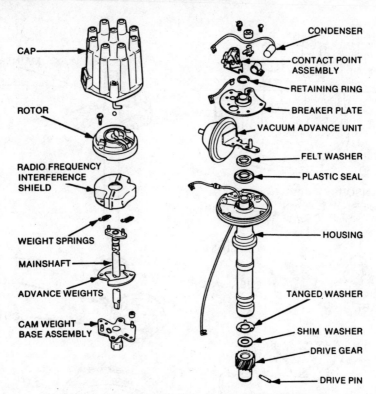

CAP

ROTOR

RADIO FREQUENCY
INTERFERENCE
SHIELD

WEIGHT SPRINGS

MAINSHAFT

ADVANCE WEIGHTS

CAM WEIGHT
BASE ASSEMBLY

CONDENSER

CONTACT POINT
ASSEMBLY

RETAINING RING

BREAKER PLATE

VACUUM ADVANCE UNIT

FELT WASHER

PLASTIC SEAL

HOUSING

TANGED WASHER

SHIM WASHER

DRIVE GEAR

DRIVE PIN

Exploded view of the V8 points-type distributor

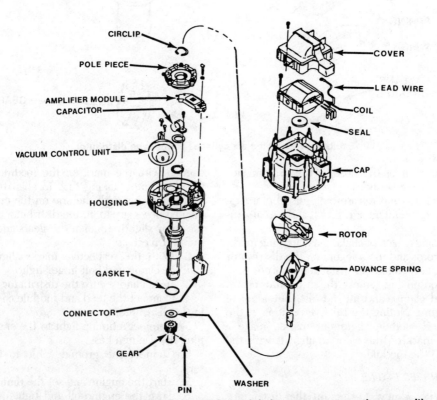

CIRCLIP

POLE PIECE

AMPLIFIER MODULE

CAPACITOR

VACUUM CONTROL UNIT

HOUSING

GASKET

CONNECTOR

GEAR

PIN

WASHER

COVER

LEAD WIRE

COIL

SEAL

CAP

ROTOR

ADVANCE SPRING

Exploded view of the HEI distributor (1981 models have no vacuum advance unit)

and unplug and connect the hose to the vacuum advance.

DISTURBED ENGINE

1. Remove the No. 1 spark plug.
2. Place a finger over the No. 1 spark plug hole and rotate the engine by hand until the compression can be felt.
3. Align the timing mark on the crankshaft pulley with the "0" mark on the timing plate.
4. Align the distributor rotor near the No. 1 spark plug tower.
5. Install the distributor, the hold down clamp, the bolt and the cap. It may be necessary to turn the rotor a little in either direction in order to engage the gears.
   NOTE: *With the distributor installed, make sure that the rotor is aligned with the No. 1 spark plug tower of the cap.*
6. Check the ignition timing.

Alternator

The alternating current generator (alternator) supplies a continuous output of electrical energy at all engine speeds. The alternator generates electrical energy and recharges the battery by supplying it with electrical current. This unit consists of four main assemblies: two end frame assemblies, a rotor assembly, and a stator assembly. The rotor assembly is supported in the drive end frame by a ball bearing and at the other end by a roller bearing. These bearings are lubricated during assembly and required no maintenance. There are six diodes in the end frame assembly. These diodes are electrical check valves that also change the alternating current developed within the stator windings to a direct (DC) current at the output (BAT) terminal. Three of these diodes are negative and are mounted flush with the end frame while the other three are positive and are mounted into a strip called a heat sink. The positive diodes are easily identified as the ones within small cavities or depressions.

ALTERNATOR PRECAUTIONS

To prevent serious damage to the alternator and the rest of the charging system, the following precautions must be observed.

1. When installing a battery, make sure that the positive cable is connected to the positive terminal and the negative to the negative.
2. When jump-starting the car with another battery, make sure that like terminals are connected. This also applies when using a battery charger.
3. Never operate the alternator with the battery disconnected or otherwise on an uncontrolled open circuit. Double-check to see that all connections are tight.
4. Do not short across or ground any alternator or regulator terminals.
5. Do not try to polarize the alternator.
6. Do not apply full battery voltage to the field (brown) connector.
7. Always disconnect the battery ground cable before disconnecting the alternator lead.

REMOVAL

1. Disconnect the battery ground cable to prevent diode damage.
2. Tag and disconnect the alternator wiring.
3. Remove the alternator brace bolt. If the car is equipped with power steering loosen the pump brace and mount nuts. Detach the drive belt(s).
4. Support the alternator and remove the mount bolt(s). Remove the unit from the vehicle.

INSTALLATION AND BELT ADJUSTMENT

To install, reverse the above removal procedure. Alternator belt tension is quite critical. A belt that is too tight may cause alternator bearing failure; one that is too loose will cause a gradual battery discharge. For details on correct belt adjustment, see "Drive Belts" in Chapter One.

Regulator

The voltage regulator combines with the battery and alternator to comprise the charging system. Just as the name implies, the voltage regulator regulates the alternator voltage output to a safe amount. A properly working regulator prevents excessive voltage from burning out wiring, bulbs, or contact points, and prevents overcharging of the battery. Mechanical adjustments (air gap, point opening) must be followed by electrical adjustments and not vice versa.

Since 1973 all GM cars have been equipped with alternators which have built-in solid state voltage regulators. The regulator is in the end frame (inside) of the alternator and requires no adjustment. The following adjustments apply to pre-1973 units.
   NOTE: *Although standard since 1973, this integral alternator/regulator has been available as an option since 1969.*

REMOVAL AND INSTALLATION

1. Disconnect the battery ground cable.
2. Disconnect the wiring harness from the regulator.
3. Remove the mounting screws and remove the regulator.

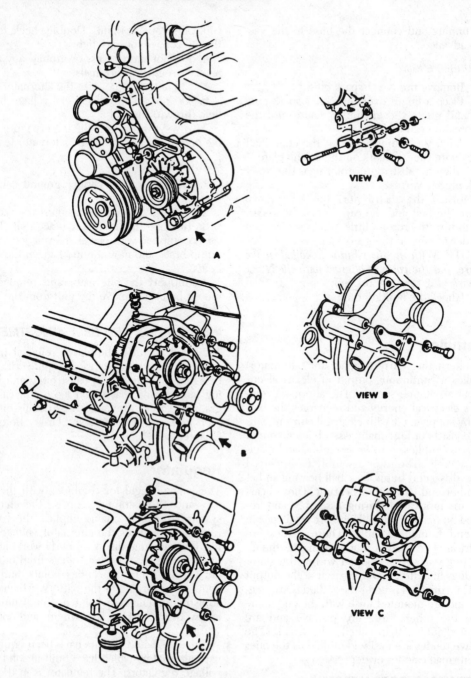

VIEW A

VIEW B

VIEW C

Typical alternator mounting—inline six cylinder (top), V6 and small-block V8 (center) and big-block V8 (bottom)

4. Make sure that the regulator base gasket is in place before installation.

5. Clean the attaching area for proper grounding.

6. Install the regulator. Do not overtighten the mounting screws, as this will cancel the cushioning effect of the rubber grommets.

ADJUSTMENT—1964–72

The standard voltage regulator is the conventional double-contact type; however, an optional transistorized regulator was available from 1964–68. Voltage adjustment procedures are the same for both except for the adjustment points. The double-contact adjustment screw is under

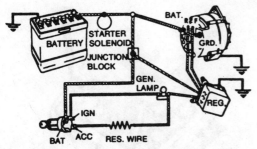

Non-integral voltage regulator charging system schematic

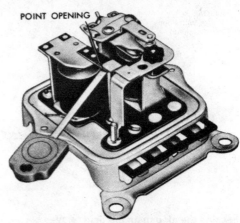

Checking the field relay point opening

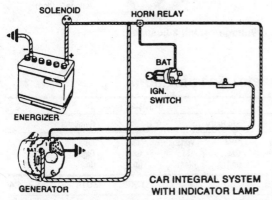

Integral voltage regulator charging system schematic

the regulator cover (also on the 1964 transistorized regulator); the 1965–68 transistorized regulator is adjusted externally after removing an Allen screw from the adjustment hole.

Field Relay Adjustments (Mechanical)

As explained earlier, mechanical adjustments must be made first and then follow by electrical adjustments.

Point Opening

Using a feeler gauge, check the point opening as illustrated. To change the opening, carefully bend the armature stop. The point opening for all regulators should be 0.014 in.

Air Gap

Check the air gap with the points just touching. The gap should be 0.067 in. If the point opening setting is correct, then the relay will operate OK even if the air gap is off. To adjust air gap, bend the flat contact spring.

Voltage Adjustment (Electrical)

1. Connect a ¼ ohm 25 watt fixed resistor (a knife blade switch using a ¼ ohm resistor) into the charging circuit (as illustrated) at the battery positive terminal. One end of the resistor connects to the battery positive terminal while the other connects to the voltmeter.

2. Operate the engine at 1,500 rpm or more for at least 15 minutes. Disconnect and reconnect the regulator connector and read the voltage on the voltmeter. If the regulator is functioning properly, the reading should be 13.5–15.2V. If the reading is not within this range, keep the engine running at 1,500 rpm and do the following:

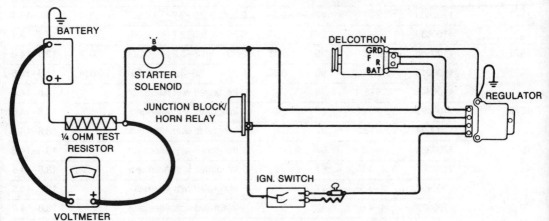

Schematic for testing the regulator voltage setting

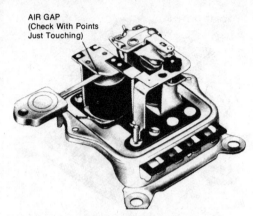

AIR GAP
(Check With Points
Just Touching)

AIR GAP
ADJUSTING NUT
ONLY

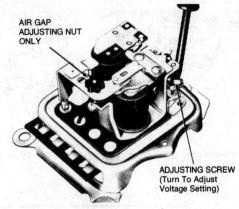

ADJUSTING SCREW
(Turn To Adjust
Voltage Setting)

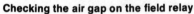

Checking the air gap on the field relay   Voltage setting adjustment

Alternator and Regulator Specifications

	Alternator			Regulator					
				Field Relay			Regulator		
Year	Part No. or Manufacturer	Field Current @ 12 V	Output (amps)	Air Gap (in.)	Point Gap (in.)	Volts to Close	Air Gap (in.)	Point Gap (in.)	Volts @ 75°
1964	1100668	1.9–2.3	42	0.15	0.30	2.3–3.7	0.067	0.014	13.5–14.4
	1100669	1.9–2.3	40	0.15	0.30	2.3–3.7	0.067	0.014	13.5–14.4
	1100670	1.9–2.3	37	0.15	0.30	2.3–3.7	0.067	0.014	13.5–14.4
	1117765	3.7–4.4	62	0.15	0.30	2.3–3.7	0.067	0.014	①
1965–67	1100693	2.2–2.6	37	0.15	0.30	2.3–2.7	0.067	0.014	13.5–14.4
	1100695	2.2–2.6	32	0.15	0.30	2.3–2.7	0.067	0.014	13.5–14.4
	1100794	2.2–2.6	37	0.15	0.30	2.3–2.7	0.067	0.014	13.5–14.4
1968	1100813	2.2–2.6	37	0.15	0.30	2.3–2.7	0.067	0.014	13.5–14.4
	1100693	2.2–2.6	37	0.15	0.30	2.3–2.7	0.067	0.014	13.5–14.4
1969	1100834	2.2–2.6	37	0.15	0.30	2.3–2.7	0.067	0.014	13.5–14.4
	1100836	2.2–2.6	37	0.15	0.30	2.3–2.7	0.067	0.014	13.5–14.4
1970	1100834	2.2–2.6	37	0.15	0.30	2.3–2.7	0.067	0.014	13.5–14.4
	1100837	2.2–2.6	37	0.15	0.30	2.3–2.7	0.067	0.014	13.5–14.4
1971	1100838	2.2–2.6	37	0.15	0.30	2.3–2.7	0.067	0.014	13.5–14.4
	1100839	2.2–2.6	37	0.15	0.30	2.3–2.7	0.067	0.014	13.5–14.4
1972	1100566	2.2–2.6	35	0.15	0.30	1.5–3.2	0.067	0.014	13.8–14.8
	1100917	2.8–3.2	59	0.30	0.30	1.5–3.2	0.067	0.014	13.8–14.8
	1100843	2.8–3.2	58	Integrated with Alternator					13.8–14.8
1973	1100497	2.8–3.2	36	Integrated with Alternator					13.8–14.8
	1100934	2.8–3.2	37	Integrated with Alternator					13.8–14.8
1974	1100934	4–4.5	37	Integrated with Alternator					13.8–14.8
	1102347	4–4.5	61	Integrated with Alternator					13.8–14.8
	1100497	4–4.5	37	Integrated with Alternator					13.8–14.8
	1100573	4–4.5	42	Integrated with Alternator					13.8–14.8
	1100597	4–4.5	61	Integrated with Alternator					13.8–14.8

Alternator and Regulator Specifications (cont.)

Year	Part No. or Manufacturer	Field Current @ 12 V	Output (amps)	Regulator					
				Field Relay			Regulator		
				Air Gap (in.)	Point Gap (in.)	Volts to Close	Air Gap (in.)	Point Gap (in.)	Volts @ 75°
1974	1100560	4–4.5	55	Integrated with Alternator					13.8–14.8
	1100575	4–4.5	55	Integrated with Alternator					13.8–14.8
1975	1100497	4–4.5	37	Integrated with Alternator					13.8–14.8
	1102397	4–4.5	37	Integrated with Alternator					13.8–14.8
	1102483	4–4.5	37	Integrated with Alternator					13.8–14.8
	1100560	4–4.5	55	Integrated with Alternator					13.8–14.8
	1100575	4–4.5	55	Integrated with Alternator					13.8–14.8
	1100597	4–4.5	61	Integrated with Alternator					13.8–14.8
	1102347	4–4.5	61	Integrated with Alternator					13.8–14.8
1976–79	1102491	4–4.5	37	Integrated with Alternator					13.8–14.8
	1102480	4–4.5	61	Integrated with Alternator					13.8–14.8
	1102486	4–4.5	61	Integrated with Alternator					13.8–14.8
	1102394	4–4.5	37	Integrated with Alternator					13.8–14.8
1980–81	1103161	4–4.5	37	Integrated with Alternator					13.8–14.8
	1103118	4–4.5	37	Integrated with Alternator					13.8–14.8
	1103043	4–4.5	42	Integrated with Alternator					13.8–14.8
	1103162	4–4.5	37	Integrated with Alternator					13.8–14.8
	1103092	4–4.5	55	Integrated with Alternator					13.8–14.8
	1103088	4–4.5	55	Integrated with Alternator					13.8–14.8
	1103100	4–4.5	55	Integrated with Alternator					13.8–14.8
	1103085	4–4.5	55	Integrated with Alternator					13.8–14.8
	1103044	4–4.5	63	Integrated with Alternator					13.8–14.8
	1103091	4–4.5	63	Integrated with Alternator					13.8–14.8
	1103169	4–4.5	63	Integrated with Alternator					13.8–14.8
	1103102	4–4.5	63	Integrated with Alternator					13.8–14.8
	1103122	4–4.5	63	Integrated with Alternator					13.8–14.8
	1101044	4–4.5	70	Integrated with Alternator					13.8–14.8
	1101071	4–4.5	70	Integrated with Alternator					13.8–14.8
1982–84	1103161	4–4.5	37	Integrated with Alternator					13.8–14.8
	1103118	4–4.5	37	Integrated with Alternator					13.8–14.8
	1103043	4–4.5	42	Integrated with Alternator					13.8–14.8
	1103162	4–4.5	37	Integrated with Alternator					13.8–14.8
	1103092	4–4.5	55	Integrated with Alternator					13.8–14.8
	1103088	4–4.5	55	Integrated with Alternator					13.8–14.8
	1103100	4–4.5	55	Integrated with Alternator					13.8–14.8
	1103085	4–4.5	55	Integrated with Alternator					13.8–14.8
	1103044	4–4.5	63	Integrated with Alternator					13.8–14.8
	1103091	4–4.5	63	Integrated with Alternator					13.8–14.8

Alternator and Regulator Specifications (cont.)

Year	Part No. or Manufacturer	Alternator Field Current @ 12 V	Output (amps)	Regulator — Field Relay / Regulator						Volts @ 75°
1982–84	1103169	4–4.5	63	Integrated with Alternator						13.8–14.8
	1101044	4–4.5	70	Integrated with Alternator						13.8–14.8
	1101066	4–4.5	70	Integrated with Alternator						13.8–14.8
	1101071	4–4.5	70	Integrated with Alternator						13.8–14.8
	1100226	4–4.5	37	Integrated with Alternator						13.8–14.8
	1100246	4–4.5	63	Integrated with Alternator						13.8–14.8
	1100270	4–4.5	78	Integrated with Alternator						13.8–14.8
	1100239	4–4.5	55	Integrated with Alternator						13.8–14.8
	1100247	4–4.5	63	Integrated with Alternator						13.8–14.8
	1100200	4–4.5	78	Integrated with Alternator						13.8–14.8
	1100230	4–4.5	42	Integrated with Alternator						13.8–14.8
	1100260	4–4.5	78	Integrated with Alternator						13.8–14.8
	1100263	4–4.5	78	Integrated with Alternator						13.8–14.8
	1105022	4–4.5	78	Integrated with Alternator						13.8–14.8
	1100237	4–4.5	55	Integrated with Alternator						13.8–14.8
	1100228	4–4.5	37	Integrated with Alternator						13.8–14.8
	1100300	4–4.5	63	Integrated with Alternator						13.8–14.8
	1105041	4–4.5	78	Integrated with Alternator						13.8–14.8
1985–86	1100246	4–4.5	66	Integrated with Alternator						13.8–14.8
	1100237	4–4.5	56	Integrated with Alternator						13.8–14.8
	1105652	4–4.5	78	Integrated with Alternator						13.8–14.8
	1105521	4–4.5	78	Integrated with Alternator						13.8–14.8
	1105523	4–4.5	56	Integrated with Alternator						13.8–14.8
	1105652	4–4.5	78	Integrated with Alternator						13.8–14.8
	1105523	4–4.5	56	Integrated with Alternator						13.8–14.8

① 13.0–13.6 @ 80°

a. Disconnect the terminal connector (four terminal connector) and remove the regulator cover. Reconnect the connector and adjust the voltage to 14.2–14.6 by turning the adjusting screw.
CAUTION: *When removing the regulator cover ALWAYS disconnect the connector first to prevent regulator damage by short circuits.*
b. Disconnect the connector, install the cover, and reconnect the connector.
c. Increase the regulator temperature by running the engine at 1,500 rpm for 10 more minutes.
d. Disconnect and reconnect the connec-

tor and read the voltmeter. A reading of 13.5–15.2 indicates a good regulator.

Battery

REMOVAL AND INSTALLATION

1. Disconnect the negative (ground) cable from the terminal, and then the positive cable. Special pullers are available to remove the cable clamps, if they seem stuck.
NOTE: *To avoid sparks, always disconnect the ground cable first, and connect it last.*
2. Remove the battery hold-down clamp.
3. Remove the battery, being careful not to spill the acid.

NOTE: *Spilled acid can be neutralized with a baking soda/water solution. If you somehow get acid into your eyes, flush it out with lots of water and get to a doctor.*

4. Clean the battery posts thoroughly before reinstalling, or when installing a new battery.

5. Clean the cable clamps, using a wire brush, both inside and out.

6. Install the battery and the hold-down clamp or strap. Connect the positive, and the negative cable (see "Note" above). Do not hammer the cables onto the terminal posts. The complete terminals should be coated lightly (externally) with petroleum jelly or grease to help prevent corrosion. There are also felt washers impregnated with an anti corrosion substance which are slipped over the battery posts before installing the cables; these are available in most auto parts stores.

CAUTION: *Make absolutely sure that the battery is connected properly (positive to positive, negative to negative) before you turn the ignition key. Reversed polarity can burn out your alternator and regulator in a matter of seconds.*

ADJUSTMENTS

Refer to Chapter One for details on battery maintenance.

Starter

REMOVAL AND INSTALLATION

NOTE: *The starters on some engines require the addition of shims to provide proper clearance between the starter pinion gear and the flywheel. These shims are available in .015 in. sizes from Pontiac dealers. Flat washers can be used if shims are unavailable.*

1. Disconnect the negative battery cable.

2. Raise the car to a convenient working height.

3. Disconnect all wiring from the starter solenoid. Replace each nut as the connector is removed, as thread sizes differ from connector to connector. Note or tag the wiring positions for installation.

Chilton Time Saver

Starter removal on certain models may necessitate the removal of the frame support. This support runs from the corner of the frame to the front crossmember. To remove:

1. Loosen the mounting bolt that attaches the support to the corner of the frame.

2. Loosen and remove the mounting bolt that attaches the support to the front crossmember and then swing the support out of the way.

3. Installation is in the reverse order of removal.

---

4. Remove the front bracket from the starter and the two mounting bolts. On engines with a solenoid heat shield, remove the front bracket upper bolt and detach the bracket from the starter.

5. Remove the front bracket bolt or nut. Lower the starter front end first, and then remove the unit from the car.

6. Reverse the removal procedures to install the starter. Torque the two mounting bolts to 25–35 ft. lbs.

SHIMMING THE STARTER

Starter noise during cranking and after the engine fires is often a result of too much or too little distance between the starter pinion gear and the flywheel. A high pitched whine during cranking (before the engine fires) can be caused by the pinion and flywheel being too far apart. Likewise, a whine after the engine starts (as the key is released) is often a result of the pinion-flywheel relationship being too close. In both cases flywheel damage can occur. Shims are available in .015 in. sizes to properly adjust the starter on its mount. You will also need a flywheel turning tool, available at most auto parts stores or from any auto tool store or salesperson.

If your car's starter emits the above noises, follow the shimming procedure below:

1. Disconnect the negative battery cable.

2. Remove the flywheel inspection cover on the bottom of the bellhousing.

3. Using the flywheel turning tool, turn the flywheel and examine the flywheel teeth. If damage is evident, the flywheel should be replaced.

4. Insert a screwdriver into the small hole in the bottom of the starter, then move the starter pinion and clutch assembly so the pinion and flywheel teeth mesh. If necessary, rotate the flywheel so that a pinion tooth is directly in the center of the two flywheel teeth and on the centerline of the two gears, as shown in the accompanying illustration.

5. Check the pinion-to-flywheel clearance by using a .020 in. wire gauge (a spark plug wire gauge may work here, or you can make your own). Make sure you center the pinion tooth between the flywheel teeth and the gauge— NOT in the corners, as you may get a false reading. If the clearance is *under* this minimum, shim the starter *away* from the flywheel by adding shim(s) one at a time to the starter mount. Check clearance after adding each shim.

6. If the clearance is a good deal *over* .020 in. (in the vicinity of .050 plus), shim the starter *towards* the flywheel. Broken or severely mangled flywheel teeth are also a good indicator that the clearance here is too great. Shimming

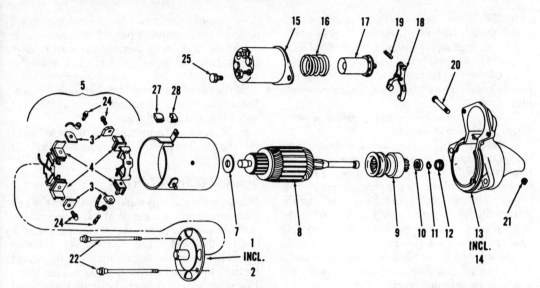

1. Frame—commutator end
2. Brush and holder pkg.
3. Brush
4. Brush holder
5. Housing—drive end
6. Frame and field asm.
7. Solenoid switch
8. Armature
9. Drive asm.
10. Plunger
11. Shift lever
12. Plunger return springer
13. Shift lever shaft
14. Lock washer
15. Screw—brush attaching
16. Screw—field lead to switch
17. Screw—switch attaching
18. Washer—brake
19. Thru bolt
20. Bushing—commutator end
21. Bushing—drive end
22. Pinion stop collar
23. Thrust collar
24. Grommet
25. Grommet
26. Plunger pin
27. Pinion stop retainer ring
28. Lever shaft retaining ring

Exploded view of the starter

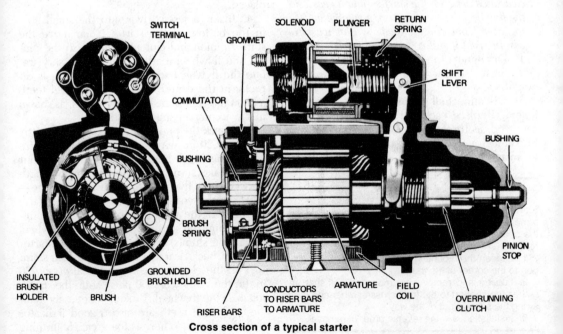

Cross section of a typical starter

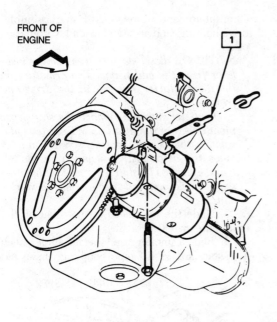

FRONT OF ENGINE

1. Use shims as required
2. Shield

Starter noise diagnostic procedure
1. Starter noise during cranking: remove 1–.015" double shim or add single .015" shim to *outer* bolt only.
2. High pitched whine after engine fires: add .015" double shims until noise disappears.

See text for complete procedure.

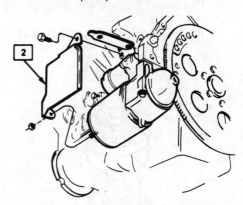

Starter motor mounting; V6 at left, diesel at right. Others similar

A .015" SHIM WILL INCREASE THE CLEARANCE APPROXIMATELY .005" MORE THAN ONE SHIM MAY BE REQUIRED.

SHIM

SCREW DRIVER

Meshing starter and flywheel teeth

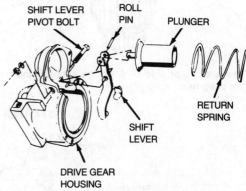

SHIFT LEVER PIVOT BOLT

ROLL PIN

PLUNGER

RETURN SPRING

SHIFT LEVER

DRIVE GEAR HOUSING

Removing shaft lever and plunger from starter

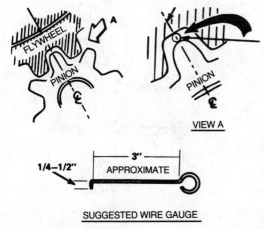

FLYWHEEL

PINION

A

PINION

VIEW A

3"
1/4–1/2"   APPROXIMATE

SUGGESTED WIRE GAUGE

Flywheel-to-pinion clearance

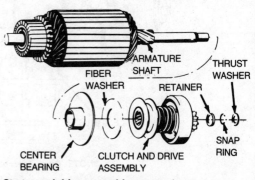

ARMATURE SHAFT

THRUST WASHER

FIBER WASHER

RETAINER

SNAP RING

CENTER BEARING

CLUTCH AND DRIVE ASSEMBLY

Starter and drive assembly removed

the starter towards the flywheel is done by adding shims to the outboard starter mounting pad only. Check the clearance after each shim is added. A shim of .015 in. at this location will decrease the clearance about .010 in.

STARTER OVERHAUL

Drive Replacement

1. Disconnect the field coil straps from the solenoid.

2. Remove the thru-bolts, and separate the commutator end frame, field frame assembly, drive housing, and armature assembly from each other.

NOTE: *On diesel starters, remove the insulator from the end frame. The armature on the diesel starter remains in the drive end frame.*

On diesel starters, remove the shift lever pivot bolt. On the diesel 25 MT starter only, remove the center bearing screws and remove the drive gear housing from the armature shaft. The shift lever and plunger assembly will now fall away from the starter clutch.

3. Slide the two piece thrust collar off the end of the armature shaft.

4. Slide a suitably sized metal cylinder, such as a standard ½ in. pipe coupling, or an old

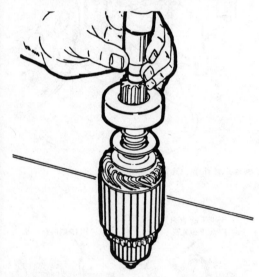

Use a piece of pipe to drive the retainer toward the snap-ring

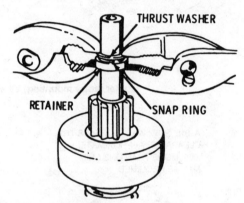

Snap-ring installation

STARTER DISASSEMBLY

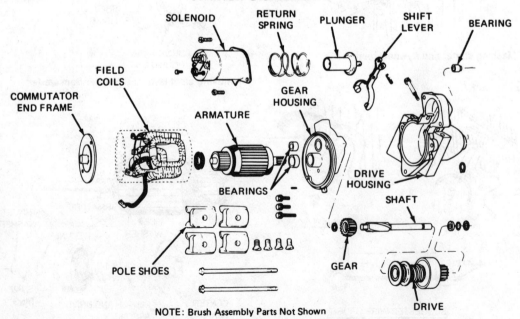

NOTE: Brush Assembly Parts Not Shown

Exploded view of the 15MT/GR starter used on the diesel engines

pinion, onto the shaft so that the end of the coupling or pinion butts up against the edge of the pinion retainer:

5. Support the lower end of the armature securely on a soft surface, such as a wooden block, and tap the end of the coupling or pinion, driving the retainer towards the armature end of the snap ring.

6. Remove the snap ring from the groove in the armature shaft with a pair of pliers. Then, slide the retainer and starter drive from the shaft.

7. To reassemble, lubricate the drive end of the armature shaft with silicone lubricant and then slide the starter drive onto the shaft *with the pinion facing outward*. Slide the retainer onto the shaft *with the cupped surface facing outward*.

8. Again support the armature on a soft surface, with the pinion at the upper end. Center the snap ring on the top of the shaft (use a new snap ring if the original was damaged during removal). Gently place a block of wood flat on top of the snap ring so as not to move it from a centered position. Tap the wooden block with a hammer in order to force the snap ring around the shaft. Then, slide the ring down into the snap ring groove.

9. Lay the armature down flat on the surface you're working on. Slide the retainer close up on to the shaft and position it and the thrust collar next to the snap ring. Using two pairs of pliers on opposite sides of the shaft, squeeze the thrust collar and the retainer together until the snap ring is forced into the retainer.

10. Lube the drive housing bushing with a silicone lubricant. Then, install the armature and the clutch assembly into the drive housing, engaging the solenoid shift lever yoke with the clutch, and positioning the front of the armature shaft into the bushing.

NOTE: *On non-diesel starters the shift lever may be installed in the drive gear housing first.*

On the 25 MT diesel starter only, install the center bearing screws and the shift lever pivot bolt, and tighten securely.

11. Apply a sealing compound approved for this application onto the drive housing; then position the field frame around the armatures shaft and against the drive housing. *Work slowly and carefully to prevent damaging the starter brushes.*

12. Lubricate the bushing in the commutator end frame with a silicone lubricant, place the leather brake washer onto the armature shaft, and then slide the commutator end frame over the shaft and into position against the field frame. Line up the bolt holes, then install and tighten the thru-bolts.

13. Reconnect the field coil straps to the "motor" terminal of the solenoid.

NOTE: *If replacement of the starter drive fails to cure improper engagement of starter pinion to flywheel, there are probably defective parts in the solenoid and/or shift lever. The best procedure would probably be to take the assembly to a shop where a pinion clearance check can be made by energizing the solenoid on a test bench. If the pinion clearance is incorrect, disassemble the solenoid and shift lever, inspect, and replace worn parts.*

Brush Replacement

1. Disassemble the starter by following Steps 1 and 2 of the "Drive Replacement" procedure above.

2. Replace the brushes one at a time to avoid having to mark the wiring. For each brush; remove the brush holding screw; remove the old brush and position the new brush in the same direction (large end toward center of field frame), position wire connector on top of brush, line up holes, and reinstall screw. Make sure the screw is snug enough to ensure good contact.

3. Reassemble starter according to Steps 10–13 above.

Solenoid Replacement

1. Remove the screw and washer from the motor connector strap terminal.

2. Remove the two solenoid retaining screws.

3. Twist the solenoid housing clockwise to remove the flange key from the keyway in the housing. Then remove the housing.

4. To re-install the unit, place the return spring on the plunger and place the solenoid body on the drive housing. Turn counterclockwise to engage the flange key. Place the two retaining screws in position, then install the screw and washer which secures the strap terminal. Install the unit on the starter.

ENGINE MECHANICAL

Design

All Chevrolet engines, whether inline sixes (L6), V6 or V8, are water-cooled, overhead valve powerplants. Most engines use cast iron blocks and heads, with the exception of some high-performance 454s, which use aluminum heads.

The crankshaft in the 230 and 250 cu. in. inline six cylinder engines is supported in seven main bearings, with the thrust being taken by the No. 7 bearing. The camshaft is low in the block and is gear-driven. Relatively long pushrods actuate the valves through ball-jointed rocker arms.

Battery and Starter Specifications

Year	Engine No. Cyl Displacement (cu in.)	Battery Ampere Hour Capacity	Battery Volts	Terminal Grounded	Lock Test Amps	Lock Test Volts	Torque (ft. lbs.)	No-Load Test Amps	No-Load Test Volts	No-Load Test RPM	Brush Spring Tension (oz)
1964–65	ALL	44	12	Neg			Not Recommended	49–76	10.6	7,800	35
1966–67	6, 8-283	44	12	Neg			Not Recommended	49–76	10.6	7,800	35
	8-327, 396	61	12	Neg			Not Recommended	65–100	10.6	4,200	35
1968–69	6, 8-307	45	12	Neg			Not Recommended	—	10.6	—	35
	8-302, 327, 350, 396	61	12	Neg			Not Recommended	—	9	—	35
1970–71	6, 8-307	45	12	Neg			Not Recommended	50–80	9	5,500–10,500	35
	8-350	61	12	Neg			Not Recommended	55–80	9	3,500–6,000	35
	8-402 (396)	61	12	Neg			Not Recommended	65–95	9	7,500–10,500	35
	8-454	62	12	Neg			Not Recommended	65–95	9	7,500–10,500	35
1972	6-250	45	12	Neg			Not Recommended	50–80	9	5,500–10,500	35
	8-307, 350, 402	61	12	Neg			Not Recommended	50–80 ①	9	5,500–10,500	35
	8-454	76	12	Neg			Not Recommended	65–95	9	7,500–10,500	35
1973	6-250	45	12	Neg			Not Recommended	50–80	9	5,500–10,500	35
	8-307	61	12	Neg			Not Recommended	50–80	9	5,500–10,500	35
	8-350, 454	76	12	Neg			Not Recommended	65–95	9	7,500–10,500	35
1974	6-250	2300 ②	12	Neg			Not Recommended	50–80	9	5,500–10,500	35
	8-350, 400	2900 ②	12	Neg			Not Recommended	65–95	9	7,500–10,500	35
	8-454	3750 ②	12	Neg			Not Recommended	65–95	9	7,500–10,500	35
1975–76	6-250	2500 ②	12	Neg			Not Recommended	50–80	9	5,500–10,500	35
	8-350, 400	3200 ②	12	Neg			Not Recommended	65–95	9	7,500–10,000	35
	8-454	4000 ②	12	Neg			Not Recommended	65–95	9	7,500–10,000	35
1977–78	6-250	275 ③	12	Neg			Not Recommended	50–80	9	5,500–10,500	35
	8-305	350 ③	12	Neg			Not Recommended	50–80	9	5,500–10,500	35
	8-350	350 ③	12	Neg			Not Recommended	65–95	9	7,500–10,500	35

Battery and Starter Specifications (cont.)

Year	Engine No. Cyl Displace-ment (cu in.)	Battery			Starter							Brush Spring Tension (oz)
		Ampere Hour Capacity	Volts	Terminal Grounded	Lock Test		Torque (ft. lbs.)	No-Load Test				
					Amps	Volts		Amps	Volts	RPM		
1979	6-250	275③	12	Neg	Not Recommended			60–88	10.6	6,500–10,100		35
	6-231	350③	12	Neg	Not Recommended			50–80	10.6	7,500–11,400		35
	6-200	350③	12	Neg	Not Recommended			50–80	10.6	7,500–11,400		35
	8-305	350③	12	Neg	Not Recommended			50–80	10.6	7,500–11,400		35
	8-350	350③	12	Neg	Not Recommended			65–95	10.6	7,500–10,500		35
1980–81	6-229	350③	12	Neg	Not Recommended			50–80	10.6	7,500–11,400		35
	6-231	350③	12	Neg	Not Recommended			50–80	10.6	7,500–11,400		35
	8-267	350③	12	Neg	Not Recommended			50–80	10.6	7,500–11,400		35
	8-305	350③	12	Neg	Not Recommended			50–80	10.6	7,500–11,400		35
1982–84	6-229	350③④	12	Neg	Not Recommended			60–80	10.6	7,500–11,400		35
	6-231	350③④	12	Neg	Not Recommended			60–80	10.6	7,500–11,400		35
	6-263	465③⑥	12	Neg	Not Recommended			160–220	10.6	4,000–5,500		35
	8-267	350③	12	Neg	Not Recommended			45–70	10.6	7,500–11,400		35
	8-305	350③	12	Neg	Not Recommended			44–70	10.6	7,500–11,400		35
	8-350	465③⑥	12	Neg	Not Recommended			160–220	10.6	4,000–5,500		35
1985–86	6-262	630③	12	Neg	Not Recommended			50–75	10	6,000–11,900		35
	8-305	500③	12	Neg	Not Recommended			50–75	10	6,000–11,900		35

① 350 & 402 use 454 starter   ④ 80 minute reserve capacity
② Cranking power in watts @ 0°F   ⑤ 75 minute reserve capacity
③ Cranking power in amps @ 0°F   ⑥ 115 minute reserve capacity; 2 batteries used

The small-block family of V8 engines, which has included the 267, 283, 305, 307, 327, 350 and 400 cu. in. blocks, have all evolved from the design of the 1955 265 cu. in. V8. It was this engine that introduced the ball-joint type rocker arm design which is now used by many car makers. The Chevrolet-built 229 and 262 V6s are also similar.

This line of engines features a great deal of interchangeability, and later parts may be utilized on earlier engines for increased reliability and/or performance. For example, in 1968 the 283 was dropped and replaced by the 307, which is in effect a 327 crankshaft in a 283 block. And the 267, 305 and 350 V8s all share the same stroke crankshaft, bore dimensions being the main difference between the engines.

The 396, 402 and 454 engines are known as the big-blocks, or less frequently, the Mark IV engines. They were available in the high-performance SS versions of the Chevelle, and feature many tuning modifications such as high-

ENGINE OVERHAUL

Most engine overhaul procedures are fairly standard. In addition to specific parts replacement procedures and complete specifications for your individual engine, this chapter also is a guide to accepted rebuilding procedures. Examples of standard rebuilding practice are shown and should be used along with specific details concerning your particular engine.

Competent and accurate machine shop services will ensure maximum performance, reliability and engine life. Procedures marked with the symbol shown above should be performed by a competent machine shop, and are provided so that you will be familiar with the procedures necessary to a successful overhaul.

In most instances it is more profitable for the do-it-yourself mechanic to remove, clean and inspect the component, buy the necessary parts and deliver these to a shop for actual machine work.

On the other hand, much of the rebuilding work (crankshaft, block, bearings, pistons, rods, and other components) is well within the scope of the do-it-yourself mechanic.

Tools

The tools required for an engine overhaul or parts replacement will depend on the depth of your involvement. With a few exceptions, they will be the tools found in a mechanic's tool kit (see Chapter 1). More indepth work will require any or all of the following:

- a dial indicator (reading in thousandths) mounted on a universal base
- micrometers and telescope gauges
- jaw and screw-type pullers
- scraper
- valve spring compressor
- ring groove cleaner
- piston ring expander and compressor
- ridge reamer
- cylinder hone or glaze breaker

- Plastigage®
- engine stand

Use of most of these tools is illustrated in this chapter. Many can be rented for a onetime use from a local parts jobber or tool supply house specializing in automotive work.

Occasionally, the use of special tools is called for. See the information on Special Tools and the Safety Notice in the front of this book before substituting another tool.

Inspection Techniques

Procedures and specifications are given in this chapter for inspecting, cleaning and assessing the wear limits of most major components. Other procedures such as Magnaflux and Zyglo can be used to locate material flaws and stress cracks. Magnaflux is a magnetic process applicable only to ferrous materials. The Zyglo process coats the material with a flourescent dye penetrant and can be used on any material. Check for suspected surface cracks can be more readily made using spot check dye. The dye is sprayed onto the suspected area, wiped off and the area sprayed with a developer. Cracks will show up brightly.

Overhaul Tips

Aluminum has become extremely popular for use in engines, due to its low weight. Observe the following precautions when handling aluminum parts:

- Never hot tank aluminum parts (the caustic hot-tank solution will eat the aluminum)
- Remove all aluminum parts (identification tag, etc.) from engine parts prior to hot-tanking.
- Always coat threads lightly with engine oil or anti-seize compounds before installation, to prevent seizure.
- Never over-torque bolts or spark plugs, especially in aluminum threads.

Stripped threads in any component can be repaired using any of several commercial repair kits (Heli-Coil, Microdot, Keenserts, etc.)

When assembling the engine, any parts that will be in frictional contact must be prelubed to provide lubrication at initial start-up. Any product specifically formulated for this purpose can be used, but engine oil is not recommended as a pre-lube.

When semi-permanent (locked, but removable) installation of bolts or nuts is desired, threads should be cleaned and coated with Loctite® or other similar, commercial non-hardening sealant.

Repairing Damaged Threads

Several methods of repairing damaged threads are available. Heli-Coil® (shown here), Keenserts® and Microdot® are among the most widely used. All involve basically the same principle—drilling out stripped threads, tapping the hole and installing a prewound insert—making welding, plugging and oversize fasteners unnecessary.

Two types of thread repair inserts are usually supplied—a standard type for most Inch Coarse, Inch Fine, Metric Coarse and Metric Fine thread sizes and a spark plug type to fit most spark plug port sizes. Consult the individual manufacturer's catalog to determine exact applications. Typical thread repair kits will contain a selection of prewound threaded inserts, a tap (corresponding to the outside diameter threads of the insert) and an installation tool. Spark plug inserts usually differ because they require a tap equipped with pilot threads and a combined reamer/tap section. Most manufacturers also supply blister-packed thread repair inserts separately in addition to a master kit containing a variety of taps and inserts plus installation tools.

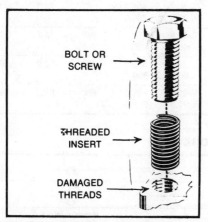

Damaged bolt holes can be repaired with thread repair inserts

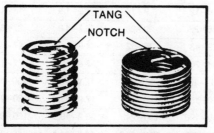

Standard thread repair insert (left) and spark plug thread insert (right)

Before effecting a repair to a threaded hole, remove any snapped, broken or damaged bolts or studs. Penetrating oil can be used to free frozen threads; the offending item can be removed with locking pliers or with a screw or stud extractor. After the hole is clear, the thread can be repaired, as follows:

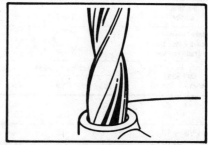

Drill out the damaged threads with specified drill. Drill completely through the hole or to the bottom of a blind hole

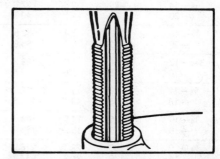

With the tap supplied, tap the hole to receive the thread insert. Keep the tap well oiled and back it out frequently to avoid clogging the threads

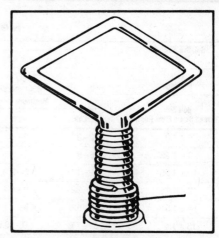

Screw the threaded insert onto the installation tool until the tang engages the slot. Screw the insert into the tapped hole until it is ¼–½ turn below the top surface, After installation break off the tang with a hammer and punch

Standard Torque Specifications and Fastener Markings

In the absence of specific torques, the following chart can be used as a guide to the maximum safe torque of a particular size/grade of fastener.
- There is no torque difference for fine or coarse threads.
- Torque values are based on clean, dry threads. Reduce the value by 10% if threads are oiled prior to assembly.
- The torque required for aluminum components or fasteners is considerably less.

U.S. Bolts

SAE Grade Number	1 or 2			5			6 or 7		
Number of lines always 2 less than the grade number.									
Bolt Size (Inches)—(Thread)	Maximum Torque			Maximum Torque			Maximum Torque		
	Ft./Lbs.	Kgm	Nm	Ft./Lbs.	Kgm	Nm	Ft./Lbs.	Kgm	Nm
¼ — 20	5	0.7	6.8	8	1.1	10.8	10	1.4	13.5
— 28	6	0.8	8.1	10	1.4	13.6			
⁵⁄₁₆ — 18	11	1.5	14.9	17	2.3	23.0	19	2.6	25.8
— 24	13	1.8	17.6	19	2.6	25.7			
⅜ — 16	18	2.5	24.4	31	4.3	42.0	34	4.7	46.0
— 24	20	2.75	27.1	35	4.8	47.5			
⁷⁄₁₆ — 14	28	3.8	37.0	49	6.8	66.4	55	7.6	74.5
— 20	30	4.2	40.7	55	7.6	74.5			
½ — 13	39	5.4	52.8	75	10.4	101.7	85	11.75	115.2
— 20	41	5.7	55.6	85	11.7	115.2			
⁹⁄₁₆ — 12	51	7.0	69.2	110	15.2	149.1	120	16.6	162.7
— 18	55	7.6	74.5	120	16.6	162.7			
⅝ — 11	83	11.5	112.5	150	20.7	203.3	167	23.0	226.5
— 18	95	13.1	128.8	170	23.5	230.5			
¾ — 10	105	14.5	142.3	270	37.3	366.0	280	38.7	379.6
— 16	115	15.9	155.9	295	40.8	400.0			
⅞ — 9	160	22.1	216.9	395	54.6	535.5	440	60.9	596.5
— 14	175	24.2	237.2	435	60.1	589.7			
1 — 8	236	32.5	318.6	590	81.6	799.9	660	91.3	894.8
— 14	250	34.6	338.9	660	91.3	849.8			

Metric Bolts

Relative Strength Marking	4.6, 4.8			8.8		
Bolt Markings						
Bolt Size Thread Size x Pitch (mm)	Maximum Torque			Maximum Torque		
	Ft./Lbs.	Kgm	Nm	Ft./Lbs.	Kgm	Nm
6 x 1.0	2–3	.2–.4	3–4	3–6	.4–.8	5–8
8 x 1.25	6–8	.8–1	8–12	9–14	1.2–1.9	13–19
10 x 1.25	12–17	1.5–2.3	16–23	20–29	2.7–4.0	27–39
12 x 1.25	21–32	2.9–4.4	29–43	35–53	4.8–7.3	47–72
14 x 1.5	35–52	4.8–7.1	48–70	57–85	7.8–11.7	77–110
16 x 1.5	51–77	7.0–10.6	67–100	90–120	12.4–16.5	130–160
18 x 1.5	74–110	10.2–15.1	100–150	130–170	17.9–23.4	180–230
20 x 1.5	110–140	15.1–19.3	150–190	190–240	26.2–46.9	160–320
22 x 1.5	150–190	22.0–26.2	200–260	250–320	34.5–44.1	340–430
24 x 1.5	190–240	26.2–46.9	260–320	310–410	42.7–56.5	420–550

CHECKING ENGINE COMPRESSION

A noticeable lack of engine power, excessive oil consumption and/or poor fuel mileage measured over an extended period are all indicators of internal engine wear. Worn piston rings, scored or worn cylinder bores, blown head gaskets, sticking or burnt valves and worn valve seats are all possible culprits here. A check of each cylinder's compression will help you locate the problems.

As mentioned in the "Tools and Equipment" section of Chapter 1, a screw-in type compression gauge is more accurate than the type you simply hold against the spark plug hole, although it takes slightly longer to use. It's worth it to obtain a more accurate reading. Follow the procedures below for gasoline and diesel-engined cars.

Gasoline Engines

1. Warm up the engine to normal operating temperature.
2. Remove all spark plugs.

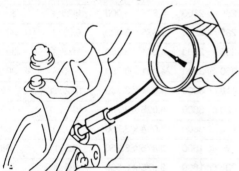

The screw-in type compression gauge is more accurate

3. Disconnect the high-tension lead from the ignition coil.
4. On carbureted cars, fully open the throttle either by operating the carburetor throttle linkage by hand or by having an assistant "floor" the accelerator pedal. On fuel-injected cars, disconnect the cold start valve and all injector connections.
5. Screw the compression gauge into the No. 1 spark plug hole until the fitting is snug.
NOTE: *Be careful not to crossthread the plug hole. On aluminum cylinder heads use extra care, as the threads in these heads are easily ruined.*
6. Ask an assistant to depress the accelerator pedal fully on both carbureted and fuel-injected cars. Then, while you read the compression gauge, ask the assistant to crank the engine two or three times in short bursts using the ignition switch.

7. Read the compression gauge at the end of each series of cranks, and record the highest of these readings. Repeat this procedure for each of the engine's cylinders. Compare the highest reading of each cylinder to the compression pressure specifications in the "Tune-Up Specifications" chart in Chapter 2. The specs in this chart are maximum values.

A cylinder's compression pressure is usually acceptable if it is not less than 80% of maximum. The difference between each cylinder should be no more than 12–14 pounds.

8. If a cylinder is unusually low, pour a tablespoon of clean engine oil into the cylinder through the spark plug hole and repeat the compression test. If the compression comes up after adding the oil, it appears that that cylinder's piston rings or bore are damaged or worn. If the pressure remains low, the valves may not be seating properly (a valve job is needed), or the head gasket may be blown near that cylinder. If compression in any two adjacent cylinders is low, and if the addition of oil doesn't help the compression, there is leakage past the head gasket. Oil and coolant water in the combustion chamber can result from this problem. There may be evidence of water droplets on the engine dipstick when a head gasket has blown.

Diesel Engines

Checking cylinder compression on diesel engines is basically the same procedure as on gasoline engines except for the following:

1. A special compression gauge adaptor suitable for diesel engines (because these engines have much greater compression pressures) must be used.
2. Remove the injector tubes and remove the injectors from each cylinder.
NOTE: *Don't forget to remove the washer underneath each injector; otherwise, it may get lost when the engine is cranked.*

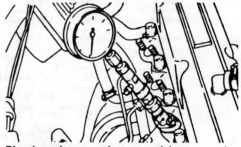

Diesel engines require a special compression gauge adaptor

3. When fitting the compression gauge adaptor to the cylinder head, make sure the bleeder of the gauge (if equipped) is closed.
4. When reinstalling the injector assemblies, install new washers underneath each injector.

General Engine Specifications

Year	Engine No. Cyl Displacement (cu in.)	Type Carburetor	Horsepower @ rpm ■	Torque @ rpm (ft. lbs.) ■	Bore and Stroke (in.)	Compression Ratio	Oil Pressure @ 2000 rpm (psi)
1964	6-194	1-bbl	120 @ 4400	177 @ 2400	3.563 x 3.250	8.5:1	35
	6-230	1-bbl	155 @ 4400	215 @ 2000	3.875 x 3.250	8.5:1	35
	6-283	2-bbl	195 @ 4800	285 @ 2800	3.875 x 3.000	9.25:1	35
	8-283	4-bbl	220 @ 4800	295 @ 3200	3.875 x 3.000	9.25:1	35
	8-327	4-bbl	250 @ 4400	350 @ 2800	4.000 x 3.250	10.5:1	35
	8-327	4-bbl	300 @ 5000	360 @ 3200	4.000 x 3.250	10.5:1	35
1965	6-194	1-bbl	120 @ 4400	177 @ 2400	3.563 x 3.250	8.5:1	35
	6-230	1-bbl	140 @ 4400	220 @ 1600	3.875 x 3.250	8.5:1	35
	8-283	2-bbl	195 @ 4800	285 @ 2400	3.875 x 3.000	9.25:1	35
	8-283	4-bbl	220 @ 4800	295 @ 3200	3.875 x 3.000	9.25:1	35
	8-327	4-bbl	250 @ 4400	350 @ 2800	4.001 x 3.250	10.5:1	35
	8-327	4-bbl	300 @ 5000	360 @ 3200	4.001 x 3.250	10.5:1	35
	8-327	4-bbl	350 @ 5800	360 @ 3600	4.001 x 3.250	11.0:1	35
1966	6-194	1-bbl	120 @ 4400	177 @ 2400	3.563 x 3.250	8.5:1	38 ①
	6-230	1-bbl	140 @ 4400	220 @ 1600	3.875 x 3.250	8.5:1	38 ①
	8-283	2-bbl	195 @ 4800	285 @ 2800	3.875 x 3.000	9.25:1	38 ①
	8-283	4-bbl	220 @ 4800	295 @ 3200	3.875 x 3.000	9.25:1	38 ①
	8-327	4-bbl	275 @ 4800	335 @ 2800	4.001 x 3.250	10.5:1	38 ①
	8-327	4-bbl	350 @ 5800	360 @ 3600	4.001 x 3.250	11.0:1	38 ①
	8-396	4-bbl	325 @ 4800	410 @ 3200	4.094 x 3.760	10.25:1	62
	8-396	4-bbl	360 @ 5200	420 @ 3600	4.096 x 3.760	10.25:1	62
	8-396	4-bbl	375 @ 5600	415 @ 3600	4.094 x 3.760	11.0:1	62
1967	6-230	1-bbl	140 @ 4400	220 @ 1600	3.875 x 3.250	8.5:1	38
	6-250	1-bbl	155 @ 4200	235 @ 1600	3.875 x 3.530	8.5:1	38 ①
	8-283	2-bbl	195 @ 4600	285 @ 2400	3.875 x 3.000	9.25:1	38 ①
	8-327	2-bbl	210 @ 4600	320 @ 2400	4.001 x 3.250	8.75:1	38 ①
	8-327	4-bbl	275 @ 4800	355 @ 3200	4.001 x 3.250	10.0:1	38 ①
	8-396	4-bbl	325 @ 4800	410 @ 3200	4.094 x 3.760	10.25:1	57
	8-396	4-bbl	350 @ 5200	415 @ 3400	4.094 x 3.760	10.25:1	57
1968	6-230	1-bbl	145 @ 4400	220 @ 1600	3.875 x 3.250	8.5:1	58
	6-250	1-bbl	155 @ 4200	235 @ 1600	3.875 x 3.530	8.5:1	58
	8-307	2-bbl	200 @ 4600	300 @ 2400	3.875 x 3.250	9.0:1	58
	8-327	2-bbl	210 @ 4600	320 @ 2400	4.001 x 3.250	8.75:1	58
	8-327	4-bbl	275 @ 4800	355 @ 3200	4.001 x 3.250	10.0:1	58
	8-396	4-bbl	325 @ 4800	410 @ 3200	4.094 x 3.760	10.25:1	62
	8-396	4-bbl	350 @ 5200	415 @ 3400	4.094 x 3.750	10.25:1	62
	8-396	4-bbl	375 @ 5600	415 @ 3600	4.094 x 3.760	11.0:1	62
1969	6-230	1-bbl	140 @ 4400	220 @ 1600	3.875 x 3.250	8.5:1	58
	6-250	1-bbl	155 @ 4200	235 @ 1600	3.875 x 3.530	8.5:1	58
	8-307	2-bbl	200 @ 4600	300 @ 2400	3.875 x 3.250	9.0:1	58
	8-350	2-bbl	250 @ 4800	345 @ 2800	4.000 x 3.480	9.0:1	62

General Engine Specifications (cont.)

Year	Engine No. Cyl Displacement (cu in.)	Type Carburetor	Horsepower @ rpm■	Torque @ rpm (ft. lbs.)■	Bore and Stroke (in.)	Compression Ratio	Oil Pressure @ 2000 rpm (psi)
1969	8-350	4-bbl	300 @ 4800	380 @ 3200	4.000 x 3.480	10.25:1	62
	8-396	4-bbl	325 @ 4800	410 @ 3200	4.094 x 3.760	10.25:1	62
	8-396	4-bbl	350 @ 5200	415 @ 3400	4.094 x 3.760	10.25:1	62
	8-396	4-bbl	375 @ 5600	415 @ 3600	4.094 x 3.760	11.0:1	62
1970	6-230	1-bbl	140 @ 4400	220 @ 1600	3.875 x 3.250	8.5:1	40
	6-250	1-bbl	155 @ 4200	235 @ 1600	3.875 x 3.530	8.5:1	40
	8-307	2-bbl	200 @ 4600	300 @ 2400	3.875 x 3.250	9.0:1	40
	8-350	2-bbl	250 @ 4800	345 @ 2800	4.000 x 3.480	9.0:1	40
	8-350	4-bbl	300 @ 4800	380 @ 3200	4.000 x 3.480	10.25:1	40
	8-400	2-bbl	265 @ 4400	400 @ 2400	4.125 x 3.760	9.0:1	40
	8-402	4-bbl	330 @ 4800	410 @ 3200	4.126 x 3.760	10.25:1	40
	8-402	4-bbl	350 @ 5200	415 @ 3400	4.126 x 3.760	10.25:1	40
	8-454	4-bbl	360 @ 4400	500 @ 3200	4.251 x 4.000	10.25:1	40
1971	6-250	1-bbl	145 @ 4200	230 @ 1600	3.875 x 3.530	8.5:1	40
	8-307	2-bbl	200 @ 4600	300 @ 2400	3.875 x 3.250	8.5:1	40
	8-350	2-bbl	245 @ 4800	350 @ 2800	4.000 x 3.480	8.5:1	40
	8-350	4-bbl	270 @ 4800	360 @ 3200	4.000 x 3.480	8.5:1	40
	8-350	4-bbl	330 @ 5000	275 @ 5600	4.000 x 3.480	9.0:1	40
	8-402	4-bbl	300 @ 4800	400 @ 3200	4.126 x 3.760	8.5:1	40
	8-454	4-bbl	365 @ 4800	465 @ 3200	4.251 x 4.000	8.5:1	40
	8-454	4-bbl	425 @ 5600	475 @ 4000	4.251 x 4.000	9.0:1	40
1972	6-250	1-bbl	110 @ 3800	185 @ 1600	3.875 x 3.530	8.5:1	40
	8-307	2-bbl	130 @ 4000	230 @ 2400	3.875 x 3.250	8.5:1	40
	8-350	2-bbl	165 @ 4000	280 @ 2400	4.000 x 3.480	8.5:1	40
	8-350	4-bbl	200 @ 4400	300 @ 2800	4.000 x 3.480	8.5:1	40
	8-350	4-bbl	225 @ 5600	280 @ 4000	4.000 x 3.480	9.0:1	40
	8-402	4-bbl	240 @ 4400	345 @ 3200	4.126 x 3.760	8.5:1	40
	8-454	4-bbl	270 @ 4000	390 @ 3200	4.251 x 4.000	8.5:1	40
1973	6-250	1-bbl	100 @ 3800	175 @ 1600	3.875 x 3.530	8.25:1	40
	8-307	2-bbl	115 @ 4000	205 @ 2000	3.875 x 3.250	8.5:1	40
	8-350	2-bbl	145 @ 4000	255 @ 2400	4.000 x 3.480	8.5:1	40
	8-350	4-bbl	175 @ 4400	270 @ 2400	4.000 x 3.480	8.5:1	40
	8-350	4-bbl	245 @ 5200	280 @ 4000	4.000 x 3.480	9.0:1	40
	8-454	4-bbl	245 @ 4000	375 @ 2800	4.251 x 4.000	8.5:1	40
1974	6-250	1-bbl	100 @ 3600	175 @ 1800	3.875 x 3.530	8.25:1	40
	8-350 ②	2-bbl	145 @ 3600	250 @ 2200	4.000 x 3.480	8.5:1	40
	8-350 ③	4-bbl	160 @ 3800	245 @ 2400	4.000 x 3.480	8.5:1	40
	8-350	4-bbl	185 @ 4000	270 @ 2600	4.000 x 3.480	8.5:1	40
	8-400 ②	2-bbl	150 @ 3200	295 @ 2600	4.126 x 3.750	8.5:1	40
	8-400 ③	4-bbl	180 @ 3800	290 @ 2400	4.126 x 3.750	8.5:1	40
	8-454	4-bbl	235 @ 4000	360 @ 2800	4.251 x 4.000	8.25:1	40

General Engine Specifications (cont.)

Year	Engine No. Cyl Displacement (cu in.)	Type Carburetor	Horsepower @ rpm ■	Torque @ rpm (ft. lbs.) ■	Bore and Stroke (in.)	Compression Ratio	Oil Pressure @ 2000 rpm (psi)
1975	6-250	1-bbl	105 @ 3800	185 @ 1200	3.875 x 3.530	8.25:1	40
	8-350 ②	2-bbl	145 @ 3800	250 @ 2200	4.000 x 3.480	8.5:1	40
	8-350 ③	4-bbl	155 @ 3800	250 @ 2400	4.000 x 3.480	8.5:1	40
	8-400	4-bbl	175 @ 3600	305 @ 2000	4.126 x 4.000	8.5:1	40
	8-454 ②	4-bbl	215 @ 4000	350 @ 2400	4.251 x 4.000	8.15:1	40
1976–77	6-250	1-bbl	105 @ 3800	185 @ 1200	3.875 x 3.530	8.25:1	40
	8-305	2-bbl	140 @ 3800	245 @ 2000	3.736 x 3.480	8.5:1	40
	8-350	2-bbl	145 @ 3800	250 @ 2200	4.000 x 3.480	8.5:1	40
	8-350	4-bbl	165 @ 3800	260 @ 2400	4.000 x 3.480	8.5:1	40
	8-400	4-bbl	175 @ 3600	305 @ 2000	4.126 x 4.000	8.5:1	40
1978–79	6-200	2-bbl	95 @ 3800	160 @ 2000	3.500 x 3.480	8.2:1	40
	6-231	2-bbl	105 @ 3400	185 @ 2000	3.800 x 3.400	8.0:1	37
	6-250	1-bbl	110 @ 3800	190 @ 1600	3.875 x 3.530	8.1:1	40
	8-305	4-bbl	155 @ 3800	260 @ 2800	3.736 x 3.480	8.4:1	45
	8-305	2-bbl	145 @ 3800	245 @ 2400	3.736 x 3.480	8.5:1	40
	8-267	2-bbl	125 @ 3800	215 @ 2400	3.500 x 3.480	8.2:1	45
	8-350	4-bbl	170 @ 3800	270 @ 2400	4.000 x 3.480	8.5:1	40
1980	6-229	2-bbl	115 @ 4000	175 @ 2000	3.736 x 3.480	8.6:1	45
	6-231	2-bbl	110 @ 3800	190 @ 1600	3.800 x 3.400	8.0:1	45
	6-231	Turbo	170 @ 4000	265 @ 2400	3.800 x 3.400	8.0:1	37
	8-267	2-bbl	120 @ 3600	215 @ 2000	3.500 x 3.480	8.3:1	45
	8-305	4-bbl	155 @ 4000	240 @ 1600	3.736 x 3.480	8.6:1	45
	8-305 (Calif.)	4-bbl	155 @ 4000	230 @ 2400	3.736 x 3.480	8.6:1	45
1981	6-229	2-bbl	110 @ 4200	170 @ 2000	3.736 x 3.480	8.6:1	45
	6-231	2-bbl	110 @ 3800	190 @ 1600	3.800 x 3.400	8.0:1	45
	6-231	Turbo	170 @ 4000	275 @ 2400	3.800 x 3.400	8.0:1	37
	8-267	2-bbl	115 @ 4000	200 @ 2400	3.500 x 3.480	8.3:1	45
	8-305	4-bbl	150 @ 3800	240 @ 2400	3.736 x 3.480	8.6:1	45
1982–84	6-229	2-bbl	110 @ 4200	170 @ 2000	3.736 x 3.480	8.6:1	45
	6-231	2-bbl	110 @ 3800	190 @ 1600	3.800 x 3.400	8.0:1	45
	6-263	Diesel	85 @ 3600	165 @ 1600	4.057 x 3.385	22.5:1	45 ①
	8-267	2-bbl	115 @ 4000	205 @ 2400	3.50 x 3.48	8.3:1	45
	8-305	4-bbl	145 @ 4000	240 @ 1600	3.736 x 3.480	8.6:1	45
	8-350	Diesel	105 @ 3200	200 @ 1600	4.057 x 3.385	22.5:1	45 ①
1985–86	6-262	TBI	130 @ 3600	218 @ 2000	4.000 x 3.480	9.3:1	45
	8-305	4 bbl	134 @ 4800	319 @ 3200	3.736 x 3.480	9.5:1	45
	8-305	4 bbl	150 @ 3800	240 @ 2400	3.736 x 3.480	8.6:1	45

■Starting 1972, horsepower and torque are SAE net figures. They are measured at the rear of the transmission with all accessories installed and operating. Since the figures vary when a given engine is installed in different models, some are representative rather than exact.
① Oil pressure at 1500 rpm   ② Not available—Calif.   ③ Calif. only

Valve Specifications

Year	Engine No. Cyl. Displacement (cu in.)	Seat Angle (deg)	Face Angle (deg)	Spring Test Pressure (lbs @ in.)	Spring Installed Height (in.)	Stem to Guide Clearance (in.) Intake	Stem to Guide Clearance (in.) Exhaust	Stem Diameter (in.) Intake	Stem Diameter (in.) Exhaust
1964–65	6-194	46	45	170 @ 1.33	1⅔	0.0010–0.0027	0.0015–0.0033	0.3404–0.3417	0.3410–0.3417
	6-230	46	45	175 @ 1.26	1⅔	0.0010–0.0027	0.0015–0.0033	0.3404–0.3417	0.3410–0.3417
	8-283	46	45	175 @ 1.26	1⅔	0.0010–0.0027	0.0015–0.0033	0.3404–0.3417	0.3410–0.3417
	8-327	46	45	175 @ 1.26	1⅔	0.0010–0.0027	0.0010–0.0027	0.3404–0.3417	0.3410–0.3417
1966	6-194	46	45	60 @ 166	1 21/32	0.0010–0.0037	0.0010–0.0047	0.3414	0.3414
	6-230	46	45	60 @ 166	1 21/32	0.0010–0.0037	0.0010–0.0047	0.3414	0.3414
	8-283	46	45	82 @ 1.66	1 21/32	0.0010–0.0037	0.0010–0.0047	0.3414	0.3414
	8-327	46	45	82 @ 1.66	1 21/32	0.0010–0.0037	0.0010–0.0047	0.3414	0.3414
	8-396 ①	46	45	90 @ 1.88	1⅞	0.0010–0.0037	0.0010–0.0047	0.3414	0.3414
	8-396 ②	46	45	100 @ 1.88	1⅞	0.0010–0.0037	0.0010–0.0047	0.3414	0.3414
1967	6-230	46 ③	45	60 @ 1.66	1 21/32	0.0010–0.0037	0.0015–0.0052	0.3414	0.3414
	6-250	46 ③	45	60 @ 1.66	1 21/32	0.0010–0.0047	0.0015–0.0052	0.3414	0.3414
	8-283	46 ③	45	80 @ 1.70	1 5/32	0.0010–0.0037	0.0010–0.0047	0.3414	0.3414
	8-327	46 ③	45	80 @ 1.70	1 5/32	0.0010–0.0037	0.0010–0.0047	0.3414	0.3414
	8-396 ①	46 ③	45	90 @ 1.88	1⅞	0.0010–0.0035	0.0012–0.0047	0.3717	0.3717
	8-396 ②	46	45	100 @ 1.88	1⅞	0.0010–0.0035	0.0012–0.0047	0.3717	0.3717
1968	6-230	46 ③	45	59 @ 1.66	1 21/32	0.0010–0.0037	0.0015–0.0052	0.3414	0.3414
	6-250	46 ③	45	59 @ 1.66	1 21/32	0.0010–0.0037	0.0015–0.0052	0.3414	0.3414
	8-307	46 ③	45	80 @ 1.70	1 5/32	0.0010–0.0037	0.0010–0.0047	0.3414	0.3414
	8-327	46 ③	45	80 @ 1.70	1 5/32	0.0010–0.0037	0.0010–0.0047	0.3414	0.3414
	8-350	46 ③	45	80 @ 1.70	1 5/32	0.0010–0.0037	0.0010–0.0047	0.3414	0.3414
	8-396	46 ③	45	90 @ 1.88	1⅞	0.0010–0.0035	0.0012–0.0047	0.3719	0.3717
1969	6-230	46 ③	45	59 @ 1.66	1 21/32	0.0010–0.0037	0.0015–0.0052	0.3414	0.3414
	6-250	46 ③	45	59 @ 1.66	1 21/32	0.0010–0.0037	0.0015–0.0052	0.3414	0.3414
	8-307	46 ③	45	80 @ 1.70	1 23/32	0.0010–0.0037	0.0012–0.0049	0.3414	0.3414

Valve Specifications (cont.)

Year	Engine No. Cyl. Displacement (cu in.)	Seat Angle (deg)	Face Angle (deg)	Spring Test Pressure (lbs @ in.)	Spring Installed Height (in.)	Stem to Guide Clearance (in.)		Stem Diameter (in.)	
						Intake	Exhaust	Intake	Exhaust
1969	8-350	46③	45	80 @ 1.70	15/32	0.0010–0.0037	0.0010–0.0047	0.3414	0.3414
	8-396①	46③	45	90 @ 1.88	17/8	0.0010–0.0035	0.0012–0.0047	0.3719	0.3719
	8-396④	46③	45	100 @ 1.88	17/8	0.0010–0.0035	0.0012–0.0047	0.3719	0.3719
1970	6-230	46③	45	59 @ 1.66	121/32	0.0010–0.0037	0.0015–0.0052	0.3414	0.3414
	6-250	46③	45	59 @ 1.66	121/32	0.0010–0.0037	0.0015–0.0052	0.3414	0.3414
	8-307	46③	45	80 @ 1.70	123/32	0.0010–0.0037	0.0012–0.0049	0.3414	0.3414
	8-350	46③	45	80 @ 1.70	123/32	0.0010–0.0037	0.0012–0.0049	0.3414	0.3414
	8-400	46③	45	80 @ 1.70	17/8	0.0010–0.0037	0.0012–0.0047	0.3414	0.3414
	8-402	46③	45	75 @ 1.88⑤	17/8	0.0010–0.0037	0.0012–0.0047	0.3719	0.3717
	8-454	46④	45	75 @ 1.88⑤	17/8	0.0010–0.0037	0.0012–0.0047	0.3717	0.3719
1971	6-250	46	45	60 @ 1.66	121/32	0.0010–0.0037	0.0015–0.0052	0.3414	0.3414
	8-307	46	45	80 @ 1.70	123/32	0.0010–0.0037	0.0012–0.0049	0.3414	0.3414
	8-350	46	45	80 @ 1.70	123/32	0.0010–0.0037	0.0012–0.0049	0.3414	0.3414
	8-402	46	45	s8175 @ 1.88⑤	17/8	0.0010–0.0037	0.0012–0.0047	0.3719	0.3717
	8-454	46	45	75 @ 1.88⑤	17/8	0.0010–0.0037	0.0012–0.0047	0.3719	0.3717
1972	6-250	46	45	60 @ 1.66	121/32	0.0010–0.0037	0.0015–0.0052	0.3414	0.3414
	8-307	46	45	80 @ 1.70	123/32	0.0010–0.0037	0.0012–0.0049	0.3414	0.3414
	8-350	46	45	80 @ 1.70	123/32	0.0010–0.0037	0.0012–0.0049	0.3414	0.3414
	8-402	46	45	75 @ 1.88⑤	17/8	0.0010–0.0037	0.0012–0.0047	0.3719	0.3717
	8-454	46	45	75 @ 1.88⑤	17/8	0.0010–0.0037	0.0012–0.0047	0.3719	0.3717
1973	6-250	46	45	60 @ 1.66	121/32	0.0010–0.0027	0.0015–0.0032	0.3414	0.3414
	8-307	46	45	80 @ 1.61	15/8	0.0010–0.0037	0.0012–0.0047	0.3414	0.3414
	8-350	46	45	80 @ 1.70	123/32	0.0012–0.0027	0.0012–0.0029	0.3414	0.3414
	8-454	46	45	80 @ 1.88	17/8	0.0010–0.0027	0.0012–0.0027	0.3719	0.3417
1974	6-250	46	45	60 @ 1.66	121/32	0.0010–0.0027	0.0012–0.0027	0.3414	0.3414

Year	Engine								
1974	8-350	46	45	80 @ 1.70	$1\frac{23}{32}$	0.0010–0.0027	0.0010–0.0027	0.3414	0.3414
	8-400	46	45	80 @ 1.70	$1\frac{23}{32}$	0.0010–0.0027	0.0010–0.0027	0.3414	0.3414
	8-454	46	45	80 @ 1.88	$1\frac{7}{8}$	0.0010–0.0027	0.0010–0.0027	0.3719	0.3719
1975–77	6-250	46	45	60 @ 1.66	$1\frac{21}{32}$	0.0010–0.0027 ⑥	0.0010–0.0027	0.3414	0.3414
	8-305	46	45	80 @ 1.70	$1\frac{23}{32}$	0.0010–0.0027	0.0010–0.0027	0.3414	0.3414
	8-350	46	45	80 @ 1.70 ⑦	$1\frac{23}{32}$	0.0010–0.0027	0.0010–0.0027	0.3414	0.3414
	8-400	46	45	80 @ 1.70 ⑦	$1\frac{23}{32}$	0.0010–0.0027	0.0010–0.0027	0.3414	0.3414
	8-454	46	45	90 @ 1.88	$1\frac{7}{8}$	0.0010–0.0027	0.0010–0.0027	0.3719	0.3719
1978–79	6-200	46	45	200 @ 1.25	$1\frac{23}{32}$ ⑧	0.0010–0.0027	0.0010–0.0027	0.3414	0.3414
	6-231	45	45	168 @ 1.33	$1\frac{47}{64}$	0.0015–0.0032	0.0015–0.0032	0.3407	0.3409
	6-250	46	45	175 @ 1.26	$1\frac{21}{32}$	0.0010–0.0027	0.0015–0.0032	0.3414	0.3414
	8-267	46	45	200 @ 1.25	$1\frac{23}{32}$	0.0010–0.0027	0.0010–0.0027	0.3414	0.3414
	8-305	46	45	200 @ 1.25	$1\frac{23}{32}$ ⑧	0.0010–0.0027	0.0010–0.0027	0.3414	0.3414
	8-350	46	45	200 @ 1.25	$1\frac{23}{32}$ ⑧	0.0010–0.0027	0.0010–0.0027	0.3414	0.3414
1980–81	6-229	46	45	200 @ 1.25	$1\frac{23}{32}$	0.0010–0.0027	0.0010–0.0027	0.3414	0.3414
	6-231	45	45	168 @ 1.33	$1\frac{47}{64}$	0.0015–0.0032	0.0015–0.0032	0.3407	0.3409
	8-267	46	45	200 @ 1.25	$1\frac{23}{32}$	0.0010–0.0027	0.0010–0.0027	0.3414	0.3414
	8-305	46	45	200 @ 1.25	$1\frac{23}{32}$	0.0010–0.0027	0.0010–0.0027	0.3414	0.3414
1982–84	6-229	46	45	200 @ 1.25	$1\frac{23}{32}$	0.0010–0.0027	0.0010–0.0027	0.3414	0.3414
	6-231	45	45	168 @ 1.33	$1\frac{47}{64}$	0.0015–0.0032	0.0015–0.0032	0.3407	0.3409
	6-263	45	46	189 @ 1.30	$1\frac{43}{64}$	0.0010–0.0027	0.0015–0.0032	0.3429	0.3423
	8-267	46	45	200 @ 1.25	$1\frac{23}{32}$	0.0010–0.0027	0.0010–0.0027	0.3414	0.3414
	8-305	46	45	200 @ 1.25	$1\frac{23}{32}$	0.0010–0.0027	0.0010–0.0027	0.3414	0.3414
	8-350	45	46	189 @ 1.30	$1\frac{43}{64}$	0.0010–0.0027	0.0015–0.0032	0.3429	0.3423
1985–86	6-262	46	45	200 @ 1.25	$1\frac{47}{64}$	0.0010–0.0027	0.0010–0.0027	0.3414	0.3414
	8-305	46	45	200 @ 1.25	$1\frac{47}{64}$	0.0010–0.0027	0.0010–0.0027	0.3414	0.3414

① 325 hp
② 360 hp and 375 hp
③ 45° on aluminum heads
④ 350 hp
⑤ Inner spring—30 @ 1.78
⑥ 1976 and later: 0.0015–0.0032
⑦ 80 @ 1.61 for exhaust
⑧ Exhaust valve—$1\frac{19}{32}$

Crankshaft and Connecting Rod Specifications
(All measurements are given in in.)

Year	Engine No. Cyl Displacement (cu in.)	Crankshaft				Journal Diameter	Connecting Rod	
		Main Brg Journal Dia	Main Brg Oil Clearance	Shaft End-Play	Thrust on No.		Oil Clearance	Side Clearance
1964	6-194	2.2983–2.2993	0.0008–0.004	0.002–0.006	7	1.999–2.000	0.0007–0.0028	0.008–0.014
	6-230	2.2983–2.2993	0.0008–0.004	0.002–0.006	7	1.999–2.000	0.0007–0.0028	0.008–0.014
	8-283	2.2978–2.2988	0.0008–0.004	0.002–0.006	5	1.999–2.000	0.0007–0.0028	0.008–0.014
1965	6-194	2.2983–2.2993	0.0003–0.0029	0.002–0.006	7	1.999–2.000	0.0007–0.0027	0.009–0.013
	6-230	2.2983–2.2993	0.0003–0.0029	0.002–0.006	7	1.999–2.000	0.0007–0.0027	0.009–0.013
	8-283	2.2978–2.2988	0.0003–0.0029*	0.002–0.006	5	1.999–2.000	0.0007–0.0027	0.009–0.013
	8-327	2.2978–2.2988	0.0008–0.0034*	0.002–0.006	5	1.999–2.000	0.0007–0.0028	0.009–0.013
1966	6-194	2.2983–2.2993	0.0003–0.0029	0.002–0.006	7	1.999–2.000	0.0007–0.0027	0.009–0.013
	6-230	2.2983–2.2993	0.0003–0.0029	0.002–0.006	7	1.999–2.000	0.0007–0.0027	0.009–0.013
	8-283	②	0.0003–0.0029①	0.003–0.011	5	1.999–2.000	0.0007–0.0027	0.009–0.013
	8-327	②	0.0003–0.0034①	0.003–0.011	5	1.999–2.000	0.0007–0.0028	0.009–0.013
	8-396	③	④	0.006–0.010	5	2.199–2.200	0.0007–0.0028	0.015–0.021
1967	6-230	2.2983–2.2993	0.0003–0.0029	0.002–0.006	7	1.999–2.000	0.0007–0.0027	0.009–0.013
	6-250	2.2983–2.2993	0.0003–0.0029	0.002–0.006	7	1.999–2.000	0.0007–0.0027	0.009–0.013
	8-283	⑤	⑦	0.003–0.011	5	1.999–2.000	0.0007–0.0027	0.009–0.013
	8-327	⑤	⑦	0.003–0.011	5	1.999–2.000	0.0007–0.0028	0.009–0.013
	8-396	③	④	0.006–0.010	5	2.1999–2.200	0.0007–0.0028	0.015–0.021
1968	6-230	2.2983–2.2993	0.0003–0.0029	0.002–0.006	7	1.999–2.000	0.0007–0.0027	0.009–0.013
	6-250	2.2983–2.2993	0.0003–0.0029	0.002–0.006	7	1.999–2.000	0.0007–0.0027	0.009–0.013
	8-307	2.4484–2.4493⑥	0.0008–0.002⑧	0.003–0.011	5	2.099–2.100	0.0007–0.0028	0.009–0.013
	8-327	2.4484–2.4493⑥	0.0008–0.002⑧	0.003–0.011	5	2.099–2.100	0.0007–0.0027	0.009–0.013
	8-350	2.4484–2.4493⑥	0.0008–0.002⑧	0.003–0.011	5	2.099–2.100	0.0007–0.0028	0.009–0.013
	8-396	⑨	⑪	0.006–0.010	5	2.199–2.200	0.0009–0.0025	0.015–0.021

Year	Engine							
1968	8-396 (375 HP)	[10]	0.0013–0.0025 [12]	0.006–0.010	5	2.1985–2.1995	0.0014–0.0030	0.019–0.025
1969	6-230	2.2983–2.2993	0.0003–0.0029	0.002–0.006	7	1.999–2.000	0.0007–0.0027	0.009–0.013
	6-250	2.2983–2.2993	0.0003–0.0029	0.002–0.006	7	1.999–2.000	0.0007–0.0027	0.009–0.013
	8-307	2.4479–2.4488	0.0008–0.002 [8]	0.003–0.011	5	2.099–2.100	0.007–0.0027	0.009–0.013
	8-350	2.4479–2.4488	0.0008–0.002 [8]	0.003–0.011	5	2.099–2.100	0.0007–0.0028	0.009–0.013
	8-396	[9]	[11]	0.006–0.010	5	2.199–2.200	0.0009–0.0025	0.015–0.021
	8-396 (375 HP)	[10]	0.0013–0.0025 [12]	0.006–0.010	5	2.1985–2.1995	0.0014–0.0030	0.019–0.025
1970	6-230	2.2983–2.2993	0.0003–0.0029	0.002–0.006	7	1.999–2.000	0.0007–0.0027	0.009–0.013
	6-250	2.2983–2.2993	0.0003–0.0029	0.002–0.006	7	1.999–2.000	0.0007–0.0027	0.009–0.013
	8-307	2.4484–2.4493 [6]	0.0003–0.0015 [13]	0.002–0.006	5	2.099–2.100	0.0007–0.0028	0.008–0.014
	8-350	2.4484–2.4493 [6]	0.0003–0.0015 [13]	0.002–0.006	5	2.099–2.100	0.0007–0.0028	0.008–0.014
	8-400 (Monte Carlo)	2.6584–2.6493 [18]	0.0008–0.0020 [21]	0.002–0.006	5	2.099–2.100	0.0009–0.0025	0.008–0.014
	8-402	2.7487–2.7496 [15]	0.0007–0.0019 [16]	0.006–0.010	5	2.199–2.200	0.0009–0.0025	0.013–0.023
	8-454	2.7485–2.7494 [10]	0.0013–0.0025 [17]	0.006–0.010	5	2.199–2.200	0.0009–0.0025	0.015–0.021
1971	6-250	2.2983–2.2993	0.0003–0.0029	0.002–0.006	7	1.999–2.000	0.0007–0.0027	0.009–0.014
	8-307	2.4484–2.4493 [20]	0.0008–0.0020 [21]	0.002–0.006	5	2.099–2.100	0.0013–0.0035	0.008–0.014
	8-350	2.4484–2.4493 [20]	0.0008–0.0020 [21]	0.002–0.006	5	2.099–2.100	0.0013–0.0035	0.008–0.014
	8-402	2.7487–2.7496 [19]	0.0007–0.0019 [16]	0.006–0.010	5	2.199–2.200	0.0009–0.0025	0.013–0.023
	8-454 (365 HP)	2.7485–2.7494 [10]	0.0013–0.0025 [17]	0.006–0.010	5	2.199–2.200	0.0009–0.0025	0.015–0.021
	8-454 (425 HP)	2.7481–2.7490 [6]	0.0013–0.0025 [19]	0.006–0.010	5	2.1985–2.1995	0.0009–0.0025	0.019–0.025
1972	6-250	2.2983–2.2993	0.0003–0.0029	0.002–0.006	7	1.999–2.000	0.0007–0.0027	0.009–0.014
	8-307	2.4484–2.4493 [20]	0.0008–0.0020 [21]	0.002–0.006	5	2.099–2.100	0.0013–0.0035	0.008–0.014
	8-350	2.4484–2.4493 [20]	0.0008–0.0020 [21]	0.002–0.006	5	2.099–2.100	0.0013–0.0035	0.008–0.014
	8-402	2.7487–2.7496 [15]	0.0007–0.0019 [16]	0.006–0.010	5	2.199–2.200	0.0009–0.0025	0.013–0.023

Crankshaft and Connecting Rod Specifications (cont.)
(All measurements are given in in.)

Year	Engine No. Cyl Displacement (cu in.)	Crankshaft				Connecting Rod		
		Main Brg Journal Dia	Main Brg Oil Clearance	Shaft End-Play	Thrust on No.	Journal Diameter	Oil Clearance	Side Clearance
1972	8-454	2.7485–2.7494 [10]	0.0013–0.0025 [17]	0.006–0.010	5	2.199–2.200	0.0009–0.0025	0.015–0.021
1973	6-250	2.3004	0.0003–0.0029	0.002–0.006	7	1.999–2.000	0.0007–0.0027	0.009–0.014
	8-307, 350	2.4502 [22]	0.0008–0.0020 [21]	0.002–0.006	5	2.099–2.100	0.0013–0.0035	0.008–0.014
1974–77	8-454	2.7492 [23]	0.0007–0.0019 [24]	0.006–0.010	5	2.199–2.200	0.0009–0.0025	0.015–0.023
	6-250	2.2988	0.0003–0.0029	0.002–0.006	7	1.9928–2.000	0.0007–0.0027	0.007–0.016
	8-305	2.4489 [26]	[25]	0.002–0.006	5	2.099–2.100	0.0013–0.0035	0.008–0.014
	8-350	2.4489 [26]	[25]	0.002–0.006	5	2.099–2.100	0.0035–0.0035	0.008–0.014
	8-400	2.6489 [27]	0.0008–0.0002 [28]	0.002–0.006	5	2.099–2.100	0.0035–0.0035	0.008–0.014
	8-454	2.7490	0.0013–0.0025 [29]	0.006–0.010	5	2.199–2.200	0.0009–0.0025	0.015–0.021
1978–79	6-200	2.4489	0.0011–0.0023 [30]	0.002–0.006	5	2.0988–2.0998	0.0013–0.0035	0.008–0.014
	6-231	2.4995	0.0004–0.0015	0.004–0.008	2	2.2487–2.2495	0.0005–0.0026	0.006–0.027
	6-250	2.2988	0.0010–0.0024	0.002–0.006	7	1.9980–2.0000	0.0010–0.0026	0.006–0.017
	8-267	2.4489 [31]	0.0020–0.0035 [27]	0.002–0.007	5	2.0978–2.0988	0.0013–0.0035	0.006–0.016
	8-305	2.4489 [31]	0.0011–0.0023 [30]	0.002–0.006	5	2.0988–2.0998	0.0013–0.0035	0.008–0.014
	8-350	2.4489 [31]	0.0011–0.0023 [30]	0.002–0.006	5	2.0988–2.0998	0.0013–0.0035	0.008–0.014
1980–81	6-229	[32]	[33]	0.002–0.006	4	2.0986–2.0998	0.0013–0.0035	0.006–0.014
	6-231	2.4995	0.0004–0.0015	0.004–0.008	2	2.2495–2.2487	0.0005–0.0026	0.006–0.027
	8-267	[32]	[33]	0.002–0.006	5	2.0986–2.0998	0.0013–0.0035	0.006–0.014
	8-305	[32]	[33]	0.002–0.006	5	2.0986–2.0998	0.0013–0.0035	0.006–0.014

	Engine							
1982–84	6-229	[32]	[33]	0.002–0.006	4	2.0986–2.0998	0.0013–0.0035	0.006–0.014
	6-231	2.4995	0.0004–0.0015	0.004–0.008	2	2.2495–2.2487	0.0005–0.0026	0.006–0.027
	6-263	2.9998	[34]	0.0035–0.0135	3	2.3742–2.375	.0003–.0025	.0082–.0214
	8-267	[32]	[33]	0.002–0.006	5	2.0986–2.0998	0.0013–0.0035	0.006–0.014
	8-305	[32]	[33]	0.002–0.006	5	2.0986–2.0998	0.0013–0.0035	0.006–0.027
	8-350	2.9998	[35]	0.0035–0.0135	3	2.1238–2.1248	0.0005–0.0026	0.006–0.020
1985–86	6-262	2.4484–2.4493 [36]	0.0008–0.0020 [37]	0.002–0.006	4	2.0986–2.0998	0.0013–0.0035	0.006–0.014
	8-305	[32]	[33]	0.002–0.006	5	2.0986–2.0998	0.0013–0.0035	0.006–0.014

* No. 5—0.0010–0.0036

[1] No. 5—0.0010–0.0036

[2] No. 1—2.2987–2.29977
Nos. 2–4—2.2983–2.2993
No. 5—2.2978–2.2988

[3] Nos. 1–2—2.7487–2.7497
Nos. 3–4—2.7482–2.7492
No. 5—2.7478–2.7488

[4] No. 1–2—0.0004–0.002
Nos. 3–4—0.0009–0.0025
No. 5—0.0013–0.0029

[5] No. 1—2.2984–2.2993
Nos. 2–4—2.2988–2.2993
No. 5—2.2978–2.2988

[6] No. 5—2.4478–2.4488

[7] No. 1—0.0008–0.002
Nos. 2–4—0.0018–0.002
No. 5—0.0010–0.0036

[8] No. 5—0.0018–0.0034

[9] Nos. 1–2—2.7484–2.7493
Nos. 3–4—2.7481–2.7490
No. 5—2.7478–2.7488

[10] No. 1—2.7484–2.7493
Nos. 2–4—2.7481–2.7490
No. 5—2.7478–2.7488

[11] Nos. 1–2—0.0010–0.0022
Nos. 3–4—0.0013–0.0025
No. 5—0.0015–0.0031

[12] No. 5—0.0015–0.0031

[13] Nos. 2–4—0.0006–0.0018
No. 5—0.0008–0.0023

[15] Nos. 3–4—2.7481–2.7490
No. 5—2.7473–2.7483

[16] Nos. 2–4—0.0013–0.0025
No. 5—0.0019–0.0025

[17] No. 5—0.0024–0.0040

[18] No. 5—2.6479–2.6488

[19] No. 5—0.0029–0.0045

[20] Nos. 2–4—2.4481–2.4490
No. 5—2.4479–2.4488

[21] Nos. 2–4—0.0011–0.0023
No. 5—0.0017–0.0033

[22] No. 5—2.4508

[23] Nos. 2–4—2.7504
No. 5—2.7499

[24] Nos. 2–4—0.0013–0.0028
No. 5—0.0019–0.0035

[25] w/Auto trans.—No. 1—0.0019–0.0031
Nos. 2–4—0.0013–0.0025
No. 5—0.0023–0.0033

[26] Nos. 2–4—2.4486
No. 5—2.4485

[27] No. 5—2.6485

[28] Nos. 2–4—0.001–0.0023
No. 5—0.0017–0.0033

[29] No. 5—0.0024–0.0070

[30] No. 1—0.0008–0.0020

[31] Nos. 2–4—2.4486
No. 5—2.4485

[32] No. 1—2.4484–2.4493
Nos. 2,3,4—2.4481–2.4490
No. 5—2.4479–2.4488

[33] No. 1—0.0008–0.0020
Nos. 2–4—0.0011–0.0023
No. 5—0.0017–0.0032

[34] Nos. 1,2,3—0.0005–0.0021
No. 4—0.0020–0.0034

[35] Nos. 1,2,3—0.0005–0.0021
No. 4—0.0015–0.0031

[36] Intermediate: 2.4481–2.4490
Rear: 2.4479–2.4488

[37] Intermediate: 0.0011–0.0023
Rear: 0.0017–0.0032

Piston and Ring Specifications

(All measurements are given in inches. To convert inches to metric units, refer to the Metric Information section.)

Year	Engine Type/ Disp. cu. in.	Piston-to-Bore Clearance	Ring Gap			Ring Side Clearance		
			Top Compression	Bottom Compression	Oil Control	Top Compression	Bottom Compression	Oil Control
1964	All Engines	—	0.010–0.020	0.010–0.020	0.015–0.055	0.0012–0.0027	0.0012–0.0032	0.0000–0.0050
1965	6-194 6-230	— —	0.010–0.020	0.010–0.020	0.015–0.055	0.0012–0.0027	0.0012–0.0032	0.0000–0.0050
	8-283 8-327	— —	0.013–0.023	0.013–0.028	0.015–0.055	0.0012–0.0027	0.0012–0.0032	0.0012–0.0050
1966	6-194	—	0.010–0.020	0.010–0.020	0.015–0.055	0.0012–0.0027	0.0012–0.0032	0.0000–0.0050
1966–69	6-230	0.0005–0.0011	0.010–0.020	0.010–0.020	0.015–0.055	0.0012–0.0027	0.0012–0.0032	0.0000–0.0050
1966–67	8-283	0.0024–0.0030	0.010–0.020	0.010–0.020	0.015–0.055	0.0012–0.0027	0.0012–0.0032	0.0000–0.0050
1966–68	8-327	0.0005–0.0011	0.013–0.023	0.013–0.025	0.015–0.055	0.0012–0.0027	0.0012–0.0032	0.0000–0.0050
1966–67	8-396	0.0007–0.0013	0.010–0.020	0.010–0.020	0.010–0.030	0.0012–0.0032	0.0012–0.0032	0.0012–0.0060
1967	6-250	0.0005–0.0011	0.010–0.020	0.010–0.020	0.015–0.055	0.0020–0.0035	0.0020–0.0040	0.0000–0.0050
1968–79	6-250	0.0005–0.0015	0.010–0.020	0.010–0.020	0.015–0.055	0.0012–0.0027	0.0012–0.0032	0.0000–0.0050
1968–73	8-307	0.0005–0.0011	0.010–0.020	0.010–0.020	0.015–0.055	0.0012–0.0032	0.0012–0.0027	0.0000–0.0050
1968–70	8-396	0.0010–0.0018 ①	0.010–0.020	0.010–0.020	0.010–0.030	0.0017–0.0032	0.0017–0.0032	0.0005–0.0065
1969	8-350	0.0005–0.0011	0.013–0.025	0.013–0.025	0.0015–0.0055	0.0012–0.0032	0.0012–0.0027	0.0000–0.0050
1970–79	8-350	0.0007–0.0013	0.010–0.020 ②	0.013–0.025 ②	0.015–0.055	0.0012–0.0032 ④	0.0012–0.0027 ⑤	0.0000–0.0050 ③⑧

1970–76	8-400	0.0034	0.010–0.020	0.010–0.020	0.015–0.055	0.0012–0.0027⑥	0.0012–0.0032⑥	0.0000–0.0050
1970–76	8-454	0.0049⑦	0.010–0.020	0.010–0.020	0.015–0.055	0.0017–0.0032	0.0017–0.0032	0.0005–0.0065
1971–72	8-402	0.0018–0.0026	0.010–0.020	0.010–0.020	0.015–0.055	0.0017–0.0032	0.0017–0.0032	0.0005–0.0065
1976–77	8-305	0.0007–0.0017	0.010–0.020	0.010–0.025	0.015–0.055	0.0012–0.0032	0.0012–0.0027	0.0000–0.0050
1978–79	6-200	0.0007–0.0017	0.010–0.020	0.010–0.025	0.010–0.030	0.0012–0.0032	0.0012–0.0032	0.002–0.007
1978–84	6-231	0.0008–0.0020	0.010–0.020	0.010–0.020	0.015–0.035	0.003–0.005	0.003–0.005	0.0035 max.
1978–86	8-305	0.0007–0.0017	0.010–0.020	0.010–0.025	0.015–0.055	0.0012–0.0032	0.0012–0.0032	0.002–0.007
1980–84	6-229	0.0007–0.0017	0.010–0.020	0.010–0.025	0.015–0.055	0.0012–0.0032	0.0012–0.0032	0.002–0.007
1979–84	8-267	0.0007–0.0017	0.010–0.020	0.010–0.025	0.015–0.055	0.0012–0.0032	0.0012–0.0032	0.002–0.007
1980–84	8-350⑨	0.005–0.006	0.015–0.025	0.015–0.025	0.015–0.055	0.005–0.007	0.0018–0.0038	0.001–0.005
1982–84	6-263⑨	0.0035–0.0045	0.015–0.025	0.015–0.025	0.015–0.055	0.005–0.007	0.003–0.005	0.001–0.005
1985–86	6-262	0.0012	0.010–0.020	0.010–0.025	0.015–0.055	0.0012–0.0032	0.0012–0.0032	0.002–0.007

① 0.0036–0.0044; 11:1 compression
② 325, 350 hp: Top 0.010–0.020
    2nd 0.013–0.023
③ 1978–82: 0.002–0.007
④ 0.0012–0.0027 on 1975 2-bbl
⑤ 165, 245, 250 hp: 0.0012–0.0032
⑥ 300 hp: Top 0.0017–0.0032
    2nd 0.0017–0.0032
⑦ 425 hp—1971: 0.0065
    1973–75: 0.0035
⑧ 1978–80: 0.015–0.050
⑨ Diesel

Torque Specifications

Year	Model	Cylinder Head Bolts (ft. lbs.)	Rod Bearing Bolts (ft. lbs.)	Main Bearing Bolts (ft. lbs.)	Crankshaft Pulley Bolt (ft. lbs.)	Flywheel to Crankshaft Bolts (ft. lbs.)	Manifold (ft. lbs.) Intake	Manifold (ft. lbs.) Exhaust
1964–65	All 6 cyl.	90–95	35–40	60–70	Press Fit	50–65	25–30	15–20
1964–65	All 8 cyl.	60–70	30–35	60–80	Press Fit	55–65	25–35	25–35
1966–75	All 6 cyl.	95	36	65	—	60	30 ⑧	25 ⑦
1966–67	8-283, 327	60–70	35	80	60 ⑥	60	30	20
1968–77	8-305, 307, 327, 350, 500	60–70	45	75 ② ⑨	60 ⑥	60	30	⑤
1966–77	8-396, 402	80 ①	50	105 ③	85 ⑥	65	30	30
	8-427, 454	80 ①	50 ④	105 ③	85	65	30	30
1978–84	6-200, 229 8-267, 305, 350	65	45	70	60	60	30	20 ⑩
1978–84	6-231	80	40	100	175	60	45	25
1982–84	6-263 ⑭	⑪	42	107	⑫	48	41 ⑬	29
1982–84	8-350 ⑭	130 ⑬	42	120	⑮	60	40	25
1985–86	6-262	60–75	45	80	70	70	45	20
	8-305	65	45	70	60	60	30 ⑯	20 ⑯

① Aluminum Heads—Short bolts 65, Long bolts 75
② Engines with 4-bolt mains—Outer bolts 65
③ 1966–68 2-bolt mains 95
　 1966–67 4-bolt mains 115
④ 7/16 Rod bolts—70
⑤ Center bolts—25–30, end bolts 15–20
⑥ Where applicable
⑦ Exhaust-to-intake
⑧ Manifold-to-head
⑨ 70 starting 1976
⑩ Inside bolts on 350—30 ft. lbs.
⑪ All bolts except Nos. 5, 6, 11, 12, 13, 14: 142 ft. lbs.
　 Nos. 5, 6, 11, 12, 13, 14: 59 ft. lbs.
⑫ Pulley-to-balancer bolts, 30 ft. lbs.
　 Balancer-to-crankshaft bolt, 160—350 ft. lbs.
⑬ Dip bolts in engine oil before torquing
⑭ Diesel engine
⑮ Pulley-to-balancer bolts, 27 ft. lbs.
　 Balancer-to-crankshaft bolt, 271–420 ft. lbs.
⑯ Inside bolts: 25 ft. lbs.

lift camshafts, solid lifters (in some cases), high compression ratios and large carburetors. These big-block engines are similar to their small-block little brothers in basic design.

The 350 V8 diesel is derived from the 350 gasoline engine, except that the cylinder block, crankshaft and main bearings, connecting rods and wrist pins are heavier duty in the diesel (due to the much higher compression ratio). The 263 V6 diesel is nearly a six-cylinder copy of the 350 V8, sharing the same bore and stroke and many engine components. Both V8 and V6 diesel cylinder heads, intake manifold, ignition and fuel systems are also different from their gasoline engine counterparts. Aircraft-type hydraulic roller valve lifters are used in the diesels.

The Buick-built 231 V6 is the only engine used in the mid-size Chevrolets which is substantially different. This engine follows Buick V8 practice in that its valve gear incorporates rocker shafts instead of the ball-joint style rockers on the other engines.

Engine

REMOVAL AND INSTALLATION

CAUTION: *Do not discharge the compressor or disconnect the A/C lines. Damage to the A/C system or personal injury could result.*

Inline 6 Cyl Gasoline Engine

1. Scribe alignment marks around the hood hinges and remove the hood.
2. Disconnect the negative battery cable and remove the air cleaner.
3. Drain the cooling system and the crankshaft.
4. Disconnect the radiator and the heater hoses, then remove the radiator and the fan shroud.

NOTE: *If equipped with an A/T, disconnect and plug the oil cooler lines at the radiator.*

5. Disconnect and label the wires at the ignition coil, the starter, the alternator, the temperature switch and the oil pressure switch.

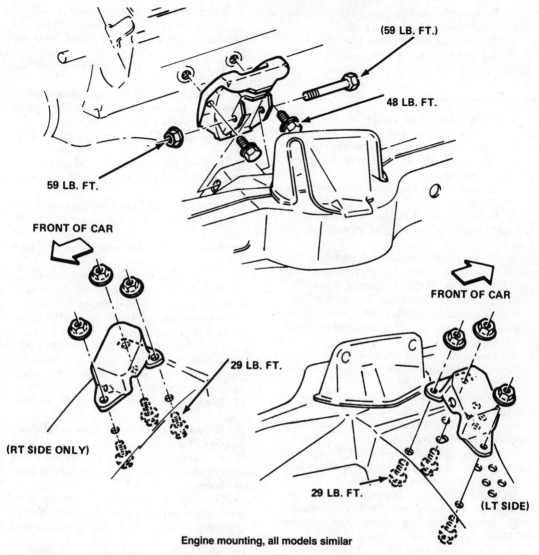

(59 LB. FT.)

48 LB. FT.

59 LB. FT.

FRONT OF CAR

FRONT OF CAR

29 LB. FT.

(RT SIDE ONLY)

29 LB. FT.

(LT SIDE)

Engine mounting, all models similar

6. Disconnect accelerator control cable at the inlet manifold, the fuel inlet line from the fuel pump, the hoses from the vapor canister and (if equipped) the power brake vacuum line from the intake manifold.

7. If equipped with power steering, remove the power steering pump and move it aside.

8. Raise and support the vehicle on jackstands.

9. Disconnect the exhaust pipe from the exhaust manifold and (if equipped) the converter bracket from the rear transmission mount.

10. Remove the starter and the flywheel splash shield or the converter housing cover.

11. If equipped with an A/T, remove the converter-to-flexplate bolts.

12. Attach a vertical hoist to the engine and support the transmission with a floor jack, then raise the engine slightly.

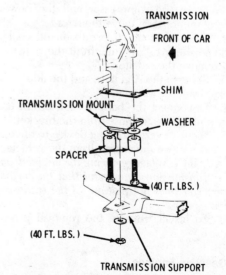

TRANSMISSION

FRONT OF CAR

SHIM

TRANSMISSION MOUNT

WASHER

SPACER

(40 FT. LBS.)

(40 FT. LBS.)

TRANSMISSION SUPPORT

Rear engine mounts on some engines are shimmed

13. Remove the engine mount through bolts and the bell housing-to-engine bolts.

14. Remove the engine from the vehicle.

15. To install, reverse the removal procedures.

V6 Gasoline Engine

1. Scribe alignment marks at the hood hinges and remove the hood.

2. Disconnect the negative battery cable.

3. Disconnect the exhaust pipe from the exhaust manifold.

4. Remove the bell housing cover and drain the transmission oil cooler lines at the oil pan.

5. Remove the left engine mount through bolt and loosen the right engine mount through bolt.

6. If equipped with an A/T, remove the torque converter cover, the converter-to-flex plate bolts and the engine-to-transmission bolts.

NOTE: *Before removing the torque converter bolts, scribe a mark to ensure the relationship between the torque converter and the flex plate.*

7. Disconnect the CCC wiring harness from the transmission and the knock sensor from the engine.

8. Disconnect the fuel hoses from the frame and the lower fan shroud.

9. Lower the vehicle and remove the windshield washer bottle.

10. Disconnect and label the CCC wiring harness, other necessary wiring connectors and the vacuum hoses from the engine.

11. Remove the air cleaner, the upper fan shroud, the accelerator and the T.V. cables.

12. Drain the cooling system, then remove the heater and the radiator hoses.

13. If equipped with A/C and power steering, remove the compressor and the power steering pump, then move them aside.

14. Disconnect the transmission oil cooler lines and the overflow tube from the radiator, then remove the radiator.

15. Remove the A/C hose and the adjusting bracket from the alternator.

16. Disconnect the battery cables from the frame and the heater hose from the bracket.

17. Secure a vertical lifting device to the engine and remove the engine from the vehicle.

CAUTION: *When removing the engine from the transmission, be careful that the torque converter does not pull out of the transmission.*

18. To install, reverse the removal procedures.

V8 Gasoline Engines

1. Scribe alignment marks on hood and remove hood from hinges.

2. Disconnect the negative battery cable.

3. Drain cooling system, then remove the heater hoses and the radiator hoses from the engine.

4. Remove the upper fan shroud and the fan assembly.

5. If equipped with A/C and power steering, remove the compressor and the power steering pump, then move them aside.

6. Disconnect the accelerator and the T.V. cables.

7. Remove the transmission oil cooler lines (if equipped) from the radiator and the radiator.

8. Disconnect and label the vacuum hoses and the CCC wiring harness connector(s) from the engine.

9. Remove the AIR pipe from the converter.

10. Remove the windshield washer bottle.

11. Disconnect and mark the wiring harness at the bulkhead and related engine wiring.

12. Remove the distributor cap and the cruise control cable (if equipped).

13. Disconnect the positive battery cable from the battery and the frame. Disconnect the negative battery cable from the A/C hose/alternator bracket.

14. Raise and support the vehicle on jackstands.

15. Remove the crossover pipe and the catalytic converter as an assembly.

16. If equipped with an A/T, remove the torque converter cover and the torque converter bolts.

NOTE: *Before removing the torque converter bolts, scribe a mark to ensure the relationship between the torque converter and the flex plate.*

17. Remove the engine-to-mount bolts.

18. Disconnect the fuel line from the fuel pump.

19. If equipped with an A/T, disconnect the torque converter clutch wiring from the transmission. Disconnect the transmission oil cooler lines from the clip at the engine oil pan.

20. Remove the engine-to-transmission bolts.

21. Lower the vehicle and support the transmission.

22. Secure a vertical lifting device to the engine and remove the engine from the vehicle.

CAUTION: *When removing the engine from the transmission, be careful that the torque converter does not pull out of the transmission.*

23. To install, reverse the removal procedures.

Diesel Engines

1. Drain the cooling system.

2. Remove the air cleaner.

3. Mark the hood-to-hinge position and remove the hood.

4. Disconnect the ground cables from the batteries.

5. Disconnect the ground wires at the fender panels and the ground strap at the cowl.

6. Disconnect the radiator hoses, cooler lines, heater hoses, vacuum hoses, power steering pump hoses, air conditioning compressor (hoses attached), fuel inlet hose and all attached wiring.

7. Remove the bellcrank clip.

8. Disconnect the throttle and transmission cables.

9. Remove the upper radiator support and the radiator.

10. Raise and support the car.

11. Disconnect the exhaust pipes at the manifold.

12. Remove the torque converter cover and the three bolts holding the converter to the flywheel.

13. Remove the engine mount bolts or nuts.

14. Remove the three right side transmission-to-engine bolts. Remove the starter.

15. Lower the car and attach a hoist to the engine.

16. Slightly raise the transmission with a jack.

17. Remove the three left side transmission-to-engine bolts and lift out the engine.

18. Installation is in the reverse order of removal. Converter cover bolts are torqued to 40 ft. lbs. on the 350 V8 and 35 ft. lbs. on the 263 V6.

Rocker Arm Cover
REMOVAL AND INSTALLATION
Inline 6 Cyl Gasoline Engine

1. At the rocker arm cover, disconnect the ventilation hoses. Remove the air cleaner.

2. Disconnect the wires, the fuel and the vacuum tubes from the rocker arm cover clips.

3. If equipped, disconnect the air injection hose from the check valve of the AIR pipe.

4. Remove the cover-to-cylinder head screws and the cover by rotating it from under the air pipe (if equipped).

NOTE: *DO NOT pry on the cover to remove it. If it sticks, use your hand palm or a rubber mallet to bump it rearwards, from the front.*

5. Using a putty knife, clean the gasket mounting surfaces.

6. To install, reverse the removal procedures. Start the engine and check for leaks.

NOTE: *When installing the cover, use a new gasket (1964–76) or an 1/8 in. bead of RTV sealant (1977–79).*

V6 Gasoline Engine
RIGHT-SIDE

1. Disconnect the negative battery cable. Remove the air cleaner.

2. Disconnect the dipstick tube bracket from the alternator bracket, then the dipstick tube head.

3. At the engine, disconnect the heater hoses from the evaporator case and bracket.

4. At the intake manifold, disconnect the heater hose and the wiring harness bracket.

5. Remove the rocker arm cover bolts and the breather pipe.

6. Disconnect the fuel lines, the clips and the spark plug wires (at the distributor).

7. Remove the rocker arm cover.

8. Using a putty knife, clean the gasket mounting surfaces.

9. To install, use a new gasket or sealant and reverse the removal procedures.

LEFT-SIDE

1. Disconnect the negative battery cable.

2. At the rocker arm cover, disconnect the PCV valve.

3. If equipped with A/C, remove the compressor and the brace.

NOTE: *When removing the A/C compressor, DO NOT disconnect the hoses.*

4. Remove the rocker arm cover bolts and the cover.

5. Using a putty knife, clean the gasket mounting surfaces.

6. To install, use a new gasket or sealant and reverse the removal procedures. Start the engine and check for leaks.

V8 Gasoline Engines
RIGHT-SIDE

1. Disconnect the negative battery cable. Remove the air cleaner.

2. On the 1985–86 models, disconnect the CCC harness from the intake manifold and the oxygen sensor.

3. At the exhaust manifold, disconnect the AIR hose.

4. Disconnect the wires from the alternator, the choke and the spark plugs, then the harness from the rocker cover (lay it aside).

5. Remove the EGR valve.

6. Remove the rocker arm cover bolts and the cover.

7. Using a putty knife, clean the gasket mounting surfaces.

8. To install, use a new gasket or sealant and reverse the removal procedures. Start the engine and check for leaks.

LEFT-SIDE

1. Disconnect the negative battery cable. Remove the air cleaner.

2. Disconnect the power brake pipe from the carburetor and the booster.

3. Disconnect the AIR hose from the exhaust manifold.

4. At the rocker arm cover, remove the PCV valve.

5. Disconnect the wire from the oxygen sensor.

6. Remove the rocker arm cover bolts and the cover.

7. Using a putty knife, clean the gasket mounting surfaces.

8. To install, use a new gasket or sealant and reverse the removal procedures. Start the engine and check for leaks.

V6 and V8 Diesel Engines

1. Refer to the "Injection Lines, Removal and Installation" procedures, in the Diesel Fuel System of Chapter 4 and remove the fuel injection lines.

2. Remove the rocker arm cover-to-cylinder head screws and any accessory mounting brackets (if necessary).

3. Using the Valve Cover Removal tool No. J-34144 or BT-8315, place it midway between the ends of the valve cover (on the upper side), then tighten the screw to lift the rocker arm cover.

4. Using a rubber mallet and a shop cloth (placed on the rocker arm cover above the removal tool to absorb the blow), strike the cover to completely remove it.

5. Using a putty knife, clean the gasket mounting surfaces.

6. Using RTV sealant, apply a ¼ in. bead to the rocker arm cover.

NOTE: *When installing the rocker arm cover, the sealant must be wet to the touch.*

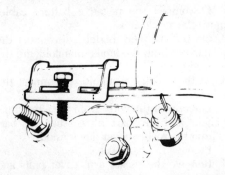

Removing the rocker arm cover on diesel engines

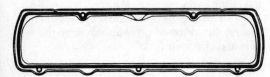

Installing RTV sealant to the rocker arm cover

7. To install, reverse the removal procedures. Start the engine and check for leaks.

Rocker Arms

REMOVAL AND INSTALLATION

All Gasoline Engines, Except 231 V6

Rocker arms are removed by removing the adjusting nut. Be sure to adjust the valve lash after replacing the rocker arms. Coat the replacement rocker arm and ball with SAE 90 gear oil before installation. Make sure the valves are closed on the cylinder you are working on before installation.

NOTE: *When replacing an exhaust rocker, move an old intake rocker to the exhaust rocker arm stud and install the new rocker arm on the intake stud. This will prevent burning of the new rocker arm on the exhaust position.*

Rocker arms studs that have damaged threads or are loose in the cylinder heads may be replaced by reaming the bore and installing oversize studs. Oversizes available are .003 and .013 in. The bore may also be tapped and screw-in studs installed. Several aftermarket companies produce complete rocker arm stud kits with installation tools. Mark IV and late high performance small block engines use screw-in studs and pushrod guide plates.

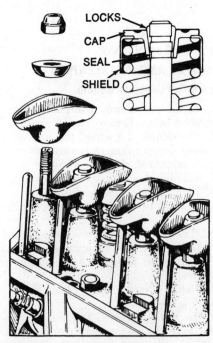

Inline six cylinder rocker arm components (V8s similar)

231 V6 Engines (Gasoline)

1. Remove the rocker arm covers.
2. Remove the rocker arm shaft assembly bolts.
3. Remove the rocker arm shaft assembly.
4. To remove the rocker arms from the shaft, the nylon arm retainers must be removed. They can be removed with a pair of water pump pliers, or they can be broken by hitting them below the head with a chisel.
5. Remove the rocker arms from the shaft. Make sure you keep them in order. Also note that the external rib on each arm points *away* from the rocker arm shaft bolt located between each pair of rocker arms.
6. If you are installing new rocker arms, note that the replacement rocker arms are marked "R" and "L" for right and left side installation. *Do not* interchange them.

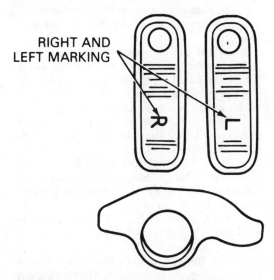

231 V6 replacement rocker arm identification

Position of rocker arms on shaft—231 V6

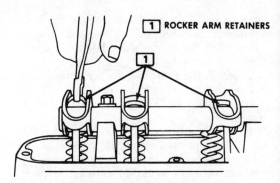

Removing nylon retainers, 231 V6 rocker shafts

7. Install the rocker arms on the shaft and lubricate them with oil.
8. Center each arm on the ¼ in. hole in the shaft. Install new nylon rocker arm retainers in the holes using a ½ in. drift.
9. Locate the push rods in the rocker arms and insert the shaft bolts. Tighten the bolts a little at a time until they are tight.
10. Install the rocker covers using new gaskets.

Diesel Engines—V6 and V8

NOTE: *When the diesel engine rocker arms are removed or loosened, the lifters must be bled down to prevent oil pressure buildup inside each lifter, which could cause it to raise up higher than normal and bring the valves within striking distance of the pistons.*

1. Remove the valve cover.
2. Remove the rocker arm pivot bolts, the bridged pivot and rocker arms.
3. Remove each rocker set as a unit.
4. To install, lubricate the pivot wear points and position each set of rocker arms in its proper location. Do not tighten the pivot bolts for fear of bending the pushrods when the engine is turned. Bleed down the valve lifters.

Diesel Engine Bleed Down

1. Before installing any removed rocker arms, rotate the crankshaft so that No. 1 cylinder is 32° BTDC. This is 50mm (2 in.) counter-clockwise from the 0° pointer on the timing indicator on the front of the engine. If only the right valve cover was removed, remove the glow plug from NO. 1 cylinder to determine if the piston is in the correct position. If the left valve cover was removed, rotate the crankshaft until the No. 5 cylinder intake valve pushrod ball is 7.0mm (.28 in.) above the No. 5 cylinder exhaust valve pushrod ball.
   CAUTION: *Use only hand wrenches to torque the rocker arm pivot bolts to avoid pushrod damage.*
2. If the No. 5 cylinder pivot and rocker arms

were removed, install them. Torque the bolts alternately between the intake and exhaust valves until the intake valve begins to open, then stop.

3. Install the remaining rocker arms except No. 3 exhaust valve for (V6) or No. 3 and No. 8 intake valves for (V8), if these rockers were removed.

4. If removed, install but do not torque the No. 3 valve pivots beyond the point that the valve would be fully open. This is indicated by a strong resistance while still turning the pivot retaining bolts. *Going beyond this will bend the pushrod.* Torque the bolts slowly, allowing the lifter to bleed down.

5. Finish torquing the No. 5 cylinder rocker arm pivot bolt slowly. Do not go beyond the point that the valve would be fully open. This is indicated by a strong resistance while still turning the pivot retaining bolts. *Going beyond this will bend the pushrod.*

6. DO NOT turn the engine crankshaft for at least 45 minutes, allowing the lifters to bleed down. *This is important.*

7. Finish reassembling the engine as the lifters are being bled.

Valve Lash Adjustment

Most engines described in this book use hydraulic lifters, which require no periodic adjustment. In the event of cylinder head removal or any operation that requires disturbing the rocker arms, the rocker arms will have to be adjusted.

SOLID LIFTERS (1964–71)

Engine Running

> NOTE: *Before adjusting solid lifters, thoroughly warm the engine. The solid lifters are generally found on certain high-performance engines.*

Oil splash stopper clips will prevent splatter when adjusting the valves with the engine running

1. Run the engine to reach normal operating temperature.

2. Remove the valve covers and gaskets by tapping the end of the cover rearward. Do not attempt to pry the cover off.

3. To avoid being splashed with hot oil, use oil deflector clips. Place one on each oil hole in the rocker arm.

4. Measure between the rocker arm and the valve stem with a flat feeler gauge, then adjust the rocker arm stud nut until clearance agrees with the specifications in the chart.

5. After adjusting all the valves, stop the engine, clean the gasket surfaces, and install the valve covers with new gaskets.

Engine Not Running

These are initial adjustments usually required after assembling an engine or doing a valve job. They should be followed up by an adjustment with the engine running as described above.

1. Set the engine to the No. 1 firing position.

2. Adjust the clearance between the valve stems and the rocker arms with a feeler gauge. Check the Chart for the proper clearance. Adjust the following valves in the No. 1 firing position: Intake No. 2, 7, Exhaust No. 4, 8.

3. Turn the crankshaft one-half revolution clockwise. Adjust the following valves: Intake No. 1, 8, Exhaust No. 3, 6.

4. Turn the crankshaft one-half revolution clockwise to No. 6 firing position. Adjust the following valves in the No. 6 firing position: Intake No. 3, 4, Exhaust No. 5, 7.

5. Turn the crankshaft one-half revolution clockwise. Adjust the following valves: Intake No. 5, 6, Exhaust No. 1, 2.

6. Run the engine until the normal operating temperature is reached. Reset all clearances, using the procedure listed above under "Engine Running."

HYDRAULIC LIFTERS

1972 and Later

1. Remove the rocker covers and gaskets.

2. Adjust the valves on inline six cylinder engines as follows:

    a. Mark the distributor housing with a piece of chalk at the No. 1 and 6 plug wire positions. Remove the distributor cap with the plug wires attached.

    b. Crank the engine until the distributor rotor points to the No. 1 cylinder and the No. 1 piston is at TDC (both No. 1 cylinder valves closed). At this point, adjust the following valves:

    • No. 1—Exhaust and Intake
    • No. 2—Intake

- No. 3—Exhaust
- No. 4—Intake
- No. 5—Exhaust

c. Back out the adjusting nut until lash is felt at the pushrod, then turn the adjusting nut in until all lash is removed. This can be determined by checking pushrod end-play while turning the adjusting nut. When all play has been removed, turn the adjusting nut in 1 full turn.

d. Crank the engine until the distributor rotor points to the No. 6 cylinder and the No. 6 piston is at TDC (both No. 6 cylinder valves closed). The following valves can be adjusted:

- No. 2—Exhaust
- No. 3—Intake
- No. 4—Exhaust
- No. 5—Intake
- No. 6—Intake and Exhaust

3. Adjust the valves on V8 and V6 engines as follows:

a. Crank the engine until the mark on the

Inline six cylinder valve adjustment (V6's and V8's similar)

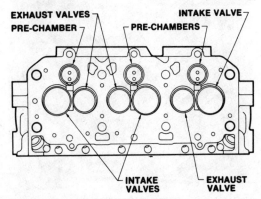

Valve arrangement, 263 V6 diesel

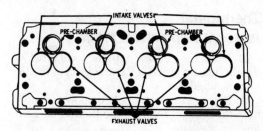

Diesel V8 valve arrangement

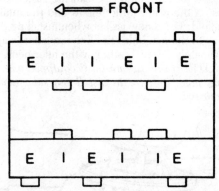

Valve arrangement of the Chevrolet-built V6 engines (E-exhaust; I-intake)

damper aligns with the TDC or 0° mark on the timing tab and the engine is in the No. 1 firing position. This can be determined by placing the fingers on the No. 1 cylinder valves as the marks align. If the valves do not move, it is in the No. 1 firing position. If the valves move, it is in the No. 6 firing position (No. 4 and V6) and the crankcase should be rotated one more revolution to the No. 1 firing position.

b. The adjustment is made in the same manner as 6 cylinder engines.

c. With the engine in thee No. 1 firing position, the following valves can be adjusted:

- V8-Exhaust—1,3,4,8
- V8-Intake—1,2,5,7
- V6-Exhaust—1,5,6
- V6-Intake—1,2,3

d. Crank the engine 1 full revolution until the marks are again in alignment. This is the No. 6 firing position (No. 4 on V6). The following valves can now be adjusted:

- V8-Exhaust—2,5,6,7
- V8-Intake—3,4,6,8
- V6-Exhaust—2,3,4
- V6-Intake—4,5,6

4. Reinstall the rocker arm covers using new gaskets or sealer.

5. Install the distributor cap and wire assembly.

6. Adjust the carburetor idle speed.

Thermostat

REMOVAL AND INSTALLATION

1. Drain the radiator until the level is below the thermostat level (below the level of the intake manifold).

2. Remove the water outlet elbow assembly from the engine. Remove the thermostat from inside the elbow.

3. Install new thermostat in the reverse order of removal, making sure the spring side is inserted into the elbow. Clean the gasket surfaces on the water outlet elbow and the intake manifold. Use a new gasket when installing the elbow to the manifold. Refill the radiator to approximately 2½ inches below the filler neck.

NOTE: *If the thermostat is equipped with a pin hole, be sure to install pin side facing upwards.*

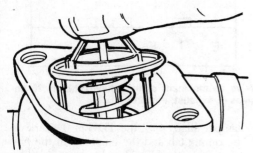

Removing thermostat from water outlet elbow

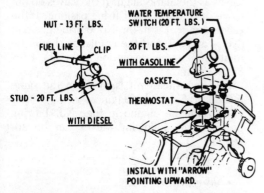

Diesel (left) and gasoline engine thermostat location and outlet elbow mounting

Intake Manifold

REMOVAL AND INSTALLATION

Inline Six Cylinder

NOTE: *The 1975–79 engines are equipped with an intake manifold which is integral with the cylinder head.*

1. Remove the air cleaner.

2. Disconnect the throttle rods at the bellcrank and remove the throttle return spring.

3. Disconnect the fuel and vacuum lines from the carburetor.

4. Disconnect the crankcase ventilation hose from the valve cover and the evaporation control hose from the carbon canister.

5. Disconnect the exhaust pipe from the manifold and throw away the packing.

6. Remove the manifold assembly and scrape off the gaskets.

7. Check the condition of the manifold. If a manifold is cracked or distorted 0.030 in. or more, it should be replaced to prevent exhaust leakage. To detect distortion, lay a straightedge along the length of the exhaust port faces. If, at any point, a gap of 0.030 in. or more exists between the straightedge and the manifold, distortion of that amount is present.

8. By removing one bolt and two nuts, the manifold can be separated.

9. To install, reverse the removal procedure using new gaskets. Replace the exhaust pipe packing.

Gasoline V6 and V8 (Except 231 V6)

1. Remove the air cleaner.

2. Drain the radiator.

3. Disconnect:

  a. Battery cables at the battery.

  b. Upper radiator and heater hoses at the manifold.

  c. Crankcase ventilation hoses as required.

  d. Fuel line at the carburetor (V8) or the fuel line clips and lines at the throttle body (if equipped with TBI-V6).

  e. Accelerator linkage and TV cables (if equipped).

  f. Vacuum hose at the distributor (if equipped).

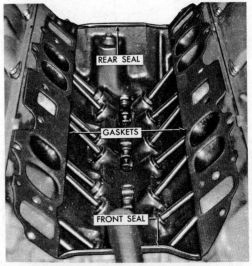

V8 intake manifold seal location

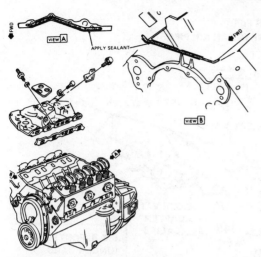

V6 intake manifold and seal location

bolts, then remove the manifold and carburetor or throttle body as an assembly.

8. If the manifold is to be replaced, transfer the carburetor (and mounting studs), water outlet and thermostat (use a new gasket) heater hose adapter, EGR valve (use new gasket) and, if applicable, TVS switch and the choke coil. 1975–79 engines use a new carburetor heat choke tube which must be transferred to a new manifold.

9. Using a putty knife clean the gasket and seal surfaces of the cylinder heads and manifold.

10. Install the manifold end seals, folding the tabs if applicable, and the manifold/head gaskets, using a sealing compound around the water passages.

NOTE: *1974–75 350 V8 engines require a new intake manifold side gasket on 4-bbl engines. The new gasket has restricted cross-over ports. The 350 2-bbl uses a restricted cross-over gasket on the right-hand side and an open gasket on the left. The 350 4-bbl uses restricted cross-over gaskets on both sides. The correct gaskets are essential.*

11. When installing the manifold, care should be taken not to dislocate the end seals. It is helpful to use a pilot in the distributor opening. Tighten the manifold bolts to 30 ft. lbs. in the sequence illustrated.

12. Install the ignition coil.

13. To complete the installation, reverse the removal procedures. Refill the cooling system. Start the engine, adjust the timing (if necessary) and check for leaks.

g. Power brake hose at the carburetor base or manifold, if applicable.

h. Ignition coil, the spark plug wires and temperature sending switch wires.

i. Water pump bypass at the water pump (Mark IV only).

j. If equipped with CCC (V8), disconnect the electrical harness and lay it aside.

4. Remove the distributor cap and scribe the rotor position relative to the distributor body.

5. Remove the distributor.

6. If applicable, remove the alternator upper bracket. As required, remove the oil filler bracket, air cleaner bracket, air conditioning compressor and bracket, and accelerator bellcrank.

7. Remove the manifold-to-head attaching

231 V6

NOTE: *A special wrench adapter, available from Snap-On and several other tool manufacturers, is necessary to remove the left front intake manifold bolt.*

1. Disconnect the battery and drain the cooling system. Remove the upper radiator hose, and the coolant bypass hose from the manifold.

2. Remove the air cleaner. Disconnect the throttle linkage from the carburetor. Remove the linkage bracket from the manifold. If the

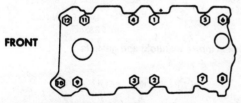

Intake manifold torque sequence—V6 (exc. 231) and small-block V8

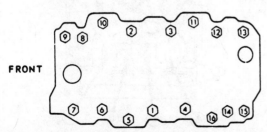

Intake manifold torque sequence—big-block V8

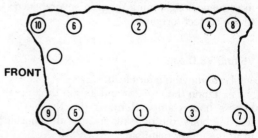

Intake manifold torque sequence—231 V6

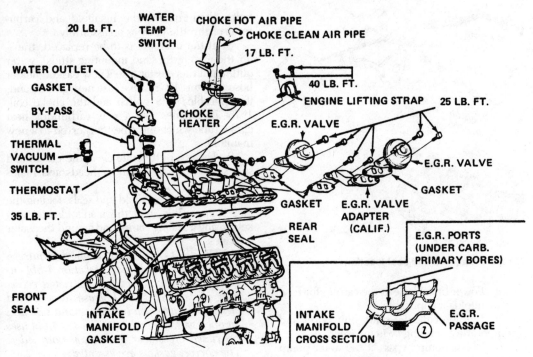

Typical gasoline V6 and V8 intake manifold installation

car is equipped with an automatic transmission, remove the downshift linkage.

3. Disconnect the fuel line from the carburetor. If equipped with power brakes, disconnect the power brake line from the manifold. Disconnect the choke pipe and all vacuum lines. Disconnect the anti-dieseling solenoid wire.

4. Remove the manifold bolts. It will be necessary to remove the distributor cap and rotor to gain access to the front left manifold bolt. This is the special bolt, known as a torx bolt. Remove the plug wires from the plugs.

5. Remove the manifold.

6. Installation is in the reverse order of removal. Use a new gasket and seals. Coat the ends of the seals with a non-hardening silicone sealer. The pointed end of the seal should be a snug fit against the block and head. When installing the manifold, start with the center bolts (numbers one and two) and slowly tighten them until *snug*. Continue with the rest of the bolts in sequence, tightening them in several stages to the correct torque.

V6 and V8 Diesel

1. Remove the air cleaner.

2. Drain the radiator and loosen the upper bypass hose clamp. Remove the thermostat housing bolts, the housing and the thermostat from the intake manifold.

3. Remove the breather pipes from the

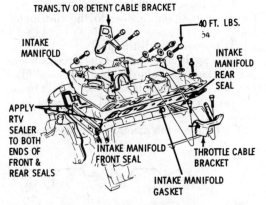

Diesel intake manifold and gaskets

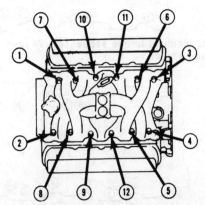

V8 diesel intake manifold bolt torque sequence

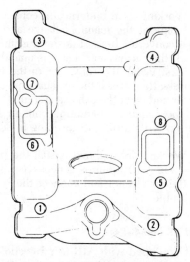

V6 diesel intake manifold bolt torque sequence

rocker covers and the air crossover. Remove the air crossover.

4. Disconnect the throttle rod and the return spring. If equipped with cruise control, remove the servo.

5. Remove the hairpin clip at the bellcrank and disconnect the cables. Remove the throttle cable from the bracket on the manifold; position the cable away from the engine. Disconnect and label any wiring as necessary.

6. Remove the alternator bracket if necessary. If equipped with air conditioning, remove the compressor mounting bolts and move the compressor aside, without disconnecting any of the hoses. Remove the compressor mounting bracket from the intake manifold.

7. Disconnect the fuel line from the pump and the fuel filter. Remove the fuel filter and bracket.

8. Remove the fuel injection pump and lines. See Chapter 4, "Fuel System," for procedures.

9. Disconnect and remove the vacuum pump or oil pump drive assembly from the rear of the engine.

10. Remove the intake manifold drain tube.

11. Remove the intake manifold bolts and the manifold. Remove the adapter seal and the injection pump adapter.

12. Clean the mating surfaces of the cylinder heads and the intake manifold using a putty knife.

13. On the V8, coat both sides of the gasket surface that seal the intake manifold to the cylinder heads with G.M. sealer #1050026 or the equivalent. On the V6, DO NOT coat the gasket or sealing surfaces with any sealer. Use an RTV sealer only on the end seals. Position the intake manifold gaskets on the cylinder heads.

Install the end seals, making sure that the ends are positioned under the cylinder heads.

14. Carefully lower the intake manifold into place on the engine.

15. Clean the intake manifold bolts thoroughly, then dip them in clean engine oil. Install the bolts and tighten to 15 ft. lbs. in the sequence shown. Next, tighten all the bolts to 30 ft. lbs., in sequence, and finally tighten to 40 ft. lbs. in sequence.

16. Install the intake manifold drain tube and clamp.

17. Install injection pump adapter. See Chapter 4. If a new adapter is not being used, skip steps 4 and 9.

18. Install the remaining components in the reverse order of removal.

Exhaust Manifold

REMOVAL AND INSTALLATION

Inline Six—1964–74

Exhaust manifold removal for these model years is covered in the "Intake Manifold, Removal and Installation" section earlier in this chapter.

Inline Six With Integral Intake Manifold—1975–76

1. Remove the air cleaner.
2. Remove the power steering and air pump brackets.
3. Remove the EFE valve bracket.
4. Disconnect the throttle linkage and return spring.
5. Unbolt the exhaust pipe from the flange.
6. Unbolt and remove the manifold.
7. Reverse the procedure for installation. Tighten the four end bolts to specifications last.

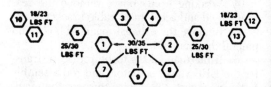

Inline six cylinder exhaust manifold torque sequence—1975–79

Inline Six With Integral Intake Manifold—1977–79

1. Disconnect negative (−) battery cable and remove air cleaner.
2. Remove the power steering and/or AIR pumps and brackets, where they are present. (You need not disconnect powersteering hoses—just support the pump out of the way.)
3. Working from below, with the vehicle safely supported, disconnect the exhaust pipe at the manifold and at the catalytic converter bracket near the transmission mount. If the car

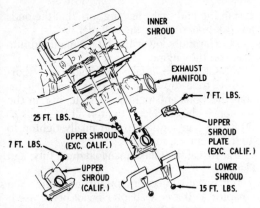

Typical exhaust manifold and hot air shrouds

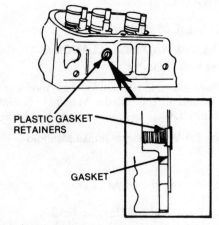

Plastic manifold gasket retainers

uses an exhaust manifold mounted converter, disconnect the pipe at the bottom of the converter and remove the converter.

4. Working from above, remove the rear heat shield and accelerator cable bracket.

5. Remove the exhaust manifold bolts, and pull off the manifold.

6. If the manifold is to be replaced, transfer the EFE valve, actuator, and rod assembly to the new part. Otherwise, inspect the manifold as described in Step 7.

7. Clean and then inspect the manifold carefully for cracks, and for free operation of the EFE valve. Repair or replace parts, and free up the EFE valve with solvent, if necessary.

8. Make sure the gasket surface is clean and free of deep scratches. Position a new gasket on the manifold, and then put the manifold in position on the block, and install the bolts hand tight.

9. Torque all bolts *in the proper order* to the specified torque (see illustration).

10. Install the rear heat shield and the accelerator cable bracket.

11. Working from underneath, connect the exhaust pipe at the manifold flange and connect the converter bracket at the transmission mount. If the car has an exhaust manifold converter, first install the converter to the manifold loosely; then attach the exhaust pipe to the converter and align the exhaust system; finally, torque the converter mounting bolts to 15 ft. lbs., in an X pattern, and torquing in several stages.

12. Working from above, install the power steering and A.I.R. pumps as necessary. Then, install the air cleaner and connect the battery ground cable.

V6 and V8 (1964–84)

1. If equipped with AIR (Air Injection Reaction), remove the air injector manifold assembly. The ¼ in. pipe threads in the manifold are straight threads. Do not use a ¼ in. tapered pipe tap to clean the threads.

2. Disconnect the battery.

3. If applicable, remove the air cleaner preheater shroud.

4. Remove the spark plug wire heat shields. On Mark IV, remove spark plugs.

5. On the left exhaust manifold, disconnect and remove the alternator.

6. Disconnect the exhaust pipe from the manifold and hang it from the frame out of the way.

7. Bend the locktabs and remove the end

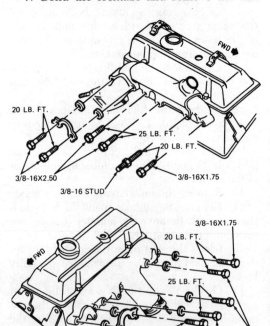

Exhaust manifold installation—V6, V8 (1980 shown, others similar)

bolts, then the center bolts. Remove the manifold.

NOTE: *A 9/16 in. thin wall 6-point socket, sharpened at the leading edge and tapped onto the head of the bolt, simplified bending the locktabs. When installing a new manifold on the right side on 1978–84 V8s you must transfer the heat stove from the old manifold to the new one.*

8. Installation is the reverse of removal. Clean all mating surfaces and use new gaskets. Torque all bolts to specifications from the inside working out.

V6 Engines–1985 and Later

RIGHT-SIDE

1. Disconnect the negative battery cable.
2. Raise and support the vehicle on jackstands.
3. Remove the exhaust pipe bolts, then lower the vehicle.
4. If equipped with air management valve, disconnect the bracket.
5. If equipped with AIR, disconnect the hoses, then the pipes to the converter, the cylinder head and the exhaust manifold.
6. Disconnect the spark plug wires.
7. Remove the exhaust manifold bolts and the manifold.
8. Using a putty knife, clean the gasket mounting surfaces.
9. To install, use new gaskets and reverse the removal procedures. Adjust the drive belts. Start the engine and check for leaks.

LEFT-SIDE

1. Disconnect the negative battery cable.
2. Raise and support the vehicle on jackstands.
3. Remove the exhaust pipe bolts, then lower the vehicle.
4. If equipped with A/C, remove the compressor and the rear adjusting brace.
5. If equipped with power steering, remove the power steering pump and the rear lower power steering adjusting brace.
6. Disconnect the spark plug wires from the spark plugs.
7. Remove the exhaust manifold bolts and the manifold.
8. Using a putty knife, clean the gasket mounting surfaces.
9. To install, use new gaskets and reverse the removal procedures. Adjust the drive belts. Start the engine and check for leaks.

V8 Engines—1985 and Later

RIGHT-SIDE

1. Disconnect the negative battery cable.
2. Raise and support the vehicle on jackstands.
3. Remove the exhaust pipe bolts, then lower the vehicle.
4. Remove the air cleaner.
5. Disconnect the spark plug wires from the spark plugs, the vacuum hoses from the carbon canister and the AIR hose(s).
6. Loosen the alternator belt, then remove the lower alternator bracket and the AIR valve.
7. Disconnect the converter's AIR pipe from the back of the manifold.
8. Remove the exhaust manifold bolts and the manifold.
9. Using a putty knife, clean the gasket mounting surfaces.
10. To install, use new gaskets and reverse the removal procedures. Adjust the drive belts. Start the engine and check for leaks.

LEFT-SIDE

1. Disconnect the negative battery cable.
2. Raise and support the vehicle on jackstands.
3. Remove the exhaust pipe from the manifold, then lower the vehicle.
4. Disconnect the AIR hose.
5. If equipped with A/C, loosen the bracket at the front of the head, then remove the rear bracket and the compressor.
6. If equipped with power steering, remove the power steering pump and the lower adjusting bracket.
7. Remove the exhaust manifold bolts, the wire loom holder at the valve cover and the manifold.
8. Using a putty knife, clean the gasket mounting surfaces.
9. To install, use new gaskets and reverse the removal procedures. Adjust the drive belts. Start the engine and check for leaks.

Diesel Engines

LEFT-SIDE

1. Remove the air cleaner.
2. Remove the alternator lower bracket.
3. Raise and support the car.
4. Remove the crossover pipe.
5. Lower the car.
6. Remove the exhaust manifold.
7. Installation is in the reverse order of removal.

RIGHT-SIDE

1. Raise and support the car.
2. Remove the crossover pipe.

3. Disconnect the exhaust pipe.

4. Remove the right front wheel.

5. Remove the exhaust manifold from under the car.

6. Installation is in the reverse order of removal.

Turbocharger and Actuator—231 V6

REMOVAL AND INSTALLATION

1. Disconnect the exhaust inlet and outlet pipes at the turbocharger.

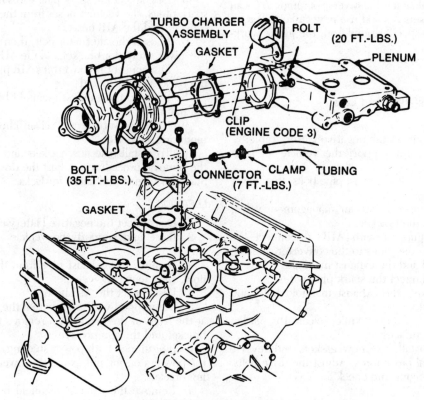

Turbocharger and plenum assembly

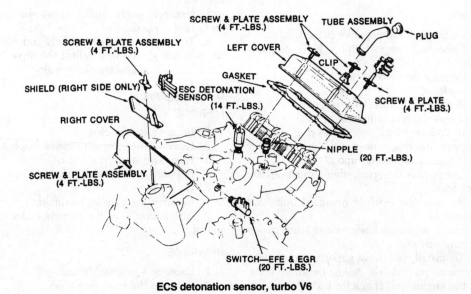

ECS detonation sensor, turbo V6

2. Disconnect the oil feed pipe from the center housing rotating assembly.

3. Remove the nut attaching the air intake elbow to the carburetor and remove the elbow; still attached to the flex tube, from the carburetor.

4. Disconnect the accelerator, cruise and detent linkages at the carb. Remove the linkage bracket from the plenum.

5. Remove the two bolts attaching the plenum to the side bracket.

6. Disconnect the fuel line and all the vacuum hoses.

7. Drain the cooling system.

8. Disconnect the coolant hoses from the front and rear of the plenum.

9. Disconnect the plenum front bracket by removing one bolt attaching the bracket to the intake manifold. Leave the bracket attached to the manifold.

10. Remove the two bolts attaching the turbine housing to the bracket on the intake manifold.

11. Unscrew the two mounting bolts and then remove the EGR valve manifold.

12. Loosen the clamp attaching the hose from the air by-pass to the pipe to the check valve.

13. Unscrew the three compressor housing-to-intake manifold mounting bolts.

14. Remove the turbocharger and actuator, still attached to the carburetor and plenum assembly from the engine.

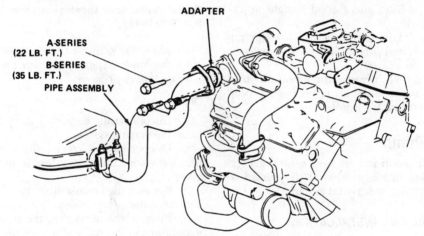

Turbo V6 exhaust pipe connections

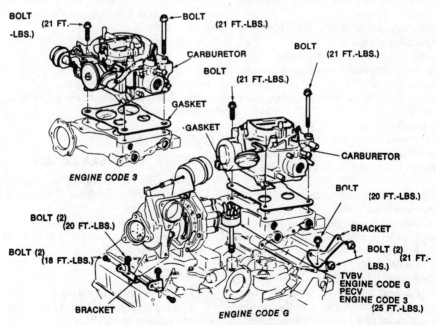

Carburetor-to-plenum installation, turbo V6

15. Unscrew the six bolts and separate the turbocharger assembly from the carburetor.

16. Remove the oil drain from the center housing rotating assembly.

17. Installation is in the reverse order of removal.

Radiator

REMOVAL AND INSTALLATION

1. Disconnect the negative battery cable and drain cooling system.

2. If necessary, remove the fan, the upper fan shroud or the upper support.

3. Disconnect upper and lower hoses.

4. Disconnect and plug the oil cooler lines, if equipped with an A/T.

5. Lift radiator and shroud straight up and out of vehicle.

NOTE: *If equipped with a clutch type fan, keep it in an upright position to prevent the fluid from leaking.*

6. To install, reverse the removal procedures. Make sure the lower cradles are properly located and A/T is full.

Water Pump

The water pump is a die cast, centrifugal-type with sealed bearings. Since it is pressed together, it must be serviced as a unit.

REMOVAL AND INSTALLATION

All Engines Except Diesel

1. Disconnect the negative battery cable and drain the cooling system.

2. If necessary, remove the fan shroud or the upper radiator support.

3. Remove the necessary drive belts.

4. Remove the fan and water pump pulley.

5. Remove the alternator and the power steering pump (if equipped) brackets, then move the units aside.

6. Remove the heater hose and the lower radiator hose from the pump.

7. Remove the water pump retaining bolts and the pump. Clean the gasket mounting surfaces.

NOTE: *Use an anti-seize compound on the water pump bolt threads.*

8. To install, use new gaskets and reverse the removal procedures. Torque the water pump, the alternator and the power steering (if equipped) mounting bolts to 30 ft. lbs. Adjust the drive belts and fill the cooling system.

NOTE: *If a belt tensioning gauge is available, adjust the belts to 100–130 lbs. of tension on new belts or to 70 lbs. on used belts. If the gauge is not available, adjust the belts*

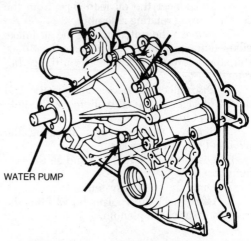

Typical V8 front cover showing water pump and pump mounting bolts

so that a 1/4–1/2 inch deflection can be made on the longest span of the belt under moderate thumb pressure.

Diesel

1. Disconnect the negative battery cable and drain the cooling system.

2. Disconnect the lower radiator hose, the heater hose and the by-pass hose from the water pump.

3. Remove the fan assembly, the drive belts and the water pump pulley.

4. Remove the alternator, the power steering pump and the A/C compressor (if equipped) brackets, than move the units aside.

5. Remove the water pump mounting bolts and the pump. Clean the gasket mounting surfaces.

6. To install, use new gaskets, sealant and reverse the removal procedures. Torque the water pump bolts to 22 ft. lbs. Adjust the belts and refill the cooling system.

NOTE: *Apply sealer to the lower water pump bolts.*

Cylinder Head

REMOVAL AND INSTALLATION

NOTE: *The engine should be "overnight" cold before the cylinder head is removed to prevent warpage.*

CAUTION: *DO NOT discharge the compressor or disconnect the A/C lines. Personal injury could result.*

Inline 6 Cyl

1. Disconnect the negative battery cable.

2. Drain cooling system. Remove air cleaner and disconnect the PCV hose.

3. Disconnect accelerator pedal rod at the

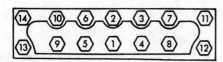

Cylinder head torque sequence—inline six cylinder

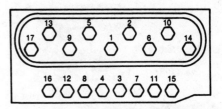

Cylinder head torque sequence—small block V8

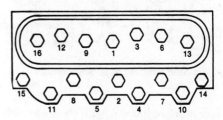

Cylinder head torque sequence—big-block V8

bellcrank on the manifold, the fuel and the vacuum lines at the carburetor.

4. Disconnect the exhaust pipe at the manifold flange, then remove the manifold bolts, the clamps, the manifolds and the carburetor as an assembly.

5. Remove the fuel and the vacuum line retaining clip from the water outlet. Disconnect the wiring harness from the temperature sending unit and the coil, leaving the harness clear of the clips on the rocker arm cover.

6. Disconnect the radiator hose at the water outlet housing and the negative battery cable from the cylinder head.

7. Disconnect the wires and remove the spark plugs.

8. Remove the rocker arm cover, then back off the rocker arm nuts. Pivot the rocker arms to clear the push rods and remove the push rods.

9. Remove the cylinder head bolts, the cylinder head and the gasket.

10. Using a putty knife, clean the gasket mounting surfaces.

11. To install, use new gaskets and reverse the removal procedures. Oil the cylinder head bolts and install them. Torque the cylinder head bolts a little at a time using the torquing sequence. Adjust the valves. Refill cooling system and check for leaks.

V8 And V6, Except 231 V-6

1. Refer to the "Intake Manifold Removal and Installation" procedures in this section and remove the intake manifold.

2. Remove the alternator's lower mounting bolt and move the unit aside.

3. Remove the exhaust manifold(s), the rocker arm cover(s) and the rocker arm assemblies.

4. Drain the cooling system.

5. Remove the diverter valve, the cylinder head bolts and the cylinder head(s).

6. Using a putty knife, clean the gasket mounting surfaces.

7. To install, use new gaskets and reverse the removal procedures. Torque the cylinder head bolts in sequence to 20–35 ft. lbs. Check and/or adjust the valve clearances, the timing and the idle speed.

231 V-6

NOTE: *On vehicles equipped with AIR, disconnect the rubber hose at the injection tubing check valve. This way the tubing will not have to be removed from the exhaust manifold.*

1. Refer to the "Intake Manifold Removal and Installation" procedures in this section and remove the intake manifold.

   a. Loosen and remove all drive belts.

   b. Tag and disconnect the wires leading from the rear of the alternator.

   c. Remove the air conditioning compressor (if so equipped) and position it out of the way with all the hoses still connected.

   d. Remove the alternator and its mounting bracket.

3. When removing the left cylinder head:

   a. Remove the oil gauge rod.

   b. Remove the power steering pump (if so equipped) and its bracket and then posi-

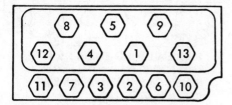

Cylinder head torque sequence—229 V6

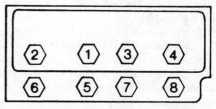

Cylinder head torque sequence—231 V6

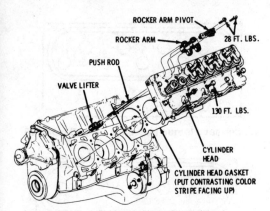

Cylinder head removal, all engines similar

tion it out of the way with the hoses still attached.

4. Tag and disconnect the spark plug wires and then remove the spark plug wire clips from the cylinder head cover studs.

5. Remove the exhaust manifold mounting bolts from the head which is being removed, and then pull the manifold away from the head.

6. Use an air hose if available, or a bunch of clean rags and clean the dirt off the head and surrounding areas thoroughly. *It is extremely important to avoid getting dirt into the hydraulic valve lifters.*

7. Remove the cylinder head cover from the top of the head that you wish to remove.

8. Remove the rocker arm and shaft assembly from the cylinder head and then remove the pushrods.

NOTE: *If the valve lifters are to be serviced, remove them at this time. Otherwise, protect the lifters and the camshaft from dust and dirt by covering the entire area with a clean cloth. Whenever the lifters or the pushrods are removed from the head it is always a good idea to place them in a wooden block with numbered holes to keep them identified as to their position in the engine.*

9. Loosen and remove all the cylinder head bolts and then lift off the head.

To install:

1. Clean the engine block gasket surface thoroughly. Make sure that no foreign material has fallen into the cylinder bores, the bolt holes or into the valve lifter area. It is always a good idea to clean out the bolt holes with an air hose if one is available.

2. Install a new head gasket with the bead facing down toward the cylinder block. The dowels in the block will hold the gasket in place.

3. Clean the gasket surface of the cylinder head and carefully set it into place on the dowels in the cylinder block.

4. Use a heavy body thread sealer on all of the head bolts since the bolt holes go all the way through into the coolant.

5. Install the head bolts. Tighten the bolts a little at a time about three times around in the sequence shown in the illustration. Tighten the bolts to a final torque equal to that given in the "torque Specifications" chart.

6. Installation of the remaining components is in the reverse order of removal.

Diesel Engines

1. Remove the intake manifold, using the procedure outlined above.

2. Remove the rocker arm cover(s), after removing any accessory brackets which interfere with cover removal.

3. Disconnect and label the glow plug wiring.

4. If the right cylinder head is being removed, remove the ground strap from the head.

5. Remove the rocker arm bolts, the bridged pivots, the rocker arms, and the pushrods, keeping all the parts in order so that they can be returned to their original locations. It is a good practice to number or mark the parts to avoid interchanging them.

6. Remove the fuel return lines from the nozzles.

7. Remove the exhaust manifold(s), using the procedure outlined above.

8. Remove the engine block drain plug on the side of the engine from which the cylinder head is being removed. On V6s, remove the pipe-thread plugs covering the upper cylinder head bolts.

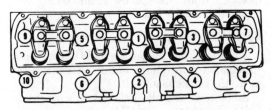

350 V8 diesel cylinder head torque sequence

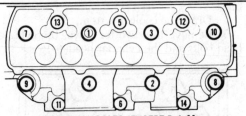

TORQUE ALL BOLTS (EXCEPT 5, 6, 11, 12, 13 & 14) TO 193 N·m (142 FT. LBS.). NUMBERS 5, 6, 11, 12, 13 & 14 TORQUE TO 80 N·m (59 FT. LBS.).

V6 diesel cylinder head torque sequence

9. Remove the head bolts. Remove the cylinder head.

10. To install, first clean the mating surfaces thoroughly. Install new head gaskets on the engine block. DO NOT coat the gaskets with any sealer. The gaskets have a special coating that eliminates the need for sealer. The use of sealer will interfere with this coating and cause leaks. Install the cylinder head onto the block.

11. Clean the head bolts (and pipe-thread plugs-V6s) thoroughly. On the V8, dip the bolts in clean engine oil and install into the cylinder block until the heads of the bolts lightly contact the cylinder head. On V6s, coat the plug threads, bolt threads and the area under the bolt threads with sealer/lubricant part No. 1052080 or equivalent.

NOTE: *The correct sealer must be used or coolant leaks and bolt torque loss will result.*

12. On the V8, tighten the bolts, in the sequence illustrated, to 100 ft. lbs. When all bolts have been tightened to this figure, begin the tightening sequence again, and torque all bolts to 130 ft. lbs.

13. On V6s, tighten all head bolts in sequence to the following torques: all except bolts 5, 6, 11, 12, 13 and 14–100 ft. lbs.; bolts 5, 6, 11, 12, 13 and 14–41 ft. lbs. Finally, tighten all bolts except 5, 6, 11, 12, 13 and 14 to 142 ft. lbs., and bolts 5, 6, 11, 12, 13 and 14 to 59 ft. lbs. in the proper sequence. Install the pipe thread plugs.

14. Install the engine block drain plug(s), the exhaust manifold(s), the fuel return lines, the glow plug wiring, and the ground strap for the right cylinder head.

15. Install the valve train assembly. Refer to "Diesel Engine, Rocker Arm Replacement," above, for valve lifter bleeding procedures.

16. Install the intake manifold.

17. Install the rocker cover(s). The valve covers are sealed with RTV (room temperature vulcanizing) silicone sealer instead of a gasket. Use GM No. 1052434 or its equivalent. Install the cover to the head within 10 minutes (while the sealer is still wet).

CLEANING AND INSPECTION

Chip carbon away from the valve heads, combustion chambers, and ports, using a chisel made of hardwood. Remove the remaining deposits with a stiff wire brush.

NOTE: *Be sure that the deposits are actually removed, rather than burnished.*

Have the cylinder head hot-tanked to remove grease, corrosion, and scale from the water passages. Clean the remaining cylinder head parts in an engine cleaning solvent. Do not remove the protective coating from the springs.

Place a straight-edge across the gasket sur-

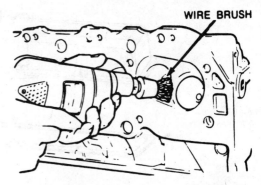

WIRE BRUSH

Removing the carbon from the cylinder head from a wire brush and an electric drill

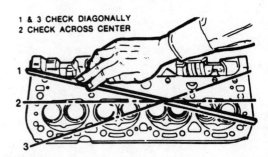

1 & 3 CHECK DIAGONALLY
2 CHECK ACROSS CENTER

Checking the cylinder head for warpage

face of the cylinder head. Using feeler gauges, determine the clearance at the center of the straightedge. If warpage exceeds .003″ in a 6″ span, or .006″ over the total length, the cylinder head must be resurfaced.

NOTE: *If warpage exceeds the manufacturer's maximum tolerance for material removal, the cylinder head must be replaced. When milling the cylinder heads of V-type engines, the intake manifold mounting position is altered, and must be corrected by milling the manifold flange a proportionate amount.*

RESURFACING

NOTE: *This procedure should only be performed by a machine shop.*

Valves and Springs
REMOVAL AND INSTALLATION

1. Remove the head(s), and place on a clean surface.

2. Using a suitable spring compressor (for pushrod-type overhead valve engines), compress the valve spring and remove the valve spring cap key. Release the spring compressor and remove the valve spring and cap (and valve rotator on some engines).

NOTE: *Use care in removing the keys; they are easily lost.*

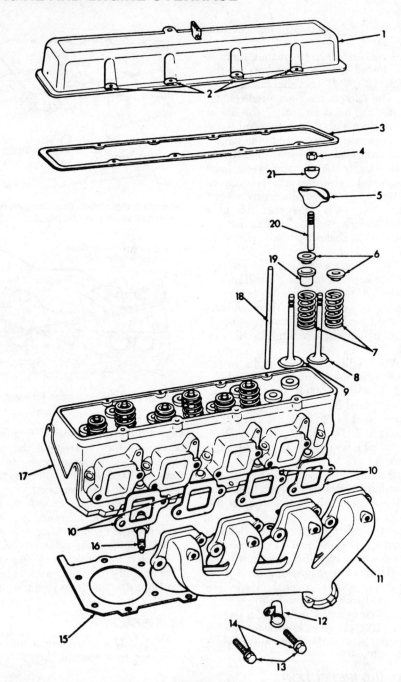

1. Valve cover	8. Exhaust valve	15. Head gasket
2. Screw reinforcements	9. Intake valve	16. Spark plug
3. Gasket	10. Gasket	17. Cylinder head
4. Adjusting nut	11. Exhaust manifold	18. Pushrod
5. Rocker arm	12. Spark plug shield	19. Spring shield
6. Valve spring retainer	13. Bolt	20. Rocker arm stud
7. Valve spring	14. Washer	21. Rocker arm ball

Exploded view of the big-block cylinder head

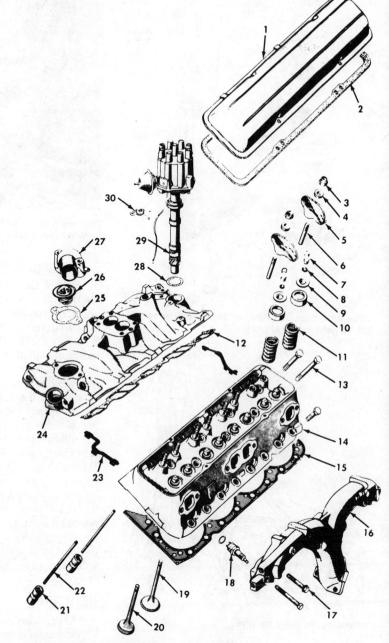

1. Rocker arm cover
2. Gasket
3. Nut
4. Ball
5. Rocker arms
6. Rocker arm studs
7. Valve keeper locks
8. O-ring seals
9. Valve spring cap
10. Shield
11. Spring
12. Gasket
13. Bolts
14. Cylinder head
15. Head gasket
16. Exhaust manifold
17. Bolts
18. Spark plug and gasket
19. Intake valve
20. Exhaust valve
21. Hydraulic lifters
22. Push rods
23. Intake manifold gaskets
24. Intake manifold
25. Gasket
26. Thermostat
27. Thermostat housing
28. Gasket
29. Distributor
30. Clamp

Exploded view of the small-block cylinder head

3. Remove the valve seals from the intake valve guides. Throw these old seals away, as you'll be installing new seals during reassembly.

4. Slide the valves out of the head from the combustion chamber side.

5. Make a holder for the valves out of a piece of wood or cardboard, as outlined for the push-rod in "Cylinder Head Removal." Make sure you number each hole in the cardboard to keep the valves in proper order. Slide the valves out

of the head from the combustion chamber side; they MUST be installed as they were removed.

INSPECTION

Inspect the valve faces and seats (in the head) for pits, burned spots and other evidence of poor seating. If a valve face is in such bad shape that the head of the valve must be ground in order to true up the face, discard the valve because the sharp edge will run too hot. The cor-

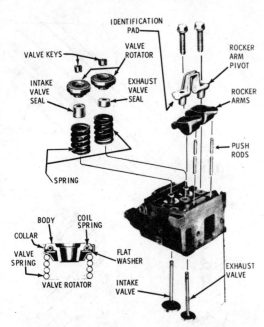

Valve train exploded view, all engine similar except 231 V6 (with rocker shafts)

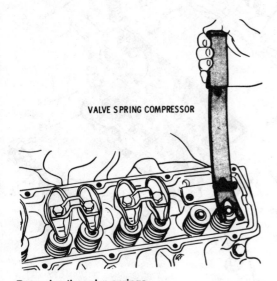

Removing the valve springs

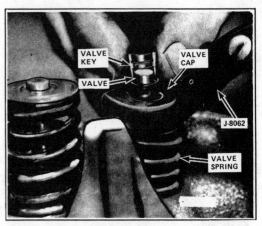

Removing the valve key and cap. A magnet is useful here in removing the keys

rect angle for valve faces is 45 degrees. We recommend the re-facing be done at a reputable machine shop.

Check the valve stem for scoring and burned spots. If not noticeably scored or damaged, clean the valve stem with solvent to remove all gum and varnish. Clean the valve guides using solvent and an expanding wire-type valve guide cleaner. If you have access to a dial indicator for measuring valve stem-to-guide clearance, mount it so that the stem of the indicator is at 90° to the valve stem, and as close to the valve guide as possible. Move the valve off its seat, and measure the valve guide-to-stem clearance by rocking the stem back and forth to actuate the dial indicator. Measure the valve stems using a micrometer, and compare to specifications to determine whether stem or guide wear is responsible for the excess clearance. If a dial indicator and micrometer are not available to you, take your cylinder head and valves to a reputable machine shop for inspection.

Some of the engines covered in this guide are equipped with valve rotators, which double as valve spring caps. In normal operation the rotators put a certain degree of wear on the tip of the valve stem; this ear appears as concentric rings on the stem tip. However, if the rotator is not working properly, the wear may appear as straight notches or "X" patterns across the valve stem tip. Whenever the valves are removed from the cylinder head, the tips should be inspected for improper pattern, which could indicate valve rotator problems. Valve stem tips will have to be ground flat if rotator patterns are severe.

REFACING

NOTE: *This procedure should only be performed by a qualified machine shop.*

Valve Guides

The engines covered in this guide use integral valve guides; that is, they are a part of the cylinder head and cannot be replaced. The guides can, however, be reamed oversize if they are found to be worn past an acceptable limit. Occasionally, a valve guide bore will be oversize as manufactured. These are marked on the inboard side of the cylinder heads on the machined surface just above the intake manifold.

If the guides must be reamed (this service is available at most machine shops), then valves

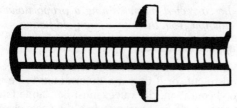

Cutaway of a knurled valve guide

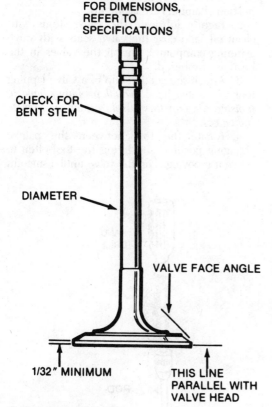

FOR DIMENSIONS, REFER TO SPECIFICATIONS

CHECK FOR BENT STEM

DIAMETER

VALVE FACE ANGLE

1/32" MINIMUM

THIS LINE PARALLEL WITH VALVE HEAD

Critical valve dimensions

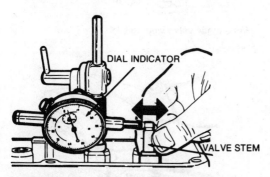

DIAL INDICATOR

VALVE STEM

Checking the valve stem-to-guide clearance

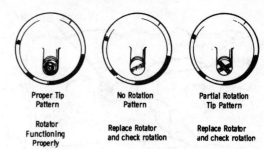

Proper Tip Pattern — Rotator Functioning Properly

No Rotation Pattern — Replace Rotator and check rotation

Partial Rotation Tip Pattern — Replace Rotator and check rotation

Valve stem wear

Have the valve seat concentricity checked at a machine shop

with oversize stems must be fitted. Valves are usually available in 0.001, 0.003 and 0.005 in. stem oversizes. Valve guides which are not excessively worn or distorted may, in some cases, be knurled rather than reamed. Knurling is a

process in which the metal on the valve guide bore is displaced and raised, thereby reducing clearance. Knurling also provides excellent oil control. The option of knurling rather than reaming valve guides should be discussed with a reputable machinist or engine specialist.

CYLINDER HEAD CLEANING AND INSPECTION

NOTE: *Any diesel cylinder head work should be handled by a reputable machine shop familiar with diesel engines. Disassembly, valve lapping, and assembly can be completed by following the gasoline engine procedures.*

Gasoline Engines

Once the complete valve train has been removed from the cylinder head(s), the head itself can be inspected, cleaned and machined (if necessary). Set the head(s) on a clean work space, so the combustion chambers are facing up. Begin cleaning the chambers and ports with a hardwood chisel or other non-metallic tool (to avoid nicking or gouging the chamber, ports, and especially the valve seats). Chip away the major carbon deposits, then remove the re-

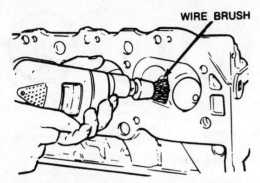

Use a wire brush and electric drill to remove carbon from the combustion chambers and exhaust ports

mainder of carbon with a wire brush fitted to an electric drill.

NOTE: *Be sure that the carbon is actually removed, rather than just burnished.*

After decarbonizing is completed, take the head(s) to a machine shop and have the head "hot tanked." In this process, the head is lowered into a hot chemical bath that very effectively cleans all grease, corrosion, and scale from all internal and external head surfaces. Also have the machinist check the valve seats and re-cut them if necessary. When you bring the clean head(s) home, place them on a clean surface. Completely clean the entire valve train with solvent.

Checking for Head Warpage

Lay the head down with the combustion chambers facing up. Place a straight-edge across the gasket surface of the head, both diagonally and straight across the center. Using a flat feeler gauge, determine the clearance at the center of the straight-edge. If warpage exceeds .003 in. in a 6 in. span, or .006 in. over the total length, the cylinder head must be resurfaced (which is akin to planing a piece of wood). Resurfacing can be performed at most machine shops.

NOTE: *When resurfacing the cylinder head(s) of V6 or V8 engines, the intake manifold mounting position is altered, and must*

be corrected by machining a proportionate amount from the intake manifold flange.

Lapping the Valves

When valve faces and seats have been re-faced and re-cut, or if they are determined to be in good condition, the valves must be "lapped in" to ensure efficient sealing when the valve closes against the sea.

1. Invert the cylinder head so that the combustion chambers are facing up.

2. Lightly lubricate the valve stems with clean oil, and coat the valve seats with valve grinding compound. Install the valves in the head as numbered.

3. Attach the suction cup of a valve lapping tool to a valve head. *You'll probably have to moisten the cup to securely attach the tool to the valve.*

4. Rotate the tool between the palms, changing position and lifting the tool often to prevent grooving. Lap the valve until a smooth,

Home-made valve lapping tool

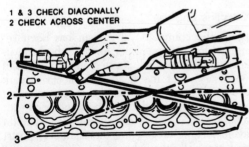

Check the cylinder head mating surface for warpage with a precision straight edge

Lapping the valves by hand

polished seat is evident (you may have to add a bit more compound after some lapping is done).

5. Remove the valve and tool, and remove ALL traces of grinding compound with solvent-soaked rag, or rinse the head with solvent.

NOTE: *Valve lapping can also be done by fastening a suction cup to a piece of drill rod in a hand "eggbeater" type drill. Proceed as above, using the drill as a lapping tool. Due to the higher speeds involved when using the hand drill, care must be exercised to avoid grooving the seat. Lift the tool and change direction of rotation often.*

Valve Springs
HEIGHT AND PRESSURE CHECK

1. Place the valve spring on a flat, clean surface next to a square.

2. Measure the height of the spring, and rotate it against the edge of the square to measure distortion (out-of-roundness). If spring height varies between springs by more than 1/16 in. or if the distortion exceeds 1/16 in., replace the spring.

A valve spring tester is needed to test spring test pressure, so the valve springs must usually be taken to a professional machine shop for this test. Spring pressure at the installed and compressed heights is checked, and a tolerance of plus or minus 5 lbs. (plus or minus 1 lb. on the 231V6) is permissible on the spring covered in this guide.

VALVE INSTALLATION

New valve seals must be installed when the valve train is put back together. Certain seals slip over the valve stem and guide boss, while others require that the boss be machined. In some applications Teflon guide seals are available. Check with a machinist and/or automotive parts store for a suggestion on the proper seals to use.

NOTE: *Remember that when installing valve seals, a small amount of oil is able to pass the seal to lubricate the valve guides; otherwise, excessive wear will result.*

To install the valves and rocker assembly:

1. Lubricate the valve stems with clean engine oil.

2. Install the valves in the cylinder head, one at a time, as numbered.

3. Lubricate and position the seals and valve springs, again a valve at a time.

4. Install the spring retainers, and compress the springs.

5. With the valve key groove exposed above the compressed valve spring, wipe some wheel bearing grease around the groove. This will retain the keys as you release the spring compressor.

6. Using needlenose pliers (or your fingers), place the keys in the key grooves. The grease should hold the keys in place. Slowly release the spring compressor; the valve cap or rotator will raise up as the compressor is released, retaining the keys.

7. Install the rocker assembly, and install the cylinder head(s).

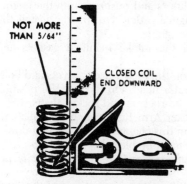

Check the valve spring free length and squareness

Have the valve spring test pressure checked professionally

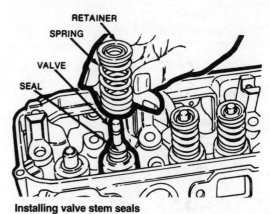

Installing valve stem seals

VALVE ADJUSTMENT

In the event of cylinder head removal or any operation that requires disturbing or removing the rocker arms, the rocker arms must be adjusted. See the "Valve Lash" procedure earlier in this chapter.

Valve Lifters

REMOVAL AND INSTALLATION

Gasoline and Diesel

NOTE: *Valve lifters and pushrods should be kept in order so they can be reinstalled in their original position. Some engines will have both standard size .010 in. oversize valve lifters as original equipment. The oversize lifters are etched with an "O" on their sides; the cylinder block will also be marked with an "O" if the oversize lifter is used.*

1. Remove the intake manifold and gasket.

2. Remove the valve covers, rocker arm assemblies and pushrods.

3. If the lifters are coated with varnish, apply carburetor cleaning solvent to the lifter body. The solvent should dissolve the varnish in about 10 minutes.

4. Remove the lifters. On diesels, remove

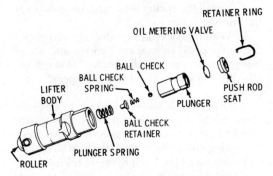

Hydraulic valve lifter, diesel roller type. Gasoline engine lifters similar but without rollers

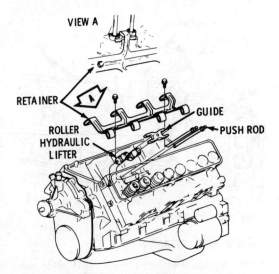

Diesel valve lifter guide and retainer

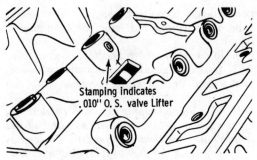

Oversize valve lifter bore marking

the lifter retainer guide bolts, and remove the guides. A special tool for removing lifters is available, and is helpful for this procedure.

5. New lifters *must* be primed before installation, *as dry lifters will seize when the engine is started.* On the diesel lifters, submerge the lifters in clean diesel fuel or kerosene and work the lifter plunger up and down to prime. On gasoline engine lifters, submerge the lifters in SAE 10 oil, which is very thin. Carefully insert the end of a ⅛ in. (3mm) drift into the lifter and push down on the plunger. Hold the plunger down while the lifter is still submerged; *do not pump the plunger.* Release the plunger. The lifter is now primed.

6. Coat the bottoms of the gasoline engine lifters, and the rollers of the diesel engine lifters with Molykote® or an equivalent molybdenum-disulfide lubricant before installation. Install the lifters and pushrods into the engine in their original order. On diesels, install the lifter retainer guide.

7. Install the intake manifold gaskets and manifold.

8. Position the rocker arms, pivots and bolts on the cylinder head. On the 231 V6, position and install the rockers and rocker shafts. Refer to the "Rocker Arm Removal and Installation" procedure in this chapter for lifter bleed-down. New lifters must be bled down; *valve-to-piston contact could occur if this procedure is neglected.*

9. Install the valve covers, connect the spark plug wires and install the air cleaner assembly.

NOTE: *An additive containing EP lube, such as EOS, should always be added to crankcase oil for break-in when new lifters or a new camshaft is installed. This additive is generally available in automotive parts stores.*

Oil Pan

REMOVAL AND INSTALLATION

Inline Six-Cylinder

NOTE: *Pan removal for all engines may be easier if the engine is turned to No. 1 cylinder firing position. This positions the crank-*

shaft in the path of least resistance for pan removal.

1. Disconnect the battery ground cable.
2. Remove the upper radiator mounting bolts or side mount bolts. Remove the upper and lower hoses from the water pump.
3. Install a piece of heavy cardboard between the fan and the radiator.
4. Disconnect the fuel suction line from the fuel pump.
5. Raise the car and drain the oil.
6. Remove the starter.
7. Remove the flywheel lower pan or converter lower pan and splash shield.
8. Rotate the crankshaft until the timing mark on the damper is at the six o'clock position.
9. Remove the brake line retaining bolts from the crossmember and move the brake line out of the way.
10. Remove the thru-bolts from the front motor mounts.
11. Remove the oil pan bolts.
12. Slowly raise the engine until the motor mounts can be removed from the frame brackets.
13. Remove the mounts and continue to raise the engine until it has been raised three inches.
14. Remove the oil pan by pulling it down from the engine and then twisting it into the opening left by the removal of the left engine mount.
15. When the pan is clear of the engine, tilt the front up and remove it by pulling it down and to the rear.
16. Install the oil pan gaskets to the engine block.
17. Install the oil pan and torque the side bolts to 6–8 ft. lbs. and the end bolts to 9–12 ft. lbs.
18. Install the motor mounts, and then install the remaining components using a reverse procedure of removal

V8 Engines

1964–68

1. Remove the engine from the chassis.
2. Remove the bellhousing or converter underpan.
3. Remove the starter.
4. Remove the oil pan.
5. Reverse the removal procedure to install the pan.

1969 396, 1969 MANUAL TRANSMISSION, AND 1970–72, 396 AND 402

1. Disconnect the battery ground cable.
2. Remove the air cleaner, dipstick, distributor cap, radiator shroud and upper mounting panel.

3. On big-block models, place a piece of heavy cardboard between the radiator and the fan.
4. Disconnect the engine ground straps. Remove the fuel pump on 307 and 350 engines.
5. Disconnect the accelerator control cable.
6. Drain the oil. Remove the filter on 307 and 350 engines.
7. Remove the driveshaft and plug the rear of transmission.
8. Remove the starter.
9. Disconnect the transmission linkage at the transmission or remove the floorshift level.
10. Disconnect the speedometer cable and the back-up switch connector.
11. On manual transmission vehicles, disconnect the clutch cross-shaft at the frame. On automatic transmission vehicles, disconnect the cooler lines, detent cable, rod or switch wire, and the modulator pipe.
12. Remove the crossmember bolts. Jack up the engine and move the crossmember rearward.
13. Remove the crossover or disconnect the dual exhaust pipes.
14. Remove:
    a. Flywheel housing cover;
    b. Transmission;
    c. Flywheel housing and throwout beating (manual transmission);
    d. Front engine mount through-bolts.
15. Raise the rear of engine approximately 4 in. Support the engine by hoist.
16. Raise the front of the engine approximately 4 in. and insert 2 in. blocks under the front engine mounts.
17. Rotate the crankshaft until the timing mark on the torsional damper is at the six o'clock position.
18. Unbolt and remove the oil pan.

1969–78

1. Disconnect the negative battery cable.
2. As a precaution, remove the distributor cap to keep it from getting broken when the engine is raised.
3. Remove the fan shroud retaining bolts.
4. On earlier models, it may be necessary to remove the radiator upper mounting panel.
5. Raise the vehicle on a hoist and drain the engine oil.
6. Disconnect the exhaust pipes or crossover pipes.
7. On automatic transmission equipped vehicles, remove the converter housing underpan and splash shield.
8. Rotate the crankshaft until the timing

mark on the torsional dampener is at the six o'clock position.

9. The starter can be swung out of the way by disconnecting the brace at the starter, removing the inboard starter bolt and loosening the outboard starter bolt. On 1970 small V8, remove the fuel pump.

10. Remove the front engine mount thru-bolts.

11. Raise the engine and insert blocks, at least three in. thick, under the engine mounts.

12. Remove the oil pan bolts and remove the oil pan.

13. To install, clean all gasket and seal surfaces thoroughly, use new gaskets and seals, and reverse the removal procedure.

NOTE: *If the crankshaft was rotated while the pan was off, place the timing mark at the six o'clock position.*

1979–86

1. Disconnect the negative battery cable.

2. Remove the air cleaner, the upper radiator mounting panel and the fan shroud.

3. Raise and support the vehicle on jackstands. Drain the oil from the engine.

4. Remove the distributor cap and the fan assembly.

5. Disconnect the AIR hose from the converter pipe and the AIR pipe from the exhaust manifold.

6. Remove the exhaust crossover pipe from the manifold and the catalytic converter.

NOTE: *On some models, it may be necessary to remove the starter.*

7. If equipped with an A/T, remove torque converter housing cover plate and disconnect the transmission oil cooler lines at the oil pan. If equipped with a M/T, remove the starter and the flywheel housing cover plate.

8. Rotate crankshaft until timing mark on torsional damper is at 6 o'clock position, this positions the crankshaft throw in the horizontal place.

9. Remove front engine mount through bolts.

10. Raise engine and insert blocks under engine mounts.

NOTE: *The block thickness should be 3 in.*

11. Remove the oil pan bolts and lower the pan.

12. Using a putty knife, clean the gasket mounting surfaces.

13. To install, use a new gasket, sealant and reverse the removal procedures. Torque the oil pan bolts to 7 ft. lbs. and the engine mount bolts to 50 ft. lbs.

V6 Engines

1. Disconnect the negative battery cable.

2. Remove the upper half of the radiator fan shroud.

3. Raise the front of the car and drain the oil.

4. Unscrew the exhaust pipe cross-over tube mounting nuts at the manifold. Lower the crossover tube.

5. On models which are equipped with an automatic transmission, remove the torque converter cover, and the oil cooler lines at the oil pan.

6. Remove the upper bolt on the starter brace and then remove the inboard starter bolt and swing the starter assembly aside.

NOTE: *If equipped with Air Injection Reaction (AIR) system, disconnect the AIR hose from the converter pipe and the AIR pipe from the exhaust manifold.*

7. Loosen and remove the left-hand motor mount thru-bolt and then loosen the thru-bolt on the right-hand mount.

8. Raise the engine and then reinstall the thru-bolt in the left-hand motor mount. *Do not tighten the bolt.*

9. Unscrew the attaching bolts and remove the oil pan from under the engine.

10. To install, clean all gasket and seal surfaces thoroughly, use new gaskets and seals and reverse the removed procedure.

Diesel Engines

1. Remove the vacuum pump and drive (with A/C) or the oil pump drive (without A/C).

2. Disconnect the batteries and remove the dipstick.

3. Remove the upper radiator support and fan shroud.

4. Raise and support the car. Drain the oil.

5. Remove the flywheel cover.

6. Disconnect the exhaust and crossover pipes.

7. Remove the oil cooler lines at the filter base.

8. Remove the starter assembly. Support the engine with a jack.

9. Remove the engine mounts from the block.

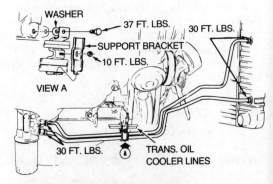

Diesel oil cooler lines, 263 V6 shown

10. Raise the front of the engine and remove the oil pan.

11. Installation is the reverse of removal.

Oil Pump

REMOVAL AND INSTALLATION

In Line Six-Cylinder

1. Remove the oil pan as previously described.

2. Remove the two flange mounting bolts, the pick-up bolt, then remove the pump and screen together.

3. To install, align the oil pump driveshafts to match with the distributor tang and position he flange over the distributor lower bushing. Install the pump mounting bolts.

4. Install the oil pan.

Gasoline and Diesel V6 and V8 (Except 231 V6)

1. Remove the oil pan as previously described.

2. Remove the pump-to-rear main bearing cap bolts and remove the pump and extension shaft.

3. To install align the slot on the top end of the extension shaft with the drive tang on the

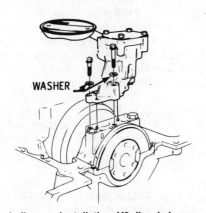

Typical oil pump installation, V6 diesel shown

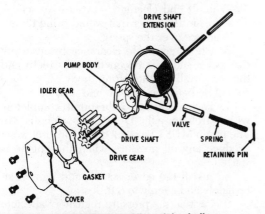

Oil pump, exploded view. All models similar

lower end of the distributor driveshaft (or until the shaft mates into the oil pump drive gear on diesels) and install the rear main bearing cap bolt.

4. Position the pump screen so that the bottom edge is parallel to the oil pan rails.

5. Install the oil pan.

231 V6

The oil pump is located in the timing chain cover and is connected by a drilled passage to the oil screen housing and pipe assembly in the oil pan. All oil is discharged from the pump to the oil pump cover assembly, on which the oil filter is mounted.

1. To remove the oil pump cover and gears, first remove the oil filter.

2. Remove the screws which attach the oil pump cover assembly to the timing chain cover.

3. Remove the cover assembly and slide out the oil pump gears. Clean the gears and inspect them for any obvious defects such as chipping or scoring.

4. Remove the oil pressure relief valve cap, spring and valve. Clean them and inspect them for wear or scoring. Check the relief valve spring to see that it is not worn on its side or collapsed. Replace the spring if it seems questionable.

5. Check the relief valve for a correct fit in its bore. It should be an easy slip fit and no more. If any perceptible shake can be felt, the valve and/or the cover should be replaced.

6. To install, lubricate the pressure relief valve and spring and place them in the cover. Install the cap and the gasket. Torque the cap to 35 ft. lbs.

7. Pack the oil pump gear cavity full of petroleum jelly. Do not use gear lube. Reinstall the oil pump gears so that the petroleum jelly is forced into every cavity of the gear pocket, and between the gear teeth. There must be no air spaces. This step is very important. Unless the pump is packed, it may not begin to pump oil as soon as the engine is started.

8. Install the cover assembly using a new gasket and sealer. Tighten the screws to 10 ft. lbs.

9. Install the oil filter.

OVERHAUL

231 V6

The oil pump is located in the timing chain cover and is connected by a drilled passage to the oil screen housing and pipe assembly in the oil pan. All oil is discharged from the pump to the oil pump cover assembly, on which the oil filter is mounted.

1. To remove the oil pump cover and gears, first remove the oil filter.

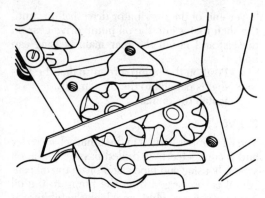

Checking oil pump end clearance

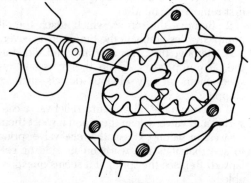

Use a feeler gauge to check oil pump side clearance

2. Remove the screws which attach the oil pump cover assembly to the timing chain cover.

3. Remove the cover assembly and slide out the oil pump gears. Clean the gears and inspect them for any obvious defects such as chipping or scoring.

4. Remove the oil pressure relief valve cap, spring and valve. Clean them and inspect them for wear or scoring. Check the relief valve spring to see that it is not worn on its side or collapsed. Replace the spring if it seems questionable.

5. Check the relief valve for a correct fit in its bore. It should be an easy slip fit and no more. If any perceptible shake can be felt the valve and/or the cover should be replaced.

6. Install the oil pump gears (if removed) and the shaft in the oil pump body section of the timing chain cover to check the gear end clearance and gear side clearance. Check gear end clearance by placing a straight edge over the gears and measure the clearance between the straight edge and the gasket surface. Clearance should be between .002 in. and .006 in. Check gear side clearance by inserting the feeler gauge between the gear teeth and the side wall of the pump body. Clearance should be between .002 in. and .005 in.

7. Check the pump cover flatness by placing a straight edge across the cover face, with a feeler gauge between the straight edge and the cover. If clearance is .001 in. or more, replace the cover.

8. To install, lubricate the pressure relief valve and spring and place them in the cover. Install the cap and the gasket. Torque the cap to 35 ft. lbs.

9. Pack the oil pump gear cavity full of petroleum jelly. *Do not use gear lube.* Reinstall the oil pump gears so that the petroleum jelly is forced into every cavity of the gear pocket, and between the gear teeth. There must be no air spaces. *This step is very important.*

CAUTION: *Unless the pump is primed this way, it won't produce any oil pressure when the engine is started.*

10. Install the cover assembly using a new gasket and sealer. Tighten the screws to 10 ft. lbs.

11. Install the oil filter.

V8 Including V6 and V8 Diesel

1. Remove the oil pump drive shaft extension.

2. Remove the cotter pin, spring and the pressure regulator valve.

NOTE: *Place your thumb over the pressure regulator bore before removing the cotter pin, as the spring is under pressure.*

3. Remove the oil pump cover attaching screws and remove the oil pump cover and gasket. Clean the pump in solvent or kerosene, and wash out the pick-up screen.

4. Remove the drive gear and idler gear from the pump body.

5. Check the gears for scoring and other damage. Install the gears if in good condition, or replace them if damaged. Check gear end clearance by placing a straight edge over the gears and measure the clearance between the straight edge and the gasket surface with a feeler gauge. End clearance for both diesels is .0005 in. to .0075 in., and other V8s is .002 in. to .0065 in. If end clearance is excessive, check for scores in the cover that would bring the total clearance over the specs.

6. Check gear side clearance by inserting the feeler gauge between the gear teeth and the side wall of the pump body. Clearance should be between .002 in. and .005 in.

7. Pack the inside of the pump completely with petroleum jelly. DO NOT use engine oil. The pump MUST be primed this way or it won't produce any oil pressure when the engine is started.

8. Install the cover screws and tighten alternately and evenly to 8 ft. lbs.

9. Position the pressure regulator valve into

the pump cover, closed end first, then install the spring and retaining pin.

NOTE: *When assembling the drive shaft extension to the drive shaft, the end of the extension nearest the washers must be inserted into the drive shaft.*

10. Insert the drive shaft extension through the opening in the main bearing cap and block until the shaft mates into the distributor drive gear.

11. Install the pump onto the rear main bearing cap and install the attaching bolts. Torque the bolts to 35 ft. lbs.

12. Install the oil pan.

Timing Gear Cover
REMOVAL AND INSTALLATION
Inline Six Cylinder

1. Drain the oil and remove the oil pan on models 1964–72.

2. Remove the radiator after draining it.

3. Remove the fan, pulley, and belt. Remove any power steering and/or AIR pump drive belts. Remove any braces for the above pumps which will interfere with cover removal and position the pumps out of the way.

4. Remove the crankshaft pulley and damper. Use the puller tool No. J-16516 to remove the damper. Do not attempt to pry or hammer the damper off, or it will be damaged.

5. Remove the retaining bolts, and remove the cover on 1964–72 models.

6. On 1973–79 models, pull the cover for-

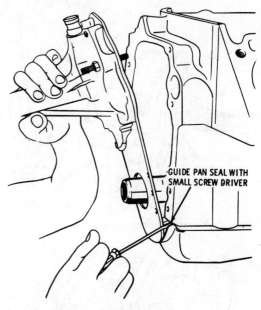

Guiding front cover into place, V8 shown

ward slightly and cut the oil pan front seal off flush with the block. Remove the cover. On installation, cut the tabs off a new oil pan front seal and install it on the cover.

7. On installation, coat the gasket with sealer and use a ⅛ in. bead of silicone sealer at the oil pan-to-cylinder block joint. Replace the damper before tightening the cover bolts down, so that the cover seal will align. The damper must be drawn into place. Hammering it will destroy it.

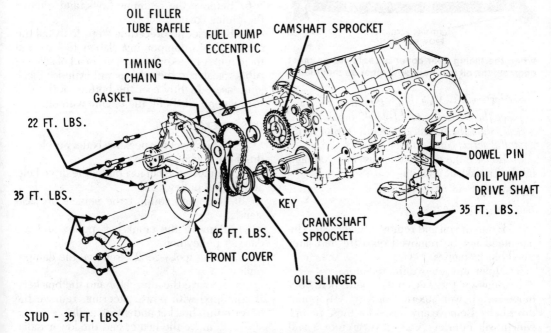

Typical front cover and timing assembly

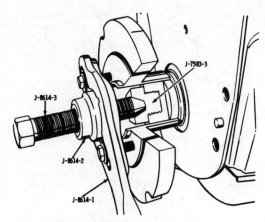

J-7583-3

J-8614-3

J-8614-2

J-8614-1

Removing harmonic balancer using puller

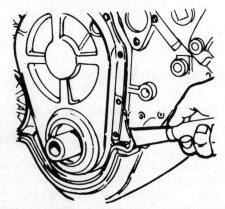

Cut the oil pan seal flush with the front of the cylinder block (V8 shown, others similar)

CUT THIS PORTION
FROM NEW SEAL

When the timing gear cover is replaced on most engines, the oil pan front seal must be modified

NOTE: *When installing the timing cover, place the centering tool J-23042 inside the oil seal, slide the timing cover into position, install 2 screws and remove the tool.*

8. Replace the oil pan if it was removed, and fill the crankshaft with oil.

V6 and V8

1964–74 (EXCEPT 231)

1. Drain the oil and remove the oil pan. The pan need not be removed on 1974 and later small block engines.

2. Drain and remove the radiator.

3. Remove the fan, pulley and belt. Remove any power steering and/or AIR pump drive belts. Remove any braces for these pumps which will interfere with cover removal and position the pumps out of the way.

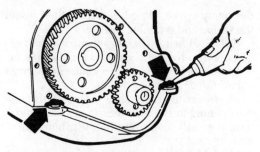

Use sealer at the timing cover-to-oil pan and the oil pan-to-cylinder block joints

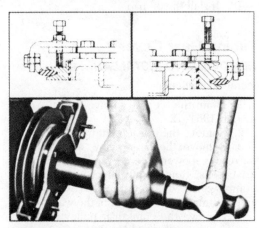

Installing the drive-on torsional damper

4. Remove the water pump.

5. Remove the crankshaft pulley and damper. Use a puller on the damper. Do not attempt to pry or hammer the damper off.

6. Remove the retaining bolts, and remove the timing cover.

7. Reverse the preceding steps to install the cover. Use a damper installation tool to pull the damper on. Apply an ⅛ in. bead of silicone rubber sealer to the oil pan and cylinder block joint faces. Lightly coat the bottom of the seal with engine oil. Refill the engine with oil.

1975–86 (EXCEPT 231)

1. Disconnect the negative battery cable and drain the cooling system.

2. Remove the fan assembly, the drive belts and the fan pulley.

3. Raise and support the vehicle on jackstands.

4. Remove the crankshaft pulley and the damper pulley bolt.

5. Using tool J-23523, remove the damper pulley.

6. Remove the alternator and the brackets. If equipped with power steering, remove the lower pump bracket and swing aside.

7. Remove the heater and the lower radiator hoses from the water pump.

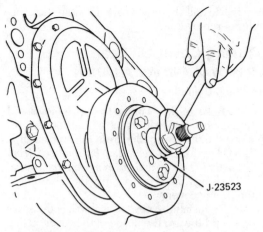

Installing the damper pulley

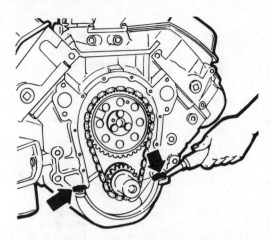

Apply sealer to the front pads at the area shown (V8)

8. Remove the water pump bolts and the pump from the engine.

9. Remove the timing cover bolts and the timing cover.

10. Using a putty knife, clean the gasket mounting surfaces.

11. To install, use new gaskets, sealant and reverse the removal procedures. Torque the timing cover bolts to 8 ft. lbs., the damper bolts to 65–75 ft. lbs. and the water pump bolts to 25–35 ft. lbs.

231 V6

1. Drain the cooling system. Remove the radiator hoses. Remove the radiator.

2. Remove all the drive belts. Remove the fan and fan pulley. Remove the bypass hose.

3. Remove the crank pulley, the fuel pump and the distributor. Note the position of the distributor rotor before you remove the distributor.

4. Remove the alternator and its bracket.

5. Remove the harmonic balancer. You'll need a puller.

6. Remove the two bolts which attach the

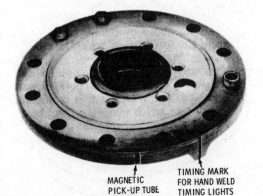

MAGNETIC
PICK-UP TUBE
TIMING MARK

TIMING MARK
FOR HAND WELD
TIMING LIGHTS

231 V6 harmonic balancer timing marks

oil pan to the front cover. Remove the bolts which attach the cover to the block.

7. Remove the cover and remove the gasket material.

8. To install, it is first necessary to remove the oil pump cover and pack the space around the oil pump gears completely full of petroleum jelly. *Do not use gear lube.* There must be no air space left inside the pump. Reinstall the pump cover using a new gasket. This step is very important since the oil pump may lose its prime any time the pump, pump cover or timing cover is disturbed. If the pump is not packed, it may not begin to pump oil as soon as the engine is started.

9. Install the cover, using a sealer and new gaskets. Make sure the dowel pins engage the dowel pin holes before starting the bolts. Apply sealer to the bolt threads.

10. Install the harmonic balancer, bolt and washer. It will be necessary to lock the flywheel in some way to torque the balancer bolt to specifications. Most mechanics remove the flywheel cover and lock the flywheel with suitable locking device.

11. The rest of the installation is in the reverse order of removal.

V8 and V6 Diesel Engines

1. Drain the cooling system and disconnect the radiator hoses.

2. Remove all belts, fan and pulley, crankshaft pulley and balancer, using a balancer puller.

CAUTION: *The use of any other type of puller, such as a universal claw type which pulls on the outside of the hub, can destroy the balancer. The outside ring of the balancer is bonded in rubber to the hub. Pulling on the outside will break the bond. The timing mark is on the outside ring. If it is sus-*

CHAMFER

Front cover dowel pin chamfer

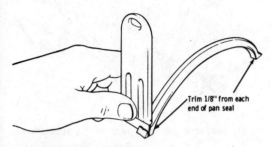

Trim 1/8" from each end of pan seal

Trimming pan seal with razor blade

pected that the bond is broken, check that the center of the keyway is 16° from the center of the timing slot. In addition, there are chiseled aligning marks between the weight and the hub.

3. Unbolt and remove the cover, timing indicator, water pump and both dowel pins.

4. It may be necessary to grind a flat on the cover for gripping purposes.

5. Grind a chamfer on one end of each dowel pin.

6. Cut the excess material from the front end of the oil pan gasket on each side of the block.

7. Clean the block, oil pan and front cover mating surfaces with solvent.

8. Trim about ⅛ in. off each end of a new front pan seal.

9. Install a new front cover gasket on the block and a new seal in the front cover.

10. Apply an R.T.V. sealer to the gasket around the coolant holes.

11. Apply an R.T.V. sealer to the block at the junction of the pan and front cover.

12. Place the cover on the block and press down to compress the seal. Rotate the cover left and right and guide the pan seal into the cavity using a small screwdriver. Oil the bolt threads and install two bolts to hold the cover in place. Install both dowel pins (chamfered end first), then install the remaining front cover bolts.

NOTE: *The front cover-to-block bolts on the V6 diesel must be coated with an adhesive, GM part #1052624 or equivalent to avoid coolant leaks and loss of bolt torque.*

13. Apply a lubricant, compatible with rubber, on the balancer seal surface.

14. Install the balancer and bolt. Torque the bolt to 200–300 ft. lbs. (160–350 ft. lbs. on V6).

15. Install the other parts in the reverse order of removal.

Timing Cover Oil Seal
REMOVAL AND INSTALLATION
Inline 6 Cylinder

1. Refer to the "Timing Cover Removal and Installation" procedures in this section and remove the damper pulley from the crankshaft.

NOTE: *The oil seal may be removed from the timing cover without removing the cover.*

2. Using a small pry bar, pry the oil seal from the timing cover.

3. To install the new oil seal, place the seal's open end toward the inside of the cover. Using the oil seal installation tool J-23042, drive the new oil seal into position.

4. To complete the installation, reverse the removal procedures. Torque the damper pulley bolt to 60 ft. lbs. and adjust the drive belts.

V8 And V6
COVER REMOVED

1. Refer to the "Timing Cover Removal and Installation" procedures in this section and remove the timing cover.

2. Using a small pry bar, pry the oil seal from the timing cover.

3. Using tool J-23042, drive the new oil seal into the timing cover.

NOTE: *When installing the new oil seal, be sure to support the rear side of the timing cover.*

4. To complete the installation, reverse the removal procedures.

COVER INSTALLED

1. Refer to the "Timing Cover Removal and Installation" procedures in this section and remove the balancer from the crankshaft.

2. Using a small pry bar, pry the oil seal from the timing cover.

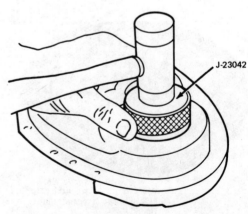

J-23042

Installing a new front oil seal

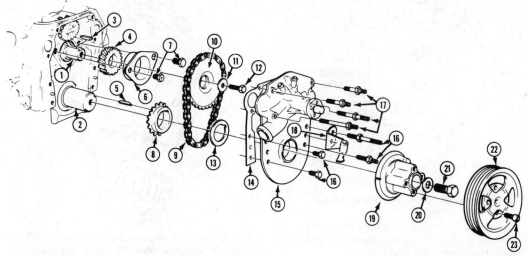

1. CAMSHAFT	9. TIMING CHAIN	17. 28 N·m (21 FT. LBS.) - APPLY ADHESIVE
2. CRANKSHAFT	10. CAMSHAFT SPROCKET	18. PROBE HOLDER (RPM COUNTER)
3. CAMSHAFT SPROCKET KEY	11. WASHER	19. CRANKSHAFT BALANCER
4. INJECTION PUMP DRIVE GEAR	12. 95 N·m (70 FT. LBS.)	20. WASHER
5. CRANKSHAFT SPROCKET KEY	13. SLINGER	21. 217-475 N·m (160 - 350 FT. LBS.)
6. FRONT CAMSHAFT BEARING RETAINER	14. GASKET	22. PULLEY ASSEMBLY
7. 65 N·m (48 FT. LBS.)	15. FRONT COVER	23. 40 N·m (30 FT. LBS.)
8. CRANKSHAFT SPROCKET	16. 57 N·m (42 FT. LBS.) - APPLY ADHESIVE	

263 V6 diesel front cover, timing assembly and bolt torque specifics

Oil seal installation with the cover removed

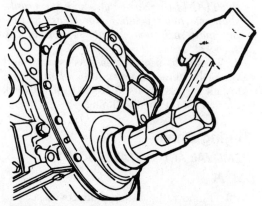

Oil seal installation with the cover installed

3. Place the new seal (open end toward the engine) on the timing cover and drive it into the cover using tool J-23042.

4. To complete the installation, reverse the removal procedures. Torque the balancer bolt to 65–75 ft. lbs.

Timing Gear

REMOVAL AND INSTALLATION

Inline 6 Cylinder

NOTE: *The timing gear is pressed onto the camshaft. To remove or install the timing gear an arbor must be used.*

1. Refer to the "Camshaft Removal and Installation" procedures in this section and remove the camshaft from the engine.

2. Using an arbor press, a press plate and a gear removal tool J-971, press the timing gear from the camshaft.

NOTE: *When pressing the timing gear from*

The inline six cylinder crankshaft gear is removed with a gear puller

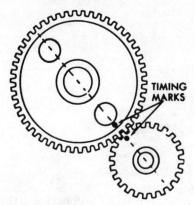

Timing gear alignment—inline six cylinder

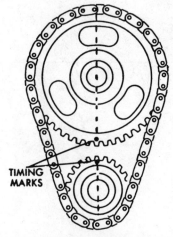

Timing sprocket alignment—V6 and V8 (1967–79) gasoline engines, plus V6 (1982–84) diesel engines

the camshaft, be certain that the position of the press plate does not contact the woodruff key.

3. To assemble, position the press plate to support the camshaft at the back of the front journal. Place the gear spacer ring and the thrust plate over the end of the camshaft, then install the woodruff key. Press the timing gear onto the camshaft, until it bottoms against the gear spacer ring.

NOTE: *The end clearance of the thrust plate should be 0.0015–0.005 inch. If less than 0.0015 in., replace the spacer ring; if more than 0.005 in., replace the thrust plate.*

4. To complete the installation, align the marks on the timing gears and reverse the removal procedures.

V8 And V6 Gasoline (Except 231 V6)

1. Refer the "Timing Cover Removal and Installation" procedures in this section and remove the water pump and the timing cover.

2. Turn the crankshaft until the mark on the camshaft sprocket aligns with the mark on the crankshaft sprocket.

3. Remove the camshaft sprocket bolts, the

V6 and V8 crankshaft sprocket removal using special puller

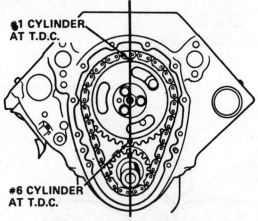

Timing sprocket alignment—V6 and V8 (1980 and later) gasoline engines, plus V8 diesel engines

camshaft sprocket, the timing chain and the crankshaft sprocket (if necessary).

NOTE: *When installing the timing chain, install the sprockets with the timing marks facing each another; this position is TDC of the No. 6 cyl. (V8) or No. 4 cyl. (V6). To locate the TDC of the No. 1 cyl., turn the crankshaft one full revolution, the camshaft timing mark will now be at the top of the sprocket.*

4. To install, use new gaskets, sealant and reverse the removal procedures. Torque the camshaft sprocket bolts to 13–23 ft. lbs. Check and/or adjust the engine timing.

Timing Chain
REMOVAL AND INSTALLATION

231 V6

1. Remove the timing chain cover.
2. Before removing anything else, make

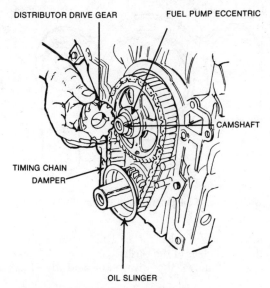

DISTRIBUTOR DRIVE GEAR   FUEL PUMP ECCENTRIC

CAMSHAFT

TIMING CHAIN
DAMPER

OIL SLINGER

Timing chain and gears—231 V6

sure the timing marks on the crankshaft and camshaft sprockets are aligned. This will greatly ease reinstallation of parts.

3. It is not necessary to remove the timing chain tensioners unless they are worn or damaged.

4. Remove the front crankshaft oil slinger.

5. Remove the bolt and the special washer that hold the camshaft distributor drive gear and fuel pump eccentric at the forward end of the camshaft.

6. Using a pair of prybars, alternately pry the camshaft sprocket, then the crankshaft sprocket forward until the camshaft sprocket is free.

7. After the camshaft sprocket and chain are removed, finish pulling the crankshaft sprocket off the crankshaft.

8. To install, if the engine has not been disturbed, proceed to Step Eleven.

9. If the engine has been disturbed, turn the crankshaft so that the number one piston is at top dead center.

10. Temporarily install the sprocket key and the camshaft sprocket on the camshaft. Turn the camshaft so that the index mark of the sprocket is pointing downward. Remove the key and the sprocket from the camshaft.

11. Assemble the timing chain and sprockets. Install the keys, sprockets, and chain assembly on the crankshaft and camshaft so that the index marks of both the sprockets are aligned. It will be necessary to hold the chain tensioners out of the way while installing the timing chain and sprocket assembly.

12. Install the front oil slinger on the crankshaft with the concave side toward the front of the engine.

13. Install the fuel pump eccentric with the oil groove forward.

14. Install the distributor drive gear on the camshaft.

15. Install the front cover.

350 V8 Diesel

1. Remove the front cover.

2. Remove the oil slinger and camshaft bolts, and remove the camshaft and crankshaft sprockets and timing chain as a unit.

3. Remove the fuel pump eccentric from the crankshaft if replacement is necessary.

4. To install, install the key in the crankshaft if removed. Also install the fuel pump eccentric if removed.

5. Install the camshaft and crankshaft sprockets and the timing chain together as a unit and align the timing marks as shown. Torque the camshaft sprocket bolt to 65 ft. lbs.

NOTE: *When the two timing marks are in alignment, number six is at T.D.C. To obtain T.D.C. for number one cylinder, slowly rotate the crankshaft one revolution. This will bring the cam mark to the top; number one will then be in firing position.*

6. Install the oil slinger and front cover.

NOTE: *Any time the timing chain and gears are replaced, it will be necessary to retime the injection system. Refer to the paragraph on Diesel Engine Injection Timing in Chapter 4.*

263 V6 Diesel

1. Remove the front cover.

2. Remove the valve covers and loosen all rocker arm pivot bolts evenly so that lash (looseness) exists between the rocker arms and the valves. See "Rocker Arm Removal" in this chapter. It is not necessary to remove the rockers completely.

3. Remove the crankshaft oil slinger.

4. Remove the camshaft-to-camshaft sprocket bolt and washer, and remove the timing chain, camshaft and crankshaft sprockets as a unit.

NOTE: *If the crank sprocket is a tight fit on the end of the crankshaft, you may have to use a sprocket puller to remove it.*

5. To install, if the camshaft sprocket-to-camshaft key should come out with the camshaft sprocket, perform the following by referring to the exploded drawing of the V6 diesel front cover.

  a. Remove the front camshaft bearing retainer.

  b. Install the key with the injection pump drive gear.

  c. Install the bearing retainer and bolts loose on the block.

d. Install the camshaft sprocket.

e. Rotate the camshaft at least 4 turns to center the retainer.

f. Remove the camshaft sprocket.

g. Torque the bearing retainer-to-block bolts evenly to 48 ft. lbs.

h. Rotate the camshaft to make sure it's free. If it is not, repeat steps a through h.

6. Install the key in the crankshaft, if removed.

7. Install the camshaft and crankshaft sprockets and the timing chain together as a unit. Align the timing marks as shown.

8. Torque the camshaft sprocket bolt to 70 ft. lbs.

9. Install the oil slinger.

10. Install the engine front cover. Bleed down the valve lifters as described in the "Rocker Arm" section in this chapter.

11. Install the valve covers and check and reset the injection pump timing.

Camshaft

REMOVAL AND INSTALLATION

Inline Six Cylinder

Due to the length of the inline six cylinder camshaft, a large amount of working room will be required in front of the engine to remove the camshaft. There are two ways to go about this task: either remove the engine from the car, or remove the radiator, grille and all supports which are mounted directly in front of the engine. If the second alternative is chosen, you must also disconnect the motor mounts and raise the front of the engine. If the second alternative is chosen, you must also disconnect the motor mounts and raise the front of the engine enough to gain the clearance necessary to remove the cam from the engine.

1. In addition to removing the timing gear cover, remove the grille and radiator.

2. Remove the valve cover and gasket,

Carefully turn camshaft slightly as you remove it.

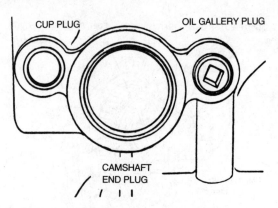

CUP PLUG   OIL GALLERY PLUG

CAMSHAFT END PLUG

Camshaft and oil gallery plugs at rear of block

loosen all the valve rocker arm nuts and pivot the arms clear of the pushrods.

3. Remove the distributor and the fuel pump.

4. Remove the coil, the side cover and its gasket. Remove the pushrods and valve lifters.

5. Remove the two camshaft thrust plate retaining screws by working through the holes in the camshaft gear.

6. Remove the camshaft and gear assembly by pulling it out through the front of the block.

NOTE: *If renewing either the camshaft or the camshaft gear, the gear must be pressed off the camshaft. The replacement parts must be assembled in the same manner (under pressure). In placing the gear on the camshaft, press the gear onto the shaft until it bottoms against the gear spacer ring. The end clearance of the thrust plate should be .001 to .005 in.*

7. Install the camshaft assembly in the engine.

NOTE: *Pre-lube the cam lobes with E.O.S. or SAE 90 gear lubricant. Do not dislodge the cam bearings when inserting the camshaft.*

8. Turn the crankshaft and the camshaft to align and bring the timing marks together. Push the camshaft into this aligned position. Install the camshaft thrust plate-to-block screws and torque them to 6–7½ ft. lbs.

9. Runout on either the crankshaft or the camshaft gear should not exceed .003 in.

10. Backlash between the two gears should be between .004 and .006 in.

11. Install the timing gear cover and its gasket.

12. Install the oil pan and gaskets.

13. Install the harmonic balancer.

14. Line up the keyway in the balancer with the key on the crankshaft and the drive balancer onto the shaft until it bottoms against the crankshaft gear.

15. Install the valve lifters and pushrods. Install the side cover with new gasket. Attach the coil wires; install the fuel pump.

16. Install the distributor and set the timing as described under "Distributor Installation" at the beginning of this section.

17. Pivot the rocker arms over the pushrods and then adjust the valves.

18. Add oil to the engine. Install and adjust the fan belt.

19. Install the radiator or shroud.

20. Install the grille assembly.

21. Fill the cooling system, start the engine and check for leaks.

22. Check and adjust the timing.

Gasoline V6 and V8 (except 231 V6)

1. Refer to the "Timing Chain Removal and Installation" procedures in this section and remove the camshaft sprocket and the timing chain.

NOTE: *If the camshaft sprocket is tight on the camshaft, use a plastic hammer to bump it loose.*

2. On the V8, remove the oil cooler lines and the hoses from the radiator, then the radiator.

3. Remove the intake manifold and the rocker arm covers.

4. On the V8, remove the AIR pump bracket and disconnect the fuel lines at the fuel pump, then remove the fuel pump.

5. If equipped with A/C on the V8, remove the compressor and the condenser, than move them aside.

6. Remove the rocker arm assemblies, the push rods and the valve lifters.

7. Install two 5/16 x 18 × 4 in. bolts in the camshaft and carefully pull it from the front of the engine.

NOTE: *When removing or replacing the camshaft, be careful not to damage the camshaft bearings.*

8. To install, reverse the removal procedures. Torque the camshaft mounting bolts to 13–23 ft. lbs. Check and/or adjust the engine timing. Refill the cooling system.

231 V6

1. Drain the engine coolant and remove the radiator and radiator hoses.

2. Remove the water pump and all the drive belts. Remove the alternator.

3. Remove the crankshaft pulley and the vibration damper.

4. Remove the intake manifold. Mark the location of the distributor and remove the distributor.

5. Remove the fuel pump. Remove the timing chain cover and the oil pump.

6. Remove the timing chain and the camshaft sprocket, along with the distributor drive gear and the fuel pump eccentric.

7. Remove the rocker arm covers and the rocker arm assemblies. Mark the pushrods and remove them. Remove the lifters. Mark them so they can be returned to their original position.

8. Carefully remove the camshaft from the engine. Make sure you don't damage the bearings.

9. Installation is in the reverse order of removal. Remember to pack the oil pump with petroleum jelly.

V8 and V6 Diesel Engine

NOTE: *If equipped with air conditioning, the system must be discharged by an air conditioning specialist before the camshaft is removed. The condenser must also be removed from the car.*

Removal of the camshaft also requires removal of the injection pump drive and driven gears, removal of the intake manifold, disassembly of the valve lifters, and re-timing of the injection pump.

1. Disconnect the negative battery cables. Drain the coolant. Remove the radiator.

2. Remove the intake manifold and gasket and the front and rear intake manifold seals. Refer to the "Intake Manifold Removal and Installation" procedure.

3. Remove the balancer pulley and the balancer. See "Caution" under "Diesel Engine Front Cover Removal and Installation," above. Remove the engine front cover using the appropriate procedure.

4. Remove the valve covers. Remove the rocker arms, pushrods and valve lifters; see the procedure earlier in this section. Be sure to keep the parts in order so that they may be returned to their original positions.

5. Remove the camshaft sprocket retaining bolt, and remove the timing chain and sprockets, using the procedure outlined earlier.

6. Position the camshaft dowel pin at the 3 o'clock position on the V8.

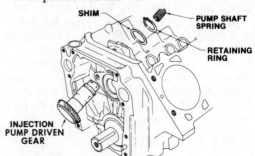

Diesel injection pump drive gear

7. On V8s, push the camshaft rearward and hold it there, being careful not to dislodge the oil gallery plug at the rear of the engine. Remove the fuel injection pump drive gear by sliding it from the camshaft while rocking the pump driven gear.

8. To remove the fuel injection pump driven gear, remove the pump adapter, the snap ring, and remove the selective washer. Remove the driven gear and spring.

9. Remove the camshaft by sliding it out the front of the engine. On the V6, install a longer bolt into the front hole on the camshaft, to act as a handle. Be extremely careful not to allow the cam lobes to contact any of the bearings, or the journals to dislodge the bearings during camshaft removal. Do not force the camshaft, or bearing damage will result.

10. If either the injection pump drive or driven gears are to be replaced, replace both gears.

11. Coat the camshaft and the cam bearings with a heavy-weight engine oil, GM lubricant #1052365 or the equivalent.

12. Carefully slide the camshaft into position in the engine.

13. Fit the crankshaft and camshaft sprockets, aligning the timing marks as shown in the timing chain removal and installation procedure, above. Remove the sprockets without disturbing the timing.

14. Install the injection pump driven gear, spring, shim, and snap ring. Check the gear end play. If the end play is not within 0.002–0.006 in. on V8s through 1979 and .002 to .015 in. on 1980–84, replace the shim to obtain the specified clearance. Shims are available in 0.003 in. increments, from 0.080 to 0.115 in.

15. Position the camshaft dowel pin at the 3 o'clock position. Align the zero marks on the pump drive gear and pump driven gear. Hold the camshaft in the rearward position and slide the pump drive gear onto the camshaft. Install the camshaft bearing retainer.

16. Install the timing chain and sprockets, making sure the timing marks are aligned.

17. Install the lifters, pushrods and rocker arms. See "Rocker Arm Replacement, Diesel Engine" for lifter bleed down procedures. *Failure to bleed down the lifters could bend valves when the engine is turned over.*

18. Install the injection pump adapter and injection pump. See the appropriate sections under "Fuel System" above for procedures.

19. Install the remaining components in the reverse order of removal.

CAMSHAFT INSPECTION

Completely clean the camshaft with solvent, paying special attention to cleaning the oil holes.

Visually inspect the cam lobes and bearing journals for excessive wear. If a lobe is questionable, have the cam checked at a reputable machine shop; if a journal or lobe is worn, the camshaft must be reground or replaced. Also have the camshaft checked for straightness on a dial indicator.

NOTE: *If a cam journal is worn, there is a good chance that the bushings are worn.*

Camshaft Bearings

REMOVAL AND INSTALLATION

If excessive camshaft wear is found, or if the engine is being completely rebuilt, the camshaft bearings should be replaced.

NOTE: *The front and rear bearings should be removed last, and installed first. Those bearings act as guides for the other bearings and pilot.*

1. Drive the camshaft rear plug from the block.

2. Assemble the removal puller with its shoulder on the bearing to be removed. Gradually tighten the puller nut until the bearing is removed.

3. Remove the remaining bearings, leaving the front and rear for last. To remove these, reverse the position of the puller, so as to pull the bearings towards the center of the block. Leave the tool in this position, pilot the new front and rear bearings on the installer, and pull them into position.

4. Return the puller to its original position and pull the remaining bearings into position.

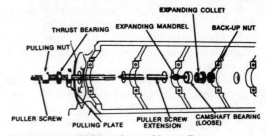

Remove camshaft bearings with a puller

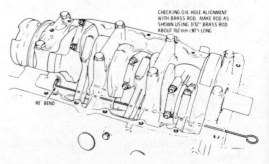

Check cam bearing alignment with this homemade tool

NOTE: *Ensure that the oil holes align when installing the bearings. This is very important! You can make a simple tool out of a piece of 3/32 in. brass rod to check alignment. See the illustration.*

5. Replace the camshaft rear plug, and stake it into position.

Pistons and Connecting Rods
REMOVAL AND INSTALLATION

Before removing the pistons, the top of the cylinder bore must be examined for a ridge. A ridge at the top of the bore is the result of normal cylinder wear, caused by the piston rings only travelling so far up the bore in the course of the piston stroke. The ridge can be felt by hand; it must be removed before the pistons are removed.

A ridge reamer is necessary for this operation. Place the piston at the bottom of its stroke, and cover it with a rag. Cut the ridge away with the ridge reamer, using extreme care to avoid cutting too deeply. Remove the rag, and remove the cuttings that remain on the piston with a magnet and a rag soaked in clean oil. *Make sure the piston top and cylinder bore are absolutely clean before moving the piston.*

1. Remove intake manifold and cylinder head or heads.
2. Remove oil pan.
3. Remove oil pump assembly if necessary.
4. Match-mark the connecting rod cap to the connecting rod with a scribe; each cap must be reinstalled on its proper rod in the proper direction. Remove the connecting rod bearing cap and the rod bearing. Number the top of each piston with silver paint or a felt-tip pen for later assembly.

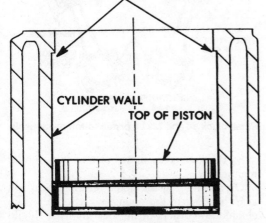

RIDGE CAUSED BY CYLINDER WEAR

CYLINDER WALL
TOP OF PISTON

This ridge must be removed before pistons are removed

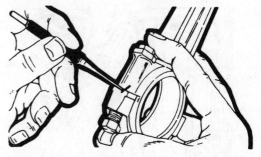

Match connecting rods to their caps with a scribe mark

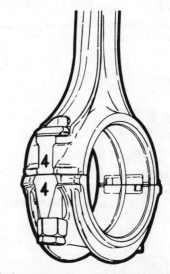

Match the connecting rods to their cylinders with a number stamp

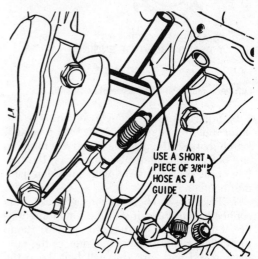

USE A SHORT PIECE OF 3/8" HOSE AS A GUIDE

Cut rubber hose for con-rod bolt guides

5. Cut lengths of 3/8 in. diameter hose to use as rod bolt guides. Install the hose over the threads of the rod bolts, to prevent the bolt threads from damaging the crankshaft journals and cylinder walls when the piston is removed.

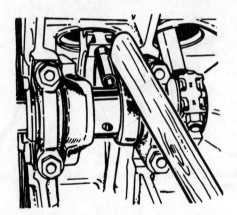

Carefully tap the piston and rod assembly out with a wooden hammer handle

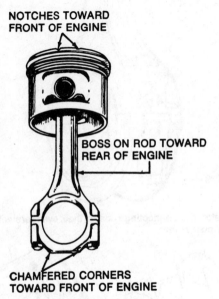

NOTCHES TOWARD FRONT OF ENGINE

BOSS ON ROD TOWARD REAR OF ENGINE

CHAMFERED CORNERS TOWARD FRONT OF ENGINE

LEFT NO. 1-3-5

Left bank piston and rod assembly, 231 V6

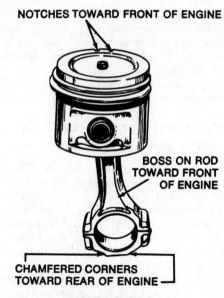

NOTCHES TOWARD FRONT OF ENGINE

BOSS ON ROD TOWARD FRONT OF ENGINE

CHAMFERED CORNERS TOWARD REAR OF ENGINE

RIGHT NO. 2-4-6

Right bank piston and rod assembly, 231 V6

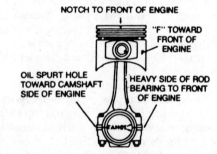

NOTCH TO FRONT OF ENGINE

"F" TOWARD FRONT OF ENGINE

OIL SPURT HOLE TOWARD CAMSHAFT SIDE OF ENGINE

HEAVY SIDE OF ROD BEARING TO FRONT OF ENGINE

Inline six cylinder piston-to-rod relationship

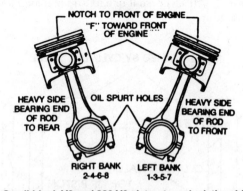

NOTCH TO FRONT OF ENGINE
"F" TOWARD FRONT OF ENGINE

HEAVY SIDE BEARING END OF ROD TO REAR

OIL SPURT HOLES

HEAVY SIDE BEARING END OF ROD TO FRONT

RIGHT BANK 2-4-6-8

LEFT BANK 1-3-5-7

Small-block V8 and 229 V6 piston-to-rod relationship

6. Squirt some clean engine oil onto the cylinder wall from above, until the wall is coated. Carefully push the piston and rod assembly up and out of the cylinder by tapping on the bottom of the connecting rod with a wooden hammer handle.

7. Place the rod bearing and cap back on the connecting rod, and install the nuts temporarily. Using a number stamp or punch, stamp the cylinder number on the side of the connecting rod and cap; this will help keep the proper piston and rod assembly on the proper cylinder.

NOTE: *On V6 engines, starting at the front the cylinders are numbered 2-4-6 on the right bank and 1-3-5 on the left. On all V8s, starting at the front the right bank cylinders are 2-4-6-8 and the left bank 1-3-5-7.*

8. Remove remaining pistons in similar manner.

On all engines, the notch on the piston will face the front of the engine for assembly. The chamfered corners of the bearing caps should face toward the front of the left bank and toward the rear of the right bank, and the boss on the

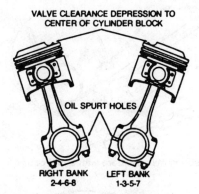

VALVE CLEARANCE DEPRESSION TO CENTER OF CYLINDER BLOCK

OIL SPURT HOLES

RIGHT BANK 2-4-6-8   LEFT BANK 1-3-5-7

Big-block (Mark IV) piston-to-rod relationship

connecting rod should face toward the front of the engine for the right bank and to the rear of the engine on the left bank.

On various engines, the piston compression rings are marked with a dimple, a letter "T", a letter "O," "GM" or the word "TOP" to identify the side of the ring which must face toward the top of the piston.

CLEANING AND INSPECTING

A piston ring expander is necessary for removing piston rings without damaging them; any other method (screwdriver blades, pliers, etc.) usually results in the rings being bent, scratched or distorted, or the piston itself being damaged. When the rings are removed, clean the ring grooves using an appropriate ring groove cleaning tool, using care not to cut too deeply. Thoroughly clean all carbon and varnish from the piston with solvent.

CAUTION: *Do not use a wire brush or caustic solvent (acids, etc.) on piston.*

Inspect the pistons for scuffing, scoring, cranks, pitting, or excessive ring groove wear. If these are evident, the piston must be replaced.

The piston should also be checked in relation to the cylinder diameter. Using a telescoping gauge and micrometer, or a dial gauge, measure the cylinder bore diameter perpendicular (90%) to the piston pin, 2½ in. below the cylinder block deck (surface where the block mates with the heads). Then, with the micrometer, measure the piston perpendicular to its wrist pin on the skirt. The difference between the two measurements is the piston clearance.

If the clearance is within specifications or slightly below (after the cylinders have been bored or honed), finish honing is all that is necessary. If the clearance is excessive, try to obtain a slightly larger piston to bring clearance to within specifications. If this is not possible obtain the first oversize piston and hone (or if necessary, bore) the cylinder to size. Gener-

ally, if the cylinder bore is tapered .005 in. or more or is out-of-round .003 in. or more, it is advisable to rebore for the smallest possible oversize piston and rings. After measuring, mark pistons with a felt-tip pen for reference and for assembly.

NOTE: *Cylinder block boring should be performed by a reputable machine shop with the proper equipment. In some cases, "cleanup" honing can be done with the cylinder block in the car, but most excessive honing and all cylinder boring must be done with the block stripped and removed from the car.*

Piston Ring and Wrist Pin
REMOVAL

Some of the engines covered in this guide utilize pistons with pressed-in wrist pins; these must be removed by a special press designed for this purpose. Other pistons have their wrist pins secured by snap rings, which are easily removed with snap ring pliers. Separate the piston from the connecting rod.

A piston ring expander is necessary for removing piston rings without damaging them; any other method (screwdriver blades, pliers, etc.) usually results in the rings being bent, scratched or distorted, or the piston itself being damaged. When the rings are removed, clean

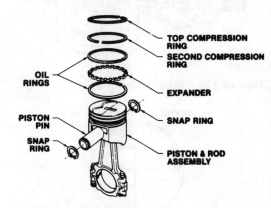

OIL RINGS

PISTON PIN

SNAP RING

TOP COMPRESSION RING

SECOND COMPRESSION RING

EXPANDER

SNAP RING

PISTON & ROD ASSEMBLY

Piston rings and wrist pin

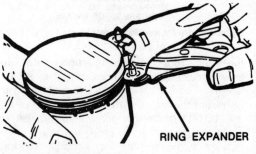

RING EXPANDER

Removing the piston rings

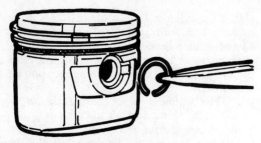

Removing wrist pin clips

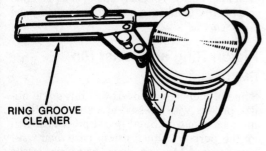

RING GROOVE CLEANER

Clean the piston ring grooves using a ring groove cleaner

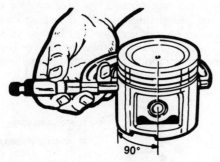

90°

Measuring the piston prior to fitting

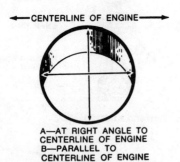

CENTERLINE OF ENGINE

A—AT RIGHT ANGLE TO CENTERLINE OF ENGINE
B—PARALLEL TO CENTERLINE OF ENGINE

Cylinder bore measuring points

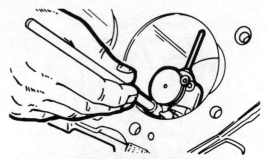

Measuring cylinder bore with a dial gauge

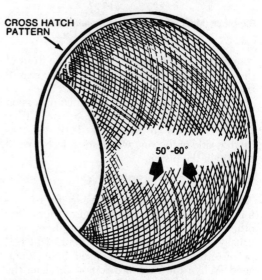

CROSS HATCH PATTERN

50°-60°

Cylinder bore cross-hatching after honing

the ring grooves using an appropriate ring groove cleaning tool, using care not to cut too deeply. Thoroughly clean all carbon and varnish from the piston with solvent.

CAUTION: *Do not use a wire brush or caustic solvent (acids, etc.) on pistons.*

Inspect the pistons for scuffing, scoring, cracks, pitting, or excessive ring groove wear. If these are evident, the piston must be replaced.

The piston should also be checked in relation to the cylinder diameter. Using a telescoping gauge and micrometer, or a dial gauge, measure the cylinder bore diameter perpendicular (90%) to the piston pin, 2½ in. below the cylinder block deck (surface where the block mates with the heads). Then, with the micrometer, measure the piston perpendicular to its wrist pin on the skirt. The difference between the two measurements is the piston clearance. If the clearance is within specifications or slightly below (after the cylinders have been bored or honed), finish honing is all that is necessary. If the clearance is excessive, try to obtain a slightly larger piston to bring clearance to within specifications. If this is not possible obtain the first oversize piston and hone (or if necessary, bore) the cylinder to size. Generally, if the cylinder bore is tapered .005 in. or more or is out-of-round .003 in. or more, it is advisable to rebore for the smallest possible oversize piston and rings.

After measuring, mark pistons with a felt-tip pen for reference and for assembly.

NOTE: *Cylinder honing and/or boring should be performed by a reputable, professional mechanic with the proper equipment. In some cases, "clean-up" honing can be done with the cylinder block in the car, but most excessive honing and all cylinder boring must be done with the block stripped and removed from the car.*

PISTON RING END GAP

Piston ring end gap should be checked while the rings are removed from the pistons. Incorrect end gap indicates the the wrong size rings are being used; *ring breakage could occur.*

Compress the piston rings to be used in a cylinder, one at a time, into that cylinder. Squirt

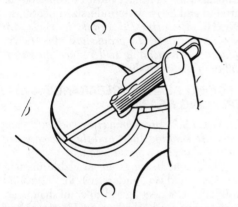

Checking piston ring end gap with a feeler gauge

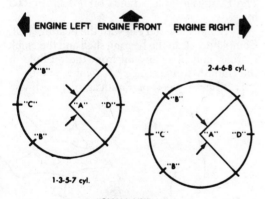

ENGINE LEFT   ENGINE FRONT   ENGINE RIGHT

2-4-6-8 cyl.

1-3-5-7 cyl.

"SMALL V8"

"A" OIL RING SPACER GAP
(Tang in Hole or Slot within Arc)

"B" OIL RING RAIL GAPS

"C" 2ND COMPRESSION RING CAP

"D" TOP COMPRESSION RING GAP

Ring gap location—all gasoline engines except 231 V6. For diesel ring gap, see diagram furnished with the new rings

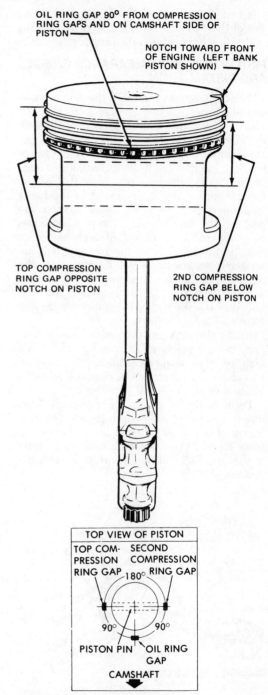

OIL RING GAP 90° FROM COMPRESSION RING GAPS AND ON CAMSHAFT SIDE OF PISTON

NOTCH TOWARD FRONT OF ENGINE (LEFT BANK PISTON SHOWN)

TOP COMPRESSION RING GAP OPPOSITE NOTCH ON PISTON

2ND COMPRESSION RING GAP BELOW NOTCH ON PISTON

TOP VIEW OF PISTON

TOP COM-PRESSION RING GAP

SECOND COMPRESSION RING GAP

180°

90°   90°

PISTON PIN   OIL RING GAP

CAMSHAFT

Piston ring gap location—231 V6

clean oil into the cylinder, so that the rings and the top 2 inches of cylinder wall are coated. Using an inverted piston, press the rings approximately 1 in. below the deck of the block (on diesels, measure ring gap clearance with the ring positioned at the *bottom* of ring travel in the bore). Measure the ring end gap with a feeler gauge, and compare to the "Ring Gap" chart in this chapter. Carefully pull the ring out of the cylinder and file the ends squarely with a fine file to obtain the proper clearance.

PISTON RING SIDE CLEARANCE CHECK AND INSTALLATION

Check the pistons to see that the ring grooves and oil return holes have been properly cleaned. Slide a piston ring into its groove, and check the side clearance with a feeler gauge. On gasoline engines, make sure you insert the gauge between the ring and its lower land (lower edge of the groove), because any wear that occurs forms a step at the inner portion of the lower land. On diesels, insert the gauge between the ring and the *upper* land. If the piston grooves have worn to the extent that relatively high steps exist on the lower land, the piston should be replaced, because these will interfere with the operation of the new rings and ring clearances will be excessive. Piston rings are not furnished in oversize widths to compensate for ring groove wear.

Install the rings on the piston, *lowest ring first,* using a piston ring expander. There is a high risk of breaking or distorting the rings, or scratching the piston, if the rings are installed by hand or other means.

Position the rings on the piston as illustrated; *spacing of the various piston ring gaps is crucial to proper oil retention and even cylinder wear.* When installing new rings, refer to the installation diagram furnished with the new parts.

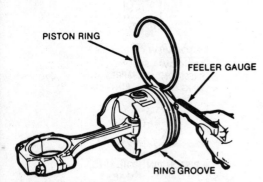

PISTON RING

FEELER GAUGE

RING GROOVE

Checking ring side clearance

Connecting Rod Bearings

Connecting rod bearings for the engines covered in this guide consist of two halves or shells which are interchangeable in the rod and cap. When the shells are placed in position, the ends extend slightly beyond the rod and cap surfaces so that when the rod bolts are torqued the shells will be clamped tightly in place to insure positive seating and to prevent turning. A tang holds the shells in place.

NOTE: *The ends of the bearing shells must never be filed flush with the mating surface of the rod and cap.*

If a rod bearing becomes noisy or is worn so that its clearance on the crank journal is sloppy, a new bearing of the correct undersize must be selected and installed since there is no provision for adjustment.

CAUTION: *Under no circumstances should the rod end or cap be filed to adjust the bearing clearance, nor should shims of any kind be used.*

Inspect the rod bearings while the rod assemblies are out of the engine. If the shells are scored or show flaking, they should be replaced. If they are in good shape check for proper clearance on the crank journal (see below). Any scoring or ridges on the crank journal means the crankshaft must be replaced, or reground and fitted with undersized bearings.

NOTE: *If turbo V6 crank journals are scored or ridged the crankshaft must be replaced, as regrinding will reduce the durability of the crankshaft.*

CHECKING BEARING CLEARANCE AND REPLACING BEARINGS

NOTE: *Make sure connecting rods and their caps are kept together, and that the caps are installed in the proper direction.*

Replacement bearings are available in standard size, and in undersizes for reground crankshafts. Connecting rod-to-crankshaft bearing clearance is checked using Plastigage® at either the top or bottom of each crank journal. The Plastigage® has a range of .001 in. to .003 in.

1. Remove the rod cap with the bearing shell. Completely clean the bearing shell and the crank journal, and blow any oil from the oil hole in the crankshaft; Plastigage® is soluble in oil.

2. Place a piece of Plastigage® lengthwise

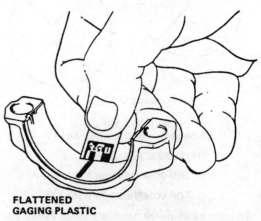

FLATTENED GAGING PLASTIC

Checking rod bearing clearance with Plastigage® or equivalent

TANG

GM M 400

8943

UNDERSIZE STAMP
IN THOUSANDS

**Undersize marks are stamped on the bearing shells.
Tangs fit in the notches in the rod and cap**

along the bottom center of the lower bearing shell, then install the cap with shell and torque the bolt or nuts to specification. DO NOT turn the crankshaft with Plastigage® in the bearing.

3. Remove the bearing cap with the shell. The flattened Plastigage® will be found sticking to either the bearing shell or crank journal. *Do not remove it yet.*

4. Use the scale printed on the Plastigage® envelope to measure the flattened material at its widest point. The number within the scale which most closely corresponds to the width of the Plastigage® indicates bearing clearance in thousandths of an inch.

5. Check the specifications chart in this chapter for the desired clearance. It is advisable to install a new bearing if clearance exceeds .003 in.; however, if the bearing is in good condition and is not being checked because of bearing noise, bearing replacement is not necessary.

6. If you are installing new bearings, try a standard size, then each undersize in order until one is found that is within the specified limits when checked for clearance with Plastigage®. Each undersize shell has its size stamped on it.

7. When the proper size shell is found, clean off the Plastigage®, oil the bearing thoroughly, reinstall the cap with its shell and torque the rod bolt units to specification.

NOTE: *With the proper bearing selected and the nuts torqued, it should be possible to move the connecting rod back and forth freely on the crank journal as allowed by the specified connecting rod end clearance. If the rod cannot be moved, either the rod bearing is too far undersize or the rod is misaligned.*

PISTON AND CONNECTING ROD ASSEMBLY AND INSTALLATION

Install the connecting rod to the piston, making sure piston installation notches and any marks on the rod are in proper relation to one another. Lubricate the wrist pin with clean engine oil, and install the pin into the rod and piston assembly, either by hand or by using a wrist pin press as required. Install snap rings of equipped, and rotate them in their grooves to make sure they are seated. To install the piston and connecting rod assembly:

1. Make sure connecting rod big-end bearings (including end cap) are of the correct size and properly installed.

2. Fit rubber hoses over the connecting rod bolts to protect the crankshaft journals, as in the "Piston Removal" procedure. Coat the rod bearings with clean oil.

3. Using the proper ring compressor, insert the piston assembly into the cylinder so that the notch in the top of the piston faces the front of the engine (this assumes that the dimple(s) or other markings on the connecting rods are in correct relation to the piston notch(s)).

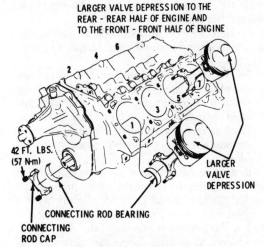

LARGER VALVE DEPRESSION TO THE
REAR - REAR HALF OF ENGINE AND
TO THE FRONT - FRONT HALF OF ENGINE

42 FT. LBS.
(57 N·m)

LARGER
VALVE
DEPRESSION

CONNECTING ROD BEARING
CONNECTING
ROD CAP

Piston locations in block, diesel shown

RING COMPRESSOR

Using a wooden hammer handle, tap the piston down through the ring compressor and into the cylinder

Checking connecting rod side clearance with a feeler gauge. Use a small pry bar to carefully spread the connecting rods

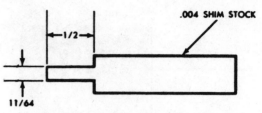

Dimensions for making an oil seal installation tool

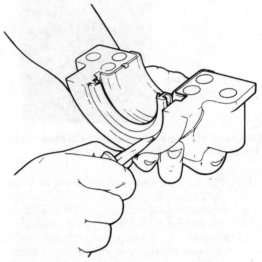

Removing the lower rear main seal

4. From beneath the engine, coat each crank journal with clean oil. Pull the connecting rod, with the bearing shell in place, into position against the crank journal.

5. Remove the rubber hoses. Install the bearing cap and cap nuts and torque to specification.

NOTE: *When more than one rod and piston assembly is being installed, the connecting rod cap attaching nuts should only be tightened enough to keep each rod in position until all have been installed. This will ease the installation of the remaining piston assemblies.*

6. Check the clearance between the sides of the connecting rods and the crankshaft using a feeler gauge. Spread the rods slightly with a screwdriver to insert the gage. If clearance is below the minimum tolerance, the rod may be machined to provide adequate clearance. If clearance is excessive, substitute an unworn rod, and recheck. If clearance is still outside specifications, the crankshaft must be welded and reground, or replaced.

7. Replace the oil pump if removed and the oil pan.

8. Install the cylinder head(s) and intake manifold.

Rear Main Oil Seal

REMOVAL AND INSTALLATION

All Engines (Except 231 and Diesel)

1. Refer to the "Oil Pan Removal and Installation" procedures in this section and remove the oil pan.

2. Remove the oil pump and the rear main bearing cap.

3. Using a small pry bar, pry the oil seal from the rear main bearing cap.

4. Using a small hammer and a brass pin punch, drive the top half of the oil seal from the rear main bearing. Drive it out far enough, so it may be removed with a pair of pliers.

5. Using a non-abrasive cleaner, clean the rear main bearing cap and the crankshaft.

6. Fabricate an oil seal installation tool from 0.004 in. shim stock, shape the end to ½ in. long by 11/64 in. wide.

7. Coat the new oil seal with engine oil; DO NOT coat the ends of the seal.

8. Position the fabricated tool between the crankshaft and the seal seat in the cylinder case.

9. Position the new half seal between the crankshaft and the tip of the tool, so that the seal bead contacts the tip of the tool.

NOTE: *Make sure that the seal lip is positioned toward the front of the engine.*

10. Using the fabricated tool as a shoe horn, to protect the seal's bead from the sharp edge of the seal seat surface in the cylinder case, roll the seal around the crankshaft. When the seal's ends are flush with the engine block, remove the installation.

11. Using the same manner of installation,

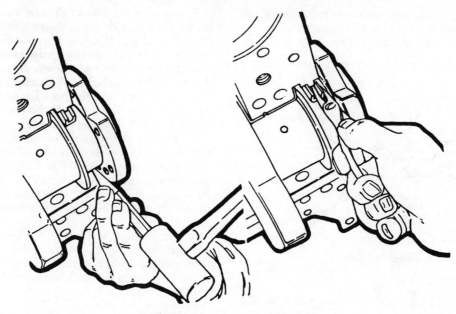

Removing the upper rear main seal

install the lower half onto the lower half of the rear main bearing cap.

12. Apply sealant to the cap-to-case mating surfaces and install the lower rear main bearing half to the engine; keep the sealant off of the seal's mating line.

13. Install the rear main bearing cap bolts and torque to 10–12 ft. lbs. Using a lead hammer, tap the crankshaft forward and rearward, to line up the thrust surfaces. Torque the main bearing bolts to 70–85 ft. lbs. (V6 and V8) or 60–75 ft. lbs. (inline 6 cyl) and reverse the removal procedures. Refill the crankshaft.

231 V6

On this engine, the upper half of the rear main bearing oil seal may be repaired, but not replaced, with the crankshaft in place. To completely replace the seal, the crankshaft must be removed. The lower part of the seal may be replaced in the conventional manner when the bearing cap is removed.

NOTE: *Place the new bearing cap neoprene seals in kerosene for two minutes before installing them. The neoprene seals will swell up once exposed to the oil and heat when in the engine. It is normal for the seals to leak for a short time, until they become properly seated. The seals must NOT be cut to fit.*

1. Remove the oil pan and the rear main bearing cap.

2. Using a blunt-edged tool, drive the upper seal into its groove until it is tightly packed. This is usually ¼–¾ in.

3. Cut pieces of a new seal ¹⁄₁₆ in. longer

than required to fill the grooves and install them, packing them into place.

4. Carefully trim any protruding edges of the seal.

5. Remove the old seal from the bearing cap, and install a new seal.

NOTE: *To help eliminate oil leakage at the joint where the cap meets the crankcase, apply RTV-type sealer to the rear main bearing cap split line. When applying sealer, use*

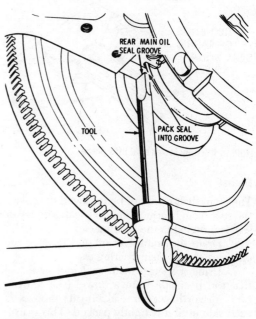

REAR MAIN OIL
SEAL GROOVE

TOOL

PACK SEAL
INTO GROOVE

Packing the rear main oil seal

only a thin coat as an overabundance will not allow the cap to seat properly.

6. Reinstall the cap and the oil pan.

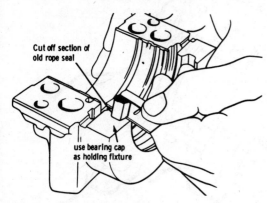

Cutting off the lower seal ends

Cut off section of old rope seal

use bearing cap as holding fixture

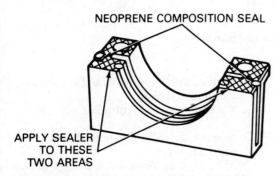

NEOPRENE COMPOSITION SEAL

APPLY SEALER TO THESE TWO AREAS

231 V6 lower main bearing cap. Sealer application. DO NOT over-apply

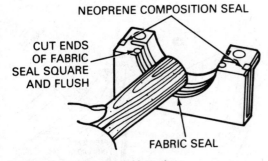

NEOPRENE COMPOSITION SEAL

CUT ENDS OF FABRIC SEAL SQUARE AND FLUSH

FABRIC SEAL

Rolling the new lower seal into place

Diesel

The crankshaft need not be removed to replace the rear main bearing upper oil seal. The lower seal is installed in the bearing cap.

1. Drain the crankshaft oil and remove the oil pan and rear main bearing cap.

2. Using a special main seal tool or a tool that can be made from a dowel (see illustration), drive the upper seal into its groove on each side until it is tightly packed. This is usually ¼–¾ in.

3. Measure the amount the seal was driven up on one side; add ¹⁄₁₆ in., then cut this length from the old seal that was removed from the main bearing cap. Use a single-edge razor blade. Measure the amount the seal was driven up on the other side; add ¹⁄₁₆ in. and cut another length from the old seal. Use the main bearing cap as a holding fixture when cutting the seal as illustrated. Carefully trim the protruding seal.

4. Work these two pieces of seal up into the cylinder block on each side with two nailsets or small screwdrivers. Using the packing tool again, pack these pieces into the block, then trim then flush with a razor blade or hobby knife as shown. *Do not scratch the bearing surface with the razor.*

5. Install a new seal in the rear main bearing cap. Run a ¹⁄₁₆ in. bead of sealer onto the outer mating surface of the bearing cap. Assemble the cap to the block and torque to specifications.

Crankshaft and Main Bearings

CRANKSHAFT REMOVAL

1. Drain the engine oil and remove the engine from the car. Mount the engine on a work stand in a suitable working area. Invert the engine, so the oil pan is facing up.

2. Remove the engine front (timing) cover.

3. Remove the timing chain and gears.

4. Remove the oil pan.

5. Remove the oil pump.

6. Stamp the cylinder number on the machined surfaces of the bolt bosses of the connecting rods and caps for identification when reinstalling. If the pistons are to be removed eventually from the connecting rod, mark the cylinder number on the pistons with silver paint or felt-tip pen for proper cylinder identification and cap-to-rod location.

7. Remove the connecting rod caps. Install lengths of rubber hose on each of the connecting rod bolts, to protect the crank journals when the crank is removed.

8. Mark the main bearing caps with a number punch or punch so that they can be reinstalled in their original positions.

9. Remove all main bearing caps.

10. Note the position of the keyway in the crankshaft so it can be installed in the same position.

11. Install rubber bands between a bolt on each connecting rod and oil pan bolts that have been reinstalled in the block (see illustration). This will keep the rods from banging on the block when the crank is removed.

12. Carefully lift the crankshaft out of the block. The rods will pivot to the center of the engine when the crank is removed.

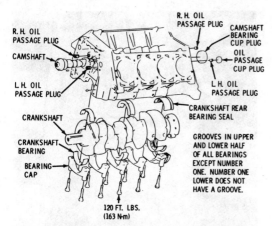

R. H. OIL PASSAGE PLUG
CAMSHAFT
L. H. OIL PASSAGE PLUG
CRANKSHAFT
CRANKSHAFT BEARING
BEARING CAP

R. H. OIL PASSAGE PLUG
CAMSHAFT BEARING CUP PLUG
OIL PASSAGE CUP PLUG
L. H. OIL PASSAGE PLUG
CRANKSHAFT REAR BEARING SEAL
GROOVES IN UPPER AND LOWER HALF OF ALL BEARINGS EXCEPT NUMBER ONE. NUMBER ONE LOWER DOES NOT HAVE A GROOVE.
120 FT. LBS. (163 N·m)

Diesel crankshaft, exploded view. Gasoline engines similar; bearing configuration may differ among engines

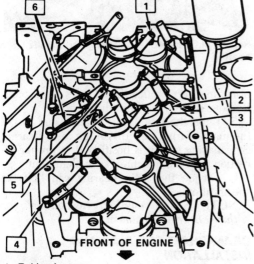

FRONT OF ENGINE

1. Rubber hose
2. #4 rod
3. #3 rod
4. Oil pan bolt
5. Note overlap of adjacent rods
6. Rubber bands

Crankshaft removal showing hose lengths on rod bolts

MAIN BEARING INSPECTION AND REPLACEMENT

Like connecting rod big-end bearings, the crankshaft main bearings are shell-type inserts that do not utilize shims and cannot be adjusted. The bearings are available in various standard and undersizes; if main bearing clearance is found to be too sloppy, a new bearing (both upper and lower halves) is required.

NOTE: *Factory-undersized crankshafts are marked, sometimes with a "9" and/or a large*

spot of light green paint; the bearing caps also will have the paint on each side of the undersized journal.

Generally, the lower half of the bearing shell (except No. 1 bearing) shows greater wear and fatigue. If the lower half only shows the effects of normal wear (no heavy scoring or discoloration), it can usually be assumed that the upper half is also in good shape; conversely, if the lower half is heavily worn or damaged, both halves should be replaced. *Never replace one bearing half without replacing the other.*

CHECKING CLEARANCE

Main bearing clearance can be checked both with the crankshaft in the car and with the engine out of the car. If the engine block is still in the car, the crankshaft should be supported both front and rear (by the damper and to remove clearance from the upper bearing. Total clearance can then be measured between the lower bearing and journal. If the block has been removed from the car, and is inverted, the crank will rest on the upper bearings and the total clearance can be measured between the lower bearing and journal. Clearance is checked in the same manner as the connecting rod bearings, with Plastigage®.

NOTE: *Crankshaft bearing caps and bearing shells should NEVER be filed flush with the cap-to-block mating surface to adjust for wear in the old bearings. Always install new bearings.*

1. If the crankshaft has been removed, install it (block removed from car). If the block is still in the car, remove the oil pan and oil pump. Starting with the rear bearing cap, remove the cap and wipe all oil from the crank journal and bearing cap.

2. Place a strip of Plastigage® the full width of the bearing, (parallel to the crankshaft), on the journal.

CAUTION: *Do not rotate the crankshaft while the gaging material is between the bearing and the journal.*

3. Install the bearing cap and evenly torque the cap bolts to specification.

4. Remove the bearing cap. The flattened Plastigage® will be sticking to either the bearing shell or the crank journal.

5. Use the graduated scale on the Plastigage® envelope to measure the material at its widest point.

NOTE: *If the flattened Plastigage® tapers towards the middle or ends, there is a difference in clearance indicating the bearing or journal has a taper, low spot or other irregularity. If this is indicated, measure the crank journal with a micrometer.*

6. If bearing clearance is within specifica-

tions, the bearing insert is in good shape. Replace the insert if the clearance is not within specifications. *Always replace both upper and lower inserts as a unit.*

7. Standard, .001in. or .002 in. undersize bearings should produce the proper clearance. If these sizes still produce too sloppy a fit, the crankshaft must be reground for use with the next undersize bearing. Recheck all clearances after installing new bearings.

8. Replace the rest of the bearings in the same manner. After all bearings have been checked, rotate the crankshaft to make sure there is no excessive drag. When checking the No. 1 main bearing, loosen the accessory drive belts (engine in car) to prevent a tapered reading with the Plastigage.®

MAIN BEARING REPLACEMENT

Engine Out of Car

1. Remove and inspect the crankshaft.
2. Remove the main bearings from the bearing saddles in the cylinder block and main bearing caps.
3. Coat the bearing surfaces of the new, correct size main bearings with clean engine oil and install them in the bearing saddles in the block and in the main bearing caps.
4. Install the crankshaft. See "Crankshaft Installation."

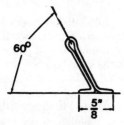

Home-made bearing roll-out pin

Engine in Car

1. With the oil pan, oil pump and spark plugs removed, remove the cap from the main bearing needing replacement and remove the bearing from the cap.
2. Make a bearing roll-out pin, using a bent cotter pin as shown in the illustration. Install the end of the pin in the oil hole in the crankshaft journal.
3. Rotate the crankshaft clockwise as viewed from the front of the engine. This will roll the upper bearing out of the block.
4. Lube the new upper bearing with clean engine oil and insert the plain (unnotched) end between the crankshaft and the indented or notched side of the block. Roll the bearing into

Roll-out pin installed for removing upper half of main bearing

place, making sure that the oil holes are aligned. Remove the roll pin from the oil hole.

5. Lube the new lower bearing and install the main bearing cap. Install the main bearing cap, making sure it is positioned in proper direction with the matchmarks in alignment.
6. Torque the main bearing cap bolts to specification.

NOTE: *See "Crankshaft Installation" for thrust bearing alignment.*

CRANKSHAFT END PLAY AND INSTALLATION

When main bearing clearance has been checked, bearings examined and/or replaced, the crankshaft can be installed. Thoroughly clean the upper and lower bearing surfaces, and lube them with clean engine oil. Install the crankshaft and main bearing caps.

Dip all main bearing cap bolts in clean oil, and torque all main bearings caps, excluding the thrust bearing cap, to specifications (see the "Crankshaft and Connecting Rod" chart in this chapter to determine which bearing is the thrust bearing). Tighten the thrust bearing bolts finger tight. To align the thrust bearing, pry the crankshaft the extent of its axial travel several times, holding the last movement toward the front of the engine. Add thrust washers if required for proper alignment. Torque the thrust bearing cap to specifications.

To check crankshaft end-play, pry the crankshaft to the extreme rear of its axial travel, then to the extreme front of its travel. Using a feeler

Measuring crankshaft-end-play with a feeler gauge

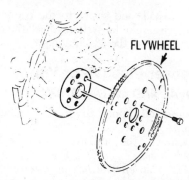
Flywheel installation. Follow torque specifications closely

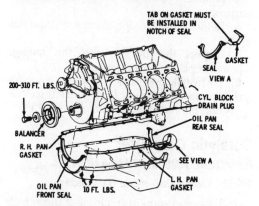
Oil pan installation. Gaskets and seals differ slightly among engines

gauge, measure the end-play at the front of the rear main bearing. End play may also be measured at the thrust bearing. Install a new rear main bearing oil seal in the cylinder block and main bearing cap. Continue to reassemble the engine.

Flywheel and Ring Gear
REMOVAL AND INSTALLATION
The ring gear is an integral part of the flywheel and is not replaceable.
1. Remove the transmission.
2. Remove the six bolts attaching the fly-

wheel to the crankshaft flange. Remove the flywheel.
3. Inspect the flywheel for cracks, and inspect the ring gear for burrs or worn teeth. Replace the flywheel if any damage is apparent. Remove burrs with a mill file.
4. Install the flywheel. The flywheel will only attach to the crankshaft in one position, as the bolt holes are unevenly spaced. Install the bolts and torque to specification.

EXHAUST SYSTEM

Before removing any component of the exhaust system, ALWAYS squirt a liquid rust busting agent onto fasteners to dissolve the rust and reduce the friction.

Tailpipe
REMOVAL AND INSTALLATION
1. Raise and support the vehicle on jackstands.
2. Remove the hanger clamps from the tailpipe.
3. Remove the tailpipe-to-muffler clamp.
4. Disengage the tailpipe from the muffler and remove the tailpipe.
5. Inspect the tailpipe hangers; replace, if necessary.

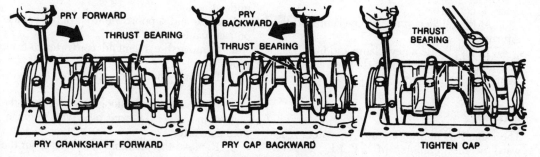
Aligning crankshaft thrust bearing

6. To install, add sealer to the connecting surfaces, assemble the system, check the clearances and tighten the attachments.

Crossover Pipe (V6 or V8)
REMOVAL AND INSTALLATION

1. Raise and support the front of vehicle on jackstands.

2. Remove the exhaust pipe-to-exhaust manifolds nuts.

NOTE: *The left-side has an extension and packing; the right-side has a heat riser valve assembly.*

3. Loosen the catalytic converter-to-transmission bracket.

4. Remove the crossover-to-catalytic converter clamp and the pipe from the converter.

NOTE: *Check and lubricate the heat riser valve to make sure that it is operating properly.*

5. To install, add sealer to the connecting surfaces, assemble the system, check the clearances and tighten all of the attachments.

Front Pipe
REMOVAL AND INSTALLATION

1. Raise and support the front of the vehicle on jackstands.

2. Remove the exhaust pipe-to-manifold nuts.

3. Support the catalytic converter and disconnect the pipe from the converter. Remove the pipe.

4. To install, use a new gasket, add sealer to the connecting surfaces, assemble the system, check the clearances and tighten the connectors.

Intermediate Pipe

The intermediate pipe is the section between the catalytic converter and the muffler.

REMOVAL AND INSTALLATION

1. Raise and support the front of the vehicle.

2. Disconnect the intermediate pipe from the catalytic converter.

3. At the muffler, remove the clamp and the intermediate pipe.

4. To install, use a new clamp and nuts/bolts, assemble the system, check the clearances and tighten the connectors.

Muffler

The exhaust system pipes and resonators rearward of the mufflers, MUST BE replaced whenever a new muffler is installed.

REMOVAL AND INSTALLATION

1. Raise and support the vehicle on jackstands.

2. On the single pipe system, cut the exhaust pipe near the front of the muffler. On the dual pipe system, remove the "U" bolt clamp at the front of the muffler and disengage the muffler from the exhaust pipe.

CAUTION: *Before cutting the exhaust pipe, measure the service muffler exhaust pipe extension and make certain to allow 1½ in. for the exhaust pipe-to-muffler extension engagement.*

3. At the rear of the muffler, remove the "U" bolt clamp and disengage the muffler from the tailpipe.

4. Remove the tailpipe clamps and the tailpipe.

5. Inspect the muffler and the tailpipe hangers; replace, if necessary.

6. To install, add sealer to the connecting surfaces, assemble the system, check the clearances and tighten all of the attachments.

Catalytic Converter
REMOVAL AND INSTALLATION
Except California—Inline 6 Cylinder

1. Raise and support the front of the vehicle on jackstands.

2. Remove the clamp at the front of the converter, then cut the pipe at the front of the converter.

3. Remove the converter-to-intermediate pipe nuts/bolts.

4. Disconnect the converter-to-transmission bracket. Remove the converter.

5. Remove the converter-to-crossover pipe or front pipe.

6. To install, add sealer to the connecting surfaces, use new clamps and nuts/bolts, assemble the system, check the clearances and tighten all of the attachments.

California—Inline 6 Cylinder

This model has a catalytic converter mounted to the exhaust manifold in addition to the one under the floor.

1. Raise and support the front of the vehicle on jackstands.

2. Remove the manifold converter-to-front pipe.

3. Remove the manifold converter-to-exhaust manifold nuts.

4. Remove the underfloor converter from the hanger and lower the front pipe with the manifold converter.

5. Remove the manifold converter from the front pipe.

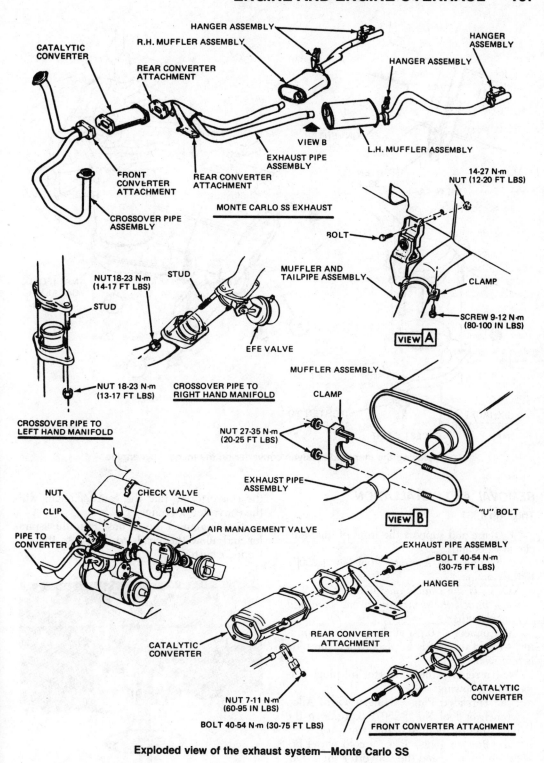

Exploded view of the exhaust system—Monte Carlo SS

6. To install, add sealer to the connecting surfaces, use new clamps and nuts/bolts, assemble the system, check the clearances and tighten all of the attachments.

Catalyst (Gasoline)

The catalyst can be replaced while the converter is on the vehicle.

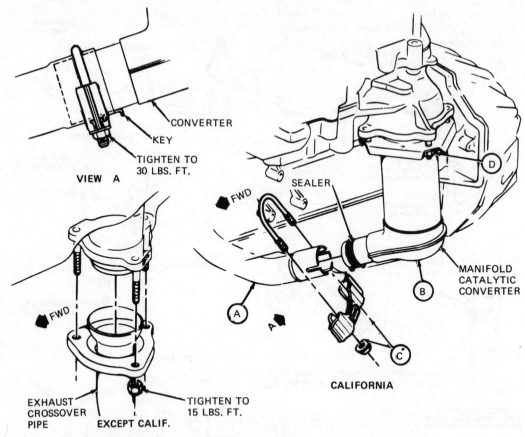

Replacing the manifold catalytic converter on the inline 6 cyl engine

REMOVAL AND INSTALLATION

Through 1981

1. Raise and support the front of the vehicle on jackstands.

2. Connect an Aspirator tool No. J-25077 to the tailpipe.

NOTE: *If the vehicle has dual exhaust systems, attach the aspirator to one pipe and plug the other.*

3. Connect a 60 psi air hose to the aspirator, to hold the beads in place when the plug is removed.

4. To remove the converter fill plug, perform the following:

   a. Threaded Plug—Using a ¾ in. Allen wrench or tool No. J-25077-3, remove the plug from the bottom of the converter.

   b. Pressed Plug—Place a cold chisel between the plug and the converter shell. Deform the plug until it can be removed with a pair of pliers.

NOTE: *When using the chisel, be careful not to damage the converter shell. DO NOT pry on the plug, for it may damage the converter's sealing opening.*

5. Connect the Vibrator tool J-25077-6 to

the converter so that the canister aligns with the converter opening.

6. Disconnect the air hose from the aspirator and allow the beads to drop into the collecting canister.

Using the fill tube to fill the converter with catalyst

7. Connect a 60 psi air hose to the vibrator and allow the excess beads to be removed from the converter, then disconnect the air hose. Remove the canister from the vibrator and discard the used catalyst.

8. Fill the container with an approved replacement catalyst.

9. Install the fill tube extension to the vibrator fixture.

10. Connect the air hoses to the aspirator and the vibrator, then attach the canister.

11. After the catalyst stops flowing, disconnect the air hose from the vibrator. Remove the vibrator from the converter and check to see if the catalyst is flush with the fill plug hole (add catalyst if necessary).

12. To install the converter plug, perform the following:

    a. Threaded Plug—Apply an anti-seize compound to the threaded fill plug; install it and torque to 60 ft. lbs.

    b. Press Plug—Use a service plug. Install the bolt into the bridge, then the bridge into the converter's hole, by moving the bridge back-and-forth to dislodge the catalyst beads until the bridge is positioned. Remove the bolt from the bridge then position the washer and the fill plug (dished side out) over the bolt. Install the assembly to the bridge 4–5 turns and release the full plug (the aspirator will pull the plug into position). Torque the bolt to 28 ft. lbs.

13. Disconnect the air hose from the aspirator.

14. Start the vehicle and check for leaks.

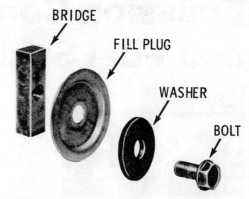

Exploded view of the replacement fill plug

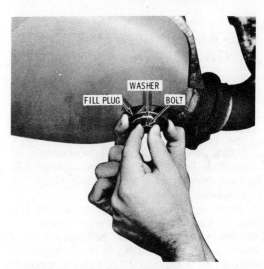

Installing the replacement fill plug

Emission Controls and Fuel System

GASOLINE ENGINE EMISSION CONTROLS

NOTE: *Due to the complex nature of modern electronic engine control systems, comprehensive diagnosis and testing procedures fall outside the confines of this repair manual. For complete information on diagnosis, testing and repair procedures concerning all modern engine and emission control systems, please refer to* **Chilton's Guide To Electronic Engine Controls**.

There are three sources of automotive pollutants: Crankcase fumes, exhaust gases and gasoline evaporation. The pollutants formed from these substances fall into three categories: unburnt hydrocarbons (HC), carbon monoxide (CO) and oxides of nitrogen (NOx). The equipment that is used to limit these pollutants is commonly called emission control equipment.

Positive Crankcase Ventilation

OPERATION

Until 1967, mid-size Chevrolets were available with two types of crankcase ventilation systems: the closed type found on all California cars and some non-California cars, or the open type. The open ventilation system (non-California cars) receives outside air through a vented oil filler cap. This filtered cap permits outside air to enter the valve cover and also allows crankcase vapors to escape from the valve cover into the atmosphere The 1967 California law and later Federal law requires that this filler cap be non-vented to prevent the emission of vapors into the air. To supply this closed system with fresh air, a hose runs from the carburetor air cleaner to an inlet hole in the valve cover. The carburetor end of the hose fits into a cup-shaped flame arrestor and filter in the air cleaner cover. In the event of a carburetor backfire, this arrestor prevents the spread of fire to the valve cover where it could create an explosion. Included in the system is a PCV (positive crankcase ventilation) valve that fits into an outlet hole in the top of the valve cover. A hose connects this valve to a vacuum outlet at the intake manifold. Contained within the valve housing is a valve (pointed at one end, flat at the other) positioned within a coiled spring. During idle or low speed operation, when manifold vacuum is highest, the valve spring tension is overcome by the high vacuum pull and, as a result, the valve is pulled up to very nearly seal off the manifold end of the valve housing. This restricts the flow of crankcase vapors to the intake manifold at a time when crankcase pressures are lowest and least disruptive to engine performance. At times of acceleration or constant speed, intake manifold vacuum is reduced to a point where it can no longer pull against the valve spring and so, spring force pulls the valve away from the housing outlet allowing crankcase vapors to escape through the hose to the intake manifold. Once inside the manifold, the gases enter the combustion chambers

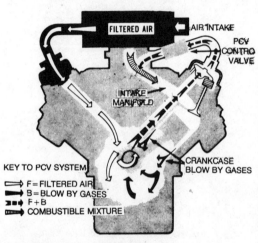

KEY TO PCV SYSTEM

F = FILTERED AIR
B = BLOW BY GASES
F + B
COMBUSTIBLE MIXTURE

Schematic of the PCV system

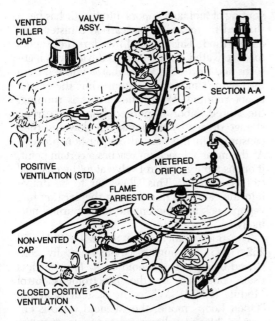

Closed and positive ventilation systems

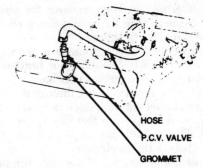

V8 PCV valve location

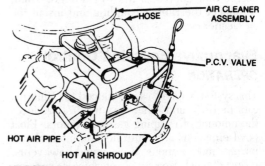

V6 PCV valve

to be reburned. At times of engine backfire (at the carburetor) or when the engine is turned off, manifold vacuum ceases permitting the spring to pull the valve against the inlet (crankcase end) of the valve housing. This seals off the inlet, thereby stopping the entrance of crankcase gases into the valve and preventing the possibility of a backfire spreading through the hose and valve to ignite these gases. The carburetor used with this system is set to provide a richer gas mixture to compensate for the additional air and gases going to the intake manifold. A valve that is clogged and stuck closed will not allow this extra air to reach the manifold. Consequently, the engine will run roughly and plugs will foul due to the creation, of an overly rich air/fuel mixture. It can be said that the PCV system performs three functions, It reduces air pollution by reburning the crankcase gases rather than releasing them to the atmosphere, and it increases engine life and gas economy. By recirculating crankcase gases, oil contamination that is harmful to engine parts is kept to a minimum. Recirculated gases returned to the intake manifold are combustible and, when combined with the air/fuel mixture from the carburetor, become fuel for operation, slightly increasing gas economy. In 1968, all cars were required to use the closed system and vented filler caps became a thing of the past. For more information on PCV, see Chapter One.

SERVICE

Inspect the PCV system hose and connections at each tune-up and replace any deteriorated hoses. Check the PCV valve at every tune-up and replace it every 24,000 miles on 1967–74 cars, and every 30,000 miles on later cars. See Chapter One for testing procedure.

REMOVAL AND INSTALLATION

The valve is inserted into a rubber grommet in the valve cover at the large end (on 1964–66 V8 engines, the valve is located in, or near the carburetor base). At the narrow end, it is inserted into a hose and clamped. To remove it, gently pull it out of the valve cover, then open the clamp with a pair of pliers. Hold the clamp open while sliding it an inch or two down the hose (away from the valve), and then remove the valve. If the end of the hose is hard or cracked where it holds the valve, it may be feasible to cut the end off if there is plenty of extra hose. Otherwise, replace the hose. Replace the grommet in the valve cover if it is cracked or hard. Replace the clamp if it is broken or weak. In replacing the valve, make sure it is fully inserted in the hose, that the clamp is moved over the ridge on the valve so that the valve will not slip out of the hose, and that the valve is fully inserted into the grommet in the valve cover.

PCV Filter

REMOVAL AND INSTALLATION

1. Slide the rubber coupling that joins the tube coming from the valve cover to the filter

off the filter nipple. Then, remove the top of the air cleaner. Slide the spring clamp off the filter, and remove the filter.

2. Inspect the rubber grommet in the valve cover and the rubber coupling for brittleness or cracking. Replace parts as necessary.

3. Insert the new PCV filter through the hole in the air cleaner with the open portion of the filter upward. Make sure that the square portion of filter behind the nipple fits into the (square) hole in the air cleaner.

4. Install a new spring clamp onto the nipple. Make sure the clamp goes under the ridge on the filter nipple all the way around. Then, reconnect the rubber coupling and install the air cleaner cover.

Evaporative Emission Control
OPERATION

This system which was introduced to California cars in 1970, and other cars in 1971, reduces the amount of escaping gasoline vapors. Float bowl emissions are controlled by internal carburetor modifications. Redesigned bowl vents, reduced bowl capacity, heat shields, and improved intake manifold-to-carburetor insulation reduce vapor loss into the atmosphere. The venting of fuel tank vapors into the air has been stopped by means of the carbon canister storage method. This method transfers fuel vapors to an activated carbon storage device which absorbs and stores the vapor that is emitted from the engine's induction system while the engine is not running. When the engine is running, the stored vapor is purged from the carbon storage device by the intake air flow and then consumed in the normal combustion process. As the manifold vacuum reaches a certain point, it opens a purge control valve atop the charcoal storage canister. This allows air to be drawn into the canister, thus forcing the existing fuel vapors back into the engine to be burned normally.

The purge function on the 231 (1981) and 262 (1985) V6 engine is electronically controlled by a purge solenoid in the line which is itself controlled by the Electronic Control Module (ECM). When the system is in the "Open Loop" mode, the solenoid valve is energized, blocking all vacuum to the purge valve. When the system is in the "Closed Loop" mode, the solenoid is deenergized, thus allowing existing vacuum to operate the purge valve. This releases the trapped fuel vapor and it is forced into the induction system.

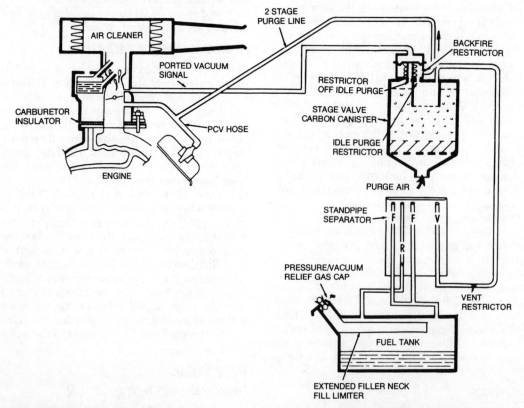

Schematic of the evaporative emission system (open)—1972. Most models are similar; open system more common than closed system

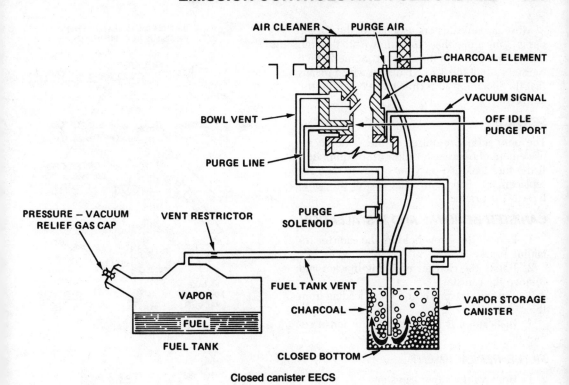

Closed canister EECS

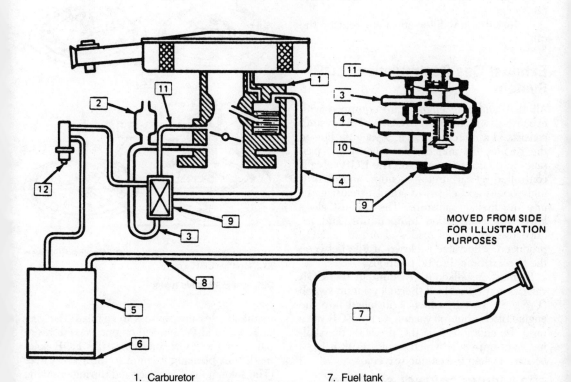

MOVED FROM SIDE
FOR ILLUSTRATION
PURPOSES

1. Carburetor
2. PCV valve
3. Manifold vacuum from PCV
4. Carburetor bowl tube
5. Vapor storage canister
6. Purge Air
7. Fuel tank
8. Fuel tank vent pipe
9. Canister control valve
10. Canister tube
11. Tube control vacuum
12. T.V.S. switch

Evaporative Emission Control System (EECS)—5.0L Engine

Most carbon canisters used are of the 'Open' design, meaning that air is drawn in through the bottom (filter) of the canister. Some 231 V6 canisters are of the 'Closed' design which means that the incoming air is drawn directly from the air cleaner.

SERVICE

The only service required is the periodic replacement of the canister filter (if so equipped). If the fuel tank cap on your car ever requires replacement, make sure that it is of the same type as the original.

CANISTER REMOVAL AND INSTALLATION

1. Loosen the screw holding the canister retaining bracket.
2. Rotate the canister retaining bracket and remove the canister.
3. Tag and disconnect the hoses leading from the canister.
4. Installation is in the reverse order of removal.

FILTER REPLACEMENT

1. Remove the vapor canister.
2. Pull the filter out from the bottom of the canister.
3. Install a new filter and then replace the canister.

Exhaust Gas Recirculation (EGR) System

All 1973 and later engines are equipped with exhaust gas recirculation (EGR). This system consists of a metering valve, a vacuum line to the carburetor, and cast-in exhaust gas passages in the intake manifold. The EGR valve is controlled by carburetor vacuum, and accordingly opens and closes to admit exhaust gases into the fuel/air moisture. The exhaust gases lower the combustion temperature, and reduce the amount of oxides of nitrogen (NO_x) produced. The valve is closed at idle between the two extreme throttle positions.

In most installations, vacuum to the EGR valve is controlled by a thermal vacuum switch (TVS); the switch, which is installed into the engine block, shuts off vacuum to the EGR valve until the engine is hot. this prevents the stalling and lumpy idle which would result if EGR occurred when the engine was cold.

EGR VACUUM CONTROL SOLENOID

To regulate EGR flow on 1981 and later models, a solenoid is used in the vacuum line, and is controlled by the Electronic Control Module (ECM). The ECM uses information from the coolant temperature, throttle position, and

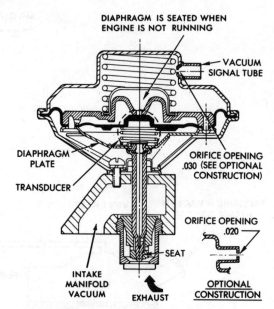

Negative backpressure EGR valve

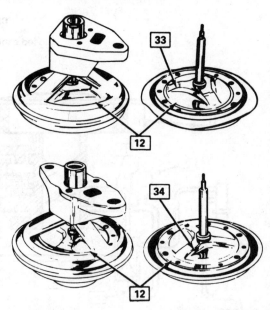

12. Diaphragm
33. Negative EGR web
34. Positive EGR web

Different EGR valve types

manifold pressure sensors to regulate the vacuum solenoid. When the engine is cold, a signal from the ECM energizes the EGR solenoid, thus blocking vacuum to the EGR valve. (The solenoid is also energized during cranking and wide-open throttle.) When the engine warms up, the EGR solenoid is turned off by the ECM, and the EGR valve operates according to normal ported vacuum and exhaust backpressure signals.

As the car accelerates, the carburetor throt-

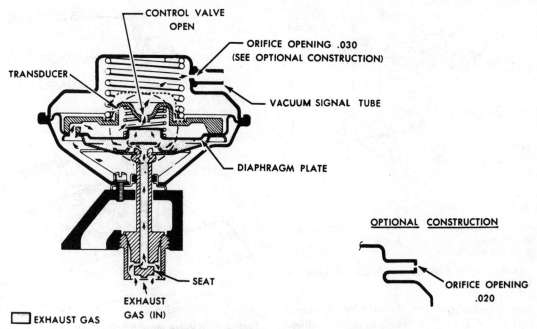

Cross section of a positive backpressure EGR valve

tle plate uncovers the vacuum port for the EGR valve. At 3–5 in. Hg, the EGR valve opens and then some of the exhaust gases are allowed to flow into the air/fuel mixture to lower the combustion temperature. At full-throttle the valve closes again.

Some California engines are equipped with a dual diaphragm EGR valve. This valve further limits the exhaust gas opening (compared to the single diaphragm EGR valve) during high intake manifold vacuum periods, such as high-speed cruising, and provides more exhaust gas recirculation during acceleration when manifold vacuum is low. In addition to the hose run-

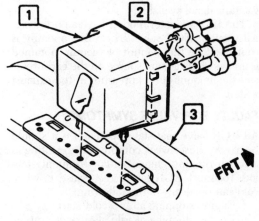

1. EGR/EFE solenoid valve
2. Harness
3. Rear rocker cover

231 V6 vacuum controlled solenoid locations

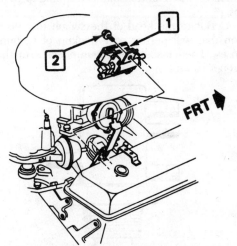

1. EGR control solenoid valve
2. Bolt (tighten to 17 N·m (12 ft. lbs.)

EGR vacuum-controlled solenoid, 229 V6, 305 V8

ning to the thermal vacuum switch, a second hose is connected directly to the intake manifold.

For 1977, all California models and cars delivered in areas above 4000 ft. are equipped with back pressure EGR valves. This valve is also used on all 1978–81 models. The EGR valve receives exhaust back pressure through its hollow shaft. This exerts a force on the bottom of the control valve diaphragm, opposed by a light spring. Under low exhaust pressure (low engine load and partial throttle), the EGR signal is reduced by an air bleed. Under conditions of high exhaust pressure (high engine load and

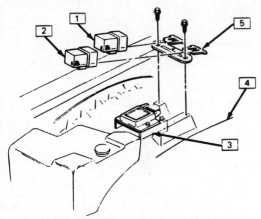

1. Fuel pump relay
2. A/C relay
3. E.S.C. module
4. R.H. wheelhouse panel
5. Bracket

Location of the EGR solenoid—262 V6 1985 and later

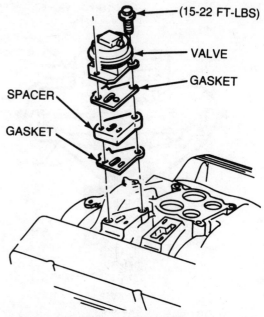

Typical EGR valve mounting location

large throttle opening), the air bleed is closed and the EGR valve responds to an unmodified vacuum signal. At wide open throttle, the EGR flow is reduced in proportion to the amount of vacuum signal available.

The 1979 and later models have a ported signal vacuum EGR valve. The valve opening is controlled by the amount of vacuum obtained from a ported vacuum source on the carburetor and the amount of backpressure in the exhaust system.

FAULTY EGR VALVE SYMPTOMS

An EGR valve that stays open when it should be closed causes weak combustion, resulting in a rough-running engine and/or frequent stalling. Too much EGR flow at idle, cruise, or when cold can cause any of the following:

• Engine stopping after a cold start
• Engine stopping at idle after deceleration
• Surging during cruising
• Rough idle

An EGR valve which is stuck closed and allows little or no EGR flow causes extreme combustion temperatures (too hot) during acceleration. Spark knock (detonation or "pinging"), engine overheating and excess engine emissions can all be a result, as well as engine damage. See the accompanying EGR system diagnosis chart for possible cause and correction procedures.

EGR VALVE REMOVAL AND INSTALLATION

1. Detach the vacuum lines from the EGR valve.
2. Unfasten the two bolts or bolt and clamp which attach the valve to the manifold. Withdraw the valve.

3. Installation is the reverse of removal. Always use a new gasket between the valve and the manifold. On dual diaphragm valves, attach the carburetor vacuum line to the tube at the top of the valve, and the manifold vacuum line to the tube at the center of the valve.

TVS SWITCH REMOVAL AND INSTALLATION

1. Drain the radiator.
2. Disconnect the vacuum lines from the switch noting their locations. Remove the switch.
3. Apply sealer to the threaded portion of the new switch, and install it, torquing to 15 ft. lbs.
4. Rotate the head of the switch to a position that will permit easy hookup of vacuum hoses. Then install the vacuum hoses to the proper connectors.

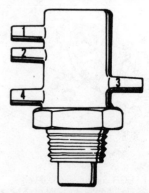

Thermostatic vacuum switch (TVS). Nipple 1 is to distributor; 2 is to TCS solenoid; 4 to intake manifold

EGR System Diagnosis

Condition	Possible Cause	Correction
Engine idles abnormally rough and/or stalls.	EGR valve vacuum hoses misrouted.	Check EGR valve vacuum hose routing. Correct as required.
	Leaking EGR valve.	Check EGR valve for correct operation.
	EGR valve gasket failed or loose EGR attaching bolts.	Check EGR attaching bolts for tightness. Tighten as required. If not loose, remove EGR valve and inspect gasket. Replace as required.
	EGR control solenoid.	Check vacuum into control solenoid from carburetor EGR port with engine at normal operating temperature and at curb idle speed. Then check the vacuum out of the EGR control solenoid to EGR valve. If the two vacuum readings are not equal within ± 1/2 in. Hg. (1.7 kPa), then problem could be within EGR solenoid or ECM unit.
	Improper vacuum to EGR valve at idle.	Check vacuum from carburetor EGR port with engine at stabilized operating temperature and at curb idle speed. Vacuum should not exceed 1.0 in. Hg. If vacuum exceeds this, check carburetor idle.
Engine runs rough on light throttle acceleration and has poor part load performance.	EGR valve vacuum hose misrouted.	Check EGR valve vacuum hose routing. Correct as required.
	Check for loose valve.	Torque valve.
	Failed EGR control solenoid.	Same as listing in "Engine Idles Rough" condition.
	Sticky or binding EGR valve.	Clean EGR passage of all deposits.
		Remove EGR valve and inspect. Replace as required.
	Wrong or no EGR gasket(s) and/or Spacer.	Check and correct as required. Install new gasket(s), install spacer (if used), torque attaching parts.
Engine stalls on decelerations.	Control valve blocked or air flow restricted.	Check internal control valve function per service procedure.
	Restriction in EGR vacuum line or control solenoid signal tube.	Check EGR vacuum lines for kinks, bends, etc. Remove or replace hoses as required. Check EGR control solenoid function.
		Check EGR valve for excessive deposits causing sticky or binding operation. Replace valve.
	Sticking or binding EGR valve.	Remove EGR valve and replace valve.
Part throttle engine detonation.	Control solenoid blocked or air flow restricted.	Check control solenoid function per check chart.
	Insufficient exhaust gas recirculation flow during part throttle accelerations.	Check EGR valve hose routing. Check EGR valve operation. Repair or replace as required. Check EGR control solenoid as listed in "Engine Idles Rough" section. Check EGR passages and valve for excessive deposit. Clean as required.

(NOTICE: Non-Functioning EGR valve could contribute to part throttle detonation.)

		Check EGR per service procedure.

(NOTICE: Detonation can be caused by several other engine variables. Perform ignition and carburetor related diagnosis.)

Condition	Possible Cause	Correction
Engine starts but immediately stalls when cold.	EGR valve hoses misrouted.	Check EGR valve hose routings.
	EGR control solenoid system malfunctioning when engine is cold.	Perform check to determine if the EGR solenoid is operational. Replace as required.

(NOTICE: Stalls after start can also be caused by carburetor problems.)

EGR VALVE CLEANING

Valves That Protrude from Mounting Face

CAUTION: *Do not wash the valve assembly in solvents or degreasers—permanent damage to the valve diaphragm may result.*

1. Remove the vacuum hose from the EGR valve assembly. Remove the two attaching bolts, remove the EGR valve from the intake manifold and discard the gasket.

2. Holding the valve assembly in hand, tap the valve lightly with a small plastic hammer to remove exhaust deposits from the valve seat. Shake out any loose particles. DO NOT put the valve in a vise.

3. Carefully remove any exhaust deposits from the mounting surface of the valve with a wire wheel or putty knife. Do not damage the mounting surface.

4. Depress the valve diaphragm and inspect the valve seating area through the valve outlet for cleanliness. If the valve and/or seat are not completely clean, repeat step 2.

5. Look for exhaust deposits in the valve outlet, and remove any deposits with an old screwdriver.

6. Clean the mounting surfaces of the intake manifold and valve assembly. Using a new gasket, install the valve assembly to the intake manifold. Torque the bolts to 25 ft. lbs. Connect the vacuum hose.

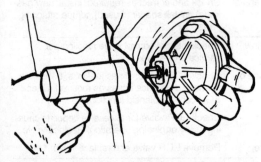

Cleaning the EGR (valve protruding). Tap lightly with hammer.

Shielded Valves or Valves That Do Not Protrude

1. Clean the base of the valve with a wire brush or wheel to remove exhaust deposits from the mounting surface.

2. Clean the valve seat and valve in an abrasive-type spark plug cleaning machine or sandblaster. Most machine shops provide this service. Make sure the valve portion is cleaned (blasted) for about 30 seconds, and that the valve is also cleaned with the diaphragm spring fully compressed (valve unseated). The cleaning should be repeated until all deposits are removed.

3. The valve must be blown out with compressed air thoroughly to ensure all abrasive material is removed from the valve.

4. Clean the mounting surface of the intake manifold and valve assembly. Using a new gasket, install the valve assembly to the intake manifold. Torque the bolts to 25 ft. lbs. Connect the vacuum hose.

Thermostatic Air Cleaner (THERMAC)

All late model engines utilize the THERMAC system (in 1978 it was called TAC, but was the same). This system is designed to warm the air entering the carburetor when underhood temperatures are low, and to maintain a controlled air temperature into the carburetor at all times. By allowing preheated air to enter the carburetor, the amount of time the choke is on is reduced, resulting in better fuel economy and lower emissions. Engine warm-up time is also reduced.

The Thermac system is composed of the air cleaner body, a filter, sensor unit, vacuum diaphragm, damper door, and associated hoses and connections. Heat radiating from the exhaust manifold is trapped by a heat stove and is ducted to the air cleaner to supply heated air to the carburetor. A movable door in the air cleaner case snorkel allows air to be drawn in from the heat stove (cold operation) or from underhood air (warm operation). The door position is controlled by the vacuum motor, which receives intake manifold vacuum as modulated by the temperature sensor.

SYSTEM CHECKS

1. Check the vacuum hoses for leaks, kinks, breaks, or improper connections and correct any defects.

2. With the engine off, check the position of the damper door within the snorkel. A mirror can be used to make this job easier. The damper door should be open to admit outside air.

3. Apply at least 7 in. Hg of vacuum to the damper diaphragm unit. The door should close. If it doesn't, check the diaphragm linkage for binding and correct hookup.

4. With vacuum still applied and the door closed, clamp the tube to trap the vacuum. If the door doesn't remain closed, there is a leak in the diaphragm assembly.

REMOVAL AND INSTALLATION

Vacuum Motor

1. Remove the air cleaner.

2. Disconnect the vacuum hose from the motor.

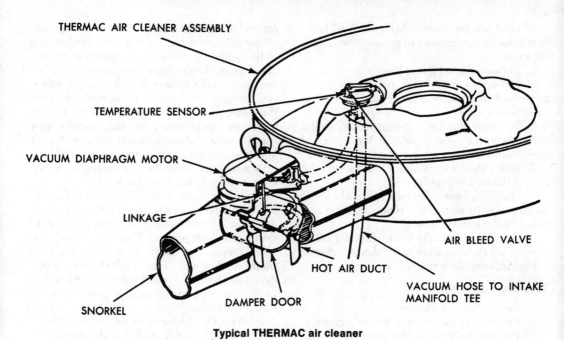

THERMAC AIR CLEANER ASSEMBLY

TEMPERATURE SENSOR

VACUUM DIAPHRAGM MOTOR

LINKAGE

AIR BLEED VALVE

HOT AIR DUCT

VACUUM HOSE TO INTAKE MANIFOLD TEE

SNORKEL

DAMPER DOOR

Typical THERMAC air cleaner

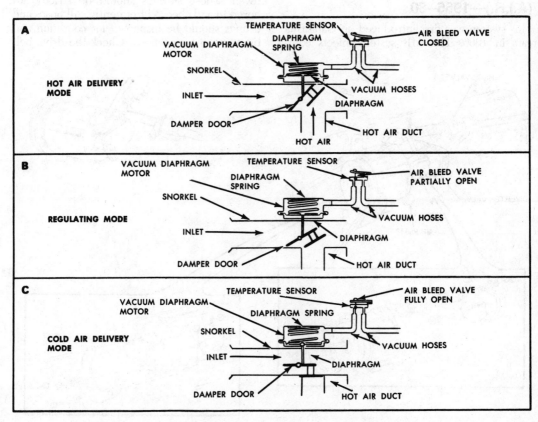

A

HOT AIR DELIVERY MODE

TEMPERATURE SENSOR

VACUUM DIAPHRAGM MOTOR

DIAPHRAGM SPRING

AIR BLEED VALVE CLOSED

SNORKEL

VACUUM HOSES

INLET

DIAPHRAGM

DAMPER DOOR

HOT AIR DUCT

HOT AIR

B

REGULATING MODE

VACUUM DIAPHRAGM MOTOR

TEMPERATURE SENSOR

DIAPHRAGM SPRING

AIR BLEED VALVE PARTIALLY OPEN

SNORKEL

VACUUM HOSES

INLET

DIAPHRAGM

DAMPER DOOR

HOT AIR DUCT

C

COLD AIR DELIVERY MODE

TEMPERATURE SENSOR

VACUUM DIAPHRAGM MOTOR

DIAPHRAGM SPRING

AIR BLEED VALVE FULLY OPEN

SNORKEL

VACUUM HOSES

INLET

DIAPHRAGM

DAMPER DOOR

HOT AIR DUCT

Schematic of the vacuum motor operation

3. Drill out the spot welds with a ⅛″ hole, then enlarge as necessary to remove the retaining strap.

4. Remove the retaining strap.

5. Lift up the motor and cock it to one side to unhook the motor linkage at the control damper assembly.

6. To install the new vacuum motor, drill a ⁷⁄₆₄″ hole in the snorkel tube as the center of the vacuum motor retaining strap.

7. Insert the vacuum motor linkage into the control damper assembly.

8. Use the motor retaining strap and a sheet metal screw to secure the retaining strap and motor to the snorkel tube.

NOTE: *Make sure the screw does not interfere with the operation of the damper assembly. Shorten the screw if necessary.*

Temperature Sensor

1. Remove the air cleaner.

2. Disconnect the hoses at the air cleaner.

3. Pry up the tabs on the sensor retaining clip and remove the clip and sensor from the air cleaner.

4. Installation is the reverse of removal.

Air Injection Reactor System (A.I.R.)—1966–80

This system was first introduced on California cars in 1966. The AIR system injects compressed air into the exhaust system, near enough to the exhaust valves to continue the burning of the normally unburned segment of the exhaust gases. To do this it employs an air injection pump and a system of hoses, valves, tubes, etc., necessary to carry the compressed air from the pump to the exhaust manifolds. Carburetors and distributors for AIR engines have specific modifications to adapt them to the air injection system; those components should not be interchanged with those intended for use on engines that do not have the system.

A diverter valve is used to prevent backfiring. The valve senses sudden increases in manifold vacuum and ceases the injection of air during fuel-rich periods. During coasting, this valve diverts the entire air flow through the pump muffler and during high engine speeds, expels it through a relief valve. Check valves in the system prevent exhaust gases from entering the pump.

NOTE: *The AIR system on the 231 V6 engine is slightly different, but its purpose remains the same.*

SERVICE

The AIR system's effectiveness depends on correct engine idle speed, ignition timing, and dwell. These settings should be strictly adhered to and checked frequently. All hoses and fittings should be inspected for condition and tightness of connections. Check the drive belt

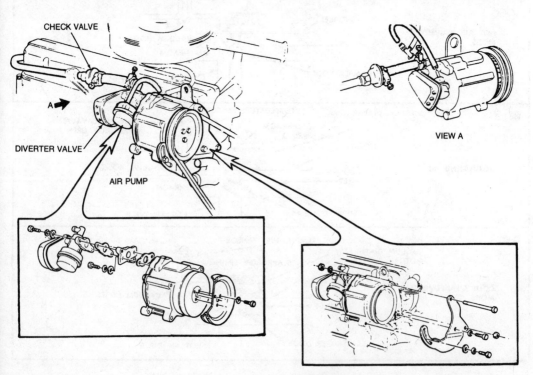

AIR system—inline six cylinder

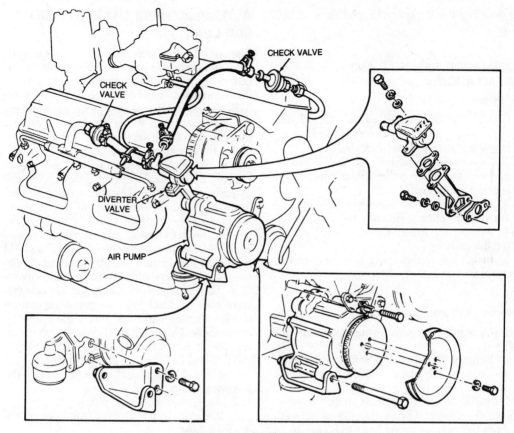

AIR system—V8 (229 V6 similar)

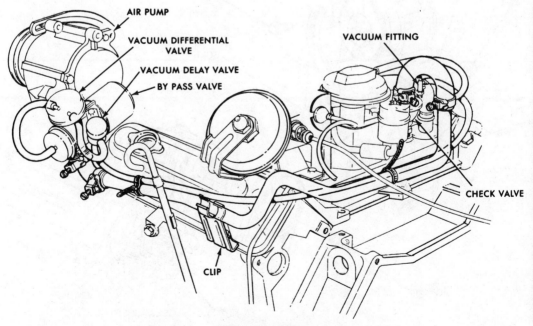

AIR system—231 V6

for wear and tension every 12 months or 12,000 miles.

COMPONENT REMOVAL AND INSTALLATION

Air Pump

CAUTION: *Do not pry on the pump housing or clamp the pump in a vise: the housing is soft and may become distorted.*

1. Disconnect the air hoses at the pump.
2. Hold the pump pulley from turning and loosen the pulley bolts.
3. Loosen the pump mounting bolt and adjustment bracket bolt. Remove the drive belt.
4. Remove the mounting bolts, and then remove the pump.
5. Install the pump using a reverse of the removal procedure.

Diverter (Anti-afterburn) Valve

1. Detach the vacuum sensing line from the valve.
2. Remove the other hose(s) from the valve.
3. Unfasten the diverter valve from the elbow or the pump body.
4. Installation is performed in the reverse order of removal. Always use a new gasket. Tighten the valve securing bolts to 85 in. lbs.

Air Management System—1981 and Later

The Air Management System is used to provide additional oxygen to continue the combustion process after the exhaust gases leave the combustion chamber; much the same as the AIR system described earlier in this chapter. Air is injected into either the exhaust port(s), the exhaust manifold(s) or the catalytic converter by an engine driven air pump. The system is in operation at all times and will bypass air only momentarily during deceleration and at high speeds. The bypass function is performed by the Air Management Valve, while the check valve protects the air pump by preventing any backflow of exhaust gases.

The AIR system helps to reduce HC and CO content in the exhaust gases by injecting air into the exhaust ports during cold engine operation. This air injection also helps the catalytic converter to reach the proper temperature quicker during warm-up. When the engine is warm (closed loop), the AIR system injects air into the beds of a three-way converter to lower the HC and CO content in the exhaust.

The Air Management System utilizes the following components:

1. An engine driven air pump
2. Air management valves (Air Control and Air Switching)

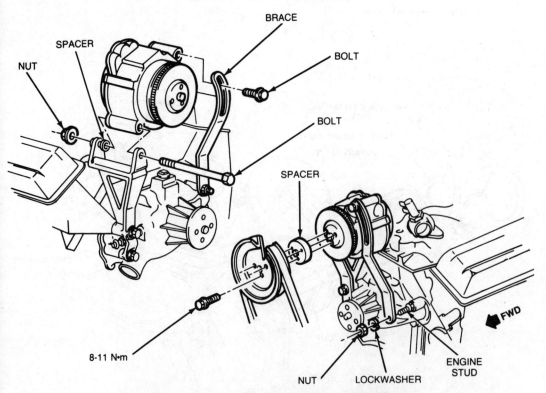

Removing the air pump; 1981 and later air management system

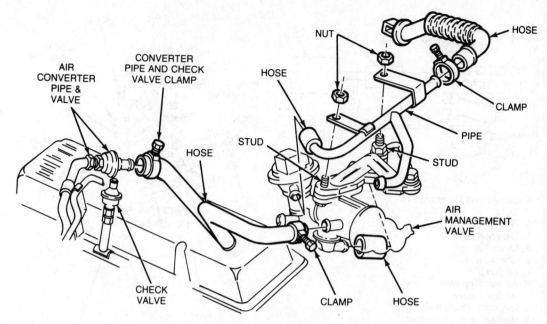

Check valve and hoses—1981 air management system

3. Airflow and control hoses

4. Check valves

5. A dual-bed, three-way catalytic converter.

The belt driven, vane-type air pump is located at the front of the engine and supplies clean air to the system for purposes already stated. When the engine is cold, the Electronic Control Module (ECM) energizes an air control solenoid. This allows air to flow to the air switching valve. The air switching valve is then energized to direct air into the exhaust port.

When the engine is warm, the ECM de-energizes the air switching valve, thus directing

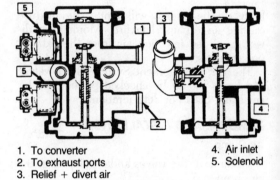

1. To converter
2. To exhaust ports
3. Relief + divert air
4. Air inlet
5. Solenoid

AIR system control valve—4.3L Engine

the air between the beds of the catalytic converter. This then provides additional oxygen for the oxidizing catalyst in the second bed to decrease HC and CO levels, while at the same time keeping oxygen levels low in the first bed, enabling the reducing catalyst to effectively decrease the levels of NOx.

If the air control valve detects a rapid increase in manifold vacuum (deceleration), certain operating modes (wide open throttle, etc.) or if the ECM self-diagnostic system detects any problems in the system, air is diverted to the air cleaner or directly into the atmosphere.

The primary purpose of the ECM's divert mode is to prevent backfiring. Throttle closure at the beginning of deceleration will temporarily create air/fuel mixtures which are too rich to burn completely. These mixtures will become burnable when they reach the exhaust if they are combined with injection air. The next

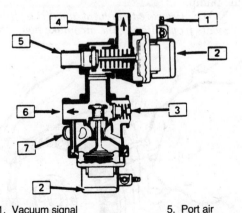

1. Vacuum signal
2. Solenoid
3. Relief valve
4. Converter air
5. Port air
6. Air from pump
7. Divert air

Electric divert/electric air switching valve (EDES)—5.0L Engine

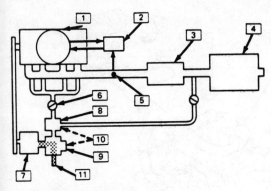

1. Closed loop fuel control
2. ECM
3. Reducing catalyst
4. Oxidizing catalyst
5. O_2 sensor
6. Check valve
7. Air pump
8. Air switching valve
9. Air divert valve
10. Electrical signals from ECM
11. By-pass air to air cleaner

AIR system operation

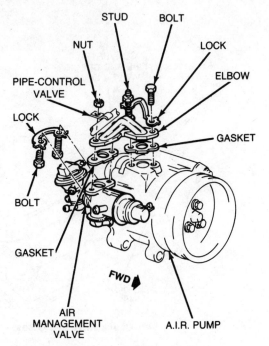

Removing the air management valve

firing of the engine will ignite the mixture causing an exhaust backfire. Momentary diverting of the injection air from the exhaust prevents this.

The Air Management System check valves and hoses should be checked periodically for any leaks, cracks or deterioration.

REMOVAL AND INSTALLATION

Air Pump

1. Remove the valves and/or adapter at the air pump.
2. Loosen the air pump adjustment bolt and remove the drive belt.
3. Unscrew the three mounting bolts and then remove the pump pulley.
4. Unscrew the pump mounting bolts and then remove the pump.
5. Installation is in the reverse order of removal. Be sure to adjust the drive belt tension after installing it.

Check Valve

1. Release the clamp and disconnect the air hoses from the valve.
2. Unscrew the check valve from the air injection pipe.
3. Installation is in the reverse order of removal.

Air Management Valve

1. Disconnect the negative battery cable.
2. Remove the air cleaner.
3. Tag and disconnect the vacuum hose from the valve.

4. Tag and disconnect the air outlet hoses from the valve.
5. Bend back the lock tabs and then remove the bolts holding the elbow to the valve.
6. Tag and disconnect any electrical connections at the valve and then remove the valve from the elbow.
7. Installation is in the reverse order of removal.

Pump Filter Removal

1. Remove the drive belt and pump pulley.
2. Using needle-nose pliers, pull the fan from the pump.
NOTE: *Use care to prevent any dirt or fragments from entering the air intake hole. DO*

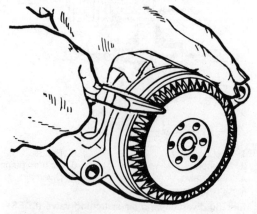

AIR filter removal

NOT insert a screwdriver between the pump and the filter, and do not attempt to remove the metal hub. It is seldom possible to remove the filter without destroying it.

3. To install a new filter, draw it on with the pulley and pulley bolts. DO NOT hammer or press the filter on the pump.

4. Draw the filter down evenly by torquing the bolts alternately. Make sure the outer edge of the filter slips into the housing. A slight amount of interference with the housing bore is normal.

NOTE: *The new filter may squeal initially until the sealing lip on the pump outer diameter has worn in.*

Anti-Dieseling Solenoid

Beginning in 1968 some models may have an idle speed solenoid on the carburetor. All 1972–75 models have idle solenoids. Due to the leaner carburetor settings required for emission control, the engine may have a tendency to "diesel" or "run-on" after the ignition is turned off. The carburetor solenoid, energized when the ignition is on, maintains the normal idle speed. When the ignition is turned off, the solenoid is de-energized and permits the throttle valves to fully close, thus preventing run-on. For adjustment of carburetors with idle solenoids see the section on carburetor adjustments later in this chapter.

Anti-dieseling solenoid

Transmission Controlled Spark (TCS)—1970–74

Introduced in 1970, this system controls exhaust emissions by eliminating vacuum advance in the lower forward gears.

The 1970 system consists of a transmission switch, solenoid vacuum switch, time delay relay, and a thermostatic water temperature switch. The solenoid vacuum switch is energized in the lower gears via the transmission switch and closes off distributor vacuum. The two-way transmission switch is activated by the

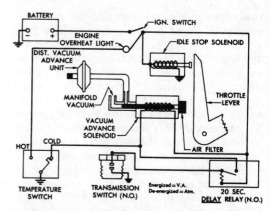

Small V8 TCS system, engine "off" mode shown. Large V8 and inline six basically similar

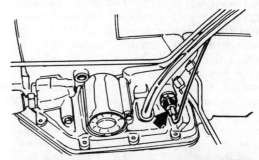

TCS switch location, Turbo Hydra-Matic 350. Location similar on other transmissions (sides may vary)

shifter shaft on manual transmissions, and by oil pressure on automatic transmissions. The switch de-energizes the solenoid in High gear, the plunger extends and uncovers the vacuum port, and the distributor receives full vacuum. The temperature switch overrides the system when engine temperature is below 63° or above 232°. This allows vacuum advance in all gears. A time delay relay opens 15 seconds after the ignition is switched on. Full vacuum advance during this delay eliminates the possibility of stalling.

The 1971 system is similar, except that the vacuum solenoid (now called a Combination Emissions Control or CEC solenoid) serves two functions. One function is to control distributor vacuum; the added function is to act as a deceleration throttle stop in High gear. This cuts down on emissions when the vehicle is coming to a stop in High gear. The CEC solenoid is controlled by a temperature switch, a transmission switch, and a 20 second time delay relay. This system also contains a reversing relay, which energizes the solenoid when the transmission switch, temperature switch or time delay completes the CEC circuit to ground. This system is directly opposite the 1970 system in operation. The 1970 vacuum solenoid was normally open to allow vacuum advance and when energized, closed to block vacuum. The 1971 system is normally closed blocking vacuum advance and when energized, opens to allow vacuum advance. The temperature switch completes the CEC circuit to ground when engine tempertaure is below 82°. The time delay relay allows vacuum advance (and raised idle speed) for 200 seconds after the ignition key is turned to the ON position. Models with an automatic transmission and air conditioning also have a solid state timing device which engages the air conditioning compressor for three seconds after the ignition key is turned to the OFF position to prevent the engine from running-on.

The 1972 six-cylinder system is similar to that used in 1971, except that an idle stop solenoid has been added to the system. In the energized position, the solenoid maintains engine speed at a predetermined fast idle. When the solenoid is de-energized by turning off the ignition, the solenoid allows the throttle plates to close beyond the normal idle position; thus cutting off their air supply and preventing engine run-on. The six-cylinder is the only 1972 engine with a C.E.C valve, which serves the same deceleration function as in 1971. The 1972 time delay relay delays full vacuum 20 seconds after the transmission is shifted into High gear. V8 engines use a vacuum advance solenoid similar to that used in 1970. This relay is normally closed to block vacuum and opens when energized to allow vacuum advance. The solenoid controls distributor vacuum advance and performs no throttle positioning function. The idle stop solenoid used operates in the same manner as the one on six-cylinder engines. All air-conditioned cars have an additional anti-diesel (run-on) solenoid which engages the compressor clutch for three seconds after the ignition is switched off. The 1973 TCS system differs from the 1972 system in three ways. The 23 second upshift delay has been replaced by a 20 second starting relay. This relay closes to complete the TCS circuit and open the TCS solenoid, allowing vacuum advance, for 20 seconds after the key is turned to the "on" position. The operating temperature of the temperature override switch has been raised to 93°, and the switch which was used to engage the A/C compressor when the key was turned OFF has been eliminated. All models are equipped with an electric throttle control solenoid to prevent run-on. The 1973 TCS system is used on all models equipped with a 307 engine and all V8 models equipped with a manual transmission.

The 1974 TCS system is used only on manual transmission models. System components remain unchanged from 1973. The vacuum ad-

vance solenoid is located on the coil bracket. The TCS system is not used in 1975 and later cars.

TESTING

If there is a TCS system malfunction, first connect a vacuum gauge in the hose between the solenoid valve and the distributor vacuum unit. Drive the vehicle or raise it on a frame lift and observe the vacuum gauge. If full vacuum is available in all gears, check for the following:

1. Blown fuse.
2. Disconnected wire at the solenoid-operated vacuum valve.
3. Disconnect wire at the transmission switch.
4. Temperature override switch energized due to low engine temperature.
5. Solenoid failure.

If no vacuum is available in any gear, check the following:

1. Solenoid valve vacuum lines switched.
2. Clogged solenoid vacuum valve.
3. Distributor or manifold vacuum lines leaking or disconnected.
4. Transmission switch or wire grounded.

Test for individual components are as follows:

Idle Stop Solenoid

This unit may be checked simply by observing it while an assistant switches the ignition on and off. It should extend further with the current switched on. The unit is not repairable.

Solenoid Vacuum Valve

Check that proper manifold vacuum is available. Connect the vacuum gauge in the line between the solenoid valve and the distributor. Apply 12 volts to the solenoid. If vacuum is still not available, the valve is defective, either mechanically or electrically. The unit is not repairable. If the valve is satisfactory, check the relay next.

Relay

1. With the engine at normal operating temperature and the ignition on, ground the solenoid vacuum valve terminal with the black lead. The solenoid should energize (no vacuum) if the relay is satisfactory.
2. With the solenoid energized as in Step 1, connect a jumper from the relay terminal with the green/white stripe lead to ground. The solenoid should de-energize (vacuum available) if the relay is satisfactory.
3. If the relay worked properly in Steps 1 and 2, check the temperature switch. The relay unit is not repairable.

Temperature Switch

The vacuum valve solenoid should be deenergized (vacuum available) with the engine cold. If it is not, ground the green/white stripe wire from the switch. If the solenoid now de-energizes, replace the switch. If the switch was satisfactory, check the transmission switch.

Transmission Switch

With the engine at normal operating temperature and the transmission in one of the no-vacuum gears, the vacuum valve solenoid should be energized (no vacuum). If not, remove and ground the switch electrical lead. If the solenoid energizes, replace the switch.

Early Fuel Evaporation System (EFE)—1975 and Later

The 1975 and later models (except TBI) are equipped with this system to reduce engine warm-up time, improve driveability, and reduce emissions. On start-up, a vacuum motor acts to close a heat valve in the exhaust manifold which causes exhaust gases to enter the intake manifold heat riser passages. Incoming fuel mixture is then heated and more complete fuel evaporation is provided during warm-up.

The system consists of a Thermal Vacuum Switch, and an Exhaust Heat Valve and actuator. The Thermal Vacuum Switch is located on the coolant outlet housing on V8s, and on the block on in-line six cylinder engines. When the engine is cold, the TVS conducts manifold vacuum to the actuator to close the valve. When engine coolant or, on 6 cylinder engines, oil warms up, vacuum is interrupted and the actuator should open the valve.

NOTE: *On the 231 V6 (1981) and 262 V6 (1985 and later) engines, the EFE system is controlled by the ECM.*

As of 1981, the 231 V6 Turbo utilizes a slightly different system. Although the function of this

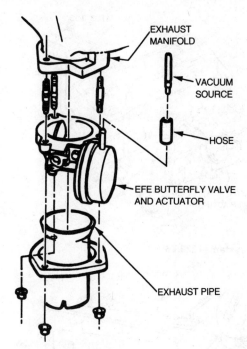

Vacuum-servo type EFE

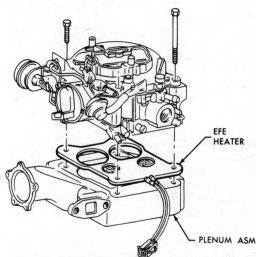

EFE heater on the 231 Turbo

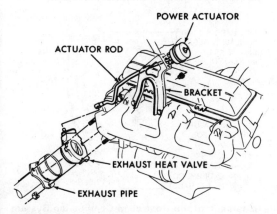

EFE system—V8 models

system remains the same—to reduce engine warm-up time, improve driveability and to reduce emissions—the operation is entirely different. The new system is electric and uses a ceramic heater grid located underneath the primary bore of the carburetor as part of the carburetor insulator/gasket. When the engine coolant is below the specified calibration level, electrical current is supplied to the heater through an ECM controlled relay.

CHECKING THE EFE SYSTEM

1. With the engine overnight cold, have someone start the engine while you observe the

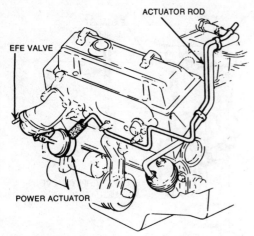

EFE system—229 V6

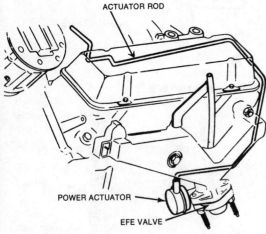

EFE system—231 V6

Exhaust Heat Valve (on some V8s, the EFE valve actuator arm is covered by a two-piece metal cover, which must be removed for service). The valve should snap to the closed position.

2. Watch the valve as the engine warms up. By the time coolant starts circulating through the radiator (V-type engines) or oil is hot (in-line engines), the valve should snap open.

3. If the valve does not close, immediately disconnect the hose at the actuator, and check for vacuum by placing your finger over the end of the hose, or with a vacuum gauge. If there is vacuum, immediately disconnect the hose leading to the TVS from the manifold *at the TVS*. If there is vacuum here, but not at the actuator, replace the TVS. If vacuum does not exist at the hose going to the TVS, check that the vacuum hose is free of cracks or breaks and tightly connected at the manifold, and that the manifold port is clear.

4. If the valve does not open when the engine coolant or oil warms up, disconnect the

hose at the actuator, and check for vacuum by placing your finger over the end of the hose or using a vacuum gauge. If there is vacuum, replace the TVS. If there is no vacuum, replace the actuator.

TVS REMOVAL AND INSTALLATION

The Thermo Vacuum Switch (TVS) is located on the engine coolant outlet housing.

On V8 engines, drain coolant until the level is below the coolant outlet housing. No oil need be drained on 6 cylinder engines. Apply sealer to threads on V8 engines. Use no sealer on 6 cylinder engines. Note that the valve must be installed until just snug (120 in. lbs.) and then turned by hand just far enough to line up the fittings for hose connection.

HEATER GRID REMOVAL AND INSTALLATION (1981 TURBO ONLY)

1. Remove the air cleaner.
2. Tag and disconnect all electrical, vacuum and fuel connections from the carburetor.
3. Disconnect the EFE heater electrical connection.
4. Remove the carburetor as detailed later in this chapter.
5. Lift off the EFE heater.
6. Installation is in the reverse order of removal.
7. Start the engine and check for any leaks.

Controlled Combustion System

The CCS system relies upon leaner air/fuel mixtures and altered ignition timing to improve combustion efficiency. A special air cleaner with a thermostatically controlled opening is used on most CCS equipped models to ensure that air entering the carburetor is kept at 100°F. This allows leaner carburetor settings and improves engine warm-up. A 15°F higher temperature thermostat is employed on CCS cars to further improve emission control.

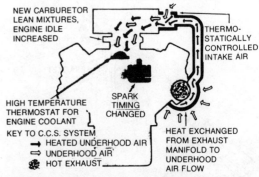

Schematic of the Controlled Combustion System (CCS)

SERVICE

Since the only extra component added with a CCS system is the thermostatically controlled air cleaner, there is no additional maintenance required; however, tune-up adjustments such as idle speed, ignition timing, and dwell become much more critical. Care must be taken to ensure that these settings are correct, both for trouble-free operation and a low emission level.

Computer Controlled Catalytic Converter System

The C-4 System, installed on certain 1979 and all 1980 cars sold in California, is an electronically controlled exhaust emission system. The purpose of the system is to maintain the ideal air/fuel ratio at which the catalytic converter is most effective.

Major components of the system include an Electronic Control Module (ECM), an oxygen sensor, an electronically controlled carburetor, and a three-way oxidation reduction catalytic converter. The system also includes a maintenance reminder flag connected to the odometer which becomes visible in the instrument cluster at regular intervals, signaling the need for oxygen sensor replacement.

The oxygen sensor, installed in the exhaust manifold, generates a voltage which varies with exhaust gas oxygen content. Lean mixtures (more oxygen) reduce voltage; rich mixtures (less oxygen) increase voltage. Voltage output is sent to the ECM.

An engine temperature sensor installed in the engine coolant outlet monitors engine coolant temperatures. Vacuum control switches and throttle position sensors also monitor engine conditions and supply signals to the ECM.

The Electronic Control Module receives input signals from all sensors. It processes these signals and generates a control signal sent to the carburetor. The control signal cycles between on (lean command) and off (rich command). The amount of on and off time is a function of the input voltage sent to the ECM by the oxygen sensor.

Rochester Dualjet (2-barrel) E2ME and E4ME (4-barrel) carburetors are used with the C-4 System. Basically, an electrically operated mixture control solenoid is installed in the carburetor float bowl. The solenoid controls the air/fuel mixture metered to the idle and main metering systems. Air metering to the idle system is controlled by an idle air bleed valve. It follows the movement of the mixture solenoid to control the amount of air bled into the idle system, enriching or leaning out the mixture as appropriate. Air/fuel mixture enrichment occurs when the fuel valve is open and the air bleed valve is closed. All cycling of this system, which occurs ten times per second, is controlled by the ECM. A throttle position switch informs the ECM of open or closed throttle operation. A number of different switches are used, varying with application. When the ECM receives a signal from the throttle switch, indicating a change of position, it immediately searches its memory for the last set of operating conditions that result in an ideal air/fuel ra-

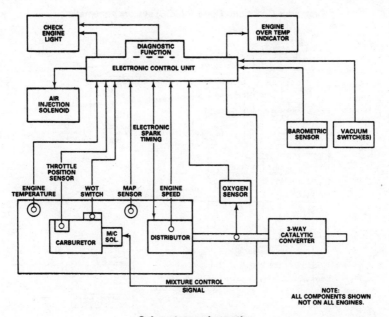

C-4 system schematic

tio, and shifts to that set of conditions. The memory is continually updated during normal operation.

A "Check-Engine" light is included in the C-4 System installation. When a fault develops, the light comes on, and a trouble code is set into the ECM memory. However, if the fault is intermittent, the light will go out, but the trouble code will remain in the ECM memory as long as the engine is running. The trouble codes are used as a diagnostic aid, and are pre-programmed.

Unless the required tools are available, troubleshooting the C-4 System should be confined to mechanical checks of electrical connectors, vacuum hoses and the like. All diagnosis and repair should be performed by a qualified mechanic.

Computer Command Control System

The Computer Command Control System, installed on all 1981 and later cars, is basically a modified version of the C-4 system. Its main advantage over its predecessor is that it can

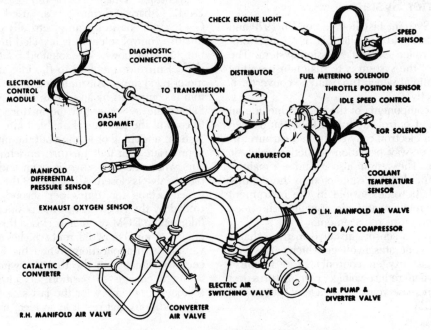

Computer Command Control (CCC) system schematic

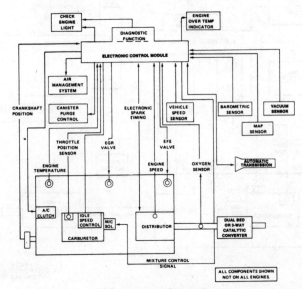

CCC system schematic

monitor and control a large number of interrelated emission control systems.

This new system can monitor up to 15 various engine/vehicle operating conditions and then use this information to control as many as 9 engine related systems. The "System" is thereby making constant adjustments to maintain good vehicle performance under all normal driving conditions while at the same time allowing the catalytic converter to effectively control the emissions of NOx, HC and CO.

In addition, the "System" has a built in di-

agnostic system that recognizes and identifies possible operational problems and alerts the driver through a "Check Engine" light in the instrument panel. The light will remain ON until the problem is corrected. The "System" also has built in back-up systems that in most cases of an operational problem will allow for the continued operation of the vehicle in a near normal manner until the repairs can be made.

The CCC system has some components in common with the C-4 system, although they are not interchangeable. These components in-

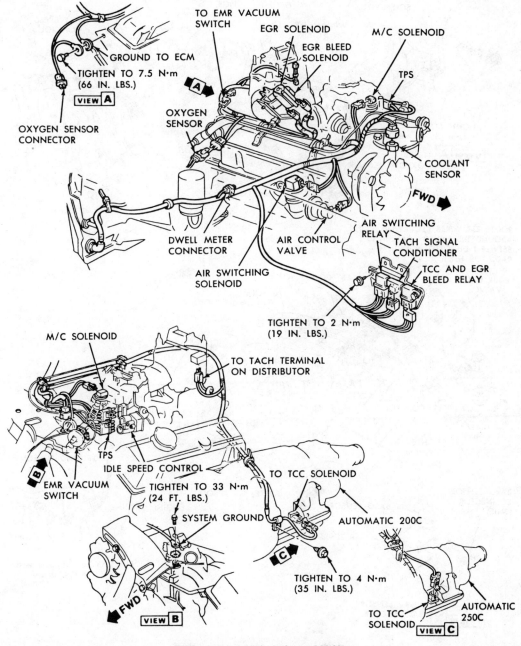

CCC component location—229 V6

clude the Electronic Control Module (ECM), which, as previously stated, controls many more functions than does its predecessor, an oxygen sensor system, an electronically controlled variable-mixture carburetor, a three-way catalytic converter, throttle position and coolant sensors, a Barometric Pressure Sensor (BARO), a Manifold Absolute Pressure Sensor (MAP) and a "Check Engine" light in the instrument panel.

Components unique to the CCC system include the Air Injection Reaction (AIR) management system, a charcoal canister purge solenoid, EGR valve controls, a vehicle speed sensor (in the instrument panel), a transmission converter clutch solenoid (only on models with automatic transmission), idle speed control and Electronic Spark Timing (EST).

The ECM, in addition to monitoring sensors and sending out a control signal to the carburetor, also controls the following components

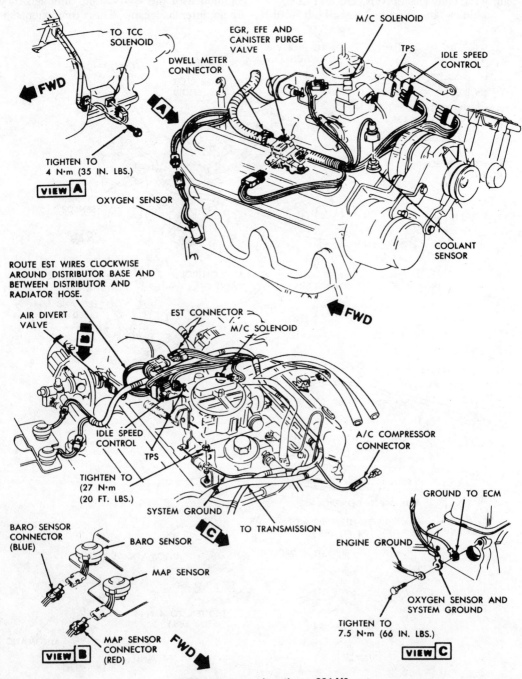

CCC component location—231 V6

or sub-systems: charcoal canister purge control, the AIR system, idle speed, automatic transmission converter lock-up, distributor ignition timing, the EGR valve, and the air conditioner converter clutch.

The EGR valve control solenoid is activated by the ECM in a fashion similar to that of the charcoal canister purge solenoid described earlier in this chapter. When the engine is cold, the ECM energizes the solenoid, which blocks the vacuum signal to the EGR valve. When the engine is warm, the ECM de-energizes the solenoid and the vacuum signal is allowed to reach and then activate the EGR valve.

The Transmission Converter Clutch (TCC) lock is controlled by the ECM through an electrical solenoid in the automatic transmission. When the vehicle speed sensor in the dash signals the ECM that the car has attained the predetermined speed, the ECM energizes the solenoid which then allows the torque converter to mechanically couple the engine to the trans-

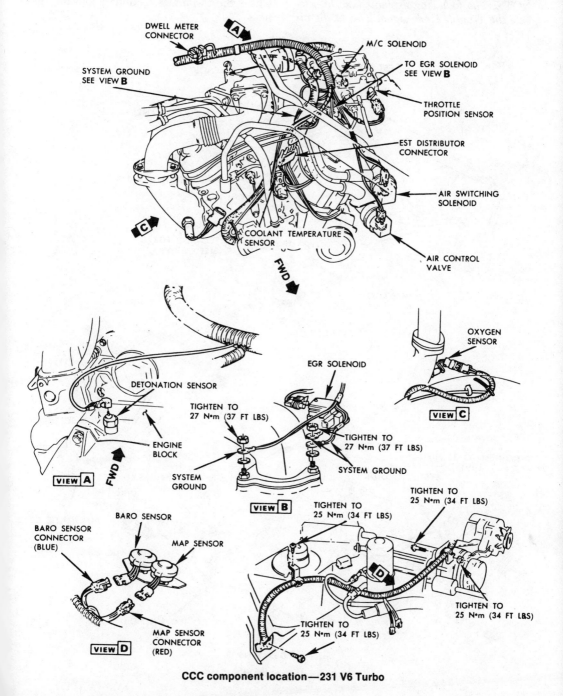

CCC component location—231 V6 Turbo

mission. When the brake pedal is pushed, or during deceleration or passing, etc., the ECM returns the transmission to fluid drive.

The idle speed control adjusts the idle speed to all particular engine load conditions and will lower the idle under no-load or low-load conditions in order to converse fuel.

NOTE: *Not all engines use all systems. Control applications may differ.*

BASIC TROUBLESHOOTING

NOTE: *The following explains how to activate the Trouble Code signal light in the in-strument cluster. This is not a full fledged C-4 or CCC system troubleshooting and isolation procedure.*

Before suspecting the C-4 or CCC system, or any of its components as being faulty, check the ignition system (distributor, timing, spark plugs and wires). Check the engine compression, the air cleaner and any of the emission control components that are not controlled by the ECM. Also check the intake manifold, the vacuum hoses and hose connectors for any leaks. Check the carburetor mounting bolts for tightness.

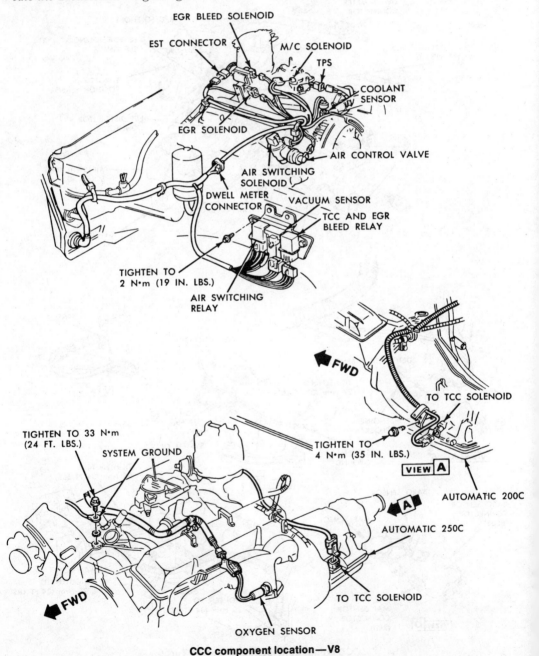

CCC component location—V8

The following symptoms could indicate a possible problem area with the C-4 or CCC systems:

1. Detonation;
2. Stalling or rough idling when the engine is cold;
3. Stalling or rough idling when the engine is hot;
4. Missing;
5. Hesitation;
6. Surging;
7. Poor gasoline mileage;
8. Sluggish or spongy performance;
9. Hard starting when engine is cold;
10. Hard starting when the engine is hot;
11. Objectionable exhaust odors;
12. Engine cuts out;
13. Improper idle speed (CCC only).

As a bulb and system check, the "Check Engine" light will come on when the ignition switch is turned to the ON position but the engine is not started.

The "Check Engine" light will also produce the trouble code/codes by a series of flashes which translate as follows: When the diagnostic test lead (C-4) or terminal (CCC) under the instrument panel is grounded, with the ignition in the ON position and the engine not running, the "Check Engine" light will flash once, pause, and then flash twice in rapid succession. This is a Code 12, which indicates that the diagnostic system is working. After a long pause, the Code 12 will repeat itself two more times. This whole cycle will then repeat itself until the engine is started or the ignition switch is turned OFF.

When the engine is started, the "Check Engine" light will remain on for a few seconds and then turn off. If the "Check Engine" light remains on, the self-diagnostic system has detected a problem. If the test lead (C-4) or test terminal (CCC) is then grounded, the trouble code will flash (3) three times. If more than one problem is found to be in existance, each trouble code will flash (3) three times and then change to the next one. Trouble codes will flash in numerical order (lowest code number to highest). The trouble code series will repeat themselves for as long as the test leads or terminal remains grounded.

A trouble code indicates a problem with a given circuit. For example, trouble code 14 indicates a problem in the cooling sensor circuit. This includes the coolant sensor, its electrical harness and the Electronic Control Module (ECM).

Since the self-diagnostic system cannot diagnose every possible fault in the system, the absence of a trouble code does not necessarily mean that the system is trouble-free. To determine whether or not a problem with the system exists that does not activate a trouble code, a system performance check must be made. This job should be left to a qualified service technician.

In the case of an intermittent fault in the system, the "Check Engine" light will go out when the fault goes away, but the trouble code will remain in the memory of the ECM. Therefore, if a trouble code can be obtained even though the "Check Engine" light is not on, it much still be evaluated. It must be determined if the fault is intermittent or if the engine must be operating under certain conditions (acceleration, deceleration, etc.) before the "Check Engine" light will come on. In some cases, certain trouble codes will not be recorded in the ECM until the engine has been operated at part throttle for at least 5 to 8 minutes.

On the C-4 system, the ECM erases all trouble codes every time that the ignition is turned off. In the case of intermittent faults, a long term memory is desirable. This can be produced by connecting the orange connector/lead from terminal "S" of the ECM directly to the battery (or to a 'hot' fuse panel terminal). This terminal must always be disconnected immediately after diagnosis as it puts an undue strain on the battery.

On the CCC system, a trouble code will be stored until the terminal 'R' at the ECM has been disconnected from the battery for at least 10 seconds.

ACTIVATING THE TROUBLE CODE

On the C-4 system, activate the trouble code by grounding the trouble code test lead. Use the illustrations to help you locate the test lead under the instrument panel (usually a white and black wire from the lead to a suitable ground).

On the CCC system, locate the test terminal under the instrument panel (see illustration). Use a jumper wire and ground only the lead.

NOTE: *Ground the test lead/terminal according to the instructions given previously in the "Basic Troubleshooting" section.*

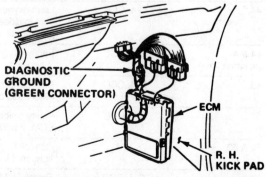

C-4 system diagnostic test lead location, above ECM

Trouble Code Identification Chart

NOTE: Always ground the test lead/terminal AFTER the engine is running

Trouble Code	Applicable System	Possible Problem Area
12	C-4, CCC	No reference pulses to the ECM. This is not stored in the memory and will only flash when the fault is present (not to be confused with the Code 12 discussed earlier).
13	C-4, CCC	Oxygen sensor circuit. The engine must run for at least 5 min. (18 min. on the C-4 equipped 231 V6) at part throttle before this code will show.
13 & 14 (at same time)	C-4	See code 43.
13 & 14 (at same time)	C-4	See code 43.
14	C-4, CCC	Shorted coolant sensor circuit. The engine must run 2–5 min. before this code will show.
15	C-4, CCC	Open coolant sensor circuit. The engine must run for at least 5 min. (18 min. on the C-4 equipped 231 V6) before this code will show.
21	C-4	Shorted wide open throttle switch and/or open closed-throttle switch circuit (when used).
	C-4, CCC	Throttle position sensor circuit. The engine must run for at least 10 sec. (25 sec.—CCC) below 800 rpm before this code will show.
21 & 22 (at same time)	C-4	Grounded wide open throttle switch circuit (231 V6).
22	C-4	Grounded closed throttle or wide open throttle switch circuit (231 V6).
23	C-4, CCC	Open or grounded carburetor mixture control (M/C) solenoid circuit.
24	CCC	Vehicle speed sensor circuit. The engine must run for at least 5 min, at normal speed before this code will show.
32	C-4, CCC	Barometric pressure sensor (BARO) circuit output is low.
32 & 55 (at same time)	C-4	Grounded +8V terminal or V(REF) terminal for BARO sensor, or a faulty ECM.
34	C-4	Manifold absolute pressure sensor (MAP) output is high. The engine must run for at least 10 sec. below 800 rpm before this code will show.
	CCC	Manifold absolute pressure sensor (MAP) circuit or vacuum sensor circuit. The engine must run for at least 5 min. below 800 rpm before this code will show.
35	CCC	Idle speed control circuit shorted. The engine must run for at least 2 sec. above ½ throttle before this code will show.
42	CCC	Electronic spark timing (EST) bypass circuit grounded.
43	C-4	Throttle position sensor adjustment. The engine must run for at least 10 sec. before this code will show.
44	C-4, CCC	Lean oxygen sensor indication. The engine must run for at least 5 min. in closed loop (oxygen sensor adjusting carburetor mixture) at part throttle under load (drive car) before this code will show.
44 & 45 (at same time)	C-4, CCC	Faulty oxygen sensor circuit.
45	C-4, CCC	Rich oxygen sensor indication. The engine must run for at least 5 min. before this code will show (see 44 for conditions).
51	C-4, CCC	Faulty calibration unit (PROM) or improper PROM installation in the ECM. It will take at least 30 sec. before this code will show.
52 & 53	C-4	"Check Engine" light off: intermittent ECM problem. "Check Engine" light on: faulty ECM—replace.
52	C-4, CCC	Faulty ECM.

Trouble Code Identification Chart (cont.)

NOTE: Always ground the test lead/terminal AFTER the engine is running

Trouble Code	Applicable System	Possible Problem Area
53	CCC	Faulty ECM.
54	C-4, CCC	Faulty mixture control solenoid circuit and/or faulty ECM.
55	C-4	Faulty throttle position sensor or ECM (all but 231 V6).
	CCC	Faulty oxygen sensor, open MAP sensor or faulty ECM (231 V6 only). Grounded +8V supply (terminal 19 on ECM connector), grounded 5V reference (terminal 21 on ECM connector), faulty oxygen sensor circuit or faulty ECM.

NOTE: *Not all codes will apply to every model.*

Mixture Control Solenoid (M/C)

The fuel flow through the carburetor idle main metering circuits is controlled by a mixture control (M/C) solenoid located in the carburetor. The M/C solenoid changes the air/fuel mixture to the engine by controlling the fuel flow through the carburetor. The ECM controls the solenoid by providing a ground. When the solenoid is energized, the fuel flow through the carburetor is reduced, providing a leaner mixture. When the ECM removes the ground, the solenoid is de-energized, increasing the fuel flow and providing a richer mixture. The M/C solenoid is energized and de-energized at a rate of 10 times per second.

Throttle Position Sensor (TPS)

The throttle position sensor is mounted in the carburetor body and is used to supply throttle position information to the ECM. The ECM memory stores an average of operation conditions with the ideal air/fuel ratios for each of those conditions. When the ECM receives a signal that indicates throttle position change, it immediately shifts to the last remembered set of operating conditions that resulted in an ideal air/fuel ratio control. The memory is continually being updated during normal operations.

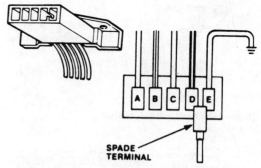

CCC system diagnostic test terminal located underneath the left side of the instrument panel

Idle Speed Control (ISC)

229, 231 V6 (Except Turbo)

The idle speed control does just what its name implies—it controls the idle. The ISC is used to maintain low engine speeds while at the same time preventing stalling due to engine load changes. The system consists of a motor assembly mounted on the carburetor which moves the throttle lever so as to open or close the throttle blades.

The whole operation is controlled by the ECM. The ECM monitors engine load to determine the proper idle speed. To prevent

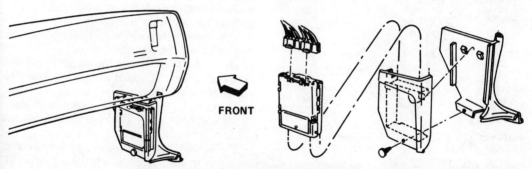

Electronic Control Module (ECM) location, all models similar

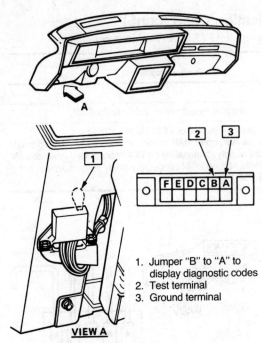

1. Jumper "B" to "A" to display diagnostic codes
2. Test terminal
3. Ground terminal

VIEW A

Under dash test terminal location

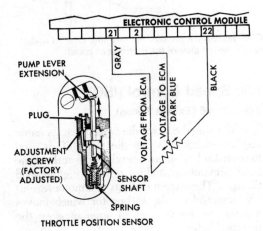

Throttle position sensor (TPS)

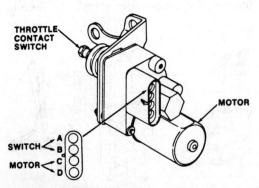

The Idle Speed Control (ISC) motor is attached to the carburetor

stalling, it monitors the air conditioning compressor switch, the transmission, the park/neutral switch and the ISC throttle switch. The ECM processes all this information and then uses it to control the ISC motor which in turn will vary the idle speed as necessary.

Electronic Spark Timing (EST)

All 1980 models with the 231 V6 engine and all 1981 and later models but those with the 229 V6 engine use EST. The EST distributor, as described in an earlier chapter, contains no vacuum or centrifugal advance mechanism and uses a seven terminal HEI module. It has four wires going to a four terminal connector in addition to the connectors normally found on HEI distributors. A reference pulse, indicating engine rpm is sent to the ECM; terminal "R" on the seven-terminal HEI provides this pulse on all models except the 229 V6. The ECM determines the proper spark advance for the engine operating conditions and then sends an 'EST' pulse back to the distributor.

NOTE: *The 1985 and later, 262 V6 distributor is equipped with a modified module which has eight terminals.*

Under most normal operating conditions, the ECM will control the spark advance. However, under certain operating conditions such as cranking or when setting base timing, the distributor is capable of operating without ECM control. This condition is called BYPASS and is determined by the BYPASS lead which runs from the ECM to the distributor. When the BYPASS lead is at the proper voltage (5), the ECM will control the spark. If the lead is grounded or open circuited, the HEI module itself will control the spark. Disconnecting the 4-terminal EST connector will also cause the engine to operate in the BYPASS mode.

Electronic Spark Control (ESC)

231 V6 Turbo (1981) and All (1984 and Later) Engines

The Electronic Spark Control (ESC) system is a closed loop system that controls engine detonation by adjusting the spark timing. There are two basic components in this system, the controller and the sensor.

The controller processes the sensor signal and remodifies the EST signal to the distributor to adjust the spark timing. The process is continuous so that the presence of detonation is monitored and controlled. The controller is not capable of memory storage.

The sensor is a magnetorestrictive device, mounted in the engine block that detects the presence, or absence, and intensity of detona-

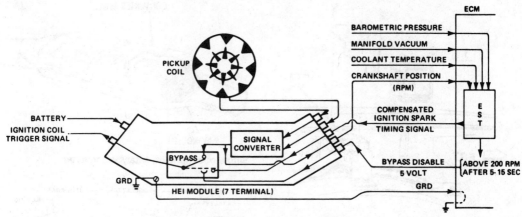

A schematic view of the EST circuitry

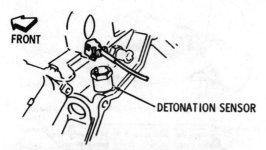

V6 turbo detonation sensor, mounted on intake manifold

tion according to the vibration characteristics of the engine. The output is an electrical signal which is sent to the controller.

Transmission Converter Clutch (TCC)

All 1981 models with an automatic transmission use TCC. The ECM controls the converter by means of a solenoid mounted in the transmission. When the vehicle speed reaches a certain level, the ECM energizes the solenoid and allows the torque converter to mechanically couple the transmission to the engine. When the operating conditions indicate that the transmission should operate as a normal fluid coupled transmission, the ECM will de-energize the solenoid. Depressing the brake will also return the transmission to normal automatic operation.

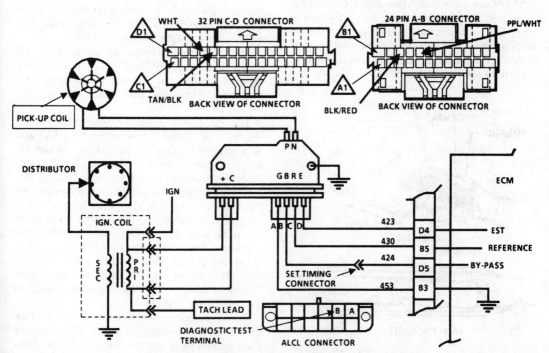

HEI system schematic with EST—262 V6, 1985 and later

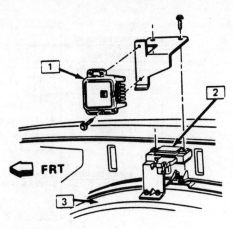

1. ESC module
2. Map sensor
3. Right wheelhouse

View of the electronic spark control module

Catalytic Converter

The catalytic converter is a muffler-like container built into the exhaust system to aid in the reduction of exhaust emissions. The catalyst element consists of individual pellets or a honeycomb monolithic substrate coated with a noble metal such as platinum, palladium, rhodium or a combination. When the exhaust gases come into contact with the catalyst, a chemical reaction occurs which will reduce the pollutants into harmless substances like water and carbon dioxide.

There are essentially two types of catalytic converters: an oxidizing type and a three-way type. The oxidizing type is used on all 1975–80 models with the exception of those 1980 models built for California. It requires the addition of oxygen to spur the catalyst into reducing the

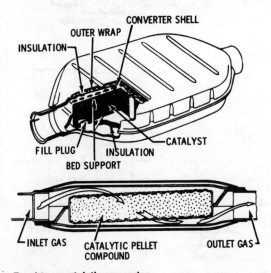

Bead-type catalytic converter

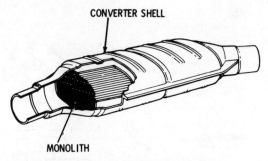

Single-bed monolith catalytic converter

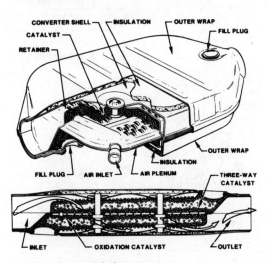

Dual-bed type catalytic converter

engine's HC and CO emissions into H_2O and CO_2. Because of this need for oxygen, the AIR system is used with all these models.

The oxidizing catalytic converter, while effectively reducing HC and CO emissions, does little, if anything in the way of reducing NO_x emissions. Thus, the three-way catalytic converter.

The three-way converter, unlike the oxidizing type, is capable of reducing HC, CO and NO_x emissions; all at the same time. In theory, it seems impossible to reduce all three pollutants in one system since the reduction of HC and CO requires the addition of oxygen, while the reduction of NO_x calls for the removal of oxygen. In actuality, the three-way system really can reduce all three pollutants, but only if the amount of oxygen in the exhaust system is precisely controlled. Due to this precise oxygen control requirement, the three-way converter system is used only in cars equipped with an oxygen sensor system.

There are no service procedures required for the catalytic converter, although the converter body should be inspected occasionally for damage. Some models with the V-6 engine require a catalyst charge at 30,000 mile intervals (consult your Owner's Manual).

PRECAUTIONS

1. Use only unleaded fuel.

2. Avoid prolonged idling; the engine should run no longer than 20 min. at curb idle and no longer than 10 min. at fast idle.

3. Do not disconnect any of the spark plug leads while the engine is running.

4. Make engine compression checks as quickly as possible.

CATALYST TESTING

At the present time there is no known way to reliably test catalytic converter operation in the field. The only reliable test is a 12 hour and 40 min. "soak" test (CVS) which must be done in a laboratory.

An infrared HC/CO tester is not sensitive enough to measure the higher tailpipe emissions from a failing converter. Thus, a bad converter may allow enough emissions to escape so that the car is no longer in compliance with Federal or state standards, but will still not cause the needle on a tester to move off zero.

The chemical reactions which occur inside a catalytic converter generate a great deal of heat. Most converter problems can be traced to fuel or ignition system problems which cause unusually high emissions. As a result of the increased intensity of the chemical reactions, the converter literally burns itself up.

A completely failed converter might cause a tester to show a slight reading. As a result, it is occasionally possible to detect one of these.

As long as you avoid severe overheating and the use of leaded fuels it is reasonably safe to assume that the converter is working properly. If you are in doubt, take the car to a diagnostic center that has a tester.

Oxygen Sensor

An oxygen sensor protrudes into the exhaust stream and monitors the oxygen content of the exhaust gases. The difference between the oxygen content of the exhaust gases and that of the outside air generates a voltage signal to the ECM. The ECM monitors this voltage and, depending upon the value of the signal received, issues a command to adjust for a rich or a lean condition.

No attempt should ever be made to measure the voltage output of the sensor. The current drain of any conventional voltmeter would be such that it would permanently damage the sensor. No jumpers, test leads or any other electrical connections should ever be made to the sensor. Use these tools ONLY on the ECM side of the wiring harness connector AFTER disconnecting it from the sensor.

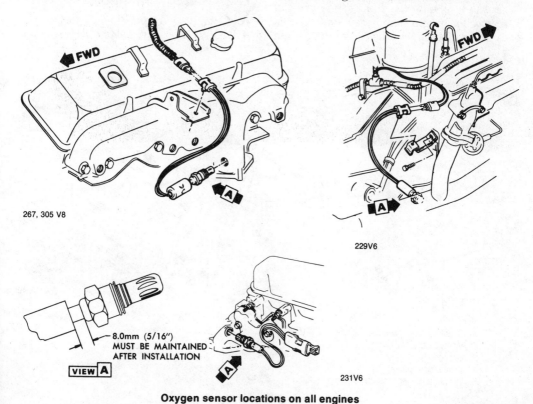

Oxygen sensor locations on all engines

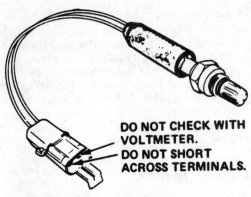

DO NOT CHECK WITH VOLTMETER.
DO NOT SHORT ACROSS TERMINALS.

Oxygen sensor assembly

REMOVAL AND INSTALLATION

The oxygen sensor must be replaced every 30,000 miles (48,000 km.). The sensor may be difficult to remove when the engine temperature is below 120°F (48°C). Excessive removal force may damage the threads in the exhaust manifold or pipe; follow the removal procedure carefully.

1. Locate the oxygen sensor. On the V8 engines, it is on the front of the left side exhaust manifold, just above the point where it connects to the exhaust pipe. On the V6 engines, it is on the inside of the exhaust pipe where it bends toward the back of the car.

NOTE: *On the V6 engine you may find it necessary to raise the front of the car and remove the oxygen sensor from underneath.*

2. Trace the wires leading from the oxygen sensor back to the first connector and then disconnect them (the connector on the V6 engine is attached to a bracket mounted on the right, rear of the engine block, while the connector in the V8 engine is attached to a bracket mounted on the top of the left side exhaust manifold).

3. Spray a commercial heat riser solvent onto the sensor threads and allow it to soak in for at least five minutes.

4. Carefully unscrew and remove the sensor.

5. To install, first coat the new sensor's threads with G.M. anti-seize compound no. 5613695 or the equivalent. This is *not* a conventional anti-seize paste. *The use of a regular compound may electrically insulate the sensor, rendering it inoperative. You must coat the threads with an electrically conductive anti-seize compound.*

6. Installation torque is 30 ft. lbs. (42 Nm.). *Do not overtighten.*

7. Reconnect the electrical connector. Be careful not to damage the electrical pigtail. Check the sensor boot for proper fit and installation. Install the air cleaner, if removed.

DIESEL ENGINE EMISSIONS CONTROLS

Crankcase Ventilation

A Crankcase Depression Regulator Valve (CDRV) is used to regulate (meter) the flow of

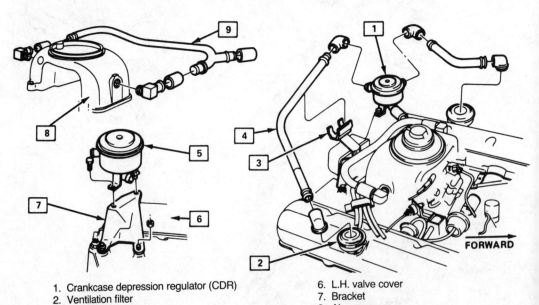

1. Crankcase depression regulator (CDR)
2. Ventilation filter
3. Brace clip
4. Ventilation pipes
5. Crankcase depression regulator (CDR)

6. L.H. valve cover
7. Bracket
8. Air crossover
9. Air crossover to regulator valve pipe

V8 diesel crankcase ventilation system

V8 Diesel EGR System Diagnosis

Condition	Possible Causes	Correction
EGR valve will not open. Engine stalls on deceleration Engine runs rough on light throttle	Binding or stuck EGR valve. No vacuum to EGR valve. Control valve blocked or air flow restricted.	Replace EGR valve. Replace EGR valve. Check VRV, RVR, solenoid, T.C.C. Operation, Vacuum Pump and connecting hoses.
EGR valve will not close. (Heavy smoke on acceleration).	Binding or stuck EGR valve. Constant high vacuum to EGR valve.	Replace EGR valve. Check VRV, RVR, solenoid, and connecting hoses.
EGR valve opens partially.	Binding EGR valve. Low vacuum at EGR valve.	Replace EGR valve. Check VRV, RVR, solenoid, vacuum pump, and connecting hoses.

V6 Diesel EGR System Diagnosis

Condition	Possible Cause	Correction
EGR valve will not open.	Binding or stuck EGR valve. No vacuum to EGR valve.	Replace EGR valve. Check VRV, RVR, solenoid TCC Operation (See Section 7A), Vacuum Pump, VMV, and connecting hoses.
EGR valve will not close, or EPR valve will not open. (Heavy smoke on acceleration).	Binding or stuck EGR or EPR valve. Constant high vacuum to EGR and EPR valve.	Replace EGR or EPR valve. Check VRV, RVR, solenoid VMV and connecting hoses.
EGR valve opens partially.	Binding EGR valve. Low vacuum at EGR valve.	Replace EGR valve. Check VRV, RVR, solenoid, vacuum pump, VMV and connecting hoses.
Loss of power and heavy smoke on acceleration, EGR valve functions normally.	Binding or stuck EPR valve, constant high vacuum to EPR valve.	Replace EPR valve. Check vacuum hose routing.

crankcase gases back into the engine to be burned. The CDRV is designed to limit vacuum in the crankcase as the gases are drawn from the valve covers through the CDRV and into the intake manifold (air crossover).

Fresh air enters the engine through the combination filter, check valve and oil fill cap. The fresh air mixes with blow-by gases and enters both valve covers. The gases pass through a filter installed on the valve covers and are drawn into connecting tubing.

Intake manifold vacuum acts against a spring loaded diaphragm to control the flow of crankcase gases. Higher intake vacuum levels pull the diaphragm closer to the top of the outlet tube. This reduces the amount of gases being drawn from the crankcase and decreases the vacuum level in the crankcase. As the intake vacuum decreases, the spring pushes the diaphragm away from the top of the outlet tube allowing more gases to flow to the intake manifold.

NOTE: *Do not allow any solvent to come in contact with the diaphragm of the Crankcase Depression Regulator Valve because the diaphragm will fail.*

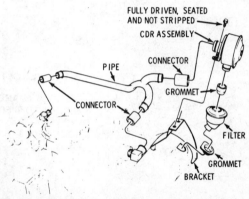

V6 diesel crankcase ventilation system

Exhaust Gas Recirculation (EGR)

To lower the formation of nitrogen oxides (NO_x) in the exhaust, it is necessary to reduce combustion temperatures. This is done in the diesel, as in the gasoline engine, by introducing exhaust gases into the cylinders through the EGR valve.

FUNCTIONAL TESTS OR COMPONENTS

Vacuum Regulator Valve (VRV)

The Vacuum Regulator Valve is attached to the side of the injection pump and regulates vacuum in proportion to throttle angle. Vacuum from the vacuum pump is supplied to port A and vacuum at port B is reduced as the throttle is opened. At closed throttle, the vacuum is 15 inches; at half throttle—6 inches; at wide open throttle there is zero vacuum.

Exhaust Gas Recirculation (EGR) Valve

Apply vacuum to vacuum port. The valve should be fully open at 10.5″ and closed below 6″.

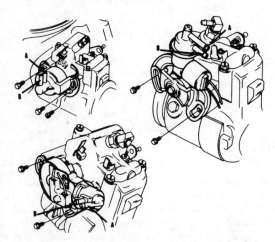

Vacuum regulator valve, mounted to diesel injection pumps

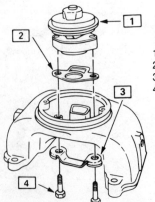

1. EGR valve
2. Gasket
3. Bolt lock
4. 24 N·m (18 ft.lbs.)

AFTER BOLTS ARE TORQUED TO SPECS BEND LOCK TABS AROUND BOLT HEADS

Diesel EGR valve location on top of intake manifold

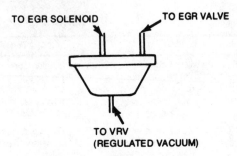

TO EGR SOLENOID   TO EGR VALVE

TO VRV
(REGULATED VACUUM)

Diesel vacuum reducer, except California

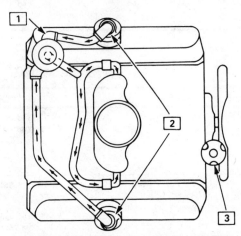

CRANKCASE VENTILATION SYSTEM SCHEMATIC V-TYPE DIESEL ENGINE WITH DEPRESSION REGULATOR VALVE

1. Crankcase depression regulator
2. Ventilation filter
3. Breather cap

Diesel crankcase ventilation flow

Response Vacuum Reducer (RVR)

Connect a vacuum gauge to the port marked "To EGR valve or T.C.C. solenoid". Connect a hand operated vacuum pump to the VRV port. Draw a 50.66 kPa (15 inch) vacuum on the pump and the reading on the vacuum gauge should be lower than the vacuum pump reading as follows:
- .75″ Except High Altitude
- 2.5″ High Altitude

Torque Converter Clutch Operated Solenoid

When the torque converter clutch is engaged, an electrical signal energizes the solenoid allowing ports 1 and 2 to be interconnected. When the solenoid is not energized, port 1 is closed and ports 2 and 3 are interconnected.

Solenoid Energized
- Ports 1 and 3 are connected.

Solenoid De-energized
- Ports 2 and 3 are connected.

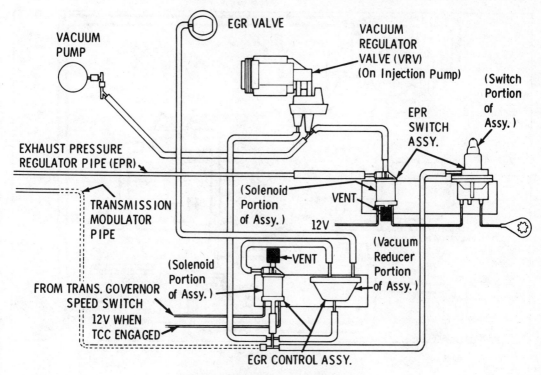

VACUUM PUMP

EGR VALVE

VACUUM REGULATOR VALVE (VRV) (On Injection Pump)

(Switch Portion of Assy.)

EPR SWITCH ASSY.

EXHAUST PRESSURE REGULATOR PIPE (EPR)

TRANSMISSION MODULATOR PIPE

(Solenoid Portion of Assy.)

VENT

12V

(Vacuum Reducer Portion of Assy.)

FROM TRANS. GOVERNOR SPEED SWITCH 12V WHEN TCC ENGAGED

(Solenoid Portion of Assy.)

VENT

EGR CONTROL ASSY.

Diesel EGR system, except California

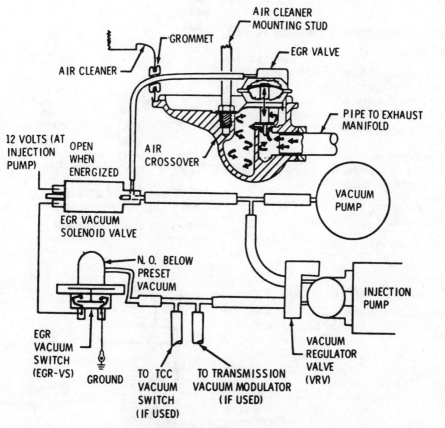

AIR CLEANER MOUNTING STUD

GROMMET

EGR VALVE

AIR CLEANER

PIPE TO EXHAUST MANIFOLD

12 VOLTS (AT INJECTION PUMP)

OPEN WHEN ENERGIZED

AIR CROSSOVER

VACUUM PUMP

EGR VACUUM SOLENOID VALVE

N. O. BELOW PRESET VACUUM

INJECTION PUMP

EGR VACUUM SWITCH (EGR-VS)

GROUND

TO TCC VACUUM SWITCH (IF USED)

TO TRANSMISSION VACUUM MODULATOR (IF USED)

VACUUM REGULATOR VALVE (VRV)

California EGR system, V8 Diesel

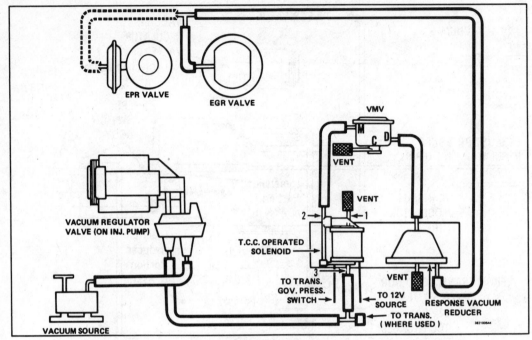

V6 diesel EGR system

Engine Temperature Sensor (ETS)

OPERATION

The engine temperature sensor has two terminals. Twelve volts are applied to one terminal and the wire from the other terminal leads to the fast idle solenoid and Housing Pressure Cold Advance solenoid that is part of the injection pump.

The switch contacts are closed below 125°F. At the calibration point, the contacts are open which turns off the solenoids.

Above Calibration
- Open circuit

Below Calibration
- Closed Circuit.

EPR Valve (California V6)

This valve is found between the right-hand exhaust manifold and the exhaust pipe on California V6 diesel cars. The EPR valve is used in the exhaust flow to increase back pressure in the exhaust system, thus increasing exhaust flow through the EGR system. The valve operates from the same vacuum source as the EGR valve. It should be fully closed at idle, and will open as the throttle is opened until, at full throttle, it will be fully open.

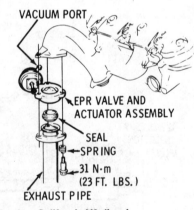

EPR valve, California V6 diesel

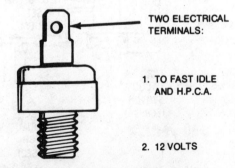

Engine Temperature Sensor (ETS), diesels

TESTING THE EPR VALVE

To test the EPR valve, apply vacuum to the vacuum port on the valve. The valve should be fully closed at 12 in. Hg of vacuum, and open below 6 in. Hg. of vacuum.

CARBURETED FUEL SYSTEM

Fuel Pump

The fuel pump is the single action AC diaphragm type. Two types of fuel pumps are used; serviceable and non-serviceable. The serviceable type is used on all 1964 and 1965 engines, 1966 inline engines without the AIR emission control system, and 1966 283 and 327 V8s. The non-serviceable type is used on all other engines.

The pump is actuated by an eccentric located on the engine camshaft. On inline engines, and the 231 V6 the eccentric actuates the pump rocker arm. On V8 and the 200 V6 engines, a pushrod between the camshaft eccentric and the fuel pump actuates the pump rocker arm.

TESTING THE FUEL PUMP

Fuel pumps should always be tested on the vehicle. The larger line between the pump and

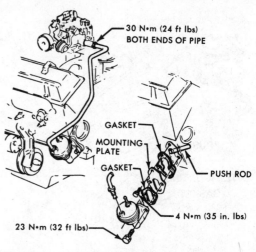

Fuel pump mounting—229 V6

tank is the suction side of the system and the smaller line, between the pump and carburetor is the pressure side. A leak in the pressure side would be apparent because of dripping fuel. A leak in the suction side is often only apparent because of the reduced volume of fuel delivered to the pressure side. However, fuel *may* leak out on the suction side when the engine is off.

1. Tighten any loose line connections and look for any kinks or restrictions. Inspect rubber hoses for cracks or leaks and replace if necessary. Inspect the fuel filter for clogging and clean or replace it as necessary.

2. Disconnect the fuel line at the carburetor. Disconnect the distributor-to-coil primary wire or, on HEI systems, the distributor connector. Place a container at the end of the fuel line and crank the engine a few revolutions. If little or no gasoline flows from the line, either the fuel pump is inoperative or the line

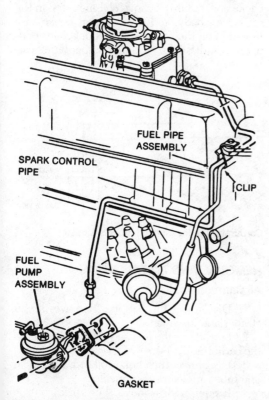

Fuel pump mounting—inline six cylinder

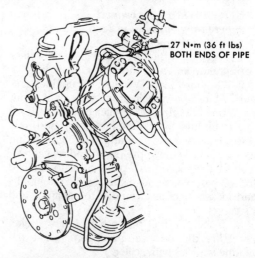

Fuel pump mounting—231 V6

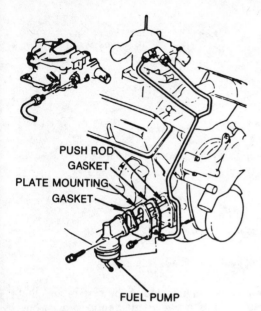

PUSH ROD
GASKET
PLATE MOUNTING
GASKET

FUEL PUMP

Fuel pump mounting—V8

is plugged. Blow through the lines with compressed air and try to the test again. Reconnect the line

3. Attach a pressure gauge to the pressure side of the fuel line with a "Tee" fitting.

4. Run the engine and note the reading on the gauge. Stop the engine and compare the reading with the specifications listed in the "Tune-Up Specifications" chart. If the pump is operating properly, the pressure will be as specified and will be constant at idle speed. If pressure varies sporadically or is too high or low, the pump should be replaced.

5. Remove the pressure gauge.

REMOVAL AND INSTALLATION

NOTE: *When you connect the fuel pump outlet fitting, always use 2 wrenches to avoid damaging the pump.*

1. Disconnect the fuel intake and outlet lines at the pump and plug the pump intake line.

2. On small-block V6 and V8 engines, remove the upper bolt from the right front mounting boss. Insert a longer bolt ($\frac{3}{8} - 16 \times 2$ in.) in this hole to hold the fuel pump pushrod.

3. Remove the two pump mounting bolts and lockwashers; remove the pump and its gasket.

4. If the rocker arm pushrod is to remove from V6 or V8, remove the two adapter bolts and lockwashers and remove the adapter and its gasket.

5. Install the fuel pump with a new gasket reversing the removal procedure. Coat the mating surfaces with sealer.

6. Connect the fuel lines and check for leaks.

Carburetors

Since their introduction in 1964, mid-size Chevrolets have used nineteen different carburetors:

- Carter AFB 4 bbl—1964–65
- Carter WCFB 4 bbl—1964–65
- Carter YF 1 bbl—1966–67
- Carter AVS 4bbl—1966
- Holley 4150 4 bbl—1965–70
- Holley 4160 bbl—1966–71
- Rochester BV 1 bbl—1964–67
- Rochester MV 1bbl—1968–76
- Rochester ME 1 bbl—1977–79
- Rochester 2GV 2 bbl—1968–74
- Rochester 2GC 2 bbl—1975–79
- Rochester M2ME 2 bbl—1980
- Rochester E2ME 2 bbl—1980 and later
- Rochester 4GC 4 bbl—1964–66
- Rochester 4MV 4 bbl—1967–74
- Rochester M4MC 4 bbl—1975–77
- Rochester 4MC 4 bbl—1977–79
- Rochester M4ME 4 bbl—1980
- Rochester E4ME 4 bbl—1980 and later

MODEL IDENTIFICATION

General Motors Rochester carburetors are identified by their model code. The first number indicates the number of barrels, while one of the last letters indicates the type of choke used. These are V for the manifold mounted choke coil, C for the choke coil mounted in the carburetor body, and E for electric choke, also mounted on the carburetor. Model codes ending in A indicate an altitude-compensating carburetor.

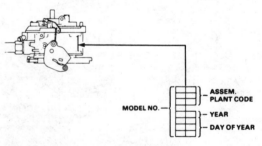

MODEL NO.—

ASSEM. PLANT CODE
YEAR
DAY OF YEAR

Carburetor I.D. location, all models similar

REMOVAL AND INSTALLATION

All Carburetors

1. Disconnect the battery. Remove the air cleaner and its gasket.

2. Disconnect the fuel and vacuum lines from the carburetor.

3. Disconnect the choke coil rod, heated air line tube, or electrical connector.

4. If equipped, remove the cruise control. Disconnect the throttle linkage.

5. On automatic transmission cars, disconnect the throttle valve linkage if so equipped.

6. If CEC equipped, remove the CEC valve vacuum hose and electrical connector. Disconnect the EGR line, if so equipped.

7. Remove the idle stop solenoid, if so equipped.

8. Remove the carburetor attaching nuts and/or bolts, gasket or insulator, and remove the carburetor.

9. Install the carburetor using the reverse of the removal procedure. Use a new gasket and fill the float bowl with gasoline to ease starting the engine.

OVERHAUL

All Types

Efficient carburetion depends greatly on careful cleaning and inspection during overhaul, since dirt, gum, water, or varnish in or on the carburetor parts are often responsible for poor performance.

Overhaul your carburetor in a clean, dust-free ares. Carefully disassemble the carburetor, referring often to the exploded views and directions packaged with the rebuilding kit. Keep all similar and look-alike parts segregated during disassembly and cleaning to avoid accidental interchange during assembly. Make a note of all jet sizes.

When the carburetor is disassembled, wash all parts (except diaphragms, electric choke units, pump plunger, and any other plastic, leather, fiber, or rubber parts) in clean carburetor solvent. Do not leave parts in the solvent any longer than is necessary to sufficiently loosen the deposits. Excessive cleaning may remove the special finish from the float bowl and choke valve bodies, leaving these parts unfit for service. Rinse all parts in clean solvent and blow them dry with compressed air or allow them to air day. Wipe clean all cork, plastic, leather, and fiber parts with a clean, lint-free cloth.

Blow out all passages and jets with compressed air and be sure that there are no restrictions or blockages. Never use wire or similar tools to clean jets, fuel passages, or air bleeds. Clean all jets and valves separately to avoid accidental interchange.

Check all parts for wear or damage. If wear or damage is found, replaced the defective parts. Especially check the following:

1. Check the float needle and seat for wear. If wear is found, replace the complete assembly.

2. Check the float hinge pin for wear and the float(s) for dents or distortion. Replace the float if fuel has leaked into it.

3. Check the throttle and choke shaft bores for wear or an out-of-round condition. Damage or wear to the throttle arm, shaft, or shaft bore will often require replacement of the throttle body. These parts require a close tolerance of fit; wear may allow air leakage, which could affect starting and idling.

NOTE: *Throttle shafts and bushings are not included in overhaul kits. They can be purchased separately.*

4. Inspect the idle mixture adjusting needles for burrs or grooves. Any such condition requires replacement of the needle, since you will not be able to obtain a satisfactory idle.

5. Test the accelerator pump check valves. They should pass air one way but not the other. Test for proper seating by blowing and sucking on the valve. Replace the valve check ball and spring as necessary. If the valve is satisfactory wash the valve parts again to remove breath moisture.

6. Check the bowl cover for warped surfaces with a straightedge.

7. Closely inspect the accelerator pump plunger for wear and damage, replacing as necessary.

8. After the carburetor is assembled, check the choke valve for freedom of operation.

Carburetor overhaul kits are recommended for each overhaul. These kits contain all gaskets and new parts to replace those which deteriorate most rapidly. Failure to replace all parts supplied with the kit (especially gaskets) can result in poor performance later.

Some carburetor manufacturers supply overhaul kits of three basic types: minor repair; major repair; and gasket kits. Basically, they contain the following:

Minor Repair Kits:
- All gaskets

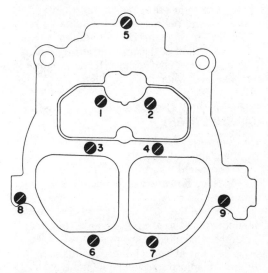

M4MC air horn tightening sequence

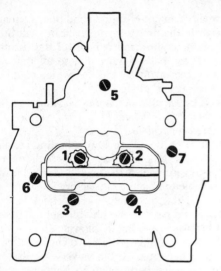

M2MC air horn tightening sequence

- Float needle valve
- All diagrams
- Spring for the pump diaphragm

Major Repair Kits:
- All jets and gaskets
- All diaphragms
- Float needle valve
- Pump ball valve
- Float
- Complete intermediate rod
- Intermediate pump lever
- Some cover hold-down screws and washers

Gasket Kits:
- All gaskets

After cleaning and checking all components, reassemble the carburetor, using new parts and referring to the exploded view. When reassembling, make sure that all screws and jets are tight in their seats, but do not overtighten as the tips will be distorted. Tighten all screws gradually, in rotation. Do not tighten needle valves into their seats; uneven jetting will result. Always use new gaskets. Be sure to adjust the float level when reassembling.

PRELIMINARY CHECKS (ALL CARBURETORS)

The following should be observed before attempting any adjustments.

1. Thoroughly warm the engine. If the engine is cold, be sure that it reaches operating temperature.

2. Check the torque of all carburetor mounting nuts and assembly screws. Also check the intake manifold-to-cylinder head bolts. If air is leaking at any of these points, any attempts at adjustment will inevitably lead to frustration.

3. Check the manifold heat control valve (if used) to be sure that it is free.

4. Check and adjust the choke as necessary.

5. Adjust the idle speed and mixture. If the mixture screws are capped, don't adjust them unless all other causes of rough idle have been eliminated. If any adjustments are performed that might possibly change the idle speed or mixture, adjust the idle and mixture again when you are finished.

Before you make any carburetor adjustments make sure that the engine is in tune. Many problems which are thought to be carburetor-related can be traced to an engine which is simply out-of-tune. Any trouble in these areas will have symptoms like those of carburetor problems.

Carter AFB—4-BBL Carburetor

AUTOMATIC CHOKE ADJUSTMENT

The automatic choke is correctly adjusted when the scribe mark on the coil housing is aligned with the center notch in the choke housing for automatic transmission cars and one notch lear for manual transmission cars.

FLOAT ADJUSTMENT

Remove the metering rods and the bowl cover. Align the float by sighting down its side to determine if it is parallel with the outer edge of the air horn. Bend the float to adjust. Float level is adjusted with the air horn inverted and the air horn gasket in place. Clearance between each float (at the outer end) and the air horn gasket should be 5/16 in. Bend to adjust.

FLOAT DROP ADJUSTMENT

Float drop is adjusted by holding the air horn in an upright position and bending the float arm

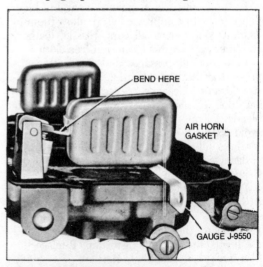

AFB float adjustment

until the vertical distance from the air horn gasket to the outer end of each float measures ¾ in.

INTERMEDIATE CHOKE ROD ADJUSTMENT

Remove the choke coil housing assembly, gasket, and baffle plate. Position a .026 in. wire gauge between the bottom of the slot in the piston and the top of the slot in the choke piston housing. Close the choke piston against the gauge and secure it with a rubber band. Bend the intermediate choke rod so that the distance between the top edge of the choke valve and the air horn divider measures .070 in.

ACCELERATOR PUMP ADJUSTMENT

The first step in adjusting the accelerator pump is to push aside the fast-idle cam and firmly seat the throttle valves. Bend the pump rod at the lower angle to obtain a ½ in. clearance between the air horn and the top of the plunger shaft.

UNLOADED, CLOSING SHOE, AND SECONDARY THROTTLE ADJUSTMENT

To adjust the unloader, hold the throttle wide open and bend the unloaded tang to obtain a ³⁄₁₆ in. clearance between the upper edge of the choke valve and the inner wall of the air horn.

The clearance between the positive closing shoes on the primary and secondary throttle valves is checked with the valves closed. Bend the secondary closing shoe as required to obtain a clearance of .020 in.

The secondary throttle opening is governed by the pick-up lever on the primary throttle shaft. It has two points of contact with the loose lever on the primary shaft. If the contact points do not simultaneously engage, bend the pick-up lever to obtain proper engagement. The primary and secondary throttle valve opening must be synchronized.

Carter AVS—4-BBL Carburetor

AIR VALVE ADJUSTMENT

1. Turn the air valve bearing retainer until the air valve freely falls open.
2. Wind the air valve bearing counterclockwise until the air valve just starts to close.
3. Continue to wind the bearing an additional 2⅛ turns, and then tighten the retainer.

ACCELERATOR PUMP ADJUSTMENT

1. With the fast idle cam out of the way, back the idle speed screw out until the throttle valves seat in their bores.
2. Hold the throttle valves closed and mea-

AVS air valve adjustment

sure the distance from the air horn to the bottom of the pump S-link.
3. If this distance is not ¹¹⁄₃₂ in., bend the pump rod to obtain it.

IDLE VENT ADJUSTMENT

Holding the choke valve open and throttle valve closed, the clearance at the idle vent valve should be .030 in. Bend the vent valve lever to adjust.

FAST IDLE CHOKE ROD ADJUSTMENT

Bend the fast idle rod at a lower angle until the fast idle cam index mark lines up with the fast idle adjustment screw. Perform this adjustment while holding the choke valve closed.

FLOAT LEVEL AND DROP ADJUSTMENT

These adjustments are made in the same manner as on the Carter AFB.

CHOKE UNLOADER ADJUSTMENT

1. Hold the throttle wide open and the choke valve toward the closed position with a rubber band.
2. Bend the unloader tang on the throttle shaft lever to obtain a clearance of .170 in. Between the upper edge of the choke valve and the dividing wall of the air horn.

CHOKE VACUUM BREAK ADJUSTMENT

1. Hold the vacuum break in against its stop and the choke valve toward the closed position with a rubber band.
2. Bend the vacuum break link at an offset to obtain .120 in. clearance between the upper edge of the choke valve and the air horn wall.

CLOSING SHOE ADJUSTMENT

1. Hold the primary and secondary throttle valves closed.
2. Bend the secondary closing shoe to obtain .020 in. clearance between the positive

closing shoes on the primary and secondary throttle levers.

SECONDARY THROTTLE OPENING

1. Check to see that the pickup lever contacts the loose lever on the primary shaft at both points simultaneously. Bend the pickup lever to obtain proper contact, if necessary.
2. If the primary and secondary throttle valves do not come to the wide open position simultaneously, bend the connecting link until they do.

SECONDARY LOCKOUT ADJUSTMENT

1. When the choke valve is closed, the lockout tang on the secondary throttle lever should engage the lockout dog. When the valve is open, the lockout dog should swing free of the tang.
2. Bend the lockout tang on the secondary throttle lever, if an adjustment is necessary.

Carter YF—1 BBL Carburetor

AUTOMATIC CHOKE ADJUSTMENT

1. Disconnect the choke rod from the choke lever.
2. Hold the choke valve closed and pull the rod up against the stop in the thermostat housing.
3. The top of the rod should be about one rod diameter above the top of the hole in the choke lever. If not, adjust the length of the rod by bending it at the bend.
4. Connect the choke rod at the lever.

HAND CHOKE ADJUSTMENT

1. Push in the hand choke knob until the knob is within 1/8 in. of the dash.
2. Loosen the cable clamp at the carburetor and adjust the cable until the choke is wide open.
3. Tighten the cable clamp and check the operation of the choke.

IDLE VENT ADJUSTMENT

1. With the choke open, back out the idle speed screw until it is free to close the throttle valve.
2. Insert a feeler gauge between the air horn and the vent valve. Adjust to get 0.065 in. clearance.

FAST IDLE AND CHOKE VALVE ADJUSTMENT

1. Hold the choke valve closed.
2. Close the throttle and mark the position of the throttle lever tang on the fast idle cam.
3. The mark on the fast idle cam should align with the upper edge of the tang on the throttle lever. If not, bend the choke rod as necessary.

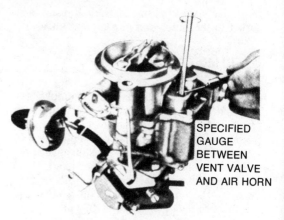

SPECIFIED GAUGE BETWEEN VENT VALVE AND AIR HORN

Adjusting the idle vent (Carter YF)

BEND ROD TO ADJUST

ALIGN MARK AND TANG AS SPECIFIED

Choke rod adjustment (Carter YF)

CHOKE UNLOADER ADJUSTMENT

1. Open the throttle to the wide open position.
2. Using a rubber band, hold the choke valve closed.
3. Bend the unloader tang on the throttle lever to get the proper clearance (0.250 in.) between the lower edge of the choke valve and the air horn wall.

VACUUM BREAK ADJUSTMENT

1. Hold the vacuum break arm against its stop and hold the choke closed with a rubber band.
2. Bend the vacuum break link to establish a clearance of 2.220 in. (automatic transmission) or 0.240 in. (standard transmission) between the lower edge of the choke valve and the air horn wall.

FLOAT LEVEL ADJUSTMENT

1. Turn the bowl cover upside down and measure the float level by measuring the distance between the float (free end) and cover.

Carter Specifications

Year	Model or Type ①	Float Level (in.)		Float Drop (in.)		Pump Travel Setting (in.)	Choke Setting			Secondary Locknut Adj.
		Prim	Sec	Prim	Sec		Unloader (in.)	Housing	
1964–65	AFB-All	7/32	7/32	3/4	3/4	1/2	1/4	1-Lean	0.020
	WCFB-All	7/32	1/4	3/4	3/4	1/2	3/16	Index	—
1966	6-Cyl-YF-4079S, 4080S	1/2	—	1 3/16	—	—	0.260	—	—
	V8-AVS-4027S, 4028S	1 15/32	—	2	—	11/32	0.170	—	—
1967	6 Cyl-YF	7/32	—	1 3/16	—	—	0.250	—	—

① Model number located on the tag or casting

This distance should be 7/32 in.; if not, bend the lip of the float, not the float arm.

2. Hold the cover in the proper position (not upside down) and measure the float drop from the cover to the float bottom at the end opposite the hinge. This distance should be 1 3/16 in.

3. Make any necessary adjustments with the stop tab on the float arm.

ACCELERATOR PUMP ADJUSTMENT

1. Seat the throttle valve by backing off the idle speed screw.

2. Hold the throttle valve closed.

3. Fully depress the diaphragm shaft and check the contact between the lower retainer and the lifter link.

4. This retainer (upper pump spring) should

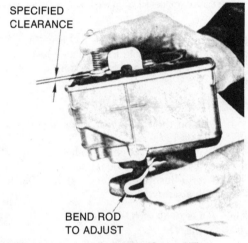

SPECIFIED CLEARANCE

BEND ROD TO ADJUST

Accelerator pump adjustment (Carter YF)

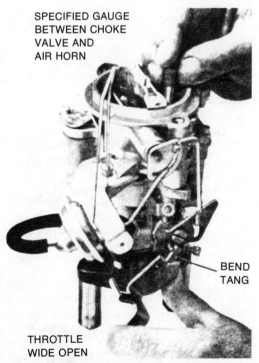

SPECIFIED GAUGE BETWEEN CHOKE VALVE AND AIR HORN

BEND TANG

THROTTLE WIDE OPEN

Choke unloader adjustment (Carter YF)

just contact the pump lifter link. Do not compress the spring.

5. Bend the pump connector link at its "U" bend to make corrections.

METERING ROD ADJUSTMENT

1. Insert the metering rod through the metering jet and close the throttle valve. Press down on the upper pump spring until the pump bottoms.

2. The metering rod arm must rest on the pump lifter link; the rod eye should just slide over the arm pin.

3. To adjust, bend the metering rod arm.

Rochester BV—1 BBL Carburetor
AUTOMATIC CHOKE ADJUSTMENT

1. Disconnect the choke rod from the choke lever at the carburetor.

2. While holding the choke valve shut, pull the choke rod up against the stop in the thermostat housing.

3. Adjust the length of the choke rod so that

Rochester BV Specifications

Year	Carburetor Identifi-cation ①	Float Level (in.)	Float Drop (in.)	Pump Rod (in.)	Idle Vent (in.)	Vacuum Break (in.)	Auto-matic Choke	Choke Rod (in.)	Choke Unloader (in.)	Fast Idle Speed
1964–66	All	1⁹⁄₃₂	1¾	—	0.050	—	—	—	0.350	—
1967	7025000	1⁹⁄₃₂	1¾	—	0.050	0.140	—	0.090	0.350	—
	7022503	1⁹⁄₃₂	1¾	—	0.050	0.160	—	0.100	0.350	—
	7026028	1⁹⁄₃₂	1¾	—	0.050	0.140	—	0.090	0.350	—
	7026027	1⁹⁄₃₂	1¾	—	0.050	0.160	—	0.100	0.350	—
	7027110	¾	1¾	—	1	0.110	—	0.060	0.215	—
	7027101	¾	1¾	—	1	0.120	—	0.060	0.215	—

① The carburetor identification tag is located at the rear of the carburetor on one of the air horn screws

the bottom edge of the choke rod is even with the top edge of the hole in the choke lever.

4. Check the linkage for freedom of operation.

IDLE VENT ADJUSTMENT

1. Position the carburetor lever on the low step of the fast idle cam.

2. The distance between the choke valve and the body casting should be 0.050 in.

3. If an adjustment is necessary, turn the valve with a screwdriver.

FAST IDLE AND CHOKE VALVE ADJUSTMENT

1. Position the end of the idle adjusting screw on the next to highest step of the fast idle cam.

2. A 0.050 in. feeler gauge should slide eas-

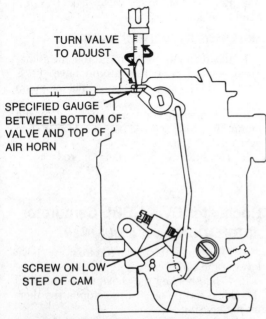

TURN VALVE TO ADJUST

SPECIFIED GAUGE BETWEEN BOTTOM OF VALVE AND TOP OF AIR HORN

SCREW ON LOW STEP OF CAM

Idle vent adjustment (Rochester BV)

ily between the lower edge of the choke valve and the carburetor bore.

3. If necessary, bend the choke rod until the correct clearance is obtained.

UNLOADER ADJUSTMENT

1. Open the throttle to the wide open position.

2. A 0.230/0.270 in. gauge should slide freely between the lower edge of the choke valve and the bore of the carburetor.

3. If necessary, bend the throttle tang to obtain the proper clearance.

VACUUM BREAK ADJUSTMENT

1. Hold the diaphragm lever against the diaphragm body.

2. The clearance between the lower edge of the choke valve and the air horn wall should be 0.136–0.154 in. on Powerglide cars and 0.154–0.173 in. on manual cars.

3. Bend the diaphragm link, if necessary.

FLOAT LEVEL ADJUSTMENT

1. Remove the air cleaner.

2. Disconnect the fuel line, fast idle rod, cam-to-choke kick lever, vacuum hose at the diaphragm, and the choke rod at the choke lever.

3. Remove the bowl cover screws and careful lift the cover off the carburetor.

4. Install a new gasket on the cover before making any adjustments.

5. Invert the cover assembly and measure the float level with a float gauge.

NOTE: *Rebuilding kits include a float level gauge.*

6. Check float centering while holding the cover sideways. Use the same gauge as in Step Five. The floats should not touch the gauge.

7. Hold the cover upright and measure the float drop. If the drop is more or less than 1¾ in., bend the stop tang until the drop is correct.

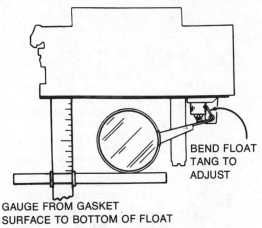

GAUGE FROM GASKET
SURFACE TO BOTTOM OF FLOAT
Adjusting the float drop (Rochester BV)

8. Install the cover and reconnect the lines and linkage in the reverse order of removal.

Rochester MV—1 BBL Carburetor

The model MV carburetor is a single bore, down-drift carburetor with an aluminum throttle body, automatic choke, internally balanced venting, and a hot idle compensating system for cars equipped with automatic transmissions. Newer models are also equipped with Combination Emission Control valves (C.E.C.) and an Exhaust Gas Recirculation (EGR) system. An electrically operated idle stop solenoid replaces the idle stop screw of older models.

The MV carburetor is used on six cylinder cars from 1968 and service procedures apply to all MV carburetors.

FAST IDLE ADJUSTMENT

NOTE: *The fast idle adjustment must be made with the transmission in Neutral.*

1. Position the fast idle lever on the high step of the fast idle cam.
2. Be sure that the choke is properly adjusted and in the wide open position with the engine warm.
3. Bend the fast idle lever until the specified speed is obtained.

CHOKE ROD (FAST IDLE CAM) ADJUSTMENT

NOTE: *Adjust the fast idle before making choke rod adjustments.*

1. Place the fast idle cam follower on the second step of the fast idle cam and hold it firmly against the rise to the high step.
2. Rotate the choke valve in the direction of a closed choke by applying force to the choke coil lever.
3. Bend the choke rod, at the point shown in the illustration, to give the specified opening

between the lower edge (upper edge—1976), of the choke valve and the inside air horn wall.
NOTE: *Measurement must be made at the center of the choke valve.*

CHOKE VACUUM BREAK ADJUSTMENT

The adjustment of the vacuum break diaphragm unit insures correct choke valve opening after engine starting.

1. Remove the air cleaner. On vehicles with the THERMAC air cleaner, plug the sensor's vacuum take off port.
2. Using an external vacuum source, apply vacuum to the vacuum break diaphragm until the plunger is fully seated.
3. When the plunger is seated, push the choke valve toward the closed position.

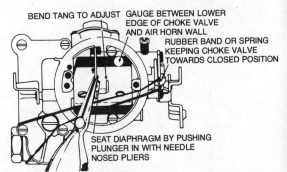

Vacuum break adjustment (MV)

CHOKE UNLOADER ADJUSTMENT

1. While holding the choke valve closed, apply pressure to the choke operating lever.
2. Turn the throttle lever to the wide open position.
3. Measure the distance between the lower edge of the choke plate and the air horn wall.
4. If an adjustment is necessary, bend the unloader tang on the throttle lever.

FLOAT LEVEL ADJUSTMENT

1. While holding the float retainer in place, push down on the outer end of the float arm.
2. Measure the distance from the top of the float bowl casting (no gasket) and the toe of the float.
3. Bend the float as necessary to obtain the specified measurement.

METERING ROD ADJUSTMENT

1. Back out the idle adjusting screw or idle stop solenoid to close the throttle valve.
2. Apply pressure to the power piston hanger and hold the piston against its stop.
3. While holding the power piston down, turn the metering rod holder over to the flat surface of the bowl casting until the metering rod lightly touches the inside edge of the bowl.

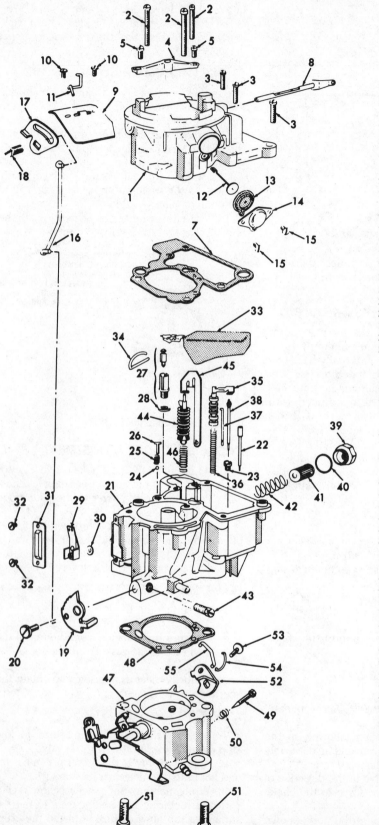

1. Air horn assembly
2. Screw—air horn—long
3. Screw—air horn—short
4. Bracket—air cleaner stud
5. Screw—bracket attaching
7. Gasket—air horn
8. Choke shaft and lever assembly
9. Choke valve
10. Screw—choke valve
11. Lever—vacuum break link
12. Vacuum break link assy.
13. Diaphragm—vacuum break
14. Cover—vacuum break
15. Screw—cover
16. Choke rod
17. Choke lever
18. Screw—choke lever
19. Cam—fast idle
20. Screw—cam attaching
21. Float bowl assembly
22. Idle tube assembly
23. Jet—main metering
24. Ball—pump discharge
25. Spring—pump discharge
26. Guide—pump discharge
27. Needle and seat assy.
28. Gasket—needle seat
29. Idle compensator assembly
30. Gasket—idle compensator
31. Cover—idle compensator
32. Screw—cover
33. Float assembly
34. Hinge pin—float
35. Power piston assembly
36. Spring—power piston
37. Rod—power piston
38. Metering rod and spring assembly
39. Filter nut—fuel inlet
40. Gasket—filter nut
41. Filter—fuel inlet
42. Spring—fuel filter
43. Screw—slow idle
44. Pump assembly
45. Lever—pump actuating
46. Spring—pump return
47. Throttle body assembly
48. Gasket—throttle body
49. Idle needle
50. Spring—idle needle
51. Screw—throttle body
52. Lever—pump and power rods—new
53. Screw—lever attaching
54. Link—power piston rod
55. Link—pump lever

Exploded view of the MV carburetor

Rochester MV Specifications

Year	Carburetor Identifi- cation ①	Float Level (in.)	Metering Rod (in.)	Pump Rod	Idle Vent (in.)	Vacuum Break (in.)	Auxiliary Vacuum Break (in.)	Fast Idle Off Car (in.)	Choke Rod (in.)	Choke Unloader (in.)	Fast Idle Speed (rpm)
1968	7028014	9/32	0.120	—	0.050	0.245	—	1½	0.150	0.350	2400 ②
	7028015	9/32	0.130	—	0.050	0.275	—	1½	0.150	0.350	2400 ②
	7028017	9/32	0.130	—	0.050	0.275	—	1½	0.150	0.350	2400 ②
1969	7029014	¼	0.070	—	0.050	0.245	—	0.100	0.170	0.350	2400 ②
	7029015	¼	0.090	—	0.050	0.275	—	0.100	0.200	0.350	2400 ②
	7029017	¼	0.090	—	0.050	0.275	—	0.100	0.200	0.350	2400 ②
1970	7040014	¼	0.070	—	—	0.200	—	0.110	0.170	0.350	2400 ②
	7040017	¼	0.090	—	—	0.160	—	0.100	0.190	0.350	2400 ②
1971	7041014	¼	0.080	—	—	0.200	—	0.100	0.160	0.350	—
	7041017	¼	0.080	—	—	0.230	—	0.100	0.180	0.350	—
	7041023	1/16	—	—	—	0.200	—	0.110	0.120	0.350	—
1972	7042014	¼	0.080	—	—	0.190	—	—	0.125	0.500	2400 ②
	7042017	¼	0.078	—	—	0.225	—	—	0.150	0.500	2400 ②
	7042984	¼	0.078	—	—	0.190	—	—	0.125	0.500	2400 ②
	7042987	¼	0.076	—	—	0.225	—	—	0.150	0.500	2400 ②
1973	7043014	¼	0.080	—	—	0.300	—	—	0.245	0.500	1800 ②
	7043017	¼	0.080	—	—	0.350	—	—	0.275	0.500	1800 ②
1974	7044014	3/10	0.079	—	—	0.275	—	—	0.230	0.500	1800 ② ③
	7044017	3/10	0.072	—	—	0.350	—	—	0.275	0.500	1800 ② ③
	7044314	3/10	0.073	—	—	0.300	—	—	0.245	0.500	1800 ② ③
1975	7045013	11/32	0.080	—	—	0.200	0.215	—	0.160	0.215	1800 ④
	7045012	11/32	0.080	—	—	0.350	0.312	—	0.275	0.275	1800 ④
	7045314	11/32	0.080	—	—	0.275	0.312	—	0.230	0.275	1800 ④
1976	17056012	11/32	0.084	—	—	0.140	0.265	—	0.100	0.260	⑤
	17056013	11/32	0.082	—	—	0.140	0.325	—	0.140	0.260	⑤
	17056014	—	—	—	—	—	—	—	—	—	—

① The carburetor identification tag is located at the rear of the carburetor on one of the air horn screws
② High step of cam
③ Without vacuum advance
④ 1700 rpm with automatic transmission in Neutral
⑤ 2100 rpm—49 states with transmission in Neutral; 2200 rpm—49 states with non-integral head; 1700 rpm—California

4. Measure the space between the bowl and the bottom of the metering rod holder. This dimension should be between 0.070 and 0.078 in.

5. Bend the metering rod holder if an adjustment is necessary.

CHOKE ROD ADJUSTMENT

1. Disconnect the choke rod from the upper choke lever and hold the choke valve closed.

2. Push the choke rod down to the bottom of its travel.

3. The top of the rod should be even with the bottom of the hole in the choke lever; bend the rod if necessary.

Rochester 1ME—1 BBL Carburetors

FLOAT LEVEL ADJUSTMENT

1. Push down on the end of the float arm and against the top of the float needle to hold the retaining pin firmly in place.

2. While holding the position of the retaining pin, gauge from the top of the casting to

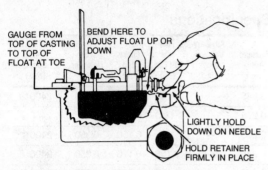

Adjusting the MV carburetor float level

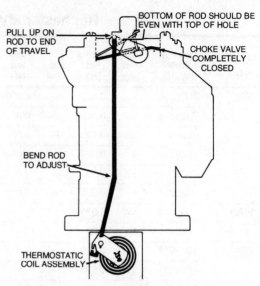

Adjusting the choke rod (MV)

the top of the index point at the toe of the float.

3. If float level needs to be changed do it by bending the float arm just on the float side of the float needle.

FAST IDLE ADJUSTMENT

1. If the carburetor has a stepped fast idle cam, put the cam follower on the high step of the cam. If the cam has a smooth contour, open the throttle slightly and rotate the cam to its highest position, then release throttle.

2. Support the lever with a pair of pliers, and bend the tang in or out to achieve specified rpm. Perform the adjustment with the engine hot and the choke open.

CHOKE COIL LEVER ADJUSTMENT

NOTE: *This adjustment requires a plug gauge or other metal rod of .120" diameter.*

1. Place the fast idle cam follower on the highest step of the cam or rotate the cam to its highest possible position. Close the choke all the way and hold.

2. Insert the plug gauge through the small hole in the outer end of the choke lever. Bend

the link at the lowest point of the curved portion until the gauge will enter the hole in the carburetor casting.

CHOKE ADJUSTMENT

1. Place the fast idle cam follower on the high step of the cam or rotate the cam until it is at the highest position.

2. Slightly loosen the three screws which retain the choke cover just enough to turn the cover—don't loosen them more than necessary, or the lever may slip out of the tang inside.

3. Turn the cover until the mark on the cover lines up with the appropriate mark on the choke housing—see specifications.

Rochester ME Specifications

Year	Carburetor Identification	Float Level (in.)	Metering Rod (in.)	Pump Rod	Idle Vent (in.)	Vacuum Break (in.)	Auxiliary Vacuum Break (in.)	Fast Idle Off Car (in.)	Choke ① Rod (in.)	Choke Unloader (in.)	Fast Idle Speed (rpm) ②
1977	17057013	3/8	.070	—	—	.125	—	—	1 CCW	.375	2000
	17057014	3/8	.070	—	—	.120	—	—	2 CCW	.325	2000
	17057310	3/8	.070	—	—	—	—	—	Index	—	1800
1978	17058013	3/8	.080	—	—	.200	—	—	Index	.200	2000
	17058014	5/16	.160	—	—	.200	—	—	Index	.200	2100
	17058314	3/8	.160	—	—	.243	—	—	Index	.245	2000
1979	17059013	—	—	Information not available							
	17059014	—	—	Information not available							
	17059314	—	—	Information not available							

① Choke adjustment—Index, CCW—counterclockwise in notches, or CW—clockwise in notches
② Transmission in Neutral

METERING ROD ADJUSTMENT

1. Hold the throttle wide open. Push downward on the metering rod until it can be slid out of the slot in the holder. Slide the rod out of the holder and remove it from the main metering jet.

2. Back out the solenoid hex screw until the throttle can be closed all the way.

3. Remove the float bowl gasket.

4. Holding power piston down and throttle closed, swing the metering rod holder over the flat surface of the bowl casting next to the throttle bore. Measure the distance from the flat surface to the outer end of the rod holder with the specified gauge (see specifications), or a metal rod of equivalent diameter.

5. Bend the horizontal portion of the rod holder where it joins the vertical portion until the gauge just passes between the holder and surface of the bowl casting with power piston bottomed.

Rochester 2GC, 2GV—2 BBL Carburetors

These procedures are for both the 1¼ and 1½ models; where there are differences these are noted. The 1½ model has larger throttle bores and an additional fuel feed circuit to make it suitable for use on the 350 V8s.

FAST IDLE ADJUSTMENT

On 2GC and 2GV models the fast idle is set automatically when the curb idle and mixture is set.

FAST IDLE CAM ADJUSTMENT

1. Turn the idle screw onto the second step of the fast idle cam, abutting against the top step.

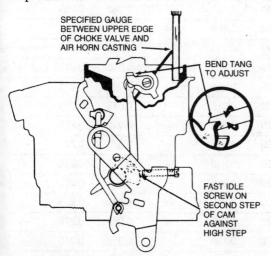

SPECIFIED GAUGE BETWEEN UPPER EDGE OF CHOKE VALVE AND AIR HORN CASTING

BEND TANG TO ADJUST

FAST IDLE SCREW ON SECOND STEP OF CAM AGAINST HIGH STEP

Adjusting the fast idle cam (2GV)

2. Hold the choke valve toward the closed position and check the clearance between the upper edge of the choke valve and the air horn wall.

3. If this measurement varies from specifications, bend the tang on the choke lever.

CHOKE UNLOADER ADJUSTMENT

1. Hold the throttle valves wide open and use a rubber band to hold the choke valve toward the closed position.

2. Measure the distance between the upper edge of the choke valve and the air horn wall.

3. If this measurement is not within specifications, bend the unloader tang on the throttle lever to correct it.

ACCELERATOR PUMP ROD ADJUSTMENT

1. Back out the idle stop screw and close the throttle valves in their bores.

2. Measure the distance from the top of the air horn to the top of the pump rod.

3. Bend the pump rod at angle to correct this dimension.

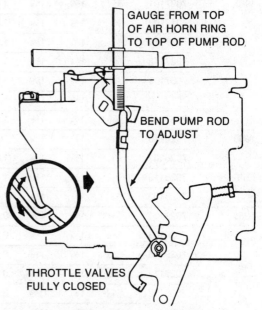

GAUGE FROM TOP OF AIR HORN RING TO TOP OF PUMP ROD

BEND PUMP ROD TO ADJUST

THROTTLE VALVES FULLY CLOSED

Adjusting the accelerator pump rod (2GV)

FLOAT LEVEL ADJUSTMENT

Invert the air horn and, with the gasket in place and the needle seated, measure the level as follows:

On nitrophyl floats, measure from the air horn gasket to the lip on the toe of the float.

On brass floats, measure the air horn gasket to the lower edge of the float seam.

Bend the float tang to adjust the level.

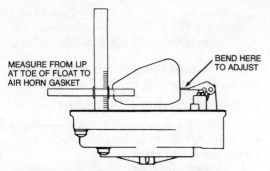

Adjusting the float level–nitrophyl (2GV)

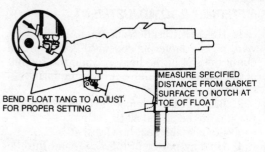

Adjusting the float drop–nitrophyl (2GV)

On nitrophyl floats, measure from the air horn gasket to the lip at the toe of the float.

On brass floats, measure from the air horn gasket to the bottom of the float.

Bend the float tang to adjust either type of float.

FLOAT DROP ADJUSTMENT

Holding the air horn right side up, measure float drop as follows:

Rochester 2GC, 2GV Specifications

Year	Carburetor Identification ①	Float Level (in.)	Float Drop (in.)	Pump Rod (in.)	Idle Vent (in.)	Vacuum Break (in.)	Automatic ② Choke	Choke Rod (in.)	Choke Unloader (in.)	Fast Idle Speed
1967	7027101	¾	1¾	1⅛	1.000	0.120	—	0.060	0.215	—
	7027103	¾	1¾	1⅛	1.000	0.120	—	0.060	0.215	—
	7027110	¾	1¾	1⅛	1.000	0.110	—	0.060	0.215	—
	7027112	¾	1¾	1⅛	1.000	0.110	—	0.060	0.215	—
	7037103	¾	1¾	1⅛	1.000	0.130	—	0.060	0.215	—
	7037110	¾	1¾	1⅛	1.000	0.110	—	0.060	0.215	—
	7037112	¾	1¾	1⅛	1.000	0.110	—	0.060	0.215	—
1968	7028110	¾	1¾	1⅛	1.000	0.100	—	0.060	0.200	—
	7028101	¾	1¾	1⅛	1.000	0.100	—	0.060	0.200	—
	7028112	¾	1¾	1⅛	1.000	0.100	—	0.060	0.200	—
	7028103	¾	1¾	1⅛	1.000	0.100	—	0.060	0.200	—
1969	7029101	27/32	1¾	1⅛	0.020	0.100	—	0.060	0.215	—
	7029103	27/32	1¾	1⅛	0.020	0.100	—	0.060	0.215	—
	7029110	27/32	1¾	1⅛	0.020	0.100	—	0.060	0.215	—
	7029112	27/32	1¾	1⅛	0.020	0.100	—	0.060	0.215	—
	7029102	¾	1¾	1 13/32	0.020	0.215	—	0.085	0.275	—
	7029104	¾	1¾	1 13/32	0.020	0.215	—	0.085	0.275	—
	7029127	¾	1¾	1 13/32	0.020	0.215	—	0.085	0.275	—
	7029129	¾	1¾	1 13/32	0.020	0.215	—	0.085	0.275	—
	7029117	¾	1¾	1 13/32	0.020	0.215	—	0.085	0.275	—
	7029118	¾	1¾	1 13/32	0.020	0.215	—	0.085	0.275	—
	7029119	⅝	1¾	1 13/32	0.020	0.215	—	0.085	0.275	—
	7029120	⅝	1¾	1 13/32	0.020	0.215	—	0.085	0.275	—
1970	7040110	27/32	1¾	1⅛	0.020	0.100	—	0.060	0.215	—
	7040112	27/32	1¾	1⅛	0.020	0.100	—	0.060	0.215	—

Rochester 2GC, 2GV Specifications (cont.)

Year	Carburetor Identification [1]	Float Level (in.)	Float Drop (in.)	Pump Rod (in.)	Idle Vent (in.)	Vacuum Break (in.)	Automatic [2] Choke	Choke Rod (in.)	Choke Unloader (in.)	Fast Idle Speed
1970	7040101	27/32	1¾	1⅛	0.020	0.125	—	0.060	0.160	—
	7040103	27/32	1¾	1⅛	0.020	0.125	—	0.060	0.225	—
	7040114	23/32	1⅜	1 17/32	0.020	0.200	—	0.085	0.325	—
	7040116	23/32	1⅜	1 17/32	0.020	0.200	—	0.085	0.325	—
	7040113	23/32	1⅜	1 17/32	0.020	0.215	—	0.085	0.275	—
	7040115	23/32	1⅜	1 17/32	0.020	0.215	—	0.085	0.275	—
	7040118	23/32	1⅜	1 17/32	0.020	0.215	—	0.085	0.325	—
	7040120	23/32	1⅜	1 17/32	0.020	0.215	—	0.085	0.325	—
	7040117	23/32	1⅜	1 17/32	0.020	0.215	—	0.085	0.325	—
	7040119	23/32	1⅜	1 17/32	0.020	0.215	—	0.085	0.325	—
1971	7041024	1/16	—	—	—	0.140	—	0.080	0.350	—
	7041101	13/16	1¾	1 3/64	—	0.110	—	0.075	0.215	—
	7041110	13/16	1¾	1 3/64	—	0.080	—	0.040	0.215	—
	7041102	25/32	1⅜	1 5/32	—	0.170	—	0.100	0.325	—
	7041114	25/32	1⅜	1 5/32	—	0.170	—	0.100	0.325	—
	7041113	23/32	1⅜	1 5/32	—	0.180	—	0.100	0.325	—
	7041127	23/32	1⅜	1 5/32	—	0.180	—	0.100	0.325	—
	7041118	23/32	1⅜	1 5/32	—	0.170	—	0.100	0.325	—
	7041181	5/8	1¾	1⅜	—	0.120	—	0.080	0.180	—
	7041182	5/8	1¾	1⅜	—	0.120	—	0.080	0.180	—
1972	7042111	23/32	1 9/32	1½	—	0.180	—	0.100	0.325	—
	7042831	23/32	1 9/32	1½	—	0.180	—	0.100	0.325	—
	7042112	23/32	1 9/32	1½	—	0.170	—	0.100	0.325	—
	7042832	23/32	1 9/32	1½	—	0.170	—	0.100	0.325	—
	7042100	25/32	1 31/32	1 5/16	—	0.080	—	0.040	0.215	—
	7042820	25/32	1 31/32	1 5/16	—	0.080	—	0.040	0.215	—
	7042101	25/32	1 31/32	1 5/16	—	0.110	—	0.075	0.215	—
	7042821	25/32	1 31/32	1 5/16	—	0.110	—	0.075	0.215	—
1973	7043100	21/32	1 9/32	1 5/16	—	0.080	—	0.150	0.215	—
	7043101	21/32	1 9/32	1 5/16	—	0.080	—	0.150	0.215	—
	7043120	21/32	1 9/32	1 5/16	—	0.080	—	0.150	0.215	—
	7043105	21/32	1 9/32	1 5/16	—	0.080	—	0.150	0.215	—
	7043112	19/32	1 9/32	1 7/16	—	0.130	—	0.245	0.325	—
	7043111	19/32	1 9/32	1 7/16	—	0.140	—	0.200	0.250	—
1974	7043100	21/32	1 9/32	1 5/16	—	0.080	—	0.150	0.215	—
	7043101	21/32	1 9/32	1 5/16	—	0.080	—	0.150	0.215	—
	7043120	21/32	1 9/32	1 5/16	—	0.080	—	0.150	0.215	—
	7043105	21/32	1 9/32	1 5/16	—	0.080	—	0.150	0.215	—
	7043112	19/32	1 9/32	1 7/16	—	0.130	—	0.245	0.325	—
	7043111	19/32	1 9/32	1 7/16	—	0.140	—	0.200	0.250	—

Rochester 2GC, 2GV Specifications (cont.)

Year	Carburetor Identification ①	Float Level (in.)	Float Drop (in.)	Pump Rod (in.)	Idle Vent (in.)	Vacuum Break (in.)	Automatic ② Choke	Choke Rod (in.)	Choke Unloader (in.)	Fast Idle Speed
1975	7045111	$2^{1}/_{32}$	$3^{1}/_{32}$	$1^{5}/_{8}$	—	0.130	—	—	0.350	—
	7045112	$2^{1}/_{32}$	$3^{1}/_{32}$	$1^{5}/_{8}$	—	0.130	—	—	0.350	—
1976	17056111	$^{9}/_{16}$	$1^{9}/_{32}$	$1^{21}/_{32}$	—	0.140	—	—	0.325	—
	17056112	$^{9}/_{16}$	$1^{9}/_{32}$	$1^{21}/_{32}$	—	0.140	—	—	0.325	—
	17056412	$^{9}/_{16}$	$1^{9}/_{32}$	$1^{11}/_{16}$	—	0.140	—	—	0.325	—
1977	17057111	$^{19}/_{32}$	$1^{9}/_{32}$	$1^{21}/_{32}$	—	0.130 ③	Index	—	0.325	—
	17057108	$^{19}/_{32}$	$1^{9}/_{32}$	$1^{21}/_{32}$	—	0.130 ③	Index	—	0.325	—
	17057412	$2^{1}/_{32}$	$1^{9}/_{32}$	$1^{21}/_{32}$	—	0.140 ③	½ CCW	—	0.325	—
1978	17058102	$^{15}/_{32}$	$1^{9}/_{32}$	$1^{17}/_{32}$	0	0.130 ④	Index	—	0.325	—
	17058103	$^{15}/_{32}$	$1^{9}/_{32}$	$1^{17}/_{32}$	0	0.130 ④	Index	—	0.325	—
	17058104	$^{15}/_{32}$	$1^{9}/_{32}$	$1^{21}/_{32}$	0	0.130 ③	Index	—	0.325	—
	17058105	$^{15}/_{32}$	$1^{9}/_{32}$	$1^{21}/_{32}$	0	0.130 ③	Index	—	0.325	—
	17058107	$^{15}/_{32}$	$1^{9}/_{32}$	$1^{17}/_{32}$	0	0.130 ③	Index	—	0.325	—
	17058109	$^{15}/_{32}$	$1^{9}/_{32}$	$1^{17}/_{32}$	0	0.130 ③	Index	—	0.325	—
	17058404	½	$1^{9}/_{32}$	$1^{21}/_{32}$	0	0.140 ③	½ CCW	—	0.325	—
	17058405	½	$1^{9}/_{32}$	$1^{21}/_{32}$	0	0.140 ③	½ CCW	—	0.325	—
1979	17059135	—	—				Information not available			
	17059134	—	—				Information not available			
	17059434	—	—				Information not available			

① The carburetor identification tag is located at the rear of the carburetor on one of the air horn screws
② Index or notches clockwise (CW) or counterclockwise (CCW)
③ .160 after 22,500 miles or first tune-up
④ .150 after 22,500 miles or first tune-up

Rochester 4GC—4-BBL Carburetor

AUTOMATIC CHOKE ADJUSTMENT

Set the cover index mark on the one notch lean mark on the housing.

INTERMEDIATE CHOKE ROD

The intermediate choke rod is adjusted with the choke cover and baffle removed.

1. Hold the choke valve closed, exert a light pressure on the choke piston to take up any lash, and then note if the choke piston is at the end of its sleeve.
2. If necessary, bend the intermediate choke rod for correct piston positioning.
3. Install the choke baffle and cover.

CHOKE ROD ADJUSTMENT

1. Turn the idle speed screw in until it just touches the second step of the fast idle cam.
2. Ensure that the choke trip lever is touching the choke counterweight lever.

3. While holding the idle speed screw on the second cam step and against the shoulder of the high step, there should be .043 in. clearance between the choke valve edge and the air horn dividing wall.
4. Bend the choke rod at a lower angle, if necessary.

CHOKE UNLOADER ADJUSTMENT

1. Hold the throttle valve wide open, while the choke trip lever touches the choke counterweight.
2. Clearance between the top of the choke valve and the dividing wall of the air horn should now be .235 in. Bend the fast idle cam tang, if necessary.

SECONDARY THROTTLE LOCKOUT ADJUSTMENT

1. Close the choke valve so that the secondary lockout tang is in the fast idle cam slot. Clearance between the fast idle cam and the tang should be .015 in.

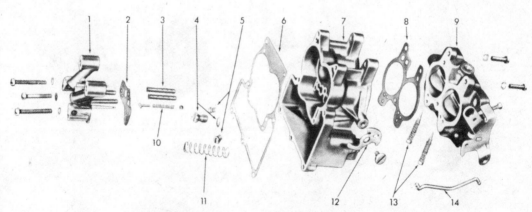

1. Pump rod	7. Power piston	13. Air horn	20. Fuel filter
2. Pump outlet lever	8. Air horn-to-bowl	14. Vent valve and shield	21. Filter spring
3. Accelerator pump	gasket	15. Vacuum diaphragm	22. Float needle and
4. Washer	9. Choke valve	16. Choke lever	seat
5. Pump inner lever	10. Choke rod	17. Diaphragm link	23. Float hinge pin
6. Pump inner lever	11. Choke shaft	18. Fuel inlet nut	24. Splash shield
retainer	12. Choke kick lever	19. Gaskets	25. Float

Exploded view of the 2GV (1¼) air horn

1. Cluster assembly
2. Gasket
3. Splash shield—main well
4. Power valve assembly
5. Main jets
6. Air horn gasket
7. Bowl assembly
8. Throttle body-to-bowl gasket
9. Throttle body assembly
10. Pump discharge check assembly
11. Accelerator pump spring
12. Fast idle cam
13. Idle mixture screws
14. Choke rod

Exploded view of the 2GV (1¼) float bowl

1. Cluster assembly
2. Cluster gasket
3. Hot idle compensator
4. Power valve assembly
5. Main jets
6. Bowl assembly
7. Throttle body-to-bowl gasket
8. Throttle body assembly
9. Idle speed screw
10. Choke rod
11. Idle mixture screws
12. Fast idle cam
13. Accelerator pump spring
14. Pump discharge check assembly

Exploded view of the 2GV (1½) float bowl

2. Bend the tang horizontally as necessary to obtain the correct clearance.

FLOAT LEVEL AND DROP ADJUSTMENT

1. Remove the bowl cover.
2. Install a new gasket on the bowl cover surface.
3. Invert the cover and install the float level gauges supplied with a carburetor rebuilding kit over the primary and secondary floats. The floats should just touch the gauges. The height from the bottom of the float to the bowl cover gasket is 1 33/64 in. for the primaries and 1 37/64 in. for the secondaries. Bend the float arms as necessary to obtain the correct level.

4. Center the floats in the level gauge,

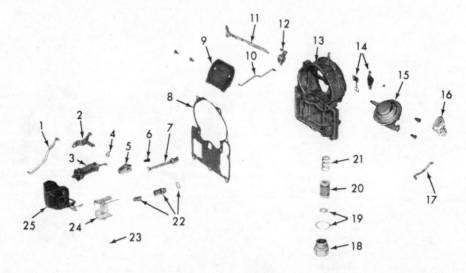

1. Pump rod
2. Pump outer lever
3. Washer
4. Accelerator pump
5. Pump inner lever
6. Pump inner lever retainer
7. Power piston
8. Air horn-to-bowl gasket
9. Choke valve
10. Choke shaft
11. Choke rod
12. Choke kick lever
13. Air horn
14. Vent valve and shield
15. Vacuum diaphragm
16. Choke lever
17. Fuel inlet nut
18. Gaskets
19. Fuel filter
20. Filter spring
21. Diaphragm link
22. Float needle and seat
23. Float hinge pin
24. Splash shields
25. Float

Exploded view of the 2GV (1½) air horn

Rochester 4GC Specifications

Year	Model or Type	Float Level (in.)		Float Drop (in.)		Pump Travel Setting (in.)	Choke Setting	
		Prim	Sec	Prim	Sec		Unloader (in.)	Housing
1964	All	1 33/64	1 33/64	2 1/4	2 1/4	1 1/16	0.235	Index
1965	All	1 33/64	1 37/64	2 1/4	2 1/4	1 1/16	0.250	Index
1966	All	1 17/32	1 19/38 1/4	2 1/4	2 1/4	1 1/16	0.250	Index

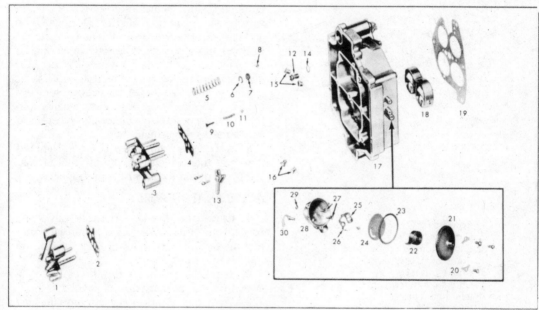

1. Secondary cluster
2. Secondary cluster gasket
3. Primary cluster
4. Primary cluster gasket
5. Pump return spring
6. Retaining ring
7. Screen
8. Check ball
9. Discharge spring guide
10. Discharge spring
11. Discharge ball
12. Power valve
13. Idle compensator
14. Power valve gasket
15. Primary main metering jets
16. Secondary main metering jets
17. Float bowl
18. Auxiliary throttle valves
19. Throttle flange gasket
20. Choke coil cover retainer
21. Choke coil cover
22. Choke coil spring
23. Choke cover gasket
24. Baffle plate
25. Choke piston and pin
26. Choke piston lever
27. Choke housing screw
28. Choke housing
29. Choke housing O-ring
30. Choke shaft

Exploded view of 4GC carburetor body

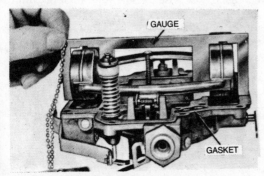

4GC float level adjustment

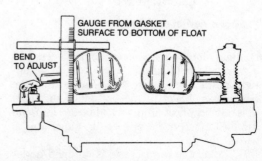

4GC float level adjustment

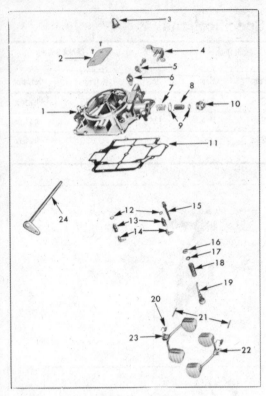

1. Bowl cover
2. Choke valve
3. Pump plunger rubber seal
4. Pump shaft and lever
5. Choke trip lever
6. Choke counterweight
7. Inlet filter spring
8. Inlet filter
9. Inlet gaskets
10. Inlet fitting
11. Bowl cover gasket
12. Float valve gasket
13. Float valve
14. Float valve needle
15. Power valve piston
16. Pump spring clip
17. Pump spring washer
18. Pump duration spring
19. Pump plunger
20. Float tension spring
21. Float hinge pin
22. Primary float
23. Secondary float
24. Choke valve shaft

Exploded view of 4GC air horn

bending them to the left or right as necessary.

5. While holding the bowl cover in an upright position, measure the distance from the bowl cover gasket to the bottom of the float. This distance, float drop, should be 2¼ in. Bend the float tang on the end of the hinge arm to correct the drop.

6. Install the bowl cover as outlined under overhaul.

Rochester 4MC, 4MV, M4MC—4 BBL Carburetors

The Rochester Quadrajet carburetor is a two stage, four-barrel downdraft carburetor. The designation MC or MV refers to the type of choke system the carburetor is designed for. The MV model is equipped with a manifold thermostatic choke coil. The MC model has a choke housing and coil mounted on the side of the float bowl.

The primary side of the carburetor is equipped with 1⅜ diameter bores and a triple venturi with plain tube nozzles. During off idle and part throttle operation, the fuel is metered through tapered metering rods operating in specially designed jets positioned by a manifold vacuum responsive piston.

The secondary side of the carburetor contains two 2¼ in. bores. An air valve is used on the secondary side for metering control and supplements the primary bores.

The secondary air valve operates tapered metering rods which regulate the fuel in constant proportion to the air being supplied.

ACCELERATOR PUMP

1. Close the primary throttle valves by backing out the slow idle screw and making sure that the fast idle cam follower is off the steps of the fast idle cam.

2. Bend the secondary throttle closing tang away from the primary throttle lever.

3. With the pump in the appropriate hole in the pump lever, measure from the top of the choke valve wall to the top of the pump stem.

4. To adjust, bend the pump lever while supporting it with a screwdriver.

5. After adjusting, reading the secondary throttle tang and the slow idle screw.

IDLE VENT ADJUSTMENT

NOTE: *This adjustment is not required on 1977–79 carburetors.*

After adjusting the accelerator pump rod as specified above, open the primary throttle valve enough to just close the idle vent. Measure from the top of the choke valve wall to the top of the pump plunger stem. If adjustment is necessary, bend the wire tang on the pump lever.

FLOAT LEVEL

With the air horn assembly upside down, measure the distance from the air horn gasket surface (gasket removed) to the top of the float at the toe. Measure at a point ³⁄₁₆″ back from the top of the float on 1977–79 carburetors.

NOTE: *Make sure the retaining pin is firmly held in place and that the tang of the float is firmly against the needle and seat assembly.*

FAST IDLE

1. Position the fast idle lever on the high step of the fast idle cam. Disconnect and plug the vacuum hose at the EGR valve.

2. Be sure that the choke is wide open and the engine warm.

3. Turn the fast idle screw to gain the proper fast idle rpm.

CHOKE ROD ADJUSTMENT

Position the cam follower on the second step of the fast idle cam, touching the high step. Close the choke valve directly on models up to 1976. On 1977 models, remove the choke thermostatic cover, and then hold the choke closed by pushing upward on the choke coil lever. Gauge the clearance between the lower edge of the choke valve and the carburetor body on models to 1975, and between the upper edge of the choke valve and the carburetor body on 1976 and 1977 models. Bend the choke rod to obtain the specified clearance. On 1977 models, install the choke thermostatic cover and adjust it to specification when the adjustment is complete. This adjustment requires sophisticated special tools on 1978 and later models, and so is not included here.

AIR VALVE DASHPOT ADJUSTMENT

Set the vacuum break diaphragm. On 1977–79 models, this requires plugging the bleed purge hole on the back of the diaphragm with tape, and the use of an external vacuum source. Hold the air valve tightly closed on all models. Gauge the clearance between the dashpot rod and the end of the slot in the air valve lever. Bend the rod to adjust. Remove the tape from the bleed purge hole.

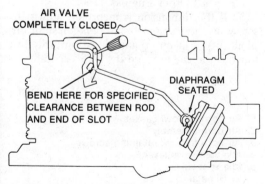

Adjusting the air valve dashpot (4MV)

CHOKE COIL ROD

1967–76

1. Close the choke valve by rotating the choke coil lever counterclockwise.

2. Disconnect the thermostatic coil rod from the upper lever.

3. Push down on the rod until it contacts the bracket of the coil.

4. The rod must fit in the notch of the upper lever.

5. If it does not, it must be bent on the curved portion just below the upper lever.

CHOKE COIL LEVER AND CHOKE THERMOSTATIC COIL

1977–79

1. Remove the three mounting screws and retainers, and pull the thermostatic coil cover assembly off the choke housing and set it aside.

2. Place the fast idle cam follower on the high step of the cam and then push up on the thermostatic coil tang in the choke housing until the choke is closed.

3. Insert a .120″ plug gauge or rod of that diameter into the hole in the housing located just below the lever. With the choke closed, the lever should just touch the gauge.

4. Adjust the choke rod by changing the angle of the bend it makes just below the choke itself, if necessary.

5. Then, install the coil cover back on the choke housing, making sure that the thermostatic coil engages the tang. Install the three retainers and screws, but do not tighten. With the fast idle cam follower still on the high step of the cam, rotate the cover assembly counterclockwise until the choke closes. Set all models 2 notches lean except 1977 models with manual transmission; set these three notches lean. Hold the position of the housing while tightening screws evenly.

VACUUM BREAK

1967–76

1. Fully seat the vacuum break diaphragm using an outside vacuum source.

2. Open the throttle valve enough to allow the fast idle cam follower to clear the fast idle cam.

3. The end of the vacuum break rod should be at the outer end of the slot in the vacuum break diaphragm plunger.

4. The specified clearance should register from the lower end of the choke valve to the inside air horn wall.

5. If the clearance is not correct, bend the vacuum break link.

1977

NOTE: *Adjustment procedures for 1978 and later models require the use of an expensive*

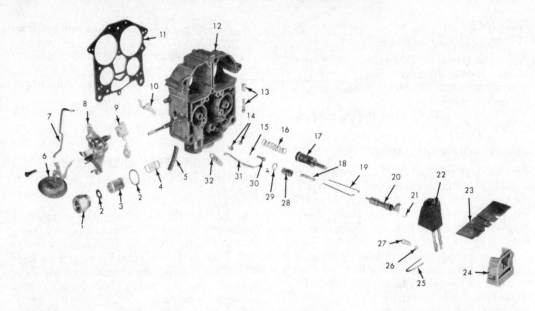

1. Fuel inlet nut
2. Gasket
3. Fuel filter
4. Fuel filter spring
5. Vacuum break hose
6. Vacuum diaphragm
7. Air valve dashpot
8. Choke control bracket
9. Fast idle cam
10. Secondary throttle lockout
11. Throttle body-to-bowl gasket

12. Float bowl assembly
13. Idle speed screw
14. Primary jets
15. Pump discharge ball
16. Pump return spring
17. Accelerator pump
18. Power piston spring
19. Primary metering rods
20. Power piston
21. Metering rod retainer
22. Float

23. Secondary air baffle
24. Float bowl insert
25. Float hinge pin
26. Float needle pull clip
27. Float needle
28. Float needle seat
29. Needle seat gasket
30. Discharge ball retainer
31. Choke rod
32. Choke lever

Exploded view of the float bowl (4MV)

and sophisticated special tool, so procedures are not included here.

1. Remove the choke thermostatic cover. Place the fast idle cam follower on the high step of the cam.

2. Where there is a purge bleed hole on the back of the choke vacuum break, put tape over the hole. Then, set the diaphragm using an outside vacuum source.

3. Push the inside choke coil lever counterclockwise until the tang on the vacuum break

lever touches the tang on the vacuum break plunger stem.

4. Place a gauge of the following diameter between the upper edge of the choke butterfly and the inside wall of the air horn:
   • California Engines: .165″
   • All Other Engines: .160″

5. If the dimension is incorrect, adjust the screw on the vacuum break plunger stem until all play is taken up and choke butterfly just touches the gauge when it's held vertically.

1. Air horn-to-bowl gasket
2. Air horn assembly
3. Air horn-to-bowl retaining screws
4. Idle vent valve lever
5. Idle vent valve
   a. Bimetal
   b. Spring
6. Choke shaft and lever
7. Choke valve
8. Idle vent shield
9. Countersunk air horn retaining screws
10. Secondary metering rods
11. Metering rod hanger

Exploded view of the air horn (4MV)

6. Reconnect the vacuum line to vacuum break port of carburetor, remove tape from purge hole (if applied) and reinstall and adjust choke thermostat (see above).

CHOKE UNLOADER ADJUSTMENT

NOTE: *Performing this adjustment on 1978 and later models requires sophisticated special tools, so the procedure is not included here.*

On 1977 models, make sure the choke thermostatic spring is properly adjusted (see above). Close the choke valve and secure it with a rubber band hooked to the vacuum break lever. Open the primary throttles all the way. Then measure the distance between the air horn and edge of the choke butterfly. On models up to and including 1976, use the bottom side of the butterfly for this measurement; on 1977 models, use the top side. Bend the fast idle lever tang to achieve the proper opening of the choke.

SECONDARY LOCKOUT ADJUSTMENT

1967–76

Completely open the choke valve and rotate the vacuum break lever clockwise. Bend the lever if the measurement between the lever and the secondary throttle exceeds specifications. Close the choke and gauge the distance between the lever and the secondary throttle shaft pin. Bend the lever to adjust.

1977–79

1. See illustration below.

AIR VALVE SPRING ADJUSTMENT

NOTE: *Loosening and tightening the locking screw to adjust the air valve spring requires a hex wrench on 1977 and later model carburetors.*

Remove all spring tension by loosening the locking screw and backing out the adjusting screw. Close the air valve and turn the adjusting screw in until the torsion spring touches

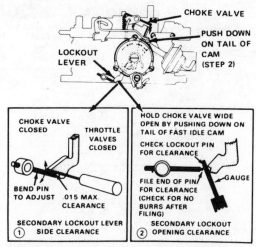

Adjusting the secondary lockout (1977–79)

the pin on the shaft, and then turn it the additional number of turns specified. Secure the locking screw.

SECONDARY CLOSING ADJUSTMENT

This adjustment assures proper closing of the secondary throttle plates.

1. Set the idle as per instructions in the appropriate section. Make sure that the fast idle cam follower is not resting on the fast idle cam.

2. There should be 0.020 in. clearance between the secondary throttle actuating rod and the front of the slot on the secondary throttle lever with the closing tang on the throttle lever resting against the actuating lever.

3. Bend the tang on the primary throttle actuating rod to adjust.

SECONDARY OPENING ADJUSTMENT

1. Open the primary throttle valves until the actuating link contacts the upper tang on the secondary lever.

2. With two point-linkage, the bottom of the link should be in the center of the secondary lever slot.

Rochester 4MV, 4MC, M4MC Specifications

Year	Carburetor Identification ①	Float Level (in.)	Air Valve Spring	Pump Rod (in.)	Idle Vent (in.)	Vacuum Break (in.)	Secondary Opening (in.)	Choke Rod (in.)	Choke Unloader (rpm)	Fast Idle Speed
1967	7027202	9/32	7/8 turn	13/32	3/8	0.160	0.015	0.100	0.260	—
	7027203	9/32	7/8 turn	13/32	3/8	0.200	0.015	0.100	0.300	—
	7027200	9/32	7/8 turn	13/32	3/8	0.160	0.015	0.100	0.300	—
	7027201	9/32	7/8 turn	13/32	3/8	0.240	0.015	0.100	0.300	—
	7027202	9/32	7/8 turn	13/32	3/8	0.160	0.015	0.100	0.260	—
	7027203	9/32	7/8 turn	13/32	3/8	0.200	0.015	0.100	0.300	—

Rochester 4MV, 4MC, M4MC Specifications (cont.)

Year	Carburetor Identifi- cation ①	Float Level (in.)	Air Valve Spring	Pump Rod (in.)	Idle Vent (in.)	Vacuum Break (in.)	Secondary Opening (in.)	Choke Rod (in.)	Choke Unloader (rpm)	Fast Idle Speed
1968	7028212	9/32	3/8 turn	9/32	3/8	0.160	0.010	0.100	0.260	—
	7028213	9/32	3/8 turn	9/32	3/8	0.245	0.010	0.100	0.300	—
	7028229	9/32	7/8 turn	9/32	3/8	0.245	0.010	0.100	0.300	—
	7028208	9/32	3/8 turn	9/32	3/8	0.160	0.010	0.100	0.260	—
	7028207	9/32	3/8 turn	9/32	3/8	0.245	0.010	0.100	0.300	—
	7028219	9/32	7/8 turn	9/32	3/8	0.245	0.010	0.100	0.300	—
	7028218	3/16	7/8 turn	9/32	3/8	0.160	0.010	0.100	0.300	—
	7028217	3/16	7/8 turn	9/32	3/8	0.245	0.010	0.100	0.300	—
	7028210	3/16	7/8 turn	9/32	3/8	0.160	0.010	0.100	0.300	—
	7028211	3/16	7/8 turn	9/32	3/8	0.245	0.010	0.100	0.300	—
	7028216	3/16	7/8 turn	9/32	3/8	0.160	0.010	0.100	0.300	—
	7028209	3/16	7/8 turn	9/32	3/8	0.245	0.010	0.100	0.300	—
1969	7029203	7/32	7/16 turn	5/16	3/8	0.245	0.015	0.100	0.450	—
	7029202	7/32	7/16 turn	5/16	3/8	0.180	0.015	0.100	0.450	—
	7029207	3/16	13/16 turn	5/16	3/8	0.245	0.015	0.100	0.450	—
	7029215	1/4	13/16 turn	5/16	3/8	0.245	0.015	0.100	0.450	—
	7029204	1/4	13/16 turn	5/16	3/8	0.180	0.015	0.100	0.450	—
1970	7040202	1/4	7/16 turn	5/16	—	0.245	—	0.100	0.450	—
	7040203	1/4	7/16 turn	5/16	—	0.275	—	0.100	0.450	—
	7040207	1/4	13/16 turn	5/16	—	0.275	—	0.100	0.450	—
	7040200	1/4	13/16 turn	5/16	—	0.245	—	0.100	0.450	—
	7040201	1/4	13/16 turn	5/16	—	0.275	—	0.100	0.450	—
	7040204	1/4	13/16 turn	5/16	—	0.245	—	0.100	0.450	—
	7040205	1/4	13/16 turn	5/16	—	0.275	—	0.100	0.450	—
1971	7041200	1/4	7/16 turn	—	—	0.260	—	0.100	—	—
	7041202	1/4	7/16 turn	—	—	0.260	—	0.100	—	—
	7041204	1/4	7/16 turn	—	—	0.260	—	0.100	—	—
	7041212	1/4	7/16 turn	—	—	0.260	—	0.100	—	—
	7041201	1/4	7/16 turn	—	—	0.275	—	0.100	—	—
	7041203	1/4	7/16 turn	—	—	0.275	—	0.100	—	—
	7041205	1/4	7/16 turn	—	—	0.275	—	0.100	—	—
	7041213	1/4	7/16 turn	—	—	0.275	—	0.100	—	—
1972	7042202	1/4	1/2 turn	3/8	—	0.215	—	0.100	0.450	—
	7042203	1/4	1/2 turn	3/8	—	0.215	—	0.100	0.450	—
	7042902	1/4	1/2 turn	3/8	—	0.215	—	0.100	0.450	—
	7042903	1/4	1/2 turn	3/8	—	0.215	—	0.100	0.450	—
1973	7043212	7/32	1 turn	13/32	—	0.250	—	0.430	0.450	—
	7043213	7/32	1 turn	13/32	—	0.250	—	0.430	0.450	—
1974	7044202	1/4	7/8 turn	13/32 ②	—	0.230	—	0.430	0.450	1600 ③–1300 ④

Rochester 4MV, 4MC, M4MC Specifications (cont.)

Year	Carburetor Identification ①	Float Level (in.)	Air Valve Spring	Pump Rod (in.)	Idle Vent (in.)	Vacuum Break (in.)	Secondary Opening (in.)	Choke Rod (in.)	Choke Unloader (rpm)	Fast Idle Speed
1974	7044203	1/4	7/8 turn	13/32 ②	—	0.230	—	0.430	0.450	1600 ③ – 1300 ④
	7044208	1/4	1 turn	13/32 ②	—	0.230	—	0.430	0.450	1600 ③ – 1300 ④
	7044209	1/4	1 turn	13/32 ②	—	0.230	—	0.430	0.450	1600 ③ – 1300 ④
	7044502	1/4	7/8 turn	13/32 ②	—	0.230	—	0.430	0.450	1600 ③ – 1300 ④
	7044503	1/4	7/8 turn	13/32 ②	—	0.230	—	0.430	0.450	1600 ③ – 1300 ④
1975	7045202	15/32	7/8 turn	0.275 ⑤	—	0.180 ⑥	—	0.300	0.325	—
	7045203	15/32	7/8 turn	0.275 ⑤	—	0.180 ⑥	—	0.300	0.325	—
	7045208	15/32	7/8 turn	0.275 ⑤	—	0.180 ⑥	—	0.300	0.325	—
	7045209	15/32	7/8 turn	0.275 ⑤	—	0.180 ⑥	—	0.300	0.325	—
1976	17056202	13/32	7/8 turn	9/32	—	0.185	—	0.325	0.325	—
	17056203	13/32	7/8 turn	9/32	—	0.170	—	0.325	0.325	—
	17056528	13/32	7/8 turn	9/32	—	0.185	—	0.325	0.325	—
1977	17057203	15/32	7/8	9/32 ⑤	—	0.160	—	0.325	0.280	1300
	17057202	15/32	—	9/32 ⑤	—	0.160	—	0.325	—	1600 ⑤
	17057502	15/32	7/8	9/32 ⑤	—	0.165	—	0.325	0.280	1600 ⑤
1978	17058203	15/32	7/8	9/32	—	0.179	—	0.314	0.277	⑦
	17058202	15/32	7/8	9/32	—	0.179	—	0.314	0.277	⑦
	17058502	15/32	7/8	9/32	—	0.187	—	0.314	0.277	⑦
1979	17059203	15/32	7/8	1/4	—	0.157	—	0.243	0.243	⑦
	17059207	15/32	7/8	1/4	—	0.157	—	0.243	0.243	⑦
	17059216	15/32	7/8	1/4	—	0.157	—	0.243	0.243	⑦
	17059217	15/32	7/8	1/4	—	0.157	—	0.243	0.243	⑦
	17059218	15/32	7/8	1/4	—	0.164	—	0.243	0.243	⑦
	17059222	15/32	7/8	1/4	—	0.164	—	0.243	0.243	⑦
	17059502	15/32	7/8	1/4	—	0.164	—	0.243	0.243	⑦
	17059504	15/32	7/8	1/4	—	0.164	—	0.243	0.243	⑦
	17059582	15/32	7/8	11/32	—	0.203	—	0.243	0.314	⑦
	17059584	15/32	7/8	11/32	—	0.203	—	0.243	0.314	⑦
	17059210	15/32	1	9/32	—	0.157	—	0.243	0.243	⑦
	17059211	15/32	1	9/32	—	0.157	—	0.243	0.243	⑦
	17029228	15/32	1	9/32	—	0.157	—	0.243	0.243	⑦

① The carburetor identification tag is located at the rear of the carburetor on one of the air horn screws
② Without vacuum advance
③ With automatic transmission; vacuum advance connected and EGR disconnected after the throttle positioned on the high step of cam
④ With manual transmission; without vacuum advance and the throttle positioned on the high step of cam
⑤ Inner pump rod location
⑥ Front vacuum break given; rear—0.170 in.
⑦ See engine compartment sticker

3. With three point linkage, there should be 0.070 in. clearance between the link and the middle tang.

4. Bend the upper tang on the secondary lever to adjust as necessary.

Holly 4150, 4160—4 BBL Carburetors

These carburetors are basically similar in design. The 4160 is an end-inlet carburetor, while the 4150 carburetor has been both an end and center inlet design.

CHOKE ADJUSTMENT

The 1965 model 4150 uses a bimetallic choke mounted on the carburetor. It is correctly set when the cover scribe mark aligns with the specified notch mark. The later model 4150 and 4160 employ a remotely located choke. To adjust, disconnect the choke rod at the choke lever and secure the choke lever shut. Bend the rod so that when the rod is depressed to the contact stop, the top is even with the bottom of the hole in the choke lever.

FLOAT LEVEL ADJUSTMENT

Position the car on a flat, level surface and start the engine. Remove the sight plugs and check to see that the fuel level reaches the bottom threads of the sight plug port. A plus or minus tolerance of ⅟₃₂ in. is acceptable. To change the level, loosen the fuel inlet needle locking screw and adjust the nut. Turning it clockwise lowers the fuel level and counterclockwise raises it. Turn the nut ⅙ of a turn for each ⅟₁₆ in. de-

sired change. Open the primary throttle slightly to assure a stabilized adjusting condition on the secondaries. There is no required float drop adjustment.

FAST IDLE ADJUSTMENT

1965 4150

Bring the engine to the normal operating temperature with the air cleaner off. Open the throttle. Place the fast idle cam on its high step and close the throttle. Adjust the fast idle screw to reach the specified idle speed.

Adjusting the float level (Holley)

1966 and Later 4150 and 4160

Open the throttle and place the choke plate fast idle lever against the top step of the fast idle cam. Bend the fast idle lever to obtain the specified throttle plate opening.

Holley 4150, 4160 Specifications

Year	Model or Type	Float Level (in.) Prim	Sec	Float Drop (in.) Prim	Sec	Pump Travel Setting (in.)	Choke Setting Unloader (in.)	Housing	Secondary Locknut Adj.
1965	327 (4150)	①	①	—	0.015		0.375	—	—
1966	327-350 hp (4150)	①	①	0.065	0.015		0.260	—	—
	327 (4160)	①	①	0.065	0.015		0.260	—	—
	396 (4160)	①	①	0.065	0.015		0.260	—	—
1967–68	327-325 hp-4 bbl (4150)	A①	A①	0.065	0.015		0.265	—	—
1967	327, 396, 427-4 bbl (4160)	A①	A①	0.065	0.015		0.265	—	—
1968–69	V8-396 (4150)	B①	B①	0.065	0.015		0.350	—	—
1970	454 (4150)	0.350		—	—	0.015	0.350	—	—
1971	454 (4160)	②		①	—	0.015	0.350	—	—

A—Primary 0.170, Secondary 0.300
B—Primary 0.350, Secondary 0.500
① Float adjustment: Fuel level should be plus or minus ⅟₃₂ in. with threads at bottom of sight holes. To adjust turn adjusting nut on top of bowl clockwise, to lower, counterclockwise to raise.
② Float centered in bowl

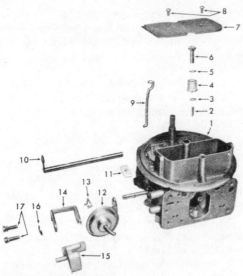

1. Main body assembly
2. Pump discharge needle
3. Pump discharge nozzle gasket
4. Pump discharge nozzle
5. Pump discharge nozzle screw gasket
6. Pump discharge nozzle screw
7. Choke valve
8. Choke valve screw
9. Choke rod
10. Choke shaft and lever
11. Choke rod seal
12. Vacuum break
13. Vacuum break link
14. Choke lever
15. Fast idle cam
16. Choke lever retainer
17. Vacuum break screw

Exploded view of the main body assembly (Holley)

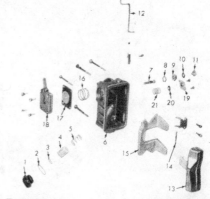

1. Fuel inlet nut
2. Inlet nut gasket
3. Fuel filter gasket
4. Fuel filter
5. Fuel filter spring
6. Fuel bowl
7. Inlet needle and seat assembly
8. Adjusting nut gasket
9. Fuel inlet adjusting nut
10. Inlet nut lock screw gasket
11. Inlet nut lock screw
12. Vent valve lever
13. Float
14. Float hinge pin
15. Fuel displacement block
16. Pump diaphragm spring
17. Pump diaphragm (primary only)
18. Pump cover
19. Vent valve cover
20. Vent valve
21. Vent valve spring

Exploded view of the fuel bowl assembly (Holley)

CHOKE UNLOADER ADJUSTMENT

Adjustment should be made with the engine not running. Fully open and secure the throttle plate. Force the choke valve toward a closed position, so that contact is made with the unloader tang. Bend the choke rod to gain the specified clearance between the main body and the lower edge of the choke valve.

ACCELERATOR PUMP ADJUSTMENT

With the engine off, block the throttle open and push the pump lever down. Clearance between the pump lever arm and the spring adjusting nut should be 0.015 in. minimum. Turn the screw or nut to adjust this clearance.

SECONDARY THROTTLE VALVE ADJUSTMENT

Close the throttle plates, and then turn the adjustment screw until it contacts the throttle lever. Advance the screw ½ turn more.

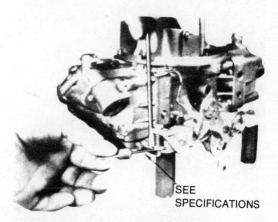

SEE SPECIFICATIONS

Adjusting the accelerator pump (Holley)

AIR VENT VALVE ADJUSTMENT

Close the throttle valves and open the choke valve so that the throttle arm is free of the idle screw. Bend the air vent valve rod to obtain the specified clearance between the choke valve and seat. Advance the idle speed screw until it touches the throttle lever, and then advance it 1½ turns.

VACUUM BREAK ADJUSTMENT

Secure the choke valve closed and the vacuum break against the stop. Bend the vacuum break link to gain the specified clearance between the

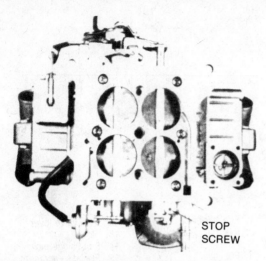

STOP SCREW

Adjusting the secondary throttle valve (Holley)

main body and the lower edge of the choke valve.

Rochester M2ME and E2ME—2 BBL Carburetors

FLOAT ADJUSTMENT

1. Remove the air horn from the throttle body.
2. Using your fingers, hold the retainer in place and then push the float down into light contact with the needle.
3. Measure the distance from the toe of the float (furthest from the hinge) to the top of the carburetor (gasket removed).
4. To adjust, remove the float and gently bend the arm to specifications. After adjustment, check the float alignment in the cham-

ber. On engines equipped with the C-4 or the CCC system, where the float level varies more than $1/16$ in. from specifications, adjust the float as follows.

FLOAT TOO HIGH:

1. Hold the retainer firmly in place and then push down the center of the float pontoon until the correct setting is obtained.

FLOAT TOO LOW:

1. Lift out the meter rods and remove the solenoid connector screw.
2. Turn the lean mixture solenoid screw clockwise until the screw is bottomed lightly in the float bowl. *Count and record the number of turns before the screw is bottomed.*
3. Turn the screw counterclockwise and remove it. Lift the solenoid and the connector from the float bowl.
4. Remove the float and bend the arm up to adjust it. Put the float back in and check its alignment.
5. Installation is in the reverse order of removal. Make sure that the solenoid lean mixture screw is backed out of the float bowl EXACTLY the same number of turns as were recorded in Step 2.

PUMP ADJUSTMENT

NOTE: *All 1980 and later engines equipped with the C-4 or the CCC system have a non-adjustable pump lever. No adjustments are either necessary or possible.*

1. With the throttle closed and the fast idle screw off the steps of the fast idle cam, measure the distance from the air horn casting to the top of the pump stem.
2. To adjust the lever, support it firmly with

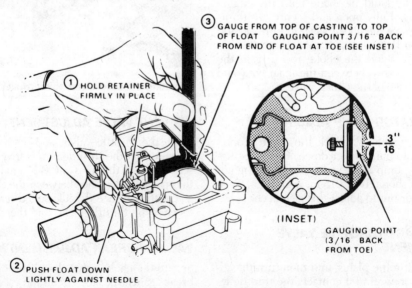

③ GAUGE FROM TOP OF CASTING TO TOP OF FLOAT   GAUGING POINT 3/16 BACK FROM END OF FLOAT AT TOE (SEE INSET)

① HOLD RETAINER FIRMLY IN PLACE

3"—16

(INSET)

GAUGING POINT (3/16 BACK FROM TOE)

② PUSH FLOAT DOWN LIGHTLY AGAINST NEEDLE

Adjusting the float—M2ME, E2ME

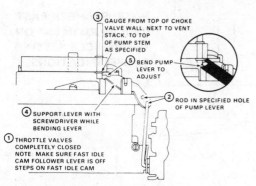

Pump adjustment—M2ME, E2ME (all but C-4 or CCC)

a screwdriver and then bend it to obtain the proper specifications.

3. When the adjustment is correct, open and close the throttle a few times to check the linkage movement and alignment.

CHOKE COIL LEVER ADJUSTMENT

NOTE: *To complete this procedure you will need a Start Cover Retainer kit; available at most auto parts suppliers.*

1. Drill out and remove the rivets. Retain the choke housing cover and then remove the thermostatic cover and coil assembly from choke housing.

2. Place the fast idle cam follower on the high step of the fast idle cam.

3. Close the choke valve by pushing up on the thermostatic coil tang (counterclockwise).

4. Insert a drill or gauge of the specified size into the hole in the choke housing. The lower edge of the choke lever should be just touching the side of the gauge.

5. If the choke lever is not touching the side of the gauge, bend the choke rod until you see that it does.

FAST IDLE ADJUSTMENT

1. Set the ignition timing and curb idle speed. Disconnect and plug any hoses as directed on the emission control sticker.

2. Place the fast idle screw on the highest step of the fast idle cam.

3. Start the engine and adjust the engine speed to specifications with the fast idle screw.

FAST IDLE CAM (CHOKE ROD) ADJUSTMENT

NOTE: *A special angle gauge should be used. If it is not available, an inch measurement can be used.*

1. Adjust the choke coil lever and the fast idle as previously detailed.

2. Rotate the degree scale until it is zeroed.

3. Close the choke valve completely and place the magnet on top of it.

4. Center the bubble.

5. Rotate the scale so that the specified degree is opposite the pointer.

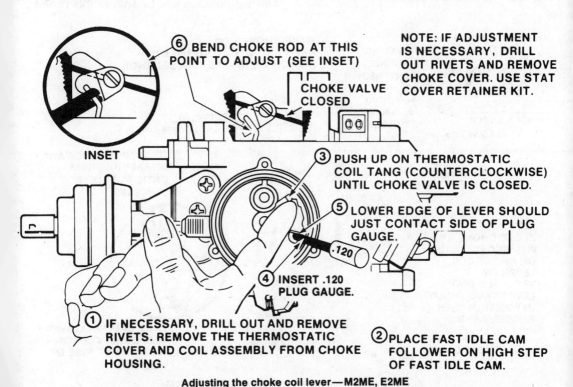

Adjusting the choke coil lever—M2ME, E2ME

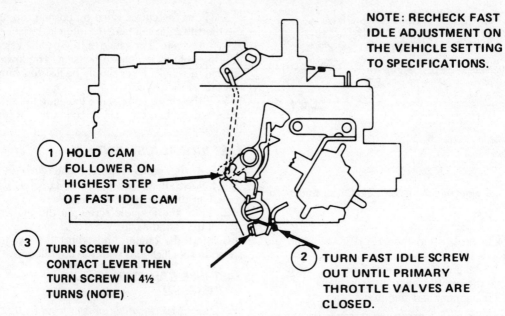

NOTE: RECHECK FAST IDLE ADJUSTMENT ON THE VEHICLE SETTING TO SPECIFICATIONS.

① HOLD CAM FOLLOWER ON HIGHEST STEP OF FAST IDLE CAM

③ TURN SCREW IN TO CONTACT LEVER THEN TURN SCREW IN 4½ TURNS (NOTE)

② TURN FAST IDLE SCREW OUT UNTIL PRIMARY THROTTLE VALVES ARE CLOSED.

Adjusting the fast idle with the carburetor off the car—M2ME, E2ME

6. Place the fast idle screw on the second step of the cam, against the rise of the high step.

7. Close the choke by pushing up on the choke coil lever or the vacuum break lever tang. You may hold it in position with a rubber band.

8. To adjust, bend the tang on the fast idle cam until the bubble is centered.

FRONT VACUUM BREAK ADJUSTMENT

1. Follow Steps 1–5 of the "Fast Idle Cam Adjustment" procedure.

2. Set the choke vacuum diaphragm using an outside vacuum source.

3. Close the choke valve by pushing up on the choke coil lever or the vacuum break lever. You may hold it in position with a rubber band.

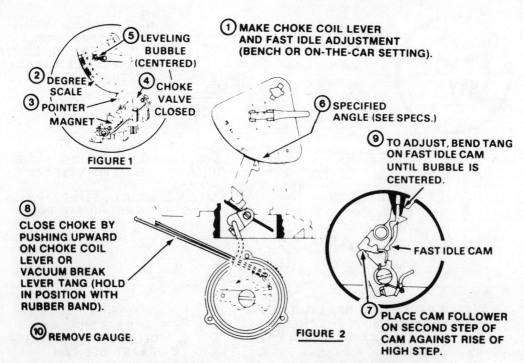

⑤ LEVELING BUBBLE (CENTERED)

② DEGREE SCALE

③ POINTER MAGNET

④ CHOKE VALVE CLOSED

FIGURE 1

① MAKE CHOKE COIL LEVER AND FAST IDLE ADJUSTMENT (BENCH OR ON-THE-CAR SETTING).

⑥ SPECIFIED ANGLE (SEE SPECS.)

⑨ TO ADJUST, BEND TANG ON FAST IDLE CAM UNTIL BUBBLE IS CENTERED.

⑧ CLOSE CHOKE BY PUSHING UPWARD ON CHOKE COIL LEVER OR VACUUM BREAK LEVER TANG (HOLD IN POSITION WITH RUBBER BAND).

⑩ REMOVE GAUGE.

FIGURE 2

— FAST IDLE CAM

⑦ PLACE CAM FOLLOWER ON SECOND STEP OF CAM AGAINST RISE OF HIGH STEP.

Fast idle cam (choke rod) adjustment—M2ME, E2ME

Rochester M2ME, E2ME Specifications

Year	Carburetor Identification ①	Float Level (in.)	Choke Rod (deg./in.)	Choke Unloader (deg./in.)	Vacuum Break Lean or Front (deg./in.)	Vacuum Break Rich or Rear (deg./in.)	Pump Rod (in.)	Choke Coil Lever (in.)	Automatic Choke (notches)
1980	17080108	⅜	38/0.243	38/0.243	25/0.142	—	5/16 ②	0.120	Fixed
	17080110	⅜	38/0.243	38/0.243	25/0.142	—	5/16 ②	0.120	Fixed
	17080130	5/16	38/0.243	38/0.243	25/0.142	—	5/16 ②	0.120	Fixed
	17080131	5/16	38/0.243	38/0.243	25/0.142	—	5/16 ②	0.120	Fixed
	17080132	5/16	38/0.243	38/0.243	25/0.142	—	5/16 ②	0.120	Fixed
	17080133	5/16	38/0.243	38/0.243	25/0.142	—	5/16 ②	0.120	Fixed
	17080138	⅜	38/0.243	38/0.243	25/0.142	—	5/16 ②	0.120	Fixed
	17080140	⅜	38/0.243	38/0.243	25/0.142	—	5/16 ②	0.120	Fixed
	17080493	5/16	38/0.139	38/0.243	25/0.117	–/0.179	Fixed	0.120	Fixed
	17080495	5/16	38/0.139	38/0.243	25/0.117	–/0.179	Fixed	0.120	Fixed
	17080496	5/16	38/0.139	38/0.243	25/0.117	–/0.203	Fixed	0.120	Fixed
	17080498	5/16	38/0.139	38/0.243	25/0.117	–/0.203	Fixed	0.120	Fixed
1981	17080185	9/32	24.5/0.139	38/0.243	19/0.103	14/0.071	¼ ②	0.120	Fixed
	17080187	9/32	24.5/0.139	38/0.243	19/0.103	14/0.071	¼ ②	0.120	Fixed
	17080191	9/32	24.5/0.139	38/0.243	18/0.096	18/0.096	¼ ②	0.120	Fixed
	17080491	5/16	24.5/0.139	38/0.243	21/0.117	35/0.220	Fixed	0.120	Fixed
	17080496	5/16	24.5/0.139	38/0.243	21/0.117	33/0.203	Fixed	0.120	Fixed
	17080498	5/16	24.5/0.139	38/0.243	21/0.117	33/0.203	Fixed	0.120	Fixed
	17081130	⅜	20/0.110	38/0.243	25/0.142	—	Fixed	0.120	Fixed
	17081131	⅜	20/0.110	38/0.243	25/0.142	—	Fixed	0.120	Fixed
	17081132	⅜	20/0.110	38/0.243	25/0.142	—	Fixed	0.120	Fixed
	17081133	⅜	20/0.110	38/0.243	25/0.142	—	Fixed	0.120	Fixed
	17081138	⅜	20/0.110	40/0.260	25/0.142	—	Fixed	0.120	Fixed
	17081140	⅜	20/0.110	40/0.260	25/0.142	—	Fixed	0.120	Fixed
	17081191	5/16	24.5/0.139	38/0.243	28/0.139	24/0.136	Fixed	0.120	Fixed
	17081192	5/16	24.5/0.139	38/0.243	28/0.139	24/0.136	Fixed	0.120	Fixed
	17081194	5/16	24.5/0.139	38/0.243	21/0.117	24/0.136	Fixed	0.120	Fixed
	17081196	5/16	24.5/0.139	38/0.243	28/0.139	24/0.136	Fixed	0.120	Fixed
	17081197	5/16	18/0.096	38/0.243	28/0.139	24/0.136	Fixed	0.120	Fixed
	17081198	⅜	24.5/0.139	38/0.243	28/0.139	24/0.136	Fixed	0.120	Fixed
	17081199	⅜	18/0.096	38/0.243	28/0.139	24/0.136	Fixed	0.120	Fixed
1982	17082130	⅜	20/–	38/0.243	27	—	Fixed	0.120	Fixed
	17082132	⅜	20/–	38/0.243	27	—	Fixed	0.120	Fixed
	17082138	⅜	20/–	38/0.243	27	—	Fixed	0.120	Fixed
	12082140	⅜	20/–	38/0.243	27	—	Fixed	0.120	Fixed
	17082497	5/16	24.5/0.139	32/–	28	24	Fixed	0.120	Fixed
1983	17082130	⅜	20/–	38/–	27	—	Fixed	0.120	Fixed
	17082132	⅜	20/–	38/–	27	—	Fixed	0.120	Fixed
	17083130	⅜	20/–	38/–	27	—	Fixed	0.120	Fixed

Rochester M2ME, E2ME Specifications (cont.)

Year	Carburetor Identification ①	Float Level (in.)	Choke Rod (deg./in.)	Choke Unloader (deg./in.)	Vacuum Break Lean or Front (deg./in.)	Vacuum Break Rich or Rear (deg./in.)	Pump Rod (in.)	Choke Coil Lever (in.)	Automatic Choke (notches)
1983	17083132	3/8	20/–	38/–	27	—	Fixed	0.120	Fixed
	17083190	5/16	18/–	32/–	28	24	Fixed	0.120	Fixed
	17083192	5/16	18/–	32/–	28	24	Fixed	0.120	Fixed
	17083193	5/16	17/–	27/–	23	28	Fixed	0.120	Fixed
1984	17082130	3/8	20/–	38/–	27	—	Fixed	0.120	Fixed
	17082132	12/32	20/–	38/–	27	—	Fixed	0.120	Fixed
	17084191	10/32	18/–	32/–	28	24	Fixed	0.120	Fixed

① The carburetor identification number is stamped on the float bowl, next to the fuel inlet nut.
② Inner hole.

4. To adjust, turn the screw in or out until the bubble in the gauge is centered.

REAR VACUUM BREAK ADJUSTMENT

1. Follow Steps 1–3 of the "Front Vacuum Break Adjustment" procedure.

2. To adjust, use a 1/8 in. Allen wrench to turn the screw in the rear cover until the bubble is centered. After adjusting, apply silicone sealant RTV over the screw head to seal the setting.

UNLOADER ADJUSTMENT

1. Follow Steps 1–5 of the "Fast Idle Cam Adjustment" procedure.

2. If they have been previously removed, install the choke thermostatic cover and the coil assembly into the choke housing.

3. Close the choke valve by pushing up on the tang on the vacuum break lever (you may hold it with a rubber band).

4. Hold the primary throttle valves wide open.

5. To adjust, bend the tang on the fast idle lever until the bubble on the gauge is centered.

Rochester M4ME and E4ME—4 BBL Carburetors

NOTE: *Float, pump, choke coil lever, fast idle, fast idle cam (choke rod), front and rear*

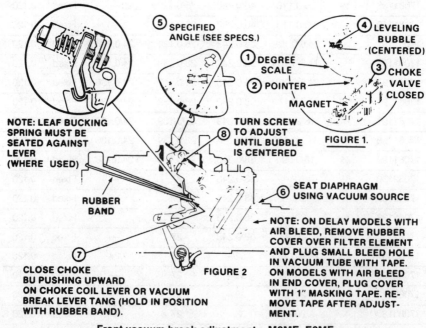

Front vacuum break adjustment—M2ME, E2ME

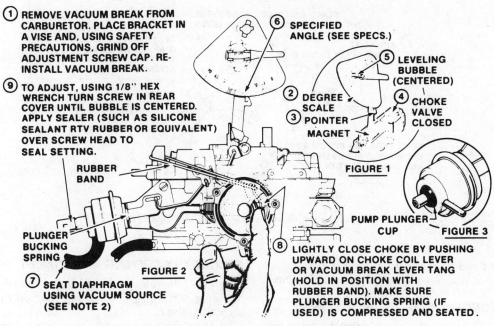

① REMOVE VACUUM BREAK FROM CARBURETOR. PLACE BRACKET IN A VISE AND, USING SAFETY PRECAUTIONS, GRIND OFF ADJUSTMENT SCREW CAP. RE-INSTALL VACUUM BREAK.

⑨ TO ADJUST, USING 1/8" HEX WRENCH TURN SCREW IN REAR COVER UNTIL BUBBLE IS CENTERED. APPLY SEALER (SUCH AS SILICONE SEALANT RTV RUBBER OR EQUIVALENT) OVER SCREW HEAD TO SEAL SETTING.

RUBBER BAND

PLUNGER BUCKING SPRING

FIGURE 2

⑦ SEAT DIAPHRAGM USING VACUUM SOURCE (SEE NOTE 2)

⑥ SPECIFIED ANGLE (SEE SPECS.)

⑤ LEVELING BUBBLE (CENTERED)

② DEGREE SCALE
③ POINTER MAGNET

④ CHOKE VALVE CLOSED

FIGURE 1

PUMP PLUNGER CUP   FIGURE 3

⑧ LIGHTLY CLOSE CHOKE BY PUSHING UPWARD ON CHOKE COIL LEVER OR VACUUM BREAK LEVER TANG (HOLD IN POSITION WITH RUBBER BAND). MAKE SURE PLUNGER BUCKING SPRING (IF USED) IS COMPRESSED AND SEATED.

Rear vacuum break adjustment—M2ME, E2ME

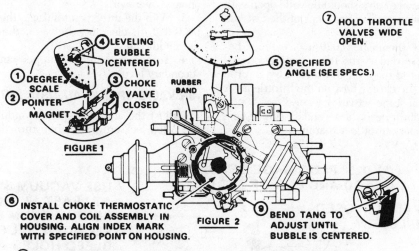

④ LEVELING BUBBLE (CENTERED)
① DEGREE SCALE
② POINTER MAGNET
③ CHOKE VALVE CLOSED
RUBBER BAND
FIGURE 1

⑦ HOLD THROTTLE VALVES WIDE OPEN.
⑤ SPECIFIED ANGLE (SEE SPECS.)
FIGURE 2
⑨ BEND TANG TO ADJUST UNTIL BUBBLE IS CENTERED.

⑥ INSTALL CHOKE THERMOSTATIC COVER AND COIL ASSEMBLY IN HOUSING. ALIGN INDEX MARK WITH SPECIFIED POINT ON HOUSING.

⑧ ON WARM ENGINE, CLOSE CHOKE VALVE BY PUSHING UP ON TANG ON VACUUM BREAK LEVER (HOLD IN POSITION WITH RUBBER BAND).

Unloader adjustment—M2ME, E2ME

vacuum break and unloader adjustments on these two carburetors are identical to those detailed in the preceding "M2ME and E2ME" section. Please refer to them. There are, however, a number of procedures that apply only to those 4 bbl carburetors.

AIR VALVE ROD ADJUSTMENT

1. Using an outside vacuum source, seat the choke vacuum diaphragm. Put a piece of tape over the purge bleed hole if so equipped.
2. Close the air valve completely.

3. Insert the gauge between the rod and the end of the slot in the lever.
4. Bend the rod to adjust the clearance.

SECONDARY LOCKOUT ADJUSTMENT

1. Pull the choke wide open by pushing out on the choke lever.
2. Open the throttle until the end of the secondary actuating lever is opposite the toe of the lockout lever.
3. Measure the clearance between the lockout lever and the secondary lever.

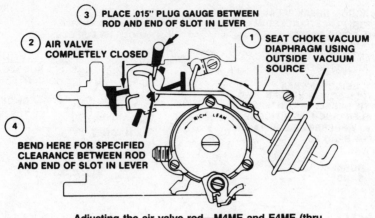

Adjusting the air valve rod—M4ME and E4ME (thru 1982)

4. Bend the lockout pin until the clearance is in accordance with the proper specifications.

SECONDARY CLOSING ADJUSTMENT

1. Make sure that the idle speed is set to the proper specifications.

2. The choke valve should be wide open with the cam follower off of the steps of the fast idle cam.

3. There should be 0.020 in. clearance between the secondary throttle actuating rod and the front of the slot on the secondary throttle lever with the closing tang on the throttle lever resting against the actuating lever.

4. To adjust, bend the secondary closing tang on the primary throttle actuating rod.

SECONDARY OPENING ADJUSTMENT

1. Open the primary throttle valves until the actuating link contacts the upper tang on the secondary lever.

2. With the two point linkage, the bottom of the link should be in the center of the secondary lever slot.

3. With the three point linkage, there should be 0.070 in. clearance between the link and the middle tang.

4. To adjust, bend the upper tang on the secondary lever.

AIR VALVE SPRING ADJUSTMENT

To adjust the air valve spring windup, loosen the Allen lockscrew and then turn the adjust-

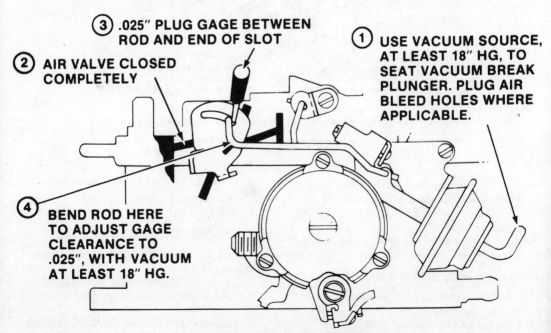

Air valve rod adjustment E4ME 1983–84

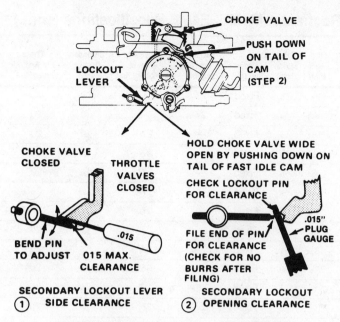

Secondary lockout adjustment—M4ME, E4ME

Rochester M4ME, E4ME Specifications

Year	Carburetor Identification ①	Float Level (in.)	Air Valve Spring (turn)	Pump Rod (in.)	Primary Vacuum Break (deg./in.)	Secondary Vacuum Break (deg./in.)	Secondary Opening (in.)	Choke Rod (deg./in.)	Choke Unloader (deg./in.)	Fast Idle Speed ② (rpm)
1980	17080202	$7/16$	$7/8$	$1/4$ ③	27/0.157	—	⑤	20/0.110	38/0.243	⑥
	17080204	$7/16$	$7/8$	$1/4$ ③	27/0.157	—	⑤	20/0.110	38/0.243	⑥
	17080207	$7/16$	$7/8$	$1/4$ ③	27/0.157	—	⑤	20/0.110	38/0.243	⑥
	17080228	$7/16$	$7/8$	$9/32$ ③	30/0.179	—	⑤	20/0.110	38/0.243	⑥
	17080243	$3/16$	$9/16$	$9/32$ ③	16/0.016	−/0.083	⑤	14.5/0.074	30/0.179	⑥
	17080274	$15/32$	$5/8$	$5/16$ ④	20/0.110	−/0.164	⑤	16/0.083	33/0.203	⑥
	17080282	$7/16$	$7/8$	$11/32$ ④	25/0.142	—	⑤	20/0.110	38/0.243	⑥
	17080284	$7/16$	$7/8$	$11/32$ ④	25/0.142	—	⑤	20/0.110	38/0.243	⑥
	17080502	$1/2$	$7/8$	Fixed	−/0.136	−/0.179	⑤	20/0.110	38/0.243	⑥
	17080504	$1/2$	$7/8$	Fixed	−/0.136	−/0.179	⑤	20/0.110	38/0.243	⑥
	17080542	$3/8$	$9/16$	Fixed	−/0.103	−/0.066	⑤	14.5/0.074	38/0.243	⑥
	17080543	$3/8$	$9/16$	Fixed	−/0.103	−/0.129	⑤	14.5/0.074	38/0.243	⑥
1981	17081202	$11/32$	$7/8$	Fixed	26/0.149	—	⑤	20/0.110	38/0.243	⑦
	17081203	$11/32$	$7/8$	Fixed	26/0.149	—	⑤	20/0.110	38/0.243	⑦
	17081204	$11/32$	$7/8$	Fixed	26/0.149	—	⑤	20/0.110	38/0.243	⑦
	17081207	$11/32$	$7/8$	Fixed	26/0.149	—	⑤	20/0.110	38/0.243	⑦
	17081216	$11/32$	$7/8$	Fixed	26/0.149	—	⑤	20/0.110	38/0.243	⑦
	17081217	$11/32$	$7/8$	Fixed	26/0.149	—	⑤	20/0.110	38/0.243	⑦
	17081218	$11/32$	$7/8$	Fixed	26/0.149	—	⑤	20/0.110	38/0.243	⑦
	17081242	$5/16$	$7/8$	Fixed	17/0.090	−/0.077	⑤	24.5/0.139	38/0.243	⑦
	17081243	$1/4$	$7/8$	Fixed	19/0.103	−/0.090	⑤	24.5/0.139	38/0.243	⑦

Rochester M4ME, E4ME Specifications (cont.)

Year	Carburetor Identification ①	Float Level (in.)	Air Valve Spring (turn)	Pump Rod (in.)	Primary Vacuum Break (deg./in.)	Secondary Vacuum Break (deg./in.)	Secondary Opening (in.)	Choke Rod (deg./in.)	Choke Unloader (deg./in.)	Fast Idle Speed ② (rpm)
1982	17082202	11/32	7/8	Fixed	27	—	⑤	20/–	38/–	⑦
	17082204	11/32	7/8	Fixed	27	—	⑤	20/–	38/–	⑦
1983	17083202	11/32	7/8	Fixed	—	27/–	⑤	20/–	38/–	⑦
	17083203	11/32	7/8	Fixed	—	27/–	⑤	38/–	38/–	⑦
	17083204	11/32	7/8	Fixed	—	27/–	⑤	20/–	38/–	⑦
	17083207	11/32	7/8	Fixed	—	27/–	⑤	38/–	38/–	⑦
	17083216	11/32	7/8	Fixed	—	27/–	⑤	20/–	38/–	⑦
	17083218	11/32	7/8	Fixed	—	27/–	⑤	20/–	38/–	⑦
	17083236	11/32	7/8	Fixed	—	27/–	⑤	20/–	38/–	⑦
	17083506	7/16	7/8	Fixed	27/–	36/–	⑤	20/–	36/–	⑦
	17083508	7/16	7/8	Fixed	27/–	36/–	⑤	20/–	36/–	⑦
	17083524	7/16	7/8	Fixed	25/–	36/–	⑤	20/–	36/–	⑦
	17083526	7/16	7/8	Fixed	25/–	36/–	⑤	20/–	36/–	⑦
1984	17084201	11/32	7/8	Fixed	27/–	—	⑤	20/–	38/–	—
	17084205	11/32	7/8	Fixed	27/–	—	⑤	38/–	38/–	—
	17084208	11/32	7/8	Fixed	27/–	—	⑤	20/–	38/–	—
	17084209	11/32	7/8	Fixed	27/–	—	⑤	38/–	38/–	—
	17084210	11/32	7/8	Fixed	27/–	—	⑤	20/–	38/–	—
	17084507	7/16	1	Fixed	27/–	36/–	⑤	20/–	36/–	—
	17084509	7/16	1	Fixed	27/–	36/–	⑤	20/–	36/–	—
	17084525	7/16	1	Fixed	25/–	36/–	⑤	20/–	36/–	—
	17084527	7/16	1	Fixed	25/–	36/–	⑤	20/–	36/–	—
1985	17085202	11/32	7/8	Fixed	27/–	—	⑤	20/–	38/–	—
	17085203	11/32	7/8	Fixed	27/–	—	⑤	20/–	38/–	—
	17085204	11/32	7/8	Fixed	27/–	—	⑤	20/–	38/–	—
	17085207	11/32	7/8	Fixed	27/–	—	⑤	38/–	38/–	—
	17085218	11/32	7/8	Fixed	27/–	—	⑤	20/–	38/–	—
	17085502	7/16	7/8	Fixed	26/–	36/–	⑤	20/–	39/–	—
	17085503	7/16	7/8	Fixed	26/–	36/–	⑤	20/–	39/–	—
	17085506	7/16	1	Fixed	27/–	36/–	⑤	20/–	36/–	—
	17085508	7/16	1	Fixed	27/–	36/–	⑤	20/–	36/–	—
	17085524	7/16	1	Fixed	25/–	36/–	⑤	20/–	36/–	—
	17085526	7/16	1	Fixed	25/–	36/–	⑤	20/–	36/–	—

① The carburetor identification number is stamped on the float bowl, near the secondary throttle lever.
② With manual transmission; w/o vacuum advance and the throttle positioned on the high step of the cam
③ Inner hole
④ Outer hole
⑤ No measurement necessary on two point linkage; see text
⑥ 4 turns after contacting lever for preliminary setting
⑦ 4½ turns after contacting lever for preliminary setting

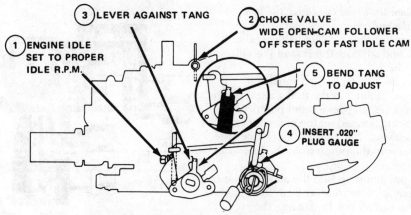

Secondary closing adjustment—M4ME, E4ME

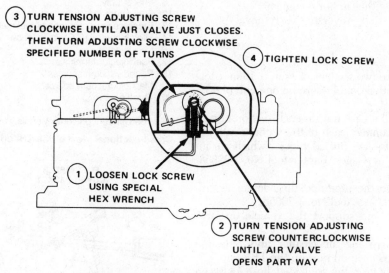

Adjusting the air valve spring—M4ME, E4ME

ing screw counterclockwise so as to remove all spring tension. With the air valve closed, turn the adjusting screw clockwise the specified number of turns after the torsion spring contacts the pin on the shaft. Hold the adjusting screw in this position and tighten the lockscrew.

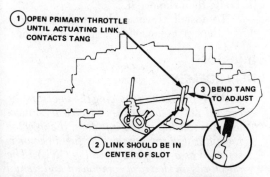

Secondary opening adjustment—M4ME, E4ME

GASOLINE FUEL INJECTION SYSTEM

NOTE: *This book contains simple testing and service procedures for your vehicles fuel injection system. More comprehensive testing and diagnosis procedures may be found in CHILTON'S GUIDE TO FUEL INJECTION AND FEEDBACK CARBURETORS, book part number 7488, available at Sears stores, most book stores and auto parts stores, or available directly from Chilton Co.*

Electric Fuel Pump
REMOVAL AND INSTALLATION
262 V6 TBI—1985 and Later

1. With the engine turned OFF, relieve the fuel pressure at the pressure regulator.
   NOTE: *The pressure regulator, located on top of the throttle body, is equipped with a*

bleed; open the bleed to reduce the fuel pressure in the system.

2. Disconnect the negative battery cable.

3. Raise and support the rear of the vehicle on jackstands.

4. Drain the fuel tank, then remove it.

5. Using a hammer and a drift punch, drive the fuel lever sending device and pump assembly locking ring (located on top of the fuel tank) counterclockwise. Lift the assembly from the tank and remove the pump from the fuel lever sending device.

6. Pull the pump up into the attaching hose while pulling it outward away from the bottom support. Be careful not to damage the rubber insulator and strainer during removal. After the pump assembly is clear of the bottom support, pull it out of the rubber connector.

7. To install, reverse the removal procedures.

Testing

1. Secure two sections of ⅜ in. x 10 in. (steel tubing), with a double-flare on one end of each section.

2. Install a flare nut on each section of tubing, then connect each of the sections into the "flare nut-to-flare nut adapters," which are included in the Gage Adapter tool No. J-29658-82.

3. Attach the pipe and the adapter assemblies to the Gage tool No. J-29658.

4. Raise and support the vehicle on jackstands.

5. Remove the air cleaner and plug the THERMAC vacuum port on the TBI.

6. Disconnect the fuel feed hose between the fuel tank and the filter, then secure the other ends of the ⅜ in. tubing into the fuel hoses with hose clamps.

7. Start the engine, check for leaks and observe the fuel pressure, it should be 9–13 psi.

8. Depressurize the fuel system, remove the testing tool, remove the plug from the THERMAC vacuum port, reconnect the fuel line, start the engine and check for fuel leaks.

Throttle Body

REMOVAL AND INSTALLATION

262 V6 TBI (1985 AND LATER)

1. Release the fuel pressure at the pressure regulator.

2. Disconnect the THERMAC hose from the engine fitting and remove the air cleaner.

3. Disconnect the electrical connectors at the idle air control, throttle position sensor and the injector.

4. Disconnect the throttle linkage, return spring and cruise control (if equipped).

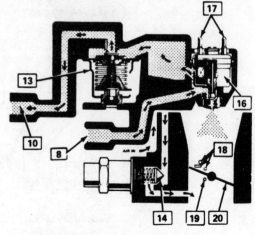

8. Fuel supply
10. Fuel return
13. Pressure regulator (part of fuel meter cover)
14. Idle air control (IAC) valve (shown open)
16. Fuel injector
17. Fuel injector terminals
18. Ported vacuum sources*
19. Manifold vacuum source*
20. Throttle valve

*May Be Different on some Models.

Cross-sectional view of the TBI operation

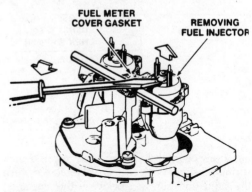

Removing the fuel injector from the throttle body

5. Disconnect the throttle body vacuum hoses, the fuel supply and fuel return lines.

6. Disconnect the bolts securing the throttle body, then remove it.

7. To install, reverse the removal procedures. Replace the manifold gaskets and O-rings.

Injector

REPLACEMENT

CAUTION: *When removing the injectors, be careful not to damage the electrical connector pins (on top of the injector), the injector fuel filter and the nozzle. The fuel injector is serviced as a complete assembly ONLY. The injector is an electrical component and should not be immersed in any kind of cleaner.*

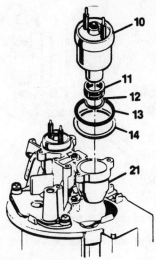

10. Injector–fuel
11. Filter–fuel injector inlet
12. "O" ring–fuel injector–lower
13. "O" ring–fuel injector–upper
14. Washer–fuel injector
21. Fuel meter body assembly

Exploded view of the fuel injector

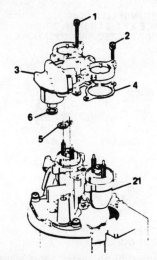

1. Screw assembly–fuel meter cover attaching–long
2. Screw assembly–fuel meter cover attaching–short
3. Fuel meter cover assembly
4. Gasket–fuel meter cover
5. Gasket–fuel meter outlet
6. Seal–pressure regulator
21. Fuel meter body assembly

Exploded view of the fuel meter cover

1. Remove the air cleaner. Relieve the fuel pressure.

2. At the injector connector, squeeze the two tabs together and pull straight up.

3. Remove the fuel meter cover and leave the cover gasket in place.

4. Using a small pry bar or tool No. J-26868, carefully lift the injector until it is free from the fuel meter body.

5. Remove the small O-ring from the nozzle end of the injector. Carefully rotate the injector's fuel filter back-and-forth to remove it from the base of the injector.

6. Discard the fuel meter cover gasket.

7. Remove the large O-ring and back-up washer from the top of the counterbore of the fuel meter body injector cavity.

8. To install, lubricate the o-rings with automatic transmission fluid and reverse the removal procedures.

Fuel Meter Cover

REPLACEMENT

1. Remove the air cleaner.

2. Disconnect the electrical connector from the fuel injector.

3. Remove the fuel meter-to-fuel meter body screws and lockwashers.

NOTE: *When removing the fuel meter cover screws note the location of the two short screws.*

4. Remove the fuel meter cover and discard the gasket.

5. To install, use a new gasket and reverse the removal procedures.

Idle Air Control Valve

REPLACEMENT

1. Remove the air cleaner.

2. Disconnect the electrical connector from the idle air control valve.

3. Using a ¼ in. (32mm) wrench or tool J-33031, remove the idle air control valve.

CAUTION: *Before installing a new idle air control valve, measure the distance that the valve extends (from the motor housing to the end of the cone); the distance should be no greater than ⅛ in. (28mm). If it extends too far, damage will occur to the valve when it is installed.*

4. To complete the installation, use a new gasket and reverse the removal procedures. Start the engine and allow it to reach operating temperature.

NOTE: *The ECM will reset the idle speed when the vehicle is driven at 30 mph.*

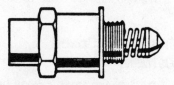

DUAL TAPER VALVE

View of the idle air control valve used with automatic transmissions

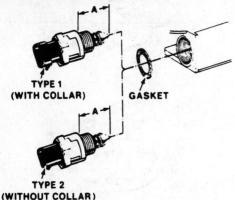

PRIOR TO INSTALLATION.
DISTANCE AT DIMENSION "A"
MUST <u>NOT</u> EXCEED SPECIFICATIONS

TYPE 1
(WITH COLLAR)   GASKET

TYPE 2
(WITHOUT COLLAR)

Installing the idle air control valve

Fuel Pump Relay

REPLACEMENT

The fuel pump relay is located in the engine compartment. Other than checking for loose electrical connections, the only service necessary is to replace the relay.

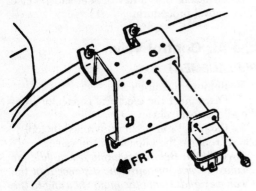

View of the fuel pump relay

Oil Pressure Switch

REPLACEMENT

The oil pressure switch is mounted to the top rear of the engine.

1. Remove the electrical connector from the switch.
2. Remove the oil pressure switch.
3. To install, reverse the removal procedures.

Minimum Idle Speed

ADJUSTMENT

Only if parts of the throttle body have been replaced, should this procedure be performed; the engine should be at operating temperature.

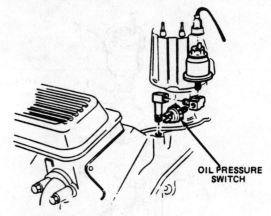

OIL PRESSURE
SWITCH

View of the oil pressure switch

1. Ground the diagnostic lead of the IAC motor.
2. Turn the ignition ON, DO NOT start the engine and wait for 30 seconds.
3. With the ignition ON, disconnect the electrical connector from the IAC motor.
4. Remove the ground from the diagnostic lead and start the engine.
5. Adjust the idle set screw to 500–600 rpm with the transmission in Drive.
6. Turn the ignition OFF and reconnect the electrical to the IAC motor.
7. Adjust the Throttle Position Sensor (TPS) to 0.450–0.600 volts.
8. Recheck the setting.
9. Start the engine and inspect for proper idle operation.

DIESEL FUEL SYSTEM

Fuel Pump

REMOVAL AND INSTALLATION

V8 Models

The fuel supply pump on the V8 engine is serviced in the same manner as the fuel pump on the gasoline engine.

V6 Models

NOTE: *The fuel pump used on the V6 diesel engine is located at the front of the engine, next to the fuel heater.*

1. Disconnect negative battery cable, remove the air cleaner, and unplug all electrical connectors from the pump.
2. Place a rag under the pump inlet and outlet fittings, and carefully unscrew the inlet and the outlet fittings. Cap all fittings to keep dirt out.
3. Remove the pump mounting bracket nut, then the fuel pump.
4. To install fuel pump, reverse above procedure, and tighten the nut of the pump

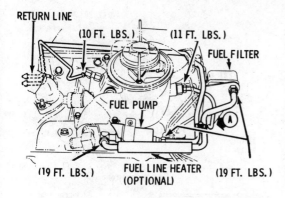

V6 diesel fuel pump and fuel filter locations; fuel filter shown below

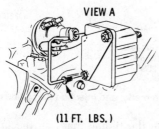

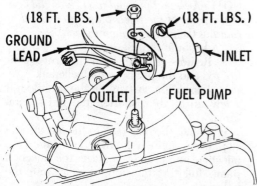

V6 diesel fuel supply pump mounted on intake manifold

mounting bracket to 18 ft. lbs. Then torque inlet and outlet line fittings to 19 ft. lbs.

NOTE: *In some cases you may have to adjust pump position slightly to align pump fittings with the fuel lines.*

5. After installing the fuel pump, position a catch basin and disconnect the fuel line at the filter and turn on the ignition switch to prime and bleed the lines. If after torquing the fuel line, the pump runs with a click-like sound, or the fuel bubbles, check for leaks in the fuel lines. When the pump quiets down, tighten the fuel line at the filter.

Fuel Filter
REMOVAL AND INSTALLATION

The fuel filter is a square assembly located at the back of the engine above the intake mani-

fold. Disconnect the fuel lines and remove the filter. Install the lines to the new filter. Start the engine and check for leaks.

Water in Fuel (Diesel)

Water is the worst enemy of the diesel fuel injection system. The injection pump, which is designed and constructed to extremely close tolerances, and the injectors can be easily damaged if enough water is forced through them in the fuel. Engine performance will also be drastically affected, and engine damage can occur.

Diesel fuel is much more susceptible than gasoline to water contamination. Diesel-engined cars are equipped with an indicator lamp system that turns on an instrument panel lamp if water (1 to 2½ gallons) is detected in the fuel tank. The lamp will come on for 2 to 5 seconds each time the ignition is turned ON, assuring the driver the lamp is working. If there is water in the fuel, the light will come back on after a 15 to 20 second off delay, and then remain ON.

Purging the Fuel Tank

Cars which have a "Water in Fuel" light may have the water removed from the tank with a siphon pump. The pump hose should be hooked up to the ¼ in. fuel return hose (the smaller of the two hoses) above the rear axle or under the hood near the fuel pump. Siphoning should continue until all water is removed from the tank. Use a clear plastic hose or observe the filter bowl on the siphon pump (if equipped) to determine when clear fuel begins to flow. Be sure to remove the cap on the fuel tank while purging. Replace the cap when finished. Discard the fuel filter and replace with a new filter.

Fuel Injection Pump And Lines
REMOVAL AND INSTALLATION

NOTE: *The V6 and V8 diesel injection systems may use either a CAV injection pump, or a Roosa-Master/Stanodyne pump.*

1. Remove the air cleaner.
2. Remove the filters and pipes from the valve covers and air crossover.
3. Remove the air crossover, then cap the intake manifold with screen covers (tool J-26996-1).
4. Disconnect the throttle rod and return spring.
5. Remove the bellcrank.
6. Remove the throttle and transmission cables from the intake manifold brackets.
7. Disconnect the fuel lines from the filter and remove the filter.

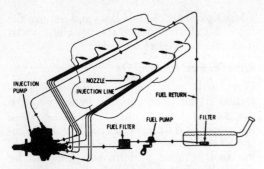

Diesel fuel injection system circuit, V8 shown

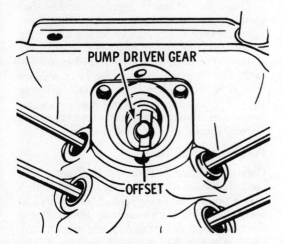

Offset on diesel injection pump driven gear

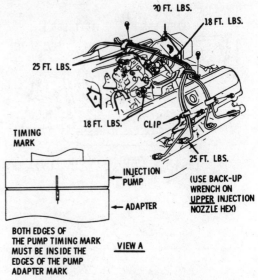

Diesel timing marks and injection pump lines, V8

8. Disconnect the fuel inlet line from the pump.

9. Remove the rear A/C compressor brace and the fuel line.

10. Disconnect the fuel return line from the injection pump.

11. Remove the clamps and pull the fuel return lines from each injection nozzle.

12. Using two wrenches, disconnect the high pressure lines from the nozzles.

13. Remove the three injection pump retaining nuts with tool J-26987 or its equivalent.

14. Remove the pump, then cap all lines and nozzles.

To install:

15. Remove the protective caps.

16. Line up the offset tang on the pump driveshaft with the pump driven gear and install the pump.

17. Install, but do not tighten the pump retaining nuts.

18. Connect the high pressure lines to the nozzles.

19. Using two wrenches, torque the high pressure line nuts to 25 ft. lbs.

20. Connect the fuel return lines to the nozzles and pump.

21. Align the timing mark on the injection pump with the line on the timing mark adaptor and torque the mounting nuts to 35 ft. lbs.

NOTE: A ¾ in. open end wrench on the boss at the front of the injection pump will aid in rotating the pump to align the marks.

22. Adjust the throttle rod:

a. Remove the clip from the cruise control rod and the rod from the bellcrank.

b. Loosen the locknut on the throttle rod a few turns, then shorten the rod several turns.

c. Rotate the bellcrank to the full throttle stop, then lengthen the throttle rod until the injection pump lever contacts the injection pump full throttle stop, then release the bellcrank.

d. Tighten the throttle rod locknut.

23. Install the fuel inlet line between the transfer pump and the filter.

24. Install the rear A/C compressor brace.

25. Install the bellcrank and clip.

26. Connect the throttle rod and return spring.

27. To adjust the transmission cable:

a. Push the snap-lock to the disengaged position.

b. Rotate the injection pump lever to the full throttle stop and hold it there.

c. Push the snap-lock until it is flush.

d. Release the injection pump lever.

28. Start the engine and check for fuel leaks.

29. Remove the screened covers and install the air crossover.

30. Install the tubes in the air flow control valve in the air crossover and install the ventilation filters in the valve covers.

31. Install the air cleaner.

CHILTON'S
FUEL ECONOMY
& TUNE-UP TIPS

Tune-up • Spark Plug Diagnosis • Emission Controls

Fuel System • Cooling System • Tires and Wheels

General Maintenance

CHILTON'S FUEL ECONOMY & TUNE-UP TIPS

Fuel economy is important to everyone, no matter what kind of vehicle you drive. The maintenance-minded motorist can save both money and fuel using these tips and the periodic maintenance and tune-up procedures in this Repair and Tune-Up Guide.

There are more than 130,000,000 cars and trucks registered for private use in the United States. Each travels an average of 10-12,000 miles per year, and, and in total they consume close to 70 billion gallons of fuel each year. This represents nearly 2/3 of the oil imported by the United States each year. The Federal government's goal is to reduce consumption 10% by 1985. A variety of methods are either already in use or under serious consideration, and they all affect you driving and the cars you will drive. In addition to "down-sizing", the auto industry is using or investigating the use of electronic fuel delivery, electronic engine controls and alternative engines for use in smaller and lighter vehicles, among other alternatives to meet the federally mandated Corporate Average Fuel Economy (CAFE) of 27.5 mpg by 1985. The government, for its part, is considering rationing, mandatory driving curtailments and tax increases on motor vehicle fuel in an effort to reduce consumption. The government's goal of a 10% reduction could be realized — and further government regulation avoided — if every private vehicle could use just 1 less gallon of fuel per week.

How Much Can You Save?

Tests have proven that almost anyone can make at least a 10% reduction in fuel consumption through regular maintenance and tune-ups. When a major manufacturer of spark plugs sur-

TUNE-UP

1. Check the cylinder compression to be sure the engine will really benefit from a tune-up and that it is capable of producing good fuel economy. A tune-up will be wasted on an engine in poor mechanical condition.

2. Replace spark plugs regularly. New spark plugs alone can increase fuel economy 3%.

3. Be sure the spark plugs are the correct type (heat range) for your vehicle. See the Tune-Up Specifications.

Heat range refers to the spark plug's ability to conduct heat away from the firing end. It must conduct the heat away in an even pattern to avoid becoming a source of pre-ignition, yet it must also operate hot enough to burn off conductive deposits that could cause misfiring.

The heat range is usually indicated by a number on the spark plug, part of the manufacturer's designation for each individual spark plug. The numbers in bold-face indicate the heat range in each manufacturer's identification system.

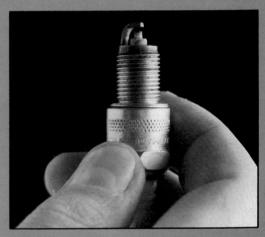

Periodically, check the spark plugs to be sure they are firing efficiently. They are excellent indicators of the internal condition of your engine.

Manufacturer	Typical Designation
AC	R **45** TS
Bosch (old)	WA **145** T30
Bosch (new)	HR **8** Y
Champion	RBL **15** Y
Fram/Autolite	**415**
Mopar	P-**62** PR
Motorcraft	BRF-**42**
NGK	BP **5** ES-15
Nippondenso	W **16** EP
Prestolite	14GR **5** 2A

On AC, Bosch (new), Champion, Fram/Autolite, Mopar, Motorcraft and Prestolite, a higher number indicates a hotter plug. On Bosch (old), NGK and Nippondenso, a higher number indicates a colder plug.

4. Make sure the spark plugs are properly gapped. See the Tune-Up Specifications in this book.

5. Be sure the spark plugs are firing efficiently. The illustrations on the next 2 pages show you how to "read" the firing end of the spark plug.

6. Check the ignition timing and set it to specifications. Tests show that almost all cars have incorrect ignition timing by more than 2°.

veyed over 6,000 cars nationwide, they found that a tune-up, on cars that needed one, increased fuel economy over 11%. Replacing worn plugs alone, accounted for a 3% increase. The same test also revealed that 8 out of every 10 vehicles will have some maintenance deficiency that will directly affect fuel economy, emissions or performance. Most of this mileage-robbing neglect could be prevented with regular maintenance.

Modern engines require that all of the functioning systems operate properly for maximum efficiency. A malfunction anywhere wastes fuel. You can keep your vehicle running as efficiently and economically as possible, by being aware of your vehicle's operating and performance characteristics. If your vehicle suddenly develops performance or fuel economy problems it could be due to one or more of the following:

PROBLEM	POSSIBLE CAUSE
Engine Idles Rough	Ignition timing, idle mixture, vacuum leak or something amiss in the emission control system.
Hesitates on Acceleration	Dirty carburetor or fuel filter, improper accelerator pump setting, ignition timing or fouled spark plugs.
Starts Hard or Fails to Start	Worn spark plugs, improperly set automatic choke, ice (or water) in fuel system.
Stalls Frequently	Automatic choke improperly adjusted and possible dirty air filter or fuel filter.
Performs Sluggishly	Worn spark plugs, dirty fuel or air filter, ignition timing or automatic choke out of adjustment.

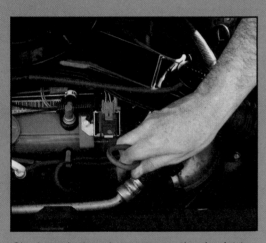

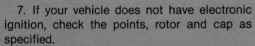

Check spark plug wires on conventional point type ignition for cracks by bending them in a loop around your finger.

Be sure that spark plug wires leading to adjacent cylinders do not run too close together. (Photo courtesy Champion Spark Plug Co.)

7. If your vehicle does not have electronic ignition, check the points, rotor and cap as specified.

8. Check the spark plug wires (used with conventional point-type ignitions) for cracks and burned or broken insulation by bending them in a loop around your finger. Cracked wires decrease fuel efficiency by failing to deliver full voltage to the spark plugs. One misfiring spark plug can cost you as much as 2 mpg.

9. Check the routing of the plug wires. Misfiring can be the result of spark plug leads to adjacent cylinders running parallel to each other and too close together. One wire tends to pick up voltage from the other causing it to fire "out of time".

10. Check all electrical and ignition circuits for voltage drop and resistance.

11. Check the distributor mechanical and/or vacuum advance mechanisms for proper functioning. The vacuum advance can be checked by twisting the distributor plate in the opposite direction of rotation. It should spring back when released.

12. Check and adjust the valve clearance on engines with mechanical lifters. The clearance should be slightly loose rather than too tight.

SPARK PLUG DIAGNOSIS

Normal

APPEARANCE: This plug is typical of one operating normally. The insulator nose varies from a light tan to grayish color with slight electrode wear. The presence of slight deposits is normal on used plugs and will have no adverse effect on engine performance. The spark plug heat range is correct for the engine and the engine is running normally.

CAUSE: Properly running engine.

RECOMMENDATION: Before reinstalling this plug, the electrodes should be cleaned and filed square. Set the gap to specifications. If the plug has been in service for more than 10-12,000 miles, the entire set should probably be replaced with a fresh set of the same heat range.

Oil Deposits

APPEARANCE: The firing end of the plug is covered with a wet, oily coating.

CAUSE: The problem is poor oil control. On high mileage engines, oil is leaking past the rings or valve guides into the combustion chamber. A common cause is also a plugged PCV valve, and a ruptured fuel pump diaphragm can also cause this condition. Oil fouled plugs such as these are often found in new or recently overhauled engines, before normal oil control is achieved, and can be cleaned and reinstalled.

RECOMMENDATION: A hotter spark plug may temporarily relieve the problem, but the engine is probably in need of work.

Incorrect Heat Range

APPEARANCE: The effects of high temperature on a spark plug are indicated by clean white, often blistered insulator. This can also be accompanied by excessive wear of the electrode, and the absence of deposits.

CAUSE: Check for the correct spark plug heat range. A plug which is too hot for the engine can result in overheating. A car operated mostly at high speeds can require a colder plug. Also check ignition timing, cooling system level, fuel mixture and leaking intake manifold.

RECOMMENDATION: If all ignition and engine adjustments are known to be correct, and no other malfunction exists, install spark plugs one heat range colder.

Photos Courtesy Fram Corporation

Carbon Deposits

APPEARANCE: Carbon fouling is easily identified by the presence of dry, soft, black, sooty deposits.

CAUSE: Changing the heat range can often lead to carbon fouling, as can prolonged slow, stop-and-start driving. If the heat range is correct, carbon fouling can be attributed to a rich fuel mixture, sticking choke, clogged air cleaner, worn breaker points, retarded timing or low compression. If only one or two plugs are carbon fouled, check for corroded or cracked wires on the affected plugs. Also look for cracks in the distributor cap between the towers of affected cylinders.

RECOMMENDATION: After the problem is corrected, these plugs can be cleaned and reinstalled if not worn severely.

MMT Fouled

APPEARANCE: Spark plugs fouled by MMT (Methycyclopentadienyl Maganese Tricarbonyl) have reddish, rusty appearance on the insulator and side electrode.

CAUSE: MMT is an anti-knock additive in gasoline used to replace lead. During the combustion process, the MMT leaves a reddish deposit on the insulator and side electrode.

RECOMMENDATION: No engine malfunction is indicated and the deposits will not affect plug performance any more than lead deposits (see Ash Deposits). MMT fouled plugs can be cleaned, regapped and reinstalled.

High Speed Glazing

APPEARANCE: Glazing appears as shiny coating on the plug, either yellow or tan in color.

CAUSE: During hard, fast acceleration, plug temperatures rise suddenly. Deposits from normal combustion have no chance to fluff-off; instead, they melt on the insulator forming an electrically conductive coating which causes misfiring.

RECOMMENDATION: Glazed plugs are not easily cleaned. They should be replaced with a fresh set of plugs of the correct heat range. If the condition recurs, using plugs with a heat range one step colder may cure the problem.

Ash (Lead) Deposits

APPEARANCE: Ash deposits are characterized by light brown or white colored deposits crusted on the side or center electrodes. In some cases it may give the plug a rusty appearance.

CAUSE: Ash deposits are normally derived from oil or fuel additives burned during normal combustion. Normally they are harmless, though excessive amounts can cause misfiring. If deposits are excessive in short mileage, the valve guides may be worn.

RECOMMENDATION: Ash-fouled plugs can be cleaned, gapped and reinstalled.

Detonation

APPEARANCE: Detonation is usually characterized by a broken plug insulator.

CAUSE: A portion of the fuel charge will begin to burn spontaneously, from the increased heat following ignition. The explosion that results applies extreme pressure to engine components, frequently damaging spark plugs and pistons.

Detonation can result by over-advanced ignition timing, inferior gasoline (low octane) lean air/fuel mixture, poor carburetion, engine lugging or an increase in compression ratio due to combustion chamber deposits or engine modification.

RECOMMENDATION: Replace the plugs after correcting the problem.

Photos Courtesy Champion Spark Plug Co.

EMISSION CONTROLS

13. Be aware of the general condition of the emission control system. It contributes to reduced pollution and should be serviced regularly to maintain efficient engine operation.

14. Check all vacuum lines for dried, cracked or brittle conditions. Something as simple as a leaking vacuum hose can cause poor performance and loss of economy.

15. Avoid tampering with the emission control system. Attempting to improve fuel econ-

FUEL SYSTEM

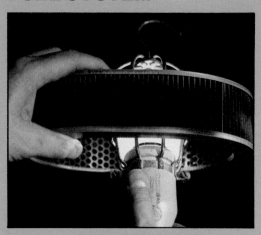

Check the air filter with a light behind it. If you can see light through the filter it can be reused.

Extremely clogged filters should be discarded and replaced with a new one.

18. Replace the air filter regularly. A dirty air filter richens the air/fuel mixture and can increase fuel consumption as much as 10%. Tests show that ⅓ of all vehicles have air filters in need of replacement.

19. Replace the fuel filter at least as often as recommended.

20. Set the idle speed and carburetor mixture to specifications.

21. Check the automatic choke. A sticking or malfunctioning choke wastes gas.

22. During the summer months, adjust the automatic choke for a leaner mixture which will produce faster engine warm-ups.

COOLING SYSTEM

29. Be sure all accessory drive belts are in good condition. Check for cracks or wear.

30. Adjust all accessory drive belts to proper tension.

31. Check all hoses for swollen areas, worn spots, or loose clamps.

32. Check coolant level in the radiator or ex-pansion tank.

33. Be sure the thermostat is operating properly. A stuck thermostat delays engine warm-up and a cold engine uses nearly twice as much fuel as a warm engine.

34. Drain and replace the engine coolant at least as often as recommended. Rust and scale

TIRES & WHEELS

38. Check the tire pressure often with a pencil type gauge. Tests by a major tire manufacturer show that 90% of all vehicles have at least 1 tire improperly inflated. Better mileage can be achieved by over-inflating tires, but never exceed the maximum inflation pressure on the side of the tire.

39. If possible, install radial tires. Radial tires deliver as much as ½ mpg more than bias belted tires.

40. Avoid installing super-wide tires. They only create extra rolling resistance and decrease fuel mileage. Stick to the manufacturer's recommendations.

41. Have the wheels properly balanced.

omy by tampering with emission controls is more likely to worsen fuel economy than improve it. Emission control changes on modern engines are not readily reversible.

16. Clean (or replace) the EGR valve and lines as recommended.

17. Be sure that all vacuum lines and hoses are reconnected properly after working under the hood. An unconnected or misrouted vacuum line can wreak havoc with engine performance.

23. Check for fuel leaks at the carburetor, fuel pump, fuel lines and fuel tank. Be sure all lines and connections are tight.

24. Periodically check the tightness of the carburetor and intake manifold attaching nuts and bolts. These are a common place for vacuum leaks to occur.

25. Clean the carburetor periodically and lubricate the linkage.

26. The condition of the tailpipe can be an excellent indicator of proper engine combustion. After a long drive at highway speeds, the inside of the tailpipe should be a light grey in color. Black or soot on the insides indicates an overly rich mixture.

27. Check the fuel pump pressure. The fuel pump may be supplying more fuel than the engine needs.

28. Use the proper grade of gasoline for your engine. Don't try to compensate for knocking or "pinging" by advancing the ignition timing. This practice will only increase plug temperature and the chances of detonation or pre-ignition with relatively little performance gain.

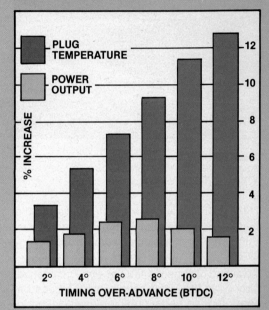

Increasing ignition timing past the specified setting results in a drastic increase in spark plug temperature with increased chance of detonation or preignition. Performance increase is considerably less. (Photo courtesy Champion Spark Plug Co.)

that form in the engine should be flushed out to allow the engine to operate at peak efficiency.

35. Clean the radiator of debris that can decrease cooling efficiency.

36. Install a flex-type or electric cooling fan, if you don't have a clutch type fan. Flex fans use curved plastic blades to push more air at low speeds when more cooling is needed; at high speeds the blades flatten out for less resistance. Electric fans only run when the engine temperature reaches a predetermined level.

37. Check the radiator cap for a worn or cracked gasket. If the cap does not seal properly, the cooling system will not function properly.

42. Be sure the front end is correctly aligned. A misaligned front end actually has wheels going in differed directions. The increased drag can reduce fuel economy by .3 mpg.

43. Correctly adjust the wheel bearings. Wheel bearings that are adjusted too tight increase rolling resistance.

Check tire pressures regularly with a reliable pocket type gauge. Be sure to check the pressure on a cold tire.

GENERAL MAINTENANCE

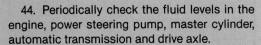

Check the fluid levels (particularly engine oil) on a regular basis. Be sure to check the oil for grit, water or other contamination.

A vacuum gauge is another excellent indicator of internal engine condition and can also be installed in the dash as a mileage indicator.

44. Periodically check the fluid levels in the engine, power steering pump, master cylinder, automatic transmission and drive axle.

45. Change the oil at the recommended interval and change the filter at every oil change. Dirty oil is thick and causes extra friction between moving parts, cutting efficiency and increasing wear. A worn engine requires more frequent tune-ups and gets progressively worse fuel economy. In general, use the lightest viscosity oil for the driving conditions you will encounter.

46. Use the recommended viscosity fluids in the transmission and axle.

47. Be sure the battery is fully charged for fast starts. A slow starting engine wastes fuel.

48. Be sure battery terminals are clean and tight.

49. Check the battery electrolyte level and add distilled water if necessary.

50. Check the exhaust system for crushed pipes, blockages and leaks.

51. Adjust the brakes. Dragging brakes or brakes that are not releasing create increased drag on the engine.

52. Install a vacuum gauge or miles-per-gallon gauge. These gauges visually indicate engine vacuum in the intake manifold. High vacuum = good mileage and low vacuum = poorer mileage. The gauge can also be an excellent indicator of internal engine conditions.

53. Be sure the clutch is properly adjusted. A slipping clutch wastes fuel.

54. Check and periodically lubricate the heat control valve in the exhaust manifold. A sticking or inoperative valve prevents engine warm-up and wastes gas.

55. Keep accurate records to check fuel economy over a period of time. A sudden drop in fuel economy may signal a need for tune-up or other maintenance.

32. Start the engine and allow it to run for two minutes. Stop the engine, let it stand for two minutes, then restart. This permits the air to bleed off within the pump.

SLOW IDLE SPEED ADJUSTMENT

1. Run the engine to normal operating temperature.

2. Insert the probe of a magnetic pickup tachometer into the timing indicator hole.

3. Set the parking brake and block the drive wheels.

4. Place the transmission in Drive and turn the A/C Off.

5. Turn the slow idle screw on the injection pump to obtain the idle specification on the emission control label.

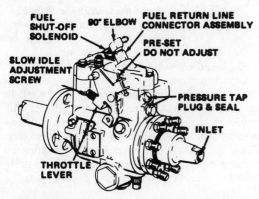

Diesel injection pump slow idle screw, Roosa Master/Stanodyne pump

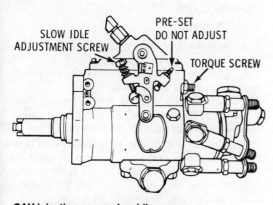

CAV injection pump slow idle screw

FAST IDLE SOLENOID ADJUSTMENT

Through 1979

1. Set the parking brake and block the drive wheels.

2. Run the engine to normal operating temperature.

3. Place the transmission in Drive, disconnect the compressor clutch wire and turn the

(6 FT. LBS.)

Fast idle solenoid adjustment. Solenoid mounted on side of injection pump

A/C On. On cars with A/C, disconnect the solenoid wire, and connect jumper wires to the solenoid terminals. Ground one of the wires and connect the other to a 12 volt power source to activate the solenoid.

4. Adjust the fast idle solenoid plunger to obtain 650 rpm.

1980 and Later

1. With the ignition OFF, disconnect the single green wire from the fast idle relay located on the front of the firewall.

2. Set the parking brake and block the drive wheels.

3. Start the engine and adjust the solenoid (energized) to the specifications on the underhood emission control label.

4. Turn the ignition switch OFF and reconnect the green wire.

CRUISE CONTROL SERVO RELAY ROD ADJUSTMENT

1. Turn the engine Off.

2. Adjust the rod to minimum slack then put the clip in the first free hole closest to the bellcrank, but within the servo bail.

Injection Timing

CHECKING

NOTE: *A special diesel timing meter is needed to check injection timing. There are a few variations of this meter, but the type desirable here uses a signal through a glow plug probe to determine combustion timing. The meter picks up the engine speed in RPM and the crankshaft position from the crankshaft balancer. This tool is available at automotive supply houses and from tool jobbers; it is the counterpart to a gasoline engine timing light, coupled with a tachometer. An intake manifold cover is also needed.*

The marks on the pump and adapter flange will normally be aligned within .030 in. on the V8 and .050 in. on the V6.

1. Place the transmission shift lever in

"Park," apply the parking brake and block the rear wheels.

2. Start the engine and let it run at idle until fully warm. Shut off the engine.

NOTE: *If the engine is not allowed to completely warm up, the probe may soot up, causing incorrect timing readings.*

3. Remove the air cleaner assembly and carefully install cover J-26996-1. *This cover over the intake is important.* Disconnect the EGR valve hose.

4. Clean away all dirt from the engine probe holder (RPM counter) and the crankshaft balancer rim.

5. Clean the lens on both ends of the glow plug probe and clean the lens in the photoelectric pick-up. Use a tooth pick to scrape the carbon from the combustion chamber side of the glow plug probe, then look through the probe to make sure it's clean. *Cleanliness is crucial for accurate readings.*

6. Install the probe into the crankshaft RPM counter (probe holder) on the engine front cover.

7. Remove the glow plug from No. 3 cylinder on the V8 and from No. 1 on the V6. Install the glow plug probe in the glow plug opening and torque to 8 ft. lbs.

8. Set the timing meter offset selector to "B" (99.5) on the V8, and to "A" (20) on the V6.

9. Connect the battery leads, red to positive, black to negative.

10. Disconnect the two-lead connector from the alternator.

11. Start the engine. Adjust the engine RPM to the speed specified on the emissions control decal.

12. Observe the timing reading, then observe it again in 2 minutes. When the readings stabilize over the 2 minutes intervals, compare that final stabilized reading to the one specified on the emissions control decal. The timing reading will be an ATDC (After Top Dead Center) reading when set to specifications.

13. Disconnect the timing meter and install the removed glow plug, torquing it to 12 ft. lbs. on the V8 and 15 ft. lbs. on the V6.

14. Connect the generator two-lead connection.

15. Install the air cleaner assembly and connect the EGR valve hose.

Adjustment

1. Shut off the engine.

2. Note the relative position of the marks on the pump flange and either the pump intermediate adapter (V6) or pump adaptor (V8).

3. Loosen the nuts or bolts holding the pump to a point where the pump can just be rotated. Use a ¾ in. open-end wrench on the boss at the front of the injection pump on the V8 and

a 1 in. open-end wrench on the V6. You may need a wrench with a slight offset to clear the fuel return line on the V6.

4. Rotate the pump to the left to advance the timing and to the right to retard the timing. On the V8 the width of the mark on the adaptor is equal to about one degree of timing. On the V6 the width of the mark on the intermediate adaptor is about ⅔ of a degree. Move the pump the amount that is needed and tighten the pump retaining nuts to 18 ft. lbs. on the V8 and 35 ft. lbs. on the V6.

5. Start the engine and recheck the timing as described earlier. Reset the timing if necessary.

6. Adjust the injection pump rod on the V8. On both engines, reset the fast and curb idle speeds.

NOTE: *Wild needle fluctuations on the timing meter indicate a cylinder not firing properly. Correction of this condition must be made prior to adjusting the timing.*

7. If after resetting the timing, the timing marks are far apart and the engine still runs poorly, the dynamic timing could still be off. It is possible that a malfunctioning cylinder will cause incorrect timing. If this occurs, it is essential that timing be checked in cylinders 2 or 3 on the V8 and 1 or 4 on the V6. If different timing exists between cylinders, try both positions to determine which timing works best.

Injection Nozzle
REMOVAL AND INSTALLATION
Through 1979

1. Remove the fuel return line from the nozzle.

2. Remove the nozzle hold-down clamp and spacer using tool No. J-26952.

3. Cap the high pressure line and nozzle tip.

NOTE: *The nozzle tip is highly susceptible to damage and must be protected at all times.*

4. If an old nozzle is to be reinstalled, a new compression seal and carbon stop seal must be installed after removal of the used seals.

5. Remove the caps and install the nozzle, spacer and clamp. Torque to 25 ft. lbs.

6. Replace return line, start the engine and check for leaks.

1982-84 Models

The injection nozzles on these engines are simply unbolted from the cylinder head, after the fuel lines are removed, in similar fashion to a spark plug. Be careful not to damage the nozzle end and make sure you remove the copper nozzle gasket from the cylinder head if it does not come off with the nozzle. Clean the carbon

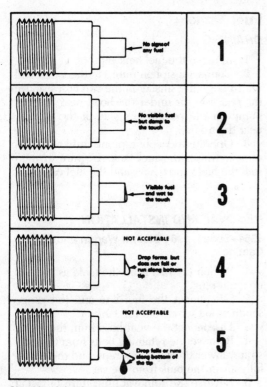

Checking injection nozzle seat tightness

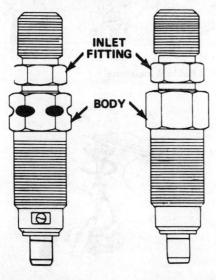

**INLET FITTING TO BODY TORQUE
DIESEL EQUIPMENT – 45 FT. LBS.
C.A.V. LUCAS – 25 FT. LBS.**

DIESEL EQUIPMENT   C.A.V. LUCAS

Injection nozzles, two types

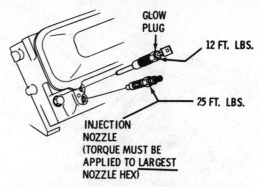

Injection nozzle and glow plug installation

off the tip of the nozzle with a soft brass wire brush and install the nozzles, with gaskets.

NOTE: *1981 and later models use two types of injectors, CAV Lucas and Diesel Equipment. When installing the inlet fittings, torque the Diesel Equipment injector fitting to 45 ft. lbs. and the CAV Lucas to 25 ft. lbs.*

Injection Pump Adapter, Adapter Seal, and New Adapter Timing Mark

REMOVAL AND INSTALLATION

NOTE: *Skip steps 4 and 9 if a new adapter is not being installed.*

1. Remove injection pump and lines as described earlier.
2. Remove the injection pump adapter.
3. Remove the seal from the adapter.
4. File the timing mark from the adapter. Do not file the mark off the pump.
5. Position the engine at TDC of No. 1 cylinder. Align the mark on the balancer with the zero mark on the indicator. The index is offset to the right when No. 1 is at TDC.
6. Apply a chassis lube to the seal areas. Install, but do not tighten the injection pump.

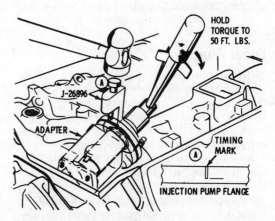

Marking injection pump adapter

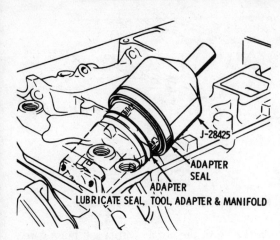

Installing adapter seal

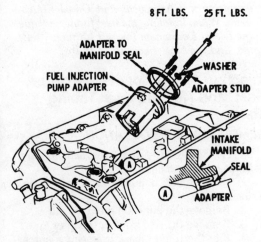

Injection pump adapter bolts

7. Install the new seal on the adapter using tool J-28425, or its equivalent.

8. Torque the adapter bolts to 25 ft. lbs.

9. Install timing tool J-26896 into the injection pump adapter. Torque the tool, toward No. 1 cylinder to 50 ft. lbs. Mark the injection pump adapter. Remove the tool.

10. Install the injection pump.

Glow Plugs

There are two types of glow plugs used on General Motors Corp. diesels; the "fast glow" type and the "slow glow" type. The fast glow type use pulsing current applied to 6 volt glow plugs while the slow glow type use continuous current applied to 12 volt glow plugs.

An easy way to tell the plugs apart is that the fast flow (6 volt) plugs have a $5/16$ in. wide electrical connector plug while the slow glow (12 volt) connector plug is $1/4$ in. wide. Do not attempt to interchange any parts of these two glow plug systems.

Fuel Tank
DRAINING

1. Remove the fuel tank cap.

2. Connect a siphon pump to the $1/4$ in. fuel return hose (the smaller of the two hoses) above the rear axle, or under the hood near the fuel pump on the passenger's side of the engine, near the front.

3. Operate the siphon pump until all fuel is removed from the fuel tank. Be sure to reinstall the fuel return hose and the fuel cap.

REMOVAL AND INSTALLATION
1964–Sedan, 1964 Station Wagon and El Camino

1. Siphon the fuel from the tank, as there is no drain plug.

2. Disconnect the fuel line and the gauge sending unit wire from the tank.

3. Disconnect the vent hose from the tank.

4. Remove the retaining bolts from the tank straps, lower the support straps, and then carefully lower the tank from the car.

5. Reverse the removal procedure to install the fuel tank.

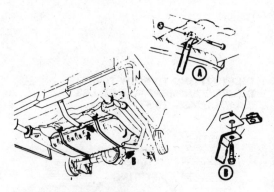

Typical fuel tank mounting

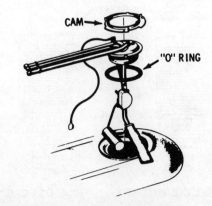

Installing fuel gauge in unit into fuel tank—typical

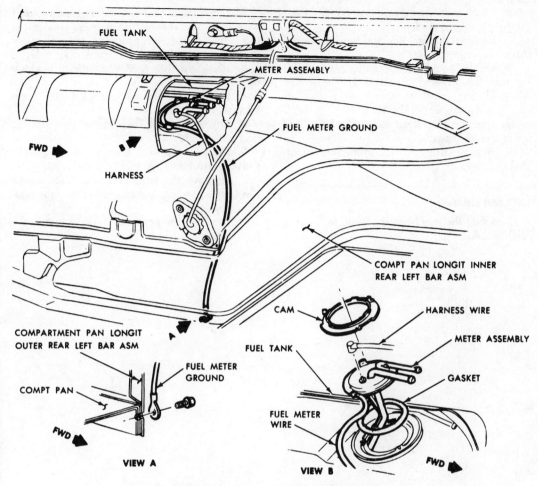

Fuel meter and wiring—Chevelle station wagon

1965–67 Station Wagon and El Camino

1. Follow Steps 1 through 3 of the preceding procedure.
2. Remove the tank support straps.
3. Remove the frame attaching screws from the front support.
4. Slide the tank forward, and then carefully lower it from the car.
5. Reverse the removal procedure to install the fuel tank.

1968–77 Sedan and El Camino

1. Siphon the fuel from the tank as there is no drain plug.
2. Disconnect the fuel gauge sending unit wire from the rear wiring harness connector. On sedans, push the grommet out and work the gauge wire through the trunk floor hole.
3. Raise the car to a convenient working height.
4. Remove the fuel gauge wire screw from the underbody.

5. Disconnect the fuel line at the sending unit pickup line.
6. Remove the vent hose (hoses for evaporative control on 1970 and later models).
7. Remove the tank filler neck bolt on the El Camino.
8. Remove the strap retaining bolts, lower the support straps, and carefully drop the tank out of the car.
9. Reverse the removal steps to install the fuel tank.

1968–77 Station Wagon

1. Siphon the fuel from the tank.
2. Jack the car up, and place the rear on stands.
3. Lower the rear axle into the full rebound position, and remove the left rear wheel assembly.
4. Disconnect the fuel gauge sending unit wire at the rear wiring harness.
5. Remove the fuel tank front shield.

6. Remove the fuel gauge ground wire from the rear quarter panel.

7. Remove the fuel line and wires from the gauge sending unit.

8. On 1974 and later models, remove the left rear shock absorber and lift the right rear wheel slightly to allow movement of the left wheel down and out of the way.

9. Remove the strap retaining bolts and lower the tank carefully.

10. Reverse the removal procedure to install the tank.

1978 and Later

1. Siphon the fuel from the tank, as there is no drain plug.

2. Disconnect the fuel gauge sending unit wire from the rear wiring harness connector. On sedans, push the grommet out and work the gauge wire through the trunk floor hole.

3. Raise the car to a convenient working height.

4. Remove the fuel gauge ground wire screw from the underbody.

5. Disconnect the fuel line at the sending unit pickup line.

6. Remove the vent hose (hoses for evaporative control on 1970 and later models).

7. Remove the strap retaining bolts, lower the support straps, and carefully lower the tank out of the car.

8. Reverse the removal steps to install the fuel tank.

Chassis Electrical

5

UNDERSTANDING AND TROUBLESHOOTING ELECTRICAL SYSTEMS

For any electrical system to operate, it must make a complete circuit. This simply means that the power flow from the battery must make a complete circle. When an electrical component is operating, power flows from the battery to the component, passes through the component causing it to perform its function (lighting a light bulb, for example) and then returns to the battery through the ground of the circuit. This ground is usually (but not always) the metal part of the car on which the electrical component is mounted.

Perhaps the easiest way to visualize this is to think of connecting a light bulb with two wires attached to it to your car battery. The battery in your car has two posts (negative and positive). If one of the two wires attached to the light bulb was attached to the negative post of the battery and the other wire was attached to the positive post of the battery, you would have a complete circuit. Current from the battery would flow out one post, through the wire attached to it and then to the light bulb, causing it to light. It would then leave the light bulb, travel through the other wire, and return to the other post of the battery.

The normal automotive circuit differs from this simple example in two ways. First, instead of having a return wire from the bulb to the battery, the light bulb returns the current to the battery through the chassis of the vehicle. Since the negative battery cable is attached to the chassis and the chassis is made of electrically conductive metal, the chassis of the vehicle can serve as a ground wire to complete the circuit. Secondly, most automotive circuits

contain switches to turn components on and off as required.

There are many types of switches, but the most common simply serves to prevent the passage of current when it is turned off. Since the switch is a part of the circle necessary for a complete circuit, it operates to leave an opening in the circuit, and thus an incomplete or open circuit, when it is turned off.

Some electrical components which require a large amount of current to operate also have a relay in their circuit. Since the circuits carry a large amount of current, the thickness of the wire (gauge size) in the circuit is also greater. If this large wire were connected from the component to the control switch on the instrument panel, and then back to the component, a voltage drop would occur in the circuit. To prevent this potential drop in voltage, an electromagnetic switch (relay) is used. The large wires in the circuit are connected from the car battery to one side of the relay, and from the opposite side of the relay to the component. The relay is normally open, preventing current from passing through the circuit. An additional, smaller, wire is connected from the relay to the control switch for the circuit. When the control switch is turned ON, it completes the circuit. This closes the relay and allows current to flow from the battery to the component. The horn, headlight, and starter circuits are three which use relays.

You have probably noticed how the car's instrument panel lights get brighter the faster you rev the engine. This happens because your alternator (which supplies the battery) puts out more current at speeds above idle. This is normal. However, it is possible for larger surges of current to pass through the electrical system of your car. If this surge of current were to reach an electrical component, it could burn the component out. To prevent this from happening, fuses are connected into the current supply wires of most of the major electrical systems of your car. The fuse serves to head off the surge at the pass. When an electrical current of excessive power passes through the component's fuse, the fuse blows out and breaks the circuit, saving it from destruction.

The fuse also protects the component from damage if the power supply wire to the component is grounded before the current reaches the component.

There is another important rule to the complete circle circuit. *Every complete circuit from a power source must include a component which is using the power from the power source.* If you were to disconnect the light bulb from the previous example of a light bulb being connected to the battery by two wires together (take our word for it—don't try it) the result would literally be shocking. A similar thing happens (on a smaller scale) when the power supply wire to a component or the electrical component itself becomes grounded before the normal ground connection for the circuit. To prevent damage to the system, the fuse for the circuit blows to interrupt the circuit—protecting the components from damage. Because grounding a wire from a power source makes a complete circuit—less the required component to use the power—this phenomenon is called a short circuit. The most common causes of short circuits are: the rubber insulation on a wire breaking or rubbing through to expose the current carrying core of the wire to a metal part of the car, or a short switch.

Some electrical systems on the car are protected by a circuit breaker which is, basically, a self-repairing fuse. When either of the above-described events takes place in a system which is protected by a circuit breaker, the circuit breaker opens the circuit the same way a fuse does. However, when either the short is removed from the circuit or the surge subsides, the circuit breaker resets itself and does not have to be replaced as a fuse does.

The final protective device in the chassis electrical system is a fuse link. A fuse link is a wire that acts as a fuse. It is connected between the starter relay and the main wiring harness for the car. This connection is under the hood, very near a similar fuse link which protects all chassis electrical components. It is the probable cause of trouble when none of the electrical components function, unless the battery is disconnected or dead.

Electrical problems generally fall into one of three areas:

1. The component that is not functioning is not receiving current.
2. The component itself is not functioning.
3. The component is not properly grounded.

Problems that fall into the first category are by far the most complicated. It is the current supply system to the component which contains all the switches, relays, fuses, etc.

The electrical system can be checked with a test light and a jumper wire. A test light is a device that looks like a pointed screwdriver with a wire attached to it. It has a light bulb in its handle. A jumper wire is a piece of insulated wire with an alligator clip attached to each end.

If a light bulb is not working, you must follow a systematic plan to determine which of the three causes is the villain.

1. Turn on the switch that controls the inoperable bulb.
2. Disconnect the power supply wire from the bulb.
3. Attach the ground wire on the test light to a good metal ground.
4. Touch the probe end of the test light to the end of the power supply wire that was disconnected from the bulb. If the bulb is receiving current, the test light will go on.

NOTE: *If the bulb is one which works only when the ignition key is turned ON (turn signal), make sure the key is turned ON.*

If the test light does not go ON, then the problem is in the circuit between the battery and the bulb. As mentioned before, this includes all the switches, fuses, and relays in the system. The problem is an open circuit between the battery and the bulb. If the fuse is blown and, when replaced, immediately blows again, there is a short circuit in the system which must be located and repaired. If there is a switch in the system, bypass it with a jumper wire. This is done by connecting one end of the jumper wire to the power supply wire into the switch, and the other end of the jumper wire to the wire coming out of the switch. If the test light lights with the jumper wire installed, the switch or whatever was bypassed is defective.

NOTE: *Never substitute the jumper wire for the bulb, as the bulb is the component required to use the power from the power source.*

5. If the bulb in the test light goes ON, then the current is getting to the bulb that is not working in the car. This eliminates the first of the three possible causes. Connect the power supply wire and connect a jumper wire from the bulb to a good metal ground. Do this with the switch which controls the bulb turned ON, and also the ignition switch turned ON if it is required for the light to work. If the bulb works with the jumper wire installed, then it has a bad ground. This is usually caused by the metal area on which the bulb mounts to the car being coated with some type of foreign matter or rust.

6. If neither test located the source of the

trouble, then the light bulb itself is defective.

The above test procedure can be applied to any of the components of the chassis electrical system by substituting the component that is not working for the light bulb. *Remember that for any electrical system to work, all connections must be clean and tight.*

HEATER

Blower Motor

REMOVAL AND INSTALLATION

1964–67

1. Disconnect the battery.
2. Unclip the hoses from the fender skirt.
3. Disconnect the electrical feed from the motor.
4. Turn the front wheels to the extreme right.
5. Remove the right front fender skirt bolts and allow the skirt to drop, resting it on top of tire. It may be wedged away from the fender lower flange with a block of wood to provide better access to the bolts.
6. Remove the screws attaching the motor mounting plate to the air inlet housing.
7. Remove the screws attaching the motor to the mounting plate.
8. Remove the clip attaching the cage to the shaft and remove the blower motor.
9. Install in the reverse of above.

1968–72

1. Disconnect the battery ground cable.
2. Disconnect the hoses and wiring from the fender skirt.
3. Remove all fender skirt attaching bolts except those attaching the skirt to the radiator support.
4. Pull out, then down, on the skirt. Place a block between the skirt and the fender.
5. Remove the blower-to-case attaching screws. Remove the blower assembly.
6. Remove the blower wheel retaining nut and separate the motor and the wheel.
7. Reverse the procedure to install. The open end of blower should be away from the motor.

1973 and Later

1. Disconnect the battery ground cable.
2. Disconnect the motor lead wire.
NOTE: *If equipped with A/C, disconnect the cooling tube.*
3. Remove the blower-to-case screws and the blower.
4. Remove the retaining nut to separate the motor and wheel.
5. Reverse the procedure for installation. The open end of the blower wheel should be away from the motor.

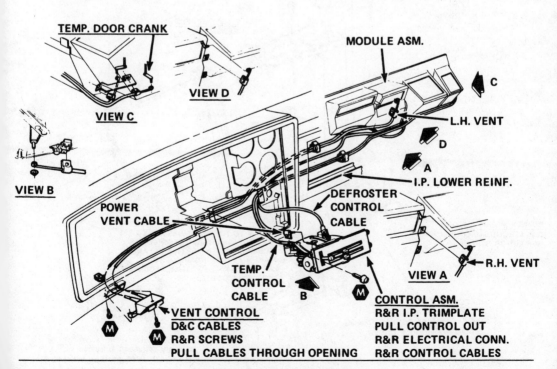

1978 heater control cable assembly

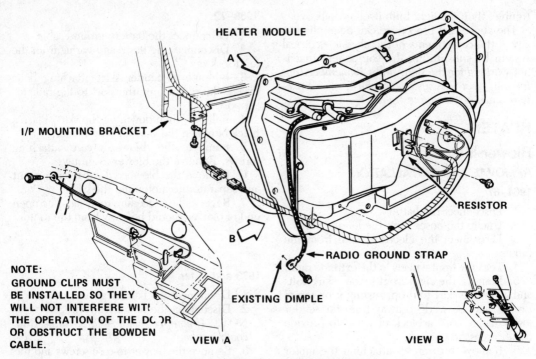

HEATER MODULE

A

I/P MOUNTING BRACKET

RESISTOR

B

RADIO GROUND STRAP

EXISTING DIMPLE

NOTE:
GROUND CLIPS MUST
BE INSTALLED SO THEY
WILL NOT INTERFERE WITH
THE OPERATION OF THE DOOR
OR OBSTRUCT THE BOWDEN
CABLE.

VIEW A

VIEW B

Heater module service, 1978 Malibu shown

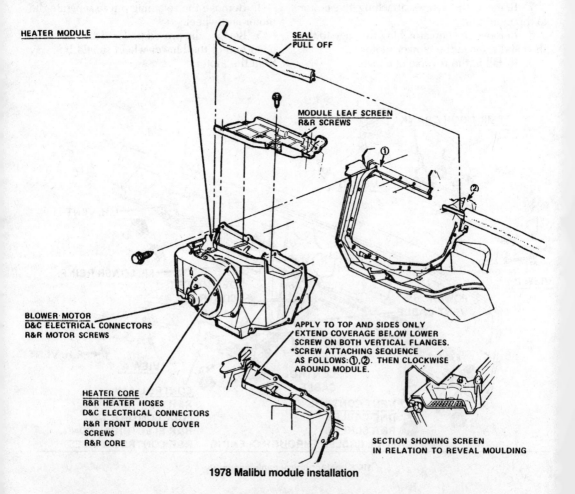

HEATER MODULE

SEAL
PULL OFF

MODULE LEAF SCREEN
R&R SCREWS

①

②

BLOWER MOTOR
D&C ELECTRICAL CONNECTORS
R&R MOTOR SCREWS

APPLY TO TOP AND SIDES ONLY
EXTEND COVERAGE BELOW LOWER
SCREW ON BOTH VERTICAL FLANGES.
*SCREW ATTACHING SEQUENCE
AS FOLLOWS: ①,②. THEN CLOCKWISE
AROUND MODULE.

HEATER CORE
R&R HEATER HOSES
D&C ELECTRICAL CONNECTORS
R&R FRONT MODULE COVER
SCREWS
R&R CORE

SECTION SHOWING SCREEN
IN RELATION TO REVEAL MOULDING

1978 Malibu module installation

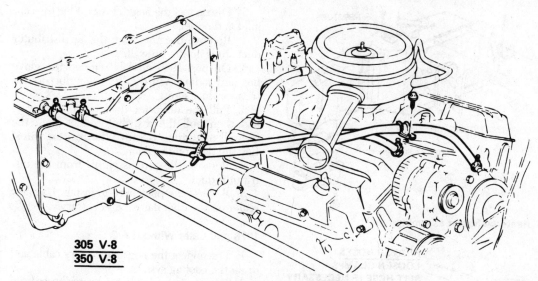

305 V-8
350 V-8

Heater hose mounting; V6 similar

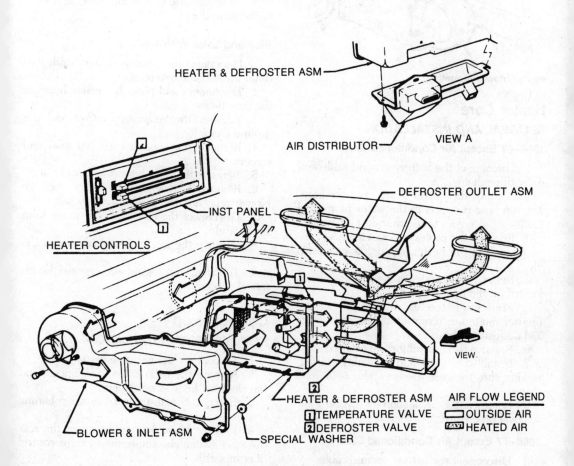

HEATER & DEFROSTER ASM

AIR DISTRIBUTOR

VIEW A

HEATER CONTROLS

INST PANEL

DEFROSTER OUTLET ASM

BLOWER & INLET ASM

SPECIAL WASHER

HEATER & DEFROSTER ASM

VIEW

AIR FLOW LEGEND

1 TEMPERATURE VALVE

2 DEFROSTER VALVE

OUTSIDE AIR

HEATED AIR

The heater air flow diagram

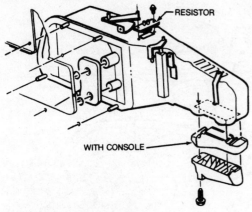

Heater/defroster assembly

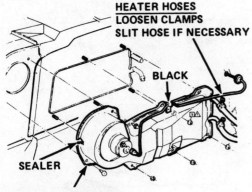

Heater blower mounting

Heater Core

REMOVAL AND INSTALLATION

1964–67 Except Air Conditioned Cars

1. Disconnect the battery ground cable and drain the radiator.
2. Remove the heater hoses from the core. The top hose connects to the water pump and the lower hose goes to the thermostat housing.
3. Remove the cables and all electrical connections from the heater and defroster assembly.
4. Remove the nuts from the core case studs located on the firewall.
5. From inside the car, remove the case-to-firewall mounting screws and also the heater and defroster assembly.
6. Remove the retaining springs and core.
7. Install the core and retaining spring, making sure the core-to-case sealer is in good shape.
8. Complete the installation by reversing the removal procedure.

1968–77 Except Air Conditioned Cars

1. Disconnect the battery ground cable.
2. Drain the radiator.

3. Disconnect the heater hoses. Plug the core inlet and outlet.
4. Remove the nuts from the air distributor duct studs on the firewall.
5. On post-1969 models remove the glove box and radio, then the defroster duct-to-distributor duct screw.
6. Pull the defroster duct out of the way, and then pull the distributor duct from the firewall mounting. Remove the resistor wires. Lay the duct on the floor.
7. Remove the core assembly from the distributor duct.
8. Reverse the procedure to install. Use new sealer on the duct flange, if necessary.

1978 and Later Without A/C

1. Disconnect the negative battery cable and drain the cooling system.
2. Disconnect and plug the heater hoses from the core tubes.
3. Disconnect the electrical connectors from the module case.
4. Unbolt and remove the module's front cover and lift out the core.
5. To install, use sealant and reverse the removal procedures.

1967 and Later With A/C

1. Disconnect the negative battery cable and drain the cooling system.
2. Disconnect and plug the heater hoses at the core tubes.
3. Remove the retaining bracket and the ground strap.
4. Remove the module's rubber seal and screen.
5. Remove the right windshield wiper arm.
6. Remove the diagnostic connector, the high blower relay and the thermostatic switch.
7. Disconnect the electrical connectors from the module.
8. Remove the module's top cover and the screen.
9. To install, use sealant and reverse the removal procedures.

Control Head

REMOVAL AND INSTALLATION

1. Disconnect the negative battery cable.
2. Remove the radio knobs (if equipped) and the clock set knob (if equipped).
3. Remove the instrument bezel retaining screws.
4. Pull the bezel out to disconnect the rear defogger switch and the remote mirror control (if equipped).
5. Remove the instrument bezel.

6. Remove the control head to dash screws and pull the head out.

7. Disconnect the electrical connectors and/or control cable(s) (if equipped), then remove the control head.

8. To install, reverse the removal procedures.

RADIO

REMOVAL AND INSTALLATION

1964–72

1. Disconnect the battery ground cable.

2. Remove the ash tray and ash tray housing as necessary.

3. Remove the knobs, controls, washers, trim plate, and nuts from radio.

4. Remove the hoses from the center air conditioning duct as necessary.

5. Disconnect all wiring leads.

6. Remove the screw from the radio rear mounting bracket and lower the radio.

7. To install, reverse the above procedure.

1973–77

1. Disconnect the battery ground cable.

2. Remove the left air conditioner lap cooler duct.

3. Pull off the knobs and bezels.

4. Remove the control shaft nuts and washers. You will probably need a deep-well socket.

5. Remove the support bracket stud nut. Disconnect the antenna, speaker, and power wires.

6. Move the radio back until the shafts clear the instrument panel. Lower it from behind the

panel. On later models, the radio can be removed through the instrument panel opening.

7. Reverse the procedure for installation. Make sure to hook up the speaker leads before turning the radio on; operating without a speaker will damage the transistors.

1978–84

1. Disconnect the negative battery cable.

2. Remove the radio control knobs by pulling them from the shafts.

3. Remove the trim plate screws and the trim plate.

4. Disconnect the electrical connectors and the antenna from the rear of the radio.

5. At the right-side of the radio bracket, remove the stud nut.

6. Remove the control knob nuts.

7. Remove the instrument panel bracket screws and the bracket from the vehicle.

8. Remove the radio through the opening in the instrument panel and detach the speaker wires.

9. To install, reverse the removal procedures.

CAUTION: *Before applying power to the radio, ALWAYS attach the speaker wiring harness.*

1985 and Later

1. Disconnect the negative battery cable.

2. To access the temperature control cable, remove the glove box, then disconnect the temperature cable from the temperature door.

3. Remove the radio, heater and A/C control panel-to-dash fasteners.

4. Pull the panel from the dash, then disconnect the A/C control vacuum and electrical connectors.

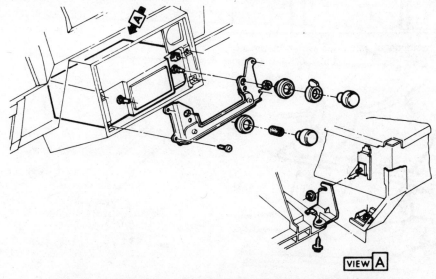

VIEW A

Radio mounting details—mounting differs between models and years

5. Remove the radio and the A/C control knobs, then the trimplate.

6. Remove the radio from the bracket.

7. To install, reverse the removal procedures. Adjust the temperature door cable.

WINDSHIELD WIPERS

Blade and Arm

REMOVAL AND INSTALLATION

If the wiper assembly has a press type release tab at the center, simply depress the tab and remove the blade. If the blade has no release tab, use a screwdriver to depress the spring at the center. This will release the assembly. To install the assembly, position the blade over the pin at the tip of the arm and press until the spring retainer engages the groove in the pin.

To remove the element, either depress the release button or squeeze the spring type retainer clip at the outer end together, and slide the blade element out. Just slide the new element in until it latches.

NOTE: *Removal of the wiper arms requires the use of a special tool, G.M. J8966 or its equivalent. Versions of this tool are generally available in auto parts stores.*

1. Insert the tool under the wiper arm and lever the arm off the shaft.

NOTE: *Raising the hood on most later models will facilitate easier wiper arm removal.*

2. Disconnect the washer hose from the arm (if so equipped). Remove the arm.

3. Installation is in the reverse order of removal. The proper park position for the arms is with the blades approximately 2 in. (50 mm) above the lower molding of the windshield. Be sure that the motor is in the park position before installing the arms.

Wiper Motor

REMOVAL AND INSTALLATION

1964–67

1. Make certain that the wiper motor is in the park position.

2. Disconnect the washer hoses and electrical connectors.

3. Remove the three motor bolts. Pull the wiper motor assembly from the cowl opening

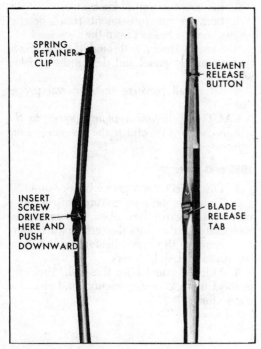

The two methods of releasing wiper blade assemblies

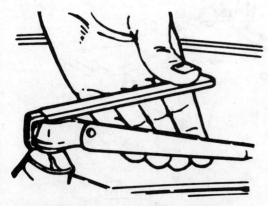

Remove the wiper arm with the special tool

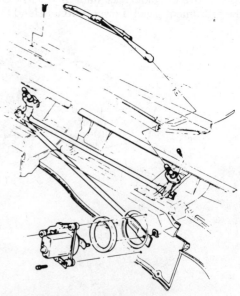

Windshield wiper motor mounting—1964–67

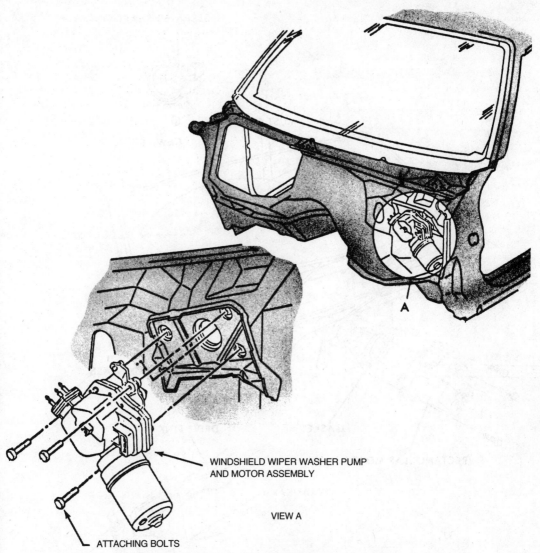

WINDSHIELD WIPER WASHER PUMP
AND MOTOR ASSEMBLY

VIEW A

ATTACHING BOLTS

Windshield wiper motor mounting—round motor

and loosen the nuts retaining the drive rod ball stud to the crank arm.

4. Reverse the procedure to install, checking the sealing gaskets at the motor. Make sure the motor is in the park position before installation.

1968–70

1. Make sure that the wiper motor is in the park position.

2. Disconnect the washer hoses and electrical connectors.

3. Remove the plenum chamber grille or access cover. Remove the nut retaining the crank arm to the motor assembly.

4. Remove the retaining screws or nuts and remove the motor. Do not allow the motor to hang by the drive link.

5. Reverse the procedure to install, check-

ing the sealing gaskets at the motor. Make sure the motor is in the park position before installation.

1971 and Later

NOTE: *Your car may be equipped with either a round motor or a rectangular motor.*

1. Remove the screen or grille that covers the cowl area.

2. Working under the hood, disconnect the motor wiring. Then, reach through the cowl opening and loosen, but do not remove, the nuts which attach the transmission drive link to the motor crank arm. Then, disconnect the drive link from the crank arm.

3. Remove the three motor attaching screws, and remove the motor, guiding the crank arm through the hole.

4. Installation is in the reverse order of re-

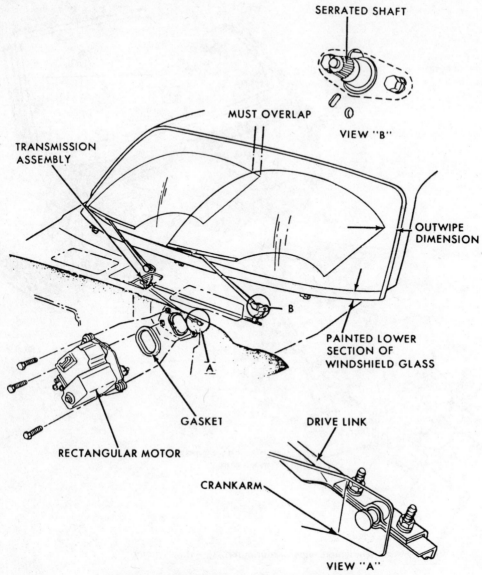

Windshield wiper motor mounting—rectangular motor

moval. The motor must be in the park position before assembling the crank arm to the transmission drive link(s).

Wiper Linkage

REMOVAL AND INSTALLATION

1964–67

1. Make certain that the wiper motor is in park position. Remove the wiper arm and blade assemblies from the transmission shaft.

2. Remove the plenum chamber grille.

3. Detach the linkage from the wiper crank arm.

4. Remove the transmission retaining screws, lower the assembly into the plenum chamber, and remove the unit.

5. Reverse the procedure to install.

1968 and Later

1. Make sure that the wiper motor is in the park position.

2. Disconnect the battery ground cable.

3. Remove the wiper arm and blade assemblies from the transmission. On the articulated left arm assemblies, remove the carburetor type clip retaining the pinned arm to the blade arm.

4. Remove the plenum chamber air intake grille or screen.

5. Loosen the nuts retaining the drive rod ball stud to the crank arm and detach the drive rod from the crank arm.

6. Remove the transmission retaining screws. Lower the transmission and drive rod assemblies into the plenum chamber.

7. Remove the transmission and linkage from

the plenum chamber through the cowl opening.

8. Reverse the procedure to install, making sure the wiper blade assemblies are installed in the park position. On recessed wiper arms, this occurs at ⅜ in. from the top of the reveal molding.

INSTRUMENTS AND SWITCHES

Instrument Cluster

REMOVAL AND INSTALLATION

1964–65

1. Disconnect the battery ground cable.
2. Remove the upper mast jacket clamp bolt and bend the clamp away from the steering column.
3. Disconnect the speedometer cable. Disconnect the oil pressure line at the gauge on the SS model.
4. Remove the screws that attach the console to the instrument panel and lean the console forward onto the mast jacket. Remove the radio knobs before removing the console from the panel.
5. Disconnect all cluster lamps, harness connectors, and the two harness retaining clips from the rear of the cluster.
6. Lift the console forward and upward to remove.
7. Unscrew and remove the cluster from the console.
8. Install by reversing the removal procedure.

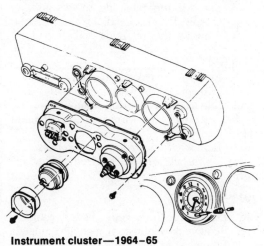

Instrument cluster—1964–65

1966–67

1. Disconnect the battery.
2. Remove the steering coupling bolt and disconnect the steering shaft from the coupling.

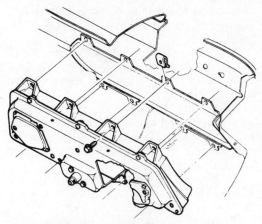

Instrument cluster—1966–67

3. Loosen the mast jacket lower clamp.
4. On air-conditioned cars, remove the air-conditioning center distribution duct.
5. Remove the radio rear support bracket screw.
6. Remove the mast jacket trim cover and the support clamp.
7. Loosen the set screw and remove the transmission dial indicator (if so equipped).
8. Disconnect the speedometer shaft at the speedometer head.
9. Remove the instrument panel attaching screws.
10. From under the console, remove the four lower retaining screws from the cluster housing.
11. With the mast jacket padded, pull the instrument panel from the console and lay forward on mast jacket.
12. Disconnect the wiring harness, cluster lamps and wiring terminals from the rear of the cluster assembly.
13. Remove the four screws holding the upper section of the cluster housing to the panel and remove the cluster from the instrument panel.
14. Install by reversing the removal procedure.

1968–69

1. Disconnect the battery ground cable.
2. Remove the ash tray and retainer.
3. Remove the radio knobs, nuts, electrical connectors, and the radio rear support. Remove the radio.
4. Remove the heater control screws, then push the control head out of the instrument panel.
5. Lower the steering column. Remove the automatic transmission indicator cable from the steering column. Protect the steering column with a cloth.
6. Remove the instrument panel retaining

screws at the top, bottom, and sides of the panel. Remove all attachments to the underside of the panel.

7. Lift the panel up and back slightly. Reach behind the cluster to remove the speedometer cable, support the panel on the protected steering column.

8. Remove the clips at the top of the cluster rear cover and remove all connectors at the rear of the cluster. Remove the oil pressure fitting from the rear of the oil pressure gauge, if so equipped.

9. Remove the screws that secure the twin window clusters to the back of the instrument panel and remove the clusters.

10. Install by reversing the procedure.

1970–72

1. Disconnect the battery ground cable.
2. Lower the steering column.
3. Disconnect the parking brake hand release.
4. Disconnect the speedometer cable.
5. Remove the instrument panel pad.
6. Disconnect the radio speaker bracket from the instrument panel. Disconnect the speaker wire from the radio.
7. Disconnect the air conditioning center outlet and the control head.
8. Remove the radio knobs, washers, bezels, and wiring.
9. Unbolt the radio braces. Roll the radio out from under the instrument panel.
10. Remove the six instrument panel bolts and roll out the instrument panel with the help of an assistant.
11. Reverse the procedure for installation.

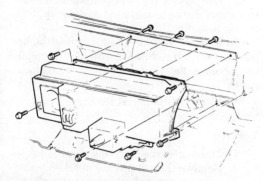

Instrument cluster—1970–72

1973–77

1. Disconnect the battery ground cable.
2. Remove the radio knobs and the clock set stem if so equipped.
3. Remove the instrument bezel retaining screws.
4. Pull the bezel out to disconnect the tail-

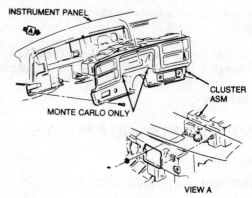

Instrument cluster—1973–75

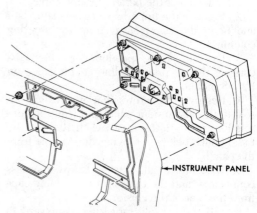

Instrument cluster—1980–81

gate release or rear defogger switch if so equipped.
5. Remove the instrument bezel.
6. Remove the retaining screws and remove the speedometer head.
7. Remove the retaining screws and remove the fuel gauge and tachometer if so equipped.
8. Remove the clock if so equipped.
9. Disconnect the transmission shift indicator cable from the steering column.
10. Disconnect the wiring and speedometer cable.
11. Remove the instrument cluster case.
12. To install, reverse the removal procedure.

1978–81

1. Disconnect the negative battery cable.
2. Remove the clock stem knob (if equipped).
3. Remove the instrument bezel mounting screws, then pull out the bezel to disconnect the rear defogger switch (if equipped).
4. Remove the bezel.
5. Remove the transmission selector indicator screws, then carefully lower the indicator assembly so that the cable can be removed.

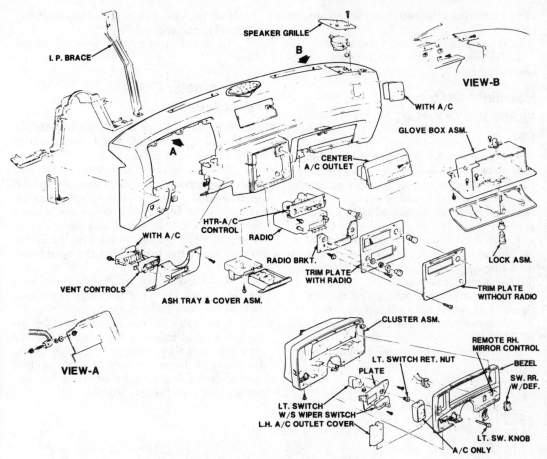

1983 Malibu instrument panel, exploded view

6. Remove the windshield/light switch mounting plate and pull the assembly rearward to provide access to the lower left cluster attaching bolt/nut. Remove the instrument panel-to-cluster nuts.

7. Pull the cluster rearward and disconnect the wiring and cables.

8. To install, reverse the removal procedures. Adjust the cable, as required.

1982 and Later

1. Disconnect the negative battery cable.

2. Remove the steering column lower cover screws and the cover.

3. At the steering column, disconnect the shift indicator cable.

4. Remove the steering column-to-instrument panel screws and lower the steering column.

5. From the perimeter of the instrument cluster lens, remove the retaining screws and the snap-in-plastic fasteners.

6. From the upper surface of the grey sheetmetal trim plate, remove the retaining screws.

7. Remove the studs nuts from the lower corner of the lens.

8. Reaching behind the instrument cluster, disconnect the speedometer cable, then remove the cluster by pulling it outward.

9. To install, reverse the removal procedures.

Windshield Wiper Switch

REMOVAL AND INSTALLATION

1978–81

Refer to the "Instrument Cluster, Removal and Installation" procedures in this section and remove the windshield wiper switch. To install, reverse the removal procedures.

1982 and Later

1. Refer to the "Instrument Cluster, Removal and Installation" procedures in this section and remove the lens and the trim.

2. Reaching behind the instrument panel, disconnect the electrical connector from the rear of the windshield wiper switch.

3. Using a prying action, remove the spring

clip which retains the switch to the instrument panel.

4. Remove the windshield wiper switch.

5. To install, reverse the removal procedures.

Headlight Switch
REMOVAL AND INSTALLATION
1964–79

1. Disconnect the negative battery cable.

2. Remove the instrument panel bezel, retained on most model years with six screws (varies among models and years).

3. Pull the headlight control knob to the ON position.

4. Remove the screws (usually three) attaching the windshield wiper switch/light switch mounting plate to the instrument cluster and pull the assembly rearward.

5. Depress the shaft retainer on the switch, then pull the knob and shaft assembly out.

6. Remove the ferrule nut and switch assembly from the mounting plate.

7. To install, reverse the removal procedures.

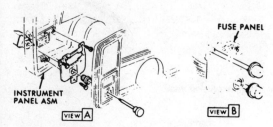

Headlight switch mounting, typical

1980–84

1. Disconnect the negative battery cable.

2. Pull the headlight control knob to the ON position.

3. Reaching up under the instrument panel, depress the switch shaft release button, then pull the shaft and the control knob out.

4. Remove the windshield wiper switch.

5. Remove the ferrule nut and the switch from the instrument panel.

6. Using a small pry bar, insert it into the side of the switch and pry the multi-contact electrical connector from the switch.

7. To install, reverse the removal procedures.

1985 and Later

1. Disconnect the negative battery cable.

2. For access, remove the steering column trim cover.

3. Remove the switch mounting screws.

4. Pull out the switch and disconnect the electrical connector.

5. To install, reverse the removal procedures.

Speedometer Cable
REPLACEMENT

NOTE: *Although not necessary, removing the instrument cluster will give better access to the speedometer cable.*

1. Reach behind the instrument cluster and push the speedometer cable casing toward the speedometer while depressing the retaining spring on the back of the instrument cluster case. Once the retaining spring has released, hold it in while pulling outward on the casing to disconnect the casing from the speedometer.

2. Remove the cable casing sealing plug from the dash panel. Then, pull the casing down from behind the dash and remove the cable.

3. If the cable is broken and cannot be entirely removed from the top, support the car securely, and then unscrew the cable casing connector at the transmission. Pull the bottom part of the cable out, and then screw the connector back onto the transmission.

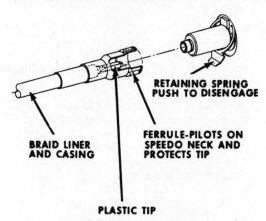

Speedo cable attachment at instrument cluster

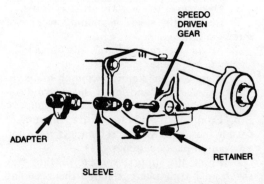

Speedometer cable-to-drive attachment, typical

4. Lubricate the new cable with a speedometer cable grease. Insert it into the casing until it bottoms. Push inward while rotating it until the square portion at the bottom engages with the coupling in the transmission, permitting the cable to move in another inch or so. Then, reconnect the cable casing to the speedometer and install the sealing plug into the dash panel.

Ignition Switch

REMOVAL AND INSTALLATION

1964–68

NOTE: *All models made in 1969 and later are equipped with ignition switches which are mounted in the steering column. Removal and installation procedures for these models can be found in Chapter 8.*

1. Disconnect the batter ground cable. Put the ignition switch in the Accessory (ACC) position.

NOTE: *Although not necessary, you may wish to remove the ashtray and radio at this point.*

2. Insert a wire into the small hole in the face of the lock cylinder. Push in on the wire to depress the plunger. Continue turning the key until the cylinder can be removed from the switch.

3. Remove the switch bezel nut, and then pull the switch out from under the dash.

4. Go in from the front of the switch with a screwdriver and unsnap the theft resistant locking tangs on the connector and then unplug the connector.

5. Installation is in the reverse order of removal.

LIGHTING

Headlights

REMOVAL AND INSTALLATION

1. Unscrew the four retaining screws and remove the headlight bezel.

2. On the 1964–77 models, remove the headlight bulb retaining screws. These are the screws which hold the retaining ring for the bulb to the front of the car. Do not touch the two headlight aiming screws, at the top and the side of the retaining ring (these screws will have different heads), or the headlight aim will have to be re-adjusted.

3. On the 1978 and later models, disengage the spring from the retaining ring, using a cotter pin removal tool, then remove the retaining ring screws.

4. Pull the bulb and ring forward and then

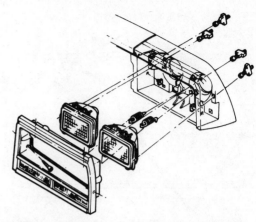

Headlight bezel and headlamp removal, 1983 Malibu shown

separate them. Unplug the electrical connector from the rear of the bulb.

5. Plug the new bulb into the electrical connector. Install the bulb into the retaining ring and then install the ring and the bulb. Install the headlight bezel.

HEADLIGHT AIMING

The headlights must be properly aimed to provide the best, safest road illumination. The lights should be checked for proper aim, and adjusted if necessary, after installing a new sealed beam unit of if the front end sheet metal has been replaced. Certain state and local authorities have requirements for headlight aiming; these should be checked before adjustment is made.

NOTE: *The car's fuel tank should be about half full when adjusting the headlights. Tires should be properly inflated, and if a heavy load is carried in the trunk or in the cargo area of station wagons, it should remain there.*

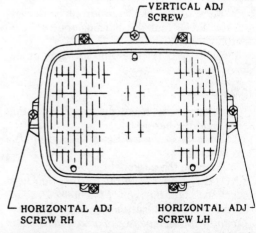

Headlight adjustment screw locations. Round headlights similar

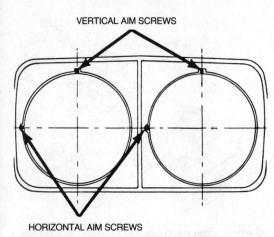

VERTICAL AIM SCREWS

HORIZONTAL AIM SCREWS

Dual headlight adjustment screw location

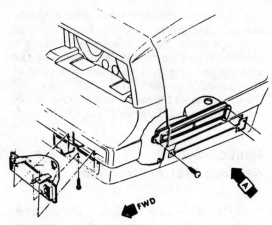

View of the parking and marker lights—1980 and later

Horizontal and vertical aiming of each sealed beam unit is provided by two adjusting screws, which move the mounting ring in the body against the body of the coil spring. There is no adjustment for focus; this is done during headlight manufacturing.

Signal And Marker Lights

NOTE: *Since the light housing capsules (on the late model vehicles) are constructed by sonic welding, the ONLY service which can be performed are the replacement of the bulbs or the light housing.*

REMOVAL AND INSTALLATION

Front Turn Signal and Parking Lights

1964–79

1. Reach up under the fender and twist out the electrical socket from the rear of the housing.
2. Remove the housing-to-front fender extension screws and the housing (pull it rearward).
3. To install, reverse the removal procedures.

1980 and Later

1. Remove the headlight bezel mounting screws and the bezel.
2. Disconnect the twist lock socket from the lens housing.
3. Remove the parking light housing.
NOTE: *To remove the bulb, turn the twist lock socket (at the rear of the housing) counterclockwise ¼ turn, then remove the socket with the bulb; replace the bulb if defective.*
4. To install, reverse the removal procedures.

Side Marker Lights

1964–79

1. Remove the headlight bezel mounting screws and the bezel.
2. Disconnect the twist lock socket from the lens housing.
3. Remove the marker light housing.
NOTE: *To remove the bulb, turn the twist lock socket (at the rear of the housing) counterclockwise ¼ turn, then remove the socket with the bulb; replace the bulb if defective.*
4. To install, reverse the removal procedures.

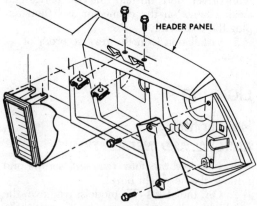

HEADER PANEL

View of the parking and marker lights—1964–79

1981 and Later

1. Remove the marker light housing screws and the housing.
2. Disconnect the twist lock socket from the lens housing.
NOTE: *To remove the bulb, turn the twist lock socket (at the rear of the housing) counterclockwise ¼ turn, then remove the socket with the bulb; replace the bulb if defective.*

3. To install, reverse the removal procedures.

Rear Turn Signal, Brake and Parking Lights

1. Remove the tail light panel screws and the panel.

2. Disconnect the twist lock socket from the lens housing.

NOTE: *To remove the bulb, turn the twist lock socket (at the rear of the housing) counterclockwise ¼ turn, then remove the socket with the bulb; replace the bulb if defective.*

3. To install, reverse the removal procedures.

CIRCUIT PROTECTION

Fusible Links

A fusible link is a protective device used in an electrical circuit. When the current increases beyond a certain amperage, the fusible metal of the wire link will melt, thus breaking the electrical circuit and preventing further damage to any other components or wiring. Whenever a fusible link is melted because of a short circuit, correct the cause before installing a new one. Most models have four fusible links.

REPLACING FUSIBLE LINKS

1. Disconnect both battery cables. If the link is connected to the junction block or starter solenoid, disconnect it.

2. Cut the wiring harness right behind the link connector(s) and remove.

3. Strip the insulation off the harness wire back ½".

4. Position a clip around the new link and wiring harness or new connector and crimp it securely. Then, solder the connection, using rosin core solder and sufficient heat to guarantee a good connection. Repeat for the remaining connection.

5. Tape all exposed wiring with electrical tape. Where necessary, connect the link to the junction block or started solenoid. Reconnect battery.

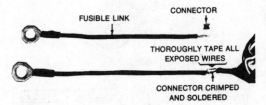

New fusible links are spliced to the wire

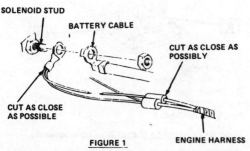

FIGURE 1
REMOVE BATTERY CABLE & FUSIBLE LINK FROM STARTER SOLENOID AND CUT OFF DEFECTIVE WIRE AS SHOWN TWO PLACES.

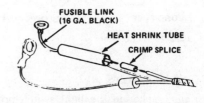

FIGURE 2
STRIP INSULATION FROM WIRE ENDS. PLACE HEAT SHRINK TUBE OVER REPLACEMENT LINK. INSERT WIRE ENDS INTO CRIMP SPLICE AS SHOWN. NOTE: PUSH WIRES IN FAR ENOUGH TO ENGAGE WIRE ENDS.

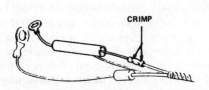

FIGURE 3
CRIMP SPLICE WITH CRIMPING TOOL TWO PLACES TO BIND BOTH WIRES.

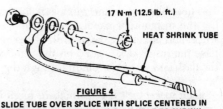

FIGURE 4
SLIDE TUBE OVER SPLICE WITH SPLICE CENTERED IN TUBE. APPLY LOW TEMPERATURE HEAT TO SHRINK TUBE AROUND WIRES & SPLICE. REASSEMBLE LINKS & BATTERY CABLE.

Fusible link repair

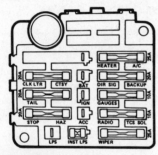

Fuse box—1971–79 (amperage figures may differ with individual models)

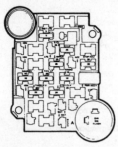

Fuse box—1981 and later

| GOOD FUSE | BLOWN FUSE |

Mini-fuses, 1978 and later

Circuit Breakers

A circuit breaker in the light switch protects the headlight circuit. A separate 30 amp breaker mounted on the firewall protects the power window, seat, and power top circuits. Circuit breakers open and close rapidly to protect the circuit if current is excessive.

Fuse Block

The fuse block on some models is located under the instrument panel next to the steering wheel and is a swing down unit. Other models have the fuse block located on the right side of the dash and access is gained through the glove box.

Each fuse block uses miniature fuses which are designed for increased circuit protection and greater reliability. The compact fuse is a blade

Fuse Color-Coding

Fuse (Amps)	Color Stripe
3	Violet
5	Tan
7.5	Brown
10	Red
20	Clear
25	White

terminal design which allows fingertip removal and replacement.

Although the fuses are interchangeable, the amperage values are molded in bold, color coded, easy to read numbers on the fuse body. Use only fuses of equal replacement value.

A blown fuse can easily be checked by visual inspection or by continuity checking.

Buzzers, Relays, and Flashers

The electrical protection devices are located in the convenience center, which is a swing down unit located under the instrument panel. All units are serviced by plug-in replacements.

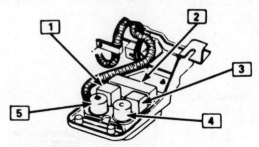

1. Horn relay
2. Seat belt–ignition key–headlight buzzer
3. Choke relay (vacant w/EFI)
4. Hazard flasher
5. Signal flasher

View of convience center and components

WIRING DIAGRAMS

Wiring diagrams have been left out of this book. As cars have become more complex, and available with longer and longer option lists, wiring diagrams have grown in size and complexity also. It has become virtually impossible to provide a readable reproduction in a reasonable number of pages. Information on ordering wiring diagrams from the vehicle manufacturer can be found in the owner's manual.

Drive Train

MANUAL TRANSMISSION

Understanding the Manual Transmission and Clutch

Because of the way the gasoline engine breathes, it can produce torque, or twisting force, only within a narrow speed range. Most modern engines must turn at about 2,500 rpm to produce their peak torque. By 4,500 rpm they are producing so little torque that continued increases in engine speed produce no power increases.

The transmission and clutch are employed to vary the relationship between engine speed and the speed of the wheels so that adequate engine power can be produced under all circumstances. The clutch allows engine torque to be applied to the transmission input shaft gradually, due to mechanical slippage. The car can, consequently, be started smoothly from a full stop.

The transmission changes the ratio between the rotating speeds of the engine and the wheels by the use of gears. Three-speed or four-speed transmissions are most common. The lower gears allow full engine power to be applied to the rear wheels during acceleration at low speeds.

The clutch driven plate is a thin disc, the center of which is splined to the transmission input shaft. Both sides of the disc are covered with a layer of material which is similar to brake lining and which is capable of allowing slippage without roughness or excessive noise.

The clutch cover is bolted to the engine flywheel and incorporates a diaphragm spring which provides the pressure to engage the clutch. The cover also houses the pressure plate. The driven disc is sandwiched between the pressure plate and the smooth surface of the flywheel when the clutch pedal is released, thus forcing it to turn at the same speed as the engine crankshaft.

The transmission contains a mainshaft which passes all the way through the transmission, from the clutch to the driveshaft. This shaft is separated at one point, so that front and rear portions can turn at different speeds.

Power is transmitted by a countershaft in the lower gears and reverse. The gears of the countershaft mesh with gears on the mainshaft, allowing power to be carried from one to the other. All the countershaft gears are integral with that shaft, while several of the mainshaft gears can either rotate independently of the shaft or be locked to it. Shifting from one gear to the next causes one of the gears to be freed from rotating with the shaft, and locks another to it. Gears are locked and unlocked by internal dog clutches which slide between the center of the gear and the shaft. The forward gears usually employ synchronizers: friction members which smoothly bring gear and shaft to the same speed before the toothed dog clutches are engaged.

The clutch is operating properly if:

1. It will stall the engine when released with the vehicle held stationary.

2. The shift lever can be moved freely between first and reverse gears when the vehicle is stationary and the clutch disengaged.

A clutch pedal free-play adjustment is incorporated in the linkage. If there is about 1–2 in. of motion before the pedal begins to release the clutch, it is adjusted properly. Inadequate free-play wears all parts of the clutch releasing mechanisms and may cause slippage. Excessive free-play may cause inadequate release and hard shifting of gears.

Some clutches use a hydraulic system in place of mechanical linkage. If the clutch fails to release, fill the clutch master cylinder with fluid to the proper level and pump the clutch pedal to fill the system with fluid. Bleed the system in the same way as a brake system. If leaks are located, tighten loose connections or overhaul the master or slave cylinder as necessary.

Identification

See Chapter 1, which lists the basic types of manual transmissions and the various locations of their serial numbers. By finding the serial number on your transmission and comparing its location with the information there, you can readily determine the type of gearbox used.

Linkage Adjustment

Column Shift

1964–66

1. Position both transmission levers in Neutral.

2. Position the column selector in Neutral. Align the First/Reverse and Second/Third shifter tube levers on the steering jacket.

3. Install the control rods on the steering jacket levers and secure them with lock clips.

4. Install a swivel on the First/Reverse shifter control rod, and adjust until the swivel can freely enter the transmission shift lever hole (rear). Install a retaining clip on the swivel, and insert the swivel in the lever hole and secure with a nut.

5. Install the Second/Third lower rod to the frame mounted idler lever and in the Second/Third transmission lever and secure with retaining clips.

6. Install the upper Second/Third shifter control rod, in the same manner as the First/Reverse shifter control rod (Step 4), to the frame idler and the jacket shifter lever.

CAUTION: *Ensure that the shifter tube levers stay in alignment.*

7. Check the adjustment by moving the shift lever through all the gear positions.

1967–68

1. Located on the left side of the transmission case are two levers. Manipulate these levers until the transmission is in neutral. Depress the clutch pedal, start the engine, and release the pedal slowly. If the car fails to move and engine is still running with the pedal fully released, the transmission is in neutral. If the car moves, the transmission is in gear and the levers should be repositioned until neutral is found. Loosen the swivel nuts on both shift rods.

2. Move the shift lever (on the column) to the neutral position. Raise the hood and locate the shifter tube levers on the steering column. Align the first and reverse lever with the second and third lever. Using a pin (use a large L-shaped Allen wrench), hold these levers in alignment (most cars have alignment holes in the levers and an alignment plate) until the linkage is connected.

3. Make the final adjustments to align the

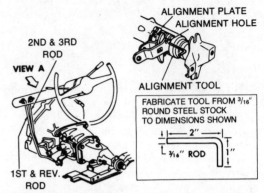

Adjusting the shift linkage (column) for 1967–69 vehicles

shift rods and levers at the transmission into the neutral position. Road-test the car and check the shifting operation. If the adjustment is correct, the alignment pin should pass freely through all alignment holes. If not, readjustment is necessary.

1969

1. Turn the ignition switch to the "off" position.

2. Loosen the swivel nuts on both shift rods.

3. Place the column-mounted shift lever in the reverse position. There are two levers located on the side of the transmission case. The lever to the front of the transmission controls second and third gears while the other lever controls first and reverse. Place this first and reverse lever into the reverse position. Push up on the first/reverse shift rod until the column lever is in the reverse detent position. Tighten the swivel nut.

4. Place the column lever and the transmission levers (located on the side of the case) in neutral (to determine neutral, see Step One for 1967–68 cars). The shift tube levers are located on the steering column mast jacket. Make sure the column lever is in neutral and hold it in this position by inserting a pin through the alignment holes in the shift tube levers (a 3/16 in. Allen wrench is perfect).

5. Hold the second/third shift rod steady (to prevent a change in adjustment) and tighten the swivel locknut.

6. Remove the alignment pin from the shift tube levers and shift the column shift lever to the reverse position. Turn the ignition key to "lock" and check the ignition interlock control. If it binds, leave the control in "lock" and readjust the first/reverse rod at the swivel.

7. Move the column lever through the gear positions and return it to neutral. The alignment pin should pass freely through the alignment holes of the shift tube levers. If it doesn't, loosen the swivel nuts and readjust.

1970–72

1. Place the shift lever (on the column) in reverse and the ignition switch in "off."

2. Raise the car and support it with floor stands.

3. Loosen the locknuts on the shift rod swivels. Pull down slightly on the first/reverse control rod on the lower steering column to remove any slack. Tighten the locknut at the transmission lever.

4. Unlock the ignition switch and shift the column lever into neutral. Position the shift tube levers (located on the lower steering column) in neutral by aligning the lever alignment holes. Hold them in this position by inserting a 3/16 in. Allen wrench through the alignment holes.

5. Hold the second/third shift rod steady and tighten the rod locknut.

6. Remove the alignment tool from the shift tube levers and check the shifting operation.

7. Place the column lever in reverse and check the movement of the ignition key. In reverse and only reverse, the key must turn freely in and out of "lock."

Floor Shift

THREE SPEED—1968–72

1. Loosen the locknuts on both shift rod swivels. The shift rods should pass freely through the swivels.

2. Move the floor shift to Neutral and install the locating gauge into the shifter bracket assembly.

NOTE: *The locating gauge is a piece of 1/8 in. thick flat stock 41/64 in. wide and 3 in. long.*

3. Position the levers on the transmission in Neutral. Turn the First/Reverse shift rod nut down against the swivel, and then tighten the locknut against the swivel.

4. Turn the Second/Third shift rod nut down against the swivel, and then tighten the locknut against the swivel.

NOTE: *On 1969 and later cars, skip Step 4 and perform Steps 5–8. Step 4 is the final step for 1968 cars.*

5. Remove the locating gauge, and shift into Reverse. Turn the ignition switch to the Lock position.

6. Loosen the swivel locknut on the backdrive control rod. Pull down slightly on the control rod to take up any slack in the column mechanism, and then tighten the clevis jam nut.

7. The ignition switch should move easily in and out of lock. If there is any binding present, keep the switch in Lock and readjust the backdrive control rod.

8. Check the shift pattern for correct operation.

FOUR-SPEED—1964–68

1. Remove the control rods from the transmission levers, and position the levers in Neutral.

2. Move the floor shift lever into Neutral and insert a locating gauge into the bracket assembly (use a 5/16 in. rod on 1964 cars. 1965–74 four-speeds use the same gauge as the three-speed floor shift).

3. Adjust the length of the control rods, and then secure the swivels with the jam nuts and install the clevis pins.

4. Remove the locating gauge, and check the shift pattern.

NOTE: *1965 and later Muncie transmission levers have two control rod holes. Attaching the control rods in the lower holes will result in reduced shift lever travel and allow faster shifting, with increased shifting effort as a minor drawback.*

FOUR-SPEED 1969–81

1. Turn the ignition switch to the Off position, except on 1970 models which should be turned to Lock.

2. Loosen the swivel lock nuts on the shift rods and backdrive control rod. Position the

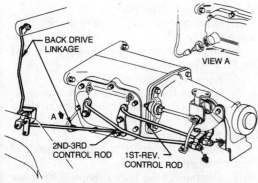

3-speed floor shift linkage (backdrive shown is on 1969–72 models)

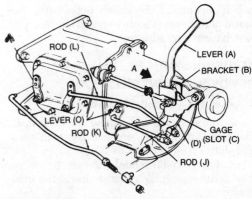

Muncie 4-speed linkage

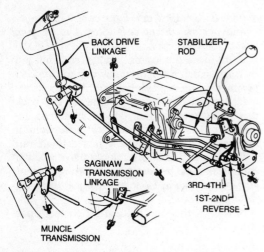

BACK DRIVE LINKAGE STABILIZER ROD

SAGINAW TRANSMISSION LINKAGE

3RD-4TH
1ST-2ND
REVERSE

MUNCIE TRANSMISSION

Saginaw 4-speed linkage

transmission side cover levers to their Neutral detent positions.

3. Place the floor shift in Neutral and insert a locating gauge (same gauge as three-speed floor shift) into the lever bracket assembly.

4. Adjust all control rods swivels for easy entry into their respective levers.

5. Tighten the shift rod locknuts and remove the gauge.

6. Shift the lever into Reverse and pull down slightly on the backdrive rod to remove the slack. Tighten the locknut.

7. The ignition switch should now be able to be moved easily into Lock, and it must not be possible to turn the key to Lock, when in any other position other than Reverse. Readjust the backdrive rod, if necessary.

8. Check the shift pattern for correctness.

CLUTCH SWITCH ADJUSTMENT AND REPLACEMENT

A clutch-operated neutral safety switch was used beginning in 1970. The ignition switch must be in the "start" position and the clutch must be fully depressed before the car will start. The switch mounts to the clutch pedal arm. Removal of this switch is obvious and simple. This switch cannot be adjusted.

Transmission
REMOVAL AND INSTALLATION

3 Speed and 4 Speed—1967–69

1. Raise the car and remove the driveshaft. On floor-shift models, remove the trim plate and shifter boot.

2. On 1968–69 models, it may be necessary to disconnect the exhaust pipe at the manifold.

3. Disconnect the speedometer cable and,

on floor-shift models, disconnect the back-up light switch.

4. Remove the crossmember-to-frame bolts. On floor-shift models, remove the bolts holding the control lever support to the crossmember.

5. Remove the transmission mount bolts.

6. Using a suitable jack and a block of wood (to be placed between the jack and the engine), raise the engine slightly and remove or relocate the crossmember.

7. Remove the shift levers from the transmission side cover.

8. On floor-shift models, remove the stabilizer rod (if so equipped) situated between the shift lever assembly and the transmission.

9. Remove the transmission-to-bellhousing bolts. Remove the top bolts first and insert guide pins into the holes, then remove the bottom bolts.

10. Remove the transmission.

11. To install, perform the following:

a. Lift the transmission into position and insert the mainshaft into the bellhousing.

b. Install the transmission-to-bellhousing bolts and lockwashers, and torque them to 50 ft. lbs.

c. Install the transmission shift levers to the side cover. On floor-shift models, install the stabilizer rod (if so equipped).

d. Raise the engine slightly, position the crossmember, and install the bolts.

e. Install the transmission mount bolts. On floor-shift models, install the bolts holding the shift lever support to the crossmember. CAUTION: *Lubricate the tailshaft bushing before the driveshafts are installed.*

f. Install the driveshaft and, if removed, install the exhaust pipe to manifold.

g. Connect the speedometer cable and, on floor-shift cars, connect the backup light.

h. Fill the transmission with lubricant.

3 Speed and 4 Speed—1970–81

1. On floor-shift models, remove the shift knob and console trim plate.

2. Raise the car and support it with floor stands.

3. Disconnect the speedometer cable and the TCS switch wiring.

4. Remove the driveshaft.

5. Remove the bolts securing the transmission mounts to the crossmember and also those bolts securing the crossmember to the frame. Remove the crossmember.

6. Remove the shift levers from the side of the transmission.

7. Disconnect the back drive rod from the bellcrank.

8. Remove the bolts from the shift control

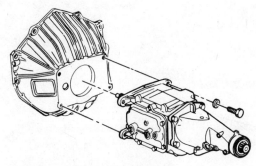

Typical transmission mounting

assembly and carefully lower the assembly until the shift lever clears the rubber shift boot. Remove the assembly from the car.

9. Remove the transmission-to-bellhousing bolts and lift the transmission from the car.

10. To install, perform the following:

a. Lift the transmission and insert the mainshaft into the bellhousing.

b. Install and torque the transmission-to-clutch housing bolts and lockwashers.

c. Install the shift lever.

d. Install the shift levers to the transmission side cover.

e. Connect the back drive rod to the bellcrank.

f. Raise the engine high enough to position the crossmember. Install and tighten the crossmember-to-frame bolts and transmission mounts to crossmember bolts.

g. Install the driveshaft.

h. Connect the speedometer cable and TCS wiring.

i. Fill the transmission with the specified lubricant. If applicable, install the console trim plate and shift knob. Adjust the linkage.

CLUTCH

Understanding the Clutch

The purpose of the clutch is to disconnect and connect engine power from the transmission. A car at rest requires a lot of engine torque to get all that weight moving. An internal-combustion engine does not develop a high starting torque (unlike steam engines), so it must be allowed to operate without any load until it builds up enough torque to move the car. Torque increases with engine rpm. The clutch allows the engine to build up torque by physically disconnecting the engine from the transmission, relieving the engine of any load or resistance. The transfer of engine power to the transmission (the load) must be smooth and gradual; if it weren't, drive line components would wear out or break quickly. This gradual power transfer is made possible by gradually releasing the clutch pedal. The clutch disc and pressure plate are the connecting link between the engine and transmission. When the clutch pedal if released, the disc and plate contact each other (clutch engagement), physically joining the engine and transmission. When the pedal is pushed in, the disc and plate separate (the clutch is disengaged), disconnecting the engine from the transmission.

The clutch assembly consists of the flywheel, the clutch disc, the clutch pressure plate, the throwout bearing and fork, the actuating linkage and the pedal. The flywheel and clutch pressure plate (driving members) are connected to the engine crankshaft and rotate with it. The clutch disc is located between the flywheel and pressure plate, and splined to the transmission shaft. A driving member is one that is attached to the engine and transfers engine power to a driven member (clutch disc) on the transmission shaft. A driving member (pressure plate) rotates (drives) a driven member (clutch disc) on contact and, in so doing, turns the transmission shaft. There is a circular diaphragm spring within the pressure plate cover (transmission side). In a relaxed state (when the clutch pedal is fully released), this spring is convex; that is, it is dished outward toward the transmission. Pushing in the clutch pedal actuates an attached linkage rod. Connected to the other end of this rod is the throwout bearing fork. The throwout bearing is attached to the fork. When the clutch pedal is depressed, the clutch linkage pushes the fork and bearing forward to contact the diaphragm spring of the pressure plate. The outer edges of the spring are secured to the pressure plate and are pivoted on rings so that when the center of the spring is compressed by the throwout bearing, the outer edges bow outward and, by so doing, pull the pressure plate in the same direction—away from the clutch disc. This action separates the disc from the plate, disengaging the clutch and allowing the transmission to be shifted into another gear. A coil type clutch return spring attached to the clutch pedal arm permits full release of the pedal. Releasing the pedal pulls the throwout bearing away from the diaphragm spring resulting in a reversal of spring position. As bearing pressure is gradually released from the spring center, the outer edges of the spring bow outward, pushing the pressure plate into closer contact with the clutch disc. As the disc and plate move closer together, friction between the two increases and slippage is reduced until, when full spring pressure is applied (by fully releasing the pedal),

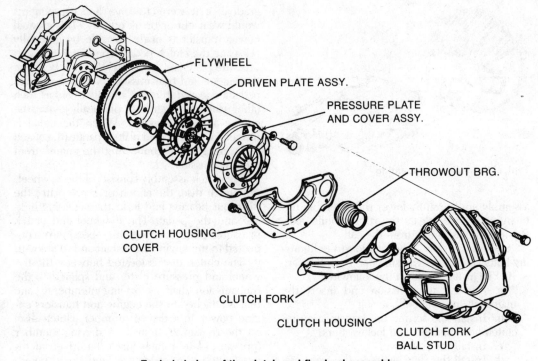

FLYWHEEL

DRIVEN PLATE ASSY.

PRESSURE PLATE
AND COVER ASSY.

THROWOUT BRG.

CLUTCH HOUSING
COVER

CLUTCH FORK

CLUTCH HOUSING

CLUTCH FORK
BALL STUD

Exploded view of the clutch and flywheel assembly

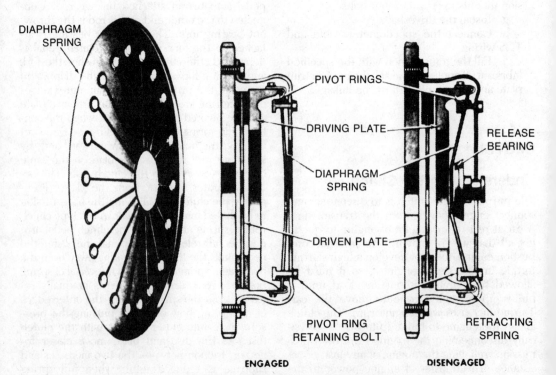

DIAPHRAGM
SPRING

PIVOT RINGS

DRIVING PLATE

RELEASE
BEARING

DIAPHRAGM
SPRING

DRIVEN PLATE

PIVOT RING
RETAINING BOLT

RETRACTING
SPRING

ENGAGED

DISENGAGED

Operation of the diaphragm spring clutch

the speed of the disc and plate are the same. This stops all slipping, creating a direct connection between the plate and disc which results in the transfer of power from the engine to the transmission. The clutch disc is now rotating with the pressure plate at engine speed and, because it is splined to the transmission shaft, the shaft now turns at the same engine speed. Understanding clutch operation can be rather difficult at first; if you're still confused after reading this, consider the following analogy. The action of the diaphragm spring can be compared to that of an oil can bottom. The bottom of an oil can is shaped very much like the clutch diaphragm spring and pushing in on the can bottom and then releasing it produces a similar effect. As mentioned earlier, the clutch pedal return spring permits full release of the pedal and reduces linkage slack due to wear. As the linkage wears, clutch free-pedal travel will increase and free-travel will decrease as the clutch wears. Free-travel is actually throwout bearing lash.

The diaphragm spring type clutches used are available in two different designs: flat diaphragm springs or bent springs. The bent fingers are bent back to create a centrifugal boost ensuring quick reengagement at higher engine speeds. This design enables pressure plate load to increase as the clutch disc wears and makes low pedal effort possible even with a heavy-duty clutch. The throwout bearing used with the bent finger design is 1¼ in. long and is shorter than the bearing used with the flat finger design. These bearings are not interchangeable. If the longer bearing is used with the bent finger clutch, free-pedal travel will not exist. This results in clutch slippage and rapid wear.

The transmission varies the gear ratio between the engine and rear wheels. It can be shifted to change engine speed as driving conditions and loads change. The transmission allows disengaging and reversing power from the engine to the wheels.

CLUTCH CROSS-SHAFT LUBRICATION

Once every 36,000 miles or sooner if necessary, remove the plug, install a fitting and lubricate with a water-resistant EP (Extreme Pressure) chassis lubricant.

LINKAGE INSPECTION

A clutch may have all the symptoms of going bad when the real trouble lies in the linkage. To avoid the unnecessary replacement of a clutch, make the following linkage checks:

a. Start the engine and depress the clutch pedal until it is about ½ in. from the floor mat and move the shift lever between first and reverse (first and second on a four-speed) several times. If this can be done smoothly without any grinding, the clutch is releasing fully. If the shifting is not smooth, the clutch is not releasing fully and adjustment is necessary.

b. Check the condition of the clutch pedal bushings for signs of sticking or excessive wear.

c. Check the throwout bearing fork for proper installation on the ball stud. The fork could possibly be pulled off the ball if not properly lubricated.

d. Check the cross-shaft levers for distortion or damage.

e. Check the car for loose or damaged motor mounts. Bad motor mounts can cause the engine to shift under acceleration and bind the clutch linkage at the cross-shaft. There must be come clearance between the cross-shaft and motor mount.

f. Check the throwout bearing clearance between the clutch spring fingers and the front bearing retainer on the transmission. If there is no clearance, the fork may be improperly installed on the ball stud or the clutch disc may be worn out.

FREE-PLAY ADJUSTMENT

This adjustment must be made under the vehicle on the clutch operating linkage. Free play is measured at the clutch pedal.

1964–67

This adjustment is made from under the car. Free-play is measured at the clutch pedal.

1. Disconnect the spring between the cross-shaft lever and the clutch fork.

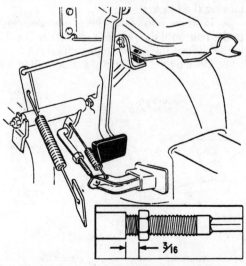

Clutch pedal free-play adjustment—1964–67

2. Loosen the pushrod locknut approximately three turns.

3. If no free travel is present, adjust the pushrod until it is free of the clutch fork.

4. While holding the clutch fork to the rear, adjust the rod until it just touches the fork seat.

5. Turn the locknut until ³⁄₁₆ in. clearance exists between the nut and the sleeve.

6. Turn the rod until the nut just contacts the sleeve, and hold the rod with a wrench and tighten the nut.

7. Free pedal clearance should be ¾–1⅛ in. (1964–65) or 1–1½ in. (1966–67).

1968–70

1. Disconnect the return spring at the clutch operating fork.

2. Use the linkage to push the clutch pedal up against its rubber bumper stop.

3. Loosen the operating rod locknut and lengthen the adjustment rod until it pushes the fork back enough that the release bearing can just be left to contact the pressure plate fingers.

4. Shorten the rod three turns and tighten the locknut.

5. Replace the spring and check the free play at the pedal pad. It should be about 1 in. or more.

1971–81

You can also use this procedure on any earlier models that have a gauge hole in the clutch pivot shaft arm.

1. Disconnect the return spring at the clutch operating fork.

2. Use the linkage to push the clutch pedal up against its rubber bumper stop. On the 1973 Chevelle, more clearance can be obtained by loosening the rubber bumper bracket and moving the bracket.

3. Push the end of the clutch operating fork to the rear until the release bearing can just be felt to contact the pressure plate fingers.

4. Detach the front end of the operating rod from the clutch pivot shaft arm and place it in the gauge hole on the arm.

5. Loosen the locknut and lengthen the rod just enough to take all the play out of the linkage. Tighten the locknut.

6. Replace the operating rod in its original location.

7. Replace the return spring and check the free play at the pedal pad. It should be about 1 in. or more.

Driven Disc And Pressure Plate
REMOVAL

CAUTION: *The clutch driven disc contains asbestos, which has been determined to be a cancer causing agent. NEVER clean the clutch surfaces with compressed air! Avoid inhaling dust from the clutch surface! When cleaning the clutch surfaces use a commercially available brake cleaning fluid.*

1. Support the engine and remove the transmission.

2. Disconnect the clutch fork push rod and spring.

3. Remove the flywheel housing.

4. Slide the clutch fork from the ball stud and remove the fork from the dust boot. The ball stud is threaded into the clutch housing and may be replaced, if necessary.

5. Install an alignment tool to support the clutch assembly during removal. Mark the flywheel and clutch cover for reinstallation, if they do not already have "X" marks.

6. Loosen the clutch-to-flywheel attaching bolts evenly, one turn at a time, until spring pressure is released. Remove the bolts and clutch assembly.

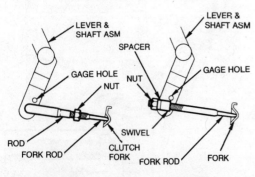

Clutch pedal free-play adjustment—1968–72

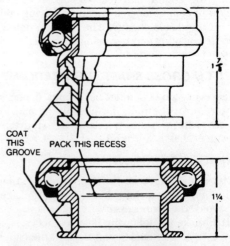

Clutch release bearing lubrication—flat finger type (top), bent finger type (bottom)

INSTALLATION

1. Clean the pressure plate and flywheel face.
2. Support the clutch disc and pressure plate with an alignment tool. The driven disc is installed with the damper springs on the transmission side. On some 1964–67 6-cylinder engines, the clutch disc is installed in a reverse manner with the damper springs to the flywheel side.
3. Turn the clutch assembly until the mark on the cover lines up with the mark on the flywheel, then install the bolts. Tighten down evenly and gradually to avoid distortion.
4. Remove the alignment tool.
5. Lubricate the ball socket and fork fingers at the release bearing end with high melting-point grease. Lubricate the recess on the inside of the throwout bearing and throwout fork groove with a light coat of graphite grease.
6. Install the clutch fork and dust boot into the housing. Install the throwout bearing to the throwout fork. Install the flywheel housing. Install the transmission.
7. Connect the fork push rod and spring. Lubricate the spring and pushrod ends.
8. Adjust the shift linkage and clutch pedal free-play.

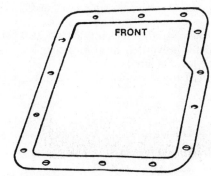

GM Powerglide

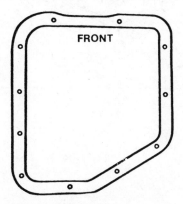

GM Turbo Hydra-Matic 200

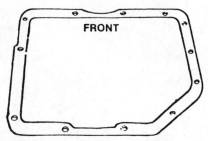

GM Turbo Hydra-Matic 250, 350, 375B

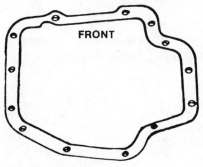

GM Turbo Hydra-Matic 400

AUTOMATIC TRANSMISSION

Identification

The four types of pan gaskets used on the automatic transmissions used in your car are pictured below for ready identification.

Fluid Pan And Filter

REMOVAL AND INSTALLATION

The fluid should be changed with the transmission warm. A 20 minute drive at highway speeds should accomplish this.

1. Raise and support the vehicle, preferably in a level attitude.
2. With the Turbo Hydra-Matic 250 or 350, support the transmission and remove the support crossmember.
3. Place a large pan under the transmission pan. Remove all the front and side pan bolts. Loosen the rear bolts about four turns.
4. Pry the pan loose and let it drain.
5. Remove the pan and gasket. Clean the pan thoroughly with solvent and air dry it. Be very careful not to get any lint from rags in the pan.
6. Remove the strainer to valve body screws, the strainer, and the gasket. Most 350 transmissions will have a throw-away filter instead of a strainer. On the 400 transmission, remove the filter retaining bolt, filter, and intake pipe O-ring.
7. If there is a strainer, clean it in solvent and air dry.

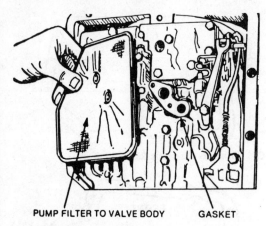

PUMP FILTER TO VALVE BODY   GASKET

Removing the filter on the Turbo 350

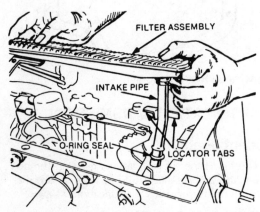

FILTER ASSEMBLY

INTAKE PIPE

O-RING SEAL

LOCATOR TABS

Removing the filter, intake pipe and O-ring on the 400

8. Install the new filter or cleaned strainer with a new gasket. Tighten the screws to 12 ft. lbs. On the 400, install a new intake pipe O-ring and a new filter, tightening the retaining bolt to 10 ft. lbs.

9. Install the pan with a new gasket. Tighten the bolts evenly to 12 ft. lbs. (8 for Powerglide and Torque Drive).

10. Lower the car and add the proper amount of DEXRON© or DEXRON© II automatic transmission fluid through the dipstick tube.

11. Start the engine in Park and let it idle. Do not race the engine. Shift into each shift lever position, shift back into Park, and check the fluid level on the dipstick. The level should be ¼ in. below ADD. Be very careful not to overfill. Recheck the level after the car has been driven long enough to thoroughly warm up the transmission. Add fluid as necessary. The level should then be at FULL

GASOLINE ENGINE SHIFT LINKAGE ADJUSTMENT

Powerglide Column Shift

1. The shift tube and lever assembly must be free in the mast jacket.

2. Lift the selector lever toward the steering wheel and allow the selector lever to be positioned in Drive by the transmission detent.

3. Release the selector lever. The lever should be prevented from engaging low, unless the lever is lifted.

4. Lift the selector lever toward the steer-

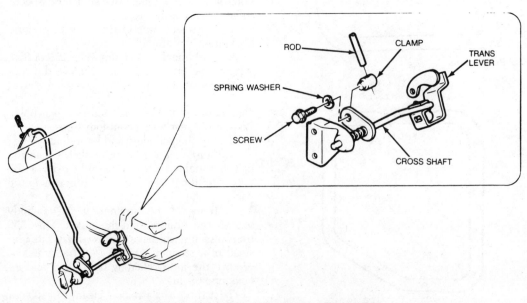

ROD   CLAMP

TRANS LEVER

SPRING WASHER

SCREW

CROSS SHAFT

Column shift linkage adjustment—Powerglide

ing wheel and allow the lever to be positioned in Neutral by the transmission detent.

5. Release the selector lever. The selector lever should now be kept from engaging. Reverse unless the lever is lifted. If the linkage is adjusted correctly, the selector lever should be prevented from moving beyond both the neutral detent and the Drive detent unless the lever is lifted to pass over the mechanical stop in the steering column.

If adjustment is necessary, perform the following steps:

6. Adjust the linkage by loosening the adjustment clamp at the cross-shaft. Place the transmission lever in Drive by rotating the lever counterclockwise to the Low detent, and then clockwise one detent to Drive.

7. Place the selector lever in Drive and remove any free-play by holding the cross-shaft up and pulling the shift rod downward.

8. Tighten the clamp and check the adjustment.

On 1969–73 cars, carry out the following additional steps:

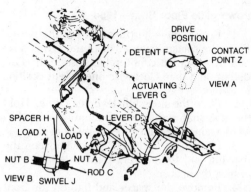

Floor shift linkage adjustment—1964–67 Powerglide

9. Place the shift lever in Park and the ignition switch in lock. Loosen the back-drive rod clamp nut. Remove any lash in the column and tighten the clamp nut.

10. When the selector lever is in Park, the ignition key should move freely into lock. Lock position should be obtainable only when the transmission is in Park.

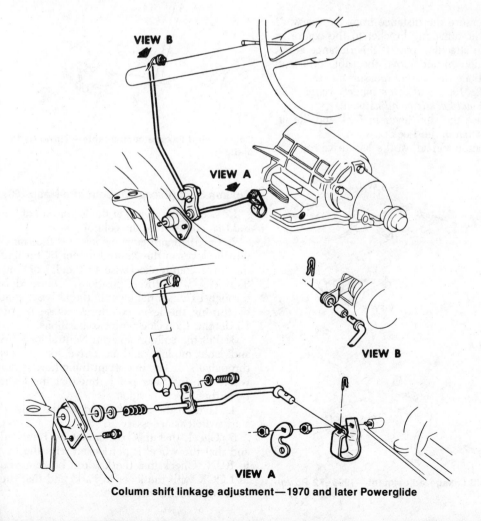

Column shift linkage adjustment—1970 and later Powerglide

Powerglide Floor Shift—1964–67

1. Loosen the adjustment nuts at the swivel. Place the transmission lever in the Drive position by moving it counterclockwise to the Low detent, and then clockwise one detent position to Drive.

2. Place the floorshift lever in Drive. Hold the floorshift unit lower operating lever forward against the shift lever detent.

3. Place a 7/64 in. (0.11) spacer between the rear nut and the swivel. Tighten the rear nut against the spacer.

4. Remove the spacer and tighten the front nut against the swivel, locking the swivel between the nuts.

Powerglide Floor Shift—1968–73

1968 and later cars use a cable-type shift linkage.

1. Place the shift lever in Drive.

2. Disconnect the cable from the transmission lever. Place the transmission lever in Drive by rotating the lever counterclockwise to the Low detent, and then clockwise one detent to Drive.

3. Measure the distance from the rearward face of the attaching bracket to the center of the cable attaching pin. If this distance is not 5.5 in., loosen and move the cable end stud nut to obtain the correct measurement.

NOTE: *1969 and later models require an additional backdrive adjustment.*

4. Place the shift lever in Park and the ignition switch in the Lock position.

5. Loosen and adjust the backdrive rod.

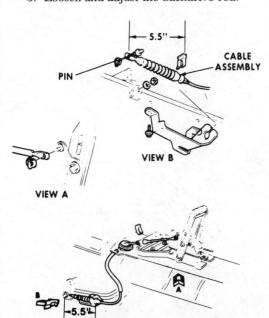

Floor shift linkage adjustment—1968–72 Powerglide

6. With the selector lever in Park, the ignition key should move freely into the Lock position. Lock position should not be obtainable in any transmission position other than Park.

Turbo Hydra-Matic Column and Floor Shift Linkage Adjustment Through 1974

Linkages used on Turbo Hydra-Matic transmissions are similar to those used on Powerglides. Adjustments are the same, except that the transmission lever is adjusted to Drive by moving the lever clockwise to the Low detent, and then counterclockwise two detent positions to Drive.

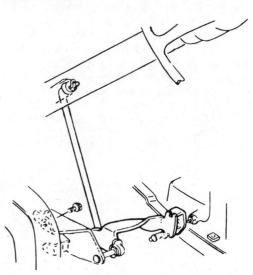

Column shift linkage components—Turbo Hydra-matic

Column Shift (Except Turbo Hydra-Matic 200)

1. Loosen the swivel at the lower end of the rod that comes from the column.

2. On 1973 and later models, set the transmission lever in the Neutral detent by turning the lever counterclockwise to the L1 detent, then clockwise three positions. On models through 1972, set the lever in the Drive detent by turning the lever counterclockwise to the L1 detent, then clockwise two positions.

3. Put the column lever in Neutral for 1973 and later models, and in Drive for models through 1972. The important thing here is not where the indicator points but that the lever be in the correct position.

4. Tighten the swivel. Readjust the neutral start switch as necessary.

5. Check that the key cannot be removed and that the wheel is not locked with the key in RUN. Check that the key can be removed in LOCK with the lever in Park, and that the steering wheel is locked.

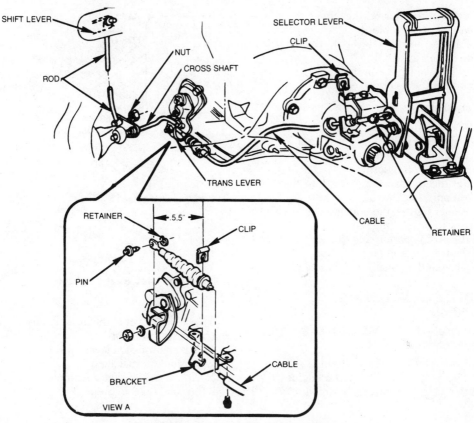

Floor shift linkage—1968–72 Powerglide

Turbo Hydra-Matic 200

1. Remove the screw and washer from the swivel assembly on the rod which activates the transmission shift lever.

2. Put the transmission shift lever in neutral by turning it counterclockwise to L1 detent and then clockwise three detent positions. Put the transmission selector lever in neutral as determined by the mechanical stop in the steering column assembly—do not use the indicator pointer.

3. Turn the swivel until it lines up directly with the hole in the shift lever, and install screw and washer. You should not have to force the transmission lever to move in either direction to install the screw.

4. Adjust the transmission indicator pointer and neutral start switch.

5. Check that the key cannot be removed from the "run" position if the transmission selector is in "Reverse" and that the key can be removed with the selector in "Park." Make sure the lever will not move from "Park" position with key out of ignition.

1975–81 Cars With Cable Linkage

1. Loosen the swivel at the lower end of the rod that comes from the steering column.

2. Loosen the pin at the transmission end of the cable.

3. Set the floorshift lever in the Drive detent.

4. Set the transmission lever in the Drive detent by moving it counterclockwise to the L1 detent, then clockwise three detent positions.

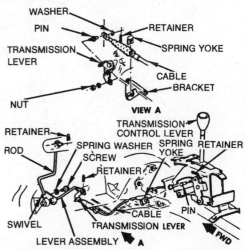

Floor shift linkage adjustment—1973 and later Turbo Hydra-matic

5. Tighten the nut on the pin at the transmission end of the cable.

6. Put the floorshift lever in Park and the ignition switch in LOCK.

7. Pull down lightly on the rod from the column and tighten its clamp nut.

1982 and Later

1. Loosen the clamping screw at the shifting rod-to-equalizer lever.

2. Position the steering column shifting lever into the Neutral position.

3. Set the transmission lever into the Neutral position.

4. Finger tighten the equalizer lever clamping screw to the shifting rod.

NOTE: *While performing this operation, DO NOT exert force in any direction.*

5. Tighten the equalizer clamping screw.

THROTTLE VALVE LINKAGE ADJUSTMENT

Powerglide—1964–66 V8, 1964–73 Six Cylinder Engines

1. Depress the accelerator pedal.

2. The bellcrank on 6 cylinder engines must be at the wide open throttle position.

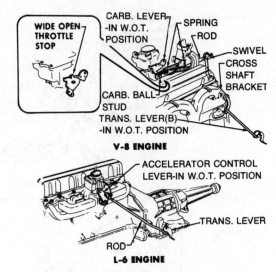

V-8 ENGINE

L-6 ENGINE

Adjusting the throttle valve linkage

3. The dash lever at the firewall must be $1/64$–$1/16$ in. off its lever stop.

4. The transmission lever must be against the transmission internal stop.

5. Adjust the linkage to simultaneously obtain the conditions in Steps 1–4.

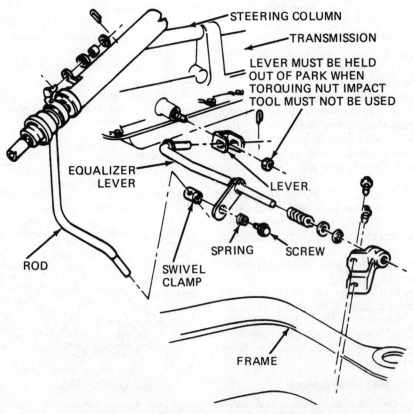

Steering column shift linkage adjustment–1982 and later

Powerglide 1967–73 V8 Engines

1. Remove the air cleaner.
2. Disconnect the accelerator linkage at the carburetor.
3. Disconnect both return springs.
4. Pull the throttle valve upper rod forward until the transmission is through the detent.
5. Open the carburetor to the wide open throttle position. Adjust the swivel on the end of the upper throttle valve rod so that the carburetor reaches wide open throttle position at the same time that the ball stud contacts the end of the slot in the upper throttle valve rod. A tolerance of ⅟₃₂ in. is allowable.

DETENT CABLE ADJUSTMENT

Turbo Hydra-Matic 250, 350

Through 1972

These transmissions utilize a downshift cable between the carburetor and the transmission.

1. Pry up on each side of the detent cable snap-lock with a small pry bar to release the lock. On cars equipped with a retaining screw, loosen the detent cable screw.
2. Squeeze the locking tabs and disconnect the snap-lock assembly from the throttle bracket.
3. Place the carburetor lever in the wide open throttle position. Make sure that the lever is against the wide open stop. On cars with Quadrajet carburetors, disengage the secondary lock-out before placing the lever in the wide open position.

NOTE: *The detent cable must be pulled through the detent position.*

4. With the carburetor lever in the wide open position, push the snap-lock on the cable or else tighten the retaining screw.

NOTE: *Do not lubricate the detent cable.*

1973 AND LATER

1. Stop the engine.
2. Locate the TV cable adjuster near the carburetor.

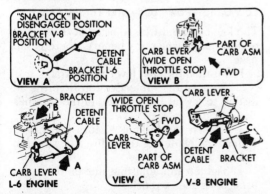

Detent cable adjustment—Turbo Hydra-matic 350 (250 similar)

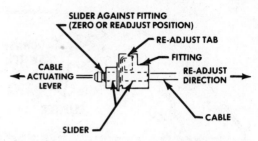

View of the TV cable adjuster—1973 and later

3. Depress and hold down the metal tab of the TV cable adjuster.
4. Move the slider until it stops against the fitting.
5. Release the adjuster tab.
6. Turn the carburetor lever to the "Full Throttle Stop" position and release it.

NOTE: *By turning the carburetor lever to the Full Throttle Stop, the TV cable will automatically adjust itself.*

DETENT SWITCH ADJUSTMENT

Turbo Hydra-Matic 400 transmissions are equipped with an electrical detent, or downshift switch operated by the throttle linkage.

1968

1. Place the carburetor lever in the wide open position.
2. Position the automatic choke so that it is off.
3. Fully depress the switch plunger.
4. Adjust the switch mounting to obtain a distance of 0.05 in. between the switch plunger and the throttle lever paddle.

1969–78

1. Pull the detent switch driver rearward until the hole in the switch body aligns with the hole in the driver. Insert a 0.092 in. diameter pin through the aligned holes to hold the driver in position.
2. Loosen the mounting bolt.

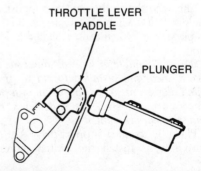

Adjusting the detent switch—1968–72 Turbo Hydra-Matic 400

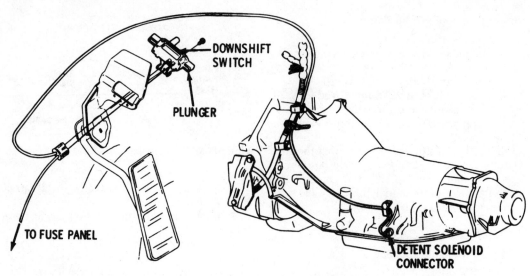

Detent (downshift) switch adjustment

3. Press the switch plunger as far forward as possible. This will preset the switch for adjustment, which will occur on the first application of wide open throttle.

4. Tighten the mounting bolt and remove the pin.

NEUTRAL SAFETY SWITCH REPLACEMENT

The neutral safety switch prevents the engine from being started in any transmission position except Neutral or Park. The switch is located on the upper side of the steering column under the instrument panel on column shift cars, and inside the shift console on floor shift models.

1. Remove the console for access on floor shift models.

2. Disconnect the electrical connectors.

3. Remove the neutral switch.

4. Place 1964–70 column shift lever models in Drive, and 1971 and later models in neutral. Locate the lever tang against the transmission selector plate on column shift models. Place 1964 through early 1972 floor shift models in Drive, and mid-1972 and later models in Park.

5. Align the slot in the contact support with the hole in the switch. Insert a 3/32 (0.90 in.) pin in place. The switch is now aligned in Drive position.

NOTE: *1973 and later neutral safety switches have a shear-pin installed to aid in proper switch alignment so that insertion of a pin is unnecessary. Moving the shift lever from Neutral shears the pin.*

6. Place the contact support drive slot over the drive tang. Install the switch mounting screws.

7. Remove the aligning pin. Connect the electrical wiring, and replace the console.

8. Set the parking brake and hold your foot on the service brake pedal. Check to see that the engine will start only in Park or Neutral.

NEUTRAL SAFETY SWITCH ADJUSTMENT

NOTE: *1977 and later cars do not have a neutral safety switch. Instead, these cars have an interlock between the lock and the transmission selector, which is nonadjustable.*

1. Place the shift lever in Neutral.

2. Move the switch until you can insert a gauge pin, 0.092 in. into the hole in the switch and through to the alignment hole.

3. Loosen the switch securing screws. Remove the console first, if necessary.

4. Tighten the screws and remove the pin.

5. Step on the brake pedal and check to see that the engine will only start in Neutral or Park.

BAND ADJUSTMENTS

There are no band adjustments possible or required for the turbo Hydra-Matic 200, 200-4R, 350 or 400.

Low Band—Powerglide and Torque Drive

The low band must be adjusted at the first required fluid change or whenever there is slippage.

1. Position the shift lever in Neutral.

2. Remove the protective cap from the adjusting screw on the left side of the transmission.

3. Loosen the locknut 1/4 turn and hold it with a wrench during the entire adjusting procedure.

4. Tighten the adjusting nut to 70 in. lbs. using a 7/32 allen wrench.

5. Back off the adjusting nut *exactly* three turns for a band used less than 6,000 miles.

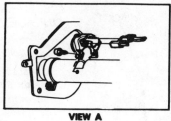

VIEW A

CONTACT SUPPORT
DRIVE SLOT IN LINE
WITH HOLE IN SWITCH

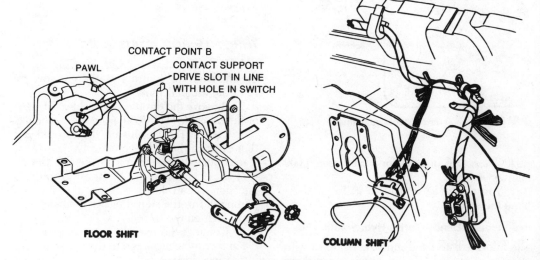

CONTACT POINT B
PAWL
CONTACT SUPPORT
DRIVE SLOT IN LINE
WITH HOLE IN SWITCH

FLOOR SHIFT

COLUMN SHIFT

Installation of the neutral safety switch (typical)

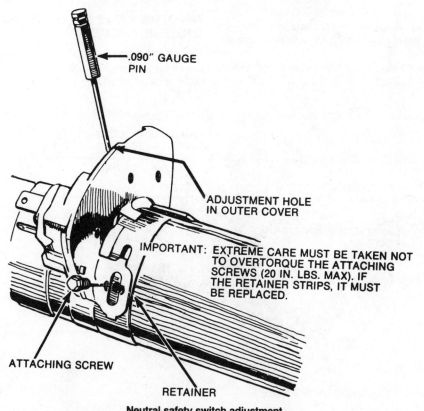

.090" GAUGE
PIN

ADJUSTMENT HOLE
IN OUTER COVER

IMPORTANT: EXTREME CARE MUST BE TAKEN NOT
TO OVERTORQUE THE ATTACHING
SCREWS (20 IN. LBS. MAX). IF
THE RETAINER STRIPS, IT MUST
BE REPLACED.

ATTACHING SCREW

RETAINER

Neutral safety switch adjustment

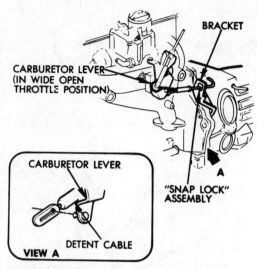

THM 200, 250, 350 detent cable adjustment

Back off *exactly* four turns for a band used 6,000 miles or more.

6. Torque the locknut to 15 ft. lbs. and replace the cap.

Intermediate Band—Turbo Hydra-Matic 250

The intermediate band must be adjusted with every required fluid change or whenever there is slippage.

1. Position the shift lever in Neutral.
2. Loosen the locknut on the right side of the transmission and tighten the adjusting screw to 30 in. lbs.
3. Back the screw out three turns and then tighten the locknut to 15 ft. lbs.

DIESEL ENGINE TRANSMISSION LINKAGE ADJUSTMENT

NOTE: *Before making any linkage adjustments, check the injection timing, and adjust if necessary. Also note that these adjustments should be performed together. The vacuum valve adjustment (THM 350s only) requires the use of special tools. If you do not have these tools at your disposal, refer the adjustment to a qualified, professional technician.*

THROTTLE ROD ADJUSTMENT

1. If equipped with cruise control, remove the clip from the control rod, then remove the rod from the bellcrank.
2. Remove the throttle valve cable (THM200) or detent cable (THM350) from the bellcrank.
3. Loosen the locknut on the throttle rod, then shorten the rod several turns.
4. Rotate the bellcrank to the full throttle stop, then lengthen the throttle rod until the injection pump lever contacts the injection pump full throttle stop. Release the bellcrank.
5. Tighten the throttle rod locknut.
6. Connect the throttle valve or detent cable and cruise control rod to the bellcrank. Adjust if necessary.

THROTTLE VALVE (TV) OR DETENT CABLE ADJUSTMENT

Refer to the previous cable adjustment procedures for gas engines. Adjust according to the style of cable which is used.

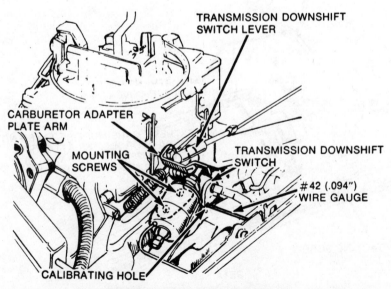

THM 400 downshift switch adjustment

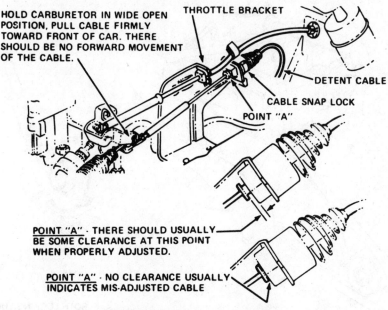

HOLD CARBURETOR IN WIDE OPEN
POSITION, PULL CABLE FIRMLY
TOWARD FRONT OF CAR. THERE
SHOULD BE NO FORWARD MOVEMENT
OF THE CABLE.

THROTTLE BRACKET

DETENT CABLE

CABLE SNAP LOCK

POINT "A"

POINT "A" · THERE SHOULD USUALLY
BE SOME CLEARANCE AT THIS POINT
WHEN PROPERLY ADJUSTED.

POINT "A" · NO CLEARANCE USUALLY
INDICATES MIS-ADJUSTED CABLE

THM 200 downshift cable adjustment

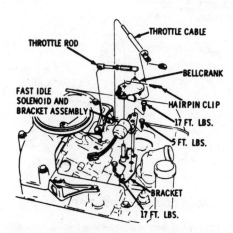

THROTTLE CABLE

THROTTLE ROD

BELLCRANK

FAST IDLE
SOLENOID AND
BRACKET ASSEMBLY

HAIRPIN CLIP

17 FT. LBS.

5 FT. LBS.

BRACKET

17 FT. LBS.

Diesel throttle linkage, V6 and V8 similar

TRANSMISSION VACUUM VALVE ADJUSTMENT

1. Remove the air cleaner assembly.
2. Remove the air intake crossover from the intake manifold. cover the intake manifold passages to prevent foreign material from entering the engine.
3. Disconnect the throttle rod from the injection pump throttle lever.
4. Loosen the transmission vacuum valve-to-injection pump bolts.
5. Mark and disconnect the vacuum lines from the vacuum valve.
6. Attach a carburetor angle gauge adapter (Kent-Moore tool J-26701-15 or its equivalent) to the injection pump throttle lever. Attach an angle gauge (J-26701 or its equivalent) to the gauge adapter.

7. Turn the throttle lever to the wide open throttle position. Set the angle gauge to zero degrees.
8. Center the bubble in the gauge level.
9. Set the angle gauge to one of the following settings, according to the year and type of engine:

Year	Engine	Setting
1980	V8	49–50°
1981	V8—Calif.	49–50°
1981	V8—non-Calif.	58°
1982	V8	58°

10. Attach a vacuum gauge to port 2 and a vacuum source (e.g. hand-held vacuum pump) to port 1 of the vacuum valve (as illustrated).
11. Apply 18–22 in. of vacuum to the valve. Slowly rotate the valve until the vacuum reading drops to one of the following values:

Year	In. Hg.
1980	7
1981 Calif.	7–8
1981 non-Calif.	8½–9
1982–83	10½

12. Tighten the vacuum valve retaining bolts.
13. Reconnect the original vacuum lines to the vacuum valve.
14. Remove the angle gauge and adapter.
15. Connect the throttle rod to the throttle lever.

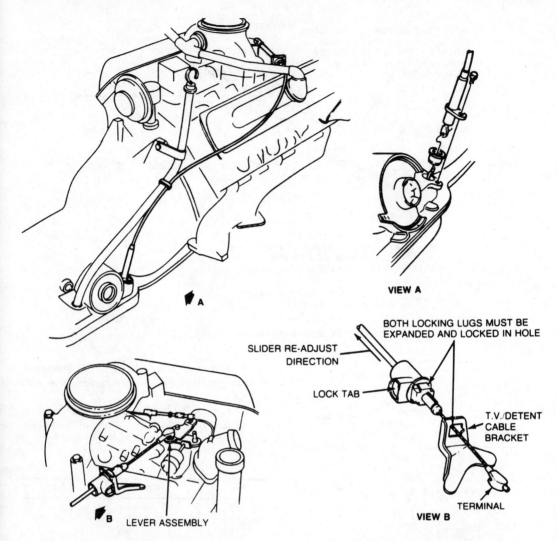

VIEW A

SLIDER RE-ADJUST
DIRECTION

BOTH LOCKING LUGS MUST BE
EXPANDED AND LOCKED IN HOLE

LOCK TAB

T.V./DETENT
CABLE
BRACKET

TERMINAL

VIEW B

B LEVER ASSEMBLY

CABLE ADJUSTMENT PROCEDURE

1. Remove pump rod from lever assembly.

2. After installation to transmission, install cable fitting into cable bracket. **CAUTION** Slider must not be adjusted before or during assembly to bracket.

3. Install cable terminal to lever assembly.

4. Rotate the lever assembly to its full throttle stop position to automatically adjust slider on cable to correct setting.

5. Release lever assembly & reconnect the pump rod to lever assembly.

CABLE RE-ADJUSTMENT PROCEDURE

In case re-adjustment is necessary because of inadvertent adjustment before or during assembly, perform the following.

1. Remove pump rod from lever assembly, depress and hold metal lock tab.

2. Move slider through fitting in direction away from lever assembly until slider stops against fitting.

3. Release metal lock tab.

4. Repeat steps 4 & 5 of adjustment procedure.

Diesel transmission vacuum Detent cable adjustment

16. Install the air intake crossover, using new gaskets.

17. Install the air cleaner assembly.

Transmission

REMOVAL AND INSTALLATION

1. Open the hood and place protectors on the fenders. Remove the air cleaner assembly and cover the air intake.

2. Disconnect the detent cable at its upper end.

3. Remove the transmission oil dipstick, and the bolt holding the dipstick tube if it is accessible.

4. Jack up the car and safety support it with jackstands.

NOTE: *If a floor pan reinforcement is used, remove it if it interferes with driveshaft removal or installation.*

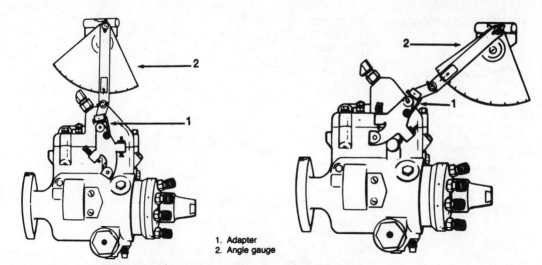

1. Adapter
2. Angle gauge

Angle gauge installation, with adaptor, for diesel vacuum valve adjustment. The gauge is positioned differently, depending on the type of throttle lever used

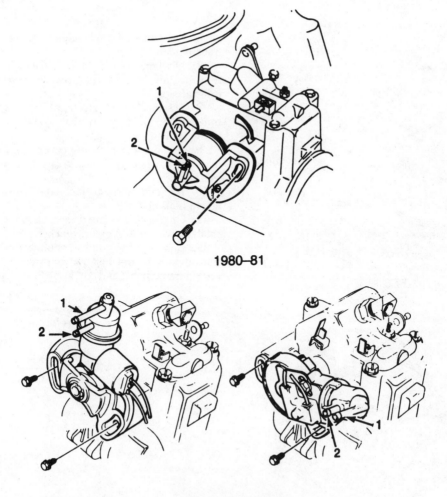

1980–81

1982 AND LATER

Diesel transmission vacuum valve adjustment

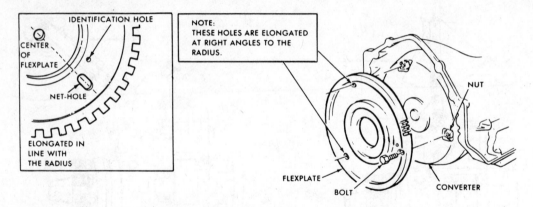

IDENTIFICATION HOLE

CENTER OF FLEXPLATE

NET-HOLE

ELONGATED IN LINE WITH THE RADIUS

NOTE: THESE HOLES ARE ELONGATED AT RIGHT ANGLES TO THE RADIUS.

NUT

FLEXPLATE

BOLT

CONVERTER

1. MOVE CONVERTER FORWARD TO CONTACT ATTACHING SURFACE ON FLEX-PLATE PRIOR TO TIGHTENING BOLTS.

2. ALIGN SLOT IN FLEXPLATE THAT HAS AN IDENTIFICATION HOLE NEAR IT, WITH AN ATTACHMENT HOLE IN CONVERTER. INSTALL BOLT AND NUT AND TIGHTEN TO SPECIFIED TORQUE. TIGHTEN ALL REMAINING BOLTS TO SPECIFIED TORQUE AS THEY ARE INSTALLED.

Typical transmission attachment, net-hole design

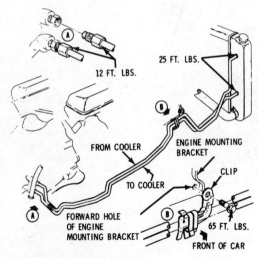

12 FT. LBS.

25 FT. LBS.

FROM COOLER

ENGINE MOUNTING BRACKET

CLIP

TO COOLER

FORWARD HOLE OF ENGINE MOUNTING BRACKET

65 FT. LBS.

FRONT OF CAR

Transmission oil cooler lines

6. Disconnect the speedometer cable at the transmission.

7. Disconnect the shift linkage at the transmission. Remove the drive shaft from the transmission.

8. Disconnect all electrical leads at the transmission and any clips that hold these leads to the transmission case.

9. Remove the flywheel cover and match-mark the flywheel and torque converter for later assembly.

10. Remove the torque converter-to-fly-wheel bolts and/or nuts.

11. On gasoline engined cars, disconnect the catalytic converter support bracket.

12. Remove the transmission support-to-transmission mount bolt and transmission support-to-frame bolts, and any insulators (if used).

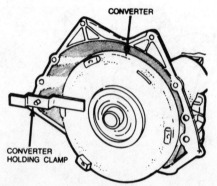

CONVERTER

CONVERTER HOLDING CLAMP

Torque converter holding fixture. A C-clamp can also be used

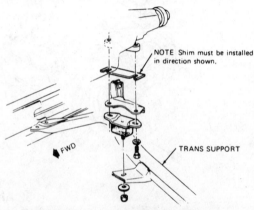

NOTE Shim must be installed in direction shown.

FWD

TRANS SUPPORT

Some transmission rear mounts are shimmed

13. Position a transmission jack under the transmission and raise it slightly.

14. Slide the transmission support rearward.

15. Loosen the transmission enough to gain access to the oil cooler lines and detent cable attachments.

16. Disconnect the oil cooler lines and detent cable. Plug all openings.

17. Support the engine and remove the engine-to-transmission bolts.

18. Disconnect the transmission assembly, being careful not to damage any cables, lines or linkage.

19. Install a C-clamp or torque converter holding tool onto the transmission housing to hold the converter in the housing. Remove the transmission assembly from the car (a hydraulic floor jack is best for this).

20. To install, reverse the removal procedure. When installing the flex plate-to-converter bolts, make sure that the weld nuts on the converter are flush with the flex plate and that the converter rotates freely by hand. Hand-start the three bolts and tighten them finger tight, then torque them evenly.

21. Install a new oil seal on the oil filler tube before installing the tube. Torque the fly-wheel-to-converter bolts to 35 ft. lbs. Torque the transmission-to-engine bolts to 35 to 40 ft. lbs. Adjust the shift linkage and detent cable following the procedures in this chapter, and check the transmission fluid if the transmission was not drained previously.

DRIVELINE

Driveshaft and U-joints

Mid-size Chevrolet driveshafts are of the conventional, open type. Located at either end of the driveshaft is a U-joint or universal joint, which allows the driveshaft to move up and down to match the motion of the rear axle. The front U-joint connects the driveshaft to a slip-jointed yoke. This yoke is internally splined, and allows the driveshaft to move in and out on the transmission splines. The rear U-joint is clamped or bolted to a companion flange fastened to the rear axle drive pinion. The rear U-joint is secured in the yoke in one of two ways. Dana and Cleveland design driveshafts use a conventional type snap-ring to hold each bearing cup in the yoke. The snap-ring fits into a groove located in each yoke end, just on top of the bearing cup. A Saginaw design driveshaft secures the U-joints differently. Nylon material is injected through a small hole in the yoke during manufacture, and flows along a circular groove between the U-joint and the yoke creating a non-metallic snap-ring.

There are two methods of attaching the rear U-joint to the rear axle. One method employs a pair of straps, while the other method is a set of bolted flanges. Bad U-joints, requiring replacement, will produce a clunking sound when the car is put into gear and when the transmission shifts from gear to gear. This is due to worn needle bearings or a scored trunnion end pos-

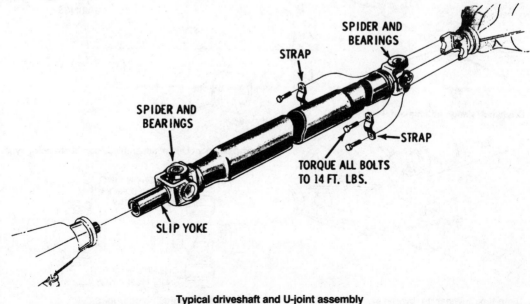

SPIDER AND BEARINGS

STRAP

SPIDER AND BEARINGS

STRAP

TORQUE ALL BOLTS TO 14 FT. LBS.

SLIP YOKE

Typical driveshaft and U-joint assembly

sibly caused by improper lubrication during assembly. U-joints require no periodic maintenance and therefore have no lubrication fittings.

Some driveshafts, generally those in heavy-duty applications, use a damper as part of the slip joint. This vibration damper cannot be serviced separately from the slip joint. If either component goes bad, the two must be replaced as a unit.

REMOVAL AND INSTALLATION

1. Raise the vehicle in the air and support it with jackstands.
2. Mark the relationship of the driveshaft to the differential flange so that they can be reassembled in the same position.
3. Disconnect the rear U-joint by removing the U-bolts or retaining straps.
4. To prevent the loss of the needle bearings, tape the bearing caps in place. If you are replacing the U-joint, this is not necessary.
5. Remove the driveshaft from the transmission by sliding it rearward. There will be some oil leakage from the rear of the transmission. It can be contained by placing a small plastic bag over the rear of the transmission and holding it in place with a rubber band.
6. To install the driveshaft, insert the front yoke into the transmission so that the driveshaft splines mesh with the transmission splines.
7. Using the reference marks made earlier,

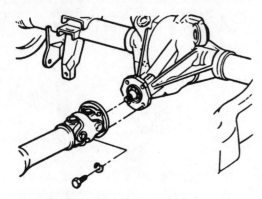

Driveshaft flange attachment

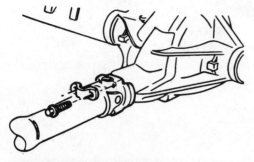

Strap-type retainer on driveshaft

align the driveshaft with the differential flange and secure it with the U-bolts or retaining straps.

U-JOINT OVERHAUL

1964–81 Cleveland Type

1. Refer to the "Driveshaft Removal & Installation" procedures in this section and remove the driveshaft.

NOTE: *NEVER clamp the driveshaft tube in a vise, for this may dent the tube. Support the driveshaft horizontally and clamp on the yokes of the universal joints.*

2. Remove the lock rings from the ends of the trunion yoke.
3. Support the driveshaft in the horizontal position with the base plate of a press, so that the lower ear of the yoke is supported on a piece of 1¼ in. I.D. pipe.
4. Place a socket on the upper bearing cup and press the lower bearing cup out of the yoke ear.

NOTE: *Since the bearing cup cannot be fully*

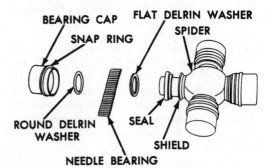

Replacement U-joint assembly, internal snap-ring type

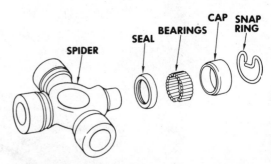

Replacement U-joint assembly, external snap-ring type

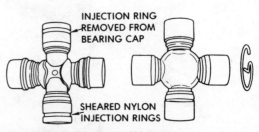

Production (original) type U-joint

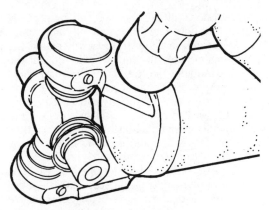

Tapping yoke-to-seat retaining ring

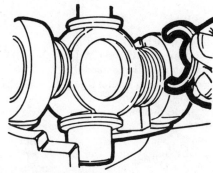

Installing retaining ring

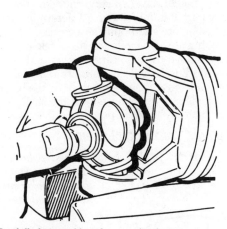

Partially inserted bearing cap (top)

pressed from the yoke ear, grasp the cup in the jaws of a vice and work it from the yoke.

5. Rotate the driveshaft to the opposite bearing cup and press the bearing cup from the yoke, using the same removal procedure.

6. With both bearing cups removed from the yoke, separate the yoke from the driveshaft.

7. Repeat the removal procedures for the other bearing cups.

8. Clean and inspect all of the parts.

NOTE: *If the used universal joints are going to be reinstalled, repack with new grease.*

9. To install, use new universal joints or repack the old ones. Place a bearing cup part way into 1 side of the yoke (place the yoke ear to the bottom).

10. Insert the cross into the yoke so that the trunnion seats freely into the bearing cup.

11. Insert the opposite bearing cup part way into the yoke ear. Install the cross into the cup, making sure that both trunnions are straight and true with the bearing cups.

12. Using an arbor press, press the bearing cups into the yoke, making sure that the cross trunnions are free to turn. Install the bearing retainers.

13. Assemble the other side of the yoke in the same manner.

14. To complete the installation, reverse the removal procedures.

1979 And Later Saginaw Type

1. Refer to the "Driveshaft Removal & Installation" procedures in this section and remove the driveshaft.

NOTE: *Never clamp the driveshaft tube in a vise, for this may dent the tube. Support the driveshaft horizontally and clamp on the yokes of the universal joints.*

2. Support the driveshaft in the horizontal position with the base plate of a press, so that the lower ear of the yoke is supported on a 1⅛ in. socket.

3. Place the cross press tool J-9522-3 on the open horizontal bearing cups and press (shear the plastic retaining ring) the lower bearing cup out of the yoke ear.

NOTE: *If the bearing cup is not completely removed, lift the cross tool and place a spacer tool J-9522-5 between the seal and the bearing cup. Repeat the pressing procedure to drive the bearing cup from the yoke.*

4. Rotate the driveshaft to the opposite bearing cup and press the bearing cup from the yoke.

5. With both bearing cups removed from the yoke, separate the yoke from the driveshaft.

6. Repeat the removal procedures for the other bearing cups.

NOTE: *Since there are no bearing retainer grooves in the production bearing cups, the universal cannot be reused.*

7. Remove the remains of the sheared bearing cups and check for nicks in the yoke ears.

8. To install, use new universal joints and place a bearing cup part way into one side of the yoke (place the yoke ear to the bottom).

9. Insert the cross into the yoke so that the trunnion seat freely into the bearing cup.

10. Insert the opposite bearing cup part way into the yoke ear. Install the cross into the cup, making sure that both trunnions are straight and true with the bearing cups.

11. Using the press, press the bearing cups into the yoke, making sure that the cross trunnions are free to turn.

12. As soon as the bearing retainer groove(s) clears the yoke, stop pressing and install the bearing retainer(s) onto the groove(s).

NOTE: *It may be necessary to strike the yoke with a hammer to align the seating of the bearing retainers.*

13. Assemble the other side of the yoke in the same manner.

14. To complete the installation, reverse the removal procedures.

REAR AXLE

Identification

The rear axle number is located in the right or left axle tube adjacent to the axle carrier (differential). See the "Rear Axle Codes" chart at the end of the chapter for information on determining axle ratio from the letter codes. Antislip differentials are identified by a tab attached to the lower right section of the axle cover.

Determining Axle Ratio

An axle ratio is obtained by dividing the number of teeth on the drive pinion gear into the number of teeth on the ring gear. For instance, on a 4.11 ratio, the driveshaft will turn 4.11 times for every turn of the rear wheel.

The most accurate way to determine the axle ratio is to drain the differential, remove the cover, and count the number of teeth on the ring and pinion.

An easier method is to jack and support the car so that both rear wheels are off the ground. Make a chalk mark on the rear wheel and the driveshaft. Block the front wheels and put the transmission in Neutral. Turn the rear wheel one complete revolution and count the number of turns made by the driveshaft. The number of driveshaft rotations is the axle ratio. More accuracy can be obtained by going more than one tire revolution and dividing the result by the number of tire rotations.

The axle ratio is also identified by the axle serial number prefix on the axle; the axle ratios are listed in dealer's parts books according to prefix number. Some axles have a tag on the cover.

Axle Shaft

Two types of axles are used on these models, the C and the non-C type. Axle shafts in the C type are retained by C-shaped locks, which fit grooves at the inner end of the shaft. Axle shafts in the non-C type are retained by the brake backing plate, which is bolted to the axle housing. Bearings in the C type axle consist of an outer race, bearing rollers, and a roller cage retained by snap-rings. The non-C type axle uses a unit roller bearing (inner race, rollers, and outer race), which is pressed onto the shaft up to a shoulder. When servicing C or non-C type axles, it is imperative to determine the axle type before attempting any service. Before attempting any service to the drive axle or axle shafts, remove the axle carrier cover and visually determine if the axle shafts are retained by C-shaped locks at the inner end, or by the brake backing plate at the outer end. If the shafts are *not* retained by C locks, proceed as follows.

REMOVAL AND INSTALLATION

CAUTION: *Brake shoes contain asbestos, which has been determined to be a cancer causing agent. Never clean the brake surfaces with compressed air! Avoid inhaling any*

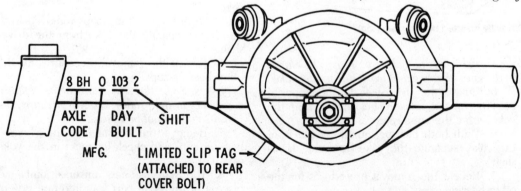

Rear axle identification. Chevrolet manufacturing codes are C Chevrolet-Buffalo; G Chevrolet Gear and Axle

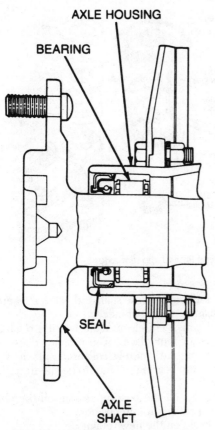

Axle shaft, cross-section

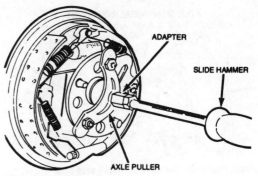

Removing the axle shaft

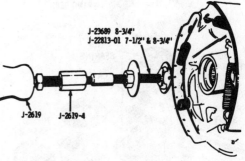

Removing axle bearing with bearing puller

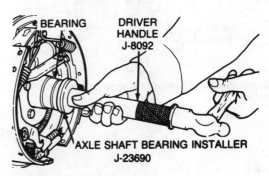

Installing axle bearing

dust from any brake surface! When cleaning brake surfaces, use a commercially available brake cleaning fluid.

1964–79 Non C-Type

Design allows for a maximum axle shaft end-play of 0.022 in., which can be measured with a dial indicator. If end-play is found to be excessive, the bearing should be replaced. Shimming the bearing is not recommended as this

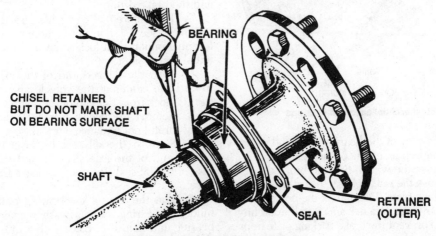

Cutting the bearing retainer, non-C-type

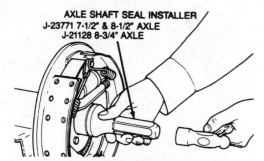

AXLE SHAFT SEAL INSTALLER
J-23771 7-1/2" & 8-1/2" AXLE
J-21128 8-3/4" AXLE

Use a seal installing tool to install axle seal

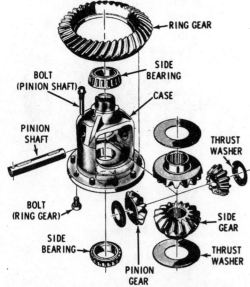

Conventional differential case assembly, all models similar

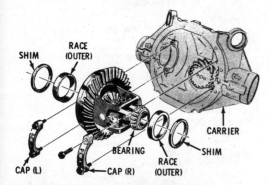

Conventional differential case and bearings

ignores end-play of the bearing itself and could result in improper seating of the bearing.

1. Remove the wheel, tire and brake drum.
2. Remove the nuts holding the retainer plate to the backing plate. Disconnect the brake line.
3. Remove the retainer and install nuts, fingertight, to prevent the brake backing plate from being dislodged.

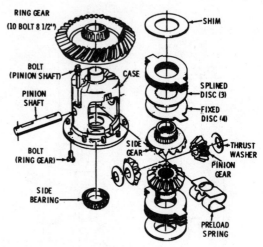

Disc-type limited slip rear axle

4. Pull out the axle shaft and bearing assembly, using a slide hammer.
5. Using a chisel, nick the bearing retainer in three or four places. The retainer does not have to be cut, merely collapsed sufficiently, to allow the bearing retainer to be slid from the shaft.
6. Press off the bearing and install the new one by pressing it into position.
7. Press on the new retainer.

NOTE: *Do not attempt to press the bearing and the retainer on at the same time.*

8. Assemble the shaft and bearing in the housing being sure that the bearing is seated properly in the housing.
9. Install the retainer, drum, wheel and tire. Bleed the brakes.

1979 and Later C-Type

If they *are* retained by C-shaped locks, proceed as follows.

1. Raise the vehicle and remove the wheel and the brake drum.
2. The differential cover has already been removed (see Caution note). Remove the differential pinion shaft lock-screw and the differential pinion shaft.
3. Push the flanged end of the axle shaft toward the center of the vehicle and remove the "C" lock from the end of the shaft.
4. Remove the axle shaft from the housing, being careful not to damage the oil seal.
5. Remove the oil seal by inserting the button end of the axle shaft behind the steel case of the oil seal. Pry the seal loose from the bore.
6. Seat the legs of the bearing puller behind the bearing. Seat a washer against the bearing and hold it in place with a nut. Use a slide hammer to pull the bearing.

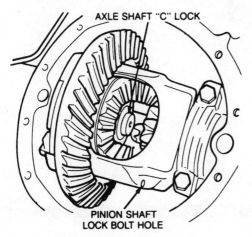

AXLE SHAFT "C" LOCK

PINION SHAFT
LOCK BOLT HOLE

View of the C-lock rear axle

7. Pack the cavity between the seal lips with wheel bearing lubricant and lubricate a new wheel bearing with same.

8. Use a suitable driver and install the bearing until it bottoms against the tube. Install the oil seal.

9. Slide the axle shaft into place. Be sure that the splines on the shaft do not damage the oil seal. Make sure that the splines engage the differential side gear.

10. Install the axle shaft C-lock on the inner end of the axle shaft and push the shaft outward so that the C-lock seats in the differential side gear counterbore.

11. Position the differential pinion shaft through the case and pinions, aligning the hole in the case with the hole for the lockscrew.

12. Use a new gasket and install the carrier cover. Be sure that the gasket surfaces are clean before installing the gasket and cover.

13. Fill the axle with lubricant to the bottom of the filler hole.

14. Install the brake drum and wheels and lower the car. Check for leaks and road test the car.

Suspension and Steering

FRONT SUSPENSION

The front suspension is designed to allow each wheel to compensate for changes in the road surface level without appreciably affecting the opposite wheel. Each wheel is independently connected to the frame by a steering knuckle, ball joint assemblies, and upper and lower control arms. The control arms are specifically designed and positioned to allow the steering knuckles to move in a prescribed three dimensional arc. The front wheels are held in proper relationship to each other by two tie rods which are connected to steering arms on the knuckles and to an intermediate rod.

Coil chassis springs are mounted between the spring housings on the frame or front end sheet metal and the lower control arms. Ride control is provided by double, direct acting, shock absorbers mounted inside the coil springs and attached to the lower control arms by bolts and nuts. The upper portion of each shock absorber extends through the upper control arm frame bracket and is secured with two grommets, two grommet retainers, and a nut.

Side role of the front suspension is controlled by a spring steel stabilizer shaft. It is mounted in rubber bushings which are held to the frame side rails by brackets. The ends of the stabilizer are connected to the lower control arms by link bolts isolated by rubber grommets.

The upper control arm is attached to a cross shaft through isolating rubber bushings. The cross shaft, in turn, is bolted to frame brackets.

A ball joint assembly is riveted to the outer end of the upper arm. It is pre-loaded by a rubber spring to insure proper seating of the ball in the socket. The upper ball joint is attached to the steering knuckle by a torque prevailing nut.

The inner ends of the lower control arm have pressed-in bushings. Bolts, passing through the bushings, attach the arm to the frame. The lower ball joint assembly is a press fit in the arm and attaches to the steering knuckle with a torque prevailing nut.

Rubber grease seals are provided at ball socket assemblies to keep dirt and moisture from entering the joint and damaging bearing surfaces.

Shock Absorbers

TESTING

Visually inspect the shock absorber. If there is evidence of leakage and the shock absorber is covered with oil, the shock is defective and should be replaced.

If there is no sign of excessive leakage (a small amount of weeping is normal) bounce the car at one corner by pressing down on the fender or bumper and releasing. When you have the car bouncing as much as you can, release the fender or bumper. The car should stop bouncing after the first rebound. If the bouncing continues past the center point of the bounce more than once, the shock absorbers are worn and should be replaced.

REMOVAL AND INSTALLATION

1. Raise the car, and with an open end wrench hold the upper stem of the shock absorber from turning. Remove the upper stem retaining nut, retainer and grommet.

2. Remove the two bolts retaining the lower shock absorber pivot to the lower control arm and then pull the shock out through the bottom of the control arm.

3. With the lower retainer and the rubber grommet in place over the upper stem, install the shock (fully extended) back through the lower control arm.

4. Install the upper grommet, retainer and nut onto the upper stem.

5. Hold the upper stem from turning with

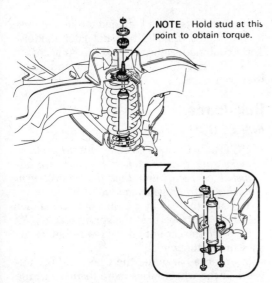

NOTE Hold stud at this point to obtain torque.

Shock absorber mounting locations

an open end wrench and then tighten the retaining nut.

6. Reinstall the retainers on the lower end of the shock.

Coil Springs

CAUTION: *The coil springs are under a considerable amount of tension. Be extremely careful when removing or installing them; they can exert enough force to cause serious injury.*

NOTE: *A coil spring compressor is needed for removal and installation. This tool can usually be rented at tool rental shops.*

REMOVAL AND INSTALLATION

1. Remove the shock absorber. Disconnect the stabilizer bar.

2. Support the car at the frame so the control arms hang free.

3. Support the inner end of the control arm using tool No. J-23028 and a floor jack.

4. Raise the jack enough to take the tension off the lower control arm pivot bolts.

5. Chain the spring to the lower control arm.

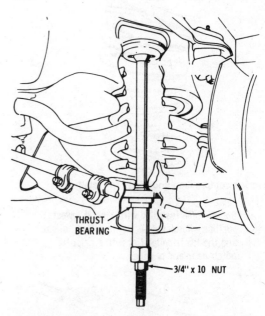

THRUST BEARING

3/4" x 10 NUT

Front coil spring removal. Make sure the lock in the top of the spring compressor is in position whenever the tool is used.

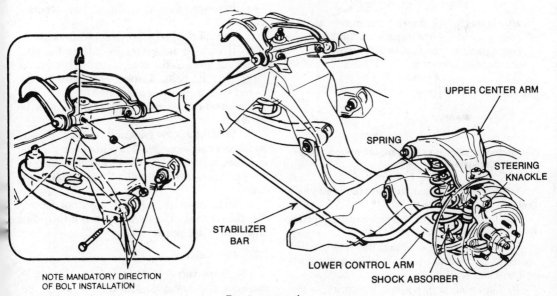

UPPER CENTER ARM

SPRING

STEERING KNUCKLE

STABILIZER BAR

NOTE MANDATORY DIRECTION OF BOLT INSTALLATION

LOWER CONTROL ARM

SHOCK ABSORBER

Front suspension

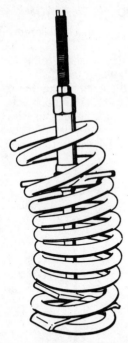

Spring compressed and ready to install

Spring to be installed with tape at lowest position. Bottom of spring is coiled helical, and the top is coiled flat with a gripper notch near end of wire.

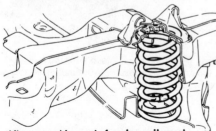

After assembly, end of spring coil must cover all or part of one inspection drain hole. The other hole must be partly exposed or completely uncovered.

Coil spring positioning, 1983 model shown. Other years similar installation

6. Remove first the rear, then the front pivot bolt.

7. Cautiously lower the jack until all spring tension is released.

8. Note the way in which the spring is installed in relation to the drain holes in the control arm and remove it.

9. On installation, position the spring to the control arm and raise it into place.

10. Install the pivot bolts and torque the nuts to 100 ft. lbs. for all 1974 and later models. Torque all models through 1973 to 85 ft. lbs.

11. Replace the shock absorber and stabilizer bar.

Ball Joints

INSPECTION

NOTE: *Before performing this inspection, make sure that the wheel bearings are adjusted correctly and that the control arm bushings are in good condition.*

1. Raise the car by placing the jack under the lower control arm at the spring seat.

2. Raise the car until there is a 1–2 in. clearance under the wheel.

3. Insert a bar under the wheel and pry upward. If the wheel raises more than ⅛ in., the ball joints are worn. Determine whether the upper or lower ball joint is worn by visual inspection while prying on the wheel.

NOTE: *Due to the distribution of forces in the suspension, the lower ball joint is usually the defective joint. Because of this, 1974 and later models are equipped with wear indicators on the lower ball joint. As long as the indicator extends below the ball stud seat, replacement is unnecessary.*

UPPER BALL JOINT REPLACEMENT

1964–70

1. Support the car by placing a jack under the outer end of the lower control arm.

2. Remove the wheel and tire assembly.

3. Remove the cotter pin and nut from the stud.

4. Remove the stud from the steering knuckle.

5. Cut off the ball joint rivets with a chisel.

6. It may be necessary to enlarge the stud attaching holes in the control arm to accept the larger ⁵⁄₁₆ in. bolts. Inspect and clean the tapered hole in the steering knuckle. If the hole is damaged or deformed, the knuckle *must* be replaced.

7. Install the new joint and connect the stud to the steering knuckle. When installing the stud nut, never back off on the nut to align the cotter pin holes; always tighten the nut to the next hole.

8. Replacement ball joints may not include the lube fitting. If not, install a self-threading fitting into the tapped hole.

1971 and Later

1. Raise the vehicle and support securely. Support the lower control arm securely. Remove the tire and wheel.

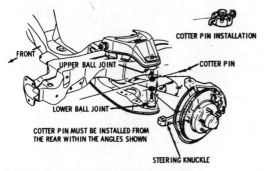

Steering knuckle cotter pin installation

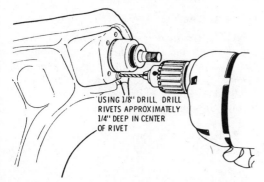

Drill the upper ball joint rivets—1971 and later

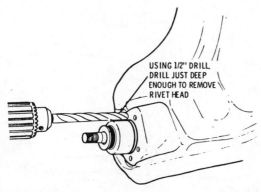

Use a ½ in. drill to drill the upper ball joint rivet heads, 1971 and later

2. Remove the upper ball stud cotter pin and loosen the ball stud nut *just one turn.*

3. Locate the tool No. J-23742 between the upper and lower ball joints and press the joints out of the steering knuckle. Remove the tool.

4. Remove the ball joint stud nut, and separate the joint from the steering knuckle. Lift the upper arm up and place a block of wood between the frame and the arm to support it.

5. With the control arm in the raised position, drill a hole ¼ in. deep into each rivet. Use a ⅛ in. drill bit.

6. Use a ½ in. drill bit and drill off the heads of each rivet.

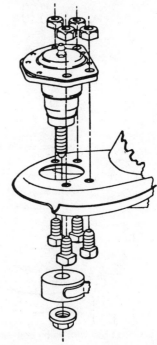

When installing the new upper ball joints, make sure that the nuts are on top (1971 and later)

7. Punch out the rivets using a small punch and then remove the ball joint.

8. Install the new ball joint using fasteners that meet Chevrolet specifications. Bolts should come in from the bottom with the nuts going on top. Torque to 10 ft. lbs.

9. Turn the ball stud cotter pin hole to the fore and aft position. Remove the block of wood from between the upper control arm and frame.

10. Clean and inspect the steering knuckle hole. Replace the steering knuckle if any out of roundness is noted.

11. Insert the ball joint stud into the steering knuckle then install and torque the stud nut to 60 ft. lbs. Install a new cotter pin. *If nut must be turned to align cotter pin holes, tighten it further. Do not back off!*

12. Install a lube fitting, and fill the joint with fresh grease.

13. Remove the lower control arm support and lower the car.

LOWER BALL JOINT REPLACEMENT
1964–1970

1. Raise the car and support securely. Support the lower control arm with a floor jack.

2. Remove the wheel. If the vehicle has disc brakes, remove the caliper assembly.

3. Remove the lower ball stud. Then, using a tool designed for such work, press the ball stud out of the steering knuckle. Wire the

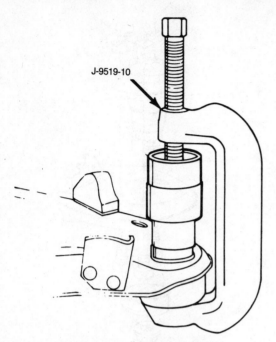

J-9519-10

Pressing out lower ball joint using ball joint tool

steering knuckle out of the way so you'll have more room.

4. Press the joint out of the control arm with a tool designed for that purpose.

5. Start the replacement joint into the control arm with the air vent in the rubber boot facing inboard.

6. Set the joint in the control arm, pressing it in with a tool designed for that purpose.

7. Install the stud into the steering knuckle, and install the attaching nut and new cotter pin.

8. Reinstall the caliper assembly (as necessary) and wheel remove the jack supporting the control arm, and lower the car.

1971 and Later

NOTE: *On models equipped with the wear indicating ball joint, Chevrolet recommends replacement of both upper and lower ball joints if only the lower ball joint is bad.*

1. Raise the vehicle and support it securely. Support the lower control arm with a jack.

2. Remove the lower ball stud cotter pin, and loosen the ball stud nut just one turn.

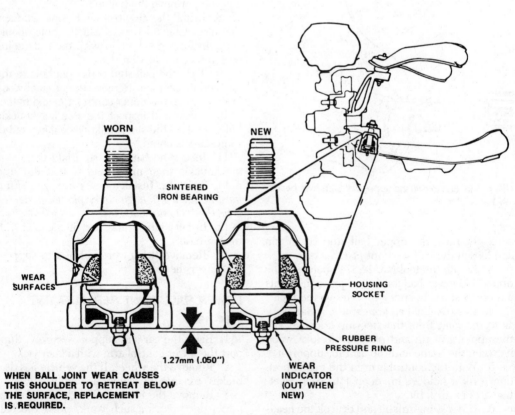

WORN

NEW

SINTERED
IRON BEARING

WEAR
SURFACES

HOUSING
SOCKET

RUBBER
PRESSURE RING

1.27mm (.050")

WHEN BALL JOINT WEAR CAUSES THIS SHOULDER TO RETREAT BELOW THE SURFACE, REPLACEMENT IS REQUIRED.

WEAR INDICATOR (OUT WHEN NEW)

Lower ball joint wear indicator—1974 and later

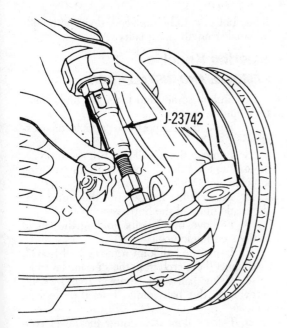

Disconnecting the lower ball joint—1980 shown, others similar

3. Install the tool No. J-23742 between the two ball studs, and press the stud downward in the steering knuckle. Then, remove the stud nut.

4. Pull the tire outward and at the same time upward, with your hands on the bottom (of the tire), to free the steering knuckle from the ball stud. Then, remove the wheel.

5. Lift up on the upper control arm and place a block of wood between it and the frame. Be careful not to put any tension on the brake hose in doing this.

6. Press the ball joint out of the lower control arm with a tool made for that purpose. You may have to disconnect the tie rod at the steering knuckle to do this.

7. To install, position the new ball joint, with the vent in the rubber boot facing inward, onto the lower control arm. Press the joint fully into the control arm with the tool No. J-9519-10 and J-9519-9.

8. Turn the ball stud cotter pin hole so it is fore and aft.

9. Remove the block of wood holding the upper control arm out of the way, and inspect the tapered hole in the steering knuckle. Remove any dirt from the hole. If the hole is out of round or there is other noticeable damage, replace the entire steering knuckle.

10. Insert the ball joint stud into the steering knuckle, install the stud nut, and torque it to 83 ft. lbs. Install a new cotter pin, aligning cotter pin holes in the nut and stud *only* through

further tightening. *Do not loosen the nut from the torque position.*

11. Install a lube fitting and lube the joint. Reconnect the tie rod (as necessary), install the wheel, remove the jack supporting the lower control arm and lower the car.

Stabilizer Bar
REMOVAL AND INSTALLATION

1. Raise and support the front of the vehicle on jackstands.

2. Disconnect the stabilizer link bolts at the lower control arms.

3. Remove the stabilizer-to-frame clamps.

4. Remove the stabilizer bar.

5. To install, reverse the removal procedures. Torque the stabilizer-to-lower control arm bolts to 13 ft. lbs. and the stabilizer-to-frame bolts to 24 ft. lbs.

Upper Control Arm
REMOVAL AND INSTALLATION

1. Raise the vehicle on a hoist.

2. Support the outer end of the lower control arm with a jack.

3. Remove the wheel.

4. Separate the upper ball joint from the steering knuckle as described above under "Upper Ball Joint Replacement."

5. Remove the control arm shaft-to-frame nuts.

NOTE: *Tape the shims together and identify them so that they can be installed in the positions from which they were removed.*

6. Remove the bolts which attach the control arm shaft to the frame and remove the control arm. Note the positions of the bolts.

7. Install in the reverse order of removal. Make sure that the shaft-to-frame bolts are installed in the same position they were in before removal and that the shims are in their original positions. Use free running nuts (not locknuts) to pull serrated bolts through the frame. Then

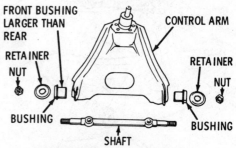

Upper control arm components (1983 shown)

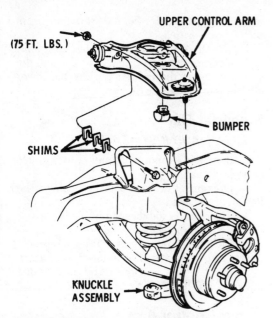

(75 FT. LBS.)

UPPER CONTROL ARM

BUMPER

SHIMS

KNUCKLE ASSEMBLY

Typical upper control arm installation

install the locknuts. Tighten the thinner shim pack first. After the car has been lowered to the ground, bounce the front end to center the bushings and then tighten the bushing collar bolts to 45 ft. lbs. Tighten the shaft-to-frame bolts to 80 ft. lbs. on models through 1973; 1974 and later models require 90 ft. lbs. The control arm shaft nuts are tightened to 65 ft. lbs. through 1974; on 1975 and later models tighten to 75 ft. lbs.

Lower Control Arm

REMOVAL AND INSTALLATION

1. Remove the spring as described earlier.
2. Remove the ball stud from the steering knuckle.
3. Remove the control arm pivot bolts and the control arm.
4. To install, reverse the above procedure.

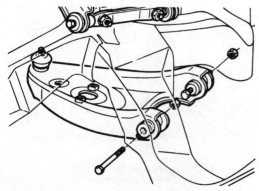

View of the lower control arm attachment bolts

If any bolts are to be replaced, do so with bolts of equal strength and quality.

Steering Knuckle

REMOVAL AND INSTALLATION

1. Siphon some fluid from the brake master cylinder.
2. Raise the support the vehicle on jackstands.
3. Remove the wheel and tire assembly.
4. Remove the caliper from the steering knuckle and support on a wire.
5. Remove the grease cup, the cotter pin, the castle nut and the hub assembly.
6. Remove the 3 bolts holding the shield to the steering knuckle.
7. Using the ball joint removal tool J-6627, disconnect the tie rod from the steering knuckle.
8. Using ball joint removal tool J-23742, disconnect the ball joints from the steering knuckle.
9. Place a floor jack under the lower control arm (near the spring seat) and disconnect the ball joint from the steering knuckle.
10. Raise the upper control arm and disconnect the ball joint from the steering knuckle.
11. Remove the steering knuckle from the vehicle.
12. To install, reverse the removal procedures. Torque the upper ball joint-to-steering knuckle nut to 65 ft. lbs., the lower ball joint-to-steering knuckle nut to 90 ft. lbs. and the tie rod-to-steering knuckle nut to 40 ft. lbs. Adjust the wheel bearing and refill the master cylinder.

Front End Alignment

CAMBER

Camber is the inward or outward tilting of the front wheels from the vertical. When the wheels tilt outward at the top, the camber is said to be positive (+). When the wheels tilt inward at the top, the camber is said to be negative (−). The amount of tilt is measured in degrees from the vertical and this measurement is called the camber angle.

CASTER

Caster is the tilting of the front steering axis either forward or backward from the vertical. A backward tilt is said to be positive (+) and a forward tilt is said to be negative (−).

TOE-IN

Toe-in is the turning in of the front wheels. The actual amount of toe-in is normally only a fraction of a degree. The purpose of toe-in is to ensure parallel rolling of the front wheels. (Excessive toe-in or toe-out will cause tire wear.)

Wheel Alignment Specifications

Year	Model	Caster Range (deg)	Caster Pref Setting (deg)	Camber Range (deg)	Camber Pref Setting (deg)	Toe-In (in.)	Steering Axis Inclination (deg)	Wheel Pivot Ratio Inner Wheel	Wheel Pivot Ratio Outer Wheel
1964	All	¼N to ¾P	¼P	¼ to 1¼P	¾P	0 to ⅛	8¼	20	18¾
1965	All	1½ to ½N	1N	¼N to ¾P	¼P	1/16 to 3/16	8	20	18¾
1966	All	1½ to ½N	1N	0 to 1P	½P	⅛ to ¼	8	20	18¾
1967	All	1½ to ½N ①	1N	0 to 1P	½P	⅛ to ¼	8¼	20	18¾
1968–69	All	1½ to ½N ①	1N	0 to 1P	½P	⅛ to ¼	8¼	20	18½
1970–71	Chevelle, Monte Carlo	1½ to ½N ①	1N	0 to 1P	½P	⅛ to ¼	7¾ to 8¾	20	NA
1972	Chevelle	1½ to ½N	1N	¼ to 1¼P	¾P	⅛ to ¼	7¾ to 8¾	NA	NA
	Monte Carlo	½N to ½P	0	¼ to 1¼P	¾P	⅛ to ¼	7¾ to 8¾	NA	NA
1973	Chevelle	1¾ to ¾N	1¼N	½ to 1½P	1P ②	⅛ to ¼	9½	NA	NA
	Monte Carlo	4¼ to 5¼P	4¾P	½ to 1½P	1P ②	0 to ⅛	9½	NA	NA
1974	Chevelle ③	1½ to ½N	1N	½ to 1½P	1P	0 to ⅛	10½	NA	NA
	Chevelle ④	½N to ½P	0	½ to 1½P	1P	0 to ⅛	10½	NA	NA
	Monte Carlo	4½ to 5½P	5	½ to 1½P	1P	0 to ⅛	10½	NA	NA
1975–77	Chevelle	1½ to 2½P	2P ⑤	½ to 1½P ②	1P	0 to ⅛	9¾	NA	NA
	Monte Carlo	4½ to 5½P	5P	¼ to 1½P ②	1P	0 to ⅛	9¾	NA	NA
1978–81	Malibu, Monte Carlo	½ to 1½P	1P	0 to 1P	½P	1/16 to 3/16	7.86	NA	NA
1983–84	Malibu, El Camino Monte Carlo	½ to 1½P ⑥	1P	0 to 1P	½P	1/16 to 3/16	7.86	NA	NA
1985–86	Monte Carlo	½ to 1½P ⑥	1P	0 to 1P	½P	1/16 to 3/16	7.86	NA	NA

① SS 396 and El Camino—0 to 1P
② Left wheel given; right wheel is ½P ± ½
③ Manual steering
④ Power steering

⑤ Radial tires—1P ± ½ with belted tires
⑥ Power steering: 2½P to 3½P, 3P
N Negative   P Positive
NA Not available

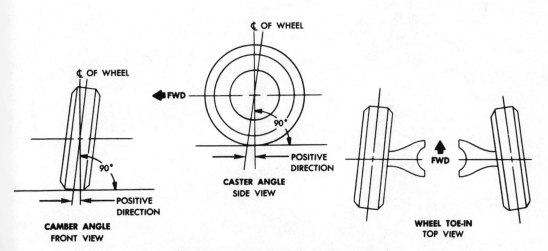

CAMBER ANGLE
FRONT VIEW

CASTER ANGLE
SIDE VIEW

WHEEL TOE-IN
TOP VIEW

Description of the camber, caster and toe-in

PIVOT SHAFT INBOARD OF FRAME

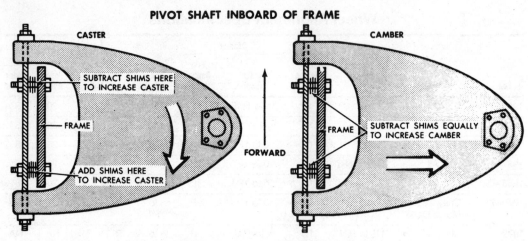

Adjustment of the caster and camber

CASTER/CAMBER ADJUSTMENT

Caster and camber can be adjusted by moving the position of the upper strut mount assembly. Moving the mount forward/rearward adjusts caster. Movement inboard/outboard adjusts camber.

TOE-IN ADJUSTMENT

1. Loosen the clamp bolts at each end of the steering tie rod adjustable sleeves.
2. With the steering wheel set straight ahead, turn the adjusting sleeves to obtain the proper adjustment.
3. When the adjustment has been com-

pleted, check to see that the number of threads showing on each end of the sleeve are equal. Also check that tie rod end housings are at the right angles to the steering arm.

REAR SUSPENSION

The rear axle assembly is attached to the frame through a link-type suspension system. Two rubber bushed lower control arms mounted between the axle assembly and the frame maintain fore and aft relationship of the axle assembly to the chassis. Two rubber bushed upper control arms, angularly mounted with respect to the centerline of the car, control

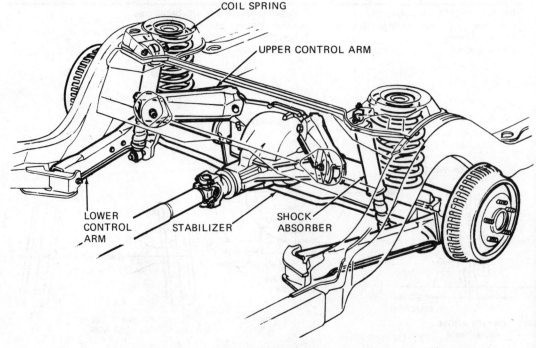

Rear suspension

driving and braking torque and sideways movement of the axle assembly. The rigid axle holds the rear wheels in proper alignment.

The upper control arms are shorter than the lower arms, causing the differential housing to "rock" or tilt forward on compression. This rocking or tilting lowers the rear propeller shaft to make possible the use of a lower tunnel in the rear floor pan area.

The rear upper control arms control drive forces, side sway and pinion nose angle. Pinion angle adjustment can greatly affect car smoothness and must be maintained as specified.

The rear chassis springs are located between brackets on the axle tube and spring seats in the frame. The springs are held in the seat pilots by the weight of the car and by the shock absorbers which limit axle movement during rebound.

Ride control is provided by two identical direct double acting shock absorbers angle-mounted between brackets attached to the axle housing and the rear spring seats. Shock absorbers are located behind the axle housing on pre-1968 models. Beginning in 1968, the shock absorbers were staggered to resist axle hop; the right shock in front of the axle and the left behind the axle.

Springs

REMOVAL AND INSTALLATION

1964–1972

1. Raise the car and support it at the frame with stands.
2. Position a hydraulic jack under the axle and support it.
3. Disconnect the shock absorber at the bottom on the side where the spring is being replaced.
4. Lower the axle to the bottom of its travel, and then pry the lower end of the spring over the axle retainer.
5. Remove the spring and its insulator.
NOTE: *On 1964–66 cars, the spring retainer must be removed to remove the spring. It is fastened to the housing with a nut and bolt.*
6. Install the spring in the frame seat with its rubber insulation.
7. Pry the spring into the axle housing retainer. Install the retainer on 1964–66 cars and torque the bolt to 45–55 ft. lbs.
8. Raise the axle and install the shock absorber. Tighten the shock absorber nuts to 12 ft. lbs.

1973–81

1. Raise the car and support it at the frame with stands.

2. Position a hydraulic jack under the axle and support it.
3. Disconnect the shock absorber at the bottom on the side where the spring is being replaced.
4. Disconnect the brake hydraulic line at the junction block located on the axle housing.
5. Disconnect the upper control arm at the axle.
6. Lower the axle to the bottom of its travel, then pry the lower end of the spring over the axle retainer and remove the spring and its insulator.
7. Install the spring in its frame seat with its rubber insulator.
8. Pry the lower end of the spring over the vertical flange of the axle bracket spring seat.
9. Position the spring so that the end of the upper coil points toward the right-side of the car.
10. Raise the axle and install the shock absorber. Tighten the nut to 12 ft. lbs.
11. Connect the upper control arm to the axle housing.
12. Connect the brake hydraulic lines and bleed the brakes.
13. Remove the jack and lower the car.

Shock Absorbers

TESTING

If the ride of your car has become increasingly bouncy or fluid leakage can be observed on the shock absorber, it's time to replace them. Push up and down on the rear bumper several times and then let go. If the car continues to move up and down the shocks aren't doing their job.

REMOVAL AND INSTALLATION

1. Jack the rear of the car up and support the axle.

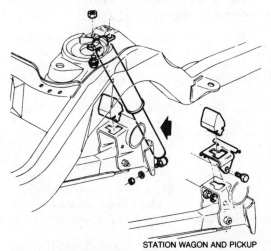

STATION WAGON AND PICKUP

Rear shock absorber mounting

2. Remove the two upper mounting bolts and disconnect the air line if equipped with superlift shock absorbers.

3. While holding the stud hex with a wrench, remove the lower mounting nut.

4. Remove the shock absorber from the car.

5. Install the upper mounting bolts hand-tight.

6. Install the lower stud into the housing bracket and loosely install the nut.

7. Tighten the two upper bolts to 12 ft. lbs.

8. While holding the stud hex, tighten the lower nut to 60 ft. lbs.

9. On superlift equipped cars, install the air hose and add approximately 10 psi of air.

10. Lower the car.

Rear Lower Control Arm
REMOVAL AND INSTALLATION

NOTE: *Remove and install ONLY one lower control arm at a time. If both arms are removed at the same time, the axle could roll or slip sideways, making installation of the arms very difficult.*

1. Raise and support the rear of the vehicle on jackstands under the rear axle.

NOTE: *If equipped with a stabilizer bar, remove it.*

2. Remove the control arm attaching fasteners and the control arm.

3. To install, reverse the removal procedures. Torque the control arm-to-frame nut to 70 ft. lbs. and the control arm-to-axle bolt to 79 ft. lbs. If equipped with a stabilizer bar, torque the mounting fasteners to 35 ft. lbs.

NOTE: *Before torquing the fasteners, the weight of the vehicle must be resting on its wheels.*

Rear Upper Control Arm
REMOVAL AND INSTALLATION

NOTE: *Remove and install ONLY one lower control arm at a time. If both arms are removed at the same time, the axle could roll or slip sideways, making installation of the arms very difficult.*

1. Raise and support the rear of the vehicle on jackstands under the axle.

2. Remove the upper control arm nut at the axle.

NOTE: *To remove the mounting bolt from the axle, it may be necessary to rock the axle. On some models, it may be necessary to remove the lower shock absorber stud to provide clearance for the upper control arm removal.*

3. Remove the upper control arm-to-frame nut and bolt, then the control arm.

4. To install, reverse the removal procedures. Torque the upper control arm-to-axle nut to 70 ft. lbs., the upper control arm-to-axle bolt to 79 ft. lbs. and the upper control arm-to-frame bolt to 70 ft. lbs.

Stabilizer Bar
REMOVAL AND INSTALLATION

1. Raise and support the rear of the vehicle on jackstands under the frame.

2. Support the axle assembly with a floor jack.

3. Remove the stabilizer bar-to-lower control arm bolts and the stabilizer bar.

4. To install, reverse the removal procedures. Torque the stabilizer bar-to-lower control arm to 35 ft. lbs.

STEERING

All models have recirculating ball type steering. Forces are transmitted from a worm to a sector gear through ball bearings. Relay type steering linkage is used with a pitman arm connected to one end of the relay rod. The other end of the relay rod is connected to an idle arm which is attached to the frame. The relay rod is connected to the steering arms by two adjustable tie rods. Most models are equipped with a collapsible steering column designed to collapse on impact, thereby reducing possible chest injuries during accidents. When making any repairs to the steering column or steering wheel, excessive pressure or force capable of collapsing the column must be avoided. Beginning 1969, the ignition lock, ignition switch, and an antitheft system were built into each column. The key cannot be removed unless the transmission is in "Park" (automatic) or Reverse (manual) with the switch in the "Lock" position. Placing the lock in the "Lock" position activates a rod within the column which locks the steering wheel and shift lever. On floorshift models, a back drive linkage between the floorshift and the column produces the same effect.

Steering Wheel

CAUTION: *Most steering columns are collapsible. When replacing the wheel, do not hammer or exert any force against the column.*

REMOVAL AND INSTALLATION
Standard Wheel
CHEVELLE—1964–69

1. Pry out the center cap and retainer.

2. Remove the three receiving cup screws

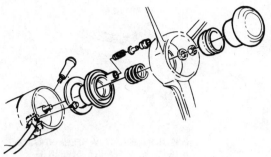

Steering wheel and horn components—1964–69

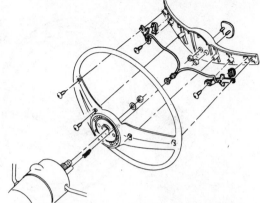

1969 deluxe and 1970–72 standard steering wheel

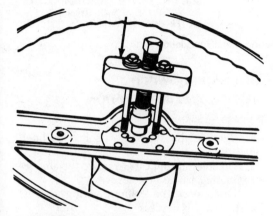

Steering wheel puller in position

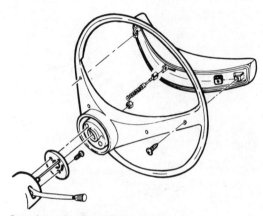

Steering wheel and horn—1973–74

and remove the cup, belleville spring, bushing, and pivot ring.

3. Remove the steering wheel nut and washer.

4. Mark the wheel-to-shaft relationship, and then remove the wheel with a puller.

5. Install the wheel on the shaft, aligning the previously made marks. Tighten the nut to 35 ft. lbs.

6. Install the belleville spring (dished side up), pivot ring, bushing, and receiving cup. Install the center cap and reconnect the battery.

NOTE: *Removal of the 1970 padded steering wheel is similar to the above.*

CHEVELLE—1969 DELUXE WHEEL AND ALL MODELS STANDARD WHEEL—1970 AND LATER

1. Remove the four trim retaining screws from behind the wheel.

2. Lift the trim off and pull the horn wires from the signal cancelling cam.

3. On 1975 models, remove the snap ring.

4. Remove the steering wheel nut.

5. Mark the wheel-to-shaft relationship, and then remove the wheel with a puller tool No. J-2927.

6. Install the wheel on the shaft, aligning the previously made marks. Tighten the nut to 30 ft. lbs.

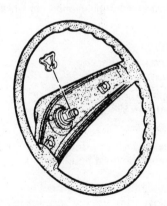

Steering wheel—1975

7. On 1975 models, install the snap-ring.

8. Insert the horn wires into the cancelling cam.

9. Install the center trim and reconnect the battery cable.

NOTE: *The 1967–69 simulated wood wheel does not require pulling for removal. Remove the center cap and horn contact assembly. The wheel is held to the hub by phil-*

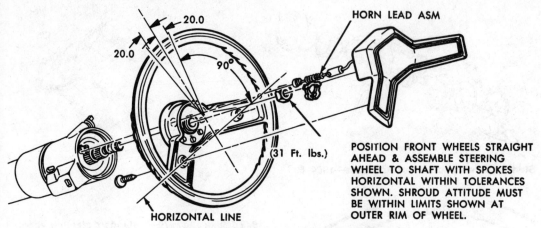

POSITION FRONT WHEELS STRAIGHT
AHEAD & ASSEMBLE STEERING
WHEEL TO SHAFT WITH SPOKES
HORIZONTAL WITHIN TOLERANCES
SHOWN. SHROUD ATTITUDE MUST
BE WITHIN LIMITS SHOWN AT
OUTER RIM OF WHEEL.

1980 and later standard steering wheel, installation

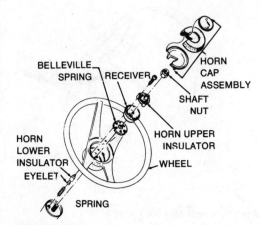

Exploded view of the cushioned rim wheel (1971 and later)

lips screws. Reverse the disassembly procedure to install the wheel.

Cushioned Rim Wheel

1971 AND LATER

1. Disconnect the battery ground cable.
2. Remove the horn button cap. Remove the snap ring.
3. Remove the steering wheel nut.
4. Remove the upper horn insulator, receiver, and belleville spring.
5. Install the wheel puller, turn the puller bolt clockwise, and remove the wheel.
6. Place the turn signal lever in a Neutral position, position the wheel to the shaft, and tighten the nut.
7. Position the horn lower insulator, eyelet, and spring in the horn contact tower. Install the belleville spring, receiver, and horn upper insulator.
8. Install the horn button cap and connect the battery cable.

Turn Signal Switch

REMOVAL AND INSTALLATION

Chevelle—1964–66

1. Remove the steering wheel as outlined above.
2. On column shift cars, remove the shift lever retaining pin and the lever.
3. Disconnect the column wiring harness from the chassis harness.
4. Remove the lower trim plate and the upper mast jacket clamp. On automatic cars, remove the indicator retaining screw and the pointer.
5. Remove the three turn signal-to-housing screws.
6. Remove the turn signal switch, housing, and shift bowl from the steering column. Separate the switch from the wiring harness.
7. Install using the reverse of the removal procedure.
NOTE: *Two different switch assemblies are used. Removal procedures are the same, but they are not interchangeable.*

1967–68

1. Disconnect the battery ground cable.
2. Disconnect the signal switch wiring from the wiring harness under the instrument panel.
3. Remove the steering wheel.
4. If applicable, remove the shift lever.
5. Remove the four-way flasher lever arm.
6. If equipped with an automatic transmission, remove the dial indicator housing and lamp assembly from the column.
7. Remove the mast jacket lower trim cover.
8. Remove the C-ring and washers from the upper steering shaft.
9. Loosen the signal switch screws, move the switch counterclockwise, and remove it from the mast jacket.

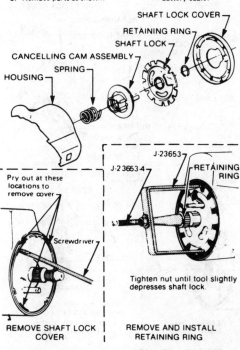

1. REMOVE AND INSTALL LOCK PLATE AND/OR CANCELLING CAM

REMOVE	INSTALL
1. Disconnect negative battery cable.	1. Install parts as shown.
2. Refer to STEERING WHEEL - Removal.	2. Refer to STEERING WHEEL - Installation.
3. Remove parts as shown.	3. Connect negative battery cable.

SHAFT LOCK COVER
RETAINING RING
SHAFT LOCK
CANCELLING CAM ASSEMBLY
SPRING
HOUSING

Pry out at these locations to remove cover
Screwdriver
J-23653
J-23653-4
RETAINING RING

Tighten nut until tool slightly depresses shaft lock.

REMOVE SHAFT LOCK COVER | REMOVE AND INSTALL RETAINING RING

2. REMOVE AND INSTALL TURN SIGNAL SWITCH

REMOVE	INSTALL
1. Remove parts as shown.	1. Install parts as shown.

SWITCH ACTUATOR ARM ASSEMBLY
SCREW
SCREW
TURN SIGNAL SWITCH ASSEMBLY
HOUSING
BOWL
WIRE PROTECTOR

Turn signal switch removal, standard steering column—1980 shown

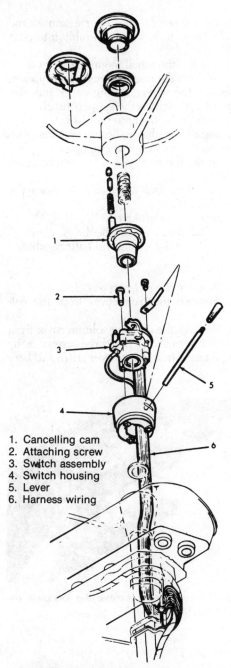

1. Cancelling cam
2. Attaching screw
3. Switch assembly
4. Switch housing
5. Lever
6. Harness wiring

Turn signal assembly—1964–66

10. Remove the upper support bracket assembly.

CAUTION: *Support the column; do not allow it to be suspended by the lower reinforcement only.*

11. Remove the wiring harness protector and clip, and then reinstall the support bracket and finger-tighten the bolts.

12. Remove the shift lever bowl from the mast jacket and disconnect it from the wiring harness.

13. Remove the three lockplate screws, being careful not to lose the three springs.

14. Disassemble the switch and upper bearing housing from the switch cover.

15. Insert the upper bearing housing assembly and switch assembly into the switch cover.

16. Align the switch and bearing housing with

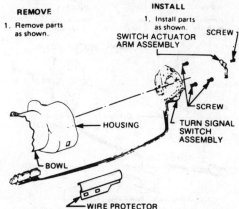

1. REMOVE AND INSTALL SHAFT LOCK AND/OR CANCELLING CAM

REMOVE	INSTALL
1. Disconnect negative battery cable.	1. Install parts as shown.
2. Refer to STEERING WHEEL - Removal.	2. Refer to STEERING WHEEL - Installation.
3. Remove parts as shown.	3. Connect negative battery cable.

SHAFT LOCK COVER
RETAINING RING
SHAFT LOCK
CANCELLING CAM ASSEMBLY
SPRING
COVER
SHAFT LOCK RETAINER
CARRIER SNAP RING RETAINER
SPACERS
RETRACTED STRG SHAFT BUMPER
*

*ON TELESCOPE STEERING ONLY

Pry out at these locations to remove cover
Screwdriver
REMOVE SHAFT LOCK COVER

J-23653
J-23653-4
RETAINING RING
Tighten nut until tool slightly depresses shaft lock
REMOVE AND INSTALL RETAINING RING

2. REMOVE AND INSTALL TURN SIGNAL SWITCH

REMOVE	INSTALL
1. Remove parts as shown.	1. Install parts as shown.

SIGNAL SWITCH ARM
SCREW
SCREW
COVER
TURN SIGNAL SWITCH
BOWL
WIRE PROTECTOR

Turn signal switch removal, adjustable column

the mounting holes in the cover and install the three mounting screws.

17. Slide the springs onto the screws and install the lockplate over the springs. Tighten the screws three turns into the lockplate.

18. Position the switch wire through the shift lever bowl and place the upper end assembly on top of the bowl.

19. Place the shift lever down and signal switch assembly on top of the jacket, inserting the lockplate tangs into the slots.

20. Push down on the cover assembly and turn clockwise to lock the assembly into position.

21. Tighten the signal mounting screws.

22. Remove the mast jacket support bracket, then install the wiring, wiring cover and clip, and install and tighten the support bracket.

23. Install a C-ring onto the shaft.

24. Install the dial indicator and lamp assembly on the column if so equipped.

25. Install the mast jacket lower trim cover if so equipped.

26. Install the four-way flasher knob and the turn signal lever.

27. Install the shift lever.

28. Install the steering wheel.

29. Connect the wiring and battery cable.

1969 and Later

1. Remove the steering wheel.

2. Remove the trim cover from the column.

3. Remove the steering column cover from the shaft by removing the three screws or by prying it out with a screwdriver (1976 and later models).

Using a special tool to remove the lockplate retaining ring (1969 and later)

Removing the turn signal switch assembly

4. Using a compressing tool No. J-23653, compress the lockplate. With the plate compressed, pry out the snap-ring from its shaft groove and throw away.

5. Slide the cancelling cam, spring, and washer off the shaft.

6. Remove the turn signal lever.

7. Push the four-way flasher knob in and unscrew it.

8. Remove the three switch mounting screws.

9. Pull the switch connector out of the bracket and wrap it with tape to prevent it from snagging.

10. If applicable, place tilt columns in the low and remove the harness cover.

11. Remove the switch.

12. To install, reverse the removal procedure, being sure to use only the specified nuts and bolts. Using screws that are slightly too long could prevent the column from collapsing during a collision.

13. When installing the cancelling cam, spring, and washer, make sure that the switch is in neutral and that the flasher knob is out.

14. Use a compressing tool No. J-23653, compress the lockplate and install a new snap-ring.

Ignition Switch

REMOVAL AND INSTALLATION

The switch is located inside the channel section of the brake pedal support and is completely inaccessible without first lowering the steering column. The switch is actuated by a rod and rack assembly. A gear on the end of the lock cylinder engages the toothed upper end of the rod.

1. Support and lower the steering column.

2. Place the ignition switch in the OFF-UNLOCKED position and move the actuating rod two detents from the top.

3. Remove the two mounting screws and the ignition switch assembly.

4. Before installing, place the new switch in the OFF-UNLOCKED position and make sure the ignition lock cylinder and the actuating rod are in the OFF-UNLOCKED (2nd detent from the top) position.

5. Install the actuating rod into the switch, mount the switch to the column and torque the mounting screws to 3 ft. lbs.

NOTE: *Use only the specified screws since over length screws could impair the collapsibility of the column.*

6. Install the steering column and torque the steering column-to-bracket nuts to 25 ft. lbs.

Lock Cylinder

REMOVAL AND INSTALLATION

1968 and Later

1. Remove the steering wheel and the directional signal switch. It is not necessary to pull the wire harness out of the column. See the applicable procedures above.

2. Place the lock cylinder in "Lock" (up to 1970), or "Run" (1971 and later).

3. Insert a small screwdriver into the turn signal housing slot. Keeping the screwdriver to the right side of the slot, break the housing flash loose and depress the spring latch at the lower end of the lock cylinder. Remove the lock cylinder.

NOTE: *Considerable force may be necessary to break this casting flash, but be careful not to damage any other parts. When ordering a new lock cylinder, specify a cylinder assembly. This will save assembling the cylinder washer, sleeve, and adaptor.*

Depressing the lock cylinder retainer (1969 and later)

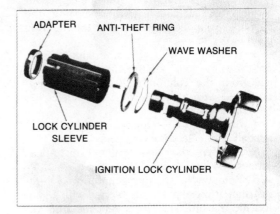

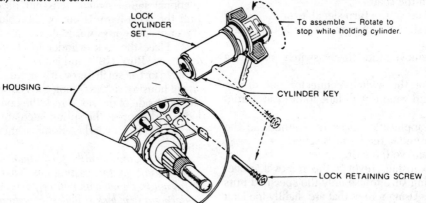

DISASSEMBLE

1. Place lock in "run".

2. Remove lock plate, turn signal switch and buzzer switch (see service manual.)

3. Remove screw & lock cylinder. **CAUTION:** *If screw is dropped on removal, it could fall into the column, requiring complete disassembly to retrieve the screw.*

ASSEMBLE

1. Rotate as shown, align cylinder key with keyway in housing.

2. Push lock all the way in.

3. Install screw. Tighten to 4.5 N·m for regular columns— 2.5 N·m for adjustable columns.

Lock cylinder removal—1979 shown, others similiar

4. To install, hold the lock cylinder sleeve and rotate the knob clockwise against the stop. Insert the cylinder into the housing, aligning the key and keyway. On 1969–76 cars hold a 0.070 in. drill between the lock bezel and the housing. On 1977 and later cars, push the cylinder into abutment of cylinder and sector. Rotate the cylinder counterclockwise, maintaining a light pressure until the drive section of the cylinder mates with the sector. Push in until the snap-ring pops into the grooves. Remove the drill. Check the operation of the cylinder. Install the direction signal switch and steering wheel.

Steering Column
REMOVAL AND INSTALLATION

1. Disconnect the negative battery cable.
NOTE: *If necessary to remove the steering wheel, be sure to use a steering wheel puller.*
2. Remove the nut/bolt from the upper intermediate shaft coupling, then separate the coupling from the lower end of the steering column.
3. If equipped with a column mounted shifter, disconnect the transmission control linkage from the column shift tube levers. If equipped with a floor shifter, disconnect the backdrive linkage.
4. At the steering column assembly, disconnect all of the electrical connectors.
5. Remove the floor pan cover-to-floor screws, the floor seal and the cover.
6. Remove the steering column bracket-to-instrument panel nuts. If equipped with an automatic transmission, disconnect the shift position indicator pointer.

NOTE: *Once the steering column has been removed from the vehicle, be careful not to drop it (especially on it's end), lean on it or damage it in any way; the column is very susceptible to damage.*
7. To install, reverse the removal procedures.

Manual Steering Gear
REMOVAL AND INSTALLATION

NOTE: *On 1964–67 models, remove the stabilizer bar-to-frame mounting brackets. Unbolt the left front bumper bracket and brace from the frame after marking their location.*
1. Raise and support the front of the vehicle on jackstands.
2. Disconnect the steering shaft coupling.

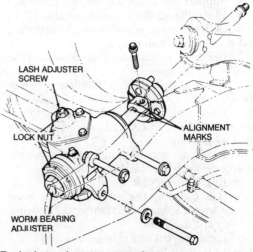

Typical steering gear mounting

3. Remove the pitman arm with a puller after marking the arm-to-shaft relationship.

4. Remove the steering gear-to-frame mounting bolts and remove the steering gear.

5. Reverse the removal steps to install the steering gear. Tighten the frame mounting bolts to 70 ft. lbs. Tighten the pitman shaft nut to 180 ft. lbs. and the steering coupling nuts to 20 ft. lbs.

ADJUSTMENT

1. Disconnect the negative battery cable.

2. At the steering wheel, remove the horn ring or button.

3. Remove the pitman arm-to-steering gear nut, then using the puller tool No. J-6632, pull the pitman arm from the steering gear.

NOTE: *Be sure to mark the relationship of the pitman arm to the steering gear before it is removed.*

4. Turn the steering wheel ½ turn from either stop, then loosen the sector shaft adjusting screw to eliminate the sector load.

CAUTION: *Turning the steering wheel too hard against the stops will damage the ball return guides.*

5. Place a 50 inch lbs. torque wrench on the steering wheel nut, then turn the wrench 90° and observe the reading. If the force is less than 5–8 inch lbs., loosen the steering gear adjuster lock nut and turn the worm thrust bearing adjuster to increase the preload.

6. Tighten the adjuster lock nut and recheck the preload.

7. To install, reverse the removal procedures.

Power Steering Gear

REMOVAL AND INSTALLATION

Installation and removal of power steering gears is the same as that described for manual steering gears above, with the addition of disconnecting and reconnecting the hydraulic lines. Cap both hoses and steering gear outlets to prevent foreign material from entering the system.

ADJUSTMENT

NOTE: *The steering gear must be removed from the vehicle in order to adjust the preload.*

1. Rotate the stub shaft several times (from stop to stop) to drain the fluid from the steering gear.

2. Mount the steering gear in a vise and remove the adjuster plug lock nut.

3. Using a spanner wrench, turn the adjuster plug clockwise until the plug and the thrust bearing are firmly bottomed (about 20 ft. lbs.).

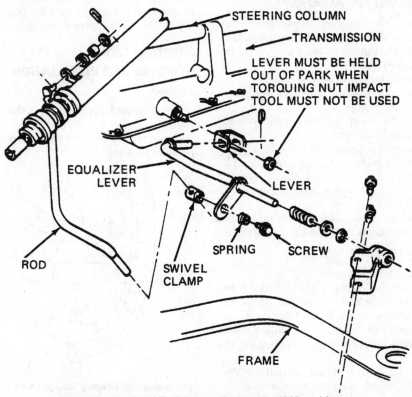

STEERING COLUMN

TRANSMISSION

LEVER MUST BE HELD OUT OF PARK WHEN TORQUING NUT IMPACT TOOL MUST NOT BE USED

EQUALIZER LEVER

LEVER

SPRING   SCREW

ROD

SWIVEL CLAMP

FRAME

Steering column shift linkage adjustment—1982 and later

4. Using the scribe mark on the housing (next to the hole in the adjuster plug), measure counterclockwise (³⁄₁₆–¼ in.) and mark the housing.

5. Turn the adjuster plug counterclockwise until the hole in the plug aligned with the second mark.

6. While holding the adjuster plug (to maintain position), tighten the lock nut.

7. Using a inch lb. torque wrench and a ¾ in. socket, turn the stub shaft to the right stop, then back ¼ turn and measure the drag. The reading must be within 4–10 inch lbs. (record the reading).

8. Rotate the stub shaft from stop to stop, then back to the center. Using the torque wrench, turn the stub shaft 45° to each side of center and check the reading.

9. Loosen the lock nut and turn the pre-load adjusting screw clockwise until the over-center (additional torque) reading of 4–8 inch lbs. (new gear, not to exceed 18 inch lbs.) or 4–5 inch lbs. (used gear, not to exceed 14 inch lbs.).

10. While holding the adjuster plug, tighten the lock nut.

11. To install the steering gear, reverse the removal procedures and bleed the system.

Power Steering Pump
REMOVAL AND INSTALLATION

1. Remove the hoses at the pump and tape the openings shut to prevent contamination. Position the disconnected lines in a raised position to prevent leakage.

2. Remove the pump belt.

3. Loosen the retaining bolts and any braces, and remove the pump.

4. Install the pump on the engine with the retaining bolts hand-tight.

5. Connect and tighten the hose fittings.

6. Refill the pump with fluid and bleed by turning the pulley counterclockwise (viewed from the front). Stop the bleeding when air bubbles no longer appear.

7. Install the pump belt on the pulley and adjust the tension as described in Chapter 1.

SYSTEM BLEEDING

1. Fill the fluid reservoir.

2. Let the fluid stand undisturbed for two minutes, then crank the engine for about two seconds. Refill reservoir if necessary.

3. Repeat Steps 1 and 2 above until the fluid level remains constant after cranking the engine.

4. Raise the front of the car until the wheels are off the ground, then start the engine. Increase the engine speed to about 1,500 rpm.

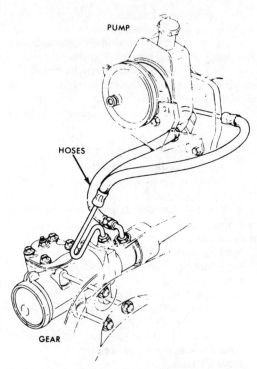

Power steering pump and lines, all models similar

5. Turn the wheels to the left and right, checking the fluid level and refilling if necessary. If the oil is extremely foamy, allow the car to stand a few minutes with the engine off, then repeat the above procedure.

Steering Linkage
REMOVAL AND INSTALLATION
Tie-Rod

1. Raise and support the vehicle on jackstands.

2. Remove the cotter pins and nuts from the tie-rod end studs.

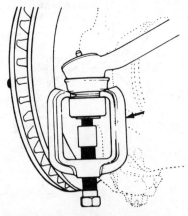

Disconnecting steering linkage using puller (arrow) or ball joint tool

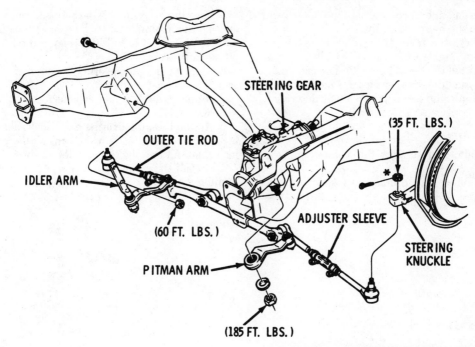

STEERING GEAR

(35 FT. LBS.)

OUTER TIE ROD

IDLER ARM

*

(60 FT. LBS.)

ADJUSTER SLEEVE

STEERING
KNUCKLE

PITMAN ARM

(185 FT. LBS.)

* AFTER REACHING TORQUE REQUIRED, NUT
MUST ALWAYS BE TIGHTENED (UP TO 1/6
TURN) FURTHER. NEVER BACK NUT OFF TO
INSERT COTTER PIN.

Steering linkage, all models similar

3. Tap on the steering arm near the tie-rod end (use another hammer as backing) or Ball Stud Puller tool No. J-6627 and pull down on the tie-rod, if necessary, to free it.

4. Remove the inner ball stud in the same manner as the outer.

NOTE: *DO NOT disengage the joint by driving a wedge between the joint and the knuckle, for damage to the seal may result.*

5. Loosen the clamp bolts and unscrew the ends if they are being replaced.

6. Lubricate the tie-rod end threads with chassis grease if they were removed. Install each end assembly an equal distance from the sleeve.

7. Ensure that the tie-rod end stud threads and nut are clean. Install new seals and install the studs into the steering arms and relay rod.

8. Install the stud nuts. Tighten the inner and outer end nuts to 35 ft. lbs.

9. Adjust the toe-in to specifications.

NOTE: *Before tightening the sleeve clamps, ensure that the clamps are positioned so that adjusting sleeve slot is covered by the clamp.*

Idler Arm

1. Raise and support the vehicle on jackstands.

2. Remove the idler arm-to-frame nut, washer, and bolt.

3. Remove the cotter pin and nut from the idler arm-to-relay rod ball end stud.

4. Tap the relay rod with a hammer, using another hammer as backing, or using the puller tool No. J-24319-01 to remove the relay rod from the idler arm.

5. Remove the idler arm.

6. Place the idler arm on the frame and install the retaining bolts and nuts. Tighten the nuts to 35 ft. lbs.

7. Position the relay rod on the idler arm. Ensure that the seal is on the stud. Install the nut and tighten to 35 ft. lbs. Install a cotter pin.

Relay Rod (Intermediate Rod)

1. Raise and support the vehicle on jackstands.

2. Remove the inner tie-rod ends from the relay rod as outlined under "Tie-Rod Removal and Installation."

3. On 1974 models with manual steering, remove the damper from the relay rod.

4. Remove the relay rod stud nut and cotter pin from the pitman arm. Free the relay rod from the pitman arm using the puller tool No. J-24319-01, moving the steering linkage if necessary. Repeat this operation to remove the relay rod from the idler arm and remove the relay rod from the car.

5. Install the relay rod on the idler arm. Tighten the nut to 35 ft. lbs.

6. Raise the relay and install it on the pitman arm. Tighten the nut to 45 ft. lbs.

7. Install the tie-rod ends to the relay rod.

8. Install the damper on 1974 models.

9. Adjust the toe-in as previously described.

Pitman Arm

1. Raise and support the vehicle on jackstands.

2. Remove the pitman arm stud nut and cotter pin.

3. Tap the relay rod off the pitman arm, using another hammer as backing or the puller tool No. J-24319-01. Pull the relay rod off the pitman arm stud.

4. Remove the pitman arm nut and mark the arm-to-shaft relationship.

5. Remove the pitman arm using a puller tool No. J-6632.

6. Install the pitman arm on the shaft, aligning the previously made marks. Install the pitman shaft nut and tighten it to 180 ft. lbs.

7. Install the relay rod on the pitman arm. Tighten the nut to 45 ft. lbs. and install a cotter pin.

BRAKE SYSTEM

All 1967 and later vehicles are equipped with independent front and rear brake systems. The systems consist of a power booster, a master cylinder, a combination valve, front and rear disc or drum assemblies.

The 1967 and later master cylinder, mounted on the left firewall or power booster, consists of two fluid reservoirs, a primary (rear) cylinder, a secondary (front) cylinder and springs. The reservoirs, being independent of one another, are contained within the same housing; fluid cannot pass from one to the other. The rear reservoir supplies fluid to the front brakes while the front reservoir supplies fluid to the rear brakes.

During operation, fluid drains from the reservoirs to the master cylinder. When the brake pedal is applied, fluid from the master cylinder is sent to the combination valve (mounted on the left front fender or frame side rail beneath the master cylinder), here it is monitored and proportionally distributed to the front or rear brake systems. Should a loss of pressure occur in one system, the other system will provide enough braking pressure to stop the vehicle. Also, should a loss of pressure in one system occur, the differential warning switch (located on the combination valve) will turn "ON" the brake warning light (located on the dash board).

As the fluid enters each brake caliper or wheel cylinder, the pistons are forced outward. The outward movement of the pistons force the brake pads against a round flat disc or brake shoes against a round metal drum. The brake lining attached to the pads or shoes comes in contact with the revolving disc or drum causing friction, which brings the wheel to a stop.

In time, the brake linings wear down. If not replaced, their metal support plates (bonded type) or rivet heads (riveted type) will come in contact with the disc or drum; damage to the disc or drum will occur. Never use brake pads or shoes with a lining thickness less than $\frac{1}{32}$ inch.

Most manufacturers provide a wear sensor, a piece of spring steel, attached to the rear edge of the inner brake pad. When the pad wears to the replacement thickness, the sensor will produce a high pitched squeal.

ADJUSTMENTS
Drum Brakes

1. Raise the car and support it with safety stands.
2. Remove the rubber plug from the adjusting slot on the backing plate.
3. Insert a brake adjusting spoon into the slot and engage the lowest possible tooth on the starwheel. Move the end of the brake spoon downward to move the starwheel upward and expand the adjusting screw. Repeat this operation until the brakes lock the wheel.
4. Insert a small screwdriver or piece of firm wire (coat-hanger wire) into the adjusting slot and push the automatic adjuster lever out and free of the starwheel on the adjusting screw.
5. Holding the adjusting lever out of the way, engage the topmost tooth possible on the starwheel with a brake adjusting spoon. Move the end of the adjusting spoon upward to move the adjusting screw starwheel downward and contact the adjusting screw. Back off the adjusting screw starwheel until the wheel spins freely with a minimum of drag. Keep track of the number of turns the starwheel is backed off.
6. Repeat this operation for the other side. When backing off the brakes on the other side, the adjusting lever must be backed off the same number of turns to prevent side-to-side brake pull.
7. Repeat this operation on the other side of brakes (front or rear).
8. When all 4 brakes are adjusted, make

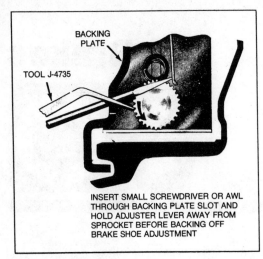

BACKING PLATE

TOOL J-4735

INSERT SMALL SCREWDRIVER OR AWL THROUGH BACKING PLATE SLOT AND HOLD ADJUSTER LEVER AWAY FROM SPROCKET BEFORE BACKING OFF BRAKE SHOE ADJUSTMENT

Brake adjustment

several stops, while backing the car, to equalize all of the wheels.

9. Road-test the car.

Brake Pedal

TRAVEL

The pedal travel is the distance which the pedal moves toward the floor from the fully released position. Inspection should be made with 50 lbs. (manual) or 100 lbs. (power) pressure on the brake pedal, when the brake system is cold. The brake pedal travel should be 2¼ inch (1964–84), 2¾ inch (1985 and later) or 3⅓ inch (hydro-boost).

NOTE: *If equipped with power brakes, be sure to pump the brakes 3 times with the engine Off, before making the travel check.*

1. Under the dash, remove the push rod-to-pedal clevis pin and separate the push rod from the brake pedal.

2. Loosen the push rod adjuster lock nut, then adjust the push rod.

3. After the correct travel is established, reverse the removal procedure.

Brake Light Switch

REMOVAL AND INSTALLATION

When the brake pedal is in the fully released position, the stop light switch plunger should be fully depressed against the pedal arm. The switch is adjusted by moving it in or out.

1. Disconnect the stop light switch electrical connector(s).

2. Remove the switch from the bracket.

3. Make sure that the tubular clip is in the brake pedal mounting bracket.

4. Depress the brake pedal and insert the switch into the tubular clip until it seats on the clip; a click will be heard.

5. Pull the brake pedal fully rearward, against the pedal stop, until the clicking sounds can no longer be heard; the switch is adjusting itself in the bracket.

6. Release the brake pedal, then pull the pedal rearward again to assure that the adjustment is complete.

Master Cylinder

REMOVAL AND INSTALLATION

NOTE: *Vehicles with disc brakes do not have a check valve in the front outlet port of the master cylinder. If one is installed, the front discs will quickly wear out due to residual hydraulic pressure holding the pads against the rotor.*

1. Disconnect the hydraulic lines from master cylinder.

2. Remove the retaining nuts and the lockwashers holding the cylinder to the cowl or the brake booster.

NOTE: *If equipped with non-power brakes, disconnect the pushrod at brake pedal.*

3. Remove the master cylinder, the gasket asnd the rubber boot.

4. To install, reverse the removal procedures. Torque the master cylinder mounting nuts to 22 ft. lbs. and the hydraulic lines to 18 ft. lbs. Refill the master cylinder, bleed the brake system and check the brake pedal freeplay.

NOTE: *On non-powered brakes, position the master cylinder on the cowl, making sure that the pushrod goes through the rubber boot into the piston. Reconnect the pushrod clevis to the brake pedal. If equipped with power brakes, install the master cylinder on the power booster.*

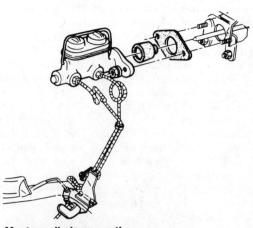

Master cylinder mounting

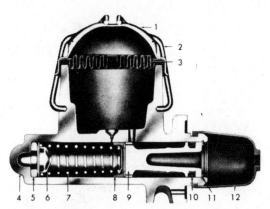

1. Reservoir cover
2. Bail wire
3. Seal
4. Body
5. Valve seat
6. Valve assembly
7. Spring
8. Primary cup
9. Piston
10. Secondary cup
11. Lock ring
12. Boot

Cutaway view of typical master cylinder—1964-66

OVERHAUL

1964-66

1. Secure the master cylinder in a vise and remove the pushrod assembly and protective boot. This exposes the lock ring which, when removed, allows extraction of the piston stop, secondary cup, and piston.

2. Remove the cylinder end plug and push out the primary cup, spring, valve assembly, and seat.

3. Wash the component parts with denatured alcohol.

4. Carefully inspect the washed metal parts and the cylinder bore. A corroded cylinder must

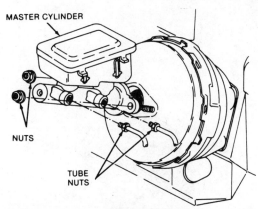

Typical master cylinder mounting for cars equipped with power brakes

be replaced. Discoloration or stains can be removed with crocus cloth. When doing this, wrap the cloth around your finger and rotate the cylinder around the cloth.

CAUTION: *Do not polish the bore lengthwise, as this can cause a fluid leak.*

5. To reassemble, moisten the cylinder bore with brake fluid and replace the valve seat, valve assembly, and spring.

CAUTION: *Be sure that the valve and seat are properly installed before proceeding. An incorrectly assembled check valve will distort and fail to provide a check valve seal, which will result in a reduction of brake pedal travel with a corresponding loss in braking.*

6. Moisten the primary cup with brake fluid and install it, flat side out, and seated over the spring. The primary cup is distinguished by a brass support ring at its base.

7. Dip the secondary cup in brake fluid and slip it over the end of the piston.

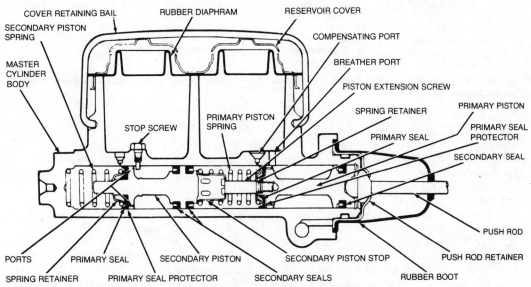

Cross section of a master cylinder

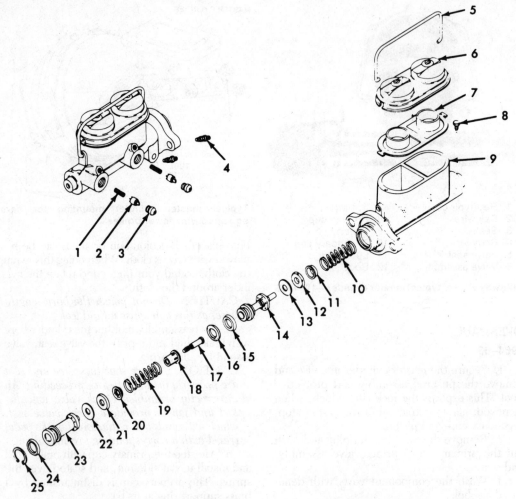

1. Spring
2. Check valve
3. Valve seat
4. Bleeder valve
5. Bail wire
6. Cover
7. Diaphragm
8. Stopscrew
9. Body
10. Spring
11. Retainer
12. Seal
13. Seal protector
14. Primary piston
15. Seal
16. Seal
17. Piston extension screw
18. Secondary piston stop
19. Spring
20. Spring retainer
21. Seal
22. Seal protector
23. Secondary piston
24. Seal
25. Retaining ring

Exploded view of a master cylinder. Some 1980 and all 1981 and later models no longer use the bails to retain the reservoir cap.

8. Insert the completed assembly, with the bleeder brake end of the piston installed first. Secure the parts with the piston stop and the snap-ring, and install the end plug.

9. Attach the rubber root and pushrod, and install the master cylinder.

10. Attach the brake pedal clevis and adjust the pushrod-to-piston clearance. Correct adjustment calls for a barely perceptible free pedal before piston/pushrod contact.

NOTE: *Overhaul of the main cylinder portion of power brake master cylinders is the same as that for manual master cylinders.*

1967 and Later

1. Remove the master cylinder from the car.

2. Remove the mounting gasket and boot, and the main cover. Empty the cylinder of all fluid.

3. Place the cylinder in a vise and remove the pushrod retainer and the secondary piston stop bolt that are found inside the front reservoir.

4. Remove the retaining ring and primary piston assembly.

5. Direct compressed air into the piston stop screw hole to force the secondary piston, spring,

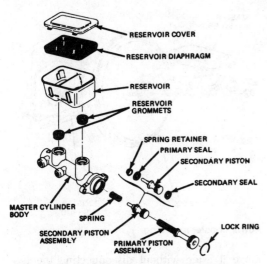

Master cylinder with plastic removable reservoir

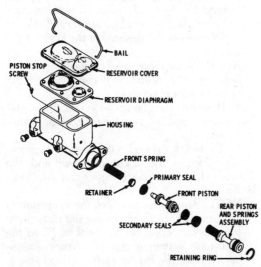

Moraine cast iron master cylinder with integral reservoir as used on 350 diesel models

and retainer from the cylinder bore. If compressed air isn't available, use a hooked wire to pull out the secondary piston.

6. Check the brass tube fitting inserts and, if damaged, remove them; if not, leave them in place.

7. If insert replacement is necessary, thread a No. 6-32 x ⅝ in. self-tapping screw into the insert. Hook the end of the screw with a claw hammer and pull out the insert.

8. An alternative (but more troublesome) way to remove the inserts is to drill out the outlet holes with a ¹³⁄₆₄ in. drill and then thread them with a ¼ in.-20 tap. Position a thick washer over the hole to serve as a spacer and then thread a ¼ in.-20 x ¾ in. hex-head bolt into

the insert and tighten the bolt until the insert is free.

9. Use only *denatured alcohol* or brake fluid and compressed air to clean the parts. Slight rust may be removed with crocus cloth.

CAUTION: *Do not polish the aluminum bore of type "A" cylinders with any type of abrasive. Never use any mineral-based solvents (gasoline, kerosene, etc.) for cleaning. It will quickly deteriorate rubber parts.*

10. Replace the brass tube inserts by positioning them in their holes and threading a brake line tube nut into the outlet hole. Turn down the nut until the insert is seated.

11. Check the piston assemblies for correct identification and, when satisfied, position the replacement secondary seals in the twin grooves of the secondary piston.

12. The outside seal is correctly placed when its lips face the flat end of the piston.

13. Slip the primary seal and its protector over the end of the secondary piston opposite the secondary seals. The flat side of this seal should face the piston's compensating hole flange.

14. Replace the primary piston assembly with the assembled piece in the overhaul kit.

15. Coat the cylinder bore and the secondary piston's inner and outer seals with brake fluid. Assemble the secondary piston spring to its retainer and place them over the end of the primary seal.

16. Insert the combined spring and piston assembly into the cylinder and, using a pencil, seat the spring against the end of the bore.

17. Coat the primary piston seals with brake fluid and push it (push rod receptacle end out) into the cylinder.

18. Hold the piston in and snap the retaining ring into place.

19. Continue to hold the piston down to make sure that all components are seated and insert the secondary piston stop screw in its hole in the bottom of the front reservoir. Torque the screw to 25–40 in. lbs.

20. Install the reservoir diaphragm and cover.

21. It will save time to bleed the cylinder before installing it in the car. Do so in the following manner:

  a. Install plugs in the outlet ports

  b. Place the unit in a vise with the front end tilted slightly downward. *DO NOT OVERTIGHTEN* the vise.

  c. Fill both reservoirs with clean fluid.

  d. Using a smooth, round rod (try the eraser end of a pencil), push in on the primary piston.

  e. Release the pressure on the rod and watch for air bubbles in the fluid. Keep repeating this until the bubbles disappear.

f. Loosen the vise and position the cylinder so the front end is tilted slightly upward. Repeat steps "d" and "e."

g. Place the diaphragm cover on the reservoir.

NOTE: *Master cylinder overhaul on cars with power brakes is the same as above.*

Combination Valve

REMOVAL AND INSTALLATION

1. Disconnect the negative battery cable.
2. Disconnect the electrical lead from the switch.
3. Place rags under the unit to absorb any spilled brake fluid.
4. Clean any dirt from the hydraulic lines and the switch/valve assembly. Disconnect the hydraulic lines from the assembly. If necessary, loosen the line connections at the master cylinder. Tape the open line ends to prevent the entrance of dirt.
5. Remove the mounting screws and remove the switch/valve assembly.
6. Make sure that the new unit is clean and free of dust and lint. If in doubt, wash the new unit in clean brake fluid.

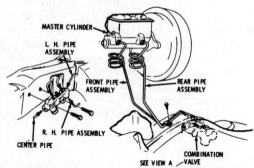

Combination valve mounting on front frame member

7. Place the new unit in position and install it to its mounting bracket with screws.
8. Remove the tape from the hydraulic lines and connect them to the unit. If necessary, tighten the line connections at the master cylinder.
9. Connect the electrical lead.
10. Connect the negative battery cable.
11. Bleed the brake systems.

Power Brake Booster

REMOVAL AND INSTALLATION

Single and Tandem

1. Disconnect the vacuum hose from the vacuum check valve.
2. Unbolt the master cylinder and carefully

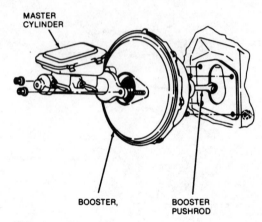

Power booster mounting

move it aside without disconnecting the hydraulic lines.

NOTE: *If sufficient booster clearance cannot be obtained, it will be necessary to disconnect the hydraulic lines from the master cylinder, then remove the master cylinder.*

3. Disconnect the pushrod at the brake pedal assembly.

NOTE: *Some Nova brake boosters may be held on with sealant; this can be easily removed with tar remover.*

4. Remove the booster-to-cowl nuts and lockwashers and the booster from engine compartment.
5. To install, reverse the removal procedures. Torque the booster-to-cowl and the master cylinder-to-booster mounting nuts to 28 ft. lbs.

NOTE: *Make sure to check the operation of the stop lights. Allow the engine vacuum to build before applying the brakes. Bleed the hydraulic system if the lines were disconnected from the master cylinder.*

Hydro-Boost

Hydro-Boost differs from conventional power brake systems, in that it operates from power steering pump fluid pressure rather than intake manifold vacuum.

The Hydro-Boost unit contains a spool valve with an open center which controls the strength of pump pressure when braking occurs. A lever assembly controls the valve's position. A boost piston provides the force necessary to operate the conventional master cylinder on the front of the booster.

A reserve of at least two assisted brake applications is supplied by an accumulator which is spring loaded on earlier and pneumatic on later models. The accumulator is an integral part of the Hydro-Boost II unit. The brakes can be applied manually if the reserve system is depleted.

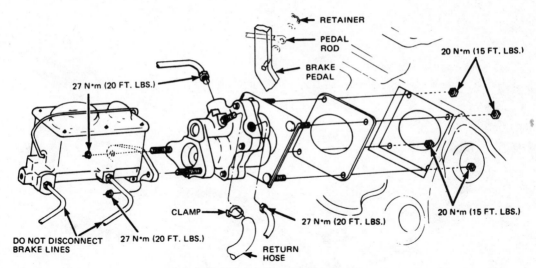

27 N•m (20 FT. LBS.)

20 N•m (15 FT. LBS.)

RETAINER

PEDAL ROD

BRAKE PEDAL

20 N•m (15 FT. LBS.)

CLAMP

DO NOT DISCONNECT BRAKE LINES

27 N•m (20 FT. LBS.)

27 N•m (20 FT. LBS.)

RETURN HOSE

20 N•m (15 FT. LBS.)

View of the Hydro-Boost brake booster

All system checks, tests and troubleshooting procedure are the same for the two systems.

1. Turn the engine off and pump the brake pedal 4 or 5 times to deplete the accumulator.

2. Remove the nuts from the master cylinder, then move the master cylinder away from the booster, with brake lines still attached.

3. Remove the hydraulic lines from the booster.

4. Remove the retainer and washer at the brake pedal.

5. Remove the attaching nuts retaining the booster fastened to the cowl and the booster.

6. To install, reverse the removal procedures. Torque the booster-to-cowl nuts to 15 ft. lbs. and the master cylinder-to-booster nuts to 20 ft. lbs. Bleed the power steering and hydro booster system.

Powermaster

The unit is a complete, integral power brake system. The assembly consists of an Electro-Hydraulic (E-H) pump, a fluid accumulator, a pressure switch, a fluid reservoir and a hydraulic booster with a dual master cylinder.

CAUTION: *Before performing any service to the brake system, depressurize the powermaster assembly.*

1. Turn the ignition OFF, then depress the brake pedal 10 times using at least 50 lbs. of force.

NOTE: *Before removing the master cylinder from the cowl, remove some of the brake fluid from the reservoir.*

2. Remove the electrical connectors from the pressure switch and the E-H pump.

3. Disconnect and plug the brake lines at the master cylinder.

4. Remove the master cylinder-to-cowl mounting nuts.

5. Disconnect the master cylinder push rod from the brake pedal.

6. Remove the powermaster unit from the vehicle.

7. To install, reverse the removal procedures. Torque the master cylinder-to-cowl nuts to 22–30 ft. lbs. Refill the master cylinder and bleed the brake system.

Bleeding

The hydraulic brake system must be bled any time one of the lines is disconnected or any time air enters the system. If the brake pedal feels spongy upon application, and goes almost to the floor but regains height when pumped, air has entered the system. It must be bled out. Check for leaks that would have allowed the entry of air and repair them before bleeding the system. The correct bleeding sequence is: right rear wheel cylinder, left rear, right front, and left front. If the master cylinder is equipped with bleeder valves, bleed them first then go to the wheel cylinder nearest the master cylinder (left front) followed by the right front, left rear, and right rear.

This method of bleeding requires two people, one to depress the brake pedal and the other to open the bleeder screws.

1. Clean the top of the master cylinder, remove the cover and fill the reservoirs with clean fluid. To prevent squirting fluid, replace the cover.

IMPORTANT: *On cars with front disc brakes, it will be necessary to hold in the metering valve pin during the bleeding pro-*

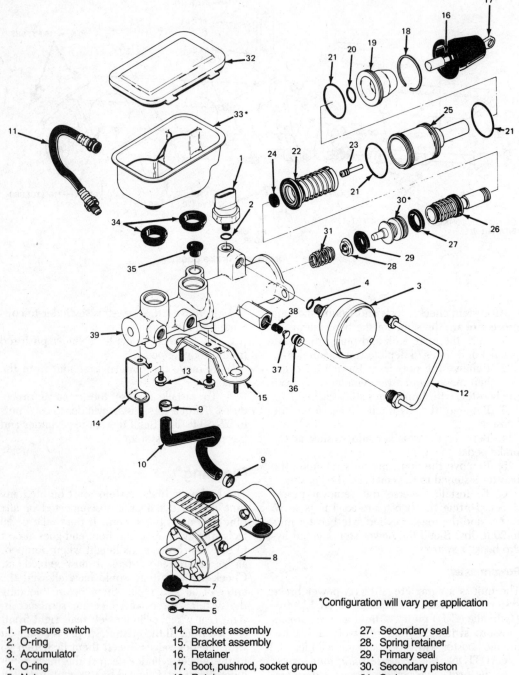

1. Pressure switch
2. O-ring
3. Accumulator
4. O-ring
5. Nut
6. Washer
7. Grommet
8. E-H pump
9. Hose clamp
10. Sump hose
11. Pressure hose assembly
12. Tube & nut assembly
13. Bolt
14. Bracket assembly
15. Bracket assembly
16. Retainer
17. Boot, pushrod, socket group
18. Retainer
19. Piston guide
20. O-ring
21. O-ring
22. Reaction body group
23. Reaction piston
24. Reaction disc
25. Power piston assembly
26. Primary piston assembly
27. Secondary seal
28. Spring retainer
29. Primary seal
30. Secondary piston
31. Spring
32. Reservoir cover and diaphragm
33. Reservoir
34. Grommet
35. Grommet
36. Valve seat and seal
37. Poppet
38. Spring
39. Powermaster body

*Configuration will vary per application

View of the Powermaster brake booster

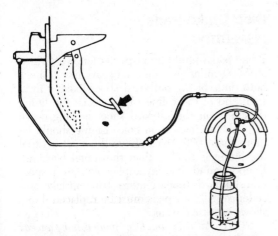

Have an assistant pump the brake pedal slowly while you bleed each wheel

cedure. The metering valve is located beneath the master cylinder and the pin is situated under the rubber boot on the end of the valve housing. This may be taped in or held by an assistant.

CAUTION: *Never reuse brake fluid which has been bled from the system.*

2. Fill the master cylinder with brake fluid.

3. Install a box-end wrench on the bleeder screw on the right rear wheel.

4. Attach a length of small diameter, clear vinyl tubing to the bleeder screw. Submerge the other end of the rubber tubing in a glass jar partially filled with clean brake fluid. Make sure the rubber tube fits on the bleeder screw snugly or you may be squirted with brake fluid when the bleeder screw is opened.

5. Have your friend slowly depress the brake pedal. As this is done, open the bleeder screw half a turn and allow the fluid to run through the tube. Close the bleeder screw, then return the brake pedal to its fully released position.

6. Repeat this procedure until no bubbles appear in the jar. Refill the master cylinder.

7. Repeat this procedure on the left rear, right front, and left front wheels, in that order.

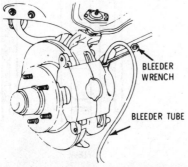

Wrench and plastic tubing fit on the bleeder nipple on each caliper

Periodically refill the master cylinder so it does not run dry.

8. If the brake warning light is on, depress the brake pedal firmly. If there is no air in the system, the light will go out.

FRONT DRUM BRAKES

CAUTION: *Brake shoes contain asbestos, which has been determined to be a cancer causing agent. Never clean the brake surfaces with compressed air! Avoid inhaling any dust from any brake surface! When cleaning brake surfaces, use a commercially available brake cleaning fluid.*

Brake Drums And Shoes

REMOVAL AND INSTALLATION

NOTE: *For information on the wheel bearings, refer to "Wheel Bearings" in Chapter 1.*

1. Raise the car and support it on jackstands.

2. Remove the front wheel and drum as a unit by removing the spindle nut and cotter pin.

3. Free the brake shoe return springs, actuator pull-back spring, hold-down pins and springs, and actuator assembly.

NOTE: *Special tools available from auto supply stores will ease removal of the spring and anchor pin, but the job may still be done with common hand tools.*

4. Disconnect the adjusting mechanism and spring, and remove the primary shoe. The primary shoe has a shorter lining than the secondary and is mounted at the front of the wheel.

5. Clean and inspect all brake parts.

6. Check the wheel cylinders for seal condition and leaking.

7. Repack wheel bearings and replace the seals.

8. Inspect the replacement shoes for nicks or burrs, lubricate the backing plate contact points, brake cable and levers, and adjusting screws and then assemble.

9. Make sure that the right and left-hand adjusting screws are not mixed. You can prevent this by working on one side at a time. This will also provide you with a reference for reassembly. The star wheel should be nearest to the secondary shoe when correctly installed.

10. To install, reverse the removal procedure. When completed, make an initial adjustment as previously described.

NOTE: *Maintenance procedures for the metallic lining option are the same as those for standard linings. Do not substitute these linings in standard drums, unless they have been honed to a 20 micro-inch finish and equipped with special heat-resistant springs.*

DRUM INSPECTION

1. Check the drums for any cracks, scores, grooves, or an out-of-round condition. Replace if cracked. Slight scores can be removed with fine emery cloth while extensive scoring requires turning the drum on a lathe.

2. Never have a drum turned more than 0.060 in.

Wheel Cylinders
REMOVAL AND INSTALLATION

1. Clean away all dirt, crud and foreign material from around wheel cylinder. It is important that dirt be kept away from the brake line when the cylinder is disconnected.

2. Disconnect the inlet tube line.

3. Wheel cylinders are retained by two types of fasteners. One type uses a round retainer with locking clips, which attaches to the wheel cylinder on the back side of the brake backing plate. The other type simply uses two bolts, which screw into the wheel cylinder from the back side of the backing plate.

4. To remove the round retainer-type cylinders, insert two awls or pins into the access slots between the wheel cylinder pilot and the retainer locking tabs. Bend both tabs away simultaneously. The wheel cylinder can be removed, as the retainer is released.

5. To remove the cylinders, loosen and remove the bolts from the back side of the backing plate, and remove the cylinder.

6. To install the retainer-type cylinder, position the wheel cylinder and hold it in place with a wooden block between the cylinder and axle flange. Install a new retainer clip, using a 1⅛ in., 12-point socket extension as shown in the illustration. This tool will seat the retainer evenly.

7. On the bolt-type cylinder, position the cylinder and install the bolts.

8. On both types of cylinders, torque the inlet type nuts to 120 ft. lbs.

9. Assemble the remaining brake components. Bleed the brakes.

FRONT DISC BRAKES

CAUTION: *Brake shoes contain asbestos, which has been determined to be a cancer causing agent. Never clean the brake surfaces with compressed air! Avoid inhaling any dust from any brake surface! When cleaning brake surfaces, use a commercially available brake cleaning fluid.*

Disc Brake Pads
INSPECTION

Brake pads should be inspected once a year or at 7,500 miles, whichever occurs first. Check both ends of the outboard shoe, looking in at each end of the caliper; then check the lining thickness on the inboard shoe, looking down through the inspection hole. Lining should be more than .020″ thick above the rivet (so that the lining is thicker than the metal backing). Keep in mind that any applicable state inspection standards that are more stringent take precedence. All four pads must be replaced if one shows excessive wear.

NOTE: *All 1979 and later models have a wear indicator that makes a noise when the linings wear to a degree where replacement is necessary. The spring clip is an integral part of the inboard shoe and lining. When the brake pad reaches a certain degree of wear, the clip will contact the rotor and produce a warning noise.*

REMOVAL AND INSTALLATION
1966–68

1. Siphon off about two-thirds of the brake fluid from a full master cylinder.

CAUTION: *The insertion of the thicker replacement pads will push the caliper pistons back into their bores and will cause a full master cylinder to overflow causing paint damage. In addition to siphoning fluid, it*

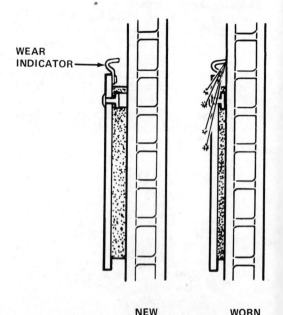

WEAR
INDICATOR→

NEW   WORN

Front disc brake pad wear indicator—1979 and later

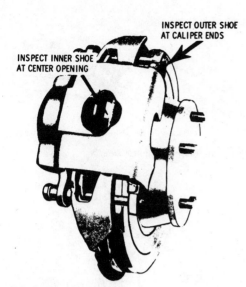

Disc brake pad inspection

NEW SHOE & LINING   READY
                         FOR REPLACEMENT

New and worn brake pads

would be wise to keep the cylinder cover on during pad replacement.

2. Raise the car and support it with jack stands. Remove the wheels.

NOTE: *Replacing the pads on just one wheel will result in uneven braking. Always replace the pads on both wheels.*

3. Extract and discard the pad retaining pin cotter key.

4. Remove the retaining pin and, while removing one pad, insert its replacement before the piston has time to move outward. If you were too slow and the pistons were too fast, it will be necessary to use a wide-bladed putty knife to hold in the pistons while inserting the new pads. If this gives you difficulty open the bleeder screw on that caliper and release some of the fluid, but do not allow the fluid to drain from the master cylinder. This may reduce the pressure and make it easier to push in on the pistons. After removing the outboard pad, inspect it and compare it with the inboard pad. They may be slightly different; if so, make sure that the replacement pads are installed correctly.

5. After installing the new pads, install the retaining pin and insert a new cotter pin.

6. Refill the master cylinder and bleed the system if necessary.

1969 and Later

1. Siphon off about two-thirds of the brake fluid from a full master cylinder.

CAUTION: *The insertion of the thicker replacement pads will push the piston back into its bore and will cause a full master cylinder to overflow causing paint damage. In addition to siphoning off fluid it would be wise to keep the cylinder cover on during pad replacement.*

2. Raise the car and support it with jackstands. Remove the wheels.

NOTE: *Replacing the pads on just one wheel will result in uneven braking. Always replace the pads on both wheels.*

3. Install a C-clamp on the caliper so that the solid side of the clamp rests against the back of the caliper and so the screw end rests against the metal part (shoe) of the outboard pad.

4. Tighten the clamp until the caliper moves enough to bottom the piston in its bore. Remove the clamp.

5. Remove the two allen-head caliper mounting bolts enough to allow the caliper to be pulled off the disc.

6. Remove the inboard pad and loosen the outboard pad. Place the caliper where it won't strain the brake hose, It would be best to wire it out of the way.

7. Remove the pad support spring clip from the piston.

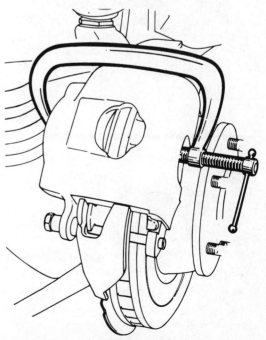

Use a C-clamp to seat the caliper piston

8. Remove the two bolt ear sleeves and the four rubber bushings from the ears.

9. Brake pads should be replaced when they are worn to within $\frac{1}{32}$ in. of the rivet heads.

10. Check the inside of the caliper for leakage and the condition of the piston dust boot.

11. Lubricate the two new sleeves and four bushings with a silicone spray.

12. Install the bushings in each caliper ear. Install the two sleeves in the two inboard ears.

13. Install the pad support spring clip and the old pad into the center of the piston. You will then push this pad down to get the piston flat against the caliper. This part of the job is a hassle and requires an assistant. While the assistant holds the caliper and loosens the bleeder valve to relieve pressure, you get a pry bar and try to force the old pad in, make the piston flush with the caliper surface. When it is flush, close the bleeder valve so that no air gets into the system.

NOTE: *On models with wear sensors, make sure the wear sensor is toward the rear of the caliper.*

14. Place the outboard pad in the caliper with its top ears over the caliper ears and the bottom tab engaged in the caliper cutout.

15. After both pads are installed, lift the caliper and place the bottom edge of the outboard pad on the outer edge of the disc to make sure

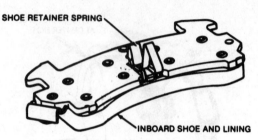

Proper retaining spring installation

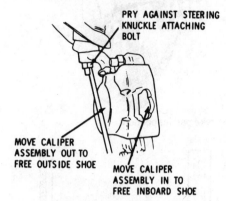

Compressing caliper with pry bar

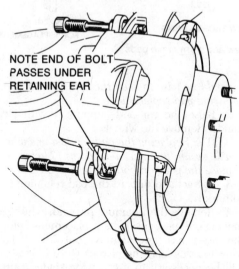

Caliper bolts must go under the pad retaining ears

that there is no clearance between the tab on the bottom of the shoes and the caliper abutment.

16. Place the caliper over the disc, lining up the hole in the caliper ears with the hole in the mounting bracket. Make sure that the brake hose is not kinked.

17. Start the caliper-to-mounting bracket bolts through the sleeves in the inboard caliper ears and through the mounting bracket making

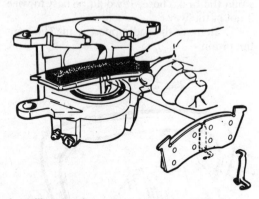

Installing the shoe support spring—1970–81

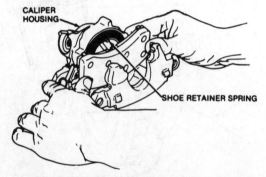

Install inboard brake shoe and linings

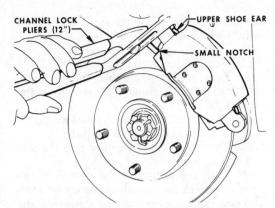

Use pliers to fit the brake pad to the caliper housing

sure that the ends of the bolts pass under the retaining ears of the inboard shoe.

18. Push the mounting bolts through to engage the holes in the outboard shoes and the outboard caliper ears and then threading them into the mounting bracket.

19. Torque the mounting bolts to 35 ft. lbs. Pump the brake pedal to seat the linings against the rotors.

20. With a pair of channel lock pliers placed on the notch on the caliper housing, bend the caliper upper ears until no clearance exists between the shoe and the caliper housing.

21. Install the wheels, lower the car, and refill the master cylinder with fluid. Pump the brake pedal to make sure that it is firm. If it is not, bleed the brakes.

Caliper
REMOVAL AND INSTALLATION

1. Raise the car and support it on jackstands.

2. Remove the tire and wheel assembly from the side on which the caliper is being removed.

3. Disconnect the brake hose at the support bracket. Tape the end of the line to prevent contamination.

4. Remove the cotter pin from the brake pad and retaining pin and remove the pin.

5. Remove the brake pads and identify them as inboard or outboard if they are being reused.

6. Remove the U-shaped retainer from the hose fitting and pull the hose from the bracket.

7. Remove the two caliper retaining bolts and also the caliper from its mounting bracket.

8. Install the brake pads. If the same pads are being reused, return them to their original places (outboard or inboard) as marked during removal. New pads will usually have an arrow on the back indicating the direction of disc ro-

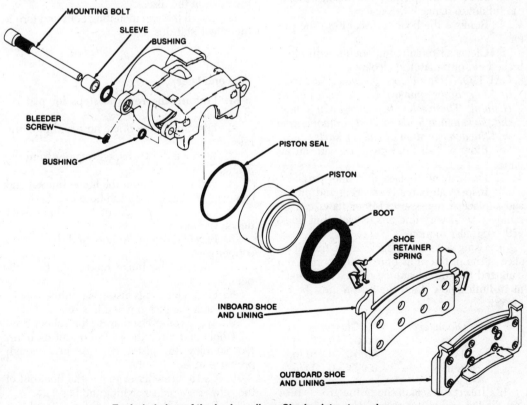

Exploded view of the brake caliper. Single piston type shown

tation. See "Brake Pad Replacement" for details.

9. Install the brake hose into the caliper, passing the female end through the support bracket.

10. Make sure that the tube line is clean and connect the brake line nut to the caliper.

11. Install the hose fitting into the support bracket and install the U-shaped retainer. Turn the steering wheel from side to side to make sure that the hose doesn't interfere with the tire. If it does, turn the hose end one or two points in the bracket until the interference is eliminated.

12. After performing the above check, install the steel tube connector and tighten it.

13. Bleed the brakes as instructed earlier in this chapter.

14. Install the wheels and lower the car.

OVERHAUL

1966–68

1. Separate the caliper halves. Remove the two O-rings from the fluid transfer holes in the caliper.

2. Push the piston all the way down into the caliper. Using the piston as a fulcrum, place a screwdriver under the steel ring in the boot and pry the boot from the caliper half.

3. Remove the pistons and springs, being careful not to damage the seal.

4. Remove the boot and seal from the piston.

5. Clean all metal components with clean brake fluid or denatured alcohol.

CAUTION: *Do not use gasoline, kerosene, or any other mineral-based solvent for cleaning. These solvents form an oily film on the parts which leads to fluid contamination and the deterioration of rubber parts.*

6. Blow out all fluid passages with an air hose.

7. Discard and replace all rubber parts.

8. Inspect all bores for scoring and pitting and replace if necessary. Minor flaws can be removed with very fine crocus cloth but do so with a circular motion.

9. Using a feeler gauge, check the clearance of the piston in its bore. If the bore is not damaged and the clearance exceeds the maximum limit below, then the piston must be replaced.

Bore Diameter	Clearance
2 1/16 in.	0.0045–0.010 in.
1 7/8	0.0045–0.010 in.
1 3/8 in.	0.0035–0.009 in.

10. Insert the seal in the piston groove nearest the flat end of the piston. The seal lip must face the large end of the piston. The lips must be in the groove and may not extend beyond.

11. Place the spring in the piston bore.

12. Coat the seal with clean brake fluid.

13. Install the piston assembly into the bore, being careful not to damage the seal lip on the edge of the bore.

14. Install the boot into the piston groove closest to the concave end of the piston.

15. The fold in the boot must face the seal end of the piston.

16. Push the pistons to the bottom of the bore and check for smooth piston movement. The end of the piston must be flush with the end of the bore. If it is not, check the installation of the seal.

17. Seat the piston boot so that its metal ring is even in the counterbore. The ring is even in the counterbore. The ring must be flush or below the machined face of the caliper. If the ring is seated unevenly dirt and moisture could get into the bore.

18. Insert the O-rings around the fluid transfer holes at both ends of the caliper halves.

19. Lubricate the bolts with brake fluid, connect the caliper halves, and torque the bolts to 130 ft. lbs.

20. While holding in the brake pistons with a putty knife, mount the caliper over the disc. Be careful not to damage the piston boots on the edge of the disc.

21. Install the two mounting bolts and torque them to 130 ft. lbs.

1969 and later

1. Perform the removal steps for pad replacement.

2. Disconnect the brake hose and plug the line.

3. Remove the U-shaped retainer from the fitting.

4. Pull the hose from the frame bracket and remove the caliper with the hose attached.

5. Clean the outside of the caliper with denatured alcohol.

6. Remove the brake hose and discard the copper gasket.

7. Remove the brake fluid from the caliper.

8. Place clean rags inside the caliper opening to catch the piston when it is released.

9. Apply compressed air to the caliper fluid inlet hole and force the piston out of its bore. Do not blow the piston out; use just enough pressure to ease it out.

10. Use a screwdriver to pry the boot out of the caliper. Avoid scratching the bore.

11. Remove the piston seal from its groove

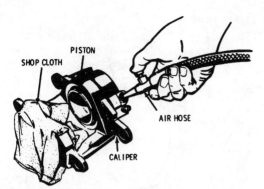

Piston removal using compressed air. Keep fingers out of the way of the piston when the air is applied

in the caliper bore. *Do not use a metal tool of any type for this operation.*

NOTE: *Replace (do not reuse) the boot, piston seal, rubber bushings, and sleeves.*

12. Blow out all passages in the caliper and bleeder valve. Clean the piston and piston bore with fresh brake fluid.

13. Examine the piston for scoring, scratches, or corrosion. If any of these conditions exist, the piston must be replaced because it is plated and cannot be refinished.

14. Examine the bore for the same defects. Light rough spots may be removed by rotating crocus cloth, using finger pressure, in the bore. Do not polish with an in-and-out motion or use any other abrasive.

15. Lubricate the piston bore and the new rubber parts with fresh brake fluid. Position the seal in the piston bore groove.

16. Lubricate the piston with brake fluid and assemble the boot into the piston groove so that the fold faces the open end of the piston.

17. Insert the piston into the bore, taking care not to unseat the seal.

18. Force the piston to the bottom of the bore (this will require as force of 40–100 lbs.). Seat the boot lip around the caliper counterbore. Proper seating of the boot is very important for sealing out contaminants.

19. Install the brake hose into the caliper with a new copper gasket.

20. Lubricate the new sleeves and rubber bushings. Install the bushings in the caliper ears. Install the sleeves so that the end toward the disc pad is flush with the machined surface.

NOTE: *Lubrication of the sleeves and bushings is essential to insure the proper operation of the sliding caliper design.*

21. Install the shoe support spring in the piston.

22. Install the disc pads in the caliper and remount the caliper on the hub (see "Disc Pad Replacement").

23. Reconnect the brake hose to the steel brake line. Install the retainer clip. Bleed the brakes (see "Brake Bleeding").

24. Replace the wheels, check the brake fluid level, check the brake pedal travel, and road-test the vehicle.

Brake disc

INSPECTION

1. Tighten the spindle nut to remove all wheel bearing play.

2. Install a dial indicator on the caliper so that its feeler will contact the disc about 1 in. below its outer edge.

3. Turn the disc and observe the runout reading. If the reading exceeds 0.002 in. (.004 in. total reading), the disc should be replaced.

4. Measure the thickness of the rotor at 5 points around the circumference. Tolerance is .0005 in.

5. Minimum thickness dimensions are cast into the caliper for reference.

REMOVAL AND INSTALLATION

1. Raise the car, support it with jackstands, and remove the wheel and tire assembly.

2. Remove the brake caliper as previously outlined.

3. Drill out the five rivets holding the disc to the hub.

4. Remove the disc.

5. Remove the rivet stubs from the hub.

6. Install the disc on the hub, aligning the lug bolts with the holes in the disc.

7. Install the brake caliper and shoes as previously outlined.

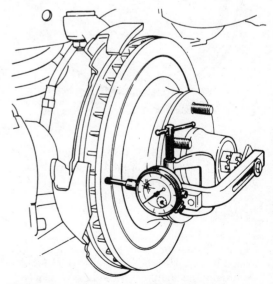

Use a dial indicator to determine brake disc runout

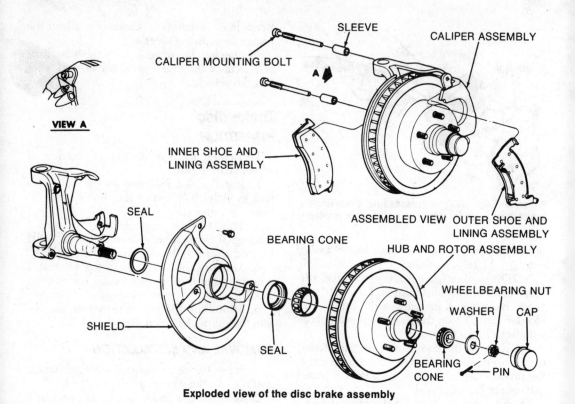

Exploded view of the disc brake assembly

Discard dimension (.965) stamped on disc hub

8. Bleed the brakes, install the wheel, and lower the car. Adjust front wheel bearings as described at the end of this chapter.

Wheel Bearings

Properly adjusted bearings have a slightly loose feeling. Wheel bearings must never be preloaded. Preloading will damage the bearings and eventually the spindles. If the bearings are too loose, they should be cleaned, inspected, and then adjusted.

Hold the tire at the top and bottom and move the wheel in and out of the spindle. If the movement is greater than 0.008 in. (0.005 in. 1974 and later), the bearings are too loose.

ADJUSTMENT

1. Raise and support the car by the lower control arm.
2. Remove the hub cap, then remove the dust cap from the hub.
3. Remove the cotter pin and spindle nut.
4. Spin the wheel forward by hand. Tighten the nut until snug to fully seat the bearings.
5. Back off the nut ¼–½ turn until it is just loose, then tighten it finger-tight.
6. Loosen the nut until either hole in the spindle lines up with a slot in the nut and then insert the cotter pin. This may appear to be too loose, but it is the correct adjustment. The spindle nut should not be even fingertight.
7. Proper adjustment creates 0.001–0.008 in. (0.001–0.005 in. 1974 and later) of endplay.

REMOVAL AND INSTALLATION
1964–69

1. Remove the wheel and tire assembly, and the brake drum or brake caliper.
2. On those cars with disc brakes, remove the hub and disc as an assembly. Remove the caliper mounting bolts and insert a block be-

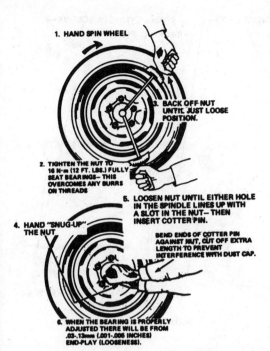

1. HAND SPIN WHEEL

3. BACK OFF NUT UNTIL JUST LOOSE POSITION.

2. TIGHTEN THE NUT TO 16 N·m (12 FT. LBS.) FULLY SEAT BEARINGS— THIS OVERCOMES ANY BURRS ON THREADS

5. LOOSEN NUT UNTIL EITHER HOLE IN THE SPINDLE LINES UP WITH A SLOT IN THE NUT— THEN INSERT COTTER PIN.

4. HAND "SNUG-UP" THE NUT

BEND ENDS OF COTTER PIN AGAINST NUT, CUT OFF EXTRA LENGTH TO PREVENT INTERFERENCE WITH DUST CAP.

6. WHEN THE BEARING IS PROPERLY ADJUSTED THERE WILL BE FROM .03-.13mm (.001-.005 INCHES) END-PLAY (LOOSENESS).

Wheel bearing adjustment

tween the brake pads as the caliper is removed. Remove the caliper and wire it out of the way.

3. Pry out the grease cap, cotter pin, spindle nut, and washer, then remove the hub. Do not drop the wheel bearings.

4. Remove the outer roller bearing assembly from the hub. The inner bearing assembly will remain in the hub and may be removed after prying out the inner seal. Discard the seal.

5. Clean all parts in solvent (air dry) and check for excessive wear or damage.

6. Using a hammer and drift, remove the bearing cups from the hub. When installing new cups, make sure they are not cocked and that they are fully seated against the hub shoulder.

7. Using a high melting point bearing lubricant, pack both inner and outer bearings.

8. Place the inner bearing in the hub and install a new inner seal, making sure the seal flange faces the bearing cup.

9. Carefully install the wheel hub over the spindle.

10. Using your hands, firmly press the outer bearing into the hub. Install the spindle washer and nut, and adjust as instructed above.

1970 and later

1. Remove the hub and disc assembly as described in Steps 1–63 above.

2. Remove the outer roller bearing assembly from the hub. The inner bearing assembly can be removed after prying out the inner seal. Discard the seal.

3. Wash all parts in solvent and check for excessive wear or damage.

4. To replace the outer or inner race, knock out the old race with a hammer and brass drift. New races must be installed squarely and evenly to avoid damage.

5. Pack the bearings with a high melting-point bearing lubricant.

6. Lightly grease the spindle and the inside of the hub.

7. Place the inner bearing in the hub race and install a new grease seal.

8. Carefully install the hub and disc assembly.

9. Install the outer wheel bearing.

10. Install the washer and nut and adjust the bearings according to the procedure outlined above.

11. Install the caliper and torque the mounting bolts to 35 ft. lbs.

12. Install the dust cap and the wheel and tire assembly, then lower the car to the ground.

PACKING

Clean the wheel bearings thoroughly with solvent and check their condition before installation.

CAUTION: *Do not blow the bearing dry with compressed air as this would allow the bearing to turn without lubrication.*

Apply a sizable daub of lubricant to the palm of one hand. Using your other hand, work the bearing into the lubricant so that the grease is pushed through the rollers and out the other side. Keep rotating the bearing while continuing to push the lubricant through it.

REAR DRUM BRAKES

CAUTION: *Brake shoes contain asbestos, which has been determined to be a cancer causing agent. Never clean the brake surfaces with compressed air! Avoid inhaling any dust from any brake surface! When cleaning brake surfaces, use a commercially available brake cleaning fluid.*

Brake Drum
REMOVAL AND INSTALLATION

1. Raise and support the car.

2. Remove the wheel or wheels.

3. Pull the brake drum off. It may be necessary to gently tap the rear edges of the drum to start it off the studs.

4. If extreme resistance to removal is encountered, it will be necessary to retract the adjusting screw. Knock out the access hole in the brake drum and turn the adjuster to retract the linings away from the drum.

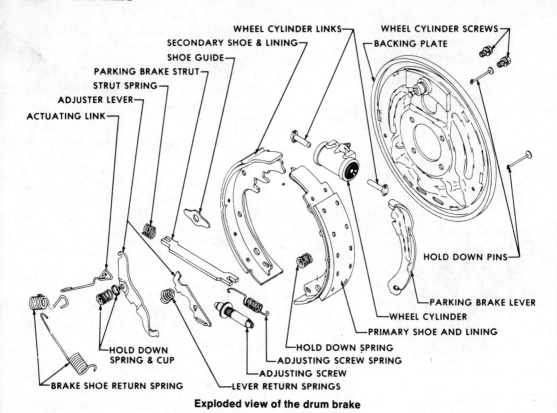

WHEEL CYLINDER LINKS
SECONDARY SHOE & LINING
SHOE GUIDE
PARKING BRAKE STRUT
STRUT SPRING
ADJUSTER LEVER
ACTUATING LINK

WHEEL CYLINDER SCREWS
BACKING PLATE

HOLD DOWN PINS
PARKING BRAKE LEVER
WHEEL CYLINDER
PRIMARY SHOE AND LINING
HOLD DOWN SPRING
ADJUSTING SCREW SPRING
ADJUSTING SCREW
LEVER RETURN SPRINGS
HOLD DOWN SPRING & CUP
BRAKE SHOE RETURN SPRING

Exploded view of the drum brake

5. Install a replacement hole cover before reinstalling drum.

6. Install the drums in the same position on the hub as removed. Adjust front wheel bearings as described at the end of this chapter.

DRUM INSPECTION

1. Check the drums for any cracks, scores, grooves, or an out-of-round condition. Replace if cracked. Slight scores can be removed with fine emery cloth while extensive scoring requires turning the drum on a lathe.

2. Never have a drum turned more than 0.060 in.

Brake Shoes

REMOVAL AND INSTALLATION

1. Raise the car and support it on jackstands.

2. Slacken the parking brake cable.

3. Remove the rear wheel and brake drum. The front wheel and drum may be removed as a unit by removing the spindle nut and cotter pin.

4. Free the brake shoe return springs, actuator pull-back spring, hold-down pins and springs, and actuator assembly.

NOTE: *Special tools available from auto supply stores will ease removal of the spring*

and anchor pin, but the job may still be done with common hand tools.

5. On the rear wheels, disconnect the adjusting mechanism and spring, and remove the primary shoe. The primary shoe has a shorter lining than the secondary and is mounted at the front of the wheel.

6. Disconnect the parking brake lever from the secondary shoe and remove the shoe. Front wheel shoes may be removed together.

7. Clean and inspect all brake parts.

8. Check the wheel cylinders for seal condition and leaking.

9. Repack wheel bearings and replace the seals.

10. Inspect the replacement shoes for nicks or burrs, lubricate the backing plate contact points, brake cable and levers, and adjusting screws and then assemble.

11. Make sure that the right and left-hand adjusting screws are not mixed. You can prevent this by working on one side at a time. This will also provide you with a reference for reassembly. The star wheel should be nearest to the secondary shoe when correctly installed.

12. To install, reverse the removal procedure. When completed, make an initial adjustment as previously described.

NOTE: *Maintenance procedures for the metallic lining option are the same as those for standard linings. Do not substitute these linings in standard drums, unless they have been honed to a 20 micro-inch finish and equipped with special heat-resistant springs.*

Wheel Cylinders

REMOVAL AND INSTALLATION

1. Clean away all dirt, crud and foreign material from around wheel cylinder. It is important that dirt be kept away from the brake line when the cylinder is disconnected.

2. Disconnect the inlet tube line.

3. Wheel cylinders are retained by two types of fasteners. One type uses a round retainer with locking clips, which attaches to the wheel cylinder on the back side of the brake backing plate. The other type simply uses two bolts, which screw into the wheel cylinder from the back side of the backing plate.

4. To remove the round retainer-type cylinders, insert two awls or pins into the access slots between the wheel cylinder pilot and the retainer locking tabs. Bend both tabs away simultaneously. The wheel cylinder can be removed, as the retainer is released.

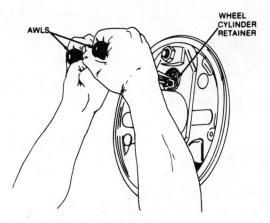

Bend retainer stubs using awls

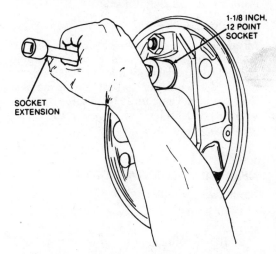

Use a socket and extension to seat the new retainer

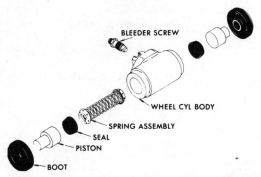

Exploded view of a typical wheel cylinder

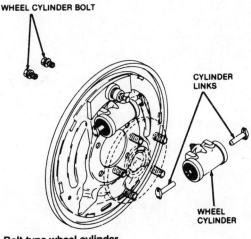

Bolt-type wheel cylinder

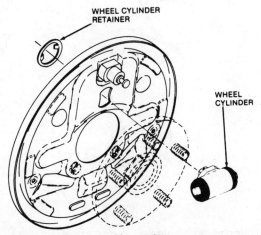

Wheel cylinder secured by retainer

5. To remove the cylinders, loosen and remove the bolts from the back side of the backing plate, and remove the cylinder.

6. To install the retainer-type cylinder, position the wheel cylinder and hold it in place

with a wooden block between the cylinder and axle flange. Install a new retainer clip, using a 1⅛ in., 12-point socket and socket extension as shown in the illustration. This tool will seat the retainer evenly.

7. On the bolt-type cylinder, position the cylinder and install the bolts.

8. On both types of cylinders, torque the inlet type nuts to 120 ft. lbs.

9. Assemble the remaining brake components. Bleed the brakes.

Wheel Bearings

Refer to the "Front Disc Brakes—Wheel Bearings" section for removal and installation, adjustment and packing procedures.

PARKING BRAKE

All models are equipped with a foot-operated ratchet-type parking brake. A cable assembly connects this pedal to an intermediate cable by means of an equalizer. Adjustment is made at the equalizer. The intermediate cable connects with two rear cables and each of these cables enters a rear wheel.

Cable

REMOVAL AND INSTALLATION

Front Cable

1. Raise the car and support it with jackstands.

2. Remove the adjusting nut at the equalizer.

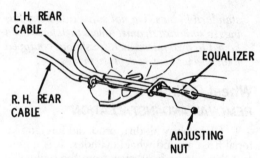

Parking brake cable adjustment

3. Remove the spring retainer clip from the bracket.

4. Lower the car. Remove the upper console cover and lower console rear screws.

5. Lift the rear of the lower console for access to the cable retainer at the hand lever.

6. Remove the cable retainer pin, cable retainer, then the cable.

7. Installation is the reverse of removal. Adjust the parking brake.

Rear Cable

1. Raise the car and support it with jackstands.

2. Loosen the adjusting nut at the equalizer.

3. Disengage the rear cable at the connector.

4. Remove the wheel assembly and brake drum.

5. Bend the retainer fingers.

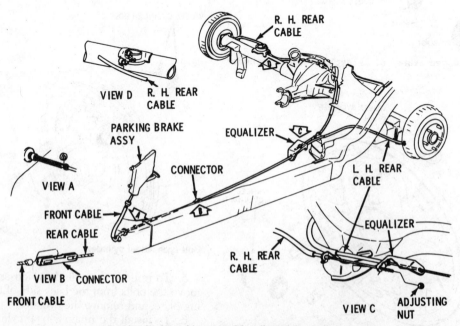

Parking brake cable assembly, all models similar

Brake Specifications

Year	Lug Nut Torque (ft. lbs.)	Master Cylinder Bore	Brake Disc		Brake Drum			Minimum Lining Thickness	
			Minimum Thickness	Maximum Run-Out	Diameter	Max Machine O/S	Max Wear Limit	Front	Rear
1964–65	80	1.0	NA	NA	9.5	9.560	9.590	²⁄₃₂	²⁄₃₂
1964–65 ②	80	.875	NA	NA	9.5	9.560	9.590	²⁄₃₂	²⁄₃₂
1966–68	80	11.125 (disc) 1.0 (drum)		.004	9.5	9.560	9.590	²⁄₃₂	²⁄₃₂
1969	80	1.0		.004	9.5	9.560	9.590	²⁄₃₂	²⁄₃₂
1970–77	80	1.125	.980	.002	9.5 ①	9.560	9.590	²⁄₃₂	²⁄₃₂
1978–83	80	1.125 (power) .9375 (manual)	.980	.002	9.5	9.560	9.590	²⁄₃₂	²⁄₃₂
1984–86	80	1.125	0.980	0.004	9.5 11.0	9.560 11.060	9.590 11.090	²⁄₃₂	²⁄₃₂

① 11.0 inches for 1973–75 station wagons
② Metallic Linings
NOTE: *Minimum lining thickness is as recommended by the manufacturer. Because of variations in state inspection regulations, the minimum allowable thickness may be different than recommended by the manufacturer.*

6. Disengage the cable at the brake shoe operating lever.

7. Installation is the reverse of removal. Adjust the parking brake.

ADJUSTMENT

1964–72

1. Jack the rear of the car up and support with jackstands.

2. Pull the parking brake on two notches from the fully released position.

3. Loosen the forward equalizer check nut, and adjust the rear nut as necessary to obtain a light drag when the rear wheel is turned.

4. Tighten both check nuts.

5. Release the parking brake lever and check to see that there is no drag present when the wheel is turned.

6. Lower the car.

1973 and Later

1. Raise the rear of the car and support it with jackstands.

2. Push down on the parking brake pedal so that it is two notches (clocks) from the fully released position.

3. Loosen the forward equalizer check nut and adjust the rear nut as necessary to obtain a light drag when the rear wheel is turned forward.

4. Tighten both check nuts.

5. Fully release the parking brake lever and check to see that there is no drag present when the rear wheel is turned forward.

6. Lower the car.

7. If the parking brake has to be forcibly released, clean and lubricate the cables and equalizer, and also the parking brake assembly, then check the cables for straightness and kinks.

Body and Trim

EXTERIOR

Doors

REMOVAL AND INSTALLATION

When removing the door, it is easier to remove the hinges because the door side hinges are very accessible.

1. Mark the position of the door hinges-to-body to make the installation easier.

2. If equipped with power operated components, remove the trim panel and detach the inner panel water deflector enough to disconnect the wiring harness from the components. Separate and remove the rubber conduit and the wiring harness from the door.

3. Using an assistant (to support the door), remove the upper and lower hinge-to-body bolts. Remove the door from the vehicle.

4. To install, reverse the removal procedures. Torque the hinge-to-body bolts to 15–21 ft. lbs.

ADJUSTMENT

The door adjustments are made possible through the use of floating anchor plates in the door and the body hinge pillars.

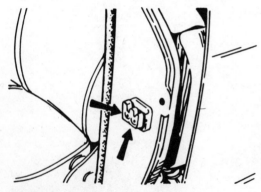

Adjusting the door striker

1. Remove the door lock striker from the body and allow the door to hang freely on it's hinges.

2. Using the Door Hinge tool No. J-28500, loosen the door hinge-to-body pillar bolts.

3. Using the body hinge pillar attachments, adjust the door up/down and fore/aft.

NOTE: *If a rearward adjustment is made, it may be necessary to replace the jamb switch.*

4. At the door hinge pillar attachments, adjust the door in and out.

5. After adjusting the door, torque the door hinge-to-body pillar bolts to 15–21 ft. lbs.

Door Locks

The door locks use a fork bolt lock design which includes a safety interlock feature. The door is

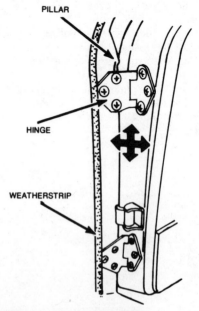

Adjusting the door hinge position

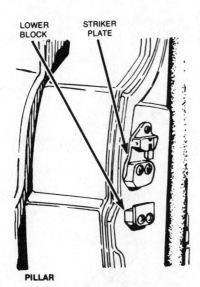

Adjusting the striker plate and lower block

securely closed when the door lock fork bolt engages the striker bolt.

REMOVAL AND INSTALLATION

NOTE: *NEVER attempt to make repairs to the lock assembly; replace it.*

1. Remove the door trim, then detach the insulator pad (if equipped) and the inner panel water deflector enough to access the door lock.

2. If working on the front doors, remove the inner panel cam.

3. If working on the rear doors, remove the stationary window and the ventilator assembly.

4. Disengage the inside handle and the power lock connecting rods (if equipped).

5. If equipped with power locks on the front door, remove the electric lock actuator by performing the following procedures:

    a. Using a center punch, drive the center pins out of pop rivets.

b. Using a ¼ in. drill bit, drill the heads off of the pop rivets.

c. Disconnect the connecting rod, the electrical connector and the actuator through the access hole.

NOTE: *On some models, it may be necessary to remove the inside handle, the lock and the connecting rod as a unit.*

6. If equipped with a remote lock button, disengage the locking rod from the door lock(s). On models with a locking button directly above the lock, remove the locking rod with the lock.

NOTE: *If working on the front door of the sedan models, disengage the lock cylinder-to-lock and the outside handle-to-lock connecting rods.*

7. Remove the lock-to-door screws and the lock through the access hole.

8. To install, attach the spring clips to the lock assembly and reverse the removal procedures. Torque the door lock-to-door screws to 80–100 inch lbs.

NOTE: *When attaching the power door lock actuator to the door, use ¼ in. x ½ in. pop rivets or nuts/bolts.*

Hood
REMOVAL AND INSTALLATION

1. Using a scratch awl, scribe the hinge onto the hood.

2. Using an assistant (to support the hood), remove the hinge-to-hood bolts and the hood.

3. To install, reverse the removal procedures. Check the hood for alignment with the hood latch.

ALIGNMENT

NOTE: *When aligning the hood and the latch, align the hood (first), then the latch (second).*

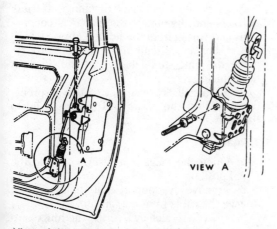

View of the power door lock actuator

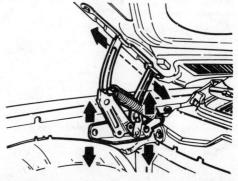

The height of the hood at the rear is adjusted by loosening the hinge-to-body bolts and moving the hood up and down

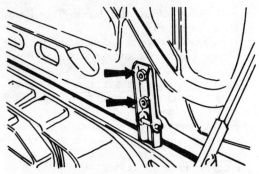

Loosen the hinge bolts to permit fore-and-aft and horizontal adjustment

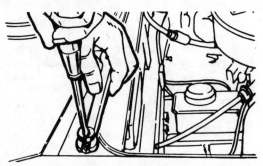

The hood is adjusted vertically by stop screws at the front and/or rear

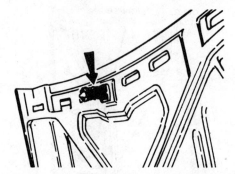

The hood pin can be adjusted for proper lock engagement

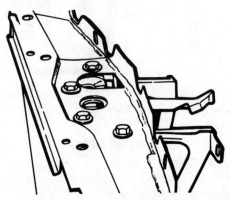

The base of the hood lock can also be repositioned slightly to give more positive lock engagement

Hood

The hood hinge-to-body mount is slotted to provide forward and rearward movement. Adjust the hood so that it is flush with the body sheetmetal.

1. Using a scratch awl, scribe the hinge outline onto the hood.

2. Loosen the appropriate screws and shift the hood into proper alignment with the vehicles sheetmetal.

CAUTION: *Make sure that the rear of the hood is properly positioned at the cowl seal; proper sealing will restrict fumes (from the engine compartment) from being pulled through the cowl vent.*

3. After adjustment, tighten the appropriate screws.

Latch

The hood latch assembly is mounted on a plate with elongated holes, which allow vertical adjustment.

Striker

The striker (on the hood) adjusts laterally to align with the hood latch assembly.

Tailgate or Trunk Lid

REMOVAL AND INSTALLATION

Trunk Lid

The trunk lid hinge is welded to the body and bolted to the lid.

1. Open the trunk lid and place protective coverings over the rear fenders (to protect the paint from damage).

2. Mark the location of the hinge-to-trunk lid bolts and disconnect the electrical connections and wiring from the lid (if equipped).

3. Using an assistant (to support the lid), remove the hinge-to-lid bolts and the lid from the vehicle.

4. To install, reverse the removal procedures. Adjust the position of the trunk lid to the body.

Tailgate

1. Open the tailgate and support it in the Open position.

2. Remove the support cable bolts and disengage the cable from the tailgate.

3. Using a scratch awl, scribe the hinge outline onto the hood.

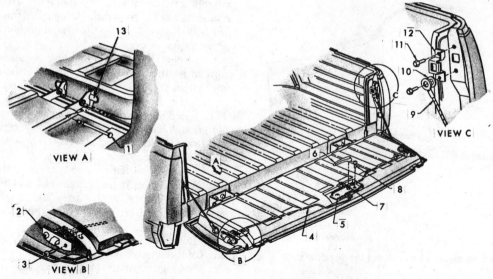

1. Pin
2. Latch assembly
3. Screw (latch assembly)
4. Rod–tailgate remote control to lock
5. Control assembly–tailgate lock remote
6. Handle tailgate lock remote
7. Spindle–remote control
8. Screw–remote control attaching
9. Cable–tailgate support
10. Washer–spacer
11. Screw–striker retainer
12. Striker–tailgate lock
13. Strap–tailgate hinge–gate side

View of the tailgate assembly

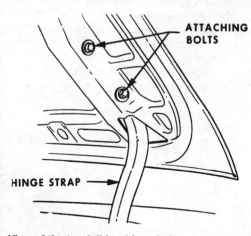

View of the trunk lid-to-hinge bolts

4. Using an assistant (to support the tailgate), remove the tailgate hinge-to-body bolts and the tailgate from the vehicle.

5. To install, reverse the removal procedures. Align the tailgate and torque the hinge-to-body bolts to 14–22 ft. lbs.

ALIGNMENT

Trunk Lid

The trunk lid can be aligned slightly by loosening the hinge-to-lid bolts and shifting the lid into position.

NOTE: *When adjusting the hinge/latch-to-body positions, be sure to use alignment marks as reference points.*

Tailgate

The tailgate can be aligned slightly by loosening the hinge and/or the latch bolts, then adjusting them.

NOTE: *When adjusting the hinge/latch-to-body positions, be sure to use alignment marks as reference points.*

Windshield

NOTE: *The bonded windshield requires special tools and procedures.*

REMOVAL

Monte Carlo

1. Place protective coverings over the hood.

2. Remove the windshield wiper arms and windshield trim.

3. If equipped with a radio antenna built into the windshield, disconnect the antenna's lead from the lower end of the windshield and tape the lead onto the outer surface of the windshield to protect it from damage.

4. Using a utility knife and the edge of the windshield as a guide, cut through the adhesive material around the entire perimeter.

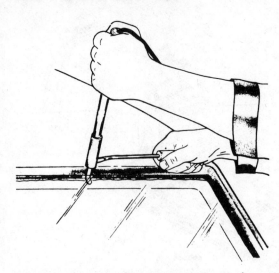

Using an electric knife to cut the window seal

5. Using a Hot Knife tool No. J-24709-1 and a cold knife, completely cut through the urethane adhesive.

6. Using an assistant (to support the windshield), remove the windshield from the vehicle.

7. If reinstalling the windshield, perform the following procedures:

a. Place the windshield onto a protective bench or holding fixture.

b. Using a razor blade or a sharp scraper, remove the excessive adhesive from the perimeter of the windshield.

c. Using denatured alcohol or lacquer thinner with a cloth, remove all traces of the adhesive from the perimeter of the windshield.

INSTALLATION

Monte Carlo

SHORT METHOD

NOTE: *This method is used when no other adhesive materials are used in the installation procedures. When using a new windshield for installation, DO NOT use kerosene or gasoline as a solvent, for a film is left which will prevent adhesion of the sealing material. When using a volatile cleaner, avoid contacting the plastic laminate material (around the edge of the glass) for discoloration and/or deterioration may occur.*

1. To prepare the windshield frame for glass installation, perform the following procedures:

a. Using a sharp scraper or a chisel, clean the excess sealing material from the windshield frame.

NOTE: *It is not necessary to remove all traces of the original material; there should be no*

mounds or loose pieces remaining. *If while removing the old material, the metal surface has been exposed, cover the area with black primer.*

b. Inspect the reveal molding retaining clips; if the upper end of the clip(s) is bent (more than 1/16 in.) away from the body metal, replace the clip(s).

NOTE: *When using weatherstrip adhesive, apply enough material to obtain a watertight seal beneath the spacer; DO NOT allow the material to squeeze out excessively.*

c. Cement the flat rubber spacers to the window opening at the pinchweld flanges; located the spacers so that they are equally spaced around the perimeter of the windshield.

d. Reinstall the metal supports at the lower edge of the windshield glass.

2. Using an assistant, lift the glass into the window opening; the windshield can be positioned without the use of suction cups. Check the position of the glass, it should not overlap the pinchweld flange (around the entire perimeter) by more than 3/16 in. The overlap across the top of the windshield can be corrected by readjusting the lower metal support spacers.

3. Check the relationship of the glass to the contour of the body. The gap between the glass and the pinchweld frame should be between 1/8–1/4 in. If there is difficulty in maintaining this distance, perform one of the following correction methods:

a. Reposition the flat spacers.

b. Apply excessive amounts of adhesive caulking material to the wide gaps.

c. Try another windshield.

d. Rework the pinchweld flange.

4. After the final adjustments have been

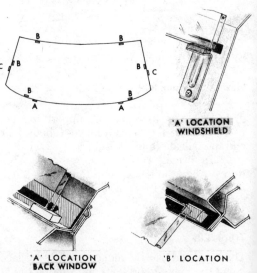

View of the glass spacer installation

made, apply pieces of masking tape over the edges of glass and the body, then slit the tape between the glass and the body. Remove the glass from opening.

NOTE: *The tape will be used for alignment of the glass upon installation and will aid in the clean up operation.*

5. If desired, apply masking tape to the inboard edge of the windshield; the tape should be placed ¼ in. (from the outer edge) around the top and sides (NOT the bottom) of the glass.

6. Using alcohol and a clean cloth, clean inner perimeter of the glass and allow it to air dry.

7. Using the Urethane Adhesive Kit No. 9636067 (two primers are provided), apply primer using the following procedures:

   a. Apply the clear primer around the entire perimeter of the glass. Allow the primer to dry for 5 minutes.

   b. If refinishing or painting operations are needed for any portions of the glass opening, apply the black primer to these portions. Allow the primer to dry for 5 minutes.

8. Using a caulking gun and an adhesive cartridge, apply a smooth continuous bead ⅜ in. high by ³⁄₁₆ in. wide around the entire perimeter of the glass.

9. Reposition the glass to the window opening using the tape as the installation guide. Apply light hand pressure to the glass to ensure a bond to the body opening. Using a small brush or flat bladed tool, paddle the bonding material around the edge of the glass to ensure a watertight seal.

10. Using a soft, warm water spray, allow the water to spill over the edges of the glass to detect water leaks. If a water leak is encountered, paddle additional material around the leak.

11. Cement rubber spacers between the right and the left sides of the windshield and the

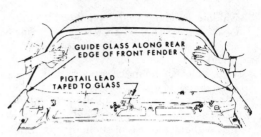

Installing the windshield

frame, to keep the glass centered during the installation procedures.

12. Install the windshield molding strips. Remove the masking tape from the inner perimeter of the windshield; pull the tape toward the center.

13. Complete the installation by replacing all of the removed parts.

NOTE: *After the windshield installation, the vehicle MUST remain at room temperature for 6 hours.*

EXTENDED METHOD

NOTE: *This method is used in conjunction with unknown adhesive materials such as butyl strips. When using a new windshield for installation, DO NOT use kerosene or gasoline as a solvent, for a film is left which will prevent adhesion of the sealing material. When using a volatile cleaner, avoid contacting the plastic laminate material (around the edge of the glass) for discoloration and/or deterioration may occur.*

1. To prepare the windshield frame for glass installation, perform the following procedures:

   a. Using a sharp scraper or a chisel, clean the excess sealing material from the windshield frame.

NOTE: *If using Butyl tape or unknown material to install the windshield, it is necessary to remove all traces of the original sealing material. If using Urethane sealing material, it is not necessary to remove all traces of the original material; there should be no mounds or loose pieces remaining. If while removing the old material, the metal surface has been exposed, cover the area with black primer.*

   b. Inspect the reveal molding retaining clips; if the upper end of the clip(s) is bent (more than ¹⁄₁₆ in.) away from the body metal, replace the clip(s).

NOTE: *If using weatherstrip adhesive, apply enough material to obtain a watertight seal beneath the spacer; DO NOT allow the material to squeeze out excessively. Weatherstrip material is not compatible with other replacement adhesives; leaks may develop where the two dissimilar materials are joined.*

   c. Cement the flat rubber spacers to the

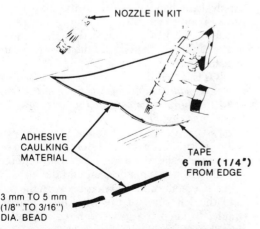

NOZZLE IN KIT

ADHESIVE CAULKING MATERIAL

TAPE 6 mm (1/4") FROM EDGE

3 mm TO 5 mm (1/8" TO 3/16") DIA. BEAD

Applying adhesive to the window—short method

window opening at the pinchweld flanges; locate the spacers so that they are equally spaced around the perimeter of the windshield.

d. Reinstall the metal supports at the lower edge of the windshield glass.

2. Using an assistant, lift the glass into the window opening; the windshield can be positioned without the use of suction cups. Check the position of the glass, it should not overlap the pinchweld flange (around the entire perimeter) by more than 3/16 in. The overlap across the top of the windshield can be corrected by readjusting the lower metal support spacers.

3. Check the relationship of the glass to the contour of the body. The gap between the glass and the pinchweld frame should be between 1/8–1/4 in. If difficulty in maintaining this distance is experienced, perform one of the following correction methods:

a. Reposition the flat spacers.

b. Apply excessive amounts of adhesive caulking material to the wide gaps.

c. Try another windshield.

d. Rework the pinchweld flange.

4. After the final adjustments have been made, apply pieces of masking tape over the edges of glass and the body, then slit the tape between the glass and the body. Remove the glass from opening.

NOTE: *The tape will be used for alignment of the glass upon installation and will aid in the clean up operation.*

5. If desired, apply masking tape to the inboard edge of the windshield; the tape should be placed 1/4 in. (from the outer edge) around the top and sides (NOT the bottom) of the glass.

6. If equipped with an embedded windshield antenna, apply an 8 in. butyl filler strip to the bottom inner center surface of the windshield. If not equipped with an embedded windshield antenna, the butyl strip is not necessary.

7. Using alcohol and a clean cloth, clean inner perimeter of the glass and allow it to air dry.

8. Using the Urethane Adhesive Kit No. 9636067 (two primers are provided), apply primer using the following procedures:

a. If equipped with an embedded antenna, apply the clear primer around the entire perimeter (except at the location of the filler strip); if not equipped with an embedded antenna, apply the clear primer around the entire perimeter of the glass. Allow the primer to dry for 5 minutes.

b. If refinishing or painting operations are needed for any portions of the glass opening, apply the black primer to these portions. Allow the primer to dry for 5 minutes.

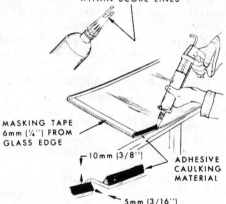

FOR EXTENDED METHOD, ENLARGE NOZZLE BY CUTTING OUT MATERIAL WITHIN SCORE LINES

MASKING TAPE 6mm (1/4") FROM GLASS EDGE

10mm (3/8")

ADHESIVE CAULKING MATERIAL

5mm (3/16")

Applying adhesive to the window—extended method

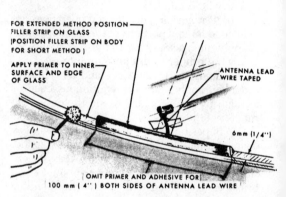

FOR EXTENDED METHOD POSITION FILLER STRIP ON GLASS (POSITION FILLER STRIP ON BODY FOR SHORT METHOD)

APPLY PRIMER TO INNER SURFACE AND EDGE OF GLASS

ANTENNA LEAD WIRE TAPED

6mm (1/4")

OMIT PRIMER AND ADHESIVE FOR 100 mm (4") BOTH SIDES OF ANTENNA LEAD WIRE

Preparing an embedded antenna windshield for installation—extended method

9. Using a caulking gun and an adhesive cartridge, apply a smooth continuous bead 3/8 in. high by 3/16 in. wide around the entire perimeter of the glass.

10. Reposition the glass to the window opening using the tape as the installation guide. Apply light hand pressure to the glass to ensure a bond to the body opening. Using a small brush or flat bladed tool, paddle the bonding material around the edge of the glass to ensure a watertight seal.

NOTE: *If equipped with an embedded antenna, paddle additional material at the edges of the butyl strip; avoid the area near the antenna pigtail.*

11. Using a soft, warm water spray, allow the water to spill over the edges of the glass to detect water leaks. If a water leak is encountered, paddle additional material around the leak.

12. Cement rubber spacers between the right and the left sides of the windshield and the frame, to keep the glass centered during the installation procedures.

13. Install the windshield molding strips. Remove the masking tape from the inner perimeter of the windshield; pull the tape toward the center.

14. Complete the installation by replacing all of the removed parts.

NOTE: *After the windshield installation, the vehicle MUST remain at room temperature for 6 hours.*

Rear Window Glass

NOTE: *The bonded windshield requires special tools and procedures.*

REMOVAL
Monte Carlo

1. Place protective coverings over the rear lid.

2. Remove the trim and the molding from around the glass.

3. If equipped with a rear window electric grid defogger (built into the glass), disconnect the wire harness connectors from the glass and tape the leads onto the outer surface of the glass to protect it from damage.

4. Using a utility knife and the edge of the windshield as a guide, cut through the adhesive material around the entire perimeter.

5. Using a Hot Knife tool No. J-24709-1 and a cold knife, completely cut through the urethane adhesive.

6. Using an assistant (to support the windshield) and suction cups, remove the window from the vehicle.

7. If reinstalling the window, perform the following procedures:

   a. Place the window onto a protective bench or holding fixture.

   b. Using a razor blade or a sharp scraper, remove the excessive adhesive from the perimeter of the window.

   c. Using denatured alcohol or lacquer thinner with a cloth, remove all traces of the adhesive from the perimeter of the window.

INSTALLATION
Monte Carlo
SHORT METHOD

NOTE: *This method is used when no other adhesive materials are used in the installation procedures. When using a new glass for installation, DO NOT use kerosene or gasoline as a solvent, for a film is left which will prevent adhesion of the sealing material. When using a volatile cleaner, avoid con-*

tacting the plastic laminate material (around the edge of the glass) for discoloration and/or deterioration may occur.

1. To prepare the window frame for glass installation, perform the following procedures:

   a. Using a sharp scraper or a chisel, clean the excess sealing material from the window frame.

NOTE: *It is not necessary to remove all traces of the original material; there should be no mounds or loose pieces remaining. If while removing the old material, the metal surface has been exposed, cover the area with black primer.*

   b. Inspect the reveal molding retaining clips; if the upper end of the clip(s) is bent (more than 1/16 in.) away from the body metal, replace the clip(s).

NOTE: *When using weatherstrip adhesive, apply enough material to obtain a watertight seal beneath the spacer; DO NOT allow the material to squeeze out excessively.*

   c. Cement the flat rubber spacers to the window opening art the pinchweld flanges; locate the spacers so that they are equally spaced around the perimeter of the window.

2. Using an assistant and suction cups, lift the glass into the window opening. Check the position of the glass, it should not overlap the pinchweld flange (around the entire perimeter) by more than 3/16 in. The overlap across the top of the window can be corrected by replacing the lower metal support spacers.

3. Check the relationship of the glass to the contour of the body. The gap between the glass and the pinchweld frame should be between 1/8–1/4 in. If there is difficulty in maintaining this distance, perform one of the following correction methods:

   a. Reposition the flat spacers.

   b. Apply excessive amounts of adhesive caulking material to the wide gaps.

   c. Try another window glass.

   d. Rework the pinchweld flange.

4. After the final adjustments have been made, apply pieces of masking tape over the edges of glass and the body, then slit the tape between the glass and the body. Remove the glass from the opening.

NOTE: *The tape will be used for alignment of the glass upon installation and will aid in the clean up operation.*

5. If desired, apply masking tape to the inboard edge of the window; the tape should be placed 1/4 in. (from the outer edge) around the top and sides (NOT the bottom) of the glass.

6. Using alcohol and a clean cloth, clean inner perimeter of the glass and allow it to air dry.

7. Using the Urethane Adhesive Kit No.

9636067 (two primers are provided), apply primer using the following procedures:

a. Apply the clear primer around the entire perimeter of the glass. Allow the primer to dry for 5 minutes.

b. If refinishing or painting operations are needed for any portions of the glass opening, apply the black primer to these portions. Allow the primer to dry for 5 minutes.

8. Using a caulking gun and an adhesive cartridge, apply a smooth continuous bead ⅜ in. high by 3/16 in. wide around the entire perimeter of the glass.

9. Reposition the glass to the window opening using the tape as the installation guide. Apply light hand pressure to the glass to ensure a bond to the body opening. Using a small brush or flat bladed tool, paddle the bonding material around the edge of the glass to ensure a watertight seal.

10. Using a soft, warm water spray, allow the water to spill over the edges of the glass to detect water leaks. If a water leak is encountered, paddle additional material around the leak.

11. Cement rubber spacers between the right and the left sides of the window and the frame, to keep the glass centered during the installation procedures.

12. Install the window molding strips. Remove the masking tape from the inner perimeter of the window; pull the tape toward the center.

13. Complete the installation by replacing all of the removed parts.

NOTE: *After the window installation, the vehicle MUST remain at room temperature for 6 hours.*

EXTENDED METHOD

NOTE: *This method is used in conjunction with unknown adhesive materials such as butyl strips. When using a new window for installation, DO NOT use kerosene or gasoline as a solvent, for a film is left which will prevent adhesion of the sealing material. When using a volatile cleaner, avoid contacting the plastic laminate material (around the edge of the glass) for discoloration and/or deterioration may occur.*

1. To prepare the window frame for glass installation, perform the following procedures:

a. Using a sharp scraper or a chisel, clean the excess sealing material from the window frame.

NOTE: *If using Butyl tape or unknown material to install the window, it is necessary to remove all traces of the original sealing material. If using Urethane sealing material, it is not necessary to remove all traces of the* original material; there should be no mounds or loose pieces remaining. If while removing the old material, the metal surface has been exposed, cover the area with black primer.

b. Inspect the reveal molding retaining clips; if the upper end of the clip(s) is bent (more than 1/16 in.) away from the body metal, replace the clip(s).

NOTE: *If using weatherstrip adhesive, apply enough material to obtain a watertight seal beneath the spacer; DO NOT allow the material to squeeze out excessively. Weatherstrip material is not compatible with other replacement adhesive; leaks may develop where the two dissimilar materials are joined.*

c. Cement the flat rubber spacers to the window opening at the pinchweld flanges; locate the spacers so that they are equally spaced around the perimeter of the window.

d. Reinstall the metal supports at the lower edge of the window glass.

2. Using an assistant and suction cups, lift the glass into the window opening. Check the position of the glass, it should not overlap the pinchweld flange (around the entire perimeter) by more than 3/16 in. The overlap across the top of the windshield can be corrected by replacing the lower metal support spacers.

3. Check the relationship of the glass to the contour of the body. The gap between the glass and the pinchweld frame should be between ⅛–¼ in. If difficulty in maintaining this distance is experienced, perform one of the following correction methods:

a. Reposition the flat spacers.

b. Apply excessive amounts of adhesive caulking material to the wide gaps.

c. Try another window.

d. Rework the pinchweld flange.

4. After the final adjustments have been made, apply pieces of masking tape over the edges of glass and the body, then slit the tape between the glass and the body. Remove the glass from opening.

NOTE: *The tape will be used for alignment of the glass upon installation and will aid in the clean up operation.*

5. If desired, apply masking tape to the inboard edge of the window; the tape should be placed ¼ in. (from the outer edge) around the top and sides (NOT the bottom) of the glass.

6. If equipped with an electric defogger, apply an 8 in. butyl filler strip to the bottom inner center surface of the window. If not equipped with an electric defogger, the butyl strip is not necessary.

7. Using alcohol and a clean cloth, clean inner perimeter of the glass and allow it to air dry.

8. Using the Urethane Adhesive Kit No.

9636067 (two primer are provided), apply primer using the following procedures:

a. If equipped with an embedded antenna, apply the clear primer around the entire perimeter (except at the location of the filler strip); if not equipped with an electric defogger, apply the clear primer around the entire perimeter of the glass. Allow the primer to dry for 5 minutes.

b. If refinishing or painting operations are needed for any portions of the glass opening, apply the black primer to these portions. Allow the primer to dry for 5 minutes.

9. Using a caulking gun and an adhesive cartridge, apply a smooth continuous bead ⅜ in. high by 3/16 in. wide around the entire perimeter of the glass.

10. Reposition the glass to the window opening using the tape as the installation guide. Apply light hand pressure to the glass to ensure a bond to the body opening. Using a small brush or flat bladed tool, paddle the bonding material around the edge of the glass to ensure a watertight seal.

NOTE: *If equipped with an electric defogger, paddle additional material at the edges of the butyl strip; avoid the area near the electrical harness.*

11. Using a soft, warm water spray, allow the water to spill over the edges of the glass to detect water leaks. If a water leak is encountered, paddle additional material around the leak.

12. Cement rubber spacers between the right and the left sides of the window glass and the frame, to keep the glass centered during the installation procedures.

13. Install the window molding strips. Remove the masking tape from the inner perimeter of the window; pull the tape toward the center.

14. Complete the installation by replacing all of the removed parts.

NOTE: *After the window installation, the vehicle MUST remain at room temperature for 6 hours.*

INTERIOR

Front Door Panels

REMOVAL AND INSTALLATION

1. Remove the door handles and the locking knob from the inside of the doors.

NOTE: *If equipped with door pull handles, remove the screws through the handle into the door inner panel.*

2. If equipped with remote control mirrors,

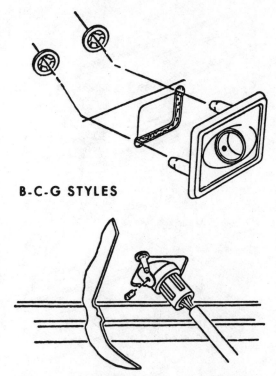

B-C-G STYLES

View of the remote mirror cable and escutcheon

remove the remote mirror escutcheon, then disengage the end of the mirror control cable from the escutcheon.

3. If equipped with a switch cover plate in the door armrest, remove the cover plate screws, then disconnect the switches and the cigar lighter (if equipped) from the electrical harness.

4. If equipped with an integral armrest, remove the screws inserted through the pull cup into the armrest hanger support. If equipped with an armrest applied after the door trim installation, remove the armrest-to-inner panel screws.

5. If equipped with two-piece trim panels, disengage the retainer clips from the front and the rear of the upper trim panel, using tool No. BT-7323A, then lift the upper door trim and slide it slightly rearward to disengage it from the door inner panel at the beltline.

NOTE: *If equipped with electric switches in the door trim panel, disconnect the electrical connectors from the switch assembly.*

6. Along the upper edge of the lower trim panel, remove the mounting screws. At the lower edge of the panel, insert tool No. BT-7323A between the inner panel and the trim panel, then disengage the retaining clips from around the outer perimeter. To remove the lower panel, push the panel down and outward to disengage it from the door.

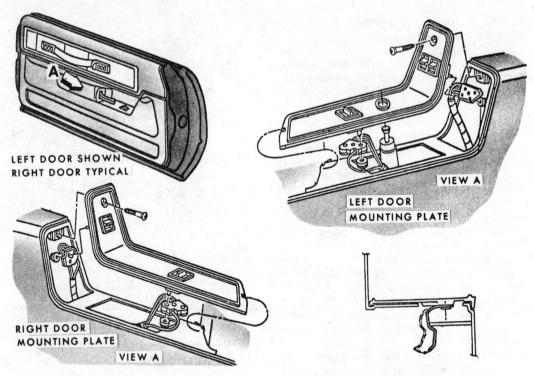

LEFT DOOR SHOWN
RIGHT DOOR TYPICAL

VIEW A

LEFT DOOR
MOUNTING PLATE

RIGHT DOOR
MOUNTING PLATE

VIEW A

View of the armrest switch cover plate and remote mirror cable attachment

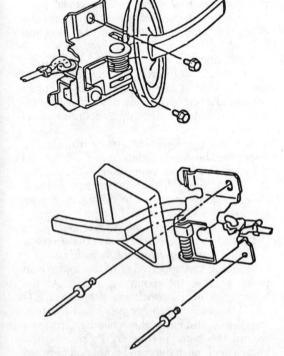

View of the door lock remote control handle

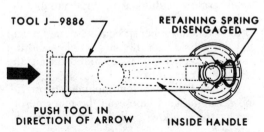

TOOL J—9886

RETAINING SPRING
DISENGAGED

PUSH TOOL IN
DIRECTION OF ARROW

INSIDE HANDLE

Removing the clip from inside the door handle

NOTE: *If equipped with courtesy lights, disconnect the wiring harness.*

7. If equipped with an insulator pad glued to the door inner panel, remove the pad (with a putty knife) by separating it from the inner panel.

8. To install, reverse the removal procedures.

NOTE: *If replacing the inner pad to the door inner panel, use 3M General Trim Adhesive No. 8080, glue it to the panel.*

Rear Door Panels
REMOVAL AND INSTALLATION

1. Remove the door handles and the locking knob from the inside of the doors.

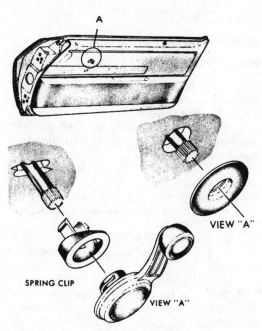

View of the window regulator handle

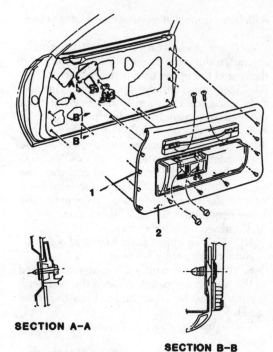

SECTION A-A

SECTION B-B

1. Trim fastener locations
2. Door trim assembly

Exploded view of the door trim panel

NOTE: *If equipped with door pull handles, remove the screws through the handle into the door inner panel.*

2. If equipped with a switch cover plate in the door armrest, remove the cover plate screws, then disconnect the switch from the electrical harness.

3. If equipped with an integral armrest, remove the screws inserted through the pull cup into the armrest hanger support. If equipped with an armrest applied after the door trim in-

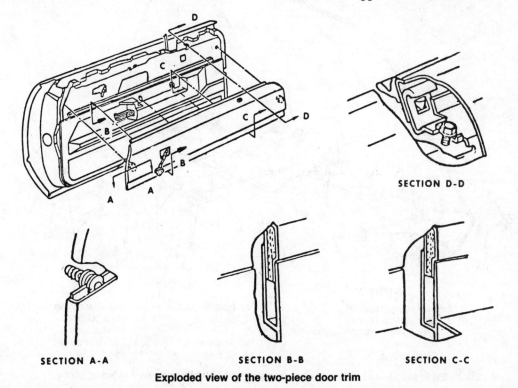

SECTION D-D

SECTION A-A   **SECTION B-B**   **SECTION C-C**

Exploded view of the two-piece door trim

stallation, remove the armrest-to-inner panel screws.

4. If equipped with two-piece trim panels, disengage the retainer clips from the front and the rear of the upper trim panel, using tool No. BT-7323A, then lift the upper door trim and slide it slightly rearward to disengage it from the door inner panel at the beltline.

5. Along the upper edge of the lower trim panel, remove the mounting screws. At the lower edge of the panel, insert tool No. BT-7323A between the inner panel and the trim panel, the disengage the retaining clips from around the outer perimeter. To remove the lower panel, push the panel down and outward to disengage it from the door.

NOTE: *If equipped with courtesy lights, disconnect the wiring harness.*

6. If equipped with an insulator pad glued to the door inner panel, remove the pad (with a putty knife) by separating it from the inner panel.

7. To install, reverse the removal procedures.

NOTE: *If replacing the inner pad to the door inner panel, use 3M General Trim Adhesive No. 8080, glue it to the panel.*

Front Door Glass

REMOVAL AND INSTALLATION

Monte Carlo–Coupe

1. Refer to the "Door Panel Removal and Installation" procedures, in this section and remove the door panel(s).

2. Remove the armrest, the trim panel(s), the insulator pad (if equipped) and the inner panel water deflector.

3. With the glass in the half raised position, mark the location of the mounting screws, then remove the following components:

   a. The front belt stabilizer and trim retainer.

   b. The rear belt stabilizer pin assembly.

   c. The front up-travel stop (on the inner panel).

   d. The rear up-travel stop (on the glass).

4. Remove the vertical guide upper and lower screws, then disengage the guide assembly from the roller and lay in the bottom of the door.

5. Position the glass to expose the lower sash channel cam nuts, then remove the nuts through the inner panel access hole.

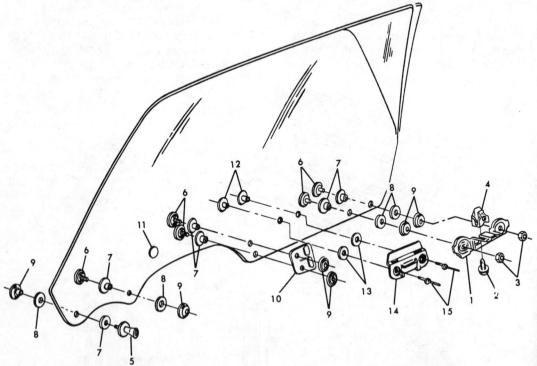

1. Rear up-stop support	6. Spanner bolt	11. Stabilizer button
2. Rear up-stop screw	7. Bushing	12. Rivet bushing
3. Rear up-stop support to glass nuts	8. Washer	13. Rivet retainer
4. Rear up-stop	9. Spanner nut	14. Stabilizer guide
5. Front up-stop	10. Spacer	15. Rivet

Exploded view of the door window assembly—stabilizer guide riveted to glass

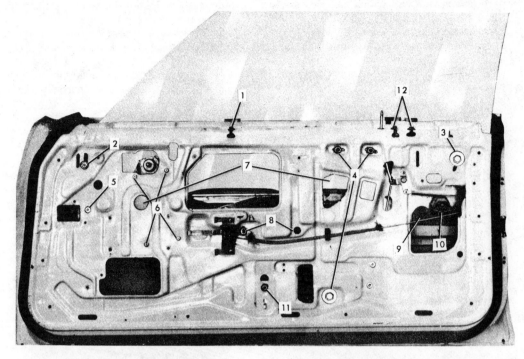

1. Front belt stabilizer and trim retainer screw
2. Front up-travel stop screw (on inner panel)
3. Rear up-travel stop screw (on inner panel)
4. Vertical guide upper and lower screws
5. Glass stabilizer rivet
6. Window regulator rivets (manual window)
7. Access holes—lower sash channel cam to glass attaching nuts
8. Inner panel cam screws
9. Rear up-stop support to glass attaching nut
10. Rear up-stop attaching screw
11. Down-travel stop screw
12. Rear belt stabilizer pin assembly screws

View of the front door hardware attachments—Monte Carlo-Coupe

6. While supporting the glass, separate it from the lower sash channel cam.

7. To remove the glass, perform the following procedures:

a. Raise the glass slowly and slide it rearward.

b. Tilt the top of the glass inboard until the front up-stop roller clears the front loading hole at the inner panel belt reinforcement.

c. Rotate the glass rearward 45°, then raise it slowly to clear the glass attaching screws through the belt loading holes.

8. To install, reverse the removal procedures. Adjust the window glass. Torque the hardware fasteners to 90–125 inch lbs.

Monte Carlo—Sedan

1. Refer to the "Door Panel Removal and Installation" procedures, in this section and remove the door panel(s).

2. To disengage the rear roller, lower the glass to ¾ of the way down, tip the nose of the glass down and slide it backward.

3. To disengage the front roller, raise the nose of the glass 45° and slide it rearward.

4. Lift the outboard of the upper frame to remove the glass. Adjust the regulator position to remove the glass.

5. To install, reverse the removal procedures. Adjust the position of the glass. Torque the fasteners to 90–125 inch lbs.

ADJUSTMENT

Monte Carlo–Coupe

1. Refer to the "Door Panel Removal and Installation" procedures, in this section and remove the door panel(s).

2. To rotate the window, loosen the front and rear up-stops, adjust the inner panel cam and the up-stops, then tighten the screws.

3. To adjust the window's upper inboard and outboard edge, perform the following procedures:

a. Position the window in the partially down position.

b. Loosen the vertical guide upper support (lower) screws, which are accessible through the inner panel access holes.

c. Loosen the pin assembly screws, the rear up-stop screw and the front belt stabilizer screw.

d. Adjust the vertical guide upper support and pin assembly (in or out) as re-

quired, then tighten the screws. Adjust and tighten the other components.

NOTE: *When adjusting the glass, make sure that it remains inboard of the blow-out clip, when cycled.*

4. If the window is too far forward or rearward, position the window partially down

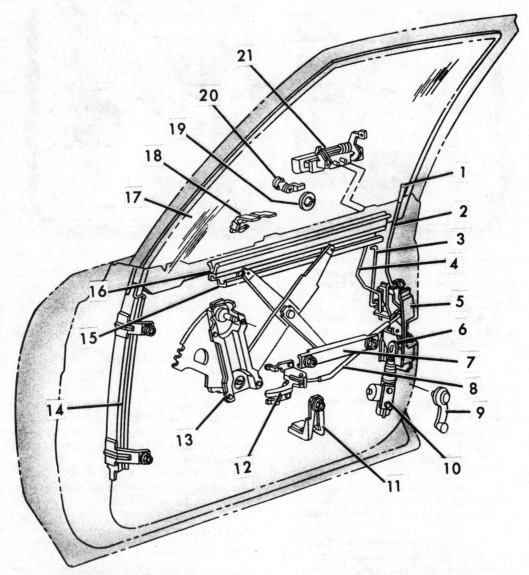

1. Inside locking rod knob
2. Inside locking rod
3. Lock cylinder to lock connecting rod
4. Outside handle to lock connecting rod
5. Door lock
6. Inside locking rod to electric actuator connecting rod
7. Inner panel cam
8. Inside remote handle to lock connecting rod
9. Manual window regulator handle
10. Power door lock actuator
11. Down-travel stop
12. Inside remote handle
13. Manual window regulator
14. Glass run channel retainer
15. Lower sash channel cam
16. Lower sash channel
17. Window glass
18. Lock cylinder retainer
19. Lock cylinder gasket
20. Lock cylinder assembly
21. Outside handle assembly

View of the front door hardware attachments—Monte Carlo-Sedan

loosen the vertical guide (upper and lower) screws, then adjust as required.

5. If the window is too high or low in it's Up position, adjust the front and rear up-travel stops.

6. If the window is too high or low in the Down position, adjust the down-travel stop.

7. If the window binds during the up and down operations, adjust the front and/or rear belt stabilizer pin assemblies.

Monte Carlo–Sedan

1. Refer to the "Door Panel Removal and Installation" procedures, in this section and remove the door panel(s).

2. If the window is rotated, loosen the inner panel cam adjusting screws, position the glass and tighten the screws.

3. If the window is too high or low in the down position, loosen the down-travel stop screws, position the glass, position the down-stop and tighten the screws.

Front Door Regulator

REMOVAL AND INSTALLATION

Monte Carlo–Coupe

1. Refer to the "Door Panel Removal and Installation" procedures, in this section and remove the door panel(s).

2. Prop the window in the half-way position by inserting rubber wedges between the window and the inner panel (at the belt) at the front and rear of the window.

NOTE: *If rubber stops are not available, remove the window.*

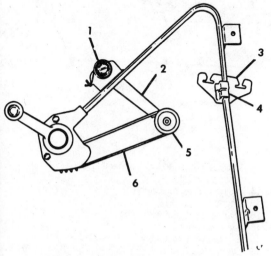

1. Counterbalance spring
2. Assist arm
3. Sash
4. Guide
5. Roller
6. Tape

View of the tape drive regulator assembly

3. Mark (locate) and remove the inner panel cam and the vertical guide screws. Remove the vertical guide through the large access hole.

4. Using a center punch and a ¼ in. drill bit, drive out the center pins and drill out the rivets of the regulator.

5. Remove the lower sash channel cam-to-glass rear nut, then slide the regulator rearward and disengage the rollers from the lower sash channel cam.

6. Remove the regulator through the largest inner panel access hole.

7. To install, reverse the removal procedures. Use ¼–20 x ½ in. nuts/to mount the regulator.

Monte Carlo–Sedan

1. Refer to the "Door Panel Removal and Installation" procedures, in this section and remove the door panel(s).

2. Position the window in the Full-Up position and tape the glass to the frame.

3. Locate and remove the inner panel cam screws and the cam.

4. Remove the remote handle-to-lock connecting rod.

5. Using a center punch and a ¼ in. drill bit, drive out the center pins and drill out the rivets of the regulator.

6. Disengage the rollers from the lower sash channel cam.

7. Remove the regulator through the largest inner panel access hole.

8. To install, reverse the removal procedures. Use ¼–20 x ½ in. nuts to mount the regulator.

Electric Window Motor–Front Door

REMOVAL AND INSTALLATION

Monte Carlo–Coupe

1. Refer to the "Door Panel Removal and Installation" procedures, in this section and remove the door panel(s).

2. Prop the window in the half-way position by inserting rubber wedges between the window and the inner panel (at the belt) at the front and rear of the window.

NOTE: *If rubber doors stops are not available, remove the window.*

3. Mark (locate) and remove the inner panel cam and the vertical guide screws. Remove the vertical guide through the large access hole. Disconnect the electrical connector from the window regulator motor.

4. Using a center punch and a ¼ in. drill bit, drive out the center pins and drill out the rivets of the regulator.

5. Remove the lower sash channel cam-to-

glass rear nut, then slide the regulator rearward and disengage the rollers from the lower sash channel cam.

6. Remove the regulator and motor through the largest inner panel access hole.

7. To install, reverse the removal procedures. Use ¼–20 x ½ in. nuts to mount the regulator.

Monte Carlo–Sedan

1. Refer to the "Door Panel Removal and Installation" procedures, in this section and remove the door panel(s).

2. Position the window in the Full-Up position and tape the glass to the frame.

3. Locate and remove the inner panel cam screws and the cam.

4. Remove the remote handle-to-lock connecting rod. Disconnect the wiring harness connector at the window regulator motor.

5. Using a center punch and a ¼ in. drill bit, drive out the center pins and drill out the rivets of the regulator.

6. Disengage the rollers from the lower sash channel cam.

7. Remove the regulator and motor through the largest inner panel access hole.

8. To install, reverse the removal procedures. Use ¼–20 x ½ in. nuts to mount the regulator.

Rear Door Glass (Sedan)
REMOVAL AND INSTALLATION
Monte Carlo

NOTE: *The rear door window is a frameless solid, safety plate glass window which is retained by two beltline support clips; the window remains in a fixed position.*

1. Refer to the "Rear Door Panel Removal and Installation" procedures, in this section and remove the door panel(s).

2. Remove the beltline support clips and the trim support retainer.

3. With the use of suction cups, slide the

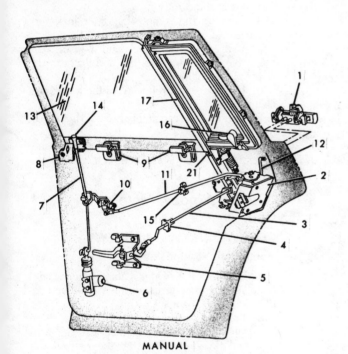

MANUAL

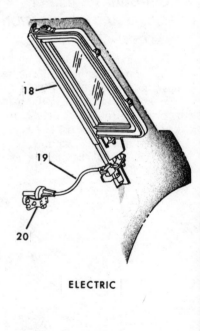

ELECTRIC

1. Outside handle assembly
2. Door lock
3. Inside handle to lock connecting rod
4. Shoe
5. Inside remote handle
6. Power door lock actuator
7. Inside locking rod
8. Trim support retainer
9. Glass support clips
10. Bell crank
11. Bell crank to lock connecting rod
12. Outside handle to lock connecting rod
13. Door glass (stationary)
14. Inside locking rod knob
15. Silencer
16. Manual vent latch assembly
17. Manual vent assembly
18. Electric vent assembly
19. Drive cable
20. Motor assembly–electric vent
21. Belt screw

View of the rear door hardware

glass down and remove it from the inboard side of the door.

4. To install, lubricate the glass channel with silicone spray of liquid soap, then reverse the removal procedures.

Rear Door Operating Vent Window Assembly

The rear doors have a movable vent window which can be either manual or electric operation. The window is held in place by mounting screws in the upper door frame and in the door belt return flange.

The manual vent window has a latch handle which locks or opens the window.

The electric vent window is operated by an electric motor and a drive cable assembly. It is controlled by the master switch on the left-front armrest or by a switch on the rear door trim panel.

REMOVAL AND INSTALLATION
Monte Carlo
MANUAL

1. Refer to the "Rear Door Glass Removal and Installation" procedures, in this section and remove the door glass.

2. Remove the frame and the belt mounting screws, then pull the top of vent assembly forward and remove it from inside of the door.

3. To install, lubricate the glass channel with silicone spray of liquid soap, then reverse the removal procedures.

ELECTRIC

1. Refer to the "Rear Door Glass and Removal and Installation" procedures, in this section and remove the door glass.

2. Disconnect the actuator rod-to-actuator lever plastic clip, by rotating the clip inward with a flat-bladed screwdriver.

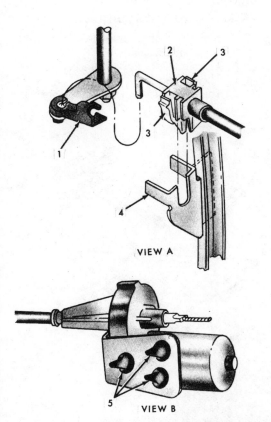

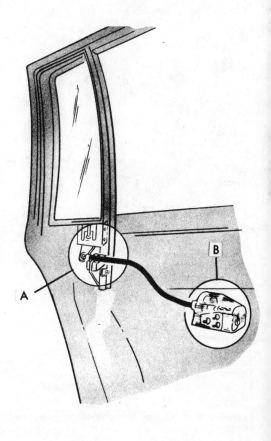

1. Retaining clip–actuator rod to actuator lever
2. Retaining clip–drive cable to retainer
3. Tabs–drive cable retaining clip
4. Retainer
5. Grommets–motor assembly to rear door inner panel

View of the door electric vent window—rear door

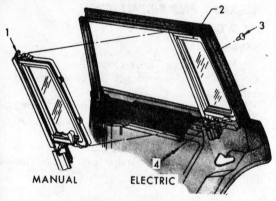

MANUAL   ELECTRIC

1. Manual vent window
2. Electric vent window
3. Upper frame attaching screw
4. Belt attaching screw

Installing the rear door vent window

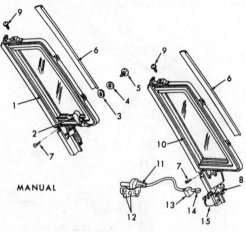

MANUAL

ELECTRIC

1. Manual vent window assembly
2. Manual latch handle
3. Washer (inboard of glass)
4. Spacer (outboard of glass)
5. Support screw
6. Reveal molding
7. Belt attaching screw
8. Actuator lever
9. Upper frame attaching screw
10. Electric vent window assembly
11. Electric actuator assembly
12. Grommets—motor assembly to rear door inner panel
13. Retaining clip—drive cable to retainer
14. Retaining clip—actuator rod to actuator lever
15. Retainer

Exploded view of the rear door hardware—vent window

3. To remove the drive cable plastic retaining clip, depress the tabs and push up.

4. Remove the upper frame screws and the belt screw.

5. Pull the top of vent assembly forward and remove it from inside of the door.

6. To install, lubricate the glass channel with silicone spray or liquid soap, then reverse the removal procedures.

Power Seat Motor
REMOVAL AND INSTALLATION

1. Disconnect the electrical harness connector and remove the seat from the vehicle, then place it upside down on a protected workbench.

2. Disconnect the motor feed wires from the motor control relay.

3. Remove the motor mounting screws and the transmission-to-motor screws, then move the motor away to disengage it from the rubber coupling.

4. To install, reverse the removal procedures.

NOTE: *When installing the motor, make sure that the rubber coupling is properly engaged at the motor and the transmission.*

Headliner
REMOVAL AND INSTALLATION

1. Remove the following items:
   a. The courtesy lamps.
   b. The sunshade support brackets.
   c. The coat hooks.
   d. The upper quarter trim finishing panels.

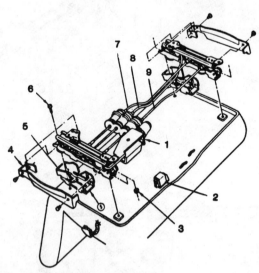

1. Transmission assembly
2. Seat relay
3. Nut
4. Adjuster track lower cover
5. Adjuster track upper cover
6. Adjuster-to-seat frame attaching bolts
7. Horizontal drive cable
8. Rear vertical drive cable
9. Front vertical drive cable

View of the six-way power seat adjusters

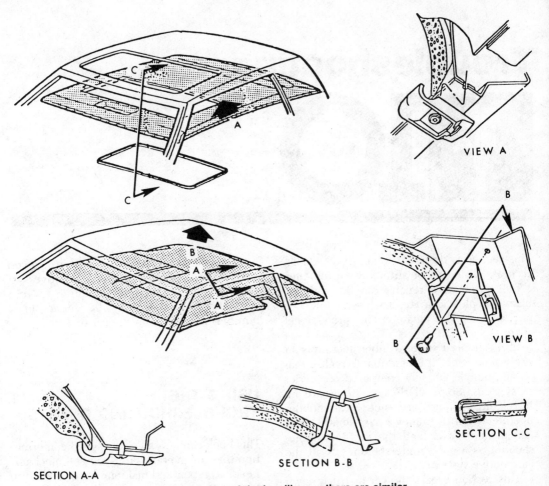

VIEW A

VIEW B

SECTION A-A

SECTION B-B

SECTION C-C

Exploded view of the headliner—others are similar

e. The side roof rail moldings.

f. The windshield and rear window garnish moldings.

g. The shoulder strap retainers and covers.

h. The windshield side garnish molding.

i. If equipped, the roof-mounted assist straps.

j. If equipped, the sun roof trim finishing lace.

k. If equipped, the twin lift-off panel roof garnish moldings.

2. On each side of the headlining assembly, disengage the tabs or clips, then move the assembly rearward enough (to provide clearance) for the front portion of the assembly to be removed through the front door opening.

NOTE: *If the replacement headlining does not have an insulator glued to the upper surface, carefully remove the insulator from the original headlining (if equipped) and spot cement it to the new headlining. DO NOT overflex the headlining, for it can become easily damaged.*

3. To install, reverse the removal procedures.

NOTE: *DO NOT attach the roof hardware until headlining has been completely installed.*

Troubleshooting

This section is designed to aid in the quick, accurate diagnosis of automotive problems. While automotive repairs can be made by many people, accurate troubleshooting is a rare skill for the amateur and professional alike.

In its simplest state, troubleshooting is an exercise in logic. It is essential to realize that an automobile is really composed of a series of systems. Some of these systems are interrelated; others are not. Automobiles operate within a framework of logical rules and physical laws, and the key to trouble-shooting is a good understanding of all the automotive systems.

This section breaks the car or truck down into its component systems, allowing the problem to be isolated. The charts and diagnostic road maps list the most common problems and the most probable causes of trouble. Obviously it would be impossible to list every possible problem that could happen along with every possible cause, but it will locate MOST problems and eliminate a lot of unnecessary guesswork. The systematic format will locate problems within a given system, but, because many automotive systems are interrelated, the solution to your particular problem may be found in a number of systems on the car or truck.

USING THE TROUBLESHOOTING CHARTS

This book contains all of the specific information that the average do-it-yourself mechanic needs to repair and maintain his or her car or truck. The troubleshooting charts are designed to be used in conjunction with the specific procedures and information in the text. For instance, troubleshooting a point-type ignition system is fairly standard for all models, but you may be directed to the text to find procedures for troubleshooting an individual type of electronic ignition. You will also have to refer to the specification charts throughout the book for specifications applicable to your car or truck.

TOOLS AND EQUIPMENT

The tools illustrated in Chapter 1 (plus two more diagnostic pieces) will be adequate to troubleshoot most problems. The two other tools needed are a voltmeter and an ohmmeter. These can be purchased separately or in combination, known as a VOM meter.

In the event that other tools are required, they will be noted in the procedures.

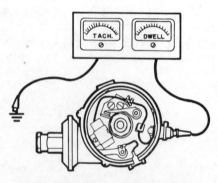

Tach-dwell hooked-up to distributor

Troubleshooting Engine Problems

See Chapters 2, 3, 4 for more information and service procedures.

Index to Systems

System	To Test	Group
Battery	Engine need not be running	1
Starting system	Engine need not be running	2
Primary electrical system	Engine need not be running	3
Secondary electrical system	Engine need not be running	4
Fuel system	Engine need not be running	5
Engine compression	Engine need not be running	6
Engine vacuum	Engine must be running	7
Secondary electrical system	Engine must be running	8
Valve train	Engine must be running	9
Exhaust system	Engine must be running	10
Cooling system	Engine must be running	11
Engine lubrication	Engine must be running	12

Index to Problems

Problem: Symptom	Begin at Specific Diagnosis, Number
Engine Won't Start:	
Starter doesn't turn	1.1, 2.1
Starter turns, engine doesn't	2.1
Starter turns engine very slowly	1.1, 2.4
Starter turns engine normally	3.1, 4.1
Starter turns engine very quickly	6.1
Engine fires intermittently	4.1
Engine fires consistently	5.1, 6.1
Engine Runs Poorly:	
Hard starting	3.1, 4.1, 5.1, 8.1
Rough idle	4.1, 5.1, 8.1
Stalling	3.1, 4.1, 5.1, 8.1
Engine dies at high speeds	4.1, 5.1
Hesitation (on acceleration from standing stop)	5.1, 8.1
Poor pickup	4.1, 5.1, 8.1
Lack of power	3.1, 4.1, 5.1, 8.1
Backfire through the carburetor	4.1, 8.1, 9.1
Backfire through the exhaust	4.1, 8.1, 9.1
Blue exhaust gases	6.1, 7.1
Black exhaust gases	5.1
Running on (after the ignition is shut off)	3.1, 8.1
Susceptible to moisture	4.1
Engine misfires under load	4.1, 7.1, 8.4, 9.1
Engine misfires at speed	4.1, 8.4
Engine misfires at idle	3.1, 4.1, 5.1, 7.1, 8.4

Sample Section

Test and Procedure	Results and Indications	Proceed to
4.1—Check for spark: Hold each spark plug wire approximately ¼″ from ground with gloves or a heavy, dry rag. Crank the engine and observe the spark.	→ If no spark is evident:	→4.2
	→ If spark is good in some cases:	→4.3
	→ If spark is good in all cases:	→4.6

Specific Diagnosis

This section is arranged so that following each test, instructions are given to proceed to another, until a problem is diagnosed.

Section 1—Battery

Test and Procedure	Results and Indications	Proceed to
1.1—Inspect the battery visually for case condition (corrosion, cracks) and water level.	If case is cracked, replace battery:	1.4
	If the case is intact, remove corrosion with a solution of baking soda and water (**CAUTION:** *do not get the solution into the battery*), and fill with water:	1.2

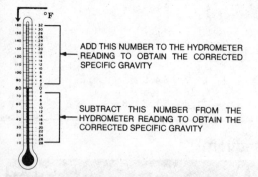

DIRT ON TOP OF BATTERY
CORROSION
PLUGGED VENT
LOOSE CABLE OR POSTS
CRACKS
LOW WATER LEVEL

Inspect the battery case

1.2—Check the battery cable connections: Insert a screwdriver between the battery post and the cable clamp. Turn the headlights on high beam, and observe them as the screwdriver is gently twisted to ensure good metal to metal contact.	If the lights brighten, remove and clean the clamp and post; coat the post with petroleum jelly, install and tighten the clamp:	1.4
	If no improvement is noted:	1.3

TESTING BATTERY CABLE CONNECTIONS USING A SCREWDRIVER

1.3—Test the state of charge of the battery using an individual cell tester or hydrometer.	If indicated, charge the battery. **NOTE:** *If no obvious reason exists for the low state of charge (i.e., battery age, prolonged storage), proceed to:*	1.4

°F

ADD THIS NUMBER TO THE HYDROMETER READING TO OBTAIN THE CORRECTED SPECIFIC GRAVITY

SUBTRACT THIS NUMBER FROM THE HYDROMETER READING TO OBTAIN THE CORRECTED SPECIFIC GRAVITY

Specific Gravity (@ 80° F.)

Minimum	Battery Charge
1.260	100% Charged
1.230	75% Charged
1.200	50% Charged
1.170	25% Charged
1.140	Very Little Power Left
1.110	Completely Discharged

The effects of temperature on battery specific gravity (left) and amount of battery charge in relation to specific gravity (right)

1.4—Visually inspect battery cables for cracking, bad connection to ground, or bad connection to starter.	If necessary, tighten connections or replace the cables:	2.1

Section 2—Starting System
See Chapter 3 for service procedures

Test and Procedure	Results and Indications	Proceed to
Note: Tests in Group 2 are performed with coil high tension lead disconnected to prevent accidental starting.		
2.1—Test the starter motor and solenoid: Connect a jumper from the battery post of the solenoid (or relay) to the starter post of the solenoid (or relay).	If starter turns the engine normally:	**2.2**
	If the starter buzzes, or turns the engine very slowly:	**2.4**
	If no response, replace the solenoid (or relay).	**3.1**
	If the starter turns, but the engine doesn't, ensure that the flywheel ring gear is intact. If the gear is undamaged, replace the starter drive.	**3.1**
2.2—Determine whether ignition override switches are functioning properly (clutch start switch, neutral safety switch), by connecting a jumper across the switch(es), and turning the ignition switch to "start".	If starter operates, adjust or replace switch:	**3.1**
	If the starter doesn't operate:	**2.3**
2.3—Check the ignition switch "start" position: Connect a 12V test lamp or voltmeter between the starter post of the solenoid (or relay) and ground. Turn the ignition switch to the "start" position, and jiggle the key.	If the lamp doesn't light or the meter needle doesn't move when the switch is turned, check the ignition switch for loose connections, cracked insulation, or broken wires. Repair or replace as necessary:	**3.1**
	If the lamp flickers or needle moves when the key is jiggled, replace the ignition switch.	**3.3**

Checking the ignition switch "start" position

STARTER RELAY (IF EQUIPPED)

Test and Procedure	Results and Indications	Proceed to
2.4—Remove and bench test the starter, according to specifications in the engine electrical section.	If the starter does not meet specifications, repair or replace as needed:	**3.1**
	If the starter is operating properly:	**2.5**
2.5—Determine whether the engine can turn freely: Remove the spark plugs, and check for water in the cylinders. Check for water on the dipstick, or oil in the radiator. Attempt to turn the engine using an 18″ flex drive and socket on the crankshaft pulley nut or bolt.	If the engine will turn freely only with the spark plugs out, and hydrostatic lock (water in the cylinders) is ruled out, check valve timing:	**9.2**
	If engine will not turn freely, and it is known that the clutch and transmission are free, the engine must be disassembled for further evaluation:	**Chapter 3**

Section 3—Primary Electrical System

Test and Procedure	Results and Indications	Proceed to
3.1—Check the ignition switch "on" position: Connect a jumper wire between the distributor side of the coil and ground, and a 12V test lamp between the switch side of the coil and ground. Remove the high tension lead from the coil. Turn the ignition switch on and jiggle the key.	If the lamp lights:	3.2
	If the lamp flickers when the key is jiggled, replace the ignition switch:	3.3
	If the lamp doesn't light, check for loose or open connections. If none are found, remove the ignition switch and check for continuity. If the switch is faulty, replace it:	3.3

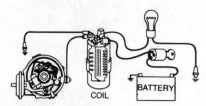

Checking the ignition switch "on" position

3.2—Check the ballast resistor or resistance wire for an open circuit, using an ohmmeter. See Chapter 3 for specific tests.	Replace the resistor or resistance wire if the resistance is zero. **NOTE:** *Some ignition systems have no ballast resistor.*	3.3

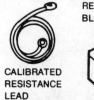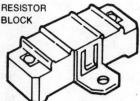

Two types of resistors

3.3—On point-type ignition systems, visually inspect the breaker points for burning, pitting or excessive wear. Gray coloring of the point contact surfaces is normal. Rotate the crankshaft until the contact heel rests on a high point of the distributor cam and adjust the point gap to specifications. On electronic ignition models, remove the distributor cap and visually inspect the armature. Ensure that the armature pin is in place, and that the armature is on tight and rotates when the engine is cranked. Make sure there are no cracks, chips or rounded edges on the armature.	If the breaker points are intact, clean the contact surfaces with fine emery cloth, and adjust the point gap to specifications. If the points are worn, replace them. On electronic systems, replace any parts which appear defective. If condition persists:	3.4

Test and Procedure	Results and Indications	Proceed to
3.4—On point-type ignition systems, connect a dwell-meter between the distributor primary lead and ground. Crank the engine and observe the point dwell angle. On electronic ignition systems, conduct a stator (magnetic pickup assembly) test. See Chapter 3.	On point-type systems, adjust the dwell angle if necessary. **NOTE:** *Increasing the point gap decreases the dwell angle and vice-versa.*	**3.6**
	If the dwell meter shows little or no reading;	**3.5**
	On electronic ignition systems, if the stator is bad, replace the stator. If the stator is good, proceed to the other tests in Chapter 3.	

Dwell is a function of point gap

3.5—On the point-type ignition systems, check the condenser for short: connect an ohmmeter across the condenser body and the pigtail lead.	If any reading other than infinite is noted, replace the condenser	**3.6**

Checking the condenser for short

3.6—Test the coil primary resistance: On point-type ignition systems, connect an ohmmeter across the coil primary terminals, and read the resistance on the low scale. Note whether an external ballast resistor or resistance wire is used. On electronic ignition systems, test the coil primary resistance as in Chapter 3.	Point-type ignition coils utilizing ballast resistors or resistance wires should have approximately 1.0 ohms resistance. Coils with internal resistors should have approximately 4.0 ohms resistance. If values far from the above are noted, replace the coil.	**4.1**

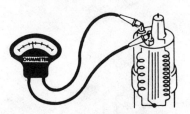

Check the coil primary resistance

Section 4—Secondary Electrical System
See Chapters 2–3 for service procedures

Test and Procedure	Results and Indications	Proceed to
4.1—Check for spark: Hold each spark plug wire approximately ¼″ from ground with gloves or a heavy, dry rag. Crank the engine, and observe the spark.	If no spark is evident:	4.2
	If spark is good in some cylinders:	4.3
	If spark is good in all cylinders:	4.6

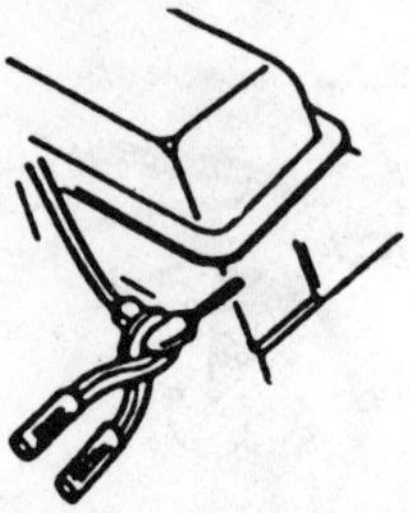

Check for spark at the plugs

4.2—Check for spark at the coil high tension lead: Remove the coil high tension lead from the distributor and position it approximately ¼″ from ground. Crank the engine and observe spark. **CAUTION: _This test should not be performed on engines equipped with electronic ignition._**	If the spark is good and consistent:	4.3
	If the spark is good but intermittent, test the primary electrical system starting at 3.3:	3.3
	If the spark is weak or non-existent, replace the coil high tension lead, clean and tighten all connections and retest. If no improvement is noted:	4.4
4.3—Visually inspect the distributor cap and rotor for burned or corroded contacts, cracks, carbon tracks, or moisture. Also check the fit of the rotor on the distributor shaft (where applicable).	If moisture is present, dry thoroughly, and retest per 4.1:	4.1
	If burned or excessively corroded contacts, cracks, or carbon tracks are noted, replace the defective part(s) and retest per 4.1:	4.1
	If the rotor and cap appear intact, or are only slightly corroded, clean the contacts thoroughly (including the cap towers and spark plug wire ends) and retest per 4.1:	
	If the spark is good in all cases:	4.6
	If the spark is poor in all cases:	4.5

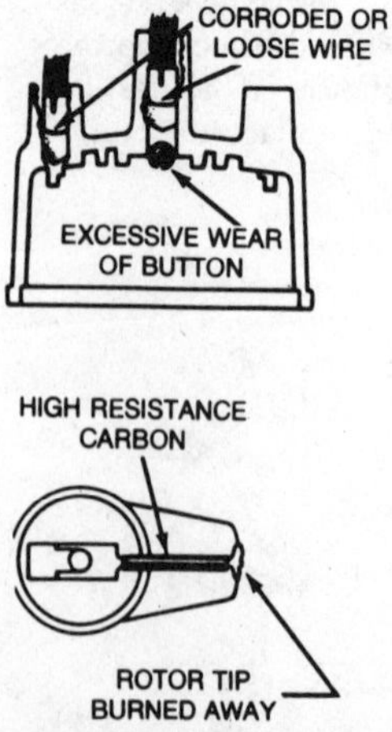

CORRODED OR LOOSE WIRE

EXCESSIVE WEAR OF BUTTON

HIGH RESISTANCE CARBON

ROTOR TIP BURNED AWAY

Inspect the distributor cap and rotor

Test and Procedure	Results and Indications	Proceed to
4.4—Check the coil secondary resistance: On point-type systems connect an ohmmeter across the distributor side of the coil and the coil tower. Read the resistance on the high scale of the ohmmeter. On electronic ignition systems, see Chapter 3 for specific tests.	The resistance of a satisfactory coil should be between 4,000 and 10,000 ohms. If resistance is considerably higher (i.e., 40,000 ohms) replace the coil and retest per 4.1. **NOTE:** *This does not apply to high performance coils.*	

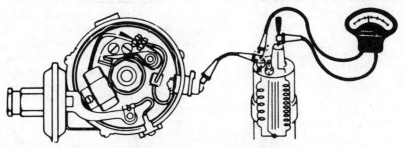

Testing the coil secondary resistance

Test and Procedure	Results and Indications	Proceed to
4.5—Visually inspect the spark plug wires for cracking or brittleness. Ensure that no two wires are positioned so as to cause induction firing (adjacent and parallel). Remove each wire, one by one, and check resistance with an ohmmeter.	Replace any cracked or brittle wires. If any of the wires are defective, replace the entire set. Replace any wires with excessive resistance (over $8000\,\Omega$ per foot for suppression wire), and separate any wires that might cause induction firing.	**4.6**

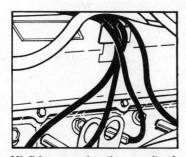

Misfiring can be the result of spark plug leads to adjacent, consecutively firing cylinders running parallel and too close together

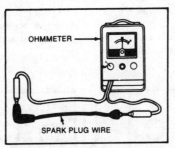

On point-type ignition systems, check the spark plug wires as shown. On electronic ignitions, do not remove the wire from the distributor cap terminal; instead, test through the cap

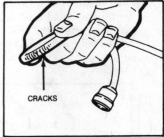

Spark plug wires can be checked visually by bending them in a loop over your finger. This will reveal any cracks, burned or broken insulation. Any wire with cracked insulation should be replaced

Test and Procedure	Results and Indications	Proceed to
4.6—Remove the spark plugs, noting the cylinders from which they were removed, and evaluate according to the color photos in the middle of this book.	See following.	**See following.**

Test and Procedure	Results and Indications	Proceed to
4.7—Examine the location of all the plugs.	The following diagrams illustrate some of the conditions that the location of plugs will reveal.	4.8

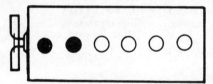

Two adjacent plugs are fouled in a 6-cylinder engine, 4-cylinder engine or either bank of a V-8. This is probably due to a blown head gasket between the two cylinders

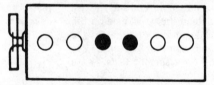

The two center plugs in a 6-cylinder engine are fouled. Raw fuel may be "boiled" out of the carburetor into the intake manifold after the engine is shut-off. Stop-start driving can also foul the center plugs, due to overly rich mixture. Proper float level, a new float needle and seat or use of an insulating spacer may help this problem

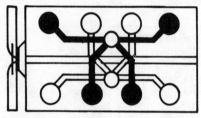

An unbalanced carburetor is indicated. Following the fuel flow on this particular design shows that the cylinders fed by the right-hand barrel are fouled from overly rich mixture, while the cylinders fed by the left-hand barrel are normal

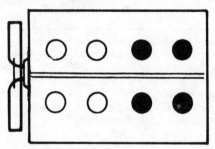

If the four rear plugs are overheated, a cooling system problem is suggested. A thorough cleaning of the cooling system may restore coolant circulation and cure the problem

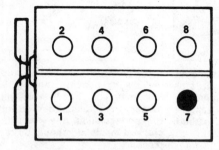

Finding one plug overheated may indicate an intake manifold leak near the affected cylinder. If the overheated plug is the second of two adjacent, consecutively firing plugs, it could be the result of ignition cross-firing. Separating the leads to these two plugs will eliminate cross-fire

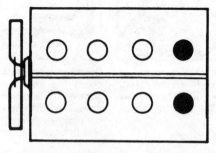

Occasionally, the two rear plugs in large, lightly used V-8's will become oil fouled. High oil consumption and smoky exhaust may also be noticed. It is probably due to plugged oil drain holes in the rear of the cylinder head, causing oil to be sucked in around the valve stems. This usually occurs in the rear cylinders first, because the engine slants that way

Test and Procedure	Results and Indications	Proceed to
4.8—Determine the static ignition timing. Using the crankshaft pulley timing marks as a guide, locate top dead center on the compression stroke of the number one cylinder.	The rotor should be pointing toward the No. 1 tower in the distributor cap, and, on electronic ignitions, the armature spoke for that cylinder should be lined up with the stator.	**4.8**
4.9—Check coil polarity: Connect a voltmeter negative lead to the coil high tension lead, and the positive lead to ground (**NOTE: _Reverse the hook-up for positive ground systems_**). Crank the engine momentarily. **Checking coil polarity**	If the voltmeter reads up-scale, the polarity is correct: If the voltmeter reads down-scale, reverse the coil polarity (switch the primary leads):	**5.1** **5.1**

Section 5—Fuel System
See Chapter 4 for service procedures

Test and Procedure	Results and Indications	Proceed to
5.1—Determine that the air filter is functioning efficiently: Hold paper elements up to a strong light, and attempt to see light through the filter.	Clean permanent air filters in solvent (or manufacturer's recommendation), and allow to dry. Replace paper elements through which light cannot be seen:	**5.2**
5.2—Determine whether a flooding condition exists: Flooding is identified by a strong gasoline odor, and excessive gasoline present in the throttle bore(s) of the carburetor.	If flooding is not evident: If flooding is evident, permit the gasoline to dry for a few moments and restart. If flooding doesn't recur: If flooding is persistent:	**5.3** **5.7** **5.5**

If the engine floods repeatedly, check the choke butterfly flap

Test and Procedure	Results and Indications	Proceed to
5.3—Check that fuel is reaching the carburetor: Detach the fuel line at the carburetor inlet. Hold the end of the line in a cup (not styrofoam), and crank the engine.	If fuel flows smoothly: If fuel doesn't flow (**NOTE: _Make sure that there is fuel in the tank_**), or flows erratically:	**5.7** **5.4**

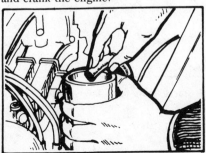

Check the fuel pump by disconnecting the output line (fuel pump-to-carburetor) at the carburetor and operating the starter briefly

Test and Procedure	Results and Indications	Proceed to
5.4—Test the fuel pump: Disconnect all fuel lines from the fuel pump. Hold a finger over the input fitting, crank the engine (with electric pump, turn the ignition or pump on); and feel for suction.	If suction is evident, blow out the fuel line to the tank with low pressure compressed air until bubbling is heard from the fuel filler neck. Also blow out the carburetor fuel line (both ends disconnected):	5.7
	If no suction is evident, replace or repair the fuel pump: **NOTE:** *Repeated oil fouling of the spark plugs, or a no-start condition, could be the result of a ruptured vacuum booster pump diaphragm, through which oil or gasoline is being drawn into the intake manifold (where applicable).*	5.7
5.5—Occasionally, small specks of dirt will clog the small jets and orifices in the carburetor. With the engine cold, hold a flat piece of wood or similar material over the carburetor, where possible, and crank the engine.	If the engine starts, but runs roughly the engine is probably not run enough. If the engine won't start:	5.9
5.6—Check the needle and seat: Tap the carburetor in the area of the needle and seat.	If flooding stops, a gasoline additive (e.g., Gumout) will often cure the problem:	5.7
	If flooding continues, check the fuel pump for excessive pressure at the carburetor (according to specifications). If the pressure is normal, the needle and seat must be removed and checked, and/or the float level adjusted:	5.7
5.7—Test the accelerator pump by looking into the throttle bores while operating the throttle.	If the accelerator pump appears to be operating normally:	5.8
	If the accelerator pump is not operating, the pump must be reconditioned. Where possible, service the pump with the carburetor(s) installed on the engine. If necessary, remove the carburetor. Prior to removal:	5.8

Check for gas at the carburetor by looking down the carburetor throat while someone moves the accelerator

Test and Procedure	Results and Indications	Proceed to
5.8—Determine whether the carburetor main fuel system is functioning: Spray a commercial starting fluid into the carburetor while attempting to start the engine.	If the engine starts, runs for a few seconds, and dies:	5.9
	If the engine doesn't start:	6.1

Test and Procedure	Results and Indications	Proceed to
5.9—Uncommon fuel system malfunctions: See below:	If the problem is solved:	**6.1**
	If the problem remains, remove and recondition the carburetor.	

Condition	Indication	Test	Prevailing Weather Conditions	Remedy
Vapor lock	Engine will not restart shortly after running.	Cool the components of the fuel system until the engine starts. Vapor lock can be cured faster by draping a wet cloth over a mechanical fuel pump.	Hot to very hot	Ensure that the exhaust manifold heat control valve is operating. Check with the vehicle manufacturer for the recommended solution to vapor lock on the model in question.
Carburetor icing	Engine will not idle, stalls at low speeds.	Visually inspect the throttle plate area of the throttle bores for frost.	High humidity, 32–40° F.	Ensure that the exhaust manifold heat control valve is operating, and that the intake manifold heat riser is not blocked.
Water in the fuel	Engine sputters and stalls; may not start.	Pump a small amount of fuel into a glass jar. Allow to stand, and inspect for droplets or a layer of water.	High humidity, extreme temperature changes.	For droplets, use one or two cans of commercial gas line anti-freeze. For a layer of water, the tank must be drained, and the fuel lines blown out with compressed air.

Section 6—Engine Compression
See Chapter 3 for service procedures

6.1—Test engine compression: Remove all spark plugs. Block the throttle wide open. Insert a compression gauge into a spark plug port, crank the engine to obtain the maximum reading, and record.	If compression is within limits on all cylinders:	**7.1**
	If gauge reading is extremely low on all cylinders:	**6.2**
	If gauge reading is low on one or two cylinders: (If gauge readings are identical and low on two or more adjacent cylinders, the head gasket must be replaced.)	**6.2**

Checking compression

6.2—Test engine compression (wet): Squirt approximately 30 cc. of engine oil into each cylinder, and retest per 6.1.	If the readings improve, worn or cracked rings or broken pistons are indicated:	**See Chapter 3**
	If the readings do not improve, burned or excessively carboned valves or a jumped timing chain are indicated: NOTE: *A jumped timing chain is often indicated by difficult cranking.*	**7.1**

Section 7—Engine Vacuum
See Chapter 3 for service procedures

Test and Procedure	Results and Indications	Proceed to
7.1—Attach a vacuum gauge to the intake manifold beyond the throttle plate. Start the engine, and observe the action of the needle over the range of engine speeds.	See below.	See below

INDICATION: normal engine in good condition

Proceed to: 8.1

Normal engine
Gauge reading: steady, from 17–22 in./Hg.

INDICATION: sticking valves or ignition miss

Proceed to: 9.1, 8.3

Sticking valves
Gauge reading: intermittent fluctuation at idle

INDICATION: late ignition or valve timing, low compression, stuck throttle valve, leaking carburetor or manifold gasket

Proceed to: 6.1

Incorrect valve timing
Gauge reading: low (10–15 in./Hg) but steady

INDICATION: improper carburetor adjustment or minor intake leak.

Proceed to: 7.2

Carburetor requires adjustment
Gauge reading: drifting needle

INDICATION: ignition miss, blown cylinder head gasket, leaking valve or weak valve spring

Proceed to: 8.3, 6.1

Blown head gasket
Gauge reading: needle fluctuates as engine speed increases

INDICATION: burnt valve or faulty valve clearance. Needle will fall when defective valve operates

Proceed to: 9.1

Burnt or leaking valves
Gauge reading: steady needle, but drops regularly

INDICATION: choked muffler, excessive back pressure in system

Proceed to: 10.1

Clogged exhaust system
Gauge reading: gradual drop in reading at idle

INDICATION: worn valve guides

Proceed to: 9.1

Worn valve guides
Gauge reading: needle vibrates excessively at idle, but steadies as engine speed increases

White pointer = steady gauge hand | Black pointer = fluctuating gauge hand

CHILTON'S
AUTO BODY
REPAIR TIPS

Tools and Materials • Step-by-Step Illustrated Procedures
How To Repair Dents, Scratches and Rust Holes
Spray Painting and Refinishing Tips

With a little practice, basic body repair procedures can be mastered by any do-it-yourself mechanic. The step-by-step repairs shown here can be applied to almost any type of auto body repair.

TOOLS & MATERIALS

You may already have basic tools, such as hammers and electric drills. Other tools unique to body repair — body hammers, grinding attachments, sanding blocks, dent puller, half-round plastic file and plastic spreaders — are relatively inexpensive and can be obtained wherever auto parts or auto body repair parts are sold. Portable air compressors and paint spray guns can be purchased or rented.

Auto Body Repair Kits

The best and most often used products are available to the do-it-yourselfer in kit form, from major manufacturers of auto body repair products. The same manufacturers also merchandise the individual products for use by pros.

Kits are available to make a wide variety of repairs, including holes, dents and scratches and fiberglass, and offer the advantage of buying the materials you'll need for the job. There is little waste or chance of materials going bad from not being used. Many kits may also contain basic body-working tools such as body files, sanding blocks and spreaders. Check the contents of the kit before buying your tools.

BODY REPAIR TIPS

Safety

Many of the products associated with auto body repair and refinishing contain toxic chemicals. Read all labels before opening containers and store them in a safe place and manner.
• Wear eye protection (safety goggles) when using power tools or when performing any operation that involves the removal of any type of material.
• Wear lung protection (disposable mask or respirator) when grinding, sanding or painting.

Sanding

1 Sand off paint before using a dent puller. When using a non-adhesive sanding disc, cover the back of the disc with an overlapping layer or two of masking tape and trim the edges. The disc will last considerably longer.

2 Use the circular motion of the sanding disc to grind *into* the edge of the repair. Grinding or sanding away from the jagged edge will only tear the sandpaper.

3 Use the palm of your hand flat on the panel to detect high and low spots. Do not use your fingertips. Slide your hand slowly back and forth.

WORKING WITH BODY FILLER

Mixing The Filler

Cleanliness and proper mixing and application are extremely important. Use a clean piece of plastic or glass or a disposable artist's palette to mix body filler.

1 Allow plenty of time and follow directions. No useful purpose will be served by adding more hardener to make it cure (set-up) faster. Less hardener means more curing time, but the mixture dries harder; more hardener means less curing time but a softer mixture.

2 Both the hardener and the filler should be thoroughly kneaded or stirred before mixing. Hardener should be a solid paste and dispense like thin toothpaste. Body filler should be smooth, and free of lumps or thick spots.

Getting the proper amount of hardener in the filler is the trickiest part of preparing the filler. Use the same amount of hardener in cold or warm weather. For contour filler (thick coats), a bead of hardener twice the diameter of the filler is about right. There's about a 15% margin on either side, but, if in doubt use less hardener.

3 Mix the body filler and hardener by wiping across the mixing surface, picking the mixture up and wiping it again. Colder weather requires longer mixing times. Do not mix in a circular motion; this will trap air bubbles which will become holes in the cured filler.

Applying The Filler

1 For best results, filler should not be applied over ¼″ thick.

Apply the filler in several coats. Build it up to above the level of the repair surface so that it can be sanded or grated down.

The first coat of filler must be pressed on with a firm wiping motion.

Apply the filler in one direction only. Working the filler back and forth will either pull it off the metal or trap air bubbles.

REPAIRING DENTS

Before you start, take a few minutes to study the damaged area. Try to visualize the shape of the panel before it was damaged. If the damage is on the left fender, look at the right fender and use it as a guide. If there is access to the panel from behind, you can reshape it with a body hammer. If not, you'll have to use a dent puller. Go slowly and work the metal a little at a time. Get the panel as straight as possible before applying filler.

1 This dent is typical of one that can be pulled out or hammered out from behind. Remove the headlight cover, headlight assembly and turn signal housing.

2 Drill a series of holes ½ the size of the end of the dent puller along the stress line. Make some trial pulls and assess the results. If necessary, drill more holes and try again. Do not hurry.

3 If possible, use a body hammer and block to shape the metal back to its original contours. Get the metal back as close to its original shape as possible. Don't depend on body filler to fill dents.

4 Using an 80-grit grinding disc on an electric drill, grind the paint from the surrounding area down to bare metal. Use a new grinding pad to prevent heat buildup that will warp metal.

5 The area should look like this when you're finished grinding. Knock the drill holes in and tape over small openings to keep plastic filler out.

6 Mix the body filler (see Body Repair Tips). Spread the body filler evenly over the entire area (see Body Repair Tips). Be sure to cover the area completely.

7 Let the body filler dry until the surface can just be scratched with your fingernail. Knock the high spots from the body filler with a body file ("Cheese-grater"). Check frequently with the palm of your hand for high and low spots.

8 Check to be sure that trim pieces that will be installed later will fit exactly. Sand the area with 40-grit paper.

9 If you wind up with low spots, you may have to apply another layer of filler.

10 Knock the high spots off with 40-grit paper. When you are satisfied with the contours of the repair, apply a thin coat of filler to cover pin holes and scratches.

11 Block sand the area with 40-grit paper to a smooth finish. Pay particular attention to body lines and ridges that must be well-defined.

12 Sand the area with 400 paper and then finish with a scuff pad. The finished repair is ready for priming and painting (see Painting Tips).

Materials and photos courtesy of Ritt Jones Auto Body, Prospect Park, PA.

REPAIRING RUST HOLES

There are many ways to repair rust holes. The fiberglass cloth kit shown here is one of the most cost efficient for the owner because it provides a strong repair that resists cracking and moisture and is relatively easy to use. It can be used on large and small holes (with or without backing) and can be applied over contoured areas. Remember, however, that short of replacing an entire panel, no repair is a guarantee that the rust will not return.

1 Remove any trim that will be in the way. Clean away all loose debris. Cut away all the rusted metal. But be sure to leave enough metal to retain the contour or body shape.

2 Grind away all traces of rust with a 24-grit grinding disc. Be sure to grind back 3-4 inches from the edge of the hole down to bare metal and be sure all traces of paint, primer and rust are removed.

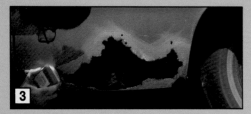

3 Block sand the area with 80 or 100 grit sandpaper to get a clear, shiny surface and feathered paint edge. Tap the edges of the hole inward with a ball peen hammer.

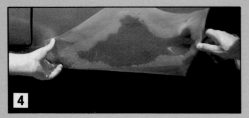

4 If you are going to use release film, cut a piece about 2-3″ larger than the area you have sanded. Place the film over the repair and mark the sanded area on the film. Avoid any unnecessary wrinkling of the film.

5 Cut 2 pieces of fiberglass matte to match the shape of the repair. One piece should be about 1″ smaller than the sanded area and the second piece should be 1″ smaller than the first. Mix enough filler and hardener to saturate the fiberglass material (see Body Repair Tips).

6 Lay the release sheet on a flat surface and spread an even layer of filler, large enough to cover the repair. Lay the smaller piece of fiberglass cloth in the center of the sheet and spread another layer of filler over the fiberglass cloth. Repeat the operation for the larger piece of cloth.

7 Place the repair material over the repair area, with the release film facing outward. Use a spreader and work from the center outward to smooth the material, following the body contours. Be sure to remove all air bubbles.

8 Wait until the repair has dried tack-free and peel off the release sheet. The ideal working temperature is 60°-90° F. Cooler or warmer temperatures or high humidity may require additional curing time. Wait longer, if in doubt.

9 Sand and feather-edge the entire area. The initial sanding can be done with a sanding disc on an electric drill if care is used. Finish the sanding with a block sander. Low spots can be filled with body filler; this may require several applications.

10 When the filler can just be scratched with a fingernail, knock the high spots down with a body file and smooth the entire area with 80-grit. Feather the filled areas into the surrounding areas.

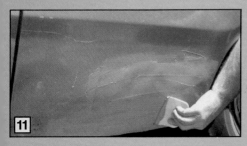

11 When the area is sanded smooth, mix some topcoat and hardener and apply it directly with a spreader. This will give a smooth finish and prevent the glass matte from showing through the paint.

12 Block sand the topcoat smooth with finishing sandpaper (200 grit), and 400 grit. The repair is ready for masking, priming and painting (see Painting Tips).

Materials and photos courtesy Marson Corporation, Chelsea, Massachusetts

PAINTING TIPS

Preparation

1 SANDING — Use a 400 or 600 grit wet or dry sandpaper. Wet-sand the area with a 1/4 sheet of sandpaper soaked in clean water. Keep the paper wet while sanding. Sand the area until the repaired area tapers into the original finish.

2 CLEANING — Wash the area to be painted thoroughly with water and a clean rag. Rinse it thoroughly and wipe the surface dry until you're sure it's completely free of dirt, dust, fingerprints, wax, detergent or other foreign matter.

3 MASKING — Protect any areas you don't want to overspray by covering them with masking tape and newspaper. Be careful not get fingerprints on the area to be painted.

4 PRIMING — All exposed metal should be primed before painting. Primer protects the metal and provides an excellent surface for paint adhesion. When the primer is dry, wet-sand the area again with 600 grit wet-sandpaper. Clean the area again after sanding.

Painting Techniques

P aint applied from either a spray gun or a spray can (for small areas) will provide good results. Experiment on an old piece of metal to get the right combination before you begin painting.

SPRAYING VISCOSITY (SPRAY GUN ONLY) — Paint should be thinned to spraying viscosity according to the directions on the can. Use only the recommended thinner or reducer and the same amount of reduction regardless of temperature.

AIR PRESSURE (SPRAY GUN ONLY) — This is extremely important. Be sure you are using the proper recommended pressure.

TEMPERATURE — The surface to be painted should be approximately the same temperature as the surrounding air. Applying warm paint to a cold surface, or vice versa, will completely upset the paint characteristics.

THICKNESS — Spray with smooth strokes. In general, the thicker the coat of paint, the longer the drying time. Apply several thin coats about 30 seconds apart. The paint should remain wet long enough to flow out and no longer; heavier coats will only produce sags or wrinkles. Spray a light (fog) coat, followed by heavier color coats.

DISTANCE — The ideal spraying distance is 8″-12″ from the gun or can to the surface. Shorter distances will produce ripples, while greater distances will result in orange peel, dry film and poor color match and loss of material due to overspray.

OVERLAPPING — The gun or can should be kept at right angles to the surface at all times. Work to a wet edge at an even speed, using a 50% overlap and direct the center of the spray at the lower or nearest edge of the previous stroke.

RUBBING OUT (BLENDING) FRESH PAINT — Let the paint dry thoroughly. Runs or imperfections can be sanded out, primed and repainted.

Don't be in too big a hurry to remove the masking. This only produces paint ridges. When the finish has dried for at least a week, apply a small amount of fine grade rubbing compound with a clean, wet cloth. Use lots of water and blend the new paint with the surrounding area.

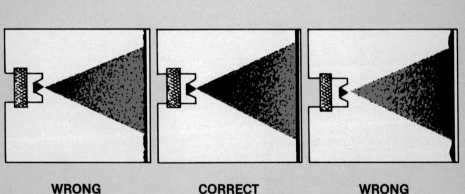

WRONG	CORRECT	WRONG
Thin coat. Stroke too fast, not enough overlap, gun too far away.	*Medium coat. Proper distance, good stroke, proper overlap.*	*Heavy coat. Stroke too slow, too much overlap, gun too close.*

Test and Procedure	Results and Indications	Proceed to
7.2—Attach a vacuum gauge per 7.1, and test for an intake manifold leak. Squirt a small amount of oil around the intake manifold gaskets, carburetor gaskets, plugs and fittings. Observe the action of the vacuum gauge.	If the reading improves, replace the indicated gasket, or seal the indicated fitting or plug: If the reading remains low:	8.1 7.3
7.3—Test all vacuum hoses and accessories for leaks as described in 7.2. Also check the carburetor body (dashpots, automatic choke mechanism, throttle shafts) for leaks in the same manner.	If the reading improves, service or replace the offending part(s): If the reading remains low:	8.1 6.1

Section 8—Secondary Electrical System
See Chapter 2 for service procedures

Test and Procedure	Results and Indications	Proceed to
8.1—Remove the distributor cap and check to make sure that the rotor turns when the engine is cranked. Visually inspect the distributor components.	Clean, tighten or replace any components which appear defective.	8.2
8.2—Connect a timing light (per manufacturer's recommendation) and check the dynamic ignition timing. Disconnect and plug the vacuum hose(s) to the distributor if specified, start the engine, and observe the timing marks at the specified engine speed.	If the timing is not correct, adjust to specifications by rotating the distributor in the engine: (Advance timing by rotating distributor opposite normal direction of rotor rotation, retard timing by rotating distributor in same direction as rotor rotation.)	8.3
8.3—Check the operation of the distributor advance mechanism(s): To test the mechanical advance, disconnect the vacuum lines from the distributor advance unit and observe the timing marks with a timing light as the engine speed is increased from idle. If the mark moves smoothly, without hesitation, it may be assumed that the mechanical advance is functioning properly. To test vacuum advance and/or retard systems, alternately crimp and release the vacuum line, and observe the timing mark for movement. If movement is noted, the system is operating.	If the systems are functioning: If the systems are not functioning, remove the distributor, and test on a distributor tester:	8.4 8.4
8.4—Locate an ignition miss: With the engine running, remove each spark plug wire, one at a time, until one is found that doesn't cause the engine to roughen and slow down.	When the missing cylinder is identified:	4.1

Section 9—Valve Train
See Chapter 3 for service procedures

Test and Procedure	Results and Indications	Proceed to
9.1—Evaluate the valve train: Remove the valve cover, and ensure that the valves are adjusted to specifications. A mechanic's stethoscope may be used to aid in the diagnosis of the valve train. By pushing the probe on or near push rods or rockers, valve noise often can be isolated. A timing light also may be used to diagnose valve problems. Connect the light according to manufacturer's recommendations, and start the engine. Vary the firing moment of the light by increasing the engine speed (and therefore the ignition advance), and moving the trigger from cylinder to cylinder. Observe the movement of each valve.	Sticking valves or erratic valve train motion can be observed with the timing light. The cylinder head must be disassembled for repairs.	**See Chapter 3**
9.2—Check the valve timing: Locate top dead center of the No. 1 piston, and install a degree wheel or tape on the crankshaft pulley or damper with zero corresponding to an index mark on the engine. Rotate the crankshaft in its direction of rotation, and observe the opening of the No. 1 cylinder intake valve. The opening should correspond with the correct mark on the degree wheel according to specifications.	If the timing is not correct, the timing cover must be removed for further investigation.	**See Chapter 3**

Section 10—Exhaust System

Test and Procedure	Results and Indications	Proceed to
10.1—Determine whether the exhaust manifold heat control valve is operating: Operate the valve by hand to determine whether it is free to move. If the valve is free, run the engine to operating temperature and observe the action of the valve, to ensure that it is opening.	If the valve sticks, spray it with a suitable solvent, open and close the valve to free it, and retest. If the valve functions properly: If the valve does not free, or does not operate, replace the valve:	**10.2** **10.2**
10.2—Ensure that there are no exhaust restrictions: Visually inspect the exhaust system for kinks, dents, or crushing. Also note that gases are flowing freely from the tailpipe at all engine speeds, indicating no restriction in the muffler or resonator.	Replace any damaged portion of the system:	**11.1**

Section 11—Cooling System
See Chapter 3 for service procedures

Test and Procedure	Results and Indications	Proceed to
11.1—Visually inspect the fan belt for glazing, cracks, and fraying, and replace if necessary. Tighten the belt so that the longest span has approximately ½″ play at its midpoint under thumb pressure (see Chapter 1).	Replace or tighten the fan belt as necessary:	**11.2**

Checking belt tension

11.2—Check the fluid level of the cooling system.	If full or slightly low, fill as necessary:	**11.5**
	If extremely low:	**11.3**
11.3—Visually inspect the external portions of the cooling system (radiator, radiator hoses, thermostat elbow, water pump seals, heater hoses, etc.) for leaks. If none are found, pressurize the cooling system to 14–15 psi.	If cooling system holds the pressure:	**11.5**
	If cooling system loses pressure rapidly, reinspect external parts of the system for leaks under pressure. If none are found, check dipstick for coolant in crankcase. If no coolant is present, but pressure loss continues:	**11.4**
	If coolant is evident in crankcase, remove cylinder head(s), and check gasket(s). If gaskets are intact, block and cylinder head(s) should be checked for cracks or holes.	
	If the gasket(s) is blown, replace, and purge the crankcase of coolant:	**12.6**
	NOTE: *Occasionally, due to atmospheric and driving conditions, condensation of water can occur in the crankcase. This causes the oil to appear milky white. To remedy, run the engine until hot, and change the oil and oil filter.*	
11.4—Check for combustion leaks into the cooling system: Pressurize the cooling system as above. Start the engine, and observe the pressure gauge. If the needle fluctuates, remove each spark plug wire, one at a time, noting which cylinder(s) reduce or eliminate the fluctuation.	Cylinders which reduce or eliminate the fluctuation, when the spark plug wire is removed, are leaking into the cooling system. Replace the head gasket on the affected cylinder bank(s).	

Pressurizing the cooling system

Test and Procedure	Results and Indications	Proceed to
11.5—Check the radiator pressure cap: Attach a radiator pressure tester to the radiator cap (wet the seal prior to installation). Quickly pump up the pressure, noting the point at which the cap releases.	If the cap releases within ± 1 psi of the specified rating, it is operating properly:	**11.6**
	If the cap releases at more than ± 1 psi of the specified rating, it should be replaced:	**11.6**

Checking radiator pressure cap

Test and Procedure	Results and Indications	Proceed to
11.6—Test the thermostat: Start the engine cold, remove the radiator cap, and insert a thermometer into the radiator. Allow the engine to idle. After a short while, there will be a sudden, rapid increase in coolant temperature. The temperature at which this sharp rise stops is the thermostat opening temperature.	If the thermostat opens at or about the specified temperature:	**11.7**
	If the temperature doesn't increase: (If the temperature increases slowly and gradually, replace the thermostat.)	**11.7**
11.7—Check the water pump: Remove the thermostat elbow and the thermostat, disconnect the coil high tension lead (to prevent starting), and crank the engine momentarily.	If coolant flows, replace the thermostat and retest per 11.6:	**11.6**
	If coolant doesn't flow, reverse flush the cooling system to alleviate any blockage that might exist. If system is not blocked, and coolant will not flow, replace the water pump.	

Section 12—Lubrication
See Chapter 3 for service procedures

Test and Procedure	Results and Indications	Proceed to
12.1—Check the oil pressure gauge or warning light: If the gauge shows low pressure, or the light is on for no obvious reason, remove the oil pressure sender. Install an accurate oil pressure gauge and run the engine momentarily.	If oil pressure builds normally, run engine for a few moments to determine that it is functioning normally, and replace the sender.	—
	If the pressure remains low:	**12.2**
	If the pressure surges:	**12.3**
	If the oil pressure is zero:	**12.3**
12.2—Visually inspect the oil: If the oil is watery or very thin, milky, or foamy, replace the oil and oil filter.	If the oil is normal:	**12.3**
	If after replacing oil the pressure remains low:	**12.3**
	If after replacing oil the pressure becomes normal:	—

Test and Procedure	Results and Indications	Proceed to
12.3—Inspect the oil pressure relief valve and spring, to ensure that it is not sticking or stuck. Remove and thoroughly clean the valve, spring, and the valve body.	If the oil pressure improves: If no improvement is noted:	— **12.4**
12.4—Check to ensure that the oil pump is not cavitating (sucking air instead of oil): See that the crankcase is neither over nor underfull, and that the pickup in the sump is in the proper position and free from sludge.	Fill or drain the crankcase to the proper capacity, and clean the pickup screen in solvent if necessary. If no improvement is noted:	**12.5**
12.5—Inspect the oil pump drive and the oil pump:	If the pump drive or the oil pump appear to be defective, service as necessary and retest per 12.1: If the pump drive and pump appear to be operating normally, the engine should be disassembled to determine where blockage exists:	**12.1** **See Chapter 3**
12.6—Purge the engine of ethylene glycol coolant: Completely drain the crankcase and the oil filter. Obtain a commercial butyl cellosolve base solvent, designated for this purpose, and follow the instructions precisely. Following this, install a new oil filter and refill the crankcase with the proper weight oil. The next oil and filter change should follow shortly thereafter (1000 miles).		

TROUBLESHOOTING EMISSION CONTROL SYSTEMS

See Chapter 4 for procedures applicable to individual emission control systems used on specific combinations of engine/transmission/model.

TROUBLESHOOTING THE CARBURETOR
See Chapter 4 for service procedures

Carburetor problems cannot be effectively isolated unless all other engine systems (particularly ignition and emission) are functioning properly and the engine is properly tuned.

Condition	Possible Cause
Engine cranks, but does not start	1. Improper starting procedure 2. No fuel in tank 3. Clogged fuel line or filter 4. Defective fuel pump 5. Choke valve not closing properly 6. Engine flooded 7. Choke valve not unloading 8. Throttle linkage not making full travel 9. Stuck needle or float 10. Leaking float needle or seat 11. Improper float adjustment
Engine stalls	1. Improperly adjusted idle speed or mixture **Engine hot** 2. Improperly adjusted dashpot 3. Defective or improperly adjusted solenoid 4. Incorrect fuel level in fuel bowl 5. Fuel pump pressure too high 6. Leaking float needle seat 7. Secondary throttle valve stuck open 8. Air or fuel leaks 9. Idle air bleeds plugged or missing 10. Idle passages plugged **Engine Cold** 11. Incorrectly adjusted choke 12. Improperly adjusted fast idle speed 13. Air leaks 14. Plugged idle or idle air passages 15. Stuck choke valve or binding linkage 16. Stuck secondary throttle valves 17. Engine flooding—high fuel level 18. Leaking or misaligned float
Engine hesitates on acceleration	1. Clogged fuel filter 2. Leaking fuel pump diaphragm 3. Low fuel pump pressure 4. Secondary throttle valves stuck, bent or misadjusted 5. Sticking or binding air valve 6. Defective accelerator pump 7. Vacuum leaks 8. Clogged air filter 9. Incorrect choke adjustment (engine cold)
Engine feels sluggish or flat on acceleration	1. Improperly adjusted idle speed or mixture 2. Clogged fuel filter 3. Defective accelerator pump 4. Dirty, plugged or incorrect main metering jets 5. Bent or sticking main metering rods 6. Sticking throttle valves 7. Stuck heat riser 8. Binding or stuck air valve 9. Dirty, plugged or incorrect secondary jets 10. Bent or sticking secondary metering rods. 11. Throttle body or manifold heat passages plugged 12. Improperly adjusted choke or choke vacuum break.
Carburetor floods	1. Defective fuel pump. Pressure too high. 2. Stuck choke valve 3. Dirty, worn or damaged float or needle valve/seat 4. Incorrect float/fuel level 5. Leaking float bowl

Condition	Possible Cause
Engine idles roughly and stalls	1. Incorrect idle speed 2. Clogged fuel filter 3. Dirt in fuel system or carburetor 4. Loose carburetor screws or attaching bolts 5. Broken carburetor gaskets 6. Air leaks 7. Dirty carburetor 8. Worn idle mixture needles 9. Throttle valves stuck open 10. Incorrectly adjusted float or fuel level 11. Clogged air filter
Engine runs unevenly or surges	1. Defective fuel pump 2. Dirty or clogged fuel filter 3. Plugged, loose or incorrect main metering jets or rods 4. Air leaks 5. Bent or sticking main metering rods 6. Stuck power piston 7. Incorrect float adjustment 8. Incorrect idle speed or mixture 9. Dirty or plugged idle system passages 10. Hard, brittle or broken gaskets 11. Loose attaching or mounting screws 12. Stuck or misaligned secondary throttle valves
Poor fuel economy	1. Poor driving habits 2. Stuck choke valve 3. Binding choke linkage 4. Stuck heat riser 5. Incorrect idle mixture 6. Defective accelerator pump 7. Air leaks 8. Plugged, loose or incorrect main metering jets 9. Improperly adjusted float or fuel level 10. Bent, misaligned or fuel-clogged float 11. Leaking float needle seat 12. Fuel leak 13. Accelerator pump discharge ball not seating properly 14. Incorrect main jets
Engine lacks high speed performance or power	1. Incorrect throttle linkage adjustment 2. Stuck or binding power piston 3. Defective accelerator pump 4. Air leaks 5. Incorrect float setting or fuel level 6. Dirty, plugged, worn or incorrect main metering jets or rods 7. Binding or sticking air valve 8. Brittle or cracked gaskets 9. Bent, incorrect or improperly adjusted secondary metering rods 10. Clogged fuel filter 11. Clogged air filter 12. Defective fuel pump

TROUBLESHOOTING FUEL INJECTION PROBLEMS

Each fuel injection system has its own unique components and test procedures, for which it is impossible to generalize. Refer to Chapter 4 of this Repair & Tune-Up Guide for specific test and repair procedures, if the vehicle is equipped with fuel injection.

TROUBLESHOOTING ELECTRICAL PROBLEMS

See Chapter 5 for service procedures

For any electrical system to operate, it must make a complete circuit. This simply means that the power flow from the battery must make a complete circle. When an electrical component is operating, power flows from the battery to the component, passes through the component causing it to perform its function (lighting a light bulb), and then returns to the battery through the ground of the circuit. This ground is usually (but not always) the metal part of the car or truck on which the electrical component is mounted.

Perhaps the easiest way to visualize this is to think of connecting a light bulb with two wires attached to it to the battery. If one of the two wires attached to the light bulb were attached to the negative post of the battery and the other were attached to the positive post of the battery, you would have a complete circuit. Current from the battery would flow to the light bulb, causing it to light, and return to the negative post of the battery.

The normal automotive circuit differs from this simple example in two ways. First, instead of having a return wire from the bulb to the battery, the light bulb returns the current to the battery through the chassis of the vehicle. Since the negative battery cable is attached to the chassis and the chassis is made of electrically conductive metal, the chassis of the vehicle can serve as a ground wire to complete the circuit. Secondly, most automotive circuits contain switches to turn components on and off as required.

Every complete circuit from a power source must include a component which is using the power from the power source. If you were to disconnect the light bulb from the wires and touch the two wires together (don't do this) the power supply wire to the component would be grounded before the normal ground connection for the circuit.

Because grounding a wire from a power source makes a complete circuit—less the required component to use the power—this phenomenon is called a short circuit. Common causes are: broken insulation (exposing the metal wire to a metal part of the car or truck), or a shorted switch.

Some electrical components which require a large amount of current to operate also have a relay in their circuit. Since these circuits carry a large amount of current, the thickness of the wire in the circuit (gauge size) is also greater. If this large wire were connected from the component to the control switch on the instrument panel, and then back to the component, a voltage drop would occur in the circuit. To prevent this potential drop in voltage, an electromagnetic switch (relay) is used. The large wires in the circuit are connected from the battery to one side of the relay, and from the opposite side of the relay to the component. The relay is normally open, preventing current from passing through the circuit. An additional, smaller, wire is connected from the relay to the control switch for the circuit. When the control switch is turned on, it grounds the smaller wire from the relay and completes the circuit. This closes the relay and allows current to flow from the battery to the component. The horn, headlight, and starter circuits are three which use relays.

It is possible for larger surges of current to pass through the electrical system of your car or truck. If this surge of current were to reach an electrical component, it could burn it out. To prevent this, fuses, circuit breakers or fusible links are connected into the current supply wires of most of the major electrical systems. When an electrical current of excessive power passes through the component's fuse, the fuse blows out and breaks the circuit, saving the component from destruction.

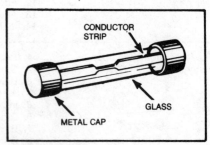

Typical automotive fuse

A circuit breaker is basically a self-repairing fuse. The circuit breaker opens the circuit the same way a fuse does. However, when either the short is removed from the circuit or the surge subsides, the circuit breaker resets itself and does not have to be replaced as a fuse does.

A fuse link is a wire that acts as a fuse. It is normally connected between the starter relay and the main wiring harness. This connection is usually under the hood. The fuse link (if installed) protects all the

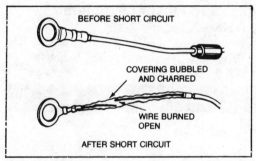

Most fusible links show a charred, melted insulation when they burn out

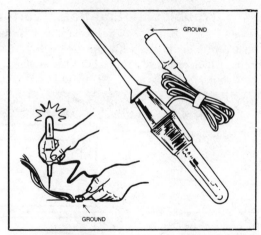

The test light will show the presence of current when touched to a hot wire and grounded at the other end

chassis electrical components, and is the probable cause of trouble when none of the electrical components function, unless the battery is disconnected or dead.

Electrical problems generally fall into one of three areas:

1. The component that is not functioning is not receiving current.

2. The component itself is not functioning.

3. The component is not properly grounded.

The electrical system can be checked with a test light and a jumper wire. A test light is a device that looks like a pointed screwdriver with a wire attached to it and has a light bulb in its handle. A jumper wire is a piece of insulated wire with an alligator clip attached to each end.

If a component is not working, you must follow a systematic plan to determine which of the three causes is the villain.

1. Turn on the switch that controls the inoperable component.

2. Disconnect the power supply wire from the component.

3. Attach the ground wire on the test light to a good metal ground.

4. Touch the probe end of the test light to the end of the power supply wire that was disconnected from the component. If the component is receiving current, the test light will go on.

NOTE: *Some components work only when the ignition switch is turned on.*

If the test light does not go on, then the problem is in the circuit between the battery and the component. This includes all the switches, fuses, and relays in the system. Follow the wire that runs back to the battery. The problem is an open circuit between the

battery and the component. If the fuse is blown and, when replaced, immediately blows again, there is a short circuit in the system which must be located and repaired. If there is a switch in the system, bypass it with a jumper wire. This is done by connecting one end of the jumper wire to the power supply wire into the switch and the other end of the jumper wire to the wire coming out of the switch. If the test light lights with the jumper wire installed, the switch or whatever was bypassed is defective.

NOTE: *Never substitute the jumper wire for the component, since it is required to use the power from the power source.*

5. If the bulb in the test light goes on, then the current is getting to the component that is not working. This eliminates the first of the three possible causes. Connect the power supply wire and connect a jumper wire from the component to a good metal ground. Do this with the switch which controls the component turned on, and also the ignition switch turned on if it is required for the component to work. If the component works with the jumper wire installed, then it has a bad ground. This is usually caused by the metal area on which the component mounts to the chassis being coated with some type of foreign matter.

6. If neither test located the source of the trouble, then the component itself is defective. Remember that for any electrical system to work, all connections must be clean and tight.

Troubleshooting Basic Turn Signal and Flasher Problems
See Chapter 5 for service procedures

Most problems in the turn signals or flasher system can be reduced to defective flashers or bulbs, which are easily replaced. Occasionally, the turn signal switch will prove defective.

F = Front   R = Rear   ● = Lights off   ○ = Lights on

Condition	Possible Cause
Turn signals light, but do not flash 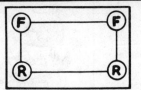	Defective flasher
No turn signals light on either side 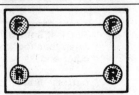	Blown fuse. Replace if defective. Defective flasher. Check by substitution. Open circuit, short circuit or poor ground.
Both turn signals on one side don't work 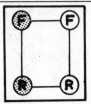	Bad bulbs. Bad ground in both (or either) housings.
One turn signal light on one side doesn't work 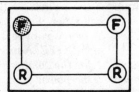	Defective bulb. Corrosion in socket. Clean contacts. Poor ground at socket.
Turn signal flashes too fast or too slowly 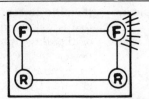	Check any bulb on the side flashing too fast. A heavy-duty bulb is probably installed in place of a regular bulb. Check the bulb flashing too slowly. A standard bulb was probably installed in place of a heavy-duty bulb. Loose connections or corrosion at the bulb socket.
Indicator lights don't work in either direction 	Check if the turn signals are working. Check the dash indicator lights. Check the flasher by substitution.
One indicator light doesn't light 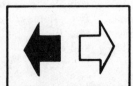	On systems with one dash indicator: See if the lights work on the same side. Often the filaments have been reversed in systems combining stoplights with taillights and turn signals. Check the flasher by substitution. On systems with two indicators: Check the bulbs on the same side. Check the indicator light bulb. Check the flasher by substitution.

Troubleshooting Lighting Problems

See Chapter 5 for service procedures

Condition	Possible Cause
One or more lights don't work, but others do	1. Defective bulb(s) 2. Blown fuse(s) 3. Dirty fuse clips or light sockets 4. Poor ground circuit
Lights burn out quickly	1. Incorrect voltage regulator setting or defective regulator 2. Poor battery/alternator connections
Lights go dim	1. Low/discharged battery 2. Alternator not charging 3. Corroded sockets or connections 4. Low voltage output
Lights flicker	1. Loose connection 2. Poor ground. (Run ground wire from light housing to frame) 3. Circuit breaker operating (short circuit)
Lights "flare"—Some flare is normal on acceleration—If excessive, see "Lights Burn Out Quickly"	High voltage setting
Lights glare—approaching drivers are blinded	1. Lights adjusted too high 2. Rear springs or shocks sagging 3. Rear tires soft

Troubleshooting Dash Gauge Problems

Most problems can be traced to a defective sending unit or faulty wiring. Occasionally, the gauge itself is at fault. See Chapter 5 for service procedures.

Condition	Possible Cause
COOLANT TEMPERATURE GAUGE	
Gauge reads erratically or not at all	1. Loose or dirty connections 2. Defective sending unit. 3. Defective gauge. To test a bi-metal gauge, remove the wire from the sending unit. Ground the wire for an instant. If the gauge registers, replace the sending unit. To test a magnetic gauge, disconnect the wire at the sending unit. With ignition ON gauge should register COLD. Ground the wire; gauge should register HOT.
AMMETER GAUGE—TURN HEADLIGHTS ON (DO NOT START ENGINE). NOTE REACTION	
Ammeter shows charge Ammeter shows discharge Ammeter does not move	1. Connections reversed on gauge 2. Ammeter is OK 3. Loose connections or faulty wiring 4. Defective gauge

Condition	Possible Cause

OIL PRESSURE GAUGE

Condition	Possible Cause
Gauge does not register or is inaccurate	1. On mechanical gauge, Bourdon tube may be bent or kinked. 2. Low oil pressure. Remove sending unit. Idle the engine briefly. If no oil flows from sending unit hole, problem is in engine. 3. Defective gauge. Remove the wire from the sending unit and ground it for an instant with the ignition ON. A good gauge will go to the top of the scale. 4. Defective wiring. Check the wiring to the gauge. If it's OK and the gauge doesn't register when grounded, replace the gauge. 5. Defective sending unit.

ALL GAUGES

Condition	Possible Cause
All gauges do not operate All gauges read low or erratically All gauges pegged	1. Blown fuse 2. Defective instrument regulator 3. Defective or dirty instrument voltage regulator 4. Loss of ground between instrument voltage regulator and frame 5. Defective instrument regulator

WARNING LIGHTS

Condition	Possible Cause
Light(s) do not come on when ignition is ON, but engine is not started Light comes on with engine running	1. Defective bulb 2. Defective wire 3. Defective sending unit. Disconnect the wire from the sending unit and ground it. Replace the sending unit if the light comes on with the ignition ON. 4. Problem in individual system 5. Defective sending unit

Troubleshooting Clutch Problems

It is false economy to replace individual clutch components. The pressure plate, clutch plate and throwout bearing should be replaced as a set, and the flywheel face inspected, whenever the clutch is overhauled. See Chapter 6 for service procedures.

Condition	Possible Cause
Clutch chatter	1. Grease on driven plate (disc) facing 2. Binding clutch linkage or cable 3. Loose, damaged facings on driven plate (disc) 4. Engine mounts loose 5. Incorrect height adjustment of pressure plate release levers 6. Clutch housing or housing to transmission adapter misalignment 7. Loose driven plate hub
Clutch grabbing	1. Oil, grease on driven plate (disc) facing 2. Broken pressure plate 3. Warped or binding driven plate. Driven plate binding on clutch shaft
Clutch slips	1. Lack of lubrication in clutch linkage or cable (linkage or cable binds, causes incomplete engagement) 2. Incorrect pedal, or linkage adjustment 3. Broken pressure plate springs 4. Weak pressure plate springs 5. Grease on driven plate facings (disc)

Troubleshooting Clutch Problems (cont.)

Condition	Possible Cause
Incomplete clutch release	1. Incorrect pedal or linkage adjustment or linkage or cable binding 2. Incorrect height adjustment on pressure plate release levers 3. Loose, broken facings on driven plate (disc) 4. Bent, dished, warped driven plate caused by overheating
Grinding, whirring grating noise when pedal is depressed	1. Worn or defective throwout bearing 2. Starter drive teeth contacting flywheel ring gear teeth. Look for milled or polished teeth on ring gear.
Squeal, howl, trumpeting noise when pedal is being released (occurs during first inch to inch and one-half of pedal travel)	Pilot bushing worn or lack of lubricant. If bushing appears OK, polish bushing with emery cloth, soak lube wick in oil, lube bushing with oil, apply film of chassis grease to clutch shaft pilot hub, reassemble. NOTE: Bushing wear may be due to misalignment of clutch housing or housing to transmission adapter
Vibration or clutch pedal pulsation with clutch disengaged (pedal fully depressed)	1. Worn or defective engine transmission mounts 2. Flywheel run out. (Flywheel run out at face not to exceed 0.005″) 3. Damaged or defective clutch components

Troubleshooting Manual Transmission Problems
See Chapter 6 for service procedures

Condition	Possible Cause
Transmission jumps out of gear	1. Misalignment of transmission case or clutch housing. 2. Worn pilot bearing in crankshaft. 3. Bent transmission shaft. 4. Worn high speed sliding gear. 5. Worn teeth or end-play in clutch shaft. 6. Insufficient spring tension on shifter rail plunger. 7. Bent or loose shifter fork. 8. Gears not engaging completely. 9. Loose or worn bearings on clutch shaft or mainshaft. 10. Worn gear teeth. 11. Worn or damaged detent balls.
Transmission sticks in gear	1. Clutch not releasing fully. 2. Burred or battered teeth on clutch shaft, or sliding sleeve. 3. Burred or battered transmission mainshaft. 4. Frozen synchronizing clutch. 5. Stuck shifter rail plunger. 6. Gearshift lever twisting and binding shifter rail. 7. Battered teeth on high speed sliding gear or on sleeve. 8. Improper lubrication, or lack of lubrication. 9. Corroded transmission parts. 10. Defective mainshaft pilot bearing. 11. Locked gear bearings will give same effect as stuck in gear.
Transmission gears will not synchronize	1. Binding pilot bearing on mainshaft, will synchronize in high gear only. 2. Clutch not releasing fully. 3. Detent spring weak or broken. 4. Weak or broken springs under balls in sliding gear sleeve. 5. Binding bearing on clutch shaft, or binding countershaft. 6. Binding pilot bearing in crankshaft. 7. Badly worn gear teeth. 8. Improper lubrication. 9. Constant mesh gear not turning freely on transmission mainshaft. Will synchronize in that gear only.

Condition	Possible Cause
Gears spinning when shifting into gear from neutral	1. Clutch not releasing fully. 2. In some cases an extremely light lubricant in transmission will cause gears to continue to spin for a short time after clutch is released. 3. Binding pilot bearing in crankshaft.
Transmission noisy in all gears	1. Insufficient lubricant, or improper lubricant. 2. Worn countergear bearings. 3. Worn or damaged main drive gear or countergear. 4. Damaged main drive gear or mainshaft bearings. 5. Worn or damaged countergear anti-lash plate.
Transmission noisy in neutral only	1. Damaged main drive gear bearing. 2. Damaged or loose mainshaft pilot bearing. 3. Worn or damaged countergear anti-lash plate. 4. Worn countergear bearings.
Transmission noisy in one gear only	1. Damaged or worn constant mesh gears. 2. Worn or damaged countergear bearings. 3. Damaged or worn synchronizer.
Transmission noisy in reverse only	1. Worn or damaged reverse idler gear or idler bushing. 2. Worn or damaged mainshaft reverse gear. 3. Worn or damaged reverse countergear. 4. Damaged shift mechanism.

TROUBLESHOOTING AUTOMATIC TRANSMISSION PROBLEMS

Keeping alert to changes in the operating characteristics of the transmission (changing shift points, noises, etc.) can prevent small problems from becoming large ones. If the problem cannot be traced to loose bolts, fluid level, misadjusted linkage, clogged filters or similar problems, you should probably seek professional service.

Transmission Fluid Indications

The appearance and odor of the transmission fluid can give valuable clues to the overall condition of the transmission. Always note the appearance of the fluid when you check the fluid level or change the fluid. Rub a small amount of fluid between your fingers to feel for grit and smell the fluid on the dipstick.

If the fluid appears:	It indicates:
Clear and red colored	Normal operation
Discolored (extremely dark red or brownish) or smells burned	Band or clutch pack failure, usually caused by an overheated transmission. Hauling very heavy loads with insufficient power or failure to change the fluid often result in overheating. Do not confuse this appearance with newer fluids that have a darker red color and a strong odor (though not a burned odor).
Foamy or aerated (light in color and full of bubbles)	1. The level is too high (gear train is churning oil) 2. An internal air leak (air is mixing with the fluid). Have the transmission checked professionally.
Solid residue in the fluid	Defective bands, clutch pack or bearings. Bits of band material or metal abrasives are clinging to the dipstick. Have the transmission checked professionally.
Varnish coating on the dipstick	The transmission fluid is overheating

TROUBLESHOOTING DRIVE AXLE PROBLEMS

First, determine when the noise is most noticeable.

Drive Noise: Produced under vehicle acceleration.

Coast Noise: Produced while coasting with a closed throttle.

Float Noise: Occurs while maintaining constant speed (just enough to keep speed constant) on a level road.

External Noise Elimination

It is advisable to make a thorough road test to determine whether the noise originates in the rear axle or whether it originates from the tires, engine, transmission, wheel bearings or road surface. Noise originating from other places cannot be corrected by servicing the rear axle.

ROAD NOISE

Brick or rough surfaced concrete roads produce noises that seem to come from the rear axle. Road noise is usually identical in Drive or Coast and driving on a different type of road will tell whether the road is the problem.

TIRE NOISE

Tire noise can be mistaken as rear axle noise, even though the tires on the front are at fault. Snow tread and mud tread tires or tires worn unevenly will frequently cause vibrations which seem to originate elsewhere; *temporarily, and for test purposes only,* inflate the tires to 40–50 lbs. This will significantly alter the noise produced by the tires, but will not alter noise from the rear axle. Noises from the rear axle will normally cease at speeds below 30 mph on coast, while tire noise will continue at lower tone as speed is decreased. The rear axle noise will usually change from drive conditions to coast conditions, while tire noise will not. Do not forget to lower the tire pressure to normal after the test is complete.

ENGINE/TRANSMISSION NOISE

Determine at what speed the noise is most pronounced, then stop in a quiet place. With the transmission in Neutral, run the engine through speeds corresponding to road speeds where the noise was noticed. Noises produced with the vehicle standing still are coming from the engine or transmission.

FRONT WHEEL BEARINGS

Front wheel bearing noises, sometimes confused with rear axle noises, will not change when comparing drive and coast conditions. While holding the speed steady, lightly apply the footbrake. This will often cause wheel bearing noise to lessen, as some of the weight is taken off the bearing. Front wheel bearings are easily checked by jacking up the wheels and spinning the wheels. Shaking the wheels will also determine if the wheel bearings are excessively loose.

REAR AXLE NOISES

Eliminating other possible sources can narrow the cause to the rear axle, which normally produces noise from worn gears or bearings. Gear noises tend to peak in a narrow speed range, while bearing noises will usually vary in pitch with engine speeds.

Noise Diagnosis

The Noise Is:	Most Probably Produced By:
1. Identical under Drive or Coast	Road surface, tires or front wheel bearings
2. Different depending on road surface	Road surface or tires
3. Lower as speed is lowered	Tires
4. Similar when standing or moving	Engine or transmission
5. A vibration	Unbalanced tires, rear wheel bearing, unbalanced driveshaft or worn U-joint
6. A knock or click about every two tire revolutions	Rear wheel bearing
7. Most pronounced on turns	Damaged differential gears
8. A steady low-pitched whirring or scraping, starting at low speeds	Damaged or worn pinion bearing
9. A chattering vibration on turns	Wrong differential lubricant or worn clutch plates (limited slip rear axle)
10. Noticed only in Drive, Coast or Float conditions	Worn ring gear and/or pinion gear

Troubleshooting Steering & Suspension Problems

Condition	Possible Cause
Hard steering (wheel is hard to turn)	1. Improper tire pressure 2. Loose or glazed pump drive belt 3. Low or incorrect fluid 4. Loose, bent or poorly lubricated front end parts 5. Improper front end alignment (excessive caster) 6. Bind in steering column or linkage 7. Kinked hydraulic hose 8. Air in hydraulic system 9. Low pump output or leaks in system 10. Obstruction in lines 11. Pump valves sticking or out of adjustment 12. Incorrect wheel alignment
Loose steering (too much play in steering wheel)	1. Loose wheel bearings 2. Faulty shocks 3. Worn linkage or suspension components 4. Loose steering gear mounting or linkage points 5. Steering mechanism worn or improperly adjusted 6. Valve spool improperly adjusted 7. Worn ball joints, tie-rod ends, etc.
Veers or wanders (pulls to one side with hands off steering wheel)	1. Improper tire pressure 2. Improper front end alignment 3. Dragging or improperly adjusted brakes 4. Bent frame 5. Improper rear end alignment 6. Faulty shocks or springs 7. Loose or bent front end components 8. Play in Pitman arm 9. Steering gear mountings loose 10. Loose wheel bearings 11. Binding Pitman arm 12. Spool valve sticking or improperly adjusted 13. Worn ball joints
Wheel oscillation or vibration transmitted through steering wheel	1. Low or uneven tire pressure 2. Loose wheel bearings 3. Improper front end alignment 4. Bent spindle 5. Worn, bent or broken front end components 6. Tires out of round or out of balance 7. Excessive lateral runout in disc brake rotor 8. Loose or bent shock absorber or strut
Noises (see also "Troubleshooting Drive Axle Problems")	1. Loose belts 2. Low fluid, air in system 3. Foreign matter in system 4. Improper lubrication 5. Interference or chafing in linkage 6. Steering gear mountings loose 7. Incorrect adjustment or wear in gear box 8. Faulty valves or wear in pump 9. Kinked hydraulic lines 10. Worn wheel bearings
Poor return of steering	1. Over-inflated tires 2. Improperly aligned front end (excessive caster) 3. Binding in steering column 4. No lubrication in front end 5. Steering gear adjusted too tight
Uneven tire wear (see "How To Read Tire Wear")	1. Incorrect tire pressure 2. Improperly aligned front end 3. Tires out-of-balance 4. Bent or worn suspension parts

HOW TO READ TIRE WEAR

The way your tires wear is a good indicator of other parts of the suspension. Abnormal wear patterns are often caused by the need for simple tire maintenance, or for front end alignment.

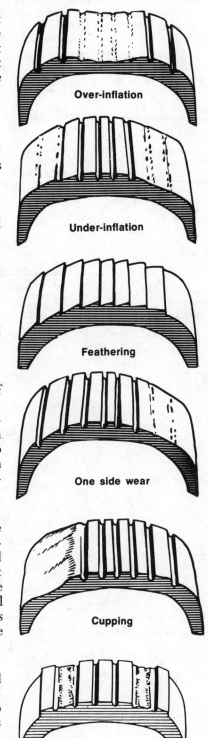

Excessive wear at the center of the tread indicates that the air pressure in the tire is consistently too high. The tire is riding on the center of the tread and wearing it prematurely. Occasionally, this wear pattern can result from outrageously wide tires on narrow rims. The cure for this is to replace either the tires or the wheels.

Over-inflation

This type of wear usually results from consistent under-inflation. When a tire is under-inflated, there is too much contact with the road by the outer treads, which wear prematurely. When this type of wear occurs, and the tire pressure is known to be consistently correct, a bent or worn steering component or the need for wheel alignment could be indicated.

Under-inflation

Feathering is a condition when the edge of each tread rib develops a slightly rounded edge on one side and a sharp edge on the other. By running your hand over the tire, you can usually feel the sharper edges before you'll be able to see them. The most common causes of feathering are incorrect toe-in setting or deteriorated bushings in the front suspension.

Feathering

When an inner or outer rib wears faster than the rest of the tire, the need for wheel alignment is indicated. There is excessive camber in the front suspension, causing the wheel to lean too much putting excessive load on one side of the tire. Misalignment could also be due to sagging springs, worn ball joints, or worn control arm bushings. Be sure the vehicle is loaded the way it's normally driven when you have the wheels aligned.

One side wear

Cups or scalloped dips appearing around the edge of the tread almost always indicate worn (sometimes bent) suspension parts. Adjustment of wheel alignment alone will seldom cure the problem. Any worn component that connects the wheel to the suspension can cause this type of wear. Occasionally, wheels that are out of balance will wear like this, but wheel imbalance usually shows up as bald spots between the outside edges and center of the tread.

Cupping

Second-rib wear is usually found only in radial tires, and appears where the steel belts end in relation to the tread. It can be kept to a minimum by paying careful attention to tire pressure and frequently rotating the tires. This is often considered normal wear but excessive amounts indicate that the tires are too wide for the wheels.

Second-rib wear

Troubleshooting Disc Brake Problems

Condition	Possible Cause
Noise—groan—brake noise emanating when slowly releasing brakes (creep-groan)	Not detrimental to function of disc brakes—no corrective action required. (This noise may be eliminated by slightly increasing or decreasing brake pedal efforts.)
Rattle—brake noise or rattle emanating at low speeds on rough roads, (front wheels only).	1. Shoe anti-rattle spring missing or not properly positioned. 2. Excessive clearance between shoe and caliper. 3. Soft or broken caliper seals. 4. Deformed or misaligned disc. 5. Loose caliper.
Scraping	1. Mounting bolts too long. 2. Loose wheel bearings. 3. Bent, loose, or misaligned splash shield.
Front brakes heat up during driving and fail to release	1. Operator riding brake pedal. 2. Stop light switch improperly adjusted. 3. Sticking pedal linkage. 4. Frozen or seized piston. 5. Residual pressure valve in master cylinder. 6. Power brake malfunction. 7. Proportioning valve malfunction.
Leaky brake caliper	1. Damaged or worn caliper piston seal. 2. Scores or corrosion on surface of cylinder bore.
Grabbing or uneven brake action—Brakes pull to one side	1. Causes listed under "Brakes Pull". 2. Power brake malfunction. 3. Low fluid level in master cylinder. 4. Air in hydraulic system. 5. Brake fluid, oil or grease on linings. 6. Unmatched linings. 7. Distorted brake pads. 8. Frozen or seized pistons. 9. Incorrect tire pressure. 10. Front end out of alignment. 11. Broken rear spring. 12. Brake caliper pistons sticking. 13. Restricted hose or line. 14. Caliper not in proper alignment to braking disc. 15. Stuck or malfunctioning metering valve. 16. Soft or broken caliper seals. 17. Loose caliper.
Brake pedal can be depressed without braking effect	1. Air in hydraulic system or improper bleeding procedure. 2. Leak past primary cup in master cylinder. 3. Leak in system. 4. Rear brakes out of adjustment. 5. Bleeder screw open.
Excessive pedal travel	1. Air, leak, or insufficient fluid in system or caliper. 2. Warped or excessively tapered shoe and lining assembly. 3. Excessive disc runout. 4. Rear brake adjustment required. 5. Loose wheel bearing adjustment. 6. Damaged caliper piston seal. 7. Improper brake fluid (boil). 8. Power brake malfunction. 9. Weak or soft hoses.

Troubleshooting Disc Brake Problems (cont.)

Condition	Possible Cause
Brake roughness or chatter (pedal pumping)	1. Excessive thickness variation of braking disc. 2. Excessive lateral runout of braking disc. 3. Rear brake drums out-of-round. 4. Excessive front bearing clearance.
Excessive pedal effort	1. Brake fluid, oil or grease on linings. 2. Incorrect lining. 3. Frozen or seized pistons. 4. Power brake malfunction. 5. Kinked or collapsed hose or line. 6. Stuck metering valve. 7. Scored caliper or master cylinder bore. 8. Seized caliper pistons.
Brake pedal fades (pedal travel increases with foot on brake)	1. Rough master cylinder or caliper bore. 2. Loose or broken hydraulic lines/connections. 3. Air in hydraulic system. 4. Fluid level low. 5. Weak or soft hoses. 6. Inferior quality brake shoes or fluid. 7. Worn master cylinder piston cups or seals.

Troubleshooting Drum Brakes

Condition	Possible Cause
Pedal goes to floor	1. Fluid low in reservoir. 2. Air in hydraulic system. 3. Improperly adjusted brake. 4. Leaking wheel cylinders. 5. Loose or broken brake lines. 6. Leaking or worn master cylinder. 7. Excessively worn brake lining.
Spongy brake pedal	1. Air in hydraulic system. 2. Improper brake fluid (low boiling point). 3. Excessively worn or cracked brake drums. 4. Broken pedal pivot bushing.
Brakes pulling	1. Contaminated lining. 2. Front end out of alignment. 3. Incorrect brake adjustment. 4. Unmatched brake lining. 5. Brake drums out of round. 6. Brake shoes distorted. 7. Restricted brake hose or line. 8. Broken rear spring. 9. Worn brake linings. 10. Uneven lining wear. 11. Glazed brake lining. 12. Excessive brake lining dust. 13. Heat spotted brake drums. 14. Weak brake return springs. 15. Faulty automatic adjusters. 16. Low or incorrect tire pressure.

Condition	Possible Cause
Squealing brakes	1. Glazed brake lining. 2. Saturated brake lining. 3. Weak or broken brake shoe retaining spring. 4. Broken or weak brake shoe return spring. 5. Incorrect brake lining. 6. Distorted brake shoes. 7. Bent support plate. 8. Dust in brakes or scored brake drums. 9. Linings worn below limit. 10. Uneven brake lining wear. 11. Heat spotted brake drums.
Chirping brakes	1. Out of round drum or eccentric axle flange pilot.
Dragging brakes	1. Incorrect wheel or parking brake adjustment. 2. Parking brakes engaged or improperly adjusted. 3. Weak or broken brake shoe return spring. 4. Brake pedal binding. 5. Master cylinder cup sticking. 6. Obstructed master cylinder relief port. 7. Saturated brake lining. 8. Bent or out of round brake drum. 9. Contaminated or improper brake fluid. 10. Sticking wheel cylinder pistons. 11. Driver riding brake pedal. 12. Defective proportioning valve. 13. Insufficient brake shoe lubricant.
Hard pedal	1. Brake booster inoperative. 2. Incorrect brake lining. 3. Restricted brake line or hose. 4. Frozen brake pedal linkage. 5. Stuck wheel cylinder. 6. Binding pedal linkage. 7. Faulty proportioning valve.
Wheel locks	1. Contaminated brake lining. 2. Loose or torn brake lining. 3. Wheel cylinder cups sticking. 4. Incorrect wheel bearing adjustment. 5. Faulty proportioning valve.
Brakes fade (high speed)	1. Incorrect lining. 2. Overheated brake drums. 3. Incorrect brake fluid (low boiling temperature). 4. Saturated brake lining. 5. Leak in hydraulic system. 6. Faulty automatic adjusters.
Pedal pulsates	1. Bent or out of round brake drum.
Brake chatter and shoe knock	1. Out of round brake drum. 2. Loose support plate. 3. Bent support plate. 4. Distorted brake shoes. 5. Machine grooves in contact face of brake drum (Shoe Knock). 6. Contaminated brake lining. 7. Missing or loose components. 8. Incorrect lining material. 9. Out-of-round brake drums. 10. Heat spotted or scored brake drums. 11. Out-of-balance wheels.

Troubleshooting Drum Brakes (cont.)

Condition	Possible Cause
Brakes do not self adjust	1. Adjuster screw frozen in thread. 2. Adjuster screw corroded at thrust washer. 3. Adjuster lever does not engage star wheel. 4. Adjuster installed on wrong wheel.
Brake light glows	1. Leak in the hydraulic system. 2. Air in the system. 3. Improperly adjusted master cylinder pushrod. 4. Uneven lining wear. 5. Failure to center combination valve or proportioning valve.

Mechanic's Data

General Conversion Table

Multiply By	To Convert	To	
		LENGTH	
2.54	Inches	Centimeters	.3937
25.4	Inches	Millimeters	.03937
30.48	Feet	Centimeters	.0328
.304	Feet	Meters	3.28
.914	Yards	Meters	1.094
1.609	Miles	Kilometers	.621
		VOLUME	
.473	Pints	Liters	2.11
.946	Quarts	Liters	1.06
3.785	Gallons	Liters	.264
.016	Cubic inches	Liters	61.02
16.39	Cubic inches	Cubic cms.	.061
28.3	Cubic feet	Liters	.0353
		MASS (Weight)	
28.35	Ounces	Grams	.035
.4536	Pounds	Kilograms	2.20
—	To obtain	From	Multiply by

Multiply By	To Convert	To	
		AREA	
.645	Square inches	Square cms.	.155
.836	Square yds.	Square meters	1.196
		FORCE	
4.448	Pounds	Newtons	.225
.138	Ft./lbs.	Kilogram/meters	7.23
1.36	Ft./lbs.	Newton-meters	.737
.112	In./lbs.	Newton-meters	8.844
		PRESSURE	
.068	Psi	Atmospheres	14.7
6.89	Psi	Kilopascals	.145
		OTHER	
1.104	Horsepower (DIN)	Horsepower (SAE)	.9861
.746	Horsepower (SAE)	Kilowatts (KW)	1.34
1.60	Mph	Km/h	.625
.425	Mpg	Km/1	2.35
—	To obtain	From	Multiply by

Tap Drill Sizes

National Coarse or U.S.S.

Screw & Tap Size	Threads Per Inch	Use Drill Number
No. 5	40	39
No. 6	32	36
No. 8	32	29
No. 10	24	25
No. 12	24	17
1/4	20	8
5/16	18	F
3/8	16	5/16
7/16	14	U
1/2	13	27/64
9/16	12	31/64
5/8	11	17/32
3/4	10	21/32
7/8	9	49/64

National Coarse or U.S.S.

Screw & Tap Size	Threads Per Inch	Use Drill Number
1	8	7/8
1 1/8	7	63/64
1 1/4	7	1 7/64
1 1/2	6	1 11/32

National Fine or S.A.E.

Screw & Tap Size	Threads Per Inch	Use Drill Number
No. 5	44	37
No. 6	40	33
No. 8	36	29
No. 10	32	21

National Fine or S.A.E.

Screw & Tap Size	Threads Per Inch	Use Drill Number
No. 12	28	15
1/4	28	3
5/16	24	1
3/8	24	Q
7/16	20	W
1/2	20	29/64
9/16	18	33/64
5/8	18	37/64
3/4	16	11/16
7/8	14	13/16
1 1/8	12	1 3/64
1 1/4	12	1 11/64
1 1/2	12	1 27/64

Drill Sizes In Decimal Equivalents

Inch	Decimal	Wire	mm	Inch	Decimal	Wire	mm	Inch	Decimal	Wire & Letter	mm	Inch	Decimal	Letter	mm	Inch	Decimal	mm
1/64	.0156		.39		.0730	49			.1614		4.1		.2717		6.9		.4331	11.0
	.0157		.4		.0748		1.9		.1654		4.2		.2720	I		7/16	.4375	11.11
	.0160	78			.0760	48			.1660	19			.2756		7.0		.4528	11.5
	.0165		.42		.0768		1.95		.1673		4.25		.2770	J		29/64	.4531	11.51
	.0173		.44	5/64	.0781		1.98		.1693		4.3		.2795		7.1	15/32	.4688	11.90
	.0177		.45		.0785	47			.1695	18			.2810	K			.4724	12.0
	.0180	77			.0787		2.0	11/64	.1719		4.36	9/32	.2812		7.14	31/64	.4844	12.30
	.0181		.46		.0807		2.05		.1730	17			.2835		7.2		.4921	12.5
	.0189		.48		.0810	46			.1732		4.4		.2854		7.25	1/2	.5000	12.70
	.0197		.5		.0820	45			.1770	16			.2874		7.3		.5118	13.0
	.0200	76			.0827		2.1		.1772		4.5		.2900	L		33/64	.5156	13.09
	.0210	75			.0846		2.15		.1800	15			.2913		7.4	17/32	.5312	13.49
	.0217		.55		.0860	44			.1811		4.6		.2950	M			.5315	13.5
	.0225	74			.0866		2.2		.1820	14			.2953		7.5	35/64	.5469	13.89
	.0236		.6		.0886		2.25		.1850	13		19/64	.2969		7.54		.5512	14.0
	.0240	73			.0890	43			.1850		4.7		.2992		7.6	9/16	.5625	14.28
	.0250	72			.0906		2.3		.1870		4.75		.3020	N			.5709	14.5
	.0256		.65		.0925		2.35	3/16	.1875		4.76		.3031		7.7	37/64	.5781	14.68
	.0260	71			.0935	42			.1890		4.8		.3051		7.75		.5906	15.0
	.0276		.7	3/32	.0938		2.38		.1890	12			.3071		7.8	19/32	.5938	15.08
	.0280	70			.0945		2.4		.1910	11			.3110		7.9	39/64	.6094	15.47
	.0292	69			.0960	41			.1929		4.9	5/16	.3125		7.93		.6102	15.5
	.0295		.75		.0965		2.45		.1935	10			.3150		8.0	5/8	.6250	15.87
	.0310	68			.0980	40			.1960	9			.3160	O			.6299	16.0
1/32	.0312		.79		.0981		2.5		.1969		5.0		.3189		8.1	41/64	.6406	16.27
	.0315		.8		.0995	39			.1990	8			.3228		8.2		.6496	16.5
	.0320	67			.1015	38			.2008		5.1		.3230	P		21/32	.6562	16.66
	.0330	66			.1024		2.6		.2010	7			.3248		8.25		.6693	17.0
	.0335		.85		.1040	37		13/64	.2031		5.16		.3268		8.3	43/64	.6719	17.06
	.0350	65			.1063		2.7		.2040	6		21/64	.3281		8.33	11/16	.6875	17.46
	.0354		.9		.1065	36			.2047		5.2		.3307		8.4		.6890	17.5
	.0360	64			.1083		2.75		.2055	5			.3320	Q		45/64	.7031	17.85
	.0370	63		7/64	.1094		2.77		.2067		5.25		.3346		8.5		.7087	18.0
	.0374		.95		.1100	35			.2087		5.3		.3386		8.6	23/32	.7188	18.25
	.0380	62			.1102		2.8		.2090	4			.3390	R			.7283	18.5
	.0390	61			.1110	34			.2126		5.4	11/32	.3438		8.73	47/64	.7344	18.65
	.0394		1.0		.1130	33			.2130	3			.3445		8.75		.7480	19.0
	.0400	60			.1142		2.9		.2165		5.5		.3465		8.8	3/4	.7500	19.05
	.0410	59			.1160	32		7/32	.2188		5.55		.3480	S		49/64	.7656	19.44
	.0413		1.05		.1181		3.0		.2205		5.6		.3504		8.9		.7677	19.5
	.0420	58			.1200	31			.2210	2			.3543		9.0	25/32	.7812	19.84
	.0430	57			.1220		3.1		.2244		5.7		.3580	T			.7874	20.0
	.0433		1.1	1/8	.1250		3.17		.2264		5.75		.3583		9.1	51/64	.7969	20.24
	.0453		1.15		.1260		3.2		.2280	1		23/64	.3594		9.12		.8071	20.5
	.0465	56			.1280		3.25		.2283		5.8		.3622		9.2	13/16	.8125	20.63
3/64	.0469		1.19		.1285	30			.2323		5.9		.3642		9.25		.8268	21.0
	.0472		1.2		.1299		3.3		.2340	A			.3661		9.3	53/64	.8281	21.03
	.0492		1.25		.1339		3.4	15/64	.2344		5.95		.3680	U		27/32	.8438	21.43
	.0512		1.3		.1360	29			.2362		6.0		.3701		9.4		.8465	21.5
	.0520	55			.1378		3.5		.2380	B			.3740		9.5	55/64	.8594	21.82
	.0531		1.35		.1405	28			.2402		6.1	3/8	.3750		9.52		.8661	22.0
	.0550	54		9/64	.1406		3.57		.2420	C			.3770	V		7/8	.8750	22.22
	.0551		1.4		.1417		3.6		.2441		6.2		.3780		9.6		.8858	22.5
	.0571		1.45		.1440	27			.2460	D			.3819		9.7	57/64	.8906	22.62
	.0591		1.5		.1457		3.7		.2461		6.25		.3839		9.75		.9055	23.0
	.0595	53			.1470	26			.2480		6.3		.3858		9.8	29/32	.9062	23.01
	.0610		1.55		.1476		3.75	1/4	.2500	E	6.35		.3860	W		59/64	.9219	23.41
1/16	.0625		1.59		.1495	25			.2520		6.4		.3898		9.9		.9252	23.5
	.0630		1.6		.1496		3.8		.2559		6.5	25/64	.3906		9.92	15/16	.9375	23.81
	.0635	52			.1520	24			.2570	F			.3937		10.0		.9449	24.0
	.0650		1.65		.1535		3.9		.2598		6.6		.3970	X		61/64	.9531	24.2
	.0669		1.7		.1540	23			.2610	G			.4040	Y			.9646	24.5
	.0670	51		5/32	.1562		3.96		.2638		6.7	13/32	.4062		10.31	31/32	.9688	24.6
	.0689		1.75		.1570	22		17/64	.2656		6.74		.4130	Z			.9843	25.0
	.0700	50			.1575		4.0		.2657		6.75		.4134		10.5	63/64	.9844	25.0
	.0709		1.8		.1590	21			.2660	H		27/64	.4219		10.71	1	1.0000	25.4
	.0728		1.85		.1610	20			.2677		6.8							

Index

Chilton's Repair & Tune-Up Guides

The Complete line covers domestic cars, imports, trucks, vans, RV's and 4-wheel drive vehicles.

RTUG Title	Part No.
AMC 1975-82	7199
Covers all U.S. and Canadian models	
Aspen/Volare 1976-80	6637
Covers all U.S. and Canadian models	
Audi 1970-73	5902
Covers all U.S. and Canadian models.	
Audi 4000/5000 1978-81	7028
Covers all U.S. and Canadian models including turbocharged and diesel engines	
Barracuda/Challenger 1965-72	5807
Covers all U.S. and Canadian models	
Blazer/Jimmy 1969-82	6931
Covers all U.S. and Canadian 2- and 4-wheel drive models, including diesel engines	
BMW 1970-82	6844
Covers U.S. and Canadian models	
Buick/Olds/Pontiac 1975-85	7308
Covers all U.S. and Canadian full size rear wheel drive models	
Cadillac 1967-84	7462
Covers all U.S. and Canadian rear wheel drive models	
Camaro 1967-81	6735
Covers all U.S. and Canadian models	
Camaro 1982-85	7317
Covers all U.S. and Canadian models	
Capri 1970-77	6695
Covers all U.S. and Canadian models	
Caravan/Voyager 1984-85	7482
Covers all U.S. and Canadian models	
Century/Regal 1975-85	7307
Covers all U.S. and Canadian rear wheel drive models, including turbocharged engines	
Champ/Arrow/Sapporo 1978-83	7041
Covers all U.S. and Canadian models	
Chevette/1000 1976-86	6836
Covers all U.S. and Canadian models	
Chevrolet 1968-85	7135
Covers all U.S. and Canadian models	
Chevrolet 1968-79 Spanish	7082
Chevrolet/GMC Pick-Ups 1970-82 Spanish	7468
Chevrolet/GMC Pick-Ups and Suburban 1970-86	6936
Covers all U.S. and Canadian $^1/_2$, $^3/_4$ and 1 ton models, including 4-wheel drive and diesel engines	
Chevrolet LUV 1972-81	6815
Covers all U.S. and Canadian models	
Chevrolet Mid-Size 1964-86	6840
Covers all U.S. and Canadian models of 1964-77 Chevelle, Malibu and Malibu SS; 1974-77 Laguna; 1978-85 Malibu; 1970-86 Monte Carlo; 1964-84 El Camino, including diesel engines	
Chevrolet Nova 1986	7658
Covers all U.S. and Canadian models	
Chevy/GMC Vans 1967-84	6930
Covers all U.S. and Canadian models of $^1/_2$, $^3/_4$, and 1 ton vans, cutaways, and motor home chassis, including diesel engines	
Chevy S-10 Blazer/GMC S-15 Jimmy 1982-85	7383
Covers all U.S. and Canadian models	
Chevy S-10/GMC S-15 Pick-Ups 1982-85	7310
Covers all U.S. and Canadian models	
Chevy II/Nova 1962-79	6841
Covers all U.S. and Canadian models	
Chrysler K- and E-Car 1981-85	7163
Covers all U.S. and Canadian front wheel drive models	
Colt/Challenger/Vista/Conquest 1971-85	7037
Corolla/Carina/Tercel/Starlet 1970-85	7036
Covers all U.S. and Canadian models	
Corona/Cressida/Crown/Mk.II/Camry/Van 1970-84	7044
Covers all U.S. and Canadian models	

RTUG Title	Part No.
Corvair 1960-69	6691
Covers all U.S. and Canadian models	
Corvette 1953-62	6576
Covers all U.S. and Canadian models	
Corvette 1963-84	6843
Covers all U.S. and Canadian models	
Cutlass 1970-85	6933
Covers all U.S. and Canadian models	
Dart/Demon 1968-76	6324
Covers all U.S. and Canadian models	
Datsun 1961-72	5790
Covers all U.S. and Canadian models of Nissan Patrol; 1500, 1600 and 2000 sports cars; Pick-Ups; 410, 411, 510, 1200 and 240Z	
Datsun 1973-80 Spanish	7083
Datsun/Nissan F-10, 310, Stanza, Pulsar 1977-86	7196
Covers all U.S. and Canadian models	
Datsun/Nissan Pick-Ups 1970-84	6816
Covers all U.S and Canadian models	
Datsun/Nissan Z & ZX 1970-86	6932
Covers all U.S. and Canadian models	
Datsun/Nissan 1200, 210, Sentra 1973-86	7197
Covers all U.S. and Canadian models	
Datsun/Nissan 200SX, 510, 610, 710, 810, Maxima 1973-84	7170
Covers all U.S. and Canadian models	
Dodge 1968-77	6554
Covers all U.S. and Canadian models	
Dodge Charger 1967-70	6486
Covers all U.S. and Canadian models	
Dodge/Plymouth Trucks 1967-84	7459
Covers all $^1/_2$, $^3/_4$, and 1 ton 2- and 4-wheel drive U.S. and Canadian models, including diesel engines	
Dodge/Plymouth Vans 1967-84	6934
Covers all $^1/_2$, $^3/_4$, and 1 ton U.S. and Canadian models of vans, cutaways and motor home chassis	
D-50/Arrow Pick-Up 1979-81	7032
Covers all U.S. and Canadian models	
Fairlane/Torino 1962-75	6320
Covers all U.S. and Canadian models	
Fairmont/Zephyr 1978-83	6965
Covers all U.S. and Canadian models	
Fiat 1969-81	7042
Covers all U.S. and Canadian models	
Fiesta 1978-80	6846
Covers all U.S. and Canadian models	
Firebird 1967-81	5996
Covers all U.S. and Canadian models	
Firebird 1982-85	7345
Covers all U.S. and Canadian models	
Ford 1968-79 Spanish	7084
Ford Bronco 1966-83	7140
Covers all U.S. and Canadian models	
Ford Bronco II 1984	7408
Covers all U.S. and Canadian models	
Ford Courier 1972-82	6983
Covers all U.S. and Canadian models	
Ford/Mercury Front Wheel Drive 1981-85	7055
Covers all U.S. and Canadian models Escort, EXP, Tempo, Lynx, LN-7 and Topaz	
Ford/Mercury/Lincoln 1968-85	6842
Covers all U.S. and Canadian models of FORD Country Sedan, Country Squire, Crown Victoria, Custom, Custom 500, Galaxie 500, LTD through 1982, Ranch Wagon, and XL; MERCURY Colony Park, Commuter, Marquis through 1982, Gran Marquis, Monterey and Park Lane; LINCOLN Continental and Towne Car	
Ford/Mercury/Lincoln Mid-Size 1971-85	6696
Covers all U.S. and Canadian models of FORD Elite, 1983-85 LTD, 1977-79 LTD II, Ranchero, Torino, Gran Torino, 1977-85 Thunderbird; MERCURY 1972-85 Cougar,	

continued on next page

RTUG Title	Part No.	RTUG Title	Part No.
1983-85 Marquis, Montego, 1980-85 XR-7; LINCOLN 1982-85 Continental, 1984-85 Mark VII, 1978-80 Versailles		Mercedes-Benz 1974-84 Covers all U.S. and Canadian models	6809
Ford Pick-Ups 1965-86	6913	**Mitsubishi, Cordia, Tredia, Starion, Galant 1983-85**	7583
Covers all ½, ¾ and 1 ton, 2- and 4-wheel drive U.S. and Canadian pick-up, chassis cab and camper models, including diesel engines		Covers all U.S. and Canadian models	
		MG 1961-81	6780
		Covers all U.S. and Canadian models	
Ford Pick-Ups 1965-82 Spanish	7469	**Mustang/Capri/Merkur 1979-85**	6963
Ford Ranger 1983-84	7338	Covers all U.S. and Canadian models	
Covers all U.S. and Canadian models		**Mustang/Cougar 1965-73**	6542
Ford Vans 1961-86	6849	Covers all U.S. and Canadian models	
Covers all U.S. and Canadian ½, ¾ and 1 ton van and cutaway chassis models, including diesel engines		**Mustang II 1974-78**	6812
		Covers all U.S. and Canadian models	
		Omni/Horizon/Rampage 1978-84	6845
GM A-Body 1982-85	7309	Covers all U.S. and Canadian models of DODGE omni, Miser, 024, Charger 2.2; PLYMOUTH Horizon, Miser, TC3, TC3 Tourismo; Rampage	
Covers all front wheel drive U.S. and Canadian models of BUICK Century, CHEVROLET Celebrity, OLDSMOBILE Cutlass Ciera and PONTIAC 6000			
		Opel 1971-75	6575
GM C-Body 1985	7587	Covers all U.S. and Canadian models	
Covers all front wheel drive U.S. and Canadian models of BUICK Electra Park Avenue and Electra T-Type, CADILLAC Fleetwood and deVille, OLDSMOBILE 98 Regency and Regency Brougham		**Peugeot 1970-74**	5982
		Covers all U.S. and Canadian models	
		Pinto/Bobcat 1971-80	7027
		Covers all U.S. and Canadian models	
		Plymouth 1968-76	6552
GM J-Car 1982-85	7059	Covers all U.S. and Canadian models	
Covers all U.S. and Canadian models of BUICK Skyhawk, CHEVROLET Cavalier, CADILLAC Cimarron, OLDSMOBILE Firenza and PONTIAC 2000 and Sunbird		**Pontiac Fiero 1984-85**	7571
		Covers all U.S. and Canadian models	
		Pontiac Mid-Size 1974-83	7346
		Covers all U.S. and Canadian models of Ventura, Grand Am, LeMans, Grand LeMans, GTO, Phoenix, and Grand Prix	
GM N-Body 1985-86	7657		
Covers all U.S. and Canadian models of front wheel drive BUICK Somerset and Skylark, OLDSMOBILE Calais, and PONTIAC Grand Am		**Porsche 924/928 1976-81**	7048
		Covers all U.S. and Canadian models	
		Renault 1975-85	7165
		Covers all U.S. and Canadian models	
GM X-Body 1980-85	7049	**Roadrunner/Satellite/Belvedere/GTX 1968-73**	5821
Covers all U.S. and Canadian models of BUICK Skylark, CHEVROLET Citation, OLDSMOBILE Omega and PONTIAC Phoenix		Covers all U.S. and Canadian models	
		RX-7 1979-81	7031
		Covers all U.S. and Canadian models	
GM Subcompact 1971-80	6935	**SAAB 99 1969-75**	5988
Covers all U.S. and Canadian models of BUICK Skyhawk (1975-80), CHEVROLET Vega and Monza, OLDSMOBILE Starfire, and PONTIAC Astre and 1975-80 Sunbird		Covers all U.S. and Canadian models	
		SAAB 900 1979-85	7572
		Covers all U.S. and Canadian models	
		Snowmobiles 1976-80	6978
Granada/Monarch 1975-82	6937	Covers Arctic Cat, John Deere, Kawasaki, Polaris, Ski-Doo and Yamaha	
Covers all U.S. and Canadian models			
		Subaru 1970-84	6982
Honda 1973-84	6980	Covers all U.S. and Canadian models	
Covers all U.S. and Canadian models		**Tempest/GTO/LeMans 1968-73**	5905
International Scout 1967-73	5912	Covers all U.S. and Canadian models	
Covers all U.S. and Canadian models		**Toyota 1966-70**	5795
Jeep 1945-87	6817	Covers all U.S. and Canadian models of Corona, MkII, Corolla, Crown, Land Cruiser, Stout and Hi-Lux	
Covers all U.S. and Canadian CJ-2A, CJ-3A, CJ-3B, CJ-5, CJ-6, CJ-7, Scrambler and Wrangler models			
		Toyota 1970-79 Spanish	7467
Jeep Wagoneer, Commando, Cherokee, Truck 1957-86	6739	**Toyota Celica/Supra 1971-85**	7043
		Covers all U.S. and Canadian models	
Covers all U.S. and Canadian models of Wagoneer, Cherokee, Grand Wagoneer, Jeepster, Jeepster Commando, J-100, J-200, J-300, J-10, J20, FC-150 and FC-170		**Toyota Trucks 1970-85**	7035
		Covers all U.S. and Canadian models of pick-ups, Land Cruiser and 4Runner	
		Valiant/Duster 1968-76	6326
Laser/Daytona 1984-85	7563	Covers all U.S. and Canadian models	
Covers all U.S. and Canadian models		**Volvo 1956-69**	6529
Maverick/Comet 1970-77	6634	Covers all U.S. and Canadian models	
Covers all U.S. and Canadian models		**Volvo 1970-83**	7040
Mazda 1971-84	6981	Covers all U.S. and Canadian models	
Covers all U.S. and Canadian models of RX-2, RX-3, RX-4, 808, 1300, 1600, Cosmo, GLC and 626		**VW Front Wheel Drive 1974-85**	6962
		Covers all U.S. and Canadian models	
		VW 1949-71	5796
Mazda Pick-Ups 1972-86	7659	Covers all U.S. and Canadian models	
Covers all U.S. and Canadian models		**VW 1970-79 Spanish**	7081
Mercedes-Benz 1959-70	6065	**VW 1970-81**	6837
Covers all U.S. and Canadian models		Covers all U.S. and Canadian Beetles, Karmann Ghia, Fastback, Squareback, Vans, 411 and 412	
Mereceds-Benz 1968-73	5907		
Covers all U.S. and Canadian models			

Chilton's Repair & Tune-Up Guides are available at your local retailer or by mailing a check or money order for **$13.50** plus **$2.50** to cover postage and handling to:

Chilton Book Company
Dept. DM
Radnor, PA 19089

NOTE: When ordering be sure to include your name & address, book part No. & title.